Encyclopaedia of
TRACK AND FIELD ATHLETICS

Sports Encyclopaedias published by Robert Hale Limited

Association Football
BY MAURICE GOLESWORTHY

Bowls
BY KEN HAWKS AND GERARD LINDLEY

Boxing
BY MAURICE GOLESWORTHY

Chess
BY ANNE SUNNUCKS

Cricket
BY MAURICE GOLESWORTHY

Flat Racing
BY ROGER MORTIMER

Golf
BY WEBSTER EVANS

Motor Cycle Sport
BY PETER CARRICK

Motor Racing
BY ANTHONY PRITCHARD AND KEITH DAVEY

Mountaineering
BY WALT UNSWORTH

Rugby Union Football
BY J. R. JONES
 (Second edition edited by Maurice Golesworthy)

Show Jumping
BY CHARLES STRATTON

Steeplechasing
BY PATRICIA SMYLY

Swimming
BY PAT BESFORD

Track and Field Athletics
BY MELVYN WATMAN

Encyclopaedia of
TRACK AND FIELD ATHLETICS

Compiled by

MEL WATMAN

ST. MARTIN'S PRESS
NEW YORK

ROBERT HALE LIMITED
LONDON

© Mel Watman 1964, 1967, 1973, 1977 and 1981

First published in Great Britain 1964
Second Edition 1967
Third Edition 1973
Fourth Edition 1977
Fifth Edition 1981

First published in the United States of America 1977
Second Edition 1981

Robert Hale Limited
Clerkenwell House
Clerkenwell Green
London EC1R 0HT

ISBN 0 7091 9242 8

St. Martin's Press, Inc.
175 Fifth Avenue
New York, N.Y. 10010

Library of Congress Catalog Card Number 81-52468

ISBN 0-312-25067-3

PRINTED IN GREAT BRITAIN BY
BRISTOL TYPESETTING CO. LTD.
BARTON MANOR - ST. PHILIPS
BRISTOL 2

Illustrations

Between pages 96 and 97

1 Jesse Owens (USA)
2 Pietro Mennea (Italy) and Allan Wells (GB)
3 Irena Szewinska (Poland) and Marita Koch (E. Germany)
4 Alberto Juantorena (Cuba), Rick Wohlhuter (USA), Ivo Van Damme (Belgium) and Willi Wulbeck (W. Germany)
5 Lee Evans (USA)
6 Edwin Moses (USA)
7 Steve Ovett (GB), Sebastian Coe (GB) and Nikolay Kirov (USSR)
8 Roger Bannister and Sebastian Coe (GB)
9 Herb Elliott (Australia)
10 Tatyana Kazankina (USSR)
11 Paavo Nurmi (Finland)
12 Ron Clarke and Derek Clayton (Australia)
13 Emil Zatopek (Czechoslovakia), Chris Chataway (GB) and Herbert Schade (W. Germany)
14 Brendan Foster (GB), Lasse Viren (Finland), Ian Stewart (GB) and Dick Quax (New Zealand)
15 Miruts Yifter (Ethiopia)
16 Henry Rono (Kenya)

Between pages 160 and 161

17 Abebe Bikila (Ethiopia)
18 Grete Waitz (Norway)
19 David Hemery (GB)
20 Bronislaw Malinowski (Poland)
21 Fanny Blankers-Koen (Netherlands), Maureen Gardner (GB) and Shirley Strickland (Australia)
22 Thomas Munkelt (E. Germany) and Renaldo Nehemiah (USA)
23 Sara Simeoni (Italy)
24 Gerd Wessig (E. Germany)
25 Bob Beamon (USA)
26 Mary Rand (GB)
27 Wladyslaw Kozakiewicz (Poland)
28 Daley Thompson (GB)
29 Viktor Sanyeyev (USSR)
30 Vladimir Golubnichiy (USSR)
31 Al Oerter (USA)
32 Mary Peters (GB and NI) and Burglinde Pollak (E. Germany)

PHOTO CREDITS

Allsport Photographic 1, 13, 17; George Herringshaw 2, 4, 7, 8, 10, 14, 28; Mike Street 3; Ed Lacey 5, 9, 25; Mark Shearman 6, 12, 15, 20, 23, 24, 29, 30; Keystone Press Agency Ltd. 11, 21; Peter Tempest 16; Paul J. Sutton/Allsport 18, 22; Tony Duffy/Allsport 19, 32; Fionnbar Callanan 26; Bob Thomas 31.

Acknowledgements

I am particularly indebted to the late Harold Abrahams, Ivan Berenyi, Ian Buchanan, John Goulstone, Stan Greenberg, Roger Gynn, Matti Hannus, Peter Hildreth, Andrew Huxtable, Richard Hymans, Peter Lovesey, Dr David E. Martin, Peter Matthews, Rich Perelman, the late Peter Pozzoli, Bob Sparks, Dave Terry and Jon Wigley for their invaluable assistance with this or previous editions.

In addition, I have referred frequently to the following magazines—*Athletics Weekly, Athletics World, Der Leichtathlet, Leichtathletik, Runner's World, The Runner, Track & Field News* and *World Athletics*—as well as the French daily sports newspaper *L'Equipe* and the publications of the Amateur Athletic Association, Association of Track & Field Statisticians, Athletics Congress, British Amateur Athletic Board, International Amateur Athletic Federation and National Union of Track Statisticians.

I would also like to thank all who have notified me of errors or omissions in the previous editions of this book.

M.W.

Metric Conversions

For the benefit of readers who might still be more familiar with measurements in feet and inches we list here key metric conversions. Note that 1 metre equals approx 3ft. 3¼in., 10 centimetres approx. 4in.

High Jump

metres	ft.	in.
1.60	5	3
1.70	5	7
1.75	5	8¾
1.80	5	10¾
1.85	6	0¾
1.90	6	2¾
1.95	6	4¾
2.00	6	6¾
2.05	6	8¾
2.10	6	10¾
2.15	7	0½
2.20	7	2½
2.25	7	4½
2.30	7	6½
2.35	7	8½
2.40	7	10½

Pole Vault

metres	ft.	in.
3.80	12	5½
4.00	13	1½
4.20	13	9¼
4.40	14	5¼
4.60	15	1
4.80	15	9
5.00	16	4¾
5.10	16	8¾
5.20	17	0¾
5.30	17	4½
5.40	17	8½
5.50	18	0½
5.60	18	4½
5.70	18	8¼
5.80	19	0¼
5.90	19	4¼

Long Jump

metres	ft.	in.
6.00	19	8¼
6.20	20	4¼
6.40	21	0
6.60	21	8
6.80	22	3¾
7.00	22	11¾
7.10	23	3½
7.25	23	9½
7.50	24	7¼
7.75	25	5¼
8.00	26	3
8.20	26	11
8.40	27	6¾
8.60	28	2¾
8.80	28	10½
9.00	29	6½

Triple Jump/Shot

metres	ft.	in.
14.00	45	11¼
14.50	47	7
15.00	49	2½
15.50	50	10¼
16.00	52	6
16.50	54	1¾
17.00	55	9¼
17.50	57	5
18.00	59	0¾
18.50	60	8½
19.00	62	4
20.00	65	7½
21.00	68	10¾
22.00	72	2¼
23.00	75	5½

Long Throws

metres	ft.	in.
40.00	131	3
45.00	147	8
50.00	164	0
55.00	180	5
60.00	196	10
65.00	213	3
67.50	221	5
70.00	229	8
75.00	246	1
77.50	254	3
80.00	262	5
85.00	278	10
90.00	295	3
95.00	311	8
100.00	328	1

I dedicate this book to the memory of Harold Abrahams (1899-1978), who so kindly contributed a foreword to the four previous editions and who helped and encouraged me so much during their compilation; and to my wife Pat for her unfailing support and understanding.

Introduction

"It has been a great pleasure for me to compile this work, which salutes the achievements of the great athletes of past and present and may, I hope, serve as an inspiration to future generations of champions."

That is how I introduced the very first edition of this book back in 1964, and those sentiments apply equally to this the fifth edition seventeen years later.

What changes we have seen in the standards of performance achieved during those years; changes which are reflected in these pages. Looking back at the list of current world records as published in the first edition, who would have thought then that, for example, Ron Clarke's 10,000 metres figures of 28 min. 15.6 sec. would be reduced by more than 50 seconds, or that the 400 metres hurdles mark of 49.2 sec. would today be fully two seconds faster. The world record for the pole vault stood at 5.28 metres, while on the women's side the fastest 200 metres was 22.9 sec., the longest discus throw was 59.28 metres . . . and no 1500 metres record was even listed! Who in 1964 could possibly have predicted, at a time when the only fully authenticated instance of a woman completing a bona fide marathon was that of Scotland's Dale Greig registering 3 hr. 27 min. 25 sec., that by 1980 the record would be over an hour faster—set in a race (the New York City Marathon) in which the 14,000 runners would include some two thousand women!

Our sport is expanding rapidly in all directions. The jogging and fun-running boom is greatly to be welcomed, as it symbolises the need by so many to return to the basics of healthy recreation; and other encouraging growth areas have been among schoolchildren at one end of the spectrum and Veterans (or Masters as they are known in the USA) at the other. At the highest international level, too, there have been many changes. Innovations since 1964 include the European Cup, World Cup, European Indoor Championships and International Cross-Country Championships for women, with the exciting prospect of World Track and Field Championships to come in 1983. On the British domestic level the advent of significant league and cup competitions has changed the structure of club athletics. All-weather competition surfaces, more sophisticated equipment and coaching, increasingly intensive training and more liberal attitudes towards athletes receiving financial support, are among the factors which have contributed to the incessant rise in standards.

Unhappily, though, there is a dark shadow over the sport . . . cast by drugs. Back in 1964 the use of drugs by athletes was practically unknown; now it is depressingly widespread and apparently growing all the time. The International Amateur Athletic Federation, as the world governing body, must accept some of the blame, for despite instituting dope control tests which have caught out many offenders the penalties meted out have been so mild as to have been no real deterrent at all. Much tougher measures are required if the fight against drug abuse is to be won—and it *must* be won. The taking of drugs to enhance athletic performance and training loads is a negation of all that athletics stands for, and those seeking to gain an unfair advantage may be irreparably damaging not only their own bodies but the sport which they would purport to love.

All material in the book has been brought completely up to date, as at May 1981, and I have attempted to strike a balance in the content between British and international, historical and topical. The 150 biographies scattered throughout the book include all the 1980 Olympic champions and current world record holders in the standard international events but the 'greats' of earlier eras—athletes like Walter George, Jim Thorpe, Paavo Nurmi, Jesse Owens, Cornelius Warmerdam, Emil Zatopek, Fanny Blankers-Koen and Roger Bannister—have not been neglected. A new feature, which I hope will be of interest, can be found in the appendix: a selection of prominent athletes who have gone on to make a name for themselves in other fields of endeavour, and of other famous figures who achieved some athletic distinction in their younger days.

MEL WATMAN

London
May 1981

ABEBE BIKILA (Ethiopia)

The first man ever to have made a successful defence of an Olympic marathon title, Abebe Bikila is still considered the greatest road runner of all time. Previously unheard of outside his own country, he created the biggest upset of the 1960 Olympic Games by winning, barefoot (" just to make history "), in a world's best time of 2 hr. 15 min. 16.2 sec. It transpired that this was his third marathon in three months, having recorded 2 hr. 39 min. 50 sec. in July and 2 hr. 21 min. 23 sec. in August at high altitude.

Four years later, in Tokyo (wearing shoes this time), he produced an even more astonishing performance by defeating the best the world could offer by a margin of over four minutes (three-quarters of a mile) in another world's best of 2 hr. 12 min. 11.2 sec.—an average of about 5 min. 2 sec. per mile for the 26 mi. 385 yd. course. Severe pains in his left leg forced him to drop out of the 1968 Olympic event after about 10 miles, a race won by Ethiopian team-mate Mamo Wolde. Tragically, he received spinal injuries in a car crash in 1969 which paralysed him from the waist down, and he died of a brain haemorrhage on Oct. 25th, 1973, aged only 41. He was born at Mout on Aug. 7th, 1932.

ABRAHAMS, Harold (GB)

In the world of athletics, Harold Abrahams distinguished himself in at least five spheres: as an active athlete, administrator, writer, broadcaster and statistician. His greatest success on the track occurred in 1924 when he won the Olympic 100 m. title—the first European and only Englishman to achieve that honour. Sprinting in an inspired fashion, he proceeded within the space of 26 hours to equal the Olympic record of 10.6 sec. in the second-round heat, semi-final (despite a dreadful start) and final. That was appreciably faster than anything he accomplished before or after the Paris Games.

One month before the Olympics, on the same day that he ran 100 yds. in a wind-assisted 9.6 sec., he long jumped 7.38 metres—a mark that stood as an English native record for 32 years. Other personal bests included 9.9 sec. for 100 yd., 21.6 sec. for 220 yd. (straight), 22.0 sec. for 200m. (turn) and 50.8 sec. for 440yd. His active career was cut short in 1925 when he broke his leg long jumping.

A leading official since 1926, he was chairman of the British Amateur Athletic Board from 1968 to 1975. In November 1976 a lifelong ambition was fulfilled when he was elected president of the AAA. Sadly he did not live to celebrate the Association's centenary in 1980 for he died on Jan. 14th, 1978.

ACKERMANN, Rosemarie (East Germany)

Prior to being bedevilled by injury, Rosi Ackermann (née Witschas) could point to a consistently brilliant record in major international high jump events. For four seasons she reigned supreme: indoors she won the European title three years running (1974–76); outdoors, she was 1974 European and 1976 Olympic champion and was winner also in the European Cup Finals of 1975 and 1977 as well as the inaugural World Cup in 1977. She made further history that year when, adding 3 cm. to her own world record, she became the first woman to jump two metres—24 cm. above her own head.

Her first significant defeat occurred at the 1978 European Championships, less than a year after an achilles tendon operation. After several seasons of playing second fiddle, Italy's Sara Simeoni at last came into her own. She equalled her pending world record of 2.01 metres to clinch the title in

Prague, with Rosi straddling a valiant 1.99 metres for second place . . . and coming within a whisker of clearing 2.01 herself.

Next year, Rosi made an even more astonishing comeback following further severe injury when, in the European Cup Final, she comfortably defeated Sara with a 1.99 metres leap, but the magic was no longer there when she sought to defend her Olympic title in Moscow. She finished fourth as Sara Simeoni lifted the crown. Rosi, who announced her retirement after the Games, was also a good sprinter (11.9 100 m.) and long jumper (6.23 metres). She was born at Lohsa on Apr. 4th, 1952.

AFRICAN GAMES and CHAMPIONSHIPS

African Games were inaugurated in Brazzaville (Congo) in 1965. The second edition, to have been held in Mali in 1969, was cancelled and the Games were not staged again until 1973, in Lagos. Algiers was the host city in 1978 and the next Games are scheduled for 1982. In order to provide more frequent major competition for the continent's top athletes, and serve also as team trials for the World Cup, African Championships—to be held every other year—were begun in 1979, Dakar (Senegal) being the first venue.

100 Metres		sec.
1965	G. Kone (Ivory Coast)	10.3
1973	O. Karikari (Ghana)	10.6
1978	A. Meite (Ivory Coast)	10.35
1979	E. Obeng (Ghana)	10.54

200 Metres		sec.
1965	G. Kone (Ivory Coast)	21.1
1973	O. Karikari (Ghana)	21.1
1978	K. Hassan (Sudan)	20.77
1979	E. Ofili (Nigeria)	20.90

400 Metres		sec.
1965	W. Kiprugut (Kenya)	46.9
1973	C. Asati (Kenya)	46.3
1978	K. Hassan (Sudan)	45.23
1979	K. Hassan (Sudan)	45.34

800 Metres		min. sec.
1965	W. Kiprugut (Kenya)	1 47.4
1973	C. Silei (Kenya)	1 45.3
1978	J. Maina (Kenya)	1 47.1
1979	J. Maina (Kenya)	1 48.8

1500 Metres		min. sec.
1965	K. Keino (Kenya)	3 41.1
1973	F. Bayi (Tanzania)	3 37.2
1978	F. Bayi (Tanzania)	3 36.2
1979	M. Boit (Kenya)	3 39.9

5000 Metres		min. sec.
1965	K. Keino (Kenya)	13 44.4
1973	B. Jipcho (Kenya)	14 07.2
1978	Y. Mohamed (Eth.)	13 44.4
1979	M. Yifter (Eth.)	14 14.0

10,000 Metres		min. sec.
1973	M. Yifter (Eth.)	29 04.6
1978	H. Rono (Kenya)	27 58.9
1979	M. Yifter (Eth.)	29 08.0

Marathon		hr. min. sec.
1973	Mamo Wolde (Eth.)	2 27 32
1978	R. Mabuza (Swaz.)	2 21 53
1979	R. Balcha (Eth.)	2 29 53

3000 m. Steeplechase		min. sec.
1965	B. Kogo (Kenya)	8 47.4
1973	B. Jipcho (Kenya)	8 20.8
1978	H. Rono (Kenya)	8 15.8
1979	K. Rono (Kenya)	8 30.9

110 Metres Hurdles		sec.
1965	F. Erinle (Nigeria)	14.6
1973	F. Kimaiyo (Kenya)	14.1
1978	F. Kimaiyo (Kenya)	13.89
1979	G. Obasogie (Nigeria)	13.76

400 Metres Hurdles		sec.
1965	K. Songok (Kenya)	51.7
1973	J. Akii-Bua (Uganda)	48.5
1978	D. Kimaiyo (Kenya)	49.48
1979	D. Kimaiyo (Kenya)	50.05

4 x 100 Metres		sec.
1965	Senegal	40.5
1973	Nigeria	39.8
1978	Ghana	39.24
1979	Ivory Coast	39.80

4 x 400 Metres		min. sec.
1965	Senegal	3 11.5
1973	Kenya	3 06.3
1978	Nigeria	3 03.2
1979	Kenya	3 08.2

High Jump		metres
1965	S. Igun (Nigeria)	2.07
1973	A. Wasughe (Somalia)	2.04
1978	N. Gadjadoum (Chad)	2.16
1979	O. Belfaa (Algeria)	2.13

AFRICAN GAMES

Pole Vault — metres
1965 B. Elloe (Ivory C.) 4.15
1973 A. Gheita (Egypt) 4.65
1978 L. Rahal (Algeria) 5.00
1979 M. Ben Saad (Algeria) 4.70

Long Jump — metres
1965 E. Akika (Nigeria) 7.49
1973 J. Owusu (Ghana) 8.00
1978 C. Ehizuelen (Nigeria) 7.92
1979 A. Agbebaku (Nigeria) 7.94

Triple Jump — metres
1965 S. Igun (Nigeria) 16.27
1973 M. Dia (Senegal) 16.53
1978 C. Ehizuelen (Nigeria) 16.51
1979 A. Agbebaku (Nigeria) 16.82

Shot — metres
1965 S. Kragbe (Ivory Coast) 16.32
1973 N. Asaad (Egypt) 19.48
1978 N. Asaad (Egypt) 18.88
1979 N. Asaad (Egypt) 20.32

Discus — metres
1965 N. Niare (Mali) 51.20
1973 N. Niare (Mali) 55.28
1978 N. Niare (Mali) 58.02
1979 A. Ben Hassine (Tunisia) 54.60

Hammer — metres
1973 Y. Ochola (Uganda) 50.64
1978 J. Benabid (Tunisia) 54.90
1979 A. Boubekeur (Algeria) 56.02

Javelin — metres
1965 A. Oyakhire (Nigeria) 71.52
1973 A. Abehi (Ivory Coast) 77.22
1978 J. Arop (Uganda) 76.94
1979 J. Aye (Ivory Coast) 76.74

Decathlon — Pts.
1978 M. Ben Saad (Algeria) 7338
1979 M. Ben Saad (Algeria) 7140

10,000 m. Walk — min. sec.
1979 B. Kachkouche (Alg.) 48 50.8

20,000 m. Walk — hr. min. sec.
1978 B. Kachkouche (Alg.) 1 39 21

WOMEN'S EVENTS

100 Metres — sec.
1965 J. Bodunrin (Nigeria) 12.4
1973 A. Annum (Ghana) 11.7
1978 H. Afriyie (Ghana) 11.50
1979 O. Nsenu (Nigeria) 11.53

200 Metres — Sec.
1973 A. Annum (Ghana) 23.8
1978 H. Afriyie (Ghana) 23.01
1979 H. Afriyie (Ghana) 23.81

400 Metres — sec.
1973 T. Chemabwai (Kenya) 54.0
1978 K. Vaughan (Nigeria) 53.86
1979 G. Bakari (Ghana) 53.33

800 Metres — min. sec.
1973 C. Anyakun (Uganda) 2 09.5
1978 T. Chemabwai (Kenya) 2 04.8
1979 M. Chemweno (Kenya) 2 08.4

1500 Metres — min. sec.
1973 P. Kesiime (Uganda) 4 38.7
1978 S. Boutamine (Algeria) 4 16.4
1979 S. Boutamine (Algeria) 4 23.6

3000 Metres — min. sec.
1979 S. Boutamine (Algeria) 9 31.1

80 Metres Hurdles — sec.
1965 R. Hart (Ghana) 11.7

100 Metres Hurdles — sec.
1973 M. Oshikoya (Nigeria) 14.2
1978 J. Bell-Gam (Nigeria) 13.67
1979 J. Bell-Gam (Nigeria) 14.13

400 Metres Hurdles — sec.
1979 F. Elfaquir (Morocco) 59.73

4 x 100 Metres — sec.
1965 Nigeria 48.0
1973 Ghana 46.2
1978 Nigeria 44.63
1979 Ghana 45.63

4 x 400 Metres — min. sec.
1973 Uganda 3 45.4
1978 Ghana 3 35.6
1979 Ghana 3 41.8

High Jump — metres
1965 A. Okoli (Nigeria) 1.62
1973 M. Oshikoya (Nigeria) 1.71
1978 M. Oshikoya (Nigeria) 1.77
1979 K. Akremi (Tunisia) 1.69

Long Jump — metres
1965 A. Annum (Ghana) 5.63
1973 M. Oshikoya (Nigeria) 6.15
1978 M. Oshikoya (Nigeria) 6.32
1979 B. Bell-Gam (Nigeria) 6.24

Shot		metres
1973	E. Okeke (Nigeria)	13.59
1978	J. Aciro (Uganda)	14.47
1979	O. Mistoul (Gabon)	13.45

Discus		metres
1973	R. Hart (Ghana)	41.06
1978	F. Jerbi (Tunisia)	46.56
1979	Z. Laayouni (Morocco)	46.18

Javelin		metres
1965	H. Okwara (Nigeria)	40.28
1973	C. Rwabiryage (Uganda)	47.50
1978	E. Nekesa (Kenya)	51.58
1979	A. Tchuinte (Camer.)	50.20

Pentathlon		Pts.
1978	B. Bell-Gam (Nigeria)	3709
1979	B. Bell-Gam (Nigeria)	3607

AKII-BUA, John (Uganda)

In spite of the disadvantage of being drawn in the sharp inside lane, a handicap in particular for a man who hurdles with a right-leg lead, John Akii-Bua not only won the 1972 Olympic 400 metres hurdles title in Munich but smashed David Hemery's prestigious world record into the bargain. The lanky Ugandan was timed in an astonishing 47.82 sec., as against the British athlete's 48.12 sec. recorded under the advantageous altitude conditions of Mexico City. He won the race by the wide margin of 0.7 sec. from Ralph Mann (USA) and Hemery.

One of 43 children (his father had eight wives), Akii-Bua took up hurdling in 1967, but it was not until 1970 that he turned seriously to the 400 m. hurdles. He quickly made an impact, finishing fourth in that year's Commonwealth Games, and the following season he won for Africa in a match against the USA in 49.0 sec., the world's second fastest time in 1971.

He topped the world rankings in 1973 with 48.5 sec. but did not compete in the Commonwealth Games early in 1974. Lacking in motivation during the intervening years it was not until the 1976 Olympics came into focus that he shaped up again as a prospective world beater, but the African withdrawal from Montreal dashed hopes of retaining his crown. In his absence, Edwin Moses (USA) seized the title . . . and Akii-Bua's world record too.

Fortunate to escape with his life from Idi Amin's crumbling regime in Uganda, he settled in West Germany in 1979 and, although far from his old form, he reached the Olympic semi-finals in Moscow.

A fine all-rounder, he has run 400 m. in 45.8 sec., clocked a wind-assisted 13.8 sec. for 110 m. hurdles and scored 6,933 pts. in his decathlon debut. He was born at Kampala on Dec. 3rd, 1949.

ALTITUDE

The effect of competing at high altitude was brought home vividly for the first time in 1955 when the Pan-American Games were held in Mexico City, at an elevation of 7,347 ft. The world records for the 400 m. and triple jump were shattered, and sprint and long jump performances were much better than expected. On the other hand, the star American miler, Wes Santee, was sensationally defeated in a slow race by a South American runner who was more familiar with such conditions, and all the long distance events were won in extremely poor times.

The reason for this disparity in performances is that at such an altitude the air is approximately 23 per cent thinner than at sea level. The consequent reduction in air resistance is favourable to sprinters and jumpers, whereas the shortage of oxygen adversely affects athletes in the endurance events (1500 m. upwards).

Long distance runners born and resident at high altitude are able to run more efficiently in those conditions than their lowland rivals—as was proved at the 1968 Olympics in Mexico City. There, such athletes from Kenya, Mexico and Ethiopia placed 1st in the 1,500 m., 2nd, 3rd and 4th in the 5,000 m., 1st, 2nd and 4th in the 10.000 m., 1st in the marathon, and 1st and 2nd in the steeplechase. Mohamed Gammoudi (Tunisia), the 5,000 m. winner, had spent considerable time training at altitude in the French Pyrenees, which helped reduce his physiological disadvantage. An unacclimatised Ron Clarke (Australia), world record holder for both events, could finish only 5th in the 5,000 m. and 6th in the 10,000 m.

The reduced air resistance contributed towards world record performances at the Games in the 100 m., 200 m., 400 m., 400 m. hurdles, 4 x 100 m. relay, 4 x 400 m. relay, long jump, triple jump and women's 100 m., 200 m., 4 x 100 m. relay and long jump.

The most astonishing feat was American Bob Beamon's long jump of 8.90 metres, a record which could survive into the 21st century. Another futuristic record was accomplished in the same stadium seven years later when Joao Carlos de Oliveira (Brazil) triple jumped 17.89 metres in the Pan-American Games, and it was in Mexico City that Italy's Pietro Mennea set a world 200 m. record of 19.72 sec. at the 1979 World University Games.

AMATEUR ATHLETIC ASSOCIATION

The AAA, which was founded in Oxford on Apr. 24th, 1880, is the governing body for men's athletics in England and Wales.

Championships

The annual AAA Championships, which have long served as the unofficial British Championships, were inaugurated at Lillie Bridge Grounds, London, on July 3rd, 1880. Previously, " English Championships " were promoted by the Amateur Athletic Club from 1866 to 1879.

The longest sequence of foreign successes in any one event occurred in the shot-put from 1927 to 1948 inclusive. During this period, the luckless Robert Howland filled second place on eight occasions!

That graceful and consistent sprinter from Trinidad, E. McDonald Bailey, holds the " record " for the greatest number of AAA titles. Excluding relays, he gained 14 victories between 1946 and 1953.

The most wins in one event is 13 by the Irish shot-putter Denis Horgan between 1893 and 1912.

Four is the highest total of championships gained in one year—by Walter George in 1882 and 1884 (880 yd., mile, 4 mi. and 10 mi.) and by William Snook in 1885 (mile, 4 mi., 10 mi. and steeplechase).

Five men have won a title seven years running: Denis Horgan (shot, 1893-99), Don Finlay (120 yd. hurdles, 1932-38), Bert Cooper (2 mi. walk, 1932-38), Harry Whittle (440 yd. hurdles, 1947-53) and Maurice Herriott (3,000 m. steeplechase, 1961-67).

Harry Edward, from British Guiana, took the 100, 220 and 440 yd. within an hour in 1922.

The Championships went metric in 1969 and moved to their present home at Crystal Palace in 1970.

For list of AAA champions from 1880 to 1955, see previous editions of this book.

100 Yards sec.
1956 J. R. C. Young 9.9
1957 K. J. Box 10.0
1958 J. S. O. Omagbemi
 (Nigeria) 9.9
1959 P. F. Radford 9.7
1960 P. F. Radford 9.7
1961 H. W. Jerome (Canada) 9.6
1962 S. Antao (Kenya) 9.8
1963 T. B. Jones 9.7
1964 E. Figuerola (Cuba) 9.4
1965 E. Figuerola (Cuba) 9.6
1966 P. Nash (S. Africa) 9.6
1967 B. H. Kelly 9.9
1968 P. Nash (S. Africa) 9.9

100 Metres
1969 R. Jones 10.7
1970 R. G. Symonds
 (Bermuda) 10.3
1971 B. W. Green 10.6
1972 V. Papageorgopoulos
 (Greece) 10.2
1973 D. G. Halliday 10.6
1974 S. Williams (USA) 10.2
1975 S. Riddick (USA) 10.39
1976 D. Quarrie (Jamaica) 10.42
1977 C. Edwards (USA) 10.48
1978 J. Sanford (USA) 10.42
1979 C. Edwards (USA) 10.35
1980 A. W. Wells 10.36

220 Yards sec.
1956 B. Shenton 21.8
1957 D. H. Segal 21.9
1958 D. H. Segal 21.4
1959 D. H. Jones 21.7
1960 D. H. Jones 21.3
1961 D. H. Jones 21.4
1962 S. Antao (Kenya) 21.1
1963 D. H. Jones 21.3
1964 W. M. Campbell 21.1
1965 P. J. A. Morrison 21.8

1966	P. Nash (S. Africa)	21.2
1967	W. M. Campbell	21.4
1968	P. Nash (S. Africa)	21.2

200 Metres

1969	D. G. Dear	21.4
1970	M. E. Reynolds	21.0
1971	A. P. Pascoe	21.1
1972	A. P. Pascoe	20.9
1973	C. L. Monk	21.1
1974	M. Lutz (USA)	20.9
1975	S. Riddick (USA)	20.81
1976	D. Quarrie (Jamaica)	20.35
1977	C. Edwards (USA)	21.05
1978	D. Quarrie (Jamaica)	20.79
1979	C. Edwards (USA)	20.77
1980	M. Lattany (USA)	20.74

440 Yards

		sec.
1956	M. K. V. Wheeler	47.7
1957	F. P. Higgins	47.6
1958	J. E. Salisbury	47.2
1959	J. D. Wrighton	47.5
1960	Milkha Singh (India)	46.5
1961	A. P. Metcalfe	47.6
1962	R. I. Brightwell	45.9
1963	A. P. Metcalfe	47.3
1964	R. I. Brightwell	47.5
1965	M. D. Larrabee (USA)	47.6
1966	W. Mottley (Trinidad)	45.9
1967	T. J. M. Graham	46.6
1968	M. J. Winbolt Lewis	46.9

400 Metres

1969	D. G. Griffiths	46.8
1970	M. Bilham	46.6
1971	D. A. Jenkins	47.1
1972	D. A. Jenkins	45.4
1973	D. A. Jenkins	46.4
1974	D. A. Jenkins	46.1
1975	D. A. Jenkins	45.87
1976	D. A. Jenkins	45.86
1977	T. Andrews (USA)	46.00
1978	M. Peoples (USA)	45.78
1979	K. Hassan (Sudan)	45.82
1980	R. B. W. Milne	46.53

880 Yards

		min. sec.
1956	M. A. Rawson	1 51.3
1957	R. Delany (Ireland)	1 49.6
1958	B. S. Hewson	1 48.3
1959	B. S. Hewson	1 52.0
1960	T. S. Farrell	1 49.3
1961	G. E. Kerr (Jamaica)	1 51.5
1962	C. Weisiger (USA)	1 50.1
1963	N. Carroll (Ireland)	1 50.3
1964	W. F. Crothers (Canada)	1 50.1
1965	T. F. Farrell (USA)	1 49.5
1966	N. Carroll (Ireland)	1 48.0
1967	J. P. Boulter	1 47.3
1968	N. Carroll (Ireland)	1 50.0

800 Metres

		min. sec.
1969	D. Cropper	1 49.0
1970	A. W. Carter	1 49.6
1971	P. M. Browne	1 47.5
1972	A. W. Carter	1 48.2
1973	A. W. Carter	1 45.1
1974	S. M. J. Ovett	1 46.8
1975	S. M. J. Ovett	1 46.1
1976	S. M. J. Ovett	1 47.3
1977	M. Savic (Yugoslavia)	1 46.3
1978	T. McLean (USA)	1 48.5
1979	S. Scott (USA)	1 47.4
1980	O. Khalifa (Sudan)	1 47.5

Mile

		min. sec.
1956	K. Wood	4 06.8
1957	B. S. Hewson	4 06.7
1958	G. E. Everett	4 06.4
1959	K. Wood	4 08.1
1960	L. Tabori (Hungary/USA)	4 01.0
1961	M. Bernard (France)	4 05.8
1962	S. G. Taylor	4 04.8
1963	A. Simpson	4 04.9
1964	A. Simpson	4 01.1
1965	A. Simpson	4 01.9
1966	J. Camien (USA)	4 01.1
1967	A. R. Green	4 00.6
1968	J. Whetton	4 06.0
1980	S. M. J. Ovett	4 04.4

1500 Metres

		min. sec.
1969	F. Murphy (Ireland)	3 40.9
1970	W. Wilkinson	3 45.3
1971	A. Polhill (NZ)	3 40.3
1972	P. J. Stewart	3 38.2
1973	R. Dixon (NZ)	3 39.0
1974	A. Waldrop (USA)	3 41.9
1975	D. Malan (S. Africa)	3 38.1
1976	R. Dixon (NZ)	3 41.4
1977	E. Coghlan (Ireland)	3 43.0
1978	D. R. Moorcroft	3 42.9
1979	S. M. J. Ovett	3 39.1

3 Miles

		min. sec.
1956	G. D. Ibbotson	13 32.6
1957	G. D. Ibbotson	13 20.8
1958	S. E. Eldon	13 22.4
1959	M. B. S. Tulloh	13 31.2
1960	F. G. J. Salvat	13 33.0
1961	D. A. G. Pirie	13 31.2
1962	M. B. S. Tulloh	13 16.0
1963	M. B. S. Tulloh	13 23.8
1964	L. Boguszewicz (Poland)	13 24.4
1965	R. W. Clarke (Australia)	12 52.4
1966	R. W. Clarke (Australia)	12 58.2

1967	R. W. Clarke (Australia)		
		12	59.6
1968	J. L. Stewart	13	28.4

5,000 Metres		min.	sec.
1969	I. Stewart	13	39.8
1970	C. R. Stewart	13	49.6
1971	M. I. Baxter	13	39.6
1972	D. C. Bedford	13	17.2
1973	B. Foster	13	23.8
1974	B. Foster	13	27.4
1975	M. Liquori (USA)	13	32.6
1976	B. Foster	13	33.0
1977	D. J. Black	13	33.2
1978	H. Rono (Kenya)	13	20.8
1979	E. Coghlan (Ireland)	13	23.6
1980	H. Hudak (W. Germ.)	13	51.8

6 Miles		min.	sec.
1956	K. L. Norris	28	13.6
1957	G. Knight	28	50.4
1958	S. E. Eldon	28	05.0
1959	S. E. Eldon	28	12.4
1960	D. A. G. Pirie	28	09.6
1961	W. D. Power (Australia)	27	57.8
1962	H. R. Fowler	27	49.8
1963	R. Hill	27	49.8
1964	M. J. Bullivant	27	26.6
1965	M. Gammoudi (Tunisia)	27	38.2
1966	M. Gammoudi (Tunisia)	27	23.4
1967	J. Haase (E. Germany)	27	33.2
1968	T. F. K. Johnston	27	22.2

10,000 Metres		min.	sec.
1969	R. G. Taylor	28	27.6
1970	D. C. Bedford	28	26.4
1971	D. C. Bedford	27	47.0
1972	D. C. Bedford	27	52.8
1973	D. C. Bedford	27	30.8
1974	D. C. Bedford	28	14.8
1975	D. J. Black	27	54.2
1976	G. Tebroke (Netherlands)	28	04.0
1977	B. Foster	27	45.7
1978	B. Foster	27	30.3
1979	J. Treacy (Ireland)	28	12.1
1980	N. H. Rose	28	12.0

10 Miles		min.	sec.
1958	F. Norris	49	39.0
1959	F. Norris	48	32.4
1960	B. B. Heatley	48	18.4
1961	B. B. Heatley	47	47.0
1962	L. G. Edelen (USA)	48	31.8
1963	M. R. Batty	48	13.4
1964	M. R. Batty	47	26.8
1965	R. Hill	48	56.0
1966	R. Hill	50	04.0
1967	R. Hill	47	38.6
1968	R. Hill	47	02.2
1969	R. Hill	47	27.0
1970	T. Wright	47	20.2
1971	T. Wright	46	51.6
1972	B. J. Plain	48	25.8
	(discontinued)		

Marathon		hr. min. sec.		
1956	H. J. Hicks	2	26	15.0
1957	E. Kirkup	2	22	27.8
1958	C. K. Kemball	2	22	27.4
1959	J. C. Fleming-Smith	2	30	11.6
1960	B. L. Kilby	2	22	48.8
1961	B. L. Kilby	2	24	37.0
1962	B. L. Kilby	2	26	15.0
1963	B. L. Kilby	2	16	45.0
1964	B. L. Kilby	2	23	01.0
1965	W. A. Adcocks	2	16	50.0
1966	G. A. H. Taylor	2	19	04.0
1967	J. N. C. Alder	2	16	08.0
1968	T. F. K. Johnston	2	15	26.0
1969	R. Hill	2	13	42.0
1970	D. K. Faircloth	2	18	15.0
1971	R. Hill	2	12	39.0
1972	L. Philipp (W. Germany)	2	12	50.0
1973	I. R. Thompson	2	12	40.0
1974	A. Usami (Japan)	2	15	16.0
1975	G. J. Norman	2	15	50.0
1976	B. J. Watson	2	15	08.0
1977	D. A. Cannon	2	15	02.0
1978	A. D. Simmons	2	12	33.0
1979	G. P. Hannon	2	13	06.0
1980	I. R. Thompson	2	14	00.0

3000 Metres Steeplechase		min.	sec.
1956	E. Shirley	8	51.6
1957	J. I. Disley	8	56.8
1958	E. Shirley	8	51.0
1959	M. Herriott	8	52.8
1960	E. Shirley	8	51.0
1961	M. Herriott	8	53.6
1962	M. Herriott	8	43.8
1963	M. Herriott	8	47.8
1964	M. Herriott	8	40.0
1965	M. Herriott	8	41.0
1966	M. Herriott	8	37.0
1967	M. Herriott	8	33.8
1968	D. G. Bryan-Jones	8	36.2
1969	J. M. Jackson	8	35.0
1970	J. A. Holden	8	38.0
1971	J. A. Holden	8	38.0
1972	S. C. Hollings	8	31.2
1973	S. C. Hollings	8	30.8
1974	J. Davies	8	26.8
1975	A. R. Staynings	8	30.0
1976	A. R. Staynings	8	34.6
1977	D. M. Coates	8	28.3
1978	D. M. Coates	8	34.4
1979	H. Tuwei (Kenya)	8	23.7
1980	R. Hackney	8	39.4

120 Yards Hurdles

Year	Athlete	sec.
1956	P. B. Hildreth	14.5
1957	E. F. Kinsella (Ireland)	14.7
1958	K. A. St. H. Gardner (Jamaica)	14.1
1959	V. C. Matthews	14.5
1960	H. G. Raziq (Pakistan)	14.6
1961	N. Svara (Italy)	14.4
1962	B. Lindgren (USA)	14.2
1963	J. L. Taitt	14.1
1964	J. M. Parker	14.2
1965	J. L. Taitt	14.3
1966	D. P. Hemery	14.0
1967	E. Ottoz (Italy)	14.0
1968	A. P. Pascoe	14.1

110 Metres Hurdles

Year	Athlete	sec.
1969	W. Coetzee (S. Africa)	14.0
1970	D. P. Hemery	13.9
1971	A. P. Pascoe	14.5
1972	A. P. Pascoe	13.9
1973	B. Price	14.1
1974	B. Price	13.9
1975	B. Price	13.94
1976	B. Price	13.80
1977	B. Price	14.17
1978	B. Price	14.14
1979	J. M. Holtom	13.78
1980	R. Milburn (USA)	13.69

220 Yards Hurdles

Year	Athlete	sec.
1956	P. A. L. Vine	24.5
1957	J. R. A. Scott-Oldfield	24.2
1958	K. S. D. Wilmshurst	24.3
1959	J. Metcalf	23.8
1960	C. W. E. Surety	24.9
1961	S. Morale (Italy)	23.9
1962	B. Lindgren (USA) (discontinued)	23.9

440 Yards Hurdles

Year	Athlete	sec.
1956	I. Savel (Romania)	52.2
1957	T. S. Farrell	52.1
1958	D. F. Lean (Australia)	51.2
1959	C. E. Goudge	52.7
1960	M. G. Boyes	52.2
1961	J. A. Rintamaki (Finland)	51.5
1962	R. Rogers (USA)	51.0
1963	W. Atterberry (USA)	51.2
1964	J. H. Cooper	51.1
1965	W. J. Cawley (USA)	50.9
1966	J. Sherwood	51.1
1967	J. Sherwood	50.9
1968	D. P. Hemery	50.2

400 Metres Hurdles

Year	Athlete	sec.
1969	J. Sherwood	50.1
1970	R. M. Roberts	52.4
1971	J. Sherwood	51.4
1972	D. P. Hemery	49.7
1973	A. P. Pascoe	49.8
1974	J. Bolding (USA)	49.1
1975	W. J. Hartley	49.65
1976	A. P. Pascoe	49.57
1977	R. Graybehl (USA)	49.96
1978	A. Pascoe	50.39
1979	E. Moses (USA)	48.58
1980	J. King (USA)	49.50

High Jump

Year	Athlete	metres
1956	I. Soeter (Romania)	1.93
1957	O. Okuwobi (Nigeria)	1.95
1958	P. Etolu (Uganda)	2.03
1959	C. W. Fairbrother	2.00
1960	R. E. Kotei (Ghana)	2.08
1961	C. W. Fairbrother	2.05
1962	K. Sugioka (Japan)	2.09
1963	K. Sugioka (Japan)	2.03
1964	C. W. Fairbrother	2.03
1965	K. A. Nilsson (Sweden)	2.03
1966	J. S. O. Kadiri (Nigeria)	1.98
1967	E. Lansdell (S. Africa)	2.00
1968	D. Mendenhall (USA)	2.08
1969	K. Lundmark (Sweden)	2.10
1970	H. Tomizawa (Japan)	2.08
1971	M. C. Campbell	2.04
1972	M. Jarmrich (West Germany)	2.08
1973	C. Dunn (USA)	2.06
1974	D. Stones (USA)	2.14
1975	R. Schiel (S. Africa)	2.10
1976	M. G. Palmer	2.06
1977	A. R. Dainton	2.14
1978	F. Jacobs (USA)	2.20
1979	T. Sakamoto (Japan)	2.15
1980	C. Thranhardt (W. Germ.)	2.23

Pole Vault

Year	Athlete	metres
1956	I. Ward	3.96
1957	I. Ward	4.09
1958	M. D. Richards (New Zealand)	4.11
1959	A. Ditta (Pakistan)	4.11
1960	S. R. Porter	4.11
1961	R. Ankio (Finland)	4.42
1962	P. K. Nikula (Finland)	4.65
1963	J. T. Pennel (USA)	5.10
1964	F. Hansen (USA)	4.57
1965	P. Wilson (USA)	4.72
1966	M. A. Bull	4.57
1967	M. A. Bull	4.57
1968	R. Dionisi (Italy)	5.03
1969	M. A. Bull	4.73
1970	K. Niwa (Japan)	5.00
1971	M. A. Bull	5.05
1972	M. A. Bull	5.21
1973	B. R. L. Hooper	5.16
1974	C. Carrigan (USA)	5.10
1975	R. Boyd (Australia)	5.00
1976	M. Tully (USA)	5.33

Year	Athlete	Mark
1977	L. Jessee (USA)	5.30
1978	R. Pullard (USA)	5.40
1979	M. Tully (USA)	5.45
1980	B. R. L. Hooper	5.59

Long Jump — metres

Year	Athlete	Mark
1956	A. R. Cruttenden	7.25
1957	A. R. Cruttenden	7.26
1958	K. A. B. Olowu (Nigeria)	7.28
1959	D. J. Whyte	7.24
1960	F. J. Alsop	7.19
1961	O. Oladitan (Nigeria)	7.41
1962	J. R. Valkama (Finland)	7.65
1963	F. J. Alsop	7.52
1964	L. Davies	7.95
1965	F. J. Alsop	7.38
1966	L. Davies	8.06
1967	L. Davies	7.93
1968	L. Davies	7.94
1969	L. Davies	7.62
1970	A. L. Lerwill	7.64
1971	H. Hines (USA)	8.01
1972	A. L. Lerwill	8.15
1973	G. J. Hignett	7.37
1974	A. L. Lerwill	7.77
1975	A. L. Lerwill	7.77
1976	R. R. Mitchell	7.93
1977	F. M. Thompson	7.52
1978	R. R. Mitchell	7.76
1979	R. Desruelles (Belgium)	7.95
1980	A. Robinson (USA)	7.92

Triple Jump — metres

Year	Athlete	Mark
1956	K. S. D. Wilmshurst	15.16
1957	K. S. D. Wilmshurst	14.86
1958	D. S. Norris (New Zealand)	15.64
1959	J. E. C. Whall	15.00
1960	F. J. Alsop	15.44
1961	F. J. Alsop	15.37
1962	T. Ota (Japan)	15.66
1963	K. Sakurai (Japan)	15.63
1964	F. J. Alsop	15.92
1965	F. J. Alsop	15.88
1966	J. Szmidt (Poland)	15.99
1967	F. J. Alsop	15.67
1968	S. Ciochina (Romania)	16.03
1969	A. E. Wadhams	15.66
1970	M. Muraki (Japan)	15.91
1971	A. E. Wadhams	15.16
1972	D. C. Johnson	15.80
1973	A. E. Wadhams	15.76
1974	T. Inoue (Japan)	16.12
1975	M. McGrath (Australia)	16.12
1976	A. L. Moore	16.30
1977	D. C. Johnson	16.07
1978	A. L. Moore	16.68
1979	K. L. Connor	15.87
1980	P. Jordan (USA)	16.49

Shot — metres

Year	Athlete	Mark
1956	W. B. L. Palmer	16.51
1957	A. Rowe	16.38
1958	A. Rowe	17.30
1959	A. Rowe	17.95
1960	A. Rowe	18.04
1961	A. Rowe	18.58
1962	L. J. Silvester (USA)	18.18
1963	M. R. Lindsay	17.64
1964	V. Varju (Hungary)	18.84
1965	V. Varju (Hungary)	19.02
1966	J. Botha (S. Africa)	17.14
1967	D. Booysen (S. Africa)	17.79
1968	J. Teale	17.74
1969	J. Teale	18.32
1970	L. R. Mills (NZ)	18.66
1971	L. R. Mills (NZ)	19.27
1972	G. L. Capes	19.47
1973	G. L. Capes	20.27
1974	A. Feuerbach (USA)	21.37
1975	G. L. Capes	20.20
1976	G. L. Capes	20.92
1977	G. L. Capes	20.70
1978	G. L. Capes	19.94
1979	G. L. Capes	19.39
1980	B. Oldfield (USA)	21.25

Discus — metres

Year	Athlete	Mark
1956	M. Pharaoh	50.02
1957	M. R. Lindsay	50.76
1958	S. J. du Plessis (S. Africa)	52.22
1959	M. R. Lindsay	53.54
1960	M. R. Lindsay	52.62
1961	E. Malan (S. Africa)	56.04
1962	L. J. Silvester (USA)	60.84
1963	D. Weill (USA)	53.90
1964	R. A. Hollingsworth (Trinidad)	54.82
1965	L. G. Haglund (Sweden)	53.94
1966	W. R. Tancred	51.76
1967	W. R. Tancred	51.74
1968	W. R. Tancred	53.06
1969	W. R. Tancred	53.08
1970	W. R. Tancred	53.88
1971	L. R. Mills (NZ)	58.62
1972	W. R. Tancred	61.06
1973	W. R. Tancred	61.22
1974	J. Powell (USA)	62.06
1975	J. Van Reenen (S. Africa)	62.26
1976	J. Powell (USA)	65.52
1977	P. A. Tancred	57.58
1978	P. A. Tancred	55.78
1979	J. Powell (USA)	61.50
1980	B. Oldfield (USA)	61.46

Hammer — metres

Year	Athlete	Mark
1956	P. C. Allday	57.28
1957	M. J. Ellis	60.28
1958	M. J. Ellis	61.92

AMATEUR ATHLETIC ASSOCIATION

1959	M. J. Ellis	61.28	1964	D. S. Clarke	6084†
1960	M. J. Ellis	64.18	1965	N. Foster	6840
1961	J. F. Lawlor (Ireland)	64.12	1966	D. S. Clarke	7001
1962	N. Okamoto (Japan)	62.18	1967	P. J. Gabbett	6533
1963	T. Sugawara (Japan)	65.56	1968	P. J. Gabbett	7247
1964	A. H. Payne	59.88	1969	P. de Villiers (S. Africa)	6960
1965	G. Zsivotzky (Hungary)	68.14	1970	P. J. Gabbett	7331
1966	G. Zsivotzky (Hungary)	66.04	1971	D. F. Kidner	6691
1967	E. Burke (USA)	67.60	1972	B. J. King	7346
1968	L. Lovasz (Hungary)	66.20	1973	D. F. Kidner	6969
1969	A. H. Payne	66.80	1974	M. Corden	7035
1970	A. H. Payne	67.66	1975	P. Zeniou	6931
1971	A. H. Payne	66.44	1976	F. M. Thompson	7684
1972	B. Williams	67.24	1977	P. Zeniou	7087
1973	A. H. Payne	67.98	1978	A. W. Drayton	7424
1974	A. Barnard (S. Africa)	70.62	1979	B. S. McStravick	7569
1975	A. Barnard (S. Africa)	73.58	1980	B. S. McStravick	7663
1976	C. F. Black	72.64		† Scored on 1950 Tables.	
1977	C. F. Black	69.50	Note: F. M. Thompson won 1975		
1978	P. Farmer (Australia)	70.72	Junior title, held in conjunction with		
1979	P. Farmer (Australia)	70.16	senior, with 7008 pts.		
1980	M. Girvan	68.72			

Javelin		metres	*12 Stage Road Relay*		
1956	P. S. Cullen	65.28	1967	Coventry Godiva H.	
1957	P. S. Cullen	72.12	1968	Coventry Godiva H.	
1958	C. G. Smith	66.48	1969	Coventry Godiva H.	
1959	C. G. Smith	69.90	1970	Coventry Godiva H.	
1960	M. Nawaz (Pakistan)	76.38	1971	Birchfield Harriers	
1961	M. Macquet (France)	77.12	1972	Tipton Harriers	
1962	J. V. McSorley	79.26	1973	Birchfield Harriers	
1963	C. G. Smith	72.46	1974	Tipton Harriers	
1964	J. FitzSimons	74.10	1975	Gateshead Harriers	
1965	D. H. Travis	73.76	1976	Gateshead Harriers	
1966	J. V. P. Kinnunen (Finland)	83.22	1977	Gateshead Harriers	
			1978	Tipton Harriers	
1967	J. B. Sanderson	73.44	1979	Gateshead Harriers	
1968	D. H. Travis	72.16	1980	Bristol AC	
1969	W. Nikiciuk (Poland)	85.08	1981	Tipton Harriers	
1970	D. H. Travis	76.90			
1971	D. H. Travis	77.00	*6 Stage Road Relay*		
1972	D. H. Travis	79.62	1969	City of Stoke AC	
1973	D. H. Travis	73.58	1970	City of Stoke AC	
1974	D. H. Travis	75.20	1971	City of Stoke AC	
1975	H. Potgieter (S. Africa)	78.14	1972	City of Stoke AC	
1976	P. Maync (Switz)	75.16	1973	Bolton United H.	
1977	D. C. Ottley	77.78	1974	Liverpool Harriers	
1978	P. D. Yates	80.10	1975	Liverpool Harriers	
1979	S. R. Osborne	81.68	1976	Liverpool Harriers	
1980	M. Nemeth (Hungary)	83.34	1977	Tipton Harriers	
			1978	Cambridge & Coleridge AC	
Decathlon		Pts.	1979	Bingley Harriers	
1956	A. G. Brown (Rhodesia)	4934†	1980	Tipton Harriers	
1957	H. L. Williams	5370†			
1958	C. J. Andrews	5113†	*2 Miles Walk*		min. sec.
1959	C. J. Andrews	5517†	1956	R. F. Goodall	14 20.8
1960	C. J. Andrews	6176†	1957	S. F. Vickers	14 05.6
1961	M. D. Burger (Rhodesia)	6343†	1958	S. F. Vickers	13 33.4
1962	Z. Sumich (Australia)	6237†	1959	K. J. Matthews	13 19.4
1963	Z. Sumich (Australia)	6538†	1960	S. F. Vickers	13 02.4

1961	K. J. Matthews	13 24.6
1962	K. J. Matthews	13 59.0
1963	K. J. Matthews	13 18.2
1964	K. J. Matthews	13 22.4
1965	V. P. Nihill	13 20.0
1966	R. E. Wallwork	13 35.0
1967	R. E. Wallwork	13 44.8
1968	A. J. Jones	13 35.6

3000 Metres Walk

1969	R. G. Mills	12 57.0
1970	V. P. Nihill	12 13.8
1971	V. P. Nihill	12 08.4
1972	R. G. Mills	12 31.6
1973	R. G. Mills	12 16.8
1974	R. G. Mills	12 27.0
1975	V. P. Nihill	12 43.2
1976	R. G. Mills	12 22.6
1977	R. G. Mills	12 08.4
1978	R. G. Mills	12 05.8
1979	R. G. Mills	12 09.1
1980	S. J. Barry	12 00.5

7 Miles Walk — min. sec.

1956	G. W. Coleman	50 19.0
1957	S. F. Vickers	51 34.4
1958	S. F. Vickers	51 10.2
1959	K. J. Matthews	50 28.8
1960	K. J. Matthews	49 42.6
1961	K. J. Matthews	49 43.6
1962	C. Williams	52 15.0
1963	K. J. Matthews	49 52.8
1964	K. J. Matthews	48 23.0
1965	V. P. Nihill	51 54.4
1966	V. P. Nihill	50 52.0
1967	M. R. Tolley	52 32.4
1968	V. P. Nihill	51 10.4

10,000 Metres Walk

1969	V. P. Nihill	44 07.0
1970	W. M. S. Sutherland	45 16.8
1971	P. B. Embleton	45 26.2
1972	P. B. Embleton	44 26.8
1973	R. G. Mills	44 38.6
1974	P. Marlow	44 58.4
1975	B. Adams	42 40.0
1976	B. Adams	42 58.0
1977	B. Adams	44 10.0
1978	B. Adams	43 44.0
1979	B. Adams	43 48.2
1980	R. G. Mills	43 21.2
1981	S. J. Barry	43 22.4

For indoor champions, see under INDOOR ATHLETICS; for road walking champions, see under WALKING.

AMERICAN CHAMPIONSHIPS
See under UNITED STATES

ANABOLIC STEROIDS
See under DOPING.

ASIAN GAMES

The Asian Games were inaugurated in New Delhi in 1951 and have been held subsequently in Manila (1954), Tokyo (1958), Djakarta (1962), Bangkok (1966 and 1970), Teheran (1974) and Bangkok again in 1978. On this last occasion the IAAF briefly suspended competitors because of the organisers' refusal to invite Israel to compete. Traditional Japanese supremacy was ended in 1978 when China won 12 gold medals to Japan's 10. The next Games will be staged in New Delhi in 1982.

100 Metres — sec.

1951	L. Pinto (India)	10.8
1954	A. Khaliq (Pakistan)	10.6
1958	A. Khaliq (Pak)	10.9
1962	M. Sarengat (Indonesia)	10.5
1966	M. Jegathesan (Malaysia)	10.5
1970	M. Jinno (Japan)	10.5
1974	R. Ratanapol (Thailand)	10.42
1978	S. Chairsuvaparb (Thai)	10.44

200 Metres — sec.

1951	L. Pinto (India)	22.0
1954	M. S. Butt (Pak)	21.9
1958	Milkha Singh (India)	21.6
1962	M. Jegathesan (Malaya)	21.3
1966	M. Jegathesan (Malaysia)	21.5
1970	A. Ratanapol (Thai)	21.1
1974	A. Ratanapol (Thai)	21.09
1978	R. Gnanasekharan (India)	21.42

400 Metres — sec.

1951	E. Okano (Japan)	50.7
1954	K. Akagi (Jap)	48.5
1958	Milkha Singh (India)	47.0
1962	Milkha Singh (India)	46.9
1966	Ajmer Singh (India)	47.1
1970	Y. Tomonaga (Japan)	46.6
1974	W. Wimaladase (Sri Lanka)	46.21
1978	A. Abbas (Iraq)	46.71

800 Metres — min. sec.

1951	Ranjit Singh (India)	1 59.3
1954	Y. Muroya (Jap)	1 54.5
1958	Y. Muroya (Jap)	1 52.1

ASIAN GAMES

1962	M. Morimoto (Jap)	1	52.6
1966	B. S. Barua (India)	1	49.4
1970	J. Crampton (Burma)	1	47.9
1974	Sri Ram Singh (India)	1	47.6
1978	Sri Ram Singh (India)	1	48.8

1500 Metres — min. sec.
1951	Nikka Singh (India)	4	04.1
1954	Yoon Chil Choi (S. Korea)	3	56.2
1958	M. Khaligh (Iran)	3	57.6
1962	Mohinder Singh (India)	3	48.6
1966	K. Sawaki (Japan)	3	47.3
1970	S. Noro (Japan)	3	53.0
1974	M. Younis (Pakistan)	3	49.3
1978	T. Ishii (Japan)	3	47.5

5000 Metres — min. sec
1951	A. Baghbanbashi (Iran)	15	54.2
1954	O. Inoue (Jap)	15	00.2
1958	O. Inoue (Jap)	14	39.4
1962	Mubarak Shah (Pak)	14	27.2
1966	K. Sawaki (Japan)	14	22.0
1970	L. Rosa (Ceylon)	14	32.2
1974	Shivnath Singh (India)	14	20.6
1978	H. Chand (India)	14	22.0

10,000 Metres — min. sec.
1951	S. Tamoi (Jap)	33	49.6
1954	Choi Chung Sik (S. Korea)	33	06.0
1958	T. Baba (Jap)	30	48.4
1962	Tarlok Singh (India)	30	21.4
1966	K. Tsuchiya (Japan)	30	27.2
1970	L. Rosa (Ceylon)	29	55.6
1974	Y. Hamada (Jap)	30	50.0
1978	H. Chand (India)	30	07.7

Marathon — hr. min. sec.
1951	Chhota Singh (India)	2	42	58.6
1954	Not held			
1958	Chang Hoon Lee (S. Korea)	2	32	55.0
1962	M. Nagata (Jap)	2	34	54.2
1966	K. Kimihara (Jap)	2	33	22.8
1970	K. Kimihara (Japan)	2	21	03.0
1974	Not held			
1978	M. Sakamoto (Japan)	2	15	29.7

3000 m. Steeplechase — min. sec.
1951	S. Takahashi (Jap)	9	30.4
1954	S. Takahashi (Jap)	9	15.0
1958	Mubarak Shah (Pak)	9	03.0
1962	Mubarak Shah (Pak)	8	57.8
1966	T. Saruwatari (Jap)	8	53.6
1970	N. Miura (Japan)	8	48.8
1974	T. Koyama (Jap)	8	58.0
1978	M. Shintaku (Japan)	8	40.7

110 Metres Hurdles — sec.
1951	Huang Liang-cheng (Singapore)	15.2
1954	Sarwan Singh (India)	14.7
1958	G. Raziq (Pak)	14.4
1962	M. Sarengat (Indonesia)	14.3
1966	G. Raziq (Pak)	14.4
1970	C. Watanabe (Japan)	14.7
1974	Tsui Lin (China)	14.26
1978	Wang Hsun-hua (China)	14.28

400 Metres Hurdles — sec.
1951	E. Okano (Japan)	54.2
1954	Mirza Khan (Pak)	54.1
1958	Tsai Cheng Fu (Taiwan)	52.4
1962	K. Ogushi (Jap)	52.2
1966	K. Yui (Japan)	51.7
1970	Y. Shigeta (Japan)	52.6
1974	T. F. Al-Saffar (Iraq)	51.69
1978	H. Kadhum (Iraq)	50.81

4 x 100 Metres — sec.
1951	Japan	42.7
1954	Japan	41.2
1958	Philippines	41.4
1962	Philippines	41.3
1966	Malaysia	40.6
1970	Thailand	40.4
1974	Thailand	40.14
1978	Thailand	40.32

4 x 400 Metres — min. sec.
1951	India	3	24.2
1954	Japan	3	17.4
1958	Japan	3	13.9
1962	India	3	10.2
1966	Japan	3	09.1
1970	Japan	3	10.0
1974	Sri Lanka	3	07.4
1978	Japan	3	08.3

High Jump — metres
1951	A. Franco (Phil)	1.95
1954	Ajit Singh (India)	1.95
1958	N. Ethirveerasingam (Ceylon)	2.03
1962	K. Sugioka (Japan)	2.08
1966	Bhim Singh (India)	2.05
1970	T. Ghiassi (Iran)	2.06
1974	T. Ghiassi (Iran)	2.21
1978	T. Sakamoto (Japan)	2.20

Pole Vault — metres
1951	B. Sawada (Jap)	4.11
1954	B. Sawada (Jap)	4.06
1958	N. Yasuda (Jap)	4.20
1962	M. Morita (Jap)	4.40
1966	T. Hirota (Japan)	4.70
1970	K. Inoue (Japan)	4.80
1974	Y. Kigawa (Jap)	5.00

ASIAN GAMES

1978	T. Takahashi (Japan)	5.10

Long Jump — metres
1951	M. Tajima (Jap)	7.14
1954	N. Sagawa (Jap)	7.02
1958	Suh Yang Joo (S. Korea)	7.54
1962	T. Okazaki (Jap)	7.41
1966	H. Yamada (Japan)	7.48
1970	S. Ogura (Japan)	7.62
1974	T. C. Yohannan (India)	8.07
1978	S. Babu (India)	7.85

Triple Jump — metres
1951	Y. Iimura (Jap)	15.18
1954	N. Sagawa (Jap)	15.13
1958	Mohinder Singh (India)	15.62
1962	K. Sakurai (Jap)	15.57
1966	K. Gushiken (Jap)	15.61
1970	Mohinder Singh Gill (India)	16.11
1974	T. Inoue (Jap)	16.45
1978	M. Nakanishi (Japan)	16.56

Shot — metres
1951	M. Lal (India)	13.78
1954	Parduman Singh (India)	14.14
1958	Parduman Singh (India)	15.04
1962	T. Itokawa (Jap)	15.57
1966	Joginder Singh (India)	16.22
1970	Joginder Singh (India)	17.09
1974	D. A. Keshmiri (Iran)	18.04
1978	Bahadur Singh (India)	17.61

Discus — metres
1951	Makhan Singh (India)	39.92
1954	Parduman Singh (India)	43.36
1958	Balkar Singh (India)	47.66
1962	S. Yanagawa (Japan)	47.70
1966	P. Kumar (India)	49.62
1970	P. Kumar (India)	52.32
1974	D. A. Keshmiri (Iran)	56.82
1978	Li Wei-nan (China)	56.26

Hammer — metres
1951	F. Kamamoto (Japan)	46.64
1954	Y. Kojima (Japan)	53.96
1958	M. Iqbal (Pak)	60.96
1962	N. Okamoto (Jap)	63.88
1966	T. Sugawara (Jap)	62.90
1970	S. Murofushi (Jap)	67.08
1974	S. Murofushi (Jap)	66.54
1978	S. Murofushi (Japan)	68.26

Javelin — metres
1951	H. Nagayasu (Jap)	63.96
1954	M. Nawaz (Pak)	64.26
1958	M. Nawaz (Pak)	69.40
1962	T. Miki (Japan)	74.56
1966	Nashatar Singh Sidhu (Malaysia)	72.92
1970	H. Yamamoto (Jap)	71.24
1974	T. Yamada (Jap)	76.12
1978	Shen Mao-Mao (China)	79.24

Decathlon — Pts.
1951	F. Nishiuchi (Jap)	6,091
1954	C. K. Yang (Taiwan)	6,111
1958	C. K. Yang (Taiwan)	7,249
1962	Gurbachan Singh (India)	7,002
1966	Wu Ah-Min (Taiwan)	7,003
1970	J. Onizuka (Japan)	7,073
1974	V. S. Chuhan (Indian)	7,375
1978	H. Iwai (Japan)	7,003

10,000m Walk — min. sec.
1951	M. Prasad (India)	52 31.4

20,000m Walk — hr. min. sec.
1978	Hakam Singh (Ind.)	1 31 55

50,000m Walk — hr. min. sec.
1951	Bakhtawar Singh (India)	5 44 08

WOMEN'S EVENTS

100 Metres — sec.
1951	K. Sugimura (Jap)	12.6
1954	A. Nambu (Jap)	12.5
1958	I. Solis (Phil)	12.5
1962	M. Sulaiman (Phil)	11.8
1966	M. Sato (Japan)	12.3
1970	Chi Cheng (Taiwan)	11.6
1974	E. Rot (Israel)	11.90
1978	Ying Ya-ping (China)	12.20

200 Metres — sec.
1951	K. Okamoto (Jap)	26.0
1954	M. Tanaka (Jap)	26.0
1958	Y. Kobayashi (Jap)	25.9
1962	M. Sulaiman (Phil)	24.5
1966	D. Markus (Israel)	25.3
1970	K. Yamada (Jap)	25.0
1974	E. Rot (Israel)	23.79
1978	U. Laopinkarn (Thai)	24.81

400 Metres — sec.
1966	M Rajamani (Malaysia)	56.3
1970	K. Sandhu (India)	57.3
1974	Chee Swee Lee (Sing)	55.08
1978	Saik Oik Cam (Malay)	55.09

800 Metres — min. sec.
1962	C. Tanaka (Jap)	2 18.2
1966	H. Shezifi (Israel)	2 10.5
1970	H. Shezifi (Israel)	2 06.5
1974	N. Kawano (Jap)	2 08.1
1978	G. Zutchi (India)	2 07.7

ASIAN GAMES

1500 Metres		min. sec.
1970	H. Shezifi (Israel)	4 25.1
1974	Sun Mei-hua (China)	4 28.7
1978	Kim Ok Sun (N. Korea)	4 18.9

3000 Metres		min. sec.
1978	Kim Ok Sun (N. Korea)	9 24.7

80 Metres Hurdles		sec.
1951	K. Yoneda (Jap)	12.8
1954	M. Iwamoto (Jap)	11.7
1958	M. Iwamoto (Jap)	11.6
1962	I. Yoda (Jap)	11.5
1966	R. Sukegawa (Jap)	11.2

100 Metres Hurdles		sec.
1970	E. Rot (Israel)	14.0
1974	E. Rot (Israel)	13.31
1978	Tsai Chien-hua (China)	13.95

400 Metres Hurdles		sec.
1978	Chen Hsin (China)	61.32

4 x 100 Metres		sec.
1951	Japan	51.4
1954	India	49.5
1958	Japan	48.6
1962	Philippines	48.6
1966	Japan	47.1
1970	Japan	47.2
1974	Japan	46.62
1978	Thailand	46.20

4 x 400 Metres		min. sec.
1974	Japan	3 43.5
1978	Japan	3 46.3

High Jump		metres
1951	K. Yoneda (Jap)	1.49
1954	A. Kraus (Israel)	1.55
1958	E. Kamiya (Jap)	1.58
1962	K. Tsutsumi (Jap)	1.60
1966	M. Takeda (Jap)	1.60
1970	M. Inaoka (Jap)	1.70
1974	O. Abramovich (Israel)	1.78
1978	Cheng Ta-chen (China)	1.88

Long Jump		metres
1951	K. Sugimura (Jap)	5.91
1954	Y. Takahashi (Jap)	5.68
1958	V. Badana (Phil)	5.64
1962	S. Kishimoto (Jap)	5.75
1966	Chi Cheng (Taiwan)	5.95
1970	H. Yamashita (Jap)	6.02
1974	Hsiao Chieh-ping (China)	6.31
1978	Tsou Wa (China)	6.28

Shot		metres
1951	T. Yoshino (Jap)	11.90
1954	T. Yoshino (Jap)	12.30
1958	S. Obonai (Jap)	13.26
1962	S. Obonai (Jap)	14.04
1966	R. Sugiyama (Jap)	14.48
1970	Ok Ja Paik (S. Kor)	14.57
1974	Ok Ja Paik (S. Kor)	16.28
1978	Shen Li-chuan (China)	17.70

Discus		metres
1951	T. Yoshino (Jap)	42.10
1954	T. Yoshino (Jap)	42.86
1958	H. Uchida (Jap)	41.90
1962	K. Murase (Jap)	45.90
1966	J. De la Vina (Phil)	47.58
1970	T. Yagishita (Jap)	47.70
1974	Kao Yu-kuei (China)	51.84
1978	Li Hsiao-hui (China)	55.92

Javelin		metres
1951	T. Yoshino (Jap)	36.22
1954	A. Kurihara (Jap)	44.04
1958	Y. Shida (Jap)	47.14
1962	H. Sato (Jap)	48.14
1966	M. Katayama (Jap)	49.44
1970	N. Morita (Jap)	49.84
1974	Chou Mao-chia (China)	53.06
1978	Yao Yui-ying (China)	57.22

Pentathlon		Pts.
1966	M. Okamoto (Jap)	4,468*
1970	E. Rot (Israel)	3,946
1974	K. Shimizu (Japan)	3,890
1978	Yeh Pei-su (China)	4,133

* old tables

BALAS, Iolanda (Romania)

Iolanda Balas, who stood 1.85 metres tall, utterly dominated the realm of women's high jumping from 1958 to 1966. Probably no other athlete in history has enjoyed such a wide measure of supremacy over such a long period. At one time she had, in 80 separate meetings, jumped higher than any other woman in history!

Miss Balas set the first of her 14 world records in July 1956. In December of that year she placed fifth at the Olympic Games, her only defeat until injury brought her career to an end in 1966.

Her championship honours include the Olympic gold in 1960 and 1964, the European title in 1958 and 1962 (having finished second in 1954), and her final world record of 1.91 metres was 7 cm. higher than the best then achieved by any other woman—a remarkable margin. She married her coach, Ion Soeter, in 1967.

Her exceptional height and phenomenally long legs would appear to have been of advantage, but on account of her physique she was unable to master either the straddle or western roll style and had to settle for a modified version of the outmoded scissors. She was born at Timosoaru on Dec. 12th, 1936.

BANNISTER, Roger (GB)

No single athletic performance either before or since has attracted quite as much publicity and acclaim as Roger Bannister's 3 min. 59.4 sec. mile at the Iffley Road track, Oxford, on May 6th, 1954. His feat of becoming the first man to break four minutes —a barrier referred to as the "Everest" of athletics—captured the headlines all over the world.

Bannister was the first to acknowledge his debt to his friends Chris Chataway and Chris Brasher, who shared pacemaking duties. The final time clipped almost two seconds from the world record set by Gunder Hagg (Sweden) in 1945, yet within seven weeks the Australian John Landy had run even faster. Such is the ephemeral nature of even the most celebrated of athletic achievements.

That first four-minute mile was the prelude to two magnificent competitive performances in 1954. At the Commonwealth Games in Vancouver in August he defeated Landy in his fastest time of 3 min. 58.8 sec. following the most dramatic miling duel in history; and later in the month he captured the European 1500 metres crown with another display of masterly tactics. This, his final season, more than made up for his Olympic disappointment of two years earlier.

Ever since 1949, when he clocked 4 min. 11.1 sec. at the age of 20, Bannister had been considered a candidate for the very highest honours. He finished a close third in the 1950 European 800 metres final and improved his mile time to 4 min. 09.9 sec. In 1951 he brought his time down to 4 min. 07.8 sec. and thrilled the crowds with his spectacular finishing powers.

Shortly before the 1952 Olympics he ran a three-quarter mile time trial in a staggering 2 min. 52.9 sec., 3.7 sec. faster than the unofficial world record held by Arne Andersson (Sweden).

The stage was set . . . but at short notice a round of semi-finals was inserted because of the large entry. It was a death blow to Bannister, a relatively delicate athlete who had not prepared for three hard, nerve-racking races on three consecutive days. In fact, he finished fourth in the UK record time of 3 min. 46.0 sec.

His personal best marks included 1 min. 50.7 sec. for 880 yd., 3 min. 42.2 sec. for 1500 m., 3 min. 58.8 sec. for the mile, and 9 min. 09.2 sec. for 2 mi. Dr. Bannister, who was born at Harrow on Mar. 23rd, 1929, was knighted in 1975.

BARDAUSKIENE, Vilma (USSR)

The world's longest jump by a woman was achieved, appropriately enough, by a woman with probably the longest name in athletics: Vilhelmina Bardauskiene (née Augustinaviciute). It was she who created history in Aug. 1978 by becoming the first female to leap beyond 7 metres, with an amazing series of jumps which included two at 7.07 metres and another of 7.06.

Eleven days later, in the qualifying round at the European Championships in Prague, she stretched out to 7.09 metres in windless conditions but in the final—during which the weather turned cold and wet—she had to settle for a winning mark of 6.88 metres. It was all a far cry from the start of the year when, mustering a mere 6.15 metres, she placed 9th out of 12 in the European Indoor Championships.

Tipped as a potential world beater when she was 16, her development was delayed first by injuries and then marriage and childbirth (1974). Prior to 1976 her best remained a modest 6.37 metres, but then her talent began to flower and in 1977 she topped the world rankings with a Soviet record of 6.82 metres.

Having reputedly reached 7.22 metres in training just before Prague, with a technique that—according to her coach—" still leaves a lot to be desired ", she set her sights on achieving 7.50 metres by, or preferably at, the Moscow Olympics. But, hindered by injuries, she never did better than 6.68 metres after 1978 and announced her retirement shortly before the Games having failed to make the Soviet team.

Very fast on the runway (she was an 11.2 sec. sprinter) and a 1.68 metres high jumper, Vilma was born in the Lithuanian village of Pakruojis on June 15th, 1953. Her annual progress: 1967—5.46 m.; 1968—5.96; 1969—6.12; 1970—6.13; 1971—6.37; 1972—6.35; 1973—6.20; 1976—6.51; 1977—6.82; 1978—7.09; 1979—6.40; 1980—6.68.

BAUTISTA, Daniel (Mexico)

Going one better than Jose Pedraza's silver medal of eight years earlier, Daniel Bautista became Mexico's first ever Olympic athletics champion by winning the 20 kilometres walk in Montreal. Not only did he emphatically defeat the finest field of walkers ever assembled but his time of 1 hr. 24 min. 40.6 sec. was the fastest yet recorded in a major championship race. Bautista himself set an unofficial world's best for the event (on the road) when returning a time of 1 hr. 23 min. 39 sec. earlier in the 1976 season.

Although a photograph of Bautista on his final lap in the Montreal stadium revealed him to be ' lifting ' (i.e. both feet were off the ground, contrary to the rules), the diminutive Mexican is generally acknowledged as a fair stylist. In the Olympic race he broke away from the East Germans, Hans-Georg Reimann and Peter Frenkel, at 18 km. to win by over half a minute.

Bautista continued to dominate the event, winning at the Lugano Cup Finals of 1977 and 1979, the latter in the phenomenal time of 1 hr. 18 min. 49 sec., but the bubble burst at the 1980 Olympics where he was disqualified and he retired soon afterwards. Other world bests of his included 1 hr. 20 min. 06.8 sec. on the track and 15,121 metres (9 mi. 697 yd.) in the hour. His best 50km. time was 3 hr. 51 min. 14 sec. He was born on Aug. 4th, 1952.

BAYI, Filbert (Tanzania)

Producing the most uncompromising run ever seen in a major international 1500 m. championship, Filbert Bayi led from gun to tape at the 1974 Commonwealth Games for a world record of 3 min. 32.2 sec., a stride ahead of New Zealand's John Walker.

Bayi's rise to fame was meteoric. As a 19-year-old novice he failed to survive his heats in the 1972 Olympics but showed promise with times of 3 min. 45.4 sec. for 1500 m. and 8 min. 41.4 sec. for the steeplechase. Within a few months he had broken into world class with 3 min. 38.9 sec. and he quickly followed this up by winning the African title in 3 min. 37.2 sec., well ahead of Kenya's Kip Keino.

He left spectators all over Europe agog in 1973 as he blazed away at unprecedented speed in his races. He passed 400 m. in 53.6 sec., 800 m. in 1 min. 51.6 sec. and 1200 m. in 2 min. 52.2 sec. when setting a Commonwealth record of 3 min. 34.6 secs., and a few days later he went even faster (52.5, 1:51.0, 2:52.0) before being overhauled by Ben Jipcho on the last lap of a mile. The Kenyan ran 3 min. 52.0 sec., Bayi 3 min. 52.6 sec. On another occasion he really overdid it, reaching 1200 m. in 2 min. 46.4 sec. before slowing drastically to 3 min. 40.7 sec. for 1500 m.

There was no misjudgment at the Commonwealth Games in Christchurch: he passed through in 54.4 sec., 1 min. 51.8 sec. and 2 min. 50.4 sec. but still had enough in hand to hold off Walker with a 55.8 sec. last lap.

Bayi accomplished his second world record in 1975, covering a mile in 3 min. 51.0 sec. in Jamaica—with quarter mile timings of 56.9, 59.7, 58.7 and 55.7 sec.—but injury cut short his eagerly awaited European tour. The record survived less than three months before Walker ran 3 min. 49.4 sec. A further setback occurred in 1976. Because of political considerations, African athletes were withdrawn from the Montreal Olympics and thus the world was deprived of what had been anticipated as the supreme duel of the Games: Bayi v. Walker.

Injuries and illness (malaria in particular) took their toll in the next three seasons, but that did not stop him making a courageous attempt to retain his Commonwealth title in 1978, losing narrowly to Dave Moorcroft after leading most of the way. However, he struck superb form in 1980 . . . as a steeplechaser. Reverting to his former speciality for the Olympics he set a devilish pace—passing 1000 m. in 2 min. 36.8 sec. and 2000 m. in a world's best of 5 min. 20.3 sec! Over 25 m. clear with two laps to go, he was eventually overhauled just before the final water jump by Poland's Bronislaw Malinowski to finish second in 8 min. 12.5 sec., proud to be his country's first ever Olympic medallist. His best marks include 1 min. 45.3 sec. for 800 m., 3 min. 32.16 sec. for 1500 m., 3 min. 51.0 sec. for the mile, 7 min. 39.3 sec. for 3000 m., 13 min. 18.2 sec. for 5000 m., 2 hr. 20 min. 35 sec. for the marathon and 8 min. 12.5 sec. for the steeplechase. He was born at Karatu on June 23rd, 1953.

BEAMON, Bob (USA)

World records are made to be broken; progress is such that few survive more than a year or two. Yet it is quite feasible that Bob Beamon's figures of 8.90 metres during the 1968 Olympic Games in Mexico City will stand as the ultimate in long jumping until the next century.

This incredible leap, widely accepted as the most astonishing single exploit in track and field history, is generations ahead of its time. It took 30 years for the record to creep up from 8.13 metres (by Jesse Owens in 1935), to the mark which Beamon beat: 8.35 metres by Ralph Boston. Suddenly not only the 28ft. (8.53 m.) barrier, but the undreamed of 29 ft. (8.84 m.) was broken. The combination of a superb take-off allied to perfect technique in ideal conditions (high altitude; following wind of 2 metres per second) resulted in a bombshell of a performance. No one, in the twelve subsequent seasons, has jumped farther than 8.54 metres.

Beamon himself was often an unreliable performer, prone to frequent no-jumping, although his prodigious talent was never in question. His best prior to Mexico was 8.33 metres but in later seasons, struggling unsuccessfully to live up to his own impossible standard, he never did better than 8.20 metres, although in fairness he did have to switch his take-off leg after seriously pulling a hamstring in his right leg early in 1969. He turned professional in 1973. A 9.5 sec. sprinter (100 yd.), he was born in New York on Aug. 29th, 1946.

BECK, Volker
(East Germany)

Volker Beck was one of the main beneficiaries of the Moscow Olympic boycott. In the enforced absence of world record holder and 1976 champion Ed Moses (USA) and European record holder Harald Schmid (West Germany), the 400 m. hurdles title became correspondingly devalued and Beck's time of 48.70 sec., although close to his personal best, was the slowest Olympic winning mark since 1964.

The 1.91 metres tall East German, the first man from his country to win an Olympic track event, initially made his mark by placing second in the 1975 European Junior Championships and created something of a sensation at the 1977 World Cup when not only did he edge out Schmid for second behind Moses in the hurdles but then won the 400 m. flat, setting national records of 48.83 sec. and 45.79 sec. in each. Following a protest on behalf of Alberto Juantorena, who was left at the start when he failed to hear the gun, the flat 400 was re-run next day with the Cuban first in 45.36 sec. and Beck ("the decision to repeat the race is a scandal") an inspired if angry second in 45.50 sec. An achilles tendon operation caused him to miss the 1978 season but he made a successful comeback in 1979.

His personal bests are 21.15 sec. for 200 m., 45.50 sec. for 400 m. and 48.58 sec. for 400 m. hurdles. Annual progress over the hurdles: 1971—42.2 (300 m.), 1972—40.4, 1973—55.3 (400 m.), 1974—52.5, 1975—51.44, 1976—49.74, 1977—48.83, 1979—48.58, 1980—48.70. He was born at Nordhausen on June 30th, 1956.

BEDFORD, Dave (GB)

A combination of flamboyant front-running and a cheeky attitude off the track made Dave Bedford the most talked-about British athlete of the early seventies. He, more than any other individual, was responsible for the return of big crowds to London's major athletics events.

His only significant international championship success was winning the International cross-country title in 1971, his reputation as one of the world's greatest distance runners having been based upon prolific record breaking.

Bedford's finest achievement was the setting of a world record of 27 min. 30.8 sec. for 10,000 m. in the 1973 AAA Championships, which cut 7.6 sec. from Lasse Viren's previous mark. He reached the 5000 m. mark in an unprecedented 13 min. 39.4 sec. (that would have been a world record for the distance prior to 1956), and then proceeded to cover the second half of the race in 13 min. 51.4 sec.—faster than the Chataway v Kuts epic!

He has at one time or another held every UK record (other than for 2 mi.) from 2000 m. to 10,000 m. inclusive, plus the steeplechase, and was only 19 when he set his first national record of 28 min. 24.4 sec. for 10,000 m. in 1969. He finished 6th at this distance in both the 1971 European Championships and 1972 Olympics, and was even more disappointed to place only 4th in the 1974 Commonwealth Games. He felt far fitter, prior to the Christchurch race, than when he accomplished the world record and anticipated a time of around 27 min. 10 sec! Unhappily, the leg injury which ruined his chances in that event persisted to such a degree that his international racing career came to a premature end although he still runs for his club.

His best marks include 4 min. 02.9 sec. for the mile, 5 min. 03.2 sec. for 2000 m., 7 min. 46.4 sec. for 3000 m., 13 min. 17.2 sec. for 5000 m., 27 min. 30.8 sec. for 10,000 m. and 8 min. 28.6 sec. for the steeplechase. He was born in London on Dec. 30th, 1949.

BEYER, Udo (East Germany)

If anyone looked destined for greatness as a shot-putter it was Udo Beyer, European junior champion in 1973 who while still a teenager had attained a distance of 20.97 metres. Nevertheless, few could have anticipated Beyer becoming Olympic champion so early in his career . . . at the age of 20. He was not added to the East German team for Montreal until the last minute, clinching his place with a put of 21.06 metres behind his colleague Heinz-Joachim Rothenburg at a final trials meeting, but at the Games he took full advantage of the relatively low standard of performance to carry off the gold medal at only 21.05 metres. That distance would have gained no higher than 5th place at the previous Olympics. A 1.95 metres, 125 kg. Colossus, he bestrode the world of shot-putting in succeeding years by winning every major event (European champion in 1978, European and World Cup winner in 1977 and 1979) as well as becoming world record holder with 22.15 metres in 1978. But at the Moscow Olympics, handicapped by a pulled back muscle, he was relegated to third place. His younger sister, Gisela, was fourth in the discus.

Beyer showed outstanding talent also as a hammer thrower (66.84 metres) before specialising. Annual progress: 1970—15.95 m. (5 kg); 1971 —15.71; 1972—17.08; 1973—19.65; 1974—20.20; 1975—20.97; 1976—21.12; 1977—21.74; 1978—22.15; 1979—21.74; 1980—21.98. He was born at Eisenhuttenstadt on Aug. 9th, 1955.

BIKILA ABEBE (Ethiopia)
See ABEBE BIKILA.

BIRYULINA, Tatyana (USSR)
Without doubt the most successful female javelin thrower in history has been Ruth Fuchs. Just one distinction eluded her—to become the first woman to throw 70 metres—and when she reached 69.96 metres in April 1980 it looked as though that honour too would fall to her. But the barrier breaker proved to be little known Tatyana Biryulina, who attained 70.08 metres at Podolsk, just outside Moscow, in July 1980. That mighty throw came in the fourth round, having thrown a personal best of 63.48 metres in the second. Her best before that remarkable competition had been a mere 61.62 metres and her international record was limited and undistinguished: in 1979 (the year she threw 59.56 metres) she was seventh in the Moscow Spartakiad and fifth in the World Student Games.

Following the out-of-the-blue world record, Tatyana's coach rhapsodised, " my protégée is reaping the harvest of a technique approaching perfection ". But, less than two weeks later at the Olympics, she only scraped through to the final as eleventh of the twelve qualifiers with 59.86 metres, and in the final she placed sixth with 65.08 metres as Cuba's Maria Colon took the gold with 68.40 metres. Biryulina was born on July 16th, 1955.

BLANKERS-KOEN, Fanny (Netherlands)
Mrs. Fanny Blankers-Koen became the most famous woman athlete in history when, at the age of 30 (13 years after she made her debut as an 800 m. runner with a time of 2 min. 29.0 sec.), she collected four gold medals at the 1948 Olympic Games in London. She triumphed in the 100 m., 200 m. and 80 m. hurdles, and anchored the Dutch 4 x 100 m. relay team to victory.

Always a superb competitor, she won eight medals in three European Championship meetings: gold in the 1946 hurdles and relay and the 1950 100 m., 200 m. and hurdles; silver in the 1950 relay; and bronze in the 1938 100 m. and 200 m.

Between 1938 and 1951 she set official world records in no fewer than seven individual events: 100 yd., 100 m., 220 yd., 80 m. hurdles, high jump, long jump and pentathlon. She unofficially equalled the 100 m. record of 11.5 sec. in 1952, the following year her hurdles time of 11.1 sec. was the fastest in the world that season, and even as late as 1956 (aged 38) she was timed at 11.3 sec. in a wind assisted hurdles race.

Her best marks included 10.8 sec. for 100 yd., 11.5 sec. for 100 m., 23.9 sec. for 200 m., 11.0 sec. for 80 m. hurdles, 1.71 m. high jump, 6.25 m. long jump, and 4.692 point pentathlon (old tables). She was born in Amsterdam on Apr. 26th, 1918.

BORZOV, Valeriy (USSR)
The only European ever to win the Olympic sprint double for men, Valeriy Borzov had an almost perfect record in major championship events during a period of nine seasons. He contested, and won, the 1968 European junior 100 and 200 m., 1969 European 100 m., 1970 and 1971 European indoor 60 m., 1971 European 100 and 200 m., 1972 European indoor 50 m., 1972 Olympic 100 and 200 m., 1974 European indoor 60 m., 1974 European 100 m., 1975 and 1976 European indoor 60 m. His only defeat was sustained at the 1976 Olympics where he finished third in the 100 m.—the first time an Olympic champion has subsequently won another medal in that event. One of the smoothest, most relaxed speedsters ever seen, he was strong in every department of sprinting—start, pick-

up, mid-race and finish, not to mention temperament.

Soviet sports authorities say that Borzov the sprinter was made rather than born. A team of scientists in Kiev studied all the facets of sprinting and, based on their findings, Prof. Valentin Petrovsky guided Borzov on his technique and training. Progress was swift and in Dec. 1968 (aged 19) he equalled the world indoor 60 m. best of 6.4 sec. In 1969 he ran his first 10.0 sec. 100 m. to tie the European record.

His Olympic victories in Munich were clear cut. The USA's two 9.9 sec. performers, Eddie Hart and Rey Robinson, failed to show up in time for their 100 m. quarter-final races, but Borzov appeared to have plenty in hand as he took the final, easing up, by a metre in 10.14 sec. In the 200 m., an event he ran infrequently, he won by 2 m. in 20.00 sec., a European record. His time in Montreal four years later again was 10.14 sec.

He continued racing until 1979, hoping to make another Olympic team, but two Achilles tendon operations prevented his regaining top form. His best marks were 10.07 and 10.0 for 100 m., 20.00 for 200 m. and 47.6 for 400 m. Born at Sambor (Ukraine) on Oct. 20th, 1949, he is married to the great Olympic gymnastics champion Lyudmila Turishcheva.

BOSTON, Ralph (USA)

Ralph Boston will be remembered by posterity not only as Olympic champion in 1960 but as the man who broke Jesse Owens' long jump world record after 25 years and became the first to leap over 27 ft. (8.23 m.).

He reached world class in 1959 and during the next two seasons carried the world record out to 8.28 metres. In 1962 he lost it to Igor Ter-Ovanesyan, his Soviet rival, but regained it in 1964 and the following season improved the mark to 8.35 metres. In 1966 he actually covered 8.56 metres but fell back for a measurement of 8.23 metres. He was placed second behind Britain's Lynn Davies in the 1964 Olympics, and third in the 1968 Games, where Bob Beamon shattered his world record.

A talented all-rounder, Boston's best marks in other events include a 9.6 sec. 100 yd., 21.0 sec. straight 220 yd., 48.5 sec. 440 yd., 13.7 sec. 120 yd. hurdles, 22.4 sec. straight 220 yd. hurdles, 2.05 m. high jump, 4.19 m. pole vault, 15.89 m. triple jump and 64 m. javelin. In 1964 he long jumped a wind-aided 8.50 m. He was born at Laurel, Mississippi, on May 9th, 1939.

BRAGINA, Lyudmila (USSR)

Incredulity was the general reaction to the news of Lyudmila Bragina's first world record. Running in the USSR Championships on July 18th, 1972, she cut 2.7 sec. off the previous mark with a time of 4 min. 06.9 sec. for 1500 m., and that was in her heat!

It was no fluke. In Munich, where the event was being staged for the first time in Olympic history, she won her heat on Sept. 4th in 4 min. 06.5 sec., her semi-final on Sept. 7th in 4 min. 05.1 sec., and the final on Sept. 9th in 4 min. 01.4 sec.—all world record runs. Usually an uncompromising front-runner, she held back in the final prior to launching a devastating last two laps, covered in an astonishing 2 min. 07.4 sec. Her winning time was faster than Albert Hill's Olympic gold medal performance in 1920!

Incredulity was the general reaction, too, to the news of her world 3000 m. record in 1976. Having lost her 1500 m. record and Olympic title to Tatyana Kazankina (USSR)—she herself placed 5th in Montreal—the 33-year-old teacher created a sensation in the USA v USSR match a few days after the closing of the Olympics. She hacked 18.3 sec. from the previous best with the phenomenal time of 8 min. 27.2 sec. She covered the kilometres in 2:47.0 ,2:53.0 and 2:47.2. No man ever ran that quickly until 1926 and it is faster than two of Paavo Nurmi's earlier world records at the distance! She was born at Sverdlovsk on July 24th, 1943.

BRASHER, Chris (GB)

The career of Chris Brasher is an inspiration to all. For years he was simply a capable middle distance runner (3 min. 54.0 sec. 1500 m. and 14 min. 22.4 sec. 3 mi. in 1951) who appeared to lack that extra something which is required of the absolute top liner.

Realising his limitations on the flat, he switched his attention to the steeplechase—an undulating event appropriate to his mountaineering skill (he was on the short list for an Everest expedition). He clocked a modest but promising 9 min. 21.8 sec. in 1951 and next year won his way into the Olympic team. At Helsinki he improved over 10 seconds on his best by returning 9 min. 03.2 sec. in his heat, and in the final he pluckily finished 11th out of 12 after injuring himself on the second lap.

Throughout the next two seasons Brasher became better known as Roger Bannister's pacemaker and training companion than as an athlete in his own right, though he did cut his mile time to 4 min. 09.0 sec. in 1954.

He returned to serious steeplechasing in 1955, and progressed to 8 min. 49.2 sec. that year. He improved to 8 min. 47.2 sec. in Aug. 1956 but he travelled to Melbourne for the Olympic Games merely as Britain's third string. Shortly before the Games though, Brasher knocked almost 13 sec. off his best 2 mi. flat time with 8 min. 45.6 sec. and in the Olympic final he ran the race of his life to win in the Olympic and U.K. record time of 8 min. 41.2 sec.

At first he was disqualified for an alleged obstruction during the race but was reinstated by the jury of appeal.

Other best marks included 3 min. 53.6 sec. for 1500 m., 4 min. 06.8 sec. for the mile and 8 min. 15.4 sec. for 3000 m. He was born in Georgetown (Guyana) on Aug. 21st, 1928. In 1981, aged 52, he ran a personal best of 2 hr. 56 min. 56 sec. in the inaugural London Marathon of which he was Race Director.

BRITISH AMATEUR ATHLETIC BOARD

The BAAB, founded in 1932, is affiliated to the International Amateur Athletic Federation as the governing athletic association for the United Kingdom of Great Britain and Northern Ireland. The Board is responsible for the control of international athletics in Britain, selects and manages teams to represent Britain, administers the United Kingdom Coaching Scheme and since 1977 has organised UK National Championships.

BRITISH ATHLETICS LEAGUE & CUP

The British (originally National) Athletics League was formed in 1969 with the purpose of providing more meaningful competition for clubs—the foundations of British athletics—and to help improve standards, particularly in the comparatively neglected field events. It proved to be an immediate success, with club spirit very much in evidence at fixtures.

The League is split into five divisions of six clubs each, with four matches per season. Each club fields two athletes per event.

Division 1 champions:
1969—Birchfield 15 pts; 1970—Thames Valley 22 pts; 1971—Thames Valley 23 pts; 1972—Cardiff 22 pts; 1973—Cardiff 22 pts; 1974—Cardiff 22 pts; 1975—Wolverhampton & Bilston 24 pts; (maximum score); 1976—Wolverhampton & Bilston 22 pts; 1977—Wolverhampton & Bilston 22 pts; 1978—Wolverhampton & Bilston 23 pts; 1979—Wolverhampton & Bilston 23 pts; 1980—Wolverhampton & Bilston 23¼ pts.

A British Women's League was launched in 1975

Division 1 champions:
1975—Edinburgh Southern 17 pts; 1976—Sale 16 pts; 1977—Sale 17 pts; 1978—Sale 17 pts; 1979—Stretford 16 pts; 1980—Bristol 15 pts.

A British club knock-out cup tournament was inaugurated in 1973, with one competitor per club per event. A women's contest was started the following year.

Cup winners: (Men) 1973—Wolverhampton & Bilston 114 pts; 1974—Cardiff 113 pts; 1975—Edinburgh Southern 126 pts; 1976—Wolverhampton & Bilston 128 pts; 1977—Wolverhampton & Bilston 142½ pts; 1978—Shaftesbury 107 pts; 1979—Wolverhampton & Bilston 131 pts; 1980—Wolverhampton & Bilston 130 pts. (Women) 1974—Mitcham 87 pts; 1975—Edinburgh Southern 104 pts; 1976—Stretford 94 pts; 1977—Stretford 105 pts; 1978—Stretford 99 pts; 1979—Stretford 98 pts; 1980—Stretford 98 pts.

BRITISH COMMONWEALTH GAMES

See COMMONWEALTH GAMES.

BRITISH COMMONWEALTH RECORDS

See APPENDIX

BRITISH RECORDS

See APPENDIX

BRUMEL, Valeriy (USSR)

Siberian-born Valeriy Brumel held the high jump world record for 10 years, his best leap—using the straddle style—being 2.28 metres in 1963. That was 43 cm. above his own head.

He began jumping at the age of 11 but progress was slow until, between 1956 and 1957, he shot up over 30 cm. While still only 18 he set a European record of 2.20 metres in 1960, and that year—in his first big international test—won the silver medal at the Olympic Games. He shared the Olympic record of 2.16 metres with his colleague Robert Shavlakadze, with the odds-on favourite John Thomas (USA) only third.

Brumel raised the outdoor world record six times between 1961 and 1963.

He won the 1964 Olympic title as expected, although John Thomas shared the winning height of 2.18 metres, but disaster struck when he sustained serious leg and foot injuries in a motor-cycle accident in the autumn of 1965. Following a series of major operations he made a miraculous comeback in 1969, and in 1970 he cleared 2.13 metres. He jumped 2.08 metres in 1976.

Other best marks include 10.5 sec. for 100 m., 4.20 m., pole vault, 7.65 m. long jump, and 15.84 m. shot. He was born at Tolbuzino on Apr. 14th, 1942.

BURGHLEY, LORD (GB)

Lord Burghley, now the 6th Marquess of Exeter, enjoyed one of the most successful careers of any British athlete. Though he made no mark on the playing fields of Eton and failed to gain his " blue " in his first year at Cambridge he did qualify at the age of 19 for the 1924 Olympic team as a 110 m. hurdler.

Equally adept at all three types of hurdle racing, he held the British records for 120 yd. from 1927 to 1936, for 220 yd. from 1925 to 1950, for 400 m. from 1928 to 1954 and for 440 yd. from 1926 to 1949.

His championship record was first class: Olympic 400 m. hurdles winner in 1928 and fourth (in his fastest time) in 1932; silver medallist in the 1932 Olympic 4 x 400 m. relay (running his stage in 46.7 sec.); triple gold medallist at the 1930 British Empire Games—120 yd. hurdles, 440 yd. hurdles and 4 x 440 yd. relay.

Best marks included 14.5 sec. for 120 yd. hurdles and 52.2 sec. for 400 m. hurdles. The Marquess was president of the AAA from 1936 to 1976 and of the International Amateur Athletic Federation from 1946 to 1976. He was born at Stamford on Feb. 9th, 1905.

CALHOUN, Lee (USA)

The only man to win the Olympic 110 m. hurdles crown twice is Lee Calhoun, who performed the trick in 1956 and 1960. As a former co-holder of world records for 110 m. and 120 yd. hurdles at 13.2 sec., he has strong claims to being considered the most successful high hurdling exponent of all-time.

He began his athletic career at the age of 17 as a high jumper and was helped by his predecessor as Olympic champion, Harrison Dillard, when he decided to switch to hurdling in 1951. After five seasons his best stood at only 14.4 sec., but in 1956 he improved sensationally to 13.5 sec.

Between his two Olympic triumphs he was suspended by the Amateur Athletic Union of the USA, after appearing with his bride on a television "give-away" show and receiving nearly £1,000 worth of gifts. Penalised for capitalising on his athletic fame, he missed the 1958 season but came back better than ever.

His best marks in other events included 9.7 sec. for 100 yd., 22.9 sec. for 220 yd. hurdles (turn) and 1.90 m. high jump. Born at Laurel, Mississippi (Ralph Boston's home town) on Feb. 23rd, 1933, he was an assistant coach to the USA Olympic team in 1976.

CHATAWAY, Chris (GB)

Few athletes have enjoyed such widespread popularity as Chris Chataway, whose personal appeal and exceptional ability contributed greatly to the British athletics boom of the 1950s. His bobbing red hair and fiery finish were characteristics that attracted thousands to the big White City meetings, and he rarely let his public down.

It is fitting, perhaps, that he was the winner of what is generally considered to be the finest race ever to grace a British track: his duel over 5000 m. with Vladimir Kuts in the London v. Moscow match of 1954. In a memorable finish he thrust his chest ahead in the last stride for victory in the world record time of 13 min. 51.6 sec. He thus gained swift revenge over his conqueror of the European Championships a few weeks earlier.

His silver medal in that race was the nearest he got to a world title (though he won the 1954 Commonwealth Games 3 mi.), for as an inexperienced 21-year-old at the 1952 Olympics he was placed fifth after tripping over while rounding the final bend and in 1956 he fell away to 11th place suffering from severe stomach cramp.

Considering it was Chataway who pulled Roger Bannister to the first four-minute mile and pushed John Landy to the second, it was only poetic justice that he himself broke the barrier in 1955.

Best marks: 3 min. 43.6 sec. for 1500 m., 3 min. 59.8 sec. for the mile, 5 min. 09.4 sec. for 2000 m., 8 min. 06.2 sec. for 3000 m., 8 min. 41.0 sec. for 2 mi., 13 min. 23.2 sec. for 3 mi. and 13 min. 51.6 sec. for 5000 m. Chataway, a Minister in Edward Heath's Government, was born at Chelsea on Jan. 31st, 1931.

CHIZHOVA, Nadyezhda (USSR)

During an entire decade following her crowning as European indoor shot-putting champion in 1964, Nadyezhda Chizhova blotted her copybook only once when a major championship was at stake: her defeat at the 1968 Olympics where, a solid favourite as world record holder (18.67 metres), she placed no higher than third behind the East Germans, Margitta Gummel and Marita Lange.

Apart from that it was titles and records all the way. She won the European gold medal in 1966, 1969, 1971 and 1974—to become the only woman ever to notch up four consecutive successes—and she made no mistake in her second crack at the Olympic title in 1972, for with her opening put she smashed the world record with 21.03 metres. In addition to being the first over 20 metres (in 1969) and 21 metres, she also inaugurated the 70 ft. era with her longest ever put of 21.45 metres (70 ft. 4¼ in.) in 1973. After missing the entire 1975 season through injury she made a good comeback in 1976 to complete a set of Olympic medals by claiming the silver. She was born at Usolye-Sibirskoye (Siberia) on Sept. 29th, 1945.

CIERPINSKI, Waldemar (East Germany)

Responsible for one of the biggest upsets of the 1976 Olympics was East German marathoner Waldemar Cierpinski. Even though the previous champion Frank Shorter (USA) ran close to the fastest time of his career he was left the best part of a minute behind by his under-rated rival.

Cierpinski was an international steeplechaser before switching to 10,000 m. in 1973. The following year he made his marathon debut, running 2 hr. 20 min. 29 sec. He progressed to 2 hr. 17 min. 31 sec. in 1975, placing 7th in the Kosice marathon, but as the 95th ranked performer in the world that year he hardly merited serious consideration as an Olympic medal contender at that stage. He made a considerable advance early in 1976, clocking 2 hr. 13 min. 58 sec. and 2 hr. 12 min. 21 sec., while in Montreal he was in unbeatable form as he pulled away from Shorter over the final 5 miles. He finished in the formidable time of 2 hr. 09 min. 55 sec., slashing over two minutes from Abebe Bikila's celebrated Olympic record.

Cierpinski hardly set the marathoning world alight in the next three seasons, running no faster than 2 hr. 12 min. 20 sec. (finishing 4th in the 1978 European championship) and failing to break even 2¼ hrs in 1977 and 1979, but—like Lasse Viren—he was transformed when Olympic titles were at stake and in Moscow in 1980 he surged clear at 36 km. to emulate Abebe Bikila's feat of winning two Olympic gold medals in the marathon. His time of 2 hr. 11 min. 03 sec. was the second fastest of his career and so fresh was he approaching the finish that he covered the last 200 m. on the track in a twinkling 33.4 sec.

Annual progress: 1974—2:20:29, 1975—2:17:31, 1976—2:09:55, 1977—2:16:00, 1978—2:12:20, 1979—2:15:50, 1980—2:11:03. Best marks at other events: 13 min. 36.6 sec. for 5000 m., 28 min. 28.2 sec. for 10,000 m. and 8 min. 32.4 sec. for the steeplechase. He was born at Neugattersleben on Aug. 3rd, 1950.

CLARKE, Ron (Australia)

Few athletes have made such an impact on the world record books as Ron Clarke, setter of global marks for 3 mi., 5000 m., 6 mi., 10,000 m., 10 mi., 20,000 m. and one hour. Only one runner before him has managed to set records in all seven of those events: the immortal Paavo Nurmi, and even he did not hold the complete set simultaneously, as did Clarke for a few months. Clarke later set world records for 2 mi. also.

It was Clarke who was mainly responsible for the astonishing upsurge in distance running standards during the sixties. As at November, 1963 the best times recorded for 5000 m. and 10,000 m. were respectively 13 min. 35.0 sec. and 28 min. 18.2 sec. Clarke produced times of 13 min. 16.6 sec. and 27 min. 39.4 sec.!

In spite of innumerable successes against the stopwatch and several brilliant victories against top opposition, Clarke never quite made his mark as a major championship competitor. He was favoured to win the Olympic 10,000 m. in 1964 but was beaten into third place; while at the 1966 Commonwealth Games he collected another two silver medals to add to the one he gained in the 3 mi. four years earlier. The problems of altitude gave him no chance at the 1968 Olympics, and he bowed out at the 1970 Commonwealth Games with yet another silver medal in the 10,000 m.

Clarke was labelled a boy wonder when he set junior world "records" of 3 min. 49.8 sec. for 1500 m., 4 min. 06.8 sec. for the mile and 9 min. 01.8 sec. for 2 mi. early in 1956 at the age of 18. He did not make the Australian Olympic team that year but was awarded the honour of carrying the Olympic torch at the opening of the Melbourne Games. He slipped into obscurity soon afterwards and it was not until 1961 that he launched his comeback.

Personal best performances include: 3 min. 44.1 sec. for 1500 m., 4 min. 00.2 sec. for the mile, 7 min. 47.2 sec. for 3000 m., 8 min. 19.6 sec. for 2 mi., 12 min. 50.4 sec. for 3 mi., 13 min. 16.6 sec. for 5000 m., 26 min. 47.0 sec. for 6 mi., 27 min. 39.4 sec. for 10,000 m., 47 min. 12.8 sec. for 10 mi., 59 min. 22.8 sec. for 20,000 m., 20,232 metres for one hour, 2 hr. 20 min. 26.8 sec. for the marathon. He was born in Melbourne on Feb. 21st, 1937. His son, Marcus, is one of Australia's most promising middle-distance runners.

CLAYTON, Derek (Australia)

Repeated leg injuries always prevented Derek Clayton from showing his true form in major championship races but he has since 1967 held the world's best time for the marathon.

This native of Lancashire, who emigrated to Australia in 1963, graduated to marathon running in 1965 but his career nearly came to a premature end when, early in 1967, he was operated on for a broken Achilles tendon. Amazingly, he recovered to such effect that in December of that year he became the first man to average under 5 min. per mile for the journey in winning a Japanese race in 2 hr. 9 min. 36.4 sec—nearly 2½ min. inside the previous world's best held by Morio Shigematsu of Japan.

Cartilage trouble destroyed his Olympic prospects in 1968 and he did well to finish 7th. Following another operation he returned in 1969 to set another world's best time of 2 hr. 8 min. 33.6 sec. in Antwerp. Some feel the course was short but Clayton, who ran up to 200 miles a week in training, has always been adamant that the performance was genuine. Further injuries prevented his finishing in the 1970 and 1974 Commonwealth Games and held him down to 13th place in the 1972 Olympics.

His best track times included 3 min. 47.8 sec. for 1500 m. 13 min. 45.6 sec. for 5000 m. and 28 min. 32.2 sec for 10.000 m. Standing 1.88 metres tall and weighing 73 kg., he was born at Barrow-in-Furness on Nov. 17th, 1942.

COE, Sebastian (GB)

The pattern of Sebastian Coe's career makes one wonder how many middle-distance runners of comparable talent never realise their potential due to an over-emphasis on training mileage and neglect in the vital area of leg speed. For it was unremitting work in this department that was largely responsible for Coe's emergence in 1979 as a world record smasher.

Coe started off as a sprinter but, facing the fact that his light build wasn't ideally suited to that activity, he switched to cross-country and 1500/3000 m. races. As AAA Youth 1500 m. and English Schools Intermediate 3000 m. champion at the age of 16, and bronze medallist in the 1975 European Junior 1500 m. two years later, he appeared to be well along the conventional path leading to the longer track events. But Seb and his father/coach, Peter Coe, came to a momentous decision: if Seb was first to approach his limits as a 1500 m. runner his basic speed had to be improved drastically.

The results of this policy became apparent in 1976 when, at 19, he slashed his best 800 m. time from 1 min. 53.8 sec. to 1 min. 47.7 sec. and clocked 3 min. 58.4 sec. for the mile. The following winter he became an international star by capturing the European indoor 800 m. title in 1 min. 46.5 sec., his light, graceful stride winning many admirers. Front running tactics kept the slightly built Coe (1.76 metres tall but only 58 kg.) out of trouble on the boards but outdoors in 1977 repeated baulking held him down to fourth place in the European Cup Final 800 m. Later he scored a famous mile victory over Filbert Bayi in 3 min. 57.7 sec., followed by a UK 800 m. record of 1 min. 45.0 sec.

The accent on speed continued in 1978 and he brought his 400 m. time down from 48.9 sec. to 47.7 sec. Shortly before the European Championships he lowered the UK 800 m. record to 1 min. 44.3 sec., but he misjudged his pace in Prague—haring through 200 m. in 24.3 sec. and 400 m. in 49.32! He led into the final straight but faded to third in 1 min. 44.8 sec.

behind East German revelation Olaf Beyer (1 min. 43.8 sec.) and Steve Ovett (1 min. 44.1 sec.). Coe bounced back to reclaim the UK record with 1 min. 44.0 sec.

Even that notable time, just 0.6 sec. outside Alberto Juantorena's world record, paled into relative insignificance when in Oslo on July 5th, 1979, Coe opened a whole new era of 800 m. running with 200 m. splits of 24.6, 26.0, 24.8 and 27.0 sec. for the prodigious time of 1 min. 42.4 sec. (actually 1 min, 42.33 sec. before rounding up). His next important race was the AAA 400 m. in which he was second (first Briton) in his fastest time of 46.87 sec., and then it was back to Oslo's Bislett Stadium for the IAAF's Golden Mile on July 17th—an event he won decisively from a glittering field in another world record of 3 min. 49.0 sec. (3 min. 48.95 sec.). His 440 yd. splits were 57.8, 57.5, 58.1 and 55.6 sec. and he passed by the 1500 m. mark in a European record of 3 min. 32.8 sec.

Still there was more to come: after a slow but devastating 800 m. win at the European Cup Final he took aim at the 1500 m. world record in Zurich on Aug. 15th. The pacemaking went awry but Coe succeeded with a time of 3 min. 32.1 sec. (3 min. 32.03 sec.) despite uneconomical laps of 54.3, 58.9 and 56.3 sec. plus 42.6 sec. for the final 300 m. Officially, Coe became the first man ever to set world records in all three events, but it should be noted that Jim Ryun held the marks for 880 yd. (with a time at least the equal of the existing 800 m. record), 1500 m. and mile.

Coe was considered a near-certainty for the Olympic 800 m. gold medal in 1980, particularly after setting a world 1000 m. record of 2 min. 13.40 sec. (1 min. 45.2 sec. at 800 m. en route) on July 1st again at Bislett, but in Moscow he ran a tactically disastrous race. Failing to show the speed of thought or movement necessary and leaving his effort far too late, he had to settle for second place in 1 min. 45.9 sec. as victory went to Ovett in 1 min. 45.4 sec. Fortunately for Coe, he had an early chance to redeem himself in the 1500 m., and he gladly seized the opportunity. The first two laps were very slow but when East German Jurgen Straub began his prolonged run for home at 800 m. the pace became a killing one. Coe thrived on it, happy to have a clear run just behind and wide of Straub. Covering the last 400 m. in 52.2 sec. he kicked, and then kicked again, to win the gold medal in 3 min. 38.4 sec. as an unusually subdued Ovett placed third. A back injury, which had troubled him all year, forced Coe to bring his post-Olympic racing schedule to a premature end but he re-emerged early in 1981 to set a world indoor 800 m. best of 1 min. 46.0 sec.

His best marks: 46.87 sec. (and 45.5 sec. in a relay) for 400 m., 1 min. 42.33 sec. for 800 m., 2 min. 13.40 sec. for 1000 m., 3 min. 32.03 sec. for 1500 m., 3 min. 48.95 sec. for the mile, 7 min. 55.2 sec. for 3000 m. and 14 min. 06.2 sec. for 5000 m. Annual progress at 800 and 1500 m.: 1970—4:31.8; 1971—2:08.4, 4:18.0; 1972—1:59.9, 4:05.9; 1973—1:56.0, 3:55.0; 1975—1:53.8, 3:45.2; 1976—1:47.7, 3:42.7 (& 3:58.4 mile); 1977—1:45.0, 3:57.7 (mile); 1978—1:44.0, 4:02.2 (mile); 1979—1:42.33, 3:32.03 (& 3:48.95 mile); 1980—1:44.7, 3:32.19. He was born in London on Sept. 29th, 1956.

COLON, Maria (Cuba)

As is so often the case in major championships, a first round throw proved to be the winner in the women's javelin at the 1980 Olympic Games. The thrower in question was not, as expected, defending champion Ruth Fuchs, nor was it the internationally unproven new world record holder Tatyana Biryulina . . . but a buxom Cuban revelling in the name of Maria Caridad Colon Ruenes. Maria Colon, as she is best known, reached a personal best of 68.40 metres to demoralise the opposition and become the first Latin American or Caribbean woman athlete to strike Olympic gold.

She first attained world class level in 1978, a year in which she improved nine metres to 63.50 metres, and she demonstrated a flair for big time competition by winning the 1979 Pan-American title. Now her sights are set on throwing 72 metres.

Annual progress: 1975—44.78 m.; 1976—50.08; 1977—54.34; 1978—63.50;

1979—64.38; 1980—68.40; She was born at Baracoa on March 25th, 1958, and is married to her coach, Angel Salzedo.

COMMONWEALTH GAMES

The first British Empire Games were staged at Hamilton, Canada, in 1930, although the idea of such an event was mooted as early as 1891 by a Mr. Astley Cooper and an "Inter-Empire Championships" was held at London's Crystal Palace in 1911. The driving force behind the Hamilton Games was Mr. M. M. (Bobby) Robinson, manager of the Canadian athletics team at the 1928 Olympic Games.

Women's events were introduced at the second Empire Games in London in 1934. Subsequent meetings were held in Sydney (1938), Auckland (1950), Vancouver (1954), Cardiff (1958), Perth, Western Australia (1962), Kingston, Jamaica (1966), Edinburgh (1970), Christchurch (1974), and Edmonton, Alberta (1978). The 1982 Games will be held in Brisbane. The Games went metric in 1970.

Champions

100 Yards sec.
1930 P. Williams (Canada) 9.9
1934 A. W. Sweeney (England) 10.0
1938 C. B. Holmes (England) 9.7
1950 J. F. Treloar (Australia) 9.7
1954 M. G. R. Agostini (Trinidad) 9.6
1958 K. A. St. H. Gardner (Jamaica) 9.4
1962 S. Antao (Kenya) 9.5
1966 H. W. Jerome (Canada) 9.4

100 Metres
1970 D. Quarrie (Jamaica) 10.2
1974 D. Quarrie (Jamaica) 10.38
1978 D. Quarrie (Jamaica) 10.03

220 Yards sec.
1930 S. E. Englehart (England) 21.8
1934 A. W. Sweeney (England) 21.9
1938 C. B. Holmes (England) 21.2
1950 J. F. Treloar (Australia) 21.5
1954 D. W. Jowett (New Zealand) 21.5
1958 T. A. Robinson (Bahamas) 21.0
1962 S. Antao (Kenya) 21.1
1966 S. F. Allotey (Ghana) 20.7

200 Metres
1970 D. Quarrie (Jamaica) 20.5
1974 D. Quarrie (Jamaica) 20.73
1978 A. W. Wells (Scotland) 20.12

440 Yards sec.
1930 A. Wilson (Canada) 48.8
1934 G. L. Rampling (England) 48.0
1938 W. Roberts (England) 47.9
1950 E. W. Carr (Australia) 47.9
1954 R. K. Gosper (Australia) 47.2
1958 Milkha Singh (India) 46.6
1962 G. E. Kerr (Jamaica) 46.7
1966 W. Mottley (Trinidad) 45.0

400 Metres
1970 C. Asati (Kenya) 45.0
1974 C. Asati (Kenya) 46.04
1978 R. Mitchell (Australia) 46.34

880 Yards min. sec.
1930 T. Hampson (England) 1 52.4
1934 P. A. Edwards (Brit. Guiana) 1 54.2
1938 V. P. Boot (New Zealand) 1 51.2
1950 H. J. Parlett (England) 1 53.1
1954 D. J. N. Johnson (England) 1 50.7
1958 H. J. Elliott (Australia) 1 49.3
1962 P. G. Snell (New Zealand) 1 47.6
1966 N. S. Clough (Australia) 1 46.9

800 Metres
1970 R. Ouko (Kenya) 1 46.8
1974 J. Kipkurgat (Kenya) 1 43.9
1978 M. Boit (Kenya) 1 46.4

Mile min. sec.
1930 R. H. Thomas (England) 4 14.0
1934 J. E. Lovelock (New Zealand) 4 12.8
1938 J. W. Ll. Alford (Wales) 4 11.6
1950 C. W. Parnell (Canada) 4 11.0
1954 R. G. Bannister (England) 3 58.8
1958 H. J. Elliott (Australia) 3 59.0
1962 P. G. Snell (New Zealand) 4 04.6
1966 K. Keino (Kenya) 3 55.3

1500 Metres
1970 K. Keino (Kenya) 3 36.6
1974 F. Bayi (Tanzania) 3 32.2
1978 D. R. Moorcroft (Eng.) 3 35.5

3 Miles min. sec.
1930 S. A. Tomlin (England) 14 27.4

1934	W. J. Beavers (England)	14	32.6
1938	C. H. Matthews (New Zealand)	13	59.6
1950	L. Eyre (England)	14	23.6
1954	C. J. Chataway (England)	13	35.2
1958	M. G. Halberg (New Zealand)	13	15.0
1962	M. G. Halberg (New Zealand)	13	34.2
1966	K. Keino (Kenya)	12	57.4

5000 Metres

1970	I. Stewart (Scotland)	13	22.8
1974	B. Jipcho (Kenya)	13	14.4
1978	H. Rono (Kenya)	13	23.0

6 Miles — min. sec.

1930	W. J. Savidan (New Zealand)	30	49.6
1934	A. W. Penny (England)	31	00.6
1938	C. H. Matthews (New Zealand)	30	14.5
1950	W. H. Nelson (New Zealand)	30	29.6
1954	P. B. Driver (England)	29	09.4
1958	W. D. Power (Australia)	28	47.8
1962	B. Kidd (Canada)	28	26.6
1966	N. Temu (Kenya)	27	14.6

10,000 Metres

1970	J. L. Stewart (Scotland)	28	11.8
1974	R. Tayler (New Zealand)	27	46.4
1978	B. Foster (England)	28	13.7

Marathon — hr. min. sec.

1930	D. McL. Wright (Scotland)	2	43	43.0
1934	H. Webster (Canada)	2	40	36.0
1938	J. L. Coleman (S. Africa)	2	30	49.8
1950	J. T. Holden (England)	2	32	57.0
1954	J. McGhee (Scotland)	2	39	36.0
1958	W. D. Power (Australia)	2	22	45.6
1962	B. L. Kilby (England)	2	21	17.0
1966	J. N. C. Alder (Scotland)	2	22	07.8
1970	R. Hill (England)	2	09	28.0
1974	I. R. Thompson (England)	2	09	12.0
1978	G. Shahanga (Tanzania)	2	15	39.8

Steeplechase — min. sec.

1930	G. W. Bailey (England)	9	52.0
1934	S. C. Scarsbrook (England)	10	23.4

3000 Metres Steeplechase — min. sec.

1962	T. A. Vincent (Australia)	8	43.4
1966	R. P. Welsh (New Zealand)	8	29.6
1970	A. P. Manning (Australia)	8	26.2
1974	B. Jipcho (Kenya)	8	20.8
1978	H. Rono (Kenya)	8	26.5

120 Yards Hurdles — sec.

1930	Lord Burghley (England)	14.6
1934	D. O. Finlay (England)	15.2
1938	T. P. Lavery (S. Africa)	14.0
1950	P. J. Gardner (Australia)	14.3
1954	K. A. St. H. Gardner (Jamaica)	14.2
1958	K. A. St. H. Gardner (Jamaica)	14.0
1962	H. G. Raziq (Pakistan)	14.3
1966	D. P. Hemery (England)	14.1

110 Metres Hurdles

1970	D. P. Hemery (England)	13.6
1974	F. Kimaiyo (Kenya)	13.69
1978	B. Price (Wales)	13.70

440 Yards Hurdles — sec.

1930	Lord Burghley (England)	54.4
1934	F. A. R. Hunter (Scotland)	55.2
1938	J. W. Loaring (Canada)	52.9
1950	D. White (Ceylon)	52.5
1954	D. F. Lean (Australia)	52.4
1958	G. C. Potgieter (S. Africa)	49.7
1962	K. J. Roche (Australia)	51.5
1966	K. J. Roche (Australia)	51.0

400 Metres Hurdles

1970	J. Sherwood (England)	50.0
1974	A. P. Pascoe (England)	48.83
1978	D. Kimaiyo (Kenya)	49.48

4 x 110 Yards Relay — sec.

1930	Canada (J. R. Brown, L. Miller, R. A. Adams J. R. Fitzpatrick)	42.2
1934	England (E. I. Davis, W. Rangeley, G. T. Saunders, A. W. Sweeney)	42.2
1938	Canada (J. Brown, P. Haley, J. W. Loaring, L. G. O'Connor)	41.6
1950	Australia (A. W. de Gruchy, D. Johnson, A. K. Gordon, J. F. Treloar)	42.2

1954	Canada (J. D. Macfarlane, D. R. Stonehouse, H. Nelson, B. Springbett)	41.3
1958	England (P. F. Radford, D. H. Segal, E. R. Sandstrom, A. Breacker)	40.7
1962	England (P. F. Radford, L. W. Carter, A. Meakin, D. H. Jones)	40.6
1966	Ghana (E. C. Addy, B. K. Mends, J. A. Addy, S. F. Allotey)	39.8

4 x 100 Metres Relay

1970	Jamaica (E. Stewart, L. Miller, C. Lawson, D. Quarrie)	39.4
1974	Australia (G. Lewis, L. D'Arcy, A. Ratcliffe, G. Haskell)	39.3
1978	Scotland (D. A. Jenkins, A. W. Wells, R. C. Sharp, A. E. McMaster)	39.24

4 x 440 Yards Relay min. sec.

1930	England (Lord Burghley, K. C. Brangwin, R. Leigh-Wood, H. S. Townend)	3 19.4
1934	England (D. L. Rathbone, C. H. Stoneley, G. N. Blake, G. L. Rampling)	3 16.8
1938	Canada (W. Dale, J. Frazer, J. W. Loaring, J. Orr)	3 16.9
1950	Australia (R. E. Price, G. V. Gedge, J. W. Humphreys, E. W. Carr)	3 17.8
1954	England (F. P. Higgins, A. Dick, P. G. Fryer, D J. N. Johnson)	3 11.2
1958	South Africa (G. R. Day, G. G. Evans, G. C. Potgieter, M. C. Spence)	3 08.1
1962	Jamaica (L. Khan, Mal Spence, Mel Spence, G. E. Kerr)	3 10.2
1966	Trinidad & Tobago (L. Yearwood, K. Bernard, E. Roberts, W. Mottley)	3 02.8

4 x 400 Metres Relay

1970	Kenya (H. Nyamau, J. Sang, R. Ouko, C. Asati)	3 03.6
1974	Kenya (C. Asati, F. Musyoki, W. Koskei, J. Sang)	3 04.4
1978	Kenya: (W. Njiri, D. Kimaiyo, W. Koskei, J. Ngetich)	3 03.5

High Jump metres

1930	J. H. Viljoen (S. Africa)	1.90
1934	E. T. Thacker (S. Africa)	1.90
1938	E. T. Thacker (S. Africa)	1.95
1950	J. A. Winter (Australia)	1.98
1954	E. A. Ifeajuna (Nigeria)	2.03
1958	E. Haisley (Jamaica)	2.05
1962	P. F. Hobson (Australia)	2.11
1966	L. Peckham (Australia)	2.08
1970	L. Peckham (Australia)	2.14
1974	G. Windeyer (Australia)	2.16
1978	C. Ferragne (Canada)	2.20

Pole Vault metres

1930	V. W. Pickard (Canada)	3.73
1934	C. J. S. Apps (Canada)	3.81
1938	A. S. du Plessis (S. Africa	4.11
1950	T. D. Anderson (England)	3.96
1954	G. M. Elliott (England)	4.26
1958	G. M. Elliott (England)	4.16
1962	T. S. Bickle (Australia)	4.49
1966	T. S. Bickle (Australia)	4.80
1970	M. A. Bull (N. Ireland)	5.10
1974	D. Baird (Australia)	5.05
1978	B. Simpson (Canada)	5.10

Long Jump metres

1930	L. Hutton (Canada)	7.20
1934	S. Richardson (Canada)	7.17
1938	H. Brown (Canada)	7.43
1950	N. G. Price (S. Africa)	7.31
1954	K. S. D. Wilmshurst (England)	7.54
1958	P. Foreman (Jamaica)	7.47
1962	M. Ahey (Ghana)	8.05
1966	L. Davies (Wales)	7.99
1970	L. Davies (Wales)	8.06
1974	A. L. Lerwill (England)	7.94
1978	R. R. Mitchell (England)	8.06

Triple Jump metres

1930	G. C. Smallacombe (Canada)	14.76
1934	J. P. Metcalfe (Australia)	15.63
1938	J. P. Metcalfe (Australia)	15.49

1950	B. T. Oliver (Australia)	15.61	
1954	K. S. D. Wilmshurst (England)	15.28	
1958	I. R. Tomlinson (Australia)	15.73	
1962	I. R. Tomlinson (Australia)	16.20	
1966	S. Igun (Nigeria)	16.40	
1970	P. J. May (Australia)	16.72	
1974	J. Owusu (Ghana)	16.50	
1978	K. L. Connor (England)	17.21	

Shot — metres
- 1930 H. B. Hart (S. Africa) 14.58
- 1934 H. B. Hart (S. Africa) 14.67
- 1938 L. A. Fouche (S. Africa) 14.48
- 1950 M. Tuicakau (Fiji) 14.63
- 1954 J. A. Savidge (England) 16.77
- 1958 A. Rowe (England) 17.57
- 1962 M. T. Lucking (England) 18.08
- 1966 D. Steen (Canada) 18.79
- 1970 D. Steen (Canada) 19.21
- 1974 G. L. Capes (England) 20.74
- 1978 G. L. Capes (England) 19.77

Discus — metres
- 1930 H. B. Hart (S. Africa) 41.44
- 1934 H. B. Hart (S. Africa) 41.54
- 1938 E. E. Coy (Canada) 44.76
- 1950 I. M. Reed (Australia) 47.72
- 1954 S. J. du Plessis (S. Africa) 51.70
- 1958 S. J. du Plessis (S. Africa) 55.94
- 1962 W. P. Selvey (Australia) 56.48
- 1966 L. R. Mills (New Zealand) 56.18
- 1970 G. Puce (Canada) 59.04
- 1974 R. Tait (New Zealand) 63.08
- 1978 B. Chambul (Canada) 59.70

Hammer — metres
- 1930 M. C. Nokes (England) 47.12
- 1934 M. C. Nokes (England) 48.24
- 1938 G. W. Sutherland (Canada) 48.72
- 1950 D. McD. M. Clark (Scotland) 49.94
- 1954 M. Iqbal (Pakistan) 55.38
- 1958 M. J. Ellis (England) 62.90
- 1962 A. H. Payne (England) 61.64
- 1966 A. H. Payne (England) 61.98
- 1970 A. H. Payne (England) 67.80
- 1974 I. A. Chipchase (England) 69.56
- 1978 P. Farmer (Australia) 71.10

Javelin — metres
- 1930 S. A. Lay (New Zealand) 63.12
- 1934 R. Dixon (Canada) 60.02
- 1938 J. A. Courtwright (Canada) 62.82
- 1950 L. J. Roininen (Canada) 57.10
- 1954 J. D. Achurch (Australia) 68.52
- 1958 C. G. Smith (England) 71.28
- 1962 A. E. Mitchell (Australia) 78.10
- 1966 J. H. P. FitzSimons (England) 79.78
- 1970 D. H. Travis (England) 79.50
- 1974 C. P. Clover (England) 84.92
- 1978 P. Olsen (Canada) 84.00

Decathlon — pts.
- 1966 R. A. Williams (New Zealand) 7270
- 1970 G. J. Smith (Australia) 7492
- 1974 M. A. Bull (N. Ireland) 7417
- 1978 F. M. Thompson (England) 8467

20 Miles Walk — hr. min. sec.
- 1966 R. Wallwork (England) 2 44 42.8
- 1970 N. F. Freeman (Australia) 2 33 33.0
- 1974 J. Warhurst (England) 2 35 23.0

30 Kilometres Walk — hr. min. sec.
- 1978 O. T. Flynn (England) 2 22 03.7

Women Champions

100 Yards — sec.
- 1934 E. M. Hiscock (England) 11.3
- 1938 D. Norman (Australia) 11.1
- 1950 M. Nelson (Australia) 10.8
- 1954 M. Nelson (Australia) 10.7
- 1958 M. J. Willard (Australia) 10.6
- 1962 D. Hyman (England) 11.2
- 1966 D. Burge (Australia) 10.6

100 Metres
- 1970 R. A. Boyle (Australia) 11.2
- 1974 R. A. Boyle (Australia) 11.27
- 1978 S. M. Lannaman (England) 11.27

220 Yards — sec.
- 1934 E. M. Hiscock (England) 25.0
- 1938 D. Norman (Australia) 24.7
- 1950 M. Nelson (Australia) 24.3
- 1954 M. Nelson (Australia) 24.0
- 1958 M. J. Willard (Australia) 23.6
- 1962 D. Hyman (England) 23.8
- 1966 D. Burge (Australia) 23.8

200 Metres
1970 R. A. Boyle (Australia) 22.7
1974 R. A. Boyle (Australia) 22.50
1978 D. Boyd (Australia) 22.82

440 Yards sec.
1966 J. Pollock (Australia) 53.0

400 Metres
1970 M. Neufville (Jamaica) 51.0
1974 Y. Saunders (Canada) 51.67
1978 D-M. L. Hartley (Eng.) 51.69

880 Yards min. sec.
1934 G. A. Lunn (England) 2 19.4
1962 D. Willis (Australia) 2 03.7
1966 A. Hoffman (Canada) 2 04.3

800 Metres
1970 R. O. Stirling (Scotland) 2 06.2
1974 C. Rendina (Australia) 2 01.1
1978 J. Peckham (Australia) 2 02.8

1500 Metres min. sec.
1970 R. Ridley (England) 4 18.8
1974 G. Reiser (Canada) 4 07.8
1978 M. Stewart (England) 4 06.3

3000 Metres min. sec.
1978 P. Fudge (England) 9 13.0

80 Metres Hurdles sec.
1934 M. R. Clark (S. Africa) 11.8
1938 B. Burke (S. Africa) 11.7
1950 S. B. Strickland (Australia) 11.6
1954 E. M. Maskell (N. Rhodesia) 10.9
1958 N. C. Thrower (Australia) 10.7
1962 P. Kilborn (Australia) 10.9
1966 P. Kilborn (Australia) 10.9

100 Metres Hurdles
1970 P. Kilborn (Australia) 13.2
1974 J. A. Vernon (England) 13.45
1978 L. M. Boothe (England) 12.98

110 x 220 x 110 Yards Relay sec.
1934 England (N. Halstead E. Maguire, E. M. Hiscock) 49.4
1938 Australia (J. Coleman, A. E. Wearne, D. Norman) 49.1
1950 Australia (M. Nelson, S. B. Strickland, V. Johnston) 47.9

4 x 110 Yards Relay
1954 Australia (G. Wallace, N. A. Fogarty, W. Cripps, M. Nelson) 46.8

1958 England (V. M. Weston, J. F. Paul, D. Hyman, H. J. Young) 45.3
1962 Australia (J. Bennett, G. Beasley, B. Cox, B. Cuthbert) 46.6
1966 Australia (J. Lamy, P. Kilborn, J. Bennett, D. Burge) 45.3

4 x 100 Metres Relay
1970 Australia (J. Lamy, P. Kilborn, M. Hoffman, R. A. Boyle) 44.1
1974 Australia (J. Lamy, D. Boyd, R. Boak, R. A. Boyle) 43.51
1978 England (B. L. Goddard, K. J. Smallwood, S. Colyear, S. M. Lannaman) 43.70

660 Yards Relay min. sec.
1934 Canada (L. Palmer, B. White, A. A. Meagher, A. Dearnley) 1 14.4
1938 Australia (J. Coleman, D. Norman, T. Peake, J. Woodland) 1 15.2
1950 Australia (S. B. Strickland, V. Johnston, M. Nelson, A. Shanley) 1 13.4

4 x 400 Metres Relay min. sec.
1974 England (S. Pettett, R. Kennedy, J. V. Roscoe, V. M. Elder) 3 29.2
1978 England (R. Kennedy, J. Y. Hoyte, V. M. Elder, D-M. L. Hartley) 3 27.2

High Jump metres
1934 M. R. Clark (S. Africa) 1.60
1938 D. J. B. Tyler (England) 1.60
1950 D. J. B. Tyler (England) 1.60
1954 T. E. Hopkins (N. Ireland) 1.67
1958 M. M. Brown (Australia) 1.70
1962 R. Woodhouse (Australia) 1.78
1966 M. M. Brown (Australia) 1.72
1970 D. Brill (Canada) 1.78
1974 B. J. Lawton (England) 1.84
1978 K. Gibbs (Australia) 1.93

Long Jump metres
1934 P. Bartholomew (England) 5.47
1938 D. Norman (Australia) 5.80

1950	Y. W. Williams (New Zealand)	5.90
1954	Y. W. Williams (New Zealand)	6.08
1958	S. H. Hoskin (England)	6.02
1962	P. Kilborn (Australia)	6.27
1966	M. D. Rand (England)	6.36
1970	S. Sherwood (England)	6.73
1974	M. Oshikoya (Nigeria)	6.46
1978	S. D. Reeve (England)	6.59

Shot — metres
1954	Y. W. Williams (New Zealand)	13.96
1958	V. I. Young (New Zealand)	15.54
1962	V. I. Young (New Zealand)	15.23
1966	V. I. Young (New Zealand)	16.50
1970	M. E. Peters (N. Ireland)	15.93
1974	J. Haist (Canada)	16.12
1978	G. Mulhall (Australia)	17.31

Discus — metres
1954	Y. W. Williams (New Zealand)	45.02
1958	S. Allday (England)	45.90
1962	V. I. Young (New Zealand)	50.20
1966	V. I. Young (New Zealand)	49.78
1970	C. R. Payne (Scotland)	54.46
1974	J. Haist (Canada)	55.52
1978	C. Ionesco (Canada)	62.16

Javelin — metres
1934	G. A. Lunn (England)	32.18
1938	R. Higgins (Canada)	38.28
1950	C. C. McGibbon (Australia)	38.84
1954	M. C. Swanepoel (S. Africa)	43.82
1958	A. Pazera (Australia)	57.40
1962	S. Platt (England)	50.24
1966	M. Parker (Australia)	51.38
1970	P. Rivers (Australia)	52.00
1974	P. Rivers (Australia)	55.48
1978	T. I. Sanderson (England)	61.34

Pentathlon — Pts.
1970	M. E. Peters (N. Ireland)	4524
1974	M. E. Peters (N. Ireland)	4455
1978	D. Konihowski (Canada)	4768

English Medallists

The following athletes, listed in alphabetical order, have won Commonwealth Games medals while representing England. G signifies gold (1st), S silver (2nd) and B bronze (3rd).

Adcocks, W. A., 1966, marathon (S).
Adey, J. A., 1966, 4 x 440 yd. (B).
Allday, P. C., 1958, hammer (B).
Allen, C. K., 1934, 3 mi. (S).
Alsop, F. J., 1962, triple jump (B); 1966, triple jump (B).
Anderson, T. D., 1950, pole vault (G).
Archer, J., 1950, 4 x 110 yd. (S).
Bailey, G. W., 1930, Steep. (G); 1934, Steep. (B).
Bannister, R. G., 1954, mile (G).
Beavers, W. J., 1934, 3 mi. (G).
Bell, D. R., 1934, discus (S).
Bilham, M., 1970, 4 x 400 m. (B).
Black, D. J., 1974, 5000 m. (B) and 10,000 m. (S).
Blake, G. N., 1934, 4 x 440 yd. (G).
Boyd, I. H., 1954, 880 yd. (B).
Brangwin, K. C., 1930, 4 x 440 yd. (G).
Breacker, A., 1958, 4 x 110 yd. (G).
Brightwell, R. I., 1962, 440 yd. (S); 4 x 440 yd. (S).
Brown, R. K., 1934, 440 hurdles (B).
Burghley, Lord, 1930, 120 yd. hurdles (G), 440 yd. hurdles (G) and 4 x 440 yd. (G).
Burns, J. A., 1934, 3 mi. (B).
Capes, G. L., 1974, shot (G); 1978, shot (G).
Carr, G. A., 1958, discus (B).
Carter, A. W., 1974, 4 x 400 m. (S).
Carter, L. W., 1962, 4 x 110 yd. (G).
Chataway, C. J., 1954, 3 mi. (G).
Chipchase, I. A., 1974, hammer (G).
Chivers, A. H., 1950, 3 mi. (B).
Clover, C. P., 1974, javelin (G).
Cohen, H. J., 1930, 4 x 110 yd. (S).
Connor, K. L., 1978 triple jump (G).
Cornes, J. F., 1930, mile (B); 1934, mile (B).
Davis, E. I., 1934, 4 x 110 yd. (G).
Dear, D. G., 1970, 4 x 100 m. (B).
Dick, A., 1954, 4 x 440 yd. (G).
Drayton, A. W., 1978 decathlon (B).
Driver, P. B., 1954, 6 mi. (G).
Duncan, K. S., 1938, 4 x 110 yd. (S).
Elliott, G. M., 1954, pole vault (G); 1958, pole vault (G).
Ellis, M. J., 1958, hammer (G).
Englehart, S. E., 1930, 220 yd. (G) and 4 x 110 yd. (S).
Evenson, T., 1930, 6 mi. (B); 1934, Steep. (G).
Eyre, L., 1950, 3 mi. (G) and mile (S).
Faircloth, D. K., 1970, marathon (B).
Ferris, S., 1930, marathon (S).

Finlay, D. O., 1934, 120 yd. hurdles (G).
FitzSimons, J. H. P., 1966, javelin (G), 1970, javelin (B).
Flynn, O. T., 1978 30 km. walk (G).
Ford, H., 1930, pole vault (S).
Foster, B., 1970, 1500 m. (B); 1974, 5000 m. (S); 1978, 10,000 m. (G), 5000 m. (B).
Fraser, B., 1970, hammer (S).
Fryer, P. G., 1954, 4 x 440 yd. (G).
Furze, A. F., 1934, 6 mi. (B).
Gabbett, P. J., 1970, decathlon (S).
Gaby, F. R., 1930, 120 yd. hurdles (B).
Graham, T. J. M., 1966, 4 x 440 yd. (B).
Green, B. W., 1970, 4 x 100 m. (B).
Green, F., 1954, 3 mi. (S).
Green, I. D., 1970, 4 x 100 m. (B).
Hampson, T., 1930, 880 yd. (G).
Handley, F. R., 1938, 880 yd. (S) and 4 x 440 yd. (S).
Hanlon, J. A. T., 1930, 4 x 110 yd. (S).
Harper, E., 1930, 6 mi. (S).
Hartley, W. J., 1974, 4 x 400 m. (S).
Hauck, M. A., 1970, 4 x 400 m. (B).
Heap, J. C., 1930, 4 x 110 yd. (S).
Hemery, D. P., 1966, 120 yd. hurdles (G), 1970, 120 yd. hurdles (G).
Herriott, M., 1962, 3000 m. steeplechase (S).
Hewson, B. S., 1954, 880 yd. (S); 1958, 880 yd. (S).
Higgins, F. P., 1954, 4 x 440 yd. (G).
Higgins, T. L., 1950, 4 x 440 yd. (S).
Higham, C. E. E., 1954, 120 yd. hurdles (S).
Hill, R., 1970, marathon (G).
Hillier, J. N., 1974, discus (B).
Holden, J. T., 1950, marathon (G).
Holmes, C. B., 1938, 100 yd. (G), 220 yd. (G) and 4 x 110 yd. (S).
Hooper, B. R. L., 1974, pole vault (B); 1978, pole vault (B).
Howland, R. L., 1930, shot (S); 1934, shot (S).
Jackson, B. D., 1962, 4 x 440 yd. (S).
Johnson, D. J. N., 1954, 880 yd. (G) and 4 x 440 yd. (G); 1958, 4 x 440 yd. (S).
Jones, D. H., 1962, 4 x 110 yd. (G) and 220 yd. (S).
Kane, H., 1954, 440 yd. hurdles (S).
Kilby, B. L., 1962, marathon (G).
King, B. J., 1970, decathlon (B); 1974, decathlon (S).
Leigh-Wood, R., 1930, 4 x 440 yd. (G) and 440 yd. hurdles (S).

Lerwill, A. L., 1970, long jump (B); 1974, long jump (G).
Lewis, L. C., 1950, 440 yd. (S), 4 x 110 yd. (S) and 4 x 440 yd. (S).
Lucking, M. T., 1958, shot (S); 1962, shot (G).
McCabe, B. F., 1938, 4 x 440 yd. (S).
McLeod, M. J., 1978, 10,000 m. (B).
McSorley, J. V., 1970, javelin (S).
Meakin, A., 1962, 4 x 110 yd. (G).
Metcalfe, A. P., 1962, 4 x 440 yd. (S).
Middleton, R. C., 1966, 20 miles walk (S).
Mitchell, R. R., 1978, long jump (G).
Moody, H. E. A., 1950, shot (S).
Moorcroft, D. R., 1978, 1500 m. (G).
Moore, A. L., 1978, triple jump (B).
Morgan, V. E., 1930, steeplechase (B).
Neame, D. M. L., 1930, 440 yd. hurdles (B).
Nokes, M. C., 1930, hammer (G); 1934, hammer (G).
Norris, A. J., 1938, marathon (S).
Pack, H. E., 1938, 4 x 440 yd. (S).
Page, E. L., 1930, 100 yd. (S).
Parker, J. M., 1966, 120 yd. hurdles (S).
Parlett, H. J., 1950, 880 yd. (G) and 4 x 440 yd. (S).
Pascoe, A. P., 1974, 400 m. hurdles (G) and 4 x 400 m. (S); 1978, 400 m. hurdles (B).
Payne, A. H., 1962, hammer (G); 1966, hammer (G); 1970, hammer (G); 1974, hammer (S).
Penny, A. W., 1934, 6 mi. (G).
Peters, J. H., 1954, 6 mi. (B).
Pharaoh, M., 1954, discus (B).
Pilbrow, A. G., 1934, 120 yd. hurdles (B).
Pridie, K. H., 1934, shot (B).
Pugh, D. C., 1950, 4 x 440 yd. (S).
Radford, P. F., 1958, 4 x 110 yd. (G); 1962, 4 x 110 yd. (G).
Rampling, G. L., 1934, 440 yd. (G) and 4 x 440 yd. (G).
Rangeley, W., 1934, 4 x 110 yd. (G) and 220 yd. (B).
Rathbone, D. L., 1934, 4 x 440 yd. (G).
Rawson, M. A., 1958, 880 yd. (B).
Revans, R. W., 1930, long jump (S) and triple jump (S).
Reynolds, M. E., 1970, 4 x 100 m. (B).
Richardson, K. J., 1938, 4 x 110 yd. (S).
Roberts, W., 1934, 440 yd. (S); 1938, 440 yd. (G) and 4 x 440 yd. (S).
Rowe, A., 1958, shot (G).

Rushmer, A. T., 1966, 3 mi. (B).
Salisbury, J. E., 1958, 4 x 440 yd. (S).
Sampson, E. J., 1958, 4 x 440 yd. (S).
Sando, F. D., 1954, 6 mi. (S) and 3 mi. (B).
Sandstrom, E. R., 1958, 4 x 110 yd. (G).
Saunders, G. T., 1934, 4 x 110 yd. (G).
Savidge, J. A., 1954, shot (G).
Scarsbrook, S. C., 1934, steeplechase (G).
Segal, D. H., 1958, 4 x 110 yd. (G).
Setti, R. E. F., 1962, 4 x 440 yd. (S)
Sheldrick, J. W., 1962, discus (B).
Shenton, B., 1950, 4 x 110 yd. (S) 1954, 220 yd. (S).
Sherwood, J., 1970, 400 m. hurdles (G), and 4 x 400 m. (B).
Simpson, A., 1966, mile (S).
Smith, C. G., 1958, javelin (G); 1962 javelin (S).
Stacey, N. D., 1950, 4 x 110 yd. (S).
Stoneley, C. H., 1934, 4 x 440 yd. (G) and 440 yd. (B).
Sweeney, A. W., 1934, 100 yd. (G), 220 yd. (G) and 4 x 110 yd. (G).
Taitt, J. L., 1962, 120 yd. hurdles (B).
Tancred, W. R., 1970, discus (B); 1974, discus (S).
Taylor, R. G., 1970, 10,000 m. (B).
Teale, J., 1970, shot (S).
Thomas, R. H., 1930, mile (G) and 880 yd. (S).
Thompson, F. M., 1978, decathlon (G).
Thompson, I. R., 1974, marathon (G).
Thorpe, R. S., 1974, 20 mi. walk (S).
Tomlin, S. A., 1930, 3 mi. (G).
Townend, H. S., 1930, 4 x 440 yd. (G.)
Travis, D. H., 1970, javelin (G); 1974, javelin (S).
Wallace, L. M., 1938, 4 x 110 yd. (S).
Wallwork, R., 1966, 20 miles walk (G).
Walters, L. B., 1970, 4 x 400 m. (B).
Ward, P. D. H., 1938, 3 mi. (S).
Warden, P., 1966, 440 yd. hurdles (B) and 4 x 440 yd. (B).
Warhurst, J., 1974, 20 mi. walk (G).
Wilkinson, P. A., 1958, marathon (B).
Williams, B., 1970, hammer (B).
Wilmshurst, K. S. D., 1954, long jump (G) and triple jump (G).
Wilson, J. A., 1974, 4 x 400 m. (S).
Winbolt Lewis, M. J., 1966, 4 x 440 yd. (B).
Winch, M. A., 1974, shot (S).
Winfield, J. W., 1930, 3 mi. (B).
Wooderson, S. C., 1934, mile (S).
Wrighton, J. D., 1958, 4 x 440 yd. (S).
Yates, P. D., 1978, javelin (B).

Women
Allday, S., 1954, discus (S); 1958, discus (G) and shot (S); 1962, shot (B).
Allison, J. F., 1970, 1500 m. (S); 1974, 1500 m. (S).
Bartholomew, P., 1934, long jump (G).
Batter, D., 1950, 660 yd. relay (S).
Bell, C., 1970, 100 m. hurdles (B).
Benning, C. M., 1978, 1500 m. (S).
Boothe, L. M., 1978, 100 m. hurdles (G).
Burgess, S., 1954, 4 x 110 yd. (S).
Butterfield, D., 1934, 880 yd. (B).
Chalmers, L., 1934, 100 yd. (B).
Cheeseman, B., 1950, 660 yd. relay (S) and 440 yd. relay (B).
Cobb, V. M., 1958, 4 x 110 yd. (G) and 100 yd. (B); 1970, 4 x 100 m. (S).
Colebrook K. J., 1978, 800 m. (B).
Colyear, S., 1978, 4 x 100 m. (G), 100 m. hurdles (B).
Corbett, S. J., 1974, javelin (B).
Cox, M., 1934, javelin (B).
Critchley, M. A., 1970, 200 m. (B) and 4 x 100 m. (S).
Crowther, B., 1950, high jump (S).
Elder, V. M., 1974, 4 x 400 m. (G), 400 m. (S); 1978, 4 x 400 m. (G), 400 m. (S).
Farquhar, A., 1970, javelin (S).
Ford, A., 1978, 3000 m. (B).
Fudge, P., 1978, 3000 m. (G).
Gardner, D. K., 1938, high jump (S).
Goddard , B. L., 1978, 4 x 100 m. (G).
Green, E., 1934, 80 m. hurdles (B).
Hall, D. G., 1950, 660 yd. relay (S) and 440 yd. relay (B).
Hall, J. A., 1966, 100 m. (B) and 4 x 110 yd. (S).
Halstead, E., 1934, javelin (S).
Halstead, N., 1934, 440 yd. relay (G), 660 yd. relay (S) and 220 yd. (B).
Hartley D-M. L., 1978, 400 m. and 4 x 400 m. (G).
Hiscock, E., 1934, 100 yd. (G), 220 yd. (G), 440 yd. relay (G) and 660 yd. relay (S).
Hoskin, S. H., 1958, long jump (G).
Hoyte, J. Y., 1978, 4 x 400 m. (G).
Hyman, D., 1958, 4 x 110 yd. (G); 1962, 100 yd. (G), 220 yd. (G) and 4 x 110 yd. (S).
Johnson, E., 1934, 660 yd. relay (S).
Jones, I., 1934, 880 yd. (S).

Jordan, J. W., 1962, 880 yd. (B).
Jordan, W., 1938, 660 yd. relay (S) and 440 yd. relay (B).
Kennedy, R., 1974, 4 x 400 m. (G); 1978, 4 x 400 m. (G).
Lannaman, S. M., 1974, 4 x 100 m. (S); 1978, 100 m. (G), 4 x 100 m. (G), 200 m. (S).
Lawton, B. J., 1974, high jump (G).
Lowe, P. B., 1970, 800 m. (S).
Lunn, G. A., 1934, 880 yd. (G) and javelin (G); 1938, javelin (B).
Lynch, J. A. C., 1974, 100 m. (S) and 4 x 100 m. (S).
Maguire, E., 1934, 440 yd. relay (G).
Mapstone, S. L., 1978, pentathlon (S).
Martin, B. A., 1974, 4 x 100 m. (S).
Moore, B. R. H., 1962, 80 m. hurdles (S) and 4 x 110 yd. (S).
Morgan, R., 1962, javelin (S).
Neil, D. A., 1970, 4 x 100 m. (S).
Oakes, J. M., 1978, shot (B).
Packer, A. E., 1962, 4 x 110 yd. (S).
Pashley, A., 1954, 4 x 110 yd. (S).
Paul, J. F., 1958, 4 x 110 yd. (G).
Peat, V., 1970, 4 x 100 m. (S).
Pettett, S., 1974, 4 x 400 m. (G).
Pickering, J. C., 1954, 80 m. hurdles (B) and long jump (B).
Pirie, S., 1954, 4 x 110 yd. (S) and 220 yd. (B).
Platt, S. M., 1962, javelin (G).
Quinton, C. L., 1958, 80 m. hurdles (S).
Raby, E., 1938, long jump (S) and 660 yd. relay (S).
Rand, M. D., 1958, long jump (S); 1966, long jump (G).
Reeve, S. D., 1978, long jump (B).
Ridley, R., 1970, 1500 m. (G).
Roscoe, J. V., 1974, 4 x 400 m. (G).
Sanderson, T. I., 1978, javelin (G).
Saunders, D., 1938, 660 yd. relay (S) and 440 yd. relay (B).
Sherwood, S. H., 1966, long jump (S); 1970, long jump (G).
Shirley, D. A., 1966, high jump (S).
Simpson, J. M., 1954, 4 x 110 yd. (S).
Slater, D., 1962, 4 x 110 yd. (S); 1966, 4 x 110 yd. (S).
Smallwood, K. J., 1978, 4 x 100 m. (G).
Smith, A. R., 1966, 880 yd. (B).
Stokes, K., 1938, 660 yd. relay (S) and 440 yd. relay (B).
Strong, S. E., 1978, 100 m. hurdles (S).
Tranter, M. D., 1966, 4 x 110 yd. (S).
Tyler, D. J. B., 1938, high jump (G); 1950, high jump (G); 1954, high jump (S).
Vernon, J. A., 1974, 100 m. hurdles (G) and 4 x 100 m. (S).
Walker, I., 1934, 660 yd. relay (S).
Walker, M., 1950, 660 yd. relay (S) and 440 yd. relay (B).
Watkinson, D. A., 1966, 440 yd. (S).
Webb, V., 1934, long jump (B).
Williams, A. M., 1958, javelin (B).
Wilson, A. S., 1970, high jump (S); long jump (S) and pentathlon (S); 1974, pentathlon (B).
Wray, Y. J., 1978, Pentathlon (B).
Young, H. J., 1954, 4 x 110 yd. (S); 1958, 4 x 110 yd. (G), 100 yd. (S) and 220 yd. (B).

Scottish Medallists

Alder, J. N. C., 1966, marathon (G) and 6 mi. (B); 1970, marathon (S).
Black, C. F., 1978, hammer (B).
Brownlee, D. A., 1934, 4 x 110 yd. (B).
Burgess, B., 1978, high jump (B).
Clark, D. McD. M., 1950, hammer (G).
Douglas, E. C. K., 1954, hammer (B).
Forbes, A., 1950, 6 mi. (S).
Hunter, F. A. R., 1934, 440 yd. hurdles (G) and 4 x 440 yd. (B).
Jenkins, D. A., 1978, 4 x 100 m. (G).
Lindsay, M. R., 1962, shot (S) and discus (S).
McCafferty, I., 1970, 5000 m. (S).
McGhee, J., 1954, marathon (G).
Mackenzie, W., 1934, hammer (B).
McMaster, A. E., 1978, 4 x 100 m. (G).
Michie, J. F., 1934, high jump (B).
Murdoch, R. L., 1934, 4 x 110 yd. (B).
Paterson, A. S., 1950, high jump (S).
Robertson, D. McN., 1934, marathon (S).
Robson, J., 1978, 1500 m. (B).
Sharp, R. C., 1978, 4 x 100 m. (G).
Stewart, I., 1970, 5000 m. (G).
Stewart, J. L., 1970, 10,000 m. (G).
Stothard, J. C., 1934, 880 yd. (B) and 4 x 440 yd. (B).
Sutherland, W. M. S., 1970, 20 mi. walk (B).
Turner, A. D., 1934, 4 x 110 yd. (B).
Wallace, R. H. H., 1934, 4 x 440 yd. (B).
Wells, A. W., 1978, 200 m. (G), 4 x 100 m. (G), 100 m. (S).
Wright, D. McL., 1930, marathon (G); 1934, marathon (B).
Wylde, R. B., 1934, 4 x 440 yd. (B).
Young, D., 1938, discus (S).
Young, I. C., 1934, 100 yd. (B) and 4 x 110 yd. (B).

COMMONWEALTH RECORDS

Women
Cunningham, J., 1934, 660 yd. relay (B).
Dobbie, S., 1934, 660 yd. relay (B).
Jackson, C., 1934, 660 yd. relay (B).
Mackenzie, M., 1934, 660 yd. relay (B).
Payne, C. R., 1970, discus (G); 1974, discus (S).
Stirling, R. O., 1970, 800 m. (G).
Walls, M. L., 1970, high jump (B).

Welsh Medallists

Alford, J. W. Ll., 1938, mile (G).
Davies, J., 1974, steeplechase (S).
Davies, L., 1966, long jump (G); 1970, long jump (G).
England, D. M., 1962, 4 x 110 yd. (B).
Jones, K. J., 1954, 220 yd. (B).
Jones, R., 1962, 4 x 110 yd. (B).
Jones, T. B., 1962, 4 x 110 yd. (B).
Longe, C. C. O., 1966, decathlon (S).
Martin-Jones, R., 1974, women's long jump (B).
Merriman, J. L., 1958, 6 mi. (S); 1962, 6 mi. (B).
Price, B., 1974, 110 m. hurdles (S); 1978, 110 m. hurdles (G).
Shaw, R. D., 1954, 440 yds. hurdles (B).
Whitehead, J. N., 1962, 4 x 110 yd. (B).

Northern Irish Medallists

Bull, M. A., 1966, pole vault (S); 1970, pole vault (G); 1974, pole vault (S) and decathlon (G).
Hopkins, T. E., 1954, Women's high jump (G) and long jump (S).
Peters, M. E., 1966, Women's shot (S); 1970, shot (G) and pentathlon (G); 1974, pentathlon (G).

Record Achievements

The most victories recorded is seven by sprinter Marjorie Nelson, *née* Jackson (Australia) in 1950 and 1954. Another Australian, Decima Norman, obtained five gold medals in 1938: 100 yards, 220 yards, long jump and two relays. Dorothy Tyler (England), who as Dorothy Odam won the 1938 high jump title, retained her laurels in 1950 and placed second in 1954—clearing 1.60 metres each time.

The most prolific male gold medallist is sprinter Don Quarrie (Jamaica) with a total of six from 1970 to 1978.

Three athletes have won three successive titles: Howard Payne (England), hammer in 1962, 1966 and 1970; Pam Kilborn (Australia), 80m. hurdles in 1962 and 1966, 100 m. hurdles in 1970; and Don Quarrie (Jamaica), 100 m. in 1970, 1974 and 1978.

COMMONWEALTH RECORDS

See APPENDIX

CROSS-COUNTRY
English:

The first English Cross-Country Championship was held in Epping Forest in 1876, but all 32 runners went off course and the race was declared void. The inaugural champion, in 1877, was Percy Stenning, who retained his title for the next three years. Only one man has equalled Stenning's feat of four consecutive victories: Alf Shrubb (1901–1904). The Championship is organised annually by the English Cross-Country Union (founded 1883).

(see previous editions for winners between 1877 and 1955)

	Individual	Team	No. of Starters
1956	K. L. Norris	Sheffield United Harriers	509
1957	F. D. Sando	South London Harriers	717
1958	A. F. Perkins	South London Harriers	574
1959	F. Norris	Sheffield United Harriers	617
1960	B. B. Heatley	Derby and County AC	662
1961	B. B. Heatley	Derby and County AC	796
1962	Gerry A. North	Derby and County AC	696
1963	B. B. Heatley	Coventry Godiva Harriers	857
1964	M. R. Batty	Portsmouth AC	840
1965	M. R. Batty	Portsmouth AC	908
1966	R. Hill	North Staffs & Stone H	919
1967	R. G. Taylor	Portsmouth AC	831

Year	Winner	Club	Time
1968	R. Hill	Coventry Godiva Harriers	944
1969	M. J. Tagg	Tipton Harriers	1046
1970	T. Wright	City of Stoke AC	1023
1971	D. C. Bedford	Shettleston Harriers	914
1972	M. Thomas	Tipton Harriers	1021
1973†	D. C. Bedford	Gateshead Harriers	1195
1974	D. J. Black	Derby and County AC	984
1975	A. D. Simmons	Gateshead Harriers	1162
1976	B. W. Ford	Gateshead Harriers	1314
1977	B. Foster	Gateshead Harriers	1458
1978	B. W. Ford	Tipton Harriers	1536
1979	M. J. McLeod	Gateshead Harriers	1672
1980	N. H. Rose	Tipton Harriers	1710
1981	J. N. Goater	Tipton Harriers	1679

† Actual winner was R. Dixon (N.Z.)

(Women champions: See under WOMEN'S AAA CHAMPIONSHIPS)

International

The first international cross-country race on record was held between England and France at Ville d'Avray on Mar. 20th, 1898. The English scored an absolute clean sweep, all eight of their runners finishing before the first Frenchman. The individual winner was S. J. Robinson.

The International Cross-Country Championship was instituted at Hamilton Park Racecourse in Scotland on Mar. 28th, 1903. Alf Shrubb was the individual winner and he led England to victory in the team race over Ireland, Scotland and Wales. France began competing in 1907 and in 1922 became the first team to defeat England. Remarkably, England has won the team title 45 times out of a possible 68.

Jack Holden (England), Alain Mimoun (France) and Gaston Roelants (Belgium) have won the race four times, one more than the next best—Jean Bouin (France). Holden and Bouin were victorious three years running. Marcel Vandewattyne (Belgium), runner-up in the 1946 race, placed 2nd again in 1962 and was a member of Belgium's winning team in 1963. The following year he made his 19th Championship appearance.

The Championships came under the jurisdiction of the IAAF in 1973 and are now referred to as the World Cross-Country Championships. Distance of the men's race has been standardised at 12 km.

Individual and Team Champions:
(note B—Belgium, E—England, F—France, I—Ireland, M—Morocco, P—Portugal, S—Scotland, Sp—Spain, T—Tunisia, Y—Yugoslavia, Fi—Finland).

Year	Individual	Team
1903	A. Shrubb (E)	England
1904	A. Shrubb (E)	England
1905	A. Aldridge (E)	England
1906	C. J. Straw (E)	England
1907	A. Underwood (E)	England
1908	A. J. Robertson (E)	England
1909	A. E. Wood (E)	England
1910	A. E. Wood (E)	England
1911	J. Bouin (F)	England
1912	J. Bouin (F)	England
1913	J. Bouin (F)	England
1914	A. H. Nicholls (E)	England
1920	J. Wilson (S)	England
1921	W. Freeman (E)	England
1922	J. Guillemot (F)	France
1923	C. E. Blewitt (E)	France
1924	W. M. Cotterell (E)	England
1925	J. E. Webster (E)	England
1926	E. Harper (E)	France
1927	L. Payne (E)	France
1928	H. Eckersley (E)	France
1929	W. M. Cotterell (E)	France
1930	T. Evenson (E)	England
1931	T. F. Smythe (I)	England
1932	T. Evenson (E)	England
1933	J. T. Holden (E)	England
1934	J. T. Holden (E)	England
1935	J. T. Holden (E)	England
1936	W. E. Eaton (E)	England
1937	J. C. Flockhart (S)	England
1938	C. A. J. Emery (E)	England
1939	J. T. Holden (E)	France
1946	R. Pujazon (F)	France
1947	R. Pujazon (F)	France
1948	J. Doms (B)	Belgium
1949	A. Mimoun (F)	France
1950	L. Theys (B)	France
1951	G. B. Saunders (E)	England

1952	A. Mimoun (F)	France
1953	F. Mihalic (Y)	England
1954	A. Mimoun (F)	England
1955	F. D. Sando (E)	England
1956	A. Mimoun (F)	France
1957	F. D. Sando (E)	Belgium
1958	S. E. Eldon (E)	England
1959	F. Norris (E)	England
1960	A. Rhadi (M)	England
1961	B. B. Heatley (E)	Belgium
1962	G. Roelants (B)	England
1963	H. R. Fowler (E)	Belgium
1964	F. Arizmendi (Sp)	England
1965	J. C. Fayolle (F)	England
1966	A. El Ghazi (M)	England
1967	G. Roelants (B)	England
1968	M. Gammoudi (T)	England
1969	G. Roelants (B)	England
1970	M. J. Tagg (E)	England
1971	D. C. Bedford (E)	England
1972	G. Roelants (B)	England
1973	P. Paivarinta (Fi)	Belgium
1974	E. De Beck (B)	Belgium
1975	I. Stewart (S)	New Zealand
1976	C. Lopes (P)	England
1977	L. Schots (B)	Belgium
1978	J. Treacy (I)	France
1979	J. Treacy (I)	England
1980	C. Virgin (USA)	England
1981	C. Virgin (USA)	Ethiopia

at the International Championships since 1961. Competitors must be under 20 on Dec. 31st in the year of the race. Individual and team champions:

	Individual	Team
1961	C. Robinson (Eng)	England
1962	A. Bouchta (Mor)	England
1963	J. Farrington (Eng)	England
1964	I. McCafferty (Sco)	England
1965	J. Dumon (Bel)	Belgium
1966	M. J. Tagg (Eng)	England
1967	E. Knox (Sco)	England
1968	J. Bednarski (Eng)	England
1969	D. C. Bedford (Eng)	England
1970	J. Hartnett (Ire)	England
1971	N. H. Rose (Eng)	England
1972	A. Tomasini (Ita)	Italy
1973	J. Brown (Sco)	Spain
1974	R. Kimball (USA)	USA
1975	R. Thomas (USA)	USA
1976	E. Hulst (USA)	USA
1977	T. Hunt (USA)	USA
1978	M. A. Morton (Eng)	England
1979	E. De Pauw (Bel)	Spain
1980	J. Garcia (Spa)	USSR
1981	M. Chouri (Tun)	USA

Women

The first women's international cross-country race on record, including English, French and Belgian runners, was held at Douai (France) in 1931. Gladys Lunn led England to victory.

Regular International Championships have been held since 1967. Individual and team champions:

	Individual	Team
1967	D. Brown (USA)	England
1968	D. Brown (USA)	USA
1969	D. Brown (USA)	USA
1970	D. Brown (USA)	England
1971	D. Brown (USA)	England
1972	J. Smith (Eng)	England
1973	P. Cacchi (Italy)	England
1974	P. Cacchi (Italy)	England
1975	J. Brown (USA)	USA
1976	C. Valero (Spain)	USSR
1977	C. Valero (Spain)	USSR
1978	G. Waitz (Norway)	Romania
1979	G. Waitz (Norway)	USA
1980	G. Waitz (Norway)	USSR
1981	G. Waitz (Norway)	USSR

Juniors

A junior men's race has been held

CUTHBERT, Betty (Australia)

As a triple gold medallist, the then 18-year-old Betty Cuthbert was naturally the heroine of the Melbourne Olympics in 1956. Her successes came in the 100 m., 200 m. and 4 x 100 m. relay.

Later championships were less rewarding. She was overshadowed by team-mate Marlene Willard at the 1958 Commonwealth Games, injured at the 1960 Olympics and showed indifferent form at the 1962 Commonwealth Games prior to anchoring the Australian relay team to victory. But at the 1964 Olympics, her final competition, she re-established herself as one of the all-time greats of women's athletics by winning the 400 m. in 52.0 sec.

She set a dozen individual world records between 1956 and 1963 at events ranging from 60 m. to 440 yd. Her best marks were 7.2 sec. for 60 m.,; 10.4 sec. for 100 yd.; 11.4 sec. for 100 m.; 23.2 sec. for 200 m. and 220 yd., 52.0 sec. for 400 m., 53.3 sec. for 440 yd. and 2 min. 17.0 sec. for 880 yd. She was born at Merrylands, near Sydney, on Apr. 20th, 1938.

DAMILANO, Maurizio (Italy)

Defending Olympic 20 km. walk champion Daniel Bautista of Mexico appeared to be on his way to a second gold medal when—nearing the finish in Moscow's Lenin Stadium—he was disqualified for 'lifting'. That left the USSR's Anatoliy Solomin out in front ... but not for long, for with victory within his grasp the judges ruled him out too! Suddenly, the unconsidered Maurizio Damilano, who had been content with the thought that he was heading for a bronze medal, found himself entering the stadium with a big lead. Winning by over a minute in the highly commendable time of 1 hr. 23 min. 35.5 sec. (shade temperature was 30° C) he added to Italy's great walking tradition established by Ugo Frigerio, Giuseppe Dordoni and Abdon Pamich.

The 1980 Olympic champion is from a remarkable walking family. His twin brother Giorgio placed 11th in Moscow, and both are coached by another brother Sandro. In previous major competitions Maurizio was fourth in the 1977 Lugano Trophy 20 km. and sixth in the 1978 European 20 km., while in the 1979 Lugano Trophy he was disqualified just 400 m. from the finish while in second place.

His best track marks are 40 min. 01.3 sec. for 10 km. and 1 hr. 21 min. 47.8 sec. for 20 km. Annual progress: 1974—46:20.2 (10 km.); 1975—44:47.8; 1976—1:29:17 (20 km.); 1977—1:25:33; 1978—1:24:58; 1979—1:22:59.1; 1980—1:21:47.8. He was born at Scarnafigi on Apr. 6th, 1957.

DA SILVA, A. F. (Brazil)

Between 1951 and 1959 Adhemar Ferreira da Silva—South America's most distinguished athlete—won every major triple jump title open to him: Olympic champion in 1952 and 1956, Pan-American titlist in 1951, 1955 and 1959. He competed in four Olympics, placing 11th in 1948 and 14th in 1960.

The lithe Brazilian held the world record from 1950 to 1953 and from 1955 to 1958, and was the first man to triple jump in excess of 16 metres. His final world record was 16.56 metres. He was undefeated from 1951 to 1956 inclusive.

Other best marks included 21.0 sec. (wind assisted) for straight 220 yd. and 7.33 m. long jump. He was born at Sao Paulo on Sept. 29th, 1927.

DAVIES, Lynn (GB)

Lynn Davies made important British athletics history in Tokyo on Oct. 18th, 1964 for in defeating Ralph Boston (USA) and Igor Ter-Ovanesyan (USSR)—the world's only 27ft. long jumpers—he became Wales' first Olympic champion and the first man from Great Britain to win an Olympic field event. Tim Ahearne, the 1908 triple jump victor, was an Irishman.

Davies' triumph was utterly unexpected; even he would have been happy with third place. The damp and desolate conditions were probably less alien to Davies than to most of his rivals but the measure of his achievement was that he was the only competitor to set a personal best, his 8.07 metres in the 5th round being accomplished off a soggy cinder runway and into an 0.7 m. per sec. breeze. Truly magnificent jumping.

He went on to complete a unique set of gold medals by capturing the Commonwealth (7.99 metres) and European (7.98 metres) titles in 1966, and the following year he won the European indoor championship. Hopes of retaining his Olympic laurels in 1968, the year in which he jumped 27 feet (8.23 m.), were dashed by Bob Beamon's awe-inspiring opening leap and a deflated Davies merely went through the motions in placing 9th.

Three more medals were added to his collection when he took 2nd place in the 1969 European Championships, indoors and out, and retained his Commonwealth title (8.06 metres wind assisted) in 1970, but injury proved too much for him in 1972 and in his Olympic farewell he failed to qualify for the final.

During his career he raised the UK record by almost two feet and jumped 8 metres or further in 22 separate competitions. He was also one of Britain's finest sprinters and, as a junior, a most promising triple jumper.

His best marks: 9.5 sec. for 100 yd., 10.4 sec. for 100 m., 21.2 sec. for 220 yd., 1.88 m. high jump (in training), 8.23 m. long jump and 15.43 m. triple jump. He served as technical director of Canadian athletics, 1973-76, and was Britain's assistant team manager at the Moscow Olympics. He was born at Nantymoel on May 20th, 1942.

DAVIS, Glenn (USA)

Glenn Davis is the only man to have won the Olympic 400 m. hurdles twice, in 1956 and 1960. He captured another gold medal in Rome, running a 45.4 sec. leg for the US team that won the 4 x 400 m. relay in the world record time of 3 min. 02.2 sec.

Previously a "one-man team" in high school, Davis made his 400 m. hurdling debut in Apr. 1956, and returned an unexceptional 54.4 sec. So swiftly did he improve, though, that only two months later he sliced no less than nine-tenths of a second off the world record with a time of 49.5 sec.!

He set further world records at 440 yd. flat (45.7 sec.), 400 m. hurdles (49.2 sec.) and 440 yd. hurdles (49.9 sec.) in 1958 and two seasons later, just prior to successfully defending his Olympic laurels, he equalled the world record of 22.5 sec. for 200 m. hurdles (turn).

Other best marks: 100 yd. in 9.7 sec., 100 m. in 10.3 sec., 200 m. (turn) in 21.0 sec., 400 m. in 45.5 sec., 120 yd. hurdles in 14.3 sec., high jump of 1.92 m. (indoors) and long jump of 7.32 m. He was born at Wellsburg, West Virginia, on Sept. 12th, 1934.

DECATHLON

A decathlon consists of ten events, four track and six field, which are held on two consecutive days in the following order. First day: 100 m., long jump, shot, high jump and 400 m. Second day: 110 m. hurdles, discus, pole vault, javelin and 1500 m.

An athlete is allowed three trials in the long jump and throwing events. A special rule applicable to the decathlon is that two (as distinct from one) false starts can be committed in the track events without incurring disqualification. The decathlon competitor must start in each of the ten events, or else he will be considered to have abandoned the competition and will not figure in the final classification.

Placings in a decathlon competition are determined by the total number of points scored by each competitor per the International Amateur Athletic Federation scoring tables. In theory it is possible for an athlete to win a decathlon without actually placing first in any of the ten events.

The current scoring tables were adopted by the IAAF in 1962 and used for the first time in 1964. Each performance recorded by a competitor is worth a certain number of points ranging from 1 to 1,200. The first class decathlon exponent averages about 800 points per event. The latest tables, published in 1977, take account of fully automatic electrical timing with points awarded for performances to a hundredth of a second in the 100 m. 400 m. and 110 m. hurdles.

The decathlon entered the Olympic programme in 1912 and right away became the centre of fierce controversy. The event was won by a handsome margin by Jim Thorpe (USA), who was later branded as a professional and whose name was deleted from the official results. His score (converted to the 1962 tables) of 6,756 points was not bettered until 1927, although it must be pointed out that the 1912 Olympic event was spread over three days.

Akilles Jarvinen (Finland), whose younger brother Matti was a world record breaker with the javelin, was the first to total over 7000 points (as re-scored on the 1962 tables); that was in 1930.

The next great name was Glenn Morris (USA), later to portray Tarzan on the screen, who won the 1936 Olympic honours with the record score of 7,421. That mark withstood all assaults until 1950 when Bob

Mathias (USA), who had two years earlier become the youngest ever male Olympic athletics champion, set the first of three records which culminated in his scoring 7,731 in defence of his title in 1952.

The distinction of cracking 8,000 points for the first time was won by Rafer Johnson (USA) in 1960. The next world record holder, Yang Chuan-kwang (Taiwan), a close 2nd to Johnson in the 1960 Olympics, caused no little embarrassment during the course of his 1963 record (9,121 on the 1950 tables then in use) by vaulting 4.84 m. The scoring tables were made redundant by this performance as points were listed only up to 4.82 m. Under the new tables, Yang's record score became 8.089 pts.

Bill Toomey (USA), winner of the 1968 Olympic title (he scored a best ever 4,499 pts. on the first day, helped by an extraordinary 45.6 sec. for 400 m.), went on to claim a world record of 8,417 the following season. He was succeeded in 1972 as Olympic champion and world record holder by Nikolay Avilov (USSR) with a score of 8,456, his winning margin of 422 pts. being the widest in the Olympics for 20 years.

Bruce Jenner (USA) amassed 8,524 in 1975, but this was intrinsically inferior to Avilov's performance (in which fully automatic electric timing was used) as his times in the 100 m., 400 m., 110 m. hurdles and 1500 m. were taken manually—an advantage of at least 100 points. Jenner improved to 8,538 in similar circumstances in the 1976 USA Olympic Trials but all confusion as to the true world record holder was swept away at the Montreal Games, where Jenner scored a remarkable 8,617 with electrical timing.

Jenner's successor both as world record holder (8,622) and Olympic champion (8,495) was Britain's Daley Thompson. Prior to Moscow, the highest British placing in an Olympic decathlon was 9th by Geoff Elliott in 1952. Guido Kratschmer (W. Ger) broke Thompson's record within a month with 8,649 pts.

See also under JENNER, Bruce; JOHNSON, Rafer; KRATSCHMER, Guido; MATHIAS, Bob; THOMPSON, Daley and THORPE, Jim.

DE LA HUNTY, Shirley (Australia)

No other woman athlete has garnered such a dazzling array of Olympic medals as Mrs. Shirley De La Hunty (*née* Strickland). The 80 m. hurdles champion in 1952 and 1956 (a unique double), having finished third in 1948, she was also 100 m. bronze medallist in 1948 and 1952 and as a member of the Australian relay team picked up a silver in 1948 and her third gold in 1956. A photo finish print of the 1948 Olympic 200 m. Final, not published until 1976, revealed that she should rightly have been placed third and not fourth in that race—which would have brought her Olympic medal haul to eight. Her Commonwealth Games tally of two gold and two silver medals adds still further lustre to her collection.

Although best known as an 80 m. hurdler (the first woman to break 11 sec.), Shirley's fastest time of 10.7 sec. was perhaps surpassed by her former world record of 11.3 sec. for 100 m. on the flat.

In 1960, when well into her thirties, she ran 100 yd. in 10.9 sec. Born at Guildford, Western Australia, on July 18th, 1925, her best marks in addition to the above are 10.6 sec. for 100 yd., 24.1 sec. for 200 m. and 56.9 sec. for 440 yd.

DE OLIVEIRA, Joao Carlos (Brazil)

For a nation with such a large population Brazil has made a relatively insignificant contribution to athletics history—that is in every event except the triple jump! The tradition established by A. F. da Silva (Olympic champion in 1952 and 1956) and maintained by Nelson Prudencio (1968 and 1972 Olympic medallist), both world record breakers in their time, reached new heights of endeavour when Joao Carlos de Oliveira achieved an astonishing exploit in the 1975 Pan-American Games. Jumping in the same stadium that was the scene of Bob Beamon's phenomenal leap of seven years earlier, the tall and lanky Brazilian took full advantage of Mexico City's high altitude to hop 6.05 metres, step 5.40 metres and jump 6.44 metres for a total distance of 17.89 metres—fully 45 cm. superior to the highly respected world record held by Viktor Sanyeyev (USSR).

Remarkably, in view of the event's highly technical nature, it transpired that he had been an athlete for only three years. Prior to the Mexican fiesta, his best stood at 16.74 metres.

Sciatica hampered his Olympic preparation in 1976 and he had to settle for the bronze medal (16.90 metres) in Montreal, but the following year he triumphed in the World Cup, while in 1978 he tied Sanyeyev's world 'low altitude' best of 17.44 m. He retained his Pan-American long and triple jump titles in 1979 but his Olympic hopes were dashed in Moscow when a series of mighty triple jumps were ruled fouls and he placed third again with 17.22 m. A formidable sprinter (10.1 100 m.), he has long jumped 8.36 m. Annual progression: 1972—14.67; 1973 15.89; 1974—16.34; 1975—17.89; 1976 —17.38; 1977—16.81; 1978—17.44; 1979—17.27; 1980—17.22. He was born near Sao Paulo on May 28th, 1954.

DILLARD, Harrison (USA)

It was the sight of Jesse Owens being cheered through the streets of Cleveland following his 1936 Olympic triumphs that inspired 13-year-old Harrison Dillard to try his luck at athletics. Helped in his formative years by Owens himself, Dillard developed after the war into a superb hurdler and sprinter.

He posted his first world record in 1946 at 220 yd. hurdles, an event in which Owens was a previous record-holder. Between May 1947 and June 1948 he won 82 successive sprint and hurdle races—an incredible run of success. His winning streak included a world record 120 yd. hurdles time of 13.6 sec. in Apr. 1948 but tragedy befell him in the US Olympic trials when he took a spill and failed to make the team as a hurdler.

Fortunately he qualified as third string in the 100 m., and at Wembley he scored a dramatic victory in 10.3 sec. to equal Jesse's Olympic record. Four years later he made up for his previous lapse by taking the high hurdles and for the second time was a member of the winning 4 x 100 m. relay team. He made a comeback at 33 in an attempt to defend his Olympic title but he finished sixth in the US trials.

His explosive start was particularly well suited to indoor racing and he won the AAU 60 yd. hurdles title seven years running.

Best marks: 9.4 sec. for 100 yd., 10.3 sec. for 100 m., 20.8 sec. for 200 m. (turn), 13.6 sec. for 120 yd. hurdles, 22.3 sec. for 220 yd. hurdles (straight), 23.0 sec. for 220 yd. hurdles (turn), 53.7 sec. for 400 m. hurdles. He was born in Cleveland on July 8th, 1923.

DISCUS

Discus throwing was popular among the ancient Greeks, but the event as it is known today dates from the closing years of the 19th century. The minimum weight of the implement was fixed at 2 Kg. (4 lb. 6½ oz.) but for some years there were three sizes of throwing area in use: a 7 ft. circle in the USA, 7 ft. square in Central Europe, 8 ft. 10¼ in. circle in Scandinavia. The inside diameter of the throwing circle was standardised at 2.50 m. (8 ft. 2½ in.) by 1912.

A throw, to be recorded as valid, must fall within a 40 deg. sector. A foul is recorded when a competitor, after he has stepped into the circle and started to make his throw, touches the ground outside the circle or the top edge of the circle with any part of his body.

The first great figure in discus throwing was Irish-born Martin Sheridan (USA), who in 1902 became the first man to reach 40 metres. He was Olympic champion in 1904 (after a throw-off with team-mate Ralph Rose) and 1908. Two other men have retained an Olympic title: Clarence Houser (USA), champion in 1924 and 1928; and Al Oerter (USA), gold medallist in 1956, 1960, 1964, and 1968.

The 50 metre landmark fell to Eric Krenz (USA) in 1930, while the pioneer 60 metre thrower was Jay Silvester (USA) in 1961. The coveted distinction (for English speaking athletes) of being the first to reach 200 ft. (60.96 m.) went, appropriately, to the greatest of them all—Al Oerter—in 1962. Silvester twice threw over 70 metres in 1971 but as these marks were never officially ratified it was Mac Wilkins (USA), five years later, who can be considered to have ushered in the 70 metre era.

Discus throwers tend to enjoy longer careers in top-flight competition than most of their athletic brethren. For example, Ludvik Danek (Czechoslovakia) won the 1972 Olympic title aged 35 and the astonishing Al Oerter ranked second in the world in 1980 with a lifetime best of 69.46 m.—at the age of 43.

Britain has little in the way of tradition in this event. The highest Olympic placing is fourth in 1956 by Mark Pharaoh, who succeeded in raising the national record nearly 7 m. in three years, whilst no UK athlete has ever won the Commonwealth title or even placed in the first six at the European Championship. Bill Tancred became the first Briton over 60 m. in 1972.

See also under OERTER, Al, RASHCHUPKIN, Viktor; SCHMIDT, Wolfgang; and WILKINS, Mac.

Women

Female competitors of all age groups use a 1 kg. discus (2 lb 3 oz.). Nina Dumbadze (USSR) was responsible for transforming the event. When she began her career in 1936 the world record stood at 48.30 metres by Gisela Mauermayer (Germany), but by 1952 she had raised the mark to 57.04 metres. Liesel Westermann (W. Germany), was the first to reach the twin landmarks of 60 m. and 200 ft. (in 1967) and eight years later Faina Melnik (USSR) threw beyond 70 Metres. Meg Ritchie became the first British 60 m. thrower in 1978.

See also under JAHL, Evelin; MELNIK, Faina; and VERGOVA, Maria.

DOMBROWSKI, Lutz
(East Germany)

The world long jump record of 8.90 metres (29 ft. 2¼ in.) by Bob Beamon has stood unchallenged since 1968 and is likely to survive for many years yet. But Beamon's legendary leap was achieved at the exceedingly helpful altitude of 7,347 ft. and there is a school of thought which suggests that separate world records should be kept for 'high altitude' and otherwise in the explosive events. The world's longest jumper at or near sea level prior to the 1980 Olympics was Larry Myricks (USA) with 8.52 metres, but in Moscow that distinction passed to Lutz Dombrowski whose gold medal performance was a European record of 8.54 metres (28 ft. 0¼ in.). The assisting wind was 0.85 metres per second, as against Beamon's 2.00 m. in Mexico City.

The powerfully built East German first made his mark in the triple jump, which remains his favourite event although he has been forbidden by his coach from tackling the event since 1977 because of the injury risk. After sitting out 1978 due to surgery on his knee, Dombrowski emerged as a world class long jumper in 1979 with 8.31 metres for victory in the European Cup Final.

Personal bests at other events: 10.4 sec. for 100 m., 2.10 metres high jump and 16.61 metres triple jump. Annual long jump progress: 1971—5.46 m.; 1973—6.41; 1974—6.35; 1975—7.13; 1976—7.55; 1977—7.80; 1979—8.31; 1980—8.54. He was born at Karl-Marx-Stadt on June 25th, 1959.

DOPING

Doping—defined by the IAAF as " the use by or distribution to an athlete of certain substances which could have the effect of improving artificially the athlete's physical and/or mental condition and so augmenting his athletic performance " —is expressly forbidden before or during competition. Anti-doping controls are carried out at major international championships and offenders are disqualified from the event and may be banned from further international competition.

Doping substances come under five main headings: psychomotor stimulant drugs (e.g. amphetamine, cocaine), sympathomimetic amines (e.g. ephedrine), miscellaneous central nervous system stimulants (e.g. strychnine), narcotic analgesics (e.g. morphine, heroin) and anabolic steroids.

The ever growing use of anabolic steroids has been a particular worry to all concerned with two of the basic tenets of athletics: fairness of competition and the sport's concern for the participant's health. Anabolic steroids are synthesised male sex hormones which can enhance muscle growth, producing a 'bulking up' effect from which throwers in particular—but, in general, athletes in all other events—can benefit. Despite persistent warnings of dire side effects (possible liver damage, loss of fertility, appearance of masculine characteristics in women, etc.), medical advice has been ignored by over-ambitious athletes and coaches.

The development of reliable testing procedures, used for the first time at the 1974 European Championships, has almost certainly led many athletes to stop taking anabolic steroids a few weeks before a major event (the tests have only a limited retrospective action), but this form of drug taking is widespread at other times.

Bulgarian discus thrower Velko Velev and Romanian woman shot putter Valentina Cioltan were the first to be found guilty of taking anabolic steroids in 1975. At Montreal in 1976 the Polish woman discus thrower Danuta Rosani became the first athlete to be disqualified at an Olympics for 'failing' a steroid test. Among others subsequently found out in doping tests are two women who went on to win Olympic titles in 1980—Ilona Slupianek (East Germany, shot) and Nadyezhda Tkachenko (USSR, pentathlon)—and three leading middle distance runners: Totka Petrova of Bulgaria and the Romanians Natalia Marasescu and Ileana Silai.

DUMAS, Charles (USA)

The first man to high jump 7 ft. (2.13 metres) in authentic competition was Charles Dumas (USA). He performed this historic feat in June 1956 aged 19, by straddling 2.15 metres (7 ft. 0½ in.). Later that year he captured the Olympic title.

Dumas was an outstanding competitor—winner of the US championship five successive years (1955-59) and Pan-American champion in 1959. He did not compete in 1961, 1962 or 1963 but made a brilliant comeback in Apr. 1964 with a leap of 2.14 m.

Far from extraordinary as a 14-year-old (best of only 1.50 metres) or 15-year-old (1.67 metres) he improved rapidly to 1.88 metres at 16, 1.97 metres at 17 and 2.09 metres at 18. He was also a useful high hurdler, with a best time of 14.1 sec. for 120 yd. He was born at Tulsa, Oklahoma, on Feb. 12th, 1937.

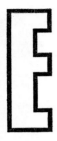

ECKERT, Barbel (East Germany)

See under WOCKEL, Barbel.

EHRHARDT, Annelie (East Germany)

European junior 80 m. hurdles (2 ft. 6 in.) champion in 1968, under her maiden name of Jahns, Annelie Ehrhardt made an unspectacular start to her career at 100 m. hurdles (2 ft. 9 in.) when this event replaced the shorter distance in 1969. She ran only a mediocre 14.1 sec. that season. Just a year later, though, she was universally acknowledged as one of the great hurdlers, with a best time of 12.9 sec. and a share in the world record of 25.8 sec. for 200 m. hurdles.

But she was still overshadowed by her illustrious East German colleague Karin Balzer, 12 years her senior, during 1971 (Annelie finished second to her in the European Championships) but in 1972 she emerged as the world's undisputed number one. Significantly faster on the flat (11.3 sec. for 100 m.), and even more efficient in her hurdling form, she cut the world record to 12.5 sec. and swept to Olympic victory by the remarkably wide margin of a quarter of a second. In Munich she was timed at 12.59 sec. (electrical) into a breeze of 0.6 metres per second.

She cut her manually timed world record to 12.3 sec. in 1973 and won the European title next year, but hampered by a back injury she failed to reach the 1976 Olympic final. She was born at Ohrsleben on June 18th, 1950.

ELLIOTT, Herb (Australia)

From 1954, when at the age of 16 he commenced serious training, until his retirement in 1962 Herb Elliott never lost a mile or 1500 m. race. The greatest mile competitor of them all won each of the three major championships he contested: the 880 yd. and mile at the 1958 Commonwealth Games and the 1960 Olympic 1500 m.

Here are some of the highlights of his glittering career:—1954: 1 min. 58.2 sec. 880 yd. and 4 min. 25.6 sec. mile (56.8 sec. first lap!) at the age of 16.

1955: Improved to 1 min. 55.8 sec. and 4 min. 20.8 sec. while still 16; later in the year ran 4 min. 20.4 sec. Percy Cerutty saw him win a 4 min. 22 sec. mile, said "this boy can be coached to break Landy's world mile record of 3 min. 57.9 sec. by the end of 1958" and proceeded to do just that.

1957: At 18, set world junior bests of 3 min. 47.8 sec. for 1500 m., 4 min. 04.3 sec. for the mile, 9 min. 01.0 sec. for 2 mi. and 14 min. 02.4 sec. for 3 mi.

1958: Ran his first four-minute mile before his 20th birthday; posted world records for the mile (3 min. 54.5 sec.) and 1500 m. (3 min. 36.0 sec.); won two titles at the Commonwealth Games in Cardiff; set Commonwealth 880 yd. record of 1 min. 47.3 sec.; in the space of eight days successively ran 3 min. 36.0 sec. for 1500 m., 3 min. 58.0 sec. mile, 3 min. 55.4 sec. mile and 3 min. 37.4 sec. 1500 m. Rejected an £89,000 offer to turn professional.

1960: Won the Olympic 1500 m. by the extraordinary margin of 20 metres in a world record of 3 min. 35.6 sec.

Elliott's personal best marks were 50.7 sec. for 440 yd., 1 min. 47.3 sec. for 880 yd., 2 min. 19.1 sec. for 1000 m., 3 min. 35.6 sec. for 1500 m., 3 min. 54.5 sec. for the mile, 8 min. 09.5 sec. for 3000 m., 8 min. 37.6 sec. for 2 mi. and 14 min. 09.9 sec. for 5000 m. He was born at Subiaco, near Perth, on Feb. 25th, 1938.

EUROPEAN CHAMPIONSHIPS

The European Championships were started in Turin in 1934. The driving force behind their establishment was a Hungarian, Szilard Stankovits. Subsequently, Championships were held in Paris (1938), Oslo (1946), Brussels (1950), Berne (1954), Stockholm (1958), Belgrade (1962), Budapest (1966), Athens (1969), Helsinki (1971), Rome (1974) and Prague (1978). The next will be staged in Athens in 1982. Britain did not send a team to the 1934 Championships; the Soviet Union competed for the first time in 1946. A separate Women's Championships took place in Vienna in 1938, but since 1946 the Championships have featured men's and women's events.

The West German team withdrew from all the individual events at the 1969 Championships in protest against the IAAF's ruling that a member of that team, Jurgen May (who defected from East Germany in 1967) was ineligible to compete.

British Medallists

The following athletes, listed in alphabetical order, have won European Championship medals while representing Britain. G signifies gold (1st), S silver (2nd) and B bronze (3rd).

Alder, J. N. C., 1969, marathon (B).
Archer, J., 1946, 100 m. (G).
Baldwin, A. G., 1938, 4 x 400 m. (S).
Bannister, R. G., 1950, 800 m. (B); 1954, 1500 m. (G).
Barnes, J. G., 1938, 4 x 400 m. (S).
Blinston, J. A., 1969, 5000 m. (B).
Box, K. J., 1954, 4 x 100 m. (S).
Breacker, A., 1958, 4 x 100 m. (S).
Brightwell, R. I., 1962, 400 m. (G) and 4 x 400 m. (S).
Brown, A. G. K., 1938, 400 m. (G), 4 x 400 m. (S) and 4 x 100 m. (B).
Capes, G. L., 1974, shot (B).
Carter, A. W., 1971, 800 m. (B).
Chataway, C. J., 1954, 5000 m. (S).
Clark, D. McD. M., 1946, hammer (B).
Coe, S. N., 1978, 800 m. (B).
Cohen, G. H., 1974, 4 x 400 m. (G).
Davies, L., 1966, long jump (G); 1969, long jump (S).
Ede, D. R., 1946, 4 x 400 m. (S).
Elliott, B. W., 1946, 4 x 400 m. (S).
Elliott, G. M., 1954, pole vault (B).
Ellis, G. S., 1954, 4 x 100 m. (S), 100 m. (B) and 200 m. (B).
Finlay, D. O., 1938, 110 m. hurdles (G).
Forbes, H., 1946, 50 km. walk (S).
Foster, B., 1971, 1500 m. (B); 1974, 5000 m. (G).
Fowler, H. R., 1962, 10,000 m. (B).
Hartley, W. J., 1974, 4 x 400 m. (G).
Hemery, D. P., 1969, 110 m. hurdles (S).
Hewson, B. S., 1958, 1500 m. (G).
Hildreth, P. B., 1950 110 m. hurdles (B).
Hill, R., 1969, marathon (G); 1971, marathon (B).
Hogan, J. J., 1966, marathon (G).
Holden, J. T., 1950, marathon (G).
Jackson, B. D., 1962, 4 x 400 m. (S).
Jenkins, D. A., 1971, 400 m. (G); 1974, 400 m. (S) and 4 x 400 m. (G).
Jones, D. H., 1962, 4 x 100 m. (B).
Jones, K. J., 1954, 4 x 100 m. (S).
Jones, R., 1962, 4 x 100 m. (B).
Jones, T. B., 1962, 4 x 100 m. (B).
Kilby, B. L., 1962, marathon (G).
Lewis, L. C., 1950, 4 x 400 m. (G).
MacIsaac, J., 1958, 4 x 400 m. (G).
Matthews, K. J., 1962, 20 km. walk (G).
Meakin, A., 1962, 4 x 100 m. (B).
Megnin, C., 1946, 50 km. walk (B).
Metcalfe, A. P., 1962, 4 x 400 m. (S).
Mills, R. G., 1974, 20 km. walk (B).
Moorcroft, D. R., 1978, 1500 m. (B).
Nankeville, G. W., 1950, 1500 m. (B).
Nihill, V. P., 1969, 20 km. walk (G); 1971, 20 km. walk (B).
Norris, F., 1958, marathon (B).
Ovett, S. M. J., 1974, 800 m. (S); 1978, 1500 m. (G) and 800 m. (S).
Page, E. L., 1938, 4 x 100 m. (B).
Parker, F. J., 1954, 110 m. hurdles (S).
Parlett, H. J., 1950, 800 m. (G).
Pascoe, A. P., 1969, 110 m. hurdles (B); 1971, 110 m. hurdles (S); 1974, 400 m. hurdles (G) and 4 x 400 m. (G).
Paterson, A. S., 1946, high jump (S); 1950, high jump (G).
Pennington, A., 1938, 4 x 400 m. (S) and 200 m. (B).
Pike, M. W., 1950, 4 x 400 m. (G).
Pirie, D. A. G., 1958, 5000 m. (B).
Pugh, D. C., 1946, 4 x 400 m. (S) and 400 m. (B); 1950, 400 m. (G) and 4 x 400 m. (G).
Radford, P. F., 1958, 4 x 100 m. (S) and 100 m. (B).
Rawson, M. A., 1958, 800 m. (G).
Roberts, W., 1946, 4 x 400 m. (S).
Rowe, A., 1958, shot (G).
Salisbury, J. E., 1958, 4 x 400 m. (G) and 400 m. (S).

Sampson, E. J., 1958, 4 x 400 m. (G).
Sando, F. D., 1954, 10,000 m. (B).
Sandstrom, E. R., 1958, 4 x 100 m. (S).
Scarr, M. M., 1938, 4 x 100 m. (B).
Scott, A. W., 1950, 4 x 400 m. (G).
Segal, D. H., 1958, 200 m. (S) and 4 x 100 m. (S).
Shenton, B., 1950, 200 m. (G); 1954, 4 x 100 m. (S).
Sherwood, J., 1969, 400 m. hurdles (S).
Simmons, A. D., 1974, 10,000 m. (S).
Stewart, I., 1969, 5000 m. (G).
Sweeney, A. W., 1938, 4 x 100 m. (B).
Tagg, M. J., 1969, 10,000 m. (S).
Thompson, D. J., 1962, 50 km. walk (B).
Thompson, F. M., 1978, decathlon (S).
Thompson, I. R., 1974, marathon (G).
Todd, A. C., 1969, 400 m. hurdles (B).
Tulloh, M. B. S., 1962, 5000 m. (G).
Vickers, S. F., 1958, 20 km. walk (G).
Whetton, J. H., 1969, 1500 m. (G).
Whitlock, H. H., 1938, 50 km. walk (G).
Whittle, H., 1950, 400 m. hurdles (B).
Wilcock, K. J., 1962, 4 x 400 m. (S).
Wooderson, S. C., 1938, 1500 m. (G); 1946, 5000 m. (G).
Wright, T., 1971, marathon (S).
Wrighton, J. D., 1958, 400 m. (G) and 4 x 400 m. (G).
Yarrow, S. S., 1938, marathon (S).

Women
Arden, D., 1962, 4 x 100 m. (B).
Board, L. B., 1969, 800 m. (G). and 4 x 400 m. (G).
Cobb, V. M., 1958, 4 x 100 m. (S).
Colyear, S., 1978, 4 x 100 m. (S).
Cooper, S. A., 1969, 4 x 100 m. (B).
Crowther, B., 1950, pentathlon (S).
Desforges, J. C., 1950, 4 x 100 m. (G); 1954, long jump (G).
Dew, M. C., 1958, 4 x 100 m. (S).
Elliott, P. G., 1954, 80 m. hurdles (B).
Gardner, M. A. J., 1950, 80 m. hurdles (S).
Goddard, B. L., 1978, 4 x 100 m. (S).
Grieveson, E. J., 1962, 400 m. (S).
Hall, D. G., 1950, 4 x 100 m. (G) and 200 m. (B).
Hay, E., 1950, 4 x 100 m. (G).
Hiscox, M. E., 1958, 400 m. (B).
Hopkins, T. E., 1954, high jump (G).
Hyman, D., 1958, 4 x 100 m. (S); 1962, 100 m. (G), 200 m. (S) and 4 x 100 m. (B).
Inkpen, B. J., 1971, high jump (S).
Jordan, W., 1946, 100 m. (S) and 200 m. (S).
Knowles, L. Y., 1962, high jump (B).
Lannaman, S. M., 1978, 4 x 100 m. (S).
Leather, D. S., 1954, 800 m. (S); 1958, 800 m. (S).
Lerwill, S. W., 1950, high jump (G).
Lowe, P. B., 1969, 4 x 400 m. (G); 1971, 800 m. (S).
Lynch, J. A. C., 1974, 100 m. (B).
Neil, D. A., 1969, 100 m. (B), and 4 x 100 m. (B).
Packer, A. E., 1962, 4 x 100 m. (B).
Pashley, A., 1954, 100 m. (B).
Paul, J. F., 1950, 4 x 100 m. (G) and 100 m. (B).
Peat, V., 1969, 200 m. (B), and 4 x 100 m. (B).
Pirie, S., 1954, 200 m. (B).
Quinton, C. L., 1958, 4 x 100 m. (S).
Ramsden, D. I., 1969, 4 x 100 m. (B).
Rand, M. D., 1962, long jump (B) and 4 x 100 m. (B).
Sanderson, T. I., 1978, javelin (S).
Shirley, D. A., 1958, high jump (B).
Simpson, J. M., 1969, 4 x 400 m. (G).
Smallwood, K. J., 1978, 4 x 100 m. (S).
Smith, J., 1974, 3000 m. (B).
Stirling, R. O., 1969, 4 x 400 m. (G); 1971, 800 m. (B).
Tyler, D. J. B., 1950, high jump (S).
Young, H. J., 1958, 100 m. (G).

Champions

100 Metres	sec.
1934 C. D. Berger (Netherlands)	10.6
1938 M. B. Osendarp (Netherlands)	10.5
1946 J. Archer (GB)	10.6
1950 E. Bally (France)	10.7
1954 H. Futterer (Germany)	10.5
1958 A. Hary (Germany)	10.3
1962 C. Piquemal (France)	10.4
1966 W. J. Maniak (Poland)	10.5
1969 V. Borzov (USSR)	10.4
1971 V. Borzov (USSR)	10.26
1974 V. Borzov (USSR)	10.27
1978 P. Mennea (Italy)	10.27

200 Metres	sec.
1934 C. D. Berger (Netherlands)	21.5
1938 M. B. Osendarp (Netherlands)	21.2
1946 N. Karakulov (USSR)	21.6
1950 B. Shenton (GB)	21.5
1954 H. Futterer (Germany)	20.9
1958 M. Germar (Germany)	21.0
1962 O. Jonsson (Sweden)	20.7

EUROPEAN CHAMPIONSHIPS 58

1966	R. Bambuck (France)	20.9	1954	V. Kuts (USSR)	13	56.6
1969	P. Clerc (Switzerland)	20.6	1958	Z. Krzyszkowiak		
1971	V. Borzov (USSR)	20.30		(Poland)	13	53.4
1974	P. Mennea (Italy)	20.60	1962	M. B. S. Tulloh (GB)	14	00.6
1978	P. Mennea (Italy)	20.16	1966	M. Jazy (France)	13	42.8
			1969	I. Stewart (GB)	13	44.8

400 Metres sec.
1934 A. Metzner (Germany) 47.9
1938 A. G. K. Brown (GB) 47.4
1946 N. Holst Sorensen
      (Denmark) 47.9
1950 D. C. Pugh (GB) 47.3
1954 A. Ignatyev (USSR) 46.6
1958 J. D. Wrighton (GB) 46.3
1962 R. I. Brightwell (GB) 45.9
1966 S. Gredzinski (Poland) 46.0
1969 J. Werner (Poland) 45.7
1971 D. A. Jenkins (GB) 45.45
1974 K. Honz (W. Germany) 45.04
1978 F-P. Hofmeister (W. Ger) 45.73

1971 J. Vaatainen (Finland) 13 32.6
1974 B. Foster (GB) 13 17.2
1978 V. Ortis (Italy) 13 28.5

10,000 Metres min. sec.
1934 I. Salminen (Finland) 31 02.6
1938 I. Salminen (Finland) 30 52.4
1946 V. J. Heino (Finland) 29 52.0
1950 E. Zatopek (Czecho-
      slovakia) 29 12.0
1954 E. Zatopek (Czecho-
      slovakia) 28 58.0
1958 Z. Krzyszkowiak
      (Poland) 28 56.0
1962 P. Bolotnikov (USSR) 28 54.0
1966 J. Haase (E. Germany) 28 26.0
1969 J. Haase (E. Germany) 28 41.6
1971 J. Vaatainen (Finland) 27 52.8
1974 M. Kuschmann
      (E. Germany) 28 25.8
1978 M. Vainio (Finland) 27 31.0

800 Metres min. sec.
1934 M. Szabo (Hungary) 1 52.0
1938 R. Harbig (Germany) 1 50.6
1946 R. Gustafsson (Sweden) 1 51.0
1950 H. J. Parlett (GB) 1 50.5
1954 L. Szentgali (Hungary) 1 47.1
1958 M. A. Rawson (GB) 1 47.8
1962 M. Matuschewski
      (Germany) 1 50.5
1966 M. Matuschewski
      (E. Germany) 1 45.9
1969 D. Fromm (E. Germany) 1 45.9
1971 Y. Arzhanov (USSR) 1 45.6
1974 L. Susanj (Yugoslavia) 1 44.1
1978 O. Beyer (E. Germany) 1 43.8

Marathon hr. min. sec.
1934 A. A. Toivonen (Fin-
      land) 2 52 29.0
1938 V. Muinonen (Fin-
      land) 2 37 28.8
1946* M. Hietanen (Fin-
      land) 2 24 55.0
1950 J. T. Holden (GB) 2 32 13.2
1954 V. L. Karvonen (Fin-
      land) 2 24 51.6
1958 S. Popov (USSR) 2 15 17.0
1962 B. L. Kilby (GB) 2 23 18.8
1966 J. J. Hogan (GB) 2 20 04.6
1969 R. Hill (GB) 2 16 47.8
1971 K. Lismont
      (Belgium) 2 13 09.0
1974 I. R. Thompson (GB) 2 13 18.8
1978 L. Moseyev (USSR) 2 11 57.5

* only 40,100 m.

1500 Metres min. sec.
1934 L. Beccali (Italy) 3 54.6
1938 S. C. Wooderson (GB) 3 53.6
1946 L. Strand (Sweden) 3 48.0
1950 W. F. Slijkhuis
      (Netherlands) 3 47.2
1954 R. G. Bannister (GB) 3 43.8
1958 B. S. Hewson (GB) 3 41.9
1962 M. Jazy (France) 3 40.9
1966 B. Tummler
      (W. Germany) 3 41.9
1969 J. H. Whetton (GB) 3 39.4
1971 F. Arese (Italy) 3 38.4
1974 K. P. Justus
      (E. Germany) 3 40.6
1978 S. M. J. Ovett (GB) 3 35.6

3000 Metres Steeplechase min. sec.
1938 L. A. Larsson (Sweden) 9 16.2
1946 R. Pujazon (France) 9 01.4
1950 J. Roudny (Czecho-
      slovakia) 9 05.4
1954 S. Rozsnyoi (Hungary) 8 49.6
1958 J. Chromik (Poland) 8 38.2
1962 G. Roelants (Belgium) 8 32.6
1966 V. Kudinskiy (USSR) 8 26.6
1969 M. Zhelev (Bulgaria) 8 25.0
1971 J-P. Villain (France) 8 25.2

5000 Metres min. sec.
1934 R. Rochard (France) 14 36.8
1938 T. A. Maki (Finland) 14 26.8
1946 S. C. Wooderson (GB) 14 08.6
1950 E. Zatopek (Czecho-
      slovakia) 14 03.0

| 1974 | B. Malinowski (Poland) | 8 | 15.0 |
| 1978 | B. Malinowski (Poland) | 8 | 15.1 |

110 Metres Hurdles — sec.
1934	J. Kovacs (Hungary)	14.8
1938	D. O. Finlay (GB)	14.3
1946	E. H. Lidman (Sweden)	14.6
1950	A. J. Marie (France)	14.6
1954	Y. Bulanchik (USSR)	14.4
1958	K. M. Lauer (Germany)	13.7
1962	A. Mikhailov (USSR)	13.8
1966	E. Ottoz (Italy)	13.7
1969	E. Ottoz (Italy)	13.5
1971	F. Siebeck (E. Germany)	14.00
1974	G. Drut (France)	13.40
1978	T. Munkelt (E. Germany)	13.54

400 Metres Hurdles — sec.
1934	H. Scheele (Germany)	53.2
1938	P. Joye (France)	53.1
1946	B. Storskrubb (Finland)	52.2
1950	A. Filiput (Italy)	51.9
1954	A. Yulin (USSR)	50.5
1958	Y. Lituyev (USSR)	51.1
1962	S. Morale (Italy)	49.2
1966	R. Frinolli (Italy)	49.8
1969	V. Skomorokhov (USSR)	49.7
1971	J-C Nallet (France)	49.2
1974	A. P. Pascoe (GB)	48.82
1978	H. Schmid (W. Germany)	48.51

4 x 100 Metres Relay — sec.
1934	Germany (E. Schein, E. Gillmeister, G. Hornberger, E. Borchmeyer)	41.0
1938	Germany (M. Kersch, G. Hornberger, K. Neckermann, J. Scheuring)	40.9
1946	Sweden (S. Danielsson, I. Nilsson, O. Laessker, S. Hakansson)	41.5
1950	USSR (V. Sukharyev, L. Kalyayev, L. Sanadze, N. Karakulov)	41.5
1954	Hungary (L. Zarandi, G. Varasdi, G. Csanyi, B. Goldovanyi)	40.6
1958	Germany (W. Mahlendorf, A. Hary, H. Futterer, M. Germar)	40.2
1962	Germany (K. Ulonska, P. Gamper, H. J. Bender, M. Germar)	39.5
1966	France (M. Berger, J. Delecour, C. Piquemal, R. Bambuck)	39.4
1969	France (A. Sarteur, P. Bourbeillon, G. Fenouil, F. Saint-Gilles)	38.8
1971	Czechoslovakia (L. Kriz, J. Demec, J. Kynos, L. Bohman)	39.3
1974	France (L. Sainte-Rose, J. Arame, B. Cherrier, D. Chauvelot)	38.69
1978	Poland (Z. Nowosz, Z. Licznerski, L. Dunecki, M. Woronin)	38.58

4 x 400 Metres Relay — min. sec.
1934	Germany (H. Hamann, H. Scheele, H. Voigt, A. Metzner)	3 14.1
1938	Germany (H. Blazejezak, M. Bues, E. Linnhoff, R. Harbig)	3 13.7
1946	France (B. Santona, Y. Cros, R. Chefd'hotel, J. Lunis)	3 14.4
1950	GB (M. W. Pike, L. C. Lewis, A. W. Scott, D. C. Pugh)	3 10.2
1954*	France (P. Haarhoff, J. Degats, J. P. Martin du Gard, J. P. Goudeau)	3 08.7
1958	GB (E. J. Sampson, J. MacIsaac, J. D. Wrighton, J. E. Salisbury)	3 07.9
1962	Germany (J. Schmitt, W. Kindermann, H. J. Reske, M. Kinder)	3 05.8
1966	Poland (J. Werner, E. Borowski, S. Gredzinski, A. Badenski)	3 04.5
1969	France (G. Bertould, C. Nicolau, J. Carette, J-C. Nallet)	3 02.3
1971	W. Germany (H-R. Schloske, T. Jordan, M. Jellinghaus, H. Kohler)	3 02.9
1974	GB (G. H. Cohen, W. J. Hartley, A. P. Pascoe, D. A. Jenkins)	3 03.3
1978	W. Germany (M. Weppler, F-P. Hofmeister, B. Herrmann, H. Schmid)	3 02.0

* GB (F. P. Higgins, A. Dick, P. G. Fryer, D. J. N. Johnson), 1st in 3 08.2, disqualified.

High Jump — metres
1934	K. Kotkas (Finland)	2.00
1938	K. Lundqvist (Sweden)	1.97
1946	A. Bolinder (Sweden)	1.99
1950	A. S. Paterson (GB)	1.96

EUROPEAN CHAMPIONSHIPS

Year	Athlete	Mark
1954	B. Nilsson (Sweden)	2.02
1958	R. Dahl (Sweden)	2.12
1962	V. Brumel (USSR)	2.21
1966	J. Madubost (France)	2.12
1969	V. Gavrilov (USSR)	2.17
1971	K. Sapka (USSR)	2.20
1974	J. Torring (Denmark)	2.25
1978	V. Yashchenko (USSR)	2.30

Pole Vault (metres)

Year	Athlete	Mark
1934	G. Wegner (Germany)	4.00
1938	K. Sutter (Germany)	4.05
1946	A. Lindberg (Sweden)	4.17
1950	R. L. Lundberg (Sweden)	4.30
1954	E. Landstrom (Finland)	4.40
1958	E. Landstrom (Finland)	4.50
1962	P. Nikula (Finland)	4.80
1966	W. Nordwig (E. Germany)	5.10
1969	W. Nordwig (E. Germany)	5.30
1971	W. Nordwig (E. Germany)	5.35
1974	V. Kishkun (USSR)	5.35
1978	V. Trofimenko (USSR)	5.55

Long Jump (metres)

Year	Athlete	Mark
1934	W. Leichum (Germany)	7.45
1938	W. Leichum (Germany)	7.65
1946	O. Laessker (Sweden)	7.42
1950	T. Bryngeirsson (Iceland)	7.32
1954	O. Foldessy (Hungary)	7.51
1958	I. Ter-Ovanesyan (USSR)	7.81
1962	I. Ter-Ovanesyan (USSR)	8.19
1966	L. Davies (GB)	7.98
1969	I. Ter-Ovanesyan (USSR)	8.17
1971	M. Klauss (E. Germany)	7.92
1974	V. Podluzhny (USSR)	8.12
1978	J. Rousseau (France)	8.18

Triple Jump (metres)

Year	Athlete	Mark
1934	W. Peters (Netherlands)	14.89
1938	O. Rajasaari (Finland)	15.32
1946	K. J. V. Rautio (Finland)	15.17
1950	L. Shcherbakov (USSR)	15.39
1954	L. Shcherbakov (USSR)	15.90
1958	J. Szmidt (Poland)	16.43
1962	J. Szmidt (Poland)	16.55
1966	G. Stoikovski (Bulgaria)	16.67
1969	V. Sanyeyev (USSR)	17.34
1971	J. Drehmel (E. Germany)	17.16
1974	V. Sanyeyev (USSR)	17.23
1978	M. Srejovic (Yugoslavia)	16.94

Shot (metres)

Year	Athlete	Mark
1934	A. Viiding (Estonia)	15.19
1938	A. Kreek (Estonia)	15.83
1946	G. Huseby (Iceland)	15.56
1950	G. Huseby (Iceland)	16.74
1954	J. Skobla (Czechoslovakia)	17.20
1958	A. Rowe (GB)	17.78
1962	V. Varju (Hungary)	19.02
1966	V. Varju (Hungary)	19.43
1969	D. Hoffmann (E. Germany)	20.12
1971	H. Briesenick (E. Germany)	21.08
1974	H. Briesenick (E. Germany)	20.50
1978	U. Beyer (E. Germany)	21.08

Discus (metres)

Year	Athlete	Mark
1934	H. Andersson (Sweden)	50.38
1938	W. Schroeder (Germany)	49.70
1946	A. Consolini (Italy)	53.22
1950	A. Consolini (Italy)	53.74
1954	A. Consolini (Italy)	53.44
1958	E. Piatkowski (Poland)	53.92
1962	V. Trusenyov (USSR)	57.10
1966	D. Thorith (E. Germany)	57.42
1969	H. Losch (E. Germany)	61.82
1971	L. Danek (Czechoslovakia)	63.90
1974	P. Kahma (Finland)	63.62
1978	W. Schmidt (E. Germany)	66.82

Hammer (metres)

Year	Athlete	Mark
1934	V. Porhola (Finland)	50.34
1938	K. Hein (Germany)	58.76
1946	B. Ericson (Sweden)	56.44
1950	S. Strandli (Norway)	55.70
1954	M. Krivonosov (USSR)	63.34
1958	T. Rut (Poland)	64.78
1962	G. Zsivotzky (Hungary)	69.64
1966	R. Klim (USSR)	70.02
1969	A. Bondarchuk (USSR)	74.68
1971	U. Beyer (W. Germany)	72.36
1974	A. Spiridonov (USSR)	74.20
1978	Y. Sedykh (USSR)	77.28

Javelin (metres)

Year	Athlete	Mark
1934	M. H. Jarvinen (Finland)	76.66
1938	M. H. Jarvinen (Finland)	76.86
1946	A. L. F. Atterwall (Sweden)	68.74
1950	T. Hyytiainen (Finland)	71.26
1954	J. Sidlo (Poland)	76.34
1958	J. Sidlo (Poland)	80.18
1962	J. Lusis (USSR)	82.04

1966	J. Lusis (USSR)	84.48
1969	J. Lusis (USSR)	91.52
1971	J. Lusis (USSR)	90.68
1974	H. Siitonen (Finland)	89.58
1978	M. Wessing (W. Germany)	89.12

Decathlon (1962 Tables)		Pts.
1934	H. H. Sievert (Germany)	6858
1938	O. Bexell (Sweden)	6870
1946	G. Holmvang (Norway)	6760
1950	I. Heinrich (France)	7009
1954	V. Kuznyetsov (USSR)	7043
1958	V. Kuznyetsov (USSR)	7697
1962	V. Kuznyetsov (USSR)	7770
1966	W. von Moltke (W. Germany)	7740
1969	J. Kirst (E. Germany)	8041
1971	J. Kirst (E. Germany)	8196
1974	R. Skowronek (Poland)	8207
1978	A. Grebenyuk (USSR)	8340

10,000 Metres Walk		min. sec.	
1946	J. F. Mikaelsson (Sweden)	46	05.2
1950	F. Schwab (Switzerland)	46	01.8
1954	J. Dolezal (Czechoslovakia)	45	01.8

20,000 Metres Walk		hr.	min.	sec.
1958	S. F. Vickers (GB)	1	33	09.0
1962	K. J. Matthews (GB)	1	35	54.8
1966	D. Lindner (E. Germany)	1	29	25.0
1969	V. P. Nihill (GB)	1	30	41.0
1971	N. Smaga (USSR)	1	27	20.2
1974	V. Golubnichiy (USSR)	1	29	30.0
1978	R. Wieser (E. Ger.)	1	23	11.5

50,000 Metres Walk		hr.	min.	sec.
1934	J. Dalins (Latvia)	4	49	52.6
1938	H. H. Whitlock (GB)	4	41	51.0
1946	J. Ljunggren (Sweden)	4	38	20.0
1950	G. Dordoni (Italy)	4	40	42.6
1954	V. Ukhov (USSR)	4	22	11.2
1958	Y. Maskinskov (USSR)	4	17	15.4
1962	A. Pamich (Italy)	4	18	46.6
1966	A. Pamich (Italy)	4	18	42.2
1969	C. Hohne (E. Germany)	4	13	32.8
1971	V. Soldatenko (USSR)	4	02	22.0
1974	C. Hohne (E. Germany)	3	59	05.6
1978	J. Llopart (Spain)	3	53	29.9

Women Champions

100 Metres		sec.
1938	S. Walasiewicz (Poland)	11.9
1946	Y. Sechenova (USSR)	11.9
1950	F. E. Blankers-Koen (Netherlands)	11.7
1954	I. Turova (USSR)	11.8
1958	H. J. Young (GB)	11.7
1962	D. Hyman (GB)	11.3
1966	E. Klobukowska (Poland)	11.5
1969	P. Vogt (E. Germany)	11.6
1971	R. Stecher (E. Germany)	11.35
1974	I. Szewinska (Poland)	11.13
1978	M. Gohr (E. Germany)	11.13

200 Metres		sec.
1938	S. Walasiewicz (Poland)	23.8
1946	Y. Sechenova (USSR)	25.4
1950	F. E. Blankers-Koen (Netherlands)	24.0
1954	M. Itkina (USSR)	24.3
1958	B. Sobotta (Poland)	24.1
1962	J. Heine (Germany)	23.5
1966	I. Szewinska (Poland)	23.1
1969	P. Vogt (E. Germany)	23.2
1971	R. Stecher (E. Germany)	22.71
1974	I. Szewinska (Poland)	22.51
1978	L. Kondratyeva (USSR)	22.52

400 Metres		sec.
1958	M. Itkina (USSR)	53.7
1962	M. Itkina (USSR)	53.4
1966	A. Chmelkova (Czechoslovakia)	52.9
1969	N. Duclos (France)	51.72
1971	H. Seidler (E. Germany)	52.1
1974	R. Salin (Finland)	50.14
1978	M. Koch (E. Germany)	48.94

800 Metres		min.	sec.
1954	N. Otkalenko (USSR)	2	08.8
1958	Y. Yermolayeva (USSR)	2	06.3
1962	G. Kraan (Netherlands)	2	02.8
1966	V. Nikolic (Yugoslavia)	2	02.8
1969	L. B. Board (GB)	2	01.4
1971	V. Nikolic (Yugoslavia)	2	00.0
1974	L. Tomova (Bulgaria)	1	58.1
1978	T. Providokhina (USSR)	1	55.8

1500 Metres		min.	sec.
1969	J. Jehlickova (Czechoslovakia)	4	10.7
1971	K. Burneleit (E. Germany)	4	09.6
1974	G. Hoffmeister (E. Germany)	4	02.3
1978	G. Romanova (USSR)	3	59.0

3000 Metres

Year	Athlete	min. sec.
1974	N. Holmen (Finland)	8 55.2
1978	S. Ulmasova (USSR)	8 33.2

80 Metres Hurdles

Year	Athlete	sec.
1938	C. Testoni (Italy)	11.6
1946	F. E. Blankers-Koen (Netherlands)	11.8
1950	F. E. Blankers-Koen (Netherlands)	11.1
1954	M. Golubnichaya (USSR)	11.0
1958	G. Bystrova (USSR)	10.9
1962	T. Ciepla (Poland)	10.6
1966	K. Balzer (E. Germany)	10.7

100 Metres Hurdles

Year	Athlete	sec.
1969	K. Balzer (E. Germany)	13.3
1971	K. Balzer (E. Germany)	12.94
1974	A. Ehrhardt (E. Germany)	12.66
1978	J. Klier (E. Germany)	12.62

400 Metres Hurdles

Year	Athlete	sec.
1978	T. Zelentsova (USSR)	54.89

4 x 100 Metres Relay

Year	Team	sec.
1938	Germany (J. Kohl, K. Krauss, E. Albus, I. Kuhnel)	46.8
1946	Netherlands (G. J. M. Koudijs, N. Timmer, M. Adema, F. E. Blankers-Koen)	47.8
1950	GB (E. Hay, J. C. Desforges, D. G. Hall, J. F. Foulds)	47.4
1954	USSR (V. Krepkina, R. Ulitkina, M. Itkina, I. Turova)	45.8
1958	USSR (V. Krepkina, L. Kepp, N. Polyakova, V. Maslovskaya)	45.3
1962	Poland (T. Ciepla, M. Piatkowska, B. Sobotta, E. Szyroka)	44.5
1966	Poland (E. Bednarek, D. Straszynska, I. Szewinska, E. Klobukowska)	44.4
1969	E. Germany (R. Hofer, R. Stecher, B. Podeswa, P. Vogt)	43.6
1971	W. Germany (E. Schittenhelm, I. Helten, A. Irrgang, I. Mickler)	43.3
1974	E. Germany (D. Maletzki, R. Stecher, C. Heinich, B. Eckert)	42.51
1978	USSR (V. Anisimova, L. Maslakova, L. Kondratyeva, L. Storoshkova)	42.54

4 x 400 Metres Relay

Year	Team	min. sec.
1969	GB (R. O. Stirling, P. B. Lowe, J. M. Simpson, L. B. Board)	3 30.8
1971	E. Germany (R. Kuhne, I. Lohse, H. Seidler, M. Zehrt)	3 29.3
1974	E. Germany (B. Rohde, W. Dietsch, A. Handt, E. Streidt)	3 25.2
1978	E. Germany (C. Marquardt, B. Krug, C. Brehmer, M. Koch)	3 21.2

High Jump

Year	Athlete	metres
1938*	I. Csak (Hungary)	1.64
1946	A. Colchen (France)	1.60
1950	S. Alexander (GB)	1.63
1954	T. E. Hopkins (GB)	1.67
1958	I. Balas (Romania)	1.77
1962	I. Balas (Romania)	1.83
1966	T. Chenchik (USSR)	1.75
1969	M. Rezkova (Czechoslovakia)	1.83
1971	I. Gusenbauer (Austria)	1.87
1974	R. Witschas (E. Germany)	1.95
1978	S. Simeoni (Italy)	2.01

* Winner at 1.70 m. D. Ratjen (Germany), disqualified after change of sex following Championships.

Long Jump

Year	Athlete	metres
1938	I. Praetz (Germany)	5.88
1946	G. J. M. Koudijs (Netherlands)	5.67
1950	V. Bogdanova (USSR)	5.82
1954	J. C. Desforges (GB)	6.04
1958	L. Jacobi (Germany)	6.14
1962	T. Shchelkanova (USSR)	6.36
1966	I. Szewinska (Poland)	6.55
1969	M. Sarna (Poland)	6.49
1971	I. Mickler (W. Germany)	6.76
1974	I. Bruzsenyak (Hungary)	6.65
1978	V. Bardauskiene (USSR)	*6.88

* 7.09 m. in qualifying

Shot

Year	Athlete	metres
1938	H. Schroder (Germany)	13.29
1946	T. Sevryukova (USSR)	14.16
1950	A. Andreyeva (USSR)	14.32
1954	G. Zybina (USSR)	15.65
1958	M. Werner (Germany)	15.74
1962	T. Press (USSR)	18.55
1966	N. Chizhova (USSR)	17.22
1969	N. Chizhova (USSR)	20.43

1971	N. Chizhova (USSR)	20.16
1974	N. Chizhova (USSR)	20.78
1978	I. Slupianek (E. Germany)	21.41

Discus		metres
1938	G. Mauermayer (Germany)	44.80
1946	N. Dumbadze (USSR)	44.52
1950	N. Dumbadze (USSR)	48.02
1954	N. Ponomaryeva (USSR)	48.02
1958	T. Press (USSR)	52.32
1962	T. Press (USSR)	56.90
1966	C. Spielberg (E. Germany)	57.76
1969	T. Danilova (USSR)	59.28
1971	F. Melnik (USSR)	64.22
1974	F. Melnik (USSR)	69.00
1978	E. Jahl (E. Germany)	66.98

Javelin		metres
1938	L. Gelius (Germany)	45.58
1946	K. Mayuchaya (USSR)	46.24
1950	N. Smirnitskaya (USSR)	47.54
1954	D. Zatopkova (Czechoslovakia)	52.90
1958	D. Zatopkova (Czechoslovakia)	56.02
1962	E. Ozolina (USSR)	54.92
1966	M. Luttge (E. Germany)	58.74
1969	A. Ranky (Hungary)	59.76
1971	D. Jaworska (Poland)	61.00
1974	R. Fuchs (E. Germany)	67.22
1978	R. Fuchs (E. Germany)	69.16

Pentathlon (Present Tables)		Pts.
1950	A. Ben Hamo (France)	3544
1954	A. Chudina (USSR)	4020
1958	G. Bystrova (USSR)	4215
1962	G. Bystrova (USSR)	4312
1966	V. Tikhomirova (USSR)	4272
1969	L. Prokop (Austria)	4419
1971	H. Rosendahl (W. Germany)	4675
1974	N. Tkachenko (USSR)	4776
1978	M. Papp (Hungary)	4655

(N. Tkachenko of USSR, 4744, disqualified after doping test)

Record Achievements

Two athletes have won a title four times running: Janis Lusis (USSR), javelin champion in 1962, 1966, 1969 and 1971, and Nadyezhda Chizhova (USSR) women's shot titlist in 1966, 1969, 1971 and 1974.

Fanny Blankers-Koen (Netherlands) —80 m. hurdles and 4 x 100 m. relay in 1946; 100 m., 200 m. and 80 m. hurdles in 1950—and Irena Szewinska (Poland)—200 m., long jump and 4 x 100 m. relay in 1966; 100 m. and 200 m. in 1974—have won five titles. Szewinska's medal tally between 1962 and 1978 was ten.

Britain's most prolific medallists, with four apiece, are Derek Pugh (400 m. and 4 x 400 m. relay in 1946 and 1950), Dorothy Hyman (relay in 1958, both sprints and relay in 1962), and Alan Pascoe (110 m. hurdles in 1969 and 1971, 400 m. hurdles and 4 x 400 m. relay in 1974).

EUROPEAN CUP

Conceived by the late Bruno Zauli, former president of the IAAF's European Committee, and named after him, a European Cup tournament was instituted in 1965. Nations are represented by one athlete per event. The tournament is now held on a two-year cycle, with the 1981 finals being staged in Zagreb. Results of finals:

1965 (Men; at Stuttgart)
1. Soviet Union 86
2. West Germany 85
3. Poland 69
4. East Germany 69
5. France 60
6. Great Britain 48

1965 (Women; at Kassel)
1. Soviet Union 56
2. East Germany 42
3. Poland 38
4. West Germany 37
5. Hungary 32
6. Netherlands 26
(GB eliminated by Hungary and Netherlands in semi-final)

1967 (Men; at Kiev)
1. Soviet Union 81
2. West Germany 80
3. East Germany 80
4. Poland 68
5. France 57
6. Hungary 53
(GB eliminated by West Germany and Hungary in semi-final)

1967 (Women; at Kiev)
1. Soviet Union 51

EUROPEAN CUP

2. East Germany 43
3. West Germany 36
4. Poland 35
5. Great Britain 34
6. Hungary 32

1970 (Men; at Stockholm)
1. East Germany 102
2. Soviet Union 92½
3. West Germany 91
4. Poland 82
5. France 77½
6. Sweden 68
7. Italy 47

(GB eliminated by France and Soviet Union in semi-final)

1970 (Women; at Budapest)
1. East Germany 70
2. West Germany 63
3. Soviet Union 43
4. Poland 33
5. Great Britain 32
6. Hungary 32

1973 (Men; at Edinburgh)
1. Soviet Union 82½
2. East Germany 78½
3. West Germany 76
4. Great Britain 71½
5. Finland 64½
6. France 45

1973 (Women; at Edinburgh)
1. East Germany 72
2. Soviet Union 52
3. Bulgaria 50
4. West Germany 36
5. Great Britain 36
6. Romania 27

1975 (Men; at Nice)
1. East Germany 112
2. Soviet Union 109
3. Poland 101
4. Great Britain 83
5. West Germany 83
6. Finland 83
7. France 80
8. Italy 68

1975 (Women; at Nice)
1. East Germany 97
2. Soviet Union 77
3. West Germany 65
4. Poland 58
5. Romania 47
6. Bulgaria 47
7. Great Britain 40
8. France 36

1977 (Men; at Helsinki)
1. East Germany 125
2. West Germany 112
3. Soviet Union 100
4. Great Britain 95
5. Poland 93
6. France 70
7. Finland 66
8. Italy 54

1977 (Women; at Helsinki)
1. East Germany 106
2. Soviet Union 94
3. Great Britain 68
4. West Germany 68
5. Poland 58
6. Romania 55
7. Bulgaria 53
8. Finland 36

1979 (Men; at Turin)
1. East Germany 125
2. Soviet Union 114
3. West Germany 110
4. Poland 90
5. Great Britain 82
6. Italy 79
7. France 70½
8. Yugoslavia 49½

1979 (Women; at Turin)
1. East Germany 102
2. Soviet Union 100
3. Bulgaria 76
4. Great Britain 62
5. Romania 58
6. West Germany 58
7. Poland 55
8. Italy 29

Individual Winners

100 Metres sec.
1965 M. Dudziak (Poland) 10.3
1967 V. Sapeya (USSR) 10.3
1970 Z. Nowosz (Poland) 10.4
1973 S. Schenke (E. Germany) 10.26
1975 V. Borzov (USSR) 10.40
1977 E. Ray (E. Germany) 10.12
1979 P. Mennea (Italy) 10.15

200 Metres sec.
1965 J. Schwarz (W. Germany) 21.1
1967 J-C. Nallet (France) 20.9
1970 S. Schenke (E. Germany) 20.7
1973 C. L. Monk (GB) 21.00
1975 P. Mennea (Italy) 20.42
1977 E. Ray (E. Germany) 20.86
1979 A. W. Wells (GB) 20.29

400 Metres sec.
1965 A. Badenski (Poland) 45.9

Year	Athlete	Time
1967	J-C. Nallet (France)	46.3
1970	J. Werner (Poland)	45.9
1973	K. Honz (W. Germany)	45.20
1975	D. A. Jenkins (GB)	45.52
1977	B. Herrmann (W. Ger)	45.92
1979	H. Schmid (W. Ger)	45.31

800 Metres — min. sec.

Year	Athlete	Time
1965	F-J. Kemper (W. Ger)	1 50.3
1967	M. Matuschewski (E. Ger)	1 46.9
1970	Y. Arzhanov (USSR)	1 47.8
1973	A. W. Carter (GB)	1 46.4
1975	S. M. J. Ovett (GB)	1 46.6
1977	W. Wulbeck (W. Ger)	1 47.2
1979	S. N. Coe (GB)	1 47.3

1500 Metres — min. sec.

Year	Athlete	Time
1965	B. Tummler (W. Ger)	3 47.4
1967	M. Matuschewski (E. Ger)	3 40.2
1970	F. Arese (Italy)	3 42.3
1973	F. J. Clement (GB)	3 40.8
1975	T. Wessinghage (W. Ger)	3 39.1
1977	S. M. J. Ovett (GB)	3 44.9
1979	J. Straub (E. Ger)	3 36.3

5000 Metres — min. sec.

Year	Athlete	Time
1965	H. Norpoth (W. Germany)	14 18.0
1967	H. Norpoth (W. Germany)	15 26.8
1970	H. Norpoth (W. Germany)	14 25.4
1973	B. Foster (GB)	13 54.8
1975	B. Foster (GB)	13 36.2
1977	N. H. Rose (GB)	13 27.8
1979	H.-J. Kunze (E. Ger)	14 12.9

10,000 Metres — min. sec.

Year	Athlete	Time
1965	N. Dutov (USSR)	28 42.2
1967	J. Haase (E. Germany)	28 54.2
1970	J. Haase (E. Germany)	28 26.8
1973	N. Sviridov (USSR)	28 44.2
1975	K-H. Leiteritz (E. Ger)	28 37.2
1977	J. Peter (E. Ger)	27 55.5
1979	B. Foster (GB)	28 22.9

3000 Metres Steeplechase — min. sec.

Year	Athlete	Time
1965	V. Kudinskiy (USSR)	8 41.0
1967	A. Kuryan (USSR)	8 38.8
1970	V. Dudin (USSR)	8 31.6
1973	T. Kantanen (Finland)	8 28.6
1975	M. Karst (W. Germany)	8 16.4
1977	M. Karst (W. Germany)	8 27.9
1979	M. Scartezzini (Italy)	8 22.8

110 Metres Hurdles — sec.

Year	Athlete	Time
1965	A. Mikhailov (USSR)	13.9
1967	V. Balikhin (USSR)	14.0
1970	G. Drut (France)	13.7
1973	G. Drut (France)	13.70
1975	G. Drut (France)	13.57
1977	T. Munkelt (E. Germany)	13.37
1979	T. Munkelt (E. Germany)	13.47

400 Metres Hurdles — sec.

Year	Athlete	Time
1965	R. Poirier (France)	50.8
1967	G. Hennige (W. Germany)	50.2
1970	J-C. Nallet (France)	50.1
1973	A. P. Pascoe (GB)	50.07
1975	A. P. Pascoe (GB)	49.00
1977	V. Beck (E. Germany)	48.90
1979	H. Schmid (W. Germany)	47.85

4 x 100 Metres Relay — sec.

Year	Team	Time
1965	USSR	39.4
1967	France	39.2
1970	East Germany	39.4
1973	East Germany	39.45
1975	East Germany	38.98
1977	East Germany	38.84
1979	Poland	38.47

4 x 400 Metres Relay — min. sec.

Year	Team	Time
1965	West Germany	3 08.3
1967	Poland	3 04.4
1970	Poland	3 05.1
1973	West Germany	3 04.3
1975	GB (G. H. Cohen, J. W. Aukett, W. J. Hartley, D. A. Jenkins)	3 02.9
1977	West Germany	3 02.7
1979	West Germany	3 02.0

High Jump — metres

Year	Athlete	Height
1965	V. Brumel (USSR)	2.15
1967	V. Gavrilov (USSR)	2.09
1970	K. Lundmark (Sweden)	2.15
1973	V. Gavrilov (USSR)	2.15
1975	A. Grigoryev (USSR)	2.24
1977	R. Beilschmidt (E. Ger)	2.31
1979	D. Mogenburg (W. Ger)	2.32

Pole Vault — metres

Year	Athlete	Height
1965	W. Nordwig (E. Germany)	5.00
1967	W. Nordwig (E. Germany)	5.10
1970	W. Nordwig (E. Germany)	5.35
1973	A. Kalliomaki (Fin) & Y. Issakov (USSR)	5.30
1975	W. Kozakiewicz (Pol)	5.45
1977	W. Kozakiewicz (Poland)	5.60
1979	K. Volkov (USSR)	5.60

Long Jump		metres
1965	I. Ter-Ovanesyan (USSR)	7.87
1967	I. Ter-Ovanesyan (USSR)	8.14
1970	J. Pani (France)	8.09
1973	V. Podluzhny (USSR)	8.20
1975	G. Cybulski (Poland)	8.15
1977	J. Rousseau (France)	8.05
1979	L. Dombrowski (E. Ger)	8.31

Triple Jump		metres
1965	H-J. Ruckborn (E. Ger)	16.51
1967	V. Sanyeyev (USSR)	16.67
1970	J. Drehmel (E. Germany)	17.13
1973	V. Sanyeyev (USSR)	16.90
1975	V. Sanyeyev (USSR)	16.97
1977	A. Piskulin (USSR)	17.09
1979	B. Lamitie (France)	16.94

Shot		metres
1965	N. Karasyov (USSR)	19.19
1967	V. Varju (Hungary)	19.25
1970	H. Briesenick (E. Ger)	20.55
1973	H. Briesenick (E. Ger)	20.95
1975	G. L. Capes (GB)	20.75
1977	U. Beyer (E. Germany)	21.65
1979	U. Beyer (E. Ger)	21.13

Discus		metres
1965	Z. Begier (Poland)	58.92
1967	E. Piatkowski (Poland)	59.10
1970	R. Bruch (Sweden)	64.88
1973	P. Kahma (Finland)	63.10
1975	W. Schmidt (E. Germany)	63.16
1977	W. Schmidt (E. Ger)*	66.86
1979	W. Schmidt (E. Germany)	66.76

* M. Tuokko (Finland), 67.06 m., disqualified after doping test.

Hammer		metres
1965	R. Klim (USSR)	67.70
1967	R. Klim (USSR)	70.58
1970	A. Bondarchuk (USSR)	70.46
1973	A. Bondarchuk (USSR)	74.08
1975	K-H. Riehm (W. Ger)	77.50
1977	K-H. Riehm (W. Ger)	75.90
1979	K-H. Riehm (W. Ger)	78.66

Javelin		metres
1965	J. Lusis (USSR)	82.56
1967	J. Lusis (USSR)	85.38
1970	W. Nikiciuk (Poland)	82.46
1973	K. Wolfermann (W. Ger)	90.68
1975	N. Grebnyev (USSR)	84.30
1977	N. Grebnyev (USSR)	87.18
1979	W. Hanisch (E. Germany)	88.68

Women

100 Metres		sec.
1965	E. Klobukowska (Pol)	11.3
1967	I. Szewinska (Poland)	11.2
1970	I. Mickler (W. Germany)	11.3
1973	R. Stecher (E. Germany)	11.25
1975	R. Stecher (E. Germany)	11.29
1977	M. Gohr (E. Germany)	11.07
1979	M. Gohr (E. Ger)	11.03

200 Metres		sec.
1965	E. Klobukowska (Pol)	23.0
1967	I. Szewinska (Poland)	23.0
1970	R. Stecher (E. Germany)	23.1
1973	R. Stecher (E. Germany)	22.81
1975	R. Stecher (E. Germany)	22.63
1977	I. Szewinska (Poland)	22.71
1979	L. Kondratyeva (USSR)	22.40

400 Metres		sec.
1965	M. Itkina (USSR)	54.0
1967	L. B. Board (GB)	53.7
1970	H. Fischer (E. Germany)	53.2
1973	M. Zehrt (E. Germany)	51.75
1975	I. Szewinska (Poland)	50.50
1977	M. Koch (E. Germany)	49.53
1979	M. Koch (E. Germany)	48.60

800 Metres		min. sec.
1965	H. Suppe (E. Germany)	2 04.3
1967	L. Erik (USSR)	2 06.8
1970	H. Falck (W. Germany)	2 04.9
1973	G. Hoffmeister (E. Ger)	1 58.9
1975	M. Suman (Romania)	2 00.6
1977	C. Liebetrau (E. Ger)	2 00.2
1979	N. Shtereva (Bulgaria)	1 56.3

1500 Metres		min. sec.
1970	E. Tittel (W. Germany)	4 16.3
1973	Tonka Petrova (Bul)	4 09.0
1975	W. Strotzer (E. Ger)	4 08.0
1977	T. Kazankina (USSR)	4 04.4
1979	Totka Petrova (Bul)	4 03.2

80 Metres Hurdles		sec.
1965	I. Press (USSR)	10.4
1967	K. Balzer (E. Germany)	10.8

100 Metres Hurdles		sec.
1970	K. Balzer (E. Germany)	13.1
1973	A. Ehrhardt (E. Germany)	12.95
1975	A. Ehrhardt (E. Germany)	12.83
1977	J. Klier (E. Germany)	12.83
1979	T. Anisimova (USSR)	12.77

EUROPEAN INDOOR CHAMPIONSHIPS

4 x 100 Metres Relay

Year	Team	sec.
1965	Poland	44.9
1967	USSR	45.0
1970	West Germany	43.9
1973	East Germany	42.95
1975	East Germany	42.81
1977	East Germany	42.62
1979	East Germany	42.09

4 x 400 Metres Relay

Year	Team	min. sec.
1970	East Germany	3 37.0
1973	East Germany	3 28.7
1975	East Germany	3 24.0
1977	East Germany	3 23.7
1979	East Germany	3 19.7

High Jump

Year	Athlete	metres
1965	T. Chenchik (USSR)	1.70
1967	A. Okorokova (USSR)	1.79
1970	R. Schmidt (E. Germany)	1.84
1973	Y. Blagoeva (Bulgaria)	1.84
1975	R. Ackermann (E. Ger)	1.94
1977	R. Ackermann (E. Ger)	1.97
1979	R. Ackermann (E. Ger)	1.99

Long Jump

Year	Athlete	metres
1965	T. Shchelkanova (USSR)	6.68
1967	I. Mickler (W. Germany)	6.63
1970	H. Rosendahl (W. Ger)	6.80
1973	A. Voigt (E. Germany)	6.63
1975	L. Alfeyeva (USSR)	6.76
1977	B. Wujak (E. Ger)	6.76
1979	B. Wujak (E. Germany)	6.89

Shot

Year	Athlete	metres
1965	T. Press (USSR)	18.59
1967	N. Chizhova (USSR)	18.24
1970	N. Chizhova (USSR)	19.42
1973	N. Chizhova (USSR)	20.77
1975	M. Adam (E. Germany)	21.32
1977	E. Wilms (W. Germany)*	20.01
1979	I. Slupianek (E. Germany)	20.93

* I. Slupianek (E. Ger.) 21.20 m. disqualified after doping test.

Discus

Year	Athlete	metres
1965	J. Kleiber (Hungary)	56.74
1967	K. Illgen (E. Germany)	58.26
1970	K. Illgen (E. Germany)	61.60
1973	F. Melnik (USSR)	69.48
1975	F. Melnik (USSR)	66.54
1977	F. Melnik (USSR)	68.08
1979	E. Jahl (E. Germany)	68.92

Javelin

Year	Athlete	metres
1965	Y. Gorchakova (USSR)	58.48
1967	D. Jaworska (Poland)	56.88
1970	R. Fuchs (E. Germany)	60.60
1973	R. Fuchs (E. Germany)	66.10
1975	R. Fuchs (E. Germany)	64.80
1977	R. Fuchs (E. Germany)	68.92
1979	E. Raduly (Romania)	66.28

The European Cup for Combined Events was instituted in 1973 and is held every other year.

1973 Results: Decathlon—1, Poland 23,578 pts.; 2, USSR 23,434; 3, East Germany 22,723. Individual winner: L. Hedmark (Sweden) 8120. Pentathlon—1, East Germany 13,924; 2, USSR 13,351; 3, Bulgaria 12,882. Individual: B. Pollak (E. Germany) 4932.

1975 Results: Decathlon—1, USSR 23,631 pts.; 2, Poland 22,824; 3, Sweden 22,763. Individual: L. Litvinyenko (USSR) 8030. Pentathlon—1, East Germany 13,754; 2, USSR 13,186; 3, West Germany 12,751. Individual: B. Pollak (E. Germany) 4672.

1977 Results: Decathlon—1, USSR 24,303 pts.; 2, West Germany 24,049; 3 East Germany 23,928. Individual: A. Grebenyuk (USSR) 8252. Pentathlon—1, USSR 13,708; 2, West Germany 12,835; 3, France 12,277 Individual: N. Tkachenko (USSR) 4839.

1979 Results: Decathlon—1, East Germany 24,070; 2 West Germany 23,755; 3, USSR 23,510. Individual: S. Stark (E. Ger) 8287. Pentathlon—1, East Germany 13,836; 2, USSR 13,620; 3, West Germany 13,325. Individual: Y. Smirnova (USSR) 4717.

EUROPEAN INDOOR CHAMPIONSHIPS

An inaugural European Indoor Games, paving the way to full-scale Championships, was held in Dortmund in 1966. Subsequent venues: 1967—Prague, 1968—Madrid, 1969—Belgrade, 1970—Vienna (First official Championships), 1971—Sofia, 1972—Grenoble, 1973—Rotterdam, 1974—Gothenburg, 1975—Katowice, 1976—Munich, 1977—San Sebastian, 1978—Milan, 1979—Vienna, 1980—Sindelfingen, 1981—Grenoble.

The most successful competitor has been Valeriy Borzov (USSR), winner of the 50 or 60 m. seven times between 1970 and 1977.

British Medallists

The following athletes, listed in alphabetical order, have won medals

EUROPEAN INDOOR CHAMPIONSHIPS

while representing Britain in the European Indoor Games or Championships. G signifies gold (1st), S silver (2nd) and B bronze (3rd).

Capes, G. L., 1974, shot (G); 1975, shot (S); 1976, shot (G); 1977 shot (S); 1978, shot (B); 1979, shot (S).
Coe, S. N., 1977, 800 m. (G).
Connor, K. L., 1978 triple jump (S).
Davies, L., 1967, long jump (G); 1969, long jump (S).
Frith, R. M., 1968, 50m. (S); 1969 50 m. (B).
Kelly, B. H., 1966 60m. (G).
Lewis, P. J., 1971, 800 m. (S).
Moore, A. L., 1981, triple jump (B).
Parker, J. M., 1966, 60 m. hurdles (S).
Pascoe, A. P., 1969, 50 m. hurdles (G).
Price, B., 1976, 60 m. hurdles (S).
Robson, J., 1979, 1500 m. (B).
Smedley, R. J., 1976, 3000 m. (B).
Stewart, I., 1969, 3000 m. (G); 1975, 3000 m. (G).
Stewart, P. J., 1971, 3000 m. (G).
Whetton, J., 1966, 1500 m. (G); 1967, 1500 m. (G); 1968, 1500 m. (G).
Wilde, R. S., 1970, 3000 m. (G).
Wilkinson, W., 1969, 1500 (B).

Women
Barnes, E. A., 1980, 800 m. (B).
Beacham, M. A., 1971, 1500 m. (G).
Cobb, V. M., 1969, 50 m. (B).
Colebrook K. J., 1977, 800 m. (G).
Elder, V. M., 1973, 400 m. (G); 1975, 400 m. (G); 1977, 400 m. (S); 1979 400 m. (G); 1981, 400 m. (B).
Knowles, L. Y., 1967, high jump (S).
Lannaman, S. M., 1976, 60 m. (S).
Lynch, J. A. C., 1974, 60 m. (S); 1975, 60 m. (S).
Neufville, M. F., 1970, 400 m. (G).
Oakes, J. M., 1979, shot (B).
Perera, C., 1969, 50 m. hurdles (B).
Rand, M. D., 1966. 60 m. (B), high jump (B), long jump (S).
Reeve, S. D., 1969, long jump (S); 1978, long jump (B).
Stewart, M., 1977, 1500 m. (G).
Stirling, R. O., 1969, 400 m. (B); 1971, 800 m. (B).

Champions

50/60 Metres		sec.
1966	B. H. Kelly (GB)	6.6
1967	P. Giannattasio (Italy)	5.7
1968	J. Hirscht (W. Germany)	5.7
1969	Z. Nowosz (Poland)	5.8
1970	V. Borzov (USSR)	6.6
1971	V. Borzov (USSR)	6.6
1972	V. Borzov (USSR)	5.8
1973	Z. Nowosz (Poland)	6.6
1974	V. Borzov (USSR)	6.58
1975	V. Borzov (USSR)	6.59
1976	V. Borzov (USSR)	6.58
1977	V. Borzov (USSR)	6.59
1978	N. Kolesnikov (USSR)	6.64
1979	M. Woronin (Poland)	6.57
1980	M. Woronin (Poland)	6.62
1981	M. Woronin (Poland)	5.65

400 Metres		sec.
1966	H. Koch (E. Germany)	47.9
1967	M. Kinder (W. Germany)	48.4
1968	A. Badenski (Poland)	47.0
1969	J. Balachowski (Poland)	47.3
1970	A. Bratchikov (USSR)	46.8
1971	A. Badenski (Poland)	46.8
1972	G. Nuckles (W. Germany)	47.2
1973	L. Susanj (Yugoslavia)	46.4
1974	A. Brydenbach (Belgium)	46.60
1975	H. Kohler (W. Germany)	48.75
1976	J. Bratanov (Bulgaria)	47.79
1977	A. Brydenbach (Belgium)	46.53
1978	P. Mennea (Italy)	46.51
1979	K. Kolar (Czech)	46.21
1980	N. Chernetsky (USSR)	46.29
1981	A. Knebel (E. Germany)	46.52

800 Metres		min. sec.
1966	N. Carroll (Ireland)	1 49.7
1967	N. Carroll (Ireland)	1 49.6
1968	N. Carroll (Ireland)	1 56.6
1969	D. Fromm (E. Germany)	1 46.6
1970	Y. Arzhanov (USSR)	1 51.0
1971	Y. Arzhanov (USSR)	1 48.7
1972	J. Plachy (Czech)	1 48.8
1973	F. Gonzalez (France)	1 49.2
1974	L. Susanj (Yugoslavia)	1 48.1
1975	G. Stolle (E. Germany)	1 49.8
1976	I. Van Damme (Belgium)	1 49.2
1977	S. N Coe (GB)	1 46.5
1978	M. Taskinen (Finland)	1 47.4
1979	A. Paez (Spain)	1 47.4
1980	R. Milhau (France)	1 50.2
1981	H. Wursthorn (W. Ger)	1 47.7

1500 Metres		min. sec.
1966	J. Whetton (GB)	3 43.8
1967	J. Whetton (GB)	3 48.7
1968	J. Whetton (GB)	3 50.9
1969	E. Salve (Belgium)	3 45.9
1970	H. Szordykowski (Poland)	3 48.8
1971	H. Szordykowski (Poland)	3 41.4
1972	J. Boxberger (France)	3 45.7
1973	H. Szordykowski (Pol)	3 43.0
1974	H. Szordykowski (Pol)	3 41.8

EUROPEAN INDOOR CHAMPIONSHIPS

1975	T. Wessinghage (W. Ger)	3 44.6
1976	P. H. Wellmann (W. Ger)	3 45.1
1977	J. Straub (E. Ger)	3 46.5
1978	A. Loikkanen (Finland)	3 38.2
1979	E. Coghlan (Ireland)	3 41.8
1980	T. Wessinghage (W. Ger)	3 37.6
1981	T. Wessinghage (W. Ger)	3 42.7

3000 Metres — min. sec.

1966	H. Norpoth (W. Germany)	7 56.0
1967	W. Girke (W. Germany)	7 58.6
1968	V. Kudinskiy (USSR)	8 10.2
1969	I. Stewart (GB)	7 55.4
1970	R. S. Wilde (GB)	7 47.0
1971	P. J. Stewart (GB)	7 53.6
1972	Y. Grustinsh (USSR)	8 03.0
1973	E. Puttemans (Bel)	7 44.6
1974	E. Puttemans (Bel)	7 48.6
1975	I. Stewart (GB)	7 58.6
1976	I. Sensburg (W. Ger)	8 01.6
1977	K. Fleschen (W. Ger)	7 57.7
1978	M. Ryffel (Swi)	7 49.5
1979	M. Ryffel (Swi)	7 44.5
1980	K. Fleschen (W. Ger)	7 57.5
1981	A. Gonzalez (France)	—

50/60 Metres Hurdles — sec.

1966	E. Ottoz (Italy)	7.7
1967	E. Ottoz (Italy)	6.4
1968	E. Ottoz (Italy)	6.5
1969	A. P. Pascoe (GB)	6.6
1970	G. Nickel (W. Germany)	7.8
1971	E. Berkes (W. Germany)	7.8
1972	G. Drut (France)	6.5
1973	F. Siebeck (E. Germany)	7.7
1974	A. Moshiashvili (USSR)	7.66
1975	L. Wodzynski (Poland)	7.69
1976	V. Myasnikov (USSR)	7.78
1977	T. Munkelt (E. Germany)	7.62
1978	T. Munkelt (E. Germany)	7.65
1979	T. Munkelt (E. Germany)	7.59
1980	Y. Chervanyov (USSR)	7.54
1981	A. Bryggare (Finland)	6.47

High Jump — metres

1966	V. Skvortsov (USSR)	2.17
1967	A. Moroz (USSR)	2.14
1968	V. Skvortsov (USSR)	2.17
1969	V. Gavrilov (USSR)	2.14
1970	V. Gavrilov (USSR)	2.20
1971	I. Major (Hungary)	2.17
1972	I. Major (Hungary)	2.24
1973	I. Major (Hungary)	2.20
1974	K. Sapka (USSR)	2.22
1975	V. Maly (Czech)	2.21
1976	S. Senyukov (USSR)	2.22
1977	J. Wszola (Poland)	2.25
1978	V. Yashchenko (USSR)	2.35
1979	V. Yashchenko (USSR)	2.26
1980	D. Mogenburg (W. Ger)	2.31
1981	R. Dalhauser (Swi)	2.28

Pole Vault — metres

1966	G. Bliznyetsov (USSR)	4.90
1967	I. Feld (USSR)	5.00
1968	W. Nordwig (E. Germany)	5.20
1969	W. Nordwig (E. Germany)	5.20
1970	F. Tracanelli (France)	5.30
1971	W. Nordwig (E. Germany)	5.40
1972	W. Nordwig (E. Germany)	5.40
1973	R. Dionisi (Italy)	5.40
1974	T. Slusarski (Poland)	5.35
1975	A. Kalliomaki (Finland)	5.35
1976	Y. Prokhorenko (USSR)	5.45
1977	W. Kozakiewicz (Poland)	5.51
1978	T. Slusarski (Poland)	5.45
1979	W. Kozakiewicz (Poland)	5.58
1980	K. Volkov (USSR)	5.60
1981	T. Vigneron (France)	5.70

Long Jump — metres

1966	I. Ter-Ovanesyan (USSR)	8.23
1967	L. Davies (GB)	7.85
1968	I. Ter-Ovanesyan (USSR)	8.16
1969	K. Beer (E. Germany)	7.77
1970	T. Lepik (USSR)	8.05
1971	H. Baumgartner (W. Germany)	8.12
1972	M. Klauss (E. Germany)	8.02
1973	H. Baumgartner (W. Germany)	7.85
1974	J-F. Bonheme (France)	8.17
1975	J. Rousseau (France)	7.94
1976	J. Rousseau (France)	7.90
1977	H. Baumgartner (W. Ger)	7.96
1978	L. Szalma (Hugary)	7.83
1979	V. Tsepelev (USSR)	7.88
1980	W. Klepsch (W. Ger)*	7.98
1981	R. Bernhard (Swi)	8.01

* R. Desruelles (Bel), 8.08 m., disqualified after doping test.

Triple Jump — metres

1966	S. Ciochina (Romania)	16.43
1967	P. Nemsovsky (Czech)	16.57
1968	N. Dudkin (USSR)	16.71
1969	N. Dudkin (USSR)	16.73
1970	V. Sanyeyev (USSR)	16.95
1971	V. Sanyeyev (USSR)	16.83
1972	V. Sanyeyev (USSR)	16.97

EUROPEAN INDOOR CHAMPIONSHIPS

1973	C. Corbu (Romania)	16.80
1974	M. Joachimowski (Poland)	17.03
1975	V. Sanyeyev (USSR)	17.01
1976	V. Sanyeyev (USSR)	17.10
1977	V. Sanyeyev (USSR)	16.65
1978	A. Piskulin (USSR)	16.82
1979	G. Valyukevich (USSR)	17.02
1980	B. Bakosi (Hungary)	16.86
1981	S. Abbyasov (USSR)	17.30

Shot — metres

1966	V. Varju (Hungary)	19.05
1967	N. Karasyov (USSR)	19.26
1968	H. Birlenbach (W. Germany)	18.65
1969	H. Birlenbach (W. Germany)	19.51
1970	H. Briesenick (E. Germany)	20.22
1971	H. Briesenick (E. Germany)	20.19
1972	H. Briesenick (E. Germany)	20.67
1973	J. Brabec (Czech)	20.29
1974	G. L. Capes (GB)	20.95
1975	V. Stoev (Bulgaria)	20.29
1976	G. L. Capes (GB)	20.64
1977	H. Halldorsson (Iceland)	20.59
1978	R. Stahlberg (Finland)	20.48
1979	R. Stahlberg (Finland)	20.47
1980	Z. Saracevic (Yugoslavia)	20.43
1981	R. Stahlberg (Finland)	19.88

Women Champions

50/60 Metres — sec.

1966	M. Nemeshazi (Hungary)	7.3
1967	M. Nemeshazi (Hungary)	6.3
1968	S. Telliez (France)	6.2
1969	I. Szewinska (Poland)	6.4
1970	R. Stecher (E. Germany)	7.4
1971	R. Stecher (E. Germany)	7.3
1972	R. Stecher (E. Germany)	6.3
1973	A. Richter (W. Germany)	7.3
1974	R. Stecher (E. Germany)	7.16
1975	J. A. C. Lynch (GB)	7.17
1976	L. Haglund (Sweden)	7.24
1977	M. Gohr (E. Germany)	7.17
1978	M. Gohr (E. Germany)	7.12
1979	M. Gohr (E. Germany)	7.16
1980	S. Popova (Bulgaria)	7.11
1981	S. Popova (Bulgaria)	6.17

400 Metres — sec.

1966	H. Henning (W. Germany)	56.9
1967	K. Wallgren (Sweden)	55.7
1968	N. Pechenkina (USSR)	55.2
1969	C. Besson (France)	54.0
1970	M. F. Neufville (GB)	53.0
1971	V. Popkova (USSR)	53.7
1972	C. Frese (W. Germany)	53.4
1973	V. M. Elder (GB)	53.0
1974	J. Pavlicic (Yug)	52.64
1975	V. M. Elder (GB)	52.68
1976	R. Wilden (W. Germany)	52.26
1977	M. Koch (E. Germany)	51.14
1978	M. Sidorova (USSR)	52.42
1979	V. M. Elder (GB)	51.80
1980	E. Decker (W. Germany)	52.28
1981	J. Kratschvilova (Cze)	50.07

800 Metres — min. sec.

1966	Z. Szabo (Hungary)	2 07.9
1967	K. Kessler (W. Germany)	2 08.2
1968	K. Burneleit (E. Germany)	2 07.6
1969	B. Wieck (E. Germany)	2 05.3
1970	M. Sykora (Austria)	2 07.0
1971	H. Falck (W. Germany)	2 06.1
1972	G. Hoffmeister (E. Germany)	2 04.8
1973	S. Yordanova (Bul)	2 02.7
1974	E. Katolik (Poland)	2 02.4
1975	A. Barkusky (E. Germany)	2 05.6
1976	N. Shtereva (Bulgaria)	2 02.2
1977	K. J. Colebrook (GB)	2 01.1
1978	U. Bruns (E. Germany)	2 02.3
1979	N. Shtereva (Bulgaria)	2 02.6
1980	J. Januchta (Poland)	2 00.6
1981	N. Shtereva (Bulgaria)	2 01.0

1500 Metres — min. sec.

1971	M. A. Beacham (GB)	4 17.2
1972	T. Pangelova (USSR)	4 14.6
1973	E. Tittel (W. Germany)	4 16.2
1974	T. Petrova (Bulgaria)	4 11.0
1975	N. Marasescu (Romania)	4 14.7
1976	B. Kraus (W. Germany)	4 15.2
1977	M. Stewart (GB)	4 09.4
1978	I. Silai (Romania)	4 07.1
1979	N. Marasescu (Romania)	4 03.5
1980	T. Koba (USSR)	4 12.5
1981	A. Possamai (Italy)	4 07.5

50/60 Metres Hurdles — sec.

1966	I. Press (USSR)	8.1
1967	K. Balzer (E. Germany)	6.9
1968	K. Balzer (E. Germany)	7.0
1969	K. Balzer (E. Germany)	7.2
1970	K. Balzer (E. Germany)	8.2
1971	K. Balzer (E. Germany)	8.1
1972	A. Ehrhardt (E. Germany)	6.9
1973	A. Ehrhardt (E Germany)	8.0

1974	A. Fiedler (E. Germany) & G. Rabsztyn (Poland)	8.08
1975	G. Rabsztyn (Poland)	8.04
1976	G. Rabsztyn (Poland)	7.96
1977	L. Nikitenko (USSR)	8.29
1978	J. Klier (E. Germany)	7.94
1979	D. Perka (Poland)	7.95
1980	Z. Bielczyk (Poland)	7.77
1981	Z. Bielczyk (Poland)	6.74

High Jump		metres
1966	I. Balas (Romania)	1.76
1967	T. Chenchik (USSR)	1.76
1968	R. Schmidt (E. Germany)	1.84
1969	R. Schmidt (E. Germany)	1.82
1970	I. Gusenbauer (Austria)	1.88
1971	M. Karbanova (Czech)	1.80
1972	R. Schmidt (E. Germany)	1.90
1973	Y. Blagoeva (Bulgaria)	1.92
1974	R. Ackermann (E. Ger)	1.90
1975	R. Ackermann (E. Ger)	1.92
1976	R. Ackermann (E. Ger)	1.92
1977	S. Simeoni (Italy)	1.92
1978	S. Simeoni (Italy)	1.94
1979	A. Matay (Hungary)	1.92
1980	S. Simeoni (Italy)	1.95
1981	S. Simeoni (Italy)	1.97

Long Jump		metres
1966	T. Shchelkanova (USSR)	6.73
1967	B. Berthelsen (Norway)	6.51
1968	B. Berthelsen (Norway)	6.43
1969	I. Szewinska (Poland)	6.38
1970	V. Viscopoleanu (Rom)	6.56
1971	H. Rosendahl (W. Germany)	6.64
1972	B. Roesen (W. Germany)	6.58
1973	D. Yorgova (Bulgaria)	6.45
1974	M. Antenen (Switz)	6.69
1975	D. Catineanu (Romania)	6.31
1976	L. Alfeyeva (USSR)	6.64
1977	J. Nygrynova (Cze)	6.63
1978	J. Nygrynova (Cze)	6.62
1979	S. Siegl (E. Germany)	6.70
1980	A. Wlodarczyk (Poland)	6.74
1981	K. Hanel (W. Germany)	6.77

Shot		metres
1966	M. Gummel (E. Germany)	17.30
1967	N. Chizhova (USSR)	17.44
1968	N. Chizhova (USSR)	18.18
1969	M. Lange (E. Germany)	17.52
1970	N. Chizhova (USSR)	18.60
1971	N. Chizhova (USSR)	19.70
1972	N. Chizhova (USSR)	19.41
1973	H. Fibingerova (Cze)	19.08
1974	H. Fibingerova (Cze)	20.75
1975	M. Adam (E. Germany)	20.05
1976	I. Khristova (Bulgaria)	20.45
1977	H. Fibingerova (Cze)	21.46
1978	H. Fibingerova (Cze)	20.67
1979	I. Slupianek (E. Ger)	21.01
1980	H. Fibingerova (Cze)	19.92
1981	I. Slupianek (E. Ger)	20.77

EUROPEAN JUNIOR CHAMPIONSHIPS

The first, unofficial, European Junior Championships were staged in Warsaw in 1964 with 14 nations represented. Their success prompted the European Committee of the IAAF to promote European Junior Games in 1966 (Odessa) and 1968 (Leipzig). The latter occasion was affected by political events in Czechoslovakia, causing 13 of the 24 nations who had accepted (including Britain, for the first time) to withdraw. European Junior Championships have been held in Paris (1970), Duisburg (1973), Athens (1975), Kiev (1977) and Bydgoszcz (1979), with the 1981 edition scheduled for Utrecht.

Eighteen European Junior title winners have gone on to gain Olympic gold medals in individual events: Valeriy Borzov, Steve Ovett, Anders Garderud, Bronislaw Malinowski, Jacek Wszola, Udo Beyer, Vladimir Kisilyev, Yuriy Sedykh, Daley Thompson, Hartwig Gauder, Irena Kirszenstein (later Szewinska), Barbel Eckert (later Wockel), Monika Zehrt, Annelie Jahns (later Ehrhardt) Nadyezhda Chizhova, Ilona Schoknecht (later Slupianek), Evelin Schlaak (later Jahl) and Mihaela Penes.

Internationally, Juniors are boys under 20 and girls under 19 on December 31st in the year of competition.

British Medallists

The following British athletes, listed in alphabetical order, have won medals. G signifies gold (1st), S silver (2nd) and B bronze (3rd).
Beaven, P. M., 1970, 400 m. (G).
Benn, R. J., 1973, 4 x 400 m. (B).
Binns, S. J., 1979, 5000 m. (G).
Boggis, J. L. A., 1970, 3000 m. (S).
Brown, P. A., 1979, 4 x 100 m. (S).
Coe, S. N., 1975, 1500 m. (B).
Cohen, G. H., 1973, 4 x 400 m. (B).
Cooke P. J., 1979, 4 x 100 m. (S).

EUROPEAN JUNIOR CHAMPIONSHIPS

Cram, S., 1979, 3000 m. (G).
Fowell, W. M., 1979, 400 m. (B).
Francis, M., 1977 4 x 400 m. (B).
Hoffmann, P., 1975, 400 m. (S).
Holtom, J. M., 1977, 110 m. hurdles (S).
Jenkins, R. A., 1973, 4 x 400 m. (B).
Kerr, A. C., 1977, 4 x 400 m. (B).
Lees, N., 1977, 5000 m. (B).
McFarlane, M. A., 1979 200 m. (G), 4 x 100 m. (S), 100 m. (B).
McKenzie, A. C. A., 1973, 110 m. hurdles (B).
Moore, A. L., 1975, triple jump (G).
Morris, M., 1975, 2000 m. steeplechase (G).
Muir, N., 1977, 5000 m. (G).
Oakes, G. J., 1977, 400 m. hurdles (B).
Ovett, S. M. J., 1973, 800 m. (G).
Powell, M., 1979, 4 x 100 m. (S).
Price, B., 1970, 110 m. hurdles (G).
Reitz, C. R., 1979, 2000 m. steeplechase (S).
Sly, C., 1977, 1500 m. (S).
Stewart, G., 1977, 4 x 400 m. (B).
Thompson, F. M., 1977 decathlon (G).
Van Rees, C., 1973, 4 x 400 m. (B).
Williamson, J. G., 1979, 1500 m. (G).
Wymark, S., 1977, 400 m. (B) 4 x 400 m. (B).

Women
Clarke, W., 1975, 100 m. (B), 200 m. (S).
Clarkson, A. R., 1975, 4 x 400 m. (B).
Golden, H., 1970, 200 m. (G), 100 m. (B).
Haskett, C., 1970, 1500 m. (S).
Hearnshaw, S. C., 1979, long jump (B).
Heath, D., 1975, 4 x 400 m. (B).
Hill, W., 1973, 4 x 100 m. (B).
Hunte, H. R., 1977 4 x 100 m. (B).
Kennedy, R., 1973, 4 x 400 m. (S); 1975, 4 x 400 m. (B).
Lannaman, S. M., 1973, 100 m. (G), 4 x 100 m. (B).
Lynch, J. A. C., 1970, 100 m. (S).
MacGregor, J., 1977, 4 x 100 m. (B).
McMeekin, E., 1973, 4 x 400 m. (B).
Mapstone, S. L., 1973, pentathlon (S).
Martin, B. A., 1973, 4 x 100 m. (B).
Murray, D. M. L., 1973, 4 x 100 m. (B).
Pettett, S., 1973, 4 x 400 m. (S).
Probert, M., 1977, 4 x 100 m. (B).
Ravenscroft, J., 1973, 4 x 400 m. (S).
Simmonds B. A., 1979, high jump (B).
Smallwood K J., 1977, 100 m. (B), 200 m. (B), 4 x 100 m. (B)
Walls, M. L., 1970 long jump (S).
Whitbread, F., 1979, javelin (G).

White, J., 1977, 800 m. (B).
Williams, K., 1975, 4 x 400 m. (B).

Champions

100 Metres		sec.
1964	Z. Traykov (Bulgaria)	10.6
1966	B. Jacob (W. Germany)	10.7
1968	V. Borzov (USSR).	10.4
1970	F-P. Hofmeister (W. Ger)	10.4
1973	K-D. Kurrat (E. Ger)	10.4
1975	W. Bastians (W. Ger)	10.52
1977	H. Panzo (France)	10.40
1979	T. Schroder (E. Ger)	10.41

200 Metres		sec.
1964	G. Fenouil (France)	21.6
1966	J. Eigenherr (W. Ger)	21.0
1968	V. Borzov (USSR)	21.0
1970	F-P. Hofmeister (W. Ger)	21.4
1973	K-D. Kurrat (E. Ger)	21.0
1975	W. Bastians (W. Ger)	21.29
1977	B. Hoff (E. Germany)	20.59
1979	M. A. McFarlane (GB)	20.89

400 Metres		sec.
1964	I. Roper (W. Germany)	48.9
1966	A. Bratchikov (USSR)	47.3
1968	M. Mahy (Belgium)	47.5
1970	P. M. Beaven (GB)	47.0
1973	A. Brydenbach (Bel)	45.9
1975	H. Galant (Poland)	46.88
1977	R. Tozzi (Italy)	47.18
1979	H. Weber (W. Germany)	45.77

800 Metres		min. sec.
1964	F-J. Kemper (W. Ger)	1 51.9
1966	B. Hebert (France)	1 51.5
1968	R. Dominik (E. Ger)	1 51.6
1970	H-H. Ohlert (E. Ger)	1 50.9
1973	S. M. J. Ovett (GB)	1 47.5
1975	G. Gabrielli (France)	1 49.8
1977	A. Busse (E. Germany)	1 47.8
1979	K. Nabein (W. Ger)	1 48.2

1500 Metres		min. sec.
1964	J. Haase (E. Germany)	3 52.4
1966	R. Gervasini (Italy)	3 51.0
1968	U. Schneider (E. Ger)	3 53.3
1970	K-P. Justus (E. Ger)	3 51.3
1973	G. Ghipu (Romania)	3 45.8
1975	A. Paunonen (Finland)	3 44.8
1977	A. Paunonen (Finland)	3 41.6
1979	J. G. Williamson (GB)	3 39.0

3000 Metres		min. sec.
1964	J. Haase (E. Germany)	8 25.4
1966	K. Tietz (E. Germany)	8 22.4
1968	I. Dima (Romania)	8 13.4
1970	H. Mignon (Belgium)	8 08.6

EUROPEAN JUNIOR CHAMPIONSHIPS

1973	H-J. Orthmann (W. Ger)	8 03.4
1975	Y. Naessens (Bel)	8 10.6
1977	J. Abascal (Spain)	7 58.3
1979	S. Cram (GB)	8 05.2

5000 Metres		min. sec.
1973	F. Cerrada (Spain)	14 01.8
1975	P. Chernuk (USSR)	14 18.0
1977	N. Muir (GB)	13 49.1
1979	S. J. Binns (GB)	13 44.4

1500 Metres Steeplechase		min. sec.
1964	A. Garderud (Sweden)	4 08.0
1966	O. Knarr (W. Germany)	4 09.7
1968	N. Baklanov (USSR)	4 05.0

2000 Metres Steeplechase		min. sec.
1970	B. Malinowski (Pol)	5 44.0
1973	F. Baumgartl (E. Ger)	5 28.2
1975	M. Morris (GB)	5 34.8
1977	V. Laukkanen (Finland)	5 30.2
1979	G. Erba (Italy)	5 27.5

110 Metres Hurdles		sec.
1964	B. Pishchulin (USSR)	14.5
1966	Y. Gorski (USSR)	14.6
1968	Y. Mazepa (USSR)	14.3
1970	B. Price (GB)	14.1
1973	V. Naidenko (USSR)	14.4
1975	A. Pouchkov (USSR)	14.07
1977	A. Bryggare (Finland)	13.84
1979	F. Rossland (E. Ger)	14.09

400 Metres Hurdles		sec.
1964	W. Martynek (Poland)	51.9
1966	M. Dolgi (USSR)	53.3
1968	Y. Gavrilenko (USSR)	51.6
1970	D. Stukalov (USSR)	50.2
1973	J. Pietrzyk (Poland)	50.1
1975	A. Muench (E. Germany)	51.26
1977	M. Konow (E. Germany)	50.61
1979	G. Vamvakas (Greece)	50.67

High Jump		metres
1964	I. Matveyev (USSR)	2.04
1966	B. Jonsson (Sweden)	2.06
1968	A. Schigin (USSR)	2.10
1970	J. Palkowsky (Cze)	2.18
1973	F. Bonnet (France)	2.14
1975	J. Wszola (Poland)	2.22
1977	V. Yashchenko (USSR)	2.30
1979	D. Mogenburg (W. Ger)	2.24

Pole Vault		metres
1964	J. E. Blomqvist (Swe)	4.40
1966	A. Kalliomaki (Fin)	4.60
1968	Y. Issakov (USSR)	4.70
1970	F. Tracanelli (Fra)	5.20
1973	S. Krivozub (USSR)	5.00
1975	A. Dolgov (USSR)	5.00

1977	V. Spassov (USSR)	5.30
1979	V. Polyakov (USSR)	5.40

Long Jump		metres
1964	J. Kobuszewski (Pol)	7.42
1966	M. Klauss (E. Germany)	7.59
1968	M. Bariban (USSR)	7.78
1970	V. Podluzhny (USSR)	7.87
1973	F. Wartenberg (E. Ger)	7.85
1975	L. Dunecki (Poland)	7.98
1977	S. Jaskulka (Poland)	7.77
1979	A. Klimaszewski (Poland)	7.83

Triple Jump		metres
1964	A. Borsenko (USSR)	15.72
1966	A. Kainov (USSR)	15.97
1968	M. Bariban (USSR)	15.94
1970	V. Podluzhny (USSR)	16.25
1973	L. Gora (E. Germany)	16.29
1975	A. L. Moore (GB)	16.16
1977	G. Valyukevich (USSR)	16.60
1979	A. Beskrovniy (USSR)	16.47

Shot		metres
1964	G. Fejer (Hungary)	17.05
1966	A. Tammert (USSR)	16.71
1968	H. Briesenick (E. Ger)	18.71
1970	W. Barthel (W. Ger)	18.10
1973	U. Beyer (E. Germany)	19.65
1975	V. Kisilyev (USSR)	18.27
1977	D. Krumm (E. Germany)	18.87
1979	R. Machura (Cze)	18.34

Discus		metres
1964	G. Fejer (Hungary)	51.50
1966	F. Tegla (Hungary)	52.92
1968	H-J. Jacobi (E. Ger)	54.22
1970	A. Nazhimov (USSR)	54.18
1973	W. Schmidt (E. Ger)	58.16
1975	H. Klink (E. Germany)	55.48
1977	Y. Dumshev (USSR)	53.30
1979	J. Schult (E. Germany)	56.18

Hammer		metres
1964	G. Costache (Romania)	62.12
1966	Y. Ashmarin (USSR)	60.94
1968	P. Przesdzing (E. Ger)	61.76
1970	T. Manolov (Bulgaria)	65.16
1973	Y. Sedykh (USSR)	67.32
1975	D. Gerstenberg (E. Ger)	70.08
1977	R. Steuk (E. Germany)	70.78
1979	I. Nikulin (USSR)	71.56

Javelin		metres
1964	W. Krupinski (Poland)	74.58
1966	R. Cramerotti (Italy)	73.32
1968	A. Szajda (Poland)	68.52
1970	A. Pusko (Finland)	76.98
1973	G. Elze (E. Germany)	75.86
1975	I. Gromov (USSR)	77.92

EUROPEAN JUNIOR CHAMPIONSHIPS

1977	K. Tafelmeier (W. Ger)	84.14
1979	J. Lange (E. Germany)	78.78

Decathlon — pts.
- 1966 V. Chelnikov (USSR) 7225
- 1968 L. Litvinyenko (USSR) 7434
- 1970 A. Blinyayev (USSR) 7632
- 1973 V. Buryakov (USSR) 7554
- 1975 E. Muller (W. Germany) 7706
- 1977 F. M. Thompson (GB) 7647
- 1979 S. Wentz (W. Germany) 7822

10,000 Metres Walk — min. sec.
- 1966 M. Efimovich (USSR) 46 53.0
- 1968 J. Dumke (E. Ger) 44 48.0
- 1970 L. Lipowski (E. Ger) 43 35.6
- 1973 H. Gauder (E. Ger) 44 13.6
- 1975 R. Wieser (E. Ger) 43 11.4
- 1977 M. Vinnitchenko (USSR) 41 31.6
- 1979 J. Pribilinec (Cze) 41 04.8

4 x 100 Metres Relay — sec.
- 1964 Poland 41.6
- 1966 France 40.5
- 1968 USSR 40.4
- 1970 USSR 40.1
- 1973 East Germany 40.0
- 1975 France 40.07
- 1977 France 39.99
- 1979 West Germany 39.86

4 x 400 Metres Relay — min. sec.
- 1966 USSR 3 14.3
- 1968 USSR 3 12.3
- 1970 USSR 3 11.2
- 1973 East Germany 3 06.8
- 1975 East Germany 3 08.7
- 1977 East Germany 3 07.8
- 1979 West Germany 3 06.8

Women

100 Metres — sec.
- 1964 E. Klobukowska (Pol) 11.5
- 1966 B. Geyer (E. Germany) 12.2
- 1968 L. Zharkova (USSR) 11.5
- 1970 H. Kerner (Poland) 12.0
- 1973 S. M. Lannaman (GB) 11.7
- 1975 P. Koppetsch (E. Ger) 11.34
- 1977 B. Lockhoff (E. Ger) 11.48
- 1979 K. Walter (E. Ger) 11.57

200 Metres — sec.
- 1964 I. Kirszenstein (Poland) 23.5
- 1966 C. Heinich (E. Germany) 24.2
- 1968 L. Zharkova (USSR) 23.9
- 1970 H. Golden (GB) 24.3
- 1973 B. Eckert (E. Germany) 22.9
- 1975 P. Koppetsch (E. Ger) 23.20
- 1977 B. Lockhoff (E. Germany) 23.12
- 1979 K. Walter (E. Germany) 23.11

400 Metres — sec.
- 1966 L. Petnjaric (Yug) 55.9
- 1968 W. Birnbaum (E. Ger) 54.0
- 1970 M. Zehrt (E. Germany) 54.0
- 1973 B. Wolfrum (E. Ger) 53.3
- 1975 C. Brehmer (E. Ger) 51.27
- 1977 G. Bussmann (W. Ger) 52.33
- 1979 D. Rubsam (E. Ger) 51.55

600 Metres — min. sec.
- 1964 G. Olausson (Swe) 1 32.3

800 Metres — min. sec.
- 1966 V. Nikolic (Yug) 2 03.4
- 1968 B. Wieck (E. Ger) 2 06.3
- 1970 W. Pohland (E. Ger) 2 05.2
- 1973 A. Barkusky (E. Ger) 2 03.3
- 1975 O. Commandeur (Neth) 2 05.8
- 1977 M. Kampfert (E. Ger) 2 01.7
- 1979 M. Hubner (E. Ger) 2 01.3

1500 Metres — min. sec.
- 1970 K. Clausnitzer (E. Ger) 4 24.0
- 1973 I. Knutsson (Swe) 4 07.5
- 1975 A. Kuhse (E. Germany) 4 18.6
- 1977 D. Rasmussen (Den) 4 20.9
- 1979 I. Nikitina (USSR) 4 10.5

80 Metres Hurdles — sec.
- 1964 E. Bednarek (Poland) 11.2
- 1966 M. Antenen (Switz) 11.2
- 1968 A. Jahns (E. Germany) 11.1

100 Metres Hurdles — sec.
- 1970 G. Rabsztyn (Poland) 13.9
- 1973 B. Eckert (E. Germany) 13.1
- 1975 L. Lebeau (France) 13.77
- 1977 K. Claus (E. Germany) 13.32
- 1979 L. Spoof (Finland) 13.24

High Jump — metres
- 1964 R. Gildemeister (E. Ger) 1.67
- 1966 A. Prackova (Czech) 1.64
- 1968 E. Kalliwoda (E. Ger) 1.72
- 1970 M. Van Doorn (Neth) 1.74
- 1973 E. Mundinger (W. Ger) 1.82
- 1975 A. Fedorchuk (USSR) 1.88
- 1977 C. Nitzsche (E. Germany) 1.88
- 1979 K. Dedner (E. Germany) 1.87

Long Jump — metres
- 1964 I. Kirszenstein (Poland) 6.19
- 1966 T. Kapisheva (USSR) 5.98
- 1968 T. Bychkova (USSR) 6.18
- 1970 J. Nygrynova (Czech) 6.27
- 1973 H. Anders (E. Germany) 6.36
- 1975 I. Shidova (USSR) 6.36
- 1977 N. Zuyeva (USSR) 6.35

1979	H. Radtke (E. Germany)		6.47

Shot — metres
1964	N. Chizhova (USSR)		16.60
1966	L. Kostuchenko (USSR)		14.25
1968	E. Syromyatnikova (USSR)		15.02
1970	G. Moritz (E. Germany)		16.91
1973	I. Schoknecht (E. Ger)		17.05
1975	V. Vasselinova (Bul)		17.30
1977	S. Michel (E. Germany)		18.10
1979	L. Schmul (E. Germany)		18.33

Discus — metres
1964	N. Chizhova (USSR)		45.86
1966	H. Friedel (E. Germany)		45.56
1968	S. Vedeneyeva (USSR)		45.94
1970	K. Pogyor (Hungary)		48.26
1973	E. Schlaak (E. Germany)		60.00
1975	K. Wenzel (E. Germany)		55.06
1977	I. Reichenbach (E. Ger)		52.06
1979	I. Meszynski (E. Ger)		60.30

Javelin — metres
1964	M. Penes (Romania)		54.54
1966	K. Launela (Finland)		51.82
1968	S. Moritz (Romania)		51.10
1970	J. Todten (E. Germany)		55.20
1973	T. Khristova (Bul)		54.84
1975	L. Blodniece (USSR)		60.62
1977	H. Repser (W. Ger)		61.96
1979	F. Whitbread (GB)		58.20

Pentathlon — pts.
1966	M. Antenen (Switz)		4609*
1968	B. Pollak (E. Germany)		4717*
1970	M. Peikert (E. Germany)		4578*
1973	B. Muller (E. Germany)		4519
1975	B. Holzapfel (W. Ger)		4450
1977	C. Nitzsche (E. Germany)		4409
1979	S. Everts (W. Germany)		4594

* old tables

4 x 100 Metres Relay — sec.
1964	Poland	46.6
1966	East Germany	46.2
1968	USSR	45.3
1970	Poland	45.2
1973	East Germany	44.4
1975	East Germany	44.05
1977	East Germany	44.17
1979	East Germany	43.95

4 x 400 Metres Relay — min. sec.
1970	East Germany		3 40.2
1973	East Germany		3 34.4
1975	East Germany		3 33.7
1977	West Germany		3 32.8
1979	East Germany		3 31.7

EUROPEAN RECORDS

See APPENDIX.

EVANS, Lee (USA)

For a period of several seasons from 1966, when he was only 19, Lee Evans was firmly entrenched as the world's leading 400 m. runner. His thrusting stride and head-rolling action would not have won him any prizes for style but they carried him to victory after victory, usually in very fast times. His powerful finish and astounding consistency in an event all too easy to misjudge became legendary.

He won many honours: Olympic champion in 1968 (with a world record of 43.86 sec. which still stood twelve years later), Pan-American champion in 1967, American champion from 1966 to 1969 and again in 1972. He gained further gold medals in the 4 x 400 m. relay at the Olympics and Pan-American Games and, but for the inability of the USA to field a relay team at the Munich Olympics following the ban imposed on Vince Matthews and Wayne Collett, another gold would probably have come his way there. In addition he set world records in the 4 x 200 m., 4 x 220 yd. and 4 x 400 m. relays, and created a world's best 600 m. time of 74.3 sec.

Even on the rare occasions he lost, he would usually turn in a sizzling performance; e.g. 45.3 for 440 yd. behind Tommie Smith and 45.1 for 400 m. behind Vince Matthews in 1967, and 45.1 for 440 yd. behind Curtis Mills in 1969. In spite of winning the American 400 m. title in 1972, defeating his eventual Olympic successor Vince Matthews, Evans was deprived of a chance of defending his crown by finishing only fourth in the US Olympic Trials. He turned professional later in the year. He was reinstated in 1980, clocking 46.5 for 400 m. that summer.

His best performances include 20.4 sec. for 200 m., 43.86 sec. for 400 m. and 50.2 sec. for 440 yd. hurdles. He was born at Madera, California, on Feb. 25th, 1947.

EXETER, MARQUESS OF

See under BURGHLEY, LORD.

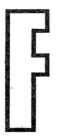

FAMILIES

Brothers

Three sets of brothers have been individual world record breakers: Tom (1.78 metres high jump, 1873) and Pat (1.90 metres high jump, 1880; 7.06 metres long jump 1883) Davin of Ireland; Tim Ahearne (14.91 metres triple jump, 1908) and Dan Ahearne (15.52 metres triple jump, 1911) of Ireland; Akilles (6719 pts. decathlon, 1930) and Matti (77.22 metres javelin, 1936) Jarvinen of Finland. In addition, Finland's Hannes Kolehmainen was world record holder at 5000 m. (14 min. 36.6 sec., 1912) and marathon (2 hr. 32 min. 36 sec. 1920), while brother Willie was the first marathoner to break 2½ hours (2 hr. 29 min. 40 sec. 1912) but as a professional.

Platt and Benjamin Adams (USA) placed first and second in the 1912 Olympic standing high jump. In standard Olympic events, the most sucessful brothers were Ireland's Patrick (2nd 1900 high jump, 3rd long jump) and Con (1st 1906 high jump and 2nd triple jump, 2nd 1908 high jump) Leahy; and Akilles (2nd 1928 and 1932 decathlon) and Matti (1st 1932 javelin) Jarvinen.

For Britain, Harold Whitlock was winner of the 1936 Olympic 50 km. walk while his brother Rex was fourth in the same event in 1952. The 1924 Olympic 100 m. champion Harold Abrahams' brother, Sidney was AAA long jump champion in 1913; Ralph Brown, brother of Godfrey (1936 Olympic 4 x 400 m. gold medallist), was third in the 1934 Empire Games 440 yd. hurdles.

Brother and sister

Ian (1969 and 1975 3000 m.), Peter (1971 3000 m.) and Mary (1977 1500 m.) Stewart of Britain were all winners of European indoor titles; in addition Ian (1970 5000 m.) and Mary (1978 1500 m.) were Commonwealth champions. Both Godfrey (4 x 400 m. gold, 400 m. silver) and Audrey (4 x 100 m. silver) Brown gained medals at the 1936 Olympics (see brothers). Roy Williams (NZ), brother of 1952 Olympic long jump champion Yvette Williams, was 1966 Commonwealth decathlon champion. Gisela Beyer (E. Germany), sister of 1976 Olympic shot champion and world record holder Udo Beyer, placed fourth in the 1980 Olympic discus. In 1981 Carl Lewis set a world indoor long jump record and sister Carol a USA indoor long jump best.

Father and daughter

The father of Jutta Stock (Germany), silver medallist in the 1966 and 1969 European 4 x 100 m., was 1936 Olympic javelin champion Gerhard Stock.

Father and son

The father of the Jarvinen brothers (see brothers), Werner, won the Greek-style discus title at the unofficial 1906 Olympics. In addition to Akilles and Matti, there were two other sons who were top class athletes: shot putter Kalle and javelin thrower Yrjo.

The only father-son Olympic gold medal combination in standard events is that of Imre (1948 hammer) and Miklos (1976 javelin) Nemeth of Hungary. Both were also world record breakers, as were Archie San Romani Snr (4 x mile relay, 1936; 2000 m., 1937) and Archie San Romani Jr (4 x mile relay 1962) of the USA.

Britain's Gordon Pirie, who set world records at 3000 m. and 5000 m. in 1956, was the son of Alick Pirie, a Scottish cross-country international in 1920.

Mother and daughter

Violet Webb (1932) and Janet Simpson (1964) both won Olympic bronze medals for Britain in the 4 x 100 m. relay. Also British Olympians were Muriel Pletts (4th 1948 4 x 100 m.)

and Sue Hearnshaw (9th 1980 long jump). The mother of world indoor high jump record breaker Andrea Matay was herself Hungarian high jump champion in 1948.

Mother and son

The mother of Russ Hodge (world record decathlon of 8230 pts. in 1966) was the former Alice Arden, who placed eighth for the USA in the 1936 Olympic high jump. Christian Haas of Germany, who set a European indoor 60 m. record in 1980, is the son of Maria Sturm bronze medallist in the 1954 European pentathlon, and Karl-Friedrich Haas, 1956 Olympic 400 m. runner-up.

Sisters

Both Irina (1960 80 m. hurdles and 1964 pentathlon) and Tamara (1960 shot, 1964 shot and discus) Press of the USSR were Olympic gold medallists and world record holders. Britain's most successful sisters have been Nellie (world 440 yd. record of 56.8 sec. in 1932) and Edith (2nd 1934 Empire Games javelin) Halstead, and Paula Fudge and Ann Ford (see twins).

Twins

Maurizio Damilano (Italy) won the 1980 Olympic 20 km. walk with his twin brother Giorgio 11th in the same race. Shigeru (2 hr. 09 min. 06 sec.) and Takeshi (2 hr. 09 min. 49 sec.) Sou of Japan both ranked among the ten fastest marathon runners of all time as at the start of 1981. When Paula Fudge (née Yeoman) of England won the 1978 Commonwealth 3000 m. title, her twin sister Ann Ford finished third. Both have held the UK record for the distance.

FIBINGEROVA, Helena (Czechoslovakia)

Once, way back in 1920, a Czech woman held the world record for shot-putting . . . the distance being a dinky 8.32 metres! Over half a century later the massive Helena Fibingerova (she weighs over 90 kg) regained the record for Czechoslovakia with a put of 21.57 metres in 1974. She lost it the following year but late in the 1976 season reclaimed the global mark with a tantalising distance of 21.99 metres. However, indoors in February 1977, she broke through the 22 metre barrier with plenty to spare as she propelled the 4 kg. shot a stunning 22.50 metres and followed up outdoors with a world record of 22.32 metres.

Fibingerova exploded into world class during 1972 when she improved her personal best from 16.77 to 19.18 metres and placed 7th in the Munich Olympics. Another major stride forward was taken in 1973, winning the European indoor title. Although she was to collect another four indoor titles between 1974 and 1980 her record in the major outdoor championships labelled her as a relatively poor competitor. She was beaten on every significant occasion.

Annual progress: 1966—13.61 m.; 1967—14.60; 1968—15.29; 1969—16.01; 1970—16.77; 1971—16.57; 1972—19.18; 1973—20.80; 1974—21.57; 1975—21.43; 1976—21.99; 1977—22.50; 1978—21.87; 1979—21.18; 1980—21.53. She was born at Vicemerice on July 13th, 1949.

FOSBURY, Dick (USA)

Although he never recaptured the form that won him the Olympic high jump title in 1968, the name of Fosbury will always be remembered and honoured. It was Dick Fosbury, a lanky 1.93 metres tall American, who hit upon the idea of propelling himself across the bar head-first on his back.

That style, known as the "Fosbury Flop", caught the imagination of the world as demonstrated so superbly by its inventor at the Mexico City Olympics, and in subsequent seasons his disciples achieved great success: both the 1980 Olympic champions and current world holders, Gerd Wessig and Sara Simeoni, are Floppers.

Fosbury's experiments with a back lay-out technique date back to when he was 16. An exponent of the unsophisticated scissors style and dissatisfied with his results, he felt he could improve by lowering his centre of gravity in going over on his back. His best jump immediately shot up from 1.62 to 1.78 metres. By the time he left high school two years later he was up to 2.00 metres and indoors in January 1968 he jumped 7 feet for the first time. He won the US Olympic Trial with a personal best of 2.21 metres and in Mexico City became the most popular champion of the Games as he cleared 2.24 metres at his final attempt. He turned professional in 1973. He was born in Portland, Oregon, on March 6th, 1947.

FOSTER, Brendan (GB)

Britain's best loved athlete of the seventies—the man who has inspired his home town of Gateshead into becoming the nation's most athletics-mad community—Brendan Foster has won every honour in the sport barring the supreme prize, an Olympic gold medal.

In his very first international appearance, the 1970 Commonwealth Games, he excelled himself by snatching the bronze medal in the 1500 metres (3 min. 40.6 sec.), and that was to set the pattern: the bigger the occasion the better he would run. He won another 1500 m. bronze, and again with a personal best (3 min. 39.2 sec.), in the 1971 European Championships; and at the following year's Olympics he took 5th place in 3 min. 39.0 sec.

From being a very good runner he emerged as a great one in 1973. He broke Lasse Viren's world 2 mi. record with 8 min. 13.7 sec. (miles of 4 min. 05.4 sec. and 4 min. 08.3 sec.) and outsmarted everyone in a tactically bizarre European Cup Final 5000 m.— and that in his first serious season at the event. He came away from the 1974 Commonwealth Games with two UK records: 13 min. 14.6 sec. for 5000 m. (finishing a close second to Kenya's Ben Jipcho) and 3 min. 37.6 sec. for 1500 m. to finish 7th in the Bayi-Walker epic.

It was in the 1974 AAA 5000 m. that Foster unveiled his new weapon —a mid race lap covered in well under 60 sec.—that was to make him such a feared opponent. He fulfilled a life's ambition three weeks later when, in front of his local fans at Gateshead, he smashed Emiel Puttemans' world record for 3000 m. with 7 min. 35.2 sec. (3 min. 49.0 sec. for 1500 m. followed by 3 min. 46.2 sec.). The following month he simply decimated the field in the European 5000 m. championship, winning by half the length of the finishing straight in 13 min. 17.2 sec.—great running in hot weather.

He was again successful in the European Cup Final 5000 m. (injecting a mid race lap of 58.2 sec!) in 1975, a year notable for his 10,000 m. debut, the fastest in history, of 27 min. 45.4 sec. He gained a bronze medal in this event at the 1976 Olympics, despite being weakened by an untimely attack of diarrhoea, and he finished 5th in the 5000 m. after setting an Olympic record of 13 mins. 20.3 sec. (which still stands) in his heat.

The finest run of his career at 10 000 m. came in the 1978 AAA Championships when he set a European record of 27 min. 30.3 sec—a time which only two weeks earlier would have constituted a world record. Foster went on to win the Commonwealth title but despite a fast time of 27 min. 32.7 sec. was just run out of the medals in the European Championships. He scored a big win in the 1979 European Cup but was below his best at the 1980 Olympics, placing 11th.

His best times include 1 min. 51.1 sec. for 800 m., 3 min. 37.6 sec. for 1500 m., 3 min. 55.9 sec. for the mile, 7 min. 35.2 sec. for 3000 m., 8 min. 13.7 sec. for 2 mi., 13 min. 14.6 sec. for 5000 m., 27 min. 30.3 sec. for 10,000 m. and 2 hr. 15 min. 49 sec. for the marathon. He was born at Hebburn on Jan. 12th, 1948.

FUCHS, Ruth (East Germany)

The world javelin record of 62.40 metres by Yelena Gorchakova (USSR) in the Olympic qualifying round at Tokyo in 1964 withstood all assaults until one day in 1972 it was broken at two separate meetings. Eva Gryziecka of Poland threw 62.70 metres in Bucharest, followed less than an hour later by what was then considered the absolutely phenomenal distance of 65.06 metres by Ruth Fuchs (née Gamm) in Potsdam.

For several years the strong but agile East German was to dominate women's javelin throwing and continually push towards new horizons. She climaxed the 1972 season by winning the Olympic gold medal and set further world records of 66.10 metres and 67.22 metres when winning the major events of 1973 (European Cup

Final) and 1974 (European Championships) respectively. She capped a fabulous career in 1976 by extending the world record to 69.12 metres and becoming the first woman to retain an Olympic javelin title.

But she hadn't finished yet. She won at the 1977 World Cup, easily defeating the USA's Kate Schmidt (who had set a world record of 69.32 metres earlier in the year); retained her European title in 1978 with a European record of 69.16 metres; won back the world record in 1979 and triumphed again in the World Cup; and came very close to becoming the first 70 metre thrower with 69.96 metres in 1980. She looked all set for a third Olympic title, but for once she succumbed to pressure and was unable to finish higher than eighth.

An adept all-rounder in her younger days, she has high jumped 1.58 metres and long jumped 5.88 metres. She was born at Egeln on Dec. 14th, 1946.

GARDERUD, Anders (Sweden)

A dazzling future was predicted for Anders Garderud when he front-ran to victory in the European Junior 1500 m. steeplechase in 1964 and a year later, aged 19, clocked the remarkable time of 4 min. 00.6 sec. for that event. The lanky Swede did indeed make good as a senior in terms of producing fast times—on the flat as well as for the steeplechase—but for much of his career he was regarded as a poor competitor on the big occasion. He was eliminated in the heats at the 1966 European Championships and at the Olympics of 1968 and 1972, while he ' choked ' again in the 1971 European steeplechase final to place 10th after clocking the fastest heat time.

He put up a better showing at the next edition of the European Championships, in 1974, to finish second behind his arch-rival Bronislaw Malinowski (Poland), and the following season he achieved a measure of immortality by becoming the first to break 8 min. 10 sec. for the 3000 m. steeplechase.

However, it was not until the 1976 Olympics that Garderud finally, and decisively, convinced doubters that he was temperamentally as well as physically equipped to land the supreme prize. Bursting ahead of Malinowski with 300 m. to go, he raced to the gold medal in a world record 8 min. 08.0 sec. Whether Frank Baumgartl (E. Germany), who was level with Garderud when he fell at the last barrier, would have won but for that mishap will long be discussed, but—as Baumgartl himself said—" the simple fact is Anders won this race ".

Best marks include 1 min. 47.2 sec. for 800 m., 3 min. 36.7 sec. for 1500 m., 3 min. 54.5 sec. for the mile, 7 min. 47.8 sec. for 3000 m., 13 min. 17.6 sec. for 5000 m., 28 min. 59.2 sec. for 10,000 m. and 8 min. 08.0 sec. for the steeplechase. He was born in Stockholm on Aug. 28th, 1946.

GAUDER, Hartwig (East Germany)

When he won the European Junior 10 km. walk title in 1973 a bright future was forecast for Hartwig Gauder. Sure enough, he developed into a world class performer at 20 km. although placing no higher than seventh in the 1978 European Championships and 1979 Lugano Trophy.

His career was transformed when, on the advice of his coach Siegfried Herrmann (3000 m. world record holder with 7 min. 46.0 sec. in 1965), he moved up to 50 km. He won the East German title in his debut (4 hr. 01 min. 20 sec.) in 1979 and just a year later—in his fourth race at the distance—he was crowned Olympic champion. In Moscow, with all around him either being disqualified or dropping out as victims of the very hot weather and fast pace, he emerged a clear winner in 3 hr. 49 min. 24 sec.

His best marks: 1 hr. 21 min. 39 sec. for 20 km. and 3 hr. 48 min. 15 sec. for 50 km. He was born at Vaihingen in West Germany (his parents moved to East Germany when he was five) on Nov. 10th, 1954.

GEORGE, W. G. (GB)

Walter George achieved enough during his amateur career to warrant lasting fame: world records in 1884 for the mile (4 min. 18.4 sec.), 2 mi. (9 min. 17.4 sec.), 3 mi. (14 min. 39.0 sec.), 6 mi. (30 min. 21.5 sec.), 10 mi. (51 min. 20.0 sec.), and one hour (11 mi. 932 yd.), together with numerous English titles at every event from 880 yd. to 10 mi. plus cross-country.

What ensured his immortality, though, was a professional mile race he won in 1886. He was pitted against the Scotsman William Cummings, holder of the professional record of 4 min. 16.2 sec., whom he had defeated in a 4 min. 20.2 sec. race the previous year.

The return match attracted enormous interest (not to mention stakes) and the large crowd was not disappointed. George ran the legs off his opponent by reeling off laps in 58.5, 63.3, 66.0 and 65.0 sec. for a total time of 4 min. 12.8 sec. (actually 4 min. 12¾ sec.). This was a phenomenal time, for it was not until 1915 that any athlete—amateur or professional—bettered it.

Indeed, in a time-trial in 1885 George had gone even faster. He was reliably timed at 4 min. 10.2 sec. for six yards over a mile—and that wasn't beaten officially until 1931. The following year he ran equally remarkable time-trials of 49 min. 29 sec. for 10 mi. (which would have been a world record right up to 1946!) and 59 min. 29 sec. for 12 mi.

Certainly, he was a man who was years ahead of his time, and in fact it was his form of training that inspired the celebrated Swedish coach Gosta Holmer to devise the popular fartlek system. Born at Calne, Wiltshire, on Sept. 9th, 1858, he lived to a great age (he died on June 4th, 1943).

GOHR, Marlies
(East Germany)

The fastest female runner yet seen, Marlies Gohr (née Oelsner) has competed in two Olympic Games and won two gold medals in the 4 x 100 m. relay, but the supreme honour—the Olympic 100 m. title—has eluded her. That was hardly surprising in Montreal in 1976; she was only 18 then and showed promise by reaching the final in which she finished eighth and last. But as the favourite in Moscow in 1980, she was unexpectedly pipped by Lyudmila Kondratyeva, the margin being just one-hundredth of a second.

Marlies achieved athletic immortality at the East German Championships in 1977 when, to general stupefaction, she became the first woman to crack 11 sec. with electrical timing. Hacking all of 13/100ths of a second off the previous world record—that's nearly a metre and a half on the track—she was timed at a stunning 10.88 sec. Superbly consistent, she has registered eight of the 11 marks of 11.00 or faster (as at the start of 1981), including a wind-assisted 10.79 sec. in 1980, and won all the important races except for the 1979 World Cup, when defeated by Evelyn Ashford (USA), and the Moscow Olympics.

A close second to Kondratyeva in the 1978 European 200 m., her best time in that event is 22.36 sec. Annual progress at 100 m.: 1971—12.8; 1972 —12.1; 1973—11.8; 1974—11.6; 1975 —11.41; 1976—11.17; 1977—10.88; 1978—10.94; 1979—10.97; 1980— 10.93. She was born at Gera on March 21st, 1958.

GOLUBNICHIY, Vladimir
(USSR)

No walker in history can rival the medal-winning achievements of Vladimir Golubnichiy. Over a 14-year span he was never worse than third in his seven Olympic and European 20 kilometre races.

He was only 19 when he set his first world record, 90 min. 02.8 sec. in 1955, but another five years went by before he made his international championship debut. And what a start: he won the 1960 Olympic title, in hot and humid conditions. He lost his crown in 1964, placing third in a race won by Britain's Ken Matthews, but he regained it in the rarefied atmosphere of Mexico City in 1968 as he prevailed in the face of a blatant late run by Mexico's Jose Pedraza. He was back again in 1972, clocking a brilliant 86 min. 55.2 sec., and failing by a mere 12.8 sec. to hold East Germany's Peter Frenkel in Munich. In his three bids for the European title, he was third in 1962, second in 1966 and winner—aged 38—in 1974. Two years later he made his fifth Olympic team, placing 7th, and clocked the fastest time of his career (83 min. 55 sec.). He was born at Sumy (Ukraine) on June 2nd, 1936.

HAGG, Gunder (Sweden)

The name of Sweden's Gunder Hagg is inextricably bound up with that of his countryman and arch-rival Arne Andersson. These two tall, powerful runners together revolutionised accepted miling standards and Hagg also accomplished phenomenal records at longer distances.

Hagg was certainly the more successful from a record point of view (he set 15 world marks against Andersson's three) but there was little between them over a mile. Andersson ran a 4 min. 01.6 sec. in 1944, Hagg 4 min. 01.3 sec. in 1945—no other runner had ever beaten 4 min. 04.6 sec. at this time.

Hagg began as a 5000 m. runner in 1936, set his first national 1500 m. record in 1940 and the following year broke Jack Lovelock's celebrated world record of 3 min. 47.8 sec. Between July and Sept. 1942 he set no fewer than ten world records at seven different distances!

One of the marks was 13 min. 58.2 sec. for 5000 m., over ten seconds faster than the previous best and destined to withstand all assaults for nearly 12 years. It was his only serious attempt at the event, his next best time being only 14 min. 24.8 sec. in 1944. Both Hagg and Andersson were disqualified for professionalism in Nov. 1945 at the height of their powers and while in training for their first European Championships.

Hagg's best performances were 1 min. 52.8 sec. for 800 m., 3 min. 43.0 sec. for 1500 m., 4 min. 01.3 sec. for the mile, 5 min. 11.8 sec. for 2000 m., 8 min. 01.2 sec. for 3000 m., 8 min. 42.8 sec. for 2 mi., 13 min. 32.4 sec. for 3 mi., 13 min. 58.2 sec. for 5000 m. and 9 min. 28.4 sec. for 3000 m. steeplechase. He was born at Sorbygden on Dec. 31st, 1918.

HAMMER

The hammer, as thrown today, consists of a metal head, a spring steel wire and a grip, weighing together not less than 7.26 kg. (16 lb.). The spherical head is of solid iron or other metal not softer than brass, or a shell of such metal filled with lead or other solid material. The implement is thrown from a circle with an inside diameter of 2.135 m. (7ft.) and must land within a 40 deg. sector.

Prior to standardisation in 1908, the hammer was thrown under several sets of rules. When the event was included at the first Oxford University Sports in 1860 the handle was wooden and an unlimited forward run was permitted, the throw being measured from the front foot at time of delivery. In 1876/77 the hammer was thrown from between two lines 7 ft. apart; from 1878 to 1886 a 7 ft. circle was used. After a 20-year period (1887-1907) with an enlarged circle of 9 ft., the AAA reverted to the current 7 ft. ring in 1908.

A dynasty of Irish-born athletes held possession of the world record from 1885 to 1949, a remarkably lengthy period of domination. The first great name was John Flanagan, who raised the record from a puny 44.46 metres in 1895 to 56.18 metres in 1909. He won the Olympic title three times to complete a perfect career.

He was succeeded as record holder and champion by Matt McGrath, whose best was 57.10 metres in 1911. McGrath hurt his knee at the 1920 Olympics and placed only fifth but in 1924, at the age of 46, he took the silver medal. The 1920 champion was Pat Ryan, who had seven years earlier relieved McGrath of the record with 57.76 metres, a performance that went unbeaten until 1937 when the last of the Irish masters, Pat O'Callaghan, reached 59.56 metres. The latter won the Olympic gold medal in 1928 and 1932.

The honour of hitting 60 metres first

in official competition fell to Jozsef Csermak (Hungary) in 1952.

It took 43 years for the record to progress from 55 to 60 metres, yet within a mere eight years Hal Connolly (USA), the 1956 Olympic champion, had reached 70 metres. Anatoliy Bondarchuk (USSR) led the way past 75 metres in 1969, and Boris Zaichuk (USSR) ushered in the 80 metre era in 1978.

Despite the successes achieved by her Irish neighbours, Britain has a fairly unimpressive record in this event. The only Olympic medallist was Malcolm Nokes, who was third in 1924, whilst Scotsman Duncan Clark placed third in the 1946 European Championships. Mike Ellis became the first Briton to surpass 60 metres in 1957, and Howard Payne, who succeeded him as the record-holder, won the Commonwealth title in 1962, 1966 and 1970. Barry Williams topped 70 metres in 1973 and Chris Black, 7th in Montreal (the highest Olympic placing since Nokes) improved the UK record to 74.98 metres in 1976.

See also under RIEHM, KARL-HANS and SEDYKH, YURIY.

HAMPSON, Tom (GB)

Tom Hampson was one of those fortunate athletes who managed to run the race of his life on the day it mattered most. Well known as an even pace runner, he kept cool in the headlong rush of the 1932 Olympic 800 m. final. The early pace was tremendously fast (24.4 sec. for the first 200 m.) and at the halfway stage Phil Edwards (Canada) led in 52.3 sec. Hampson was nearly 20 m. down in 54.8 sec. but by maintaining his speed while the leader was forced to decelerate he drew level with Edwards halfway around the second lap and fought it out with another Canadian, Alex Wilson, for the remainder of the race. The Englishman, who only three years earlier had trailed in a poor last in something over two minutes in the Oxford v. Cambridge half-mile, proved just the stronger and won by a foot or two in 1 min. 49.7 sec. to become the first man to crack 1 min. 50 sec.

Five days later he collected a silver medal in the 4 x 400 m. relay, covering his leg in 47.6 sec. Two years prior, he had won the Commonwealth 880 yd. title in his best time of 1 min. 52.4 sec. His fastest mile time was 4 min. 17.0 sec. He was born in London on Oct. 28th, 1907 and died on Sept. 4th, 1965.

HARBIG, Rudolf (Germany)

Rudolf Harbig's 1 min. 46.6 sec. for 800 m. in 1939 is widely regarded as one of the most amazing individual achievements in track and field history. No one had previously run faster than 1 min. 48.4 sec. (Britain's Sydney Wooderson) and 16 years were to pass before Roger Moens, of Belgium, finally removed the world record.

In this famous race, on the fast 500 m. track in Milan, Harbig led only for the final 100 m. (reputedly covered in just 12 sec.!)—arch rival Mario Lanzi (Italy) having set a swift pace for 700 m. Harbig broke another world record in 1939, clocking 46.0 sec. for 400 m. Two years later he set a kilometre record of 2 min. 21.5 sec.

He was only a 48.8 sec./1 min. 52.2 sec. performer in 1936 when he won a bronze medal in the Berlin Olympic 4 x 400 m., but by 1938 he had attained sufficient stature to capture the European 800 m. title, as well as assisting Germany to victory in the relay.

He won 55 consecutive races at all distances from 50 to 1000 m. between Aug. 1938 and Sept. 1940. His last race was a 1 min. 54.2 sec. 800 m. in Oct. 1942. Best marks: 10.6 sec. for 100 m., 21.5 sec. for 200 m., 46.0 sec. for 400 m., 1 min. 46.6 sec. for 800 m., 2 min. 21.5 sec. for 1000 m., 4 min. 01.0 sec. for 1500 m.

Harbig, who was born in Dresden on Nov. 8th, 1913, and was killed at the Eastern front on Mar. 5th, 1944, was trained by Waldemar Gerschler —later the coach to Josy Barthel (Luxemburg), the 1952 Olympic 1500 m. champion, and Britain's Gordon Pirie.

HARDIN, Glenn (USA)

Another athlete years ahead of his time was Glenn Hardin, whose mark of 50.6 sec. for 400 m. hurdles in a race he won by 40 m. survived as the world record from 1934 to 1953. In the same year he posted the second fastest 440 yd. on record (46.8 sec.) and unofficially tied the 220 yd. hurdles (straight) record of 22.7 sec.

Two years earlier he had experienced a somewhat bizarre season. At the American championships he broke the tape in the 400 m. hurdles only to find himself disqualified for running out of his lane. Later, in the Olympic final, because of the rules relating to the knocking down of hurdles then in force, he was credited with equalling the world record of 52.0 sec. though the race and Olympic record went to Irishman Bob Tisdall in 51.7 sec!

He won the Olympic title at the second attempt in 1936 and promptly retired. However, the name of Hardin again became prominent in athletic circles when his son Billy made the USA Olympic team in 1964 as a 400 m. hurdler.

Glenn Hardin's best marks included 21.4 sec. for 220 yd., 46.8 sec. for 440 yd., 1 min. 53.0 sec. for an 880 yd. relay leg, 15.4 sec. for 110 m. hurdles, 22.7 sec. for 220 yd. hurdles and 50.6 sec. for 400 m. hurdles. He was born at Derma, Mississippi, on July 1st, 1910 and died on March 6th, 1975.

HAYES, Bob (USA)

Bob Hayes, perhaps the fastest runner ever, began sprinting in 1959 when he was 16, and a mere two years later became the 13th man to tie Mel Patton's 100 yd. world record of 9.3 sec. That same season he was only a tenth of a second outside the straight 220 yd. record of 20.0 sec.

The following year he matched Frank Budd's new record of 9.2 sec. and in 1963 he finally made the world mark his own by streaking over 100 yd. of the rapid asphalt-rubber track in St. Louis in 9.1 sec. with the wind-gauge registering a breeze of only 0.8 m. per second behind him. Earlier in the season he had tied the then world records for 200 m. and 220 yd. (turn) of 20.5 sec.

One of his greatest displays occurred in Hanover in 1963 when, unleashing the most devastating burst of speed, he made up some 4 metres in a relay leg against Alfred Hebauf (W. Germany), who had run 100 m. in 10.3 sec. previously that day. The burly American may have exceeded 27 m.p.h.

Early in 1964 he made further history by recording 5.9 sec. for 60 yd. to become the first man to break six seconds for this classic indoor event, but the climax to a brilliant career came, appropriately, at the Olympic Games. After scorching to victory in his 100 m. semi-final in a wind assisted 9.9 sec. he recorded a legal, world record equalling 10.0 sec. (10.06 sec. on electrical timing) in the final to win by around two metres—the widest margin in Olympic 100 m. history. Six days later he produced an astonishing anchor leg to capture the 4 x 100 m. relay for the USA in world record time.

That proved to be Hayes' final race, for on returning to the United States he signed a professional football contract with the Dallas Cowboys and became one of the game's outstanding players.

Best marks: 9.1 sec. for 100 yd., 10.0/10.06 for 100 m. 20.1 sec. for 220 yd. (straight), 20.5 sec. for 220 yd. (turn). He was born in Jacksonville, Florida, on Dec. 20th, 1942.

HEMERY, David (GB)

David Hemery, who announced his retirement from amateur competition following the 1972 season, was to a unique degree a product of both British and American athletics.

Born in Gloucestershire, he moved with his family to the United States when he was 12. After graduating from high school in Massachusetts he returned to Britain in 1962. The following year he won the AAA junior 120 yd. hurdles title and, more significantly, made his 440 yd. hurdles debut—clocking 58.6 sec. for third in the Midland Championships.

He entered Boston University in the autumn of 1964 and steady progress was made at both hurdling events and on the flat. Particularly exciting were his European indoor records, early in 1966, of 1 min. 09.8 sec. for 600 yd. and 7.1 sec. for 60 yd. hurdles. Outdoors he ran only a handful of quarter hurdles (52.8 sec. in 1965 and 51.8 sec. in 1966) and concentrated on the "highs" to good effect. He won the 1966 Commonwealth title and, back in Europe, equalled the UK record of 13.9 sec.

He began his 1968 outdoor season by equalling his best 440 yd. hurdles time of 51.8 sec. and improved practically week by week so that in his final American race he won the National Collegiate 400 m. hurdles title in 49.8 sec. He trimmed that to 49.6 sec. in Britain and was ready for the Olympic challenge. Content to ease through his heat and semi-final (the latter in 49.3 sec.), he unleashed a staggering performance in the final. Running at a speed and with an attack never before witnessed in this event Hemery won by the huge margin of seven metres and, in clocking 48.12 sec., sliced seven-tenths off the previous world record!

Having achieved the ultimate in 400 m. hurdling, Hemery turned to other challenges in his next two years. He tackled the decathlon with gusto and in 1969 he cut the UK 110 m. hurdles record to 13.6 sec. and won the silver medal in the European Championships. In 1970 he retained his Commonwealth title. He took 1971 off in a repetition of his preparations of four years earlier and returned to his best event in 1972. This time he did not win the Olympic title but he ran with characteristic panache in Munich to take the bronze medal in 48.52 sec. a performance comparable to his high-altitude 48.12 sec. in Mexico City. He completed a set of Olympic medals by winning a silver in the 4 x 400 m. relay

He returned to the track in 1975 as a professional, clocking 35.5 sec. for 330 yd. hurdles.

His best marks included 10.9 sec. for 100 m., 21.8 sec. for 200 m., 47.1 sec. for 400 m. (44.8 sec. in relay), 1 min. 52 sec. for 800 m. (in training), 13.6 sec. for 110 m. hurdles, 34.6 sec. for 300 m. hurdles (best on record), 48.12 sec. for 400 m. hurdles, 1.86 m. high jump, 7.17 m. long jump and 6,893 pts. decathlon. He was born at Cirencester on July 18th, 1944.

HEPTATHLON

The seven-event heptathlon replaced the five-event pentathlon as the officially recognised all-round test for women athletes at the start of the 1981 season. The sequence of events is: (Day 1) 100 m. hurdles, shot, high jump, 200 m.; (Day 2) long jump, javelin, 800 m. The best score on record prior to 1981 was 6144 pts. by Yekaterina Gordienko (USSR) in 1980 made up of these marks: 14.06 sec., 14.80 metres, 1.74 metres, 24. 53 sec., 6.43 metres, 32. 08 metres and 2 min. 11.4 sec. Allison Manley set a UK best of 5373 pts. in March 1981.

HIGH JUMP

A high jumper may set about his task of clearing the maximum possible height in any manner he likes—except that he is obliged to take off from one foot.

Three consecutive failures result in the elimination of a competitor. Since 1927 the rules have stipulated that the crossbar must rest in such a manner that it can fall either forwards or backwards.

There are two styles of high jumping commonly in use: the straddle, where the athlete drapes himself face down across the bar (as used by Rosi Ackermann and Vladimir Yashchenko), and the Fosbury-flop, where the athlete employs a back lay-out and goes over head first (as originated by 1968 Olympic champion Dick Fosbury and used by Sara Simeoni and Gerd Wessig).

The first jumper to lift himself over six feet was the English rugby international, the Hon. Marshall Brooks, who in 1876 " cat jumped " 6 ft. 0¼ in. (1.83 metres) and subsequently 1.89 metres.

Pioneer of the eastern cut-off was Mike Sweeney, an Irish-American, who set world marks of 1.95 metres and 1.97 metres in 1895. His record stood until 1912, in which year George Horine (USA)—inventor of the western roll—went 2.00 metres.

Dave Albritton, who tied with fellow-American Cornelius Johnson at the world record height of 2.07 metres in 1936, was the first great straddle exponent. Another straddle jumper, Les Steers (USA) raised the record three times in 1941 ending with 2.11 metres.

The magical seven-foot jump could not be far away, it seemed, but in fact another 15 years were to flit past before its realisation in *bona fide* competition. The hero was Charles Dumas

(USA), whose silken straddle carried him over 7 ft. 0¼ in. (2.15 metres) in 1956.

John Thomas (USA) swept the world record upwards in four stages to 2.22 metres in 1960 and he was succeeded by another straddle jumper Valeriy Brumel (USSR) who was credited with six records culminating with 2.28 metres in 1963. Brumel's record stood until Pat Matzdorf (USA) cleared 2.29 metres in 1971, a height jumped by China's Ni Chih-chin in 1970. That leap was not ratified, as China was not a member of the IAAF. Dwight Stones (USA), a flopper, took possession of the record in 1973 (2.30 metres) and currently it stands at 2.36 metres to the credit of Gerd Wessig (E. Germany).

The man who has jumped highest over his own head is 1.73 metres (5 ft. 8 in.) tall Franklin Jacobs (USA), who cleared 2.32 metres (7 ft. 7¼ in.) indoors in 1978—a differential of 59 cm! Highest standing jump is 1.90 metres by Sweden's Rune Almen in 1980.

Most remarkable of all, Canadian Arnie Boldt, who has no right leg, has jumped 2.08 metres—by means of hopping to the bar.

Excluding a number of talented Irishmen (including the Leahy brothers, Pat and Con, who placed second in the 1900 and 1908 Olympics respectively) British high jumpers have had a lean time since the turn of the century.

The one bright exception was the Scotsman Alan Paterson, who won the European title in 1950. The first British seven-footer was Mike Butterfield, indoors in 1975.

See also under BRUMEL, VALERIY; DUMAS, CHARLES; FOSBURY, DICK; WESSIG, GERD; WSZOLA, JACEK and YASHCHENKO, VLADIMIR.

Women

It took 80 years for the men's record to climb from 6 to 7 ft., but in the women's event, where standards are roughly a foot lower, only 33 years elapsed between the first five-foot clearance by Phyllis Green (GB) in 1925 and the initial six-footer by Iolanda Balas (Romania) in 1958. Balas dominated the event for practically a decade and her final world record of 1.91 metres survived from 1961 to 1971, when Ilona Gusenbauer (Austria) added a centimetre. Yordanka Blagoeva (Bulgaria) jumped 1.94 metres in 1972, and she was succeeded by those great rivals, Rosi Ackermann (E. Germany) and Sara Simeoni (Italy), both of whom have cleared 2 metres.

Two women have jumped 26 cm. above their head: Tamami Yagi of Japan (1.64 metres tall) in 1978, and Marina Sysoyeva of USSR (1.67 metres tall) in 1980.

The three outstanding British jumpers, all world record holders in their time, have been Dorothy Tyler (*née* Odam), Sheila Lerwill (*née* Alexander), the first female straddle stylist, and Thelma Hopkins. Each of these athletes also won an Olympic silver medal (two in Mrs. Tyler's case); in fact it was Britain's misfortune to have been placed second in every Olympic competition from 1936 to 1960 inclusive! The first British-born woman to jump 6 feet (1.83 metres) was Linda Hedmark (*née* Knowles) later a Swedish citizen, in 1971.

See also under ACKERMANN, ROSEMARIE; BALAS, IOLANDA; BLANKERS-KOEN, FANNY; SIMEONI, SARA and TYLER, DOROTHY.

HILL, Albert (GB)

Albert Hill is surprisingly little remembered these days when one considers the magnitude of his achievement in winning both the 800 and 1500 m. at the 1920 Olympic Games. That double triumph came at the age of 31, fully ten years after he won his first AAA title . . . at 4 miles.

In the space of four days he ran a total of five races, winning the 800 m. by a metre in the British record time of 1 min. 53.4 sec. and the 1500 m. by four metres from his colleague Philip Baker (who as Philip Noel-Baker won the Nobel Peace Prize in 1959) in 4 min. 01.8 sec.

The following year he won the AAA mile in 4 min. 13.8 sec. to slash a full three seconds from the British record he shared with Joe Binks. Hill was coached by Sam Mussabini, the trainer of Harold Abrahams and Willie Applegarth among other notables, and he in turn later coached the great Sydney Wooderson. He was born on Mar. 24th, 1889 and died in Canada on Jan. 8th, 1969.

HINES, Jim (USA)

As the first man to better 10 sec. for 100 metres, the place of Jim Hines in the history of sprinting is assured. The occasion was the American AAU Championships at Sacramento in June 1968 and after a wind-assisted 9.8 sec. heat he established a new world record of 9.9 sec. in his semi.

The final was an anti-climax in that he suffered a bad start and lost narrowly to Charlie Greene, both clocking a windy 10.0 sec. At Mexico City later in the season he made no mistake and won the Olympic crown by a full metre in an electrically timed 9.95 sec.—which remains (at the end of 1980) the world record on fully automatic timing. He also ran a dynamic anchor leg in the 4 x 100 m. relay, taking his team both to victory and a world record 38.2 sec.

Hines, who was coached by 1956 Olympic sprint hero Bobby Morrow, also equalled the world records of 5.9 for indoor 60 yd. and 9.1 sec. for 100 yd. and was timed at 45.5 sec. for a 440 yd. relay leg. As a profesional in 1969 he ran 220 yd in 20.2 sec. . . . against a racehorse! He was born at Dumas, Arkansas, on Sep. 10th, 1946.

HISTORY OF ATHLETICS

Men have run, jumped and thrown things in competition with one another for thousands of years. The Lugnasad, or Tailteann Games, in Ireland are thought to have been founded as far back as 1829 B.C., some four and a half centuries before the Olympic Games are believed to have been started in Greece.

The first Olympic champion whose name we know is Coroebus, winner of the stade (185 m.) foot race in the Games of 776 B.C. Thirty Olympiads later, in 656 B.C., a Spartan athlete called Chionis long jumped 7.05 metres—the earliest measured performance known to posterity.

Following the abolition of the Olympic Games in A.D. 393 athletics plunged into the Dark Ages. There are reports of athletic activity in medieval England (King Henry VIII was noted for his hammer throwing among other activities) but it wasn't until the start of the 19th century that the sport as we know it today began to take shape.

Below are some of the key dates in the development of track and field athletics:—

1850 Foundation of Much Wenlock 'Olympic Games' in Shropshire.
1858 Sheffield Football Club staged what was possibly the first open amateur meeting held in England.
1862 British residents organised a meeting at Bonn, Germany, involving amateur athletes from eleven countries.
1863 Indoor meeting organised by West London Rowing Club at Ashburnham Hall, Chelsea.
1864 Annual Oxford v Cambridge match inaugurated.
1866 Amateur Athletic Club promoted the first English Championships.
1876 American Championships held for the first time. An Ireland v England match was staged in Dublin.
1877 First English cross-country championship.
1880 Formation of the Amateur Athletic Association and inauguration of AAA Championships.
1895 First women's track and field meeting held at Vassar College (USA).
1896 Olympic Games revived in Athens.
1903 First international cross-country championship.
1913 Establishment of the International Amateur Athletic Federation.
1917 First women's national governing body founded in France.
1921 First full international match between France and England held in Paris.
1922 Foundation of the Women's Amateur Athletic Association.
1928 Women's events added to the Olympic Games athletics programme.
1930 Establishment of the British Empire (later Commonwealth) Games.

HURDLES

1934 Establishment of the European Championships.
1964 Establishment of European Junior Games (Championships from 1970).
1965 Establishment of European Cup Tournament.
1966 Establishment of European Indoor Games (Championships from 1970).
1977 Establishment of World Cup Tournament.
1983 Inaugural World Championships scheduled.

HURDLES

There are currently two forms of hurdle racing for men: 110 metres over 3 ft. 6 in. (1.067 m.) barriers, and 400 metres over 3 ft. (0.914 m.) obstacles. Each comprises ten flights of hurdles.

High Hurdles

The barriers in the earliest days were crude sheep hurdles, about 3ft. 6in. high, staked in the ground. They were standardised at 3ft. 6in. in 1866.

The high hurdling pioneers used an ungainly bent-leg clearance style. Arthur Croome, an Oxford student, is credited with being the first man to lead over the hurdles with a straight leg in 1886. Alvin Kraenzlein (USA), winner of four gold medals at the 1900 Olympics, brought the record down to 15.2 sec. in 1898 but progress was slow until 1916, when Robert Simpson (USA) twice clocked 14.6 sec. The next record holder (14.4 sec. in 1920), Earl Thomson (Canada), was the first hurdler to use a double-shift arm action.

Shortly after the 1936 Olympics the biggest sensation in hurdling history occurred when Forrest Towns (USA), the newly crowned champion, cut all of four-tenths of a second from the world record with a dazzling time of 13.7 sec. for 110 m.

It was only in 1948 that this record was trimmed to 13.6 sec. by Harrison Dillard (USA), the one man to win both the Oympic 100 m. and 110 m. hurdles. Inches behind Dillard at the 1952 Games was Jack Davis (USA), who shared the winner's Olympic record. Davis ran the first 13.4 sec. in 1956 but in that year's Olympics he underwent the traumatic experience of again sharing the winner's time in second place. The championship went to Lee Calhoun (USA), who successfully defended his laurels in 1960.

Martin Lauer (W. Germany) was the first man to run 13.2 sec., in 1959, and that remained unsurpassed until Rod Milburn (USA) clocked 13.0 sec. for 120 yd. (only 10 in. less than 110 m.) in 1971 and won the Olympic 110 m. title the following year in 13.24 sec.—a world record on electrical timing. Guy Drut (France), the 1976 Olympic winner, ran a manually timed 13-flat for the metric event in 1975 and four years later Renaldo Nehemiah (USA) clocked an electrical 13.00 sec.

Britain possessed two world class high hurdlers in the 1930s in Lord Burghley, whose 14.5 sec. clocking in 1930 was only a tenth outside the existing world record, and Don Finlay, twice an Olympic medallist. Finlay was Britain's number one from 1932 to 1949 and for most of the following decade or so Peter Hildreth (once Britain's most "capped" international) was his country's first string —thus two athletes dominated the event for close on 30 years between them. Mike Parker became the first Briton to duck under 14 seconds by returning 13.9 sec. in 1963.

David Hemery won the Commonwealth title in 1966 and gained a European silver medal in 1969, a distinction achieved by Alan Pascoe in 1971.

Intermediate Hurdles

A 440 yard race over 12 flights was held at the 1860 Oxford University Sports. Although the event received Olympic recognition in 1900 it did not feature in the AAA and AAU Championships until 1914.

The four big names in pre-war intermediate hurdling tangled at the 1932 Olympics. Winner was Bob Tisdall (Ireland), whose time of 51.7 sec. for 400 m. was not officially accepted as a world record because he knocked down the final hurdle, which was against the rules for records then in force. His was one of the most startling breakthroughs in Olympic history, for he was only a novice at the event and his best time prior to the Games was but 54.2 sec.

Runner-up, but absurdly credited with the world record, was Glenn Hardin (USA), who in 1934 was to smash Tisdall's mark by over a second with a resounding 50.6 sec. and two years later was to succeed the Irishman as Olympic champion. In third place was Morgan Taylor (USA), who had won the 1924 title but like Tisdall had lost a record through clipping a hurdle. Placing fourth in 52.2 sec., a British record for 22 years, was the defending champion Lord Burghley.

Yuriy Lituyev (USSR) broke Hardin's record by a fifth of a second in 1953 but the next advance was a dramatic one. Glenn Davis (USA)—in his FIRST year of quarter mile hurdling—ran 49.5 sec. for the metric event and went on to take the Olympic title, which four years later in 1960 he retained. Davis set a new mark of 49.2 sec. in 1958, a time matched by Salvatore Morale (Italy) in winning the 1962 European crown, and bettered by the 1964 Olympic champion, American Rex Cawley (49.1 sec.).

The event's standards were transformed in 1968 when Geoff Vanderstock (USA) ran 48.8 sec. and David Hemery (GB) dominated the Olympic final in 48.12 sec—both times being run at high altitude. Hemery's record stood unchallenged until the Munich Olympics, where John Akii-Bua (Uganda) clocked 47.82 sec. at close to sea level. Hemery finished third to add to his previous gold medal and the silver gained by John Cooper in 1964.

The British successor to Hemery was Alan Pascoe, winner of the Commonwealth and European titles in 1974, but—recovering from untimely injury—he was unable to do himself justice in the 1976 Olympics, a race won by Edwin Moses (USA) in a world record of 47.64 sec. Moses has totally dominated the event ever since, cutting the record to 47.13 sec.

See also under AKII-BUA, JOHN; BECK, VOLKER; BURGHLEY, LORD; CALHOUN, LEE; DAVIS, GLENN; DILLARD, HARRISON; HARDIN, GLENN; HEMERY, DAVID; MILBURN, ROD; MOSES, EDWIN; MUNKELT, THOMAS; NEHEMIAH, RENALDO and OWENS, JESSE.

Women

The standard short hurdling event for women, since 1969, has been 100 m. over ten flights of 2 ft. 9 in. (0.84 m.) hurdles. Previously the race run at Olympic, European and Commonwealth Games was 80 m. in length, over 8 flights of 2 ft. 6 in. hurdles. The 100 m. record of 12.36 sec. is held by Grazyna Rabsztyn of Poland.

The 400 m. hurdles, comprising ten flights of 2 ft. 6 in. (0.762 m.) hurdles, has from small beginnings swiftly developed into a standard international event. Inaugural world championships were staged in 1980 and the event will be included in the 1984 Olympics. It wasn't until 1973 that 60 sec. was first beaten, but by 1980 the record stood at 54.28 sec. by Karin Rossley (E. Germany).

See also under BLANKERS-KOEN, FANNY; DELAHUNTY, SHIRLEY; EHRHARDT, ANNELIE; KOMISOVA, VERA; RABSZTYN, GRAZYNA and ROSSLEY, KARIN.

IBBOTSON, Derek (GB)

Few British athletes ever endeared themselves to the general public to quite the same degree as Derek Ibbotson. His cheerful personality, allied to exceptional running ability, made him the leading box office attraction in British athletics for several seasons.

He shot into world class as a three-miler in 1955, the following year winning the bronze medal in the Olympic 5000 m. behind Vladimir Kuts and Gordon Pirie. His most startling achievement in 1956 came over a mile, though. Despite a previous best of only 4 min. 07.0 sec. he sensationally clocked 3 min. 59.4 sec.

In July 1957 he became world record holder thanks to a scintillating run of 3 min. 57.2 sec. The race was a complete triumph for Ibbotson, for he convincingly defeated the most formidable opposition the world could offer. Ron Delany (Ireland), the Olympic champion, finished second ten metres behind, with Stanislav Jungwirth, the Czech who had broken the world 1500 m. record the previous week, and Ken Wood (Britain) also inside four minutes.

Ibbotson ran several fine races in the seasons that followed without ever quite recapturing his 1957 sparkle. Perhaps the outstanding achievement of his later years was his 1962 indoor campaign when he posted European bests at 2 and 3 mi.

Best marks: 1 min. 52.2 sec. for 880 yd., 3 min. 41.9 sec. for 1500 m., 3 min. 57.2 sec. for the mile, 5 min. 12.8 sec. for 2000 m., 8 min. 00.0 sec. for 3000 m., 8 min. 41.2 sec. for 2 mi., 13 min. 20.8 sec. for 3 mi., 13 min. 54.4 sec. for 5000 m. and 28 min. 52.0 sec. for 6 mi. He was born in Huddersfield on June 17th, 1932.

INDOOR ATHLETICS

Amateur indoor athletics meetings in England date back to 1863, and possibly earlier, but it took over 70 years for English Championships to be organised by the AAA. Meetings were held at Wembley from 1935 to 1939, and were revived in 1962. The championships have been staged at RAF Cosford since 1965. The record number of titles won is eight by pole vaulter Mike Bull between 1967 and 1977, and by Verona Elder (seven at 400 m., one at 800 m.) between 1972 and 1981.

The USA's first indoor meeting was promoted by the New York Athletic Club in 1868. Some American championships were held from 1893 but it was not until 1906 that meetings with the full range of events were instituted (women from 1927) by the AAU. The record number of titles won is ten by Henry Laskau in the mile walk (1948–57).

Inaugural European Indoor Games were held in 1966 and became official championships in 1970. For list of champions and British medallists, see EUROPEAN INDOOR CHAMPIONSHIPS.

Owing to the wide variations in the size of tracks, and the differing surfaces, indoor records are not officially ratified. For the best performances on record indoors on tracks up to 200 m. or 220 yd. in circumference, see APPENDIX.

AAA Champions (Post-War)

60 Yards		sec.
1962	D. H. Jones	6.5
1963	H. J. Bender (W. Germany)	6.4
1964	A. Meakin	6.4
1965	R. M. Frith	6.3
1966	B. H. Kelly	6.3
1967	R. M. Frith	6.3

60 Metres		sec.
1968	R. M. Frith	6.8
1969	R. M. Frith	6.9
1970	P. Pinnington	6.8
1971	D. G. Halliday	6.8
1972	B. H. Kelly	6.8
1973	B. W. Green	6.8
1974	D. G. Halliday	6.7

INDOOR ATHLETICS

Year	Athlete	Time
1975	D. L. Roberts	6.8
1976	C. L. Monk	6.9
1977	A. W. Wells	6.7
1978	P. D. Little	6.84
1979	S. M. Green	6.85
1980	R. C. Sharp	6.74
1981	S. Clarke	6.8

220 Yards — sec.
1965	D. G. Dear	22.8
1966	D. G. Dear	23.1
1967	T. J. Smith	22.7

200 Metres — sec.
1968	R. Banthorpe	22.8
1969	P. Wiltshire	22.6
1970	K. Meredith	23.0
1975	C. L. Monk	22.5
1976	A. E. McMaster	22.0
1977	G. H. Cohen	22.0
1978	M. A. McFarlane	21.9
1979	P. A. Brown	22.1
1980	P. A. Brown	22.1
1981	L. Christie	21.9

440 Yards — sec.
1965	M. A. Rawson	49.6
1966	W. Mottley (Trinidad)	47.3
1967	C. W. A. Campbell	49.8

400 Metres — sec.
1968	C. W. A. Campbell	47.9
1969	D. G. Griffiths	48.9
1970	D. G. Griffiths	49.0
1971	J. W. Aukett	48.2
1972	J. W. Aukett	48.9
1973	J. W. Aukett	47.9
1974	J. W. Aukett	47.9
1975	J. Chivers	48.4
1976	S. Scutt	49.0
1977	C. Hamilton	49.3
1978	C. Hamilton	49.3
1979	A. Bennett	48.3
1980	T. R. Whitehead	48.4
1981	A. Bennett	47.6

600 Yards — min. sec.
1962	B. H. A. Morris	1 16.3
1963	W. F. Crothers (Canada)	1 12.1
1964	W. F. Crothers (Canada)	1 10.0

880 Yards — min. sec.
1965	P. J. Beacham	1 52.5
1966	J. Gingell	1 52.3
1967	A. D. Middleton	1 51.5

800 Metres — min. sec.
1968	J. Gingell	1 52.0
1969	R. S. Adams	1 51.1
1970	C. W. A. Campbell	1 49.6
1971	P. J. Lewis	1 50.2
1972	C. F. Cusick	1 51.2
1973	A. K. Gibson	1 52.0
1974	R. Weatherburn	1 52.8
1975	P. M. Browne	1 52.4
1976	P. J. Lewis	1 50.0
1977	S. N. Coe	1 49.1
1978	P. R. W. Hoffmann	1 51.4
1979	M. R. Edwards	1 51.9
1980	S. Larder	1 51.0
1981	P. Forbes	1 50.3

1000 Yards — min. sec.
1962	T. J. B. Bryan	2 17.9
1963	W. F. Crothers (Canada)	2 14.0
1964	J. Whetton	2 12.2

Mile — min. sec.
1962	W. Olivier (S. Africa)	4 12.1
1963	J. Whetton	4 13.3
1964	J. Whetton	4 07.9
1965	J. Whetton	4 06.3
1966	J. Whetton	4 04.7
1967	J. Whetton	4 09.9

1500 Metres — min. sec.
1968	J. Whetton	3 51.0
1969	W. Wilkinson	3 49.3
1970	W. Wilkinson	3 48.0
1971	J. Davies	3 46.9
1972	F. J. Clement	3 46.4
1973	J. McGuinness	3 50.6
1974	C. J. Thomas	3 53.4
1975	P. A. Banning	3 42.2
1976	D. R. Moorcroft	3 45.6
1977	A. D. Mottershead	3 50.7
1978	T. H. Hutchings	3 48.4
1979	P. S. Williams	3 46.6
1980	M. R. Edwards	3 46.9
1981	R. Hackney	3 44.4

2 Miles — min. sec.
1962	G. D. Ibbotson	8 52.2
1963	J. Cooke	8 57.4
1964	B. Kidd (Canada)	8 39.0
1965	G. D. Ibbotson	8 42.6
1966	A. Simpson	8 45.6
1967	I. McCafferty	8 36.4

3000 Metres — min. sec.
1968	I. McCafferty	8 00.4
1969	I. McCafferty	8 08.4
1970	R. S. Wilde	7 59.2
1971	P. J. Stewart	8 00.4
1972	I. Stewart	7 50.0
1973	I. Stewart	7 58.0
1974	R. J. Smedley	8 00.0
1975	I. Stewart	8 01.0
1976	R. J. Smedley	7 59.2
1977	R. J. Smedley	7 59.2

INDOOR ATHLETICS

1978	S. J. Emson	8 05.4		1975	C. A. G. Boreham	2.00
1979	S. N. Coe	7 59.8		1976	M. Butterfield	2.16
1980	R. J. Callan	8 00.0		1977	M. Naylor	2.10
1981	S. N. Coe	7 55.2		1978	M. Naylor	2.11
				1979	M. Naylor	2.15
2000 m. Steeplechase		min. sec.		1980	A. D. McIver	2.15
1967	R. McAndrew	5 42.4		1981	M. Naylor	2.18
1968	P. A. Morris	5 35.0				
1969	B. D. Blakeley	5 36.6		*Pole Vault*		metres
1970	R. McAndrew	5 36.8		1962	T. P. Burton	4.19
1971	B. Hayward	5 34.8		1963	M. R. Higdon	3.96
1972	R. McAndrew	5 32.4		1964	R. Schmelz	
1973	R. McAndrew	5 36.8			(W. Germany)	4.70
1974	I. W. Gilmour	5 34.6		1965	D. D. Stevenson	4.49
1975	D. M. Coates	5 30.8		1966	M. R. Higdon	4.26
1976	A. Asgeirsson (Iceland)	5 38.8		1967	M. A. Bull	4.60
1977	P. J. L. Griffiths	5 34.2		1968	M. A. Bull	4.75
1978	D. M. Coates	5 24.6		1969	M. A. Bull	4.95
1979	I. W. Gilmour	5 40.2		1970	M. A. Bull	4.90
1980	P. Bettridge	5 45.3		1971	M. A. Bull	4.73
1981	R. Harris	5 32.9		1972	M. A. Bull	4.90
				1973	B. R. L. Hooper	4.80
60 Yards Hurdles		sec.		1974	M. A. Bull	5.00
1962	J. M. W. Hogan	7.7		1975	B. R. L. Hooper	5.20
1963	J. L. Taitt	7.6		1976	B. R. L. Hooper	5.05
1964	J. M. Parker	7.4		1977	M. A. Bull	4.90
1965	J. M. Parker	7.4		1978	B. R. L. Hooper	5.21
1966	J. M. Parker	7.4		1979	B. R. L. Hooper	5.35
1967	A. P. Pascoe	7.5		1980	K. F. Stock	4.80
				1981	B. R. L. Hooper	5.40
60 Metres Hurdles		sec.				
1968	A. P. Pascoe	8.1		*Long Jump*		metres
1969	A. P. Pascoe	7.8		1962	F. J. Alsop	7.19
1970	A. P. Pascoe	7.8		1963	L. Davies	7.48
1971	B. Price	7.9		1964	O. Oladitan (Nigeria)	7.33
1972	G. J. Gower	7.9		1965	F. J. Alsop	7.22
1973	A. P. Pascoe	8.0		1966	L. Davies	7.85
1974	C. J. Kirkpatrick	8.0		1967	P. S. Templeton	7.25
1975	B. Price	8.0		1968	D. Walker	7.37
1976	B. Price	8.1		1969	P. N. Scott	7.26
1977	P. C. Kelly	8.2		1970	A. L. Lerwill	7.55
1978	B. Price	7.90		1971	A. L. Lerwill	7.63
1979	J. M. Holtom	8.1		1972	L. Davies	7.51
1980	D. N. Wilson	7.99		1973	A. L. Lerwill	7.63
1981	P. C. Kelly	8.21		1974	P. N. Scott	7.33
				1975	P. N. Scott	7.28
High Jump		metres		1976	R. R. Mitchell	7.69
1962	G. A. Miller	2.03		1977	W. A. Kirkpatrick	7.23
1963	C. W. Fairbrother	2.00		1978	A. Henry	7.47
1964	H. Wadsworth (USA)	2.00		1979	W. A. Kirkpatrick	7.42
1965	G. A. Miller	2.03		1980	A. Henry	7.56
1966	C. W. Fairbrother	2.00		1981	A. L. Moore	7.49
1967	M. C. Campbell	1.95				
1968	M. C. Campbell	1.95		*Triple Jump*		metres
1969	M. C. Campbell	1.93		1965	F. J. Alsop	15.51
1970	D. N. Wilson	1.95		1966	M. Ralph	14.72
1971	D. J. Livesey	2.09		1967	F. J. Alsop	15.09
1972	M. C. Campbell	2.00		1968	F. J. Alsop	15.49
1973	A. Sneazwell (Aus)	2.10		1969	D. C. J. Boosey	15.47
1974	J. Fanning (Ireland)	2.01		1970	D. C. J. Boosey	15.68

INDOOR ATHLETICS

1971	A. E. Wadhams	15.43		*220 Yards*		sec.
1972	D. C. J. Boosey	15.17		1966	M. D. Tranter	24.8
1973	C. P. Colman	15.40		1967	J. B. Pawsey	25.2
1974	P. Blackburn	15.54				
1975	D. C. Johnson	15.54		*200 Metres*		sec.
1976	A. L. Moore	15.80		1969	D. P. James	25.5
1977	A. L. Moore	15.76		1979	C. A. Warden	25.0
1978	K. L. Connor	16.54		1980	L. T. Macdonald	24.3
1979	R. T. Philps	15.37		1981	C. V. Smart	24.5
1980	D. C. Johnson	15.64				
1981	A. L. Moore	15.90		*440 Yards*		sec.
				1966	G. Dourass	58.0
Shot		metres		1967	R. O. Wright	56.3
1962	M. T. Lucking	17.88				
1963	A. Carter	15.73		*400 Metres*		sec.
1964	M. R. Lindsay	17.54		1969	R. O. Wright	56.0
1965	A. Carter	17.44		1970	M. F. Neufville	54.9
1966	M. R. Lindsay	16.83		1971	J. V. Roscoe	56.1
1967	A. E. Elvin	16.57		1972	V. M. Elder	55.9
1968	J. Teale	17.73		1973	V. M. Elder	54.6
1969	W. R. Tancred	17.31		1974	S. Colyear	57.2
1970	J. Teale	17.19		1975	V. M. Elder	53.5
1971	G. L. Capes	18.07		1976	V. M. Elder	54.1
1972	G. L. Capes	18.65		1977	V. M. Elder	54.3
1973	M. A. Winch	18.67		1978	E. M. Eddy	54.8
1974	G. L. Capes	20.28		1979	V. M. Elder	54.3
1975	G. L. Capes	19.92		1980	E. A. Barnes	55.3
1976	W. R. Tancred	18.01		1981	V. M. Elder	53.2
1977	G. L. Capes	20.63				
1978	G. L. Capes	20.32		*600 Yards*		min. sec.
1979	M. A. Winch	18.60		1962	P. E. M. Perkins	1 28.6
1980	M. A. Winch	18.74		1963	B. J. Cook	1 28.4
1981	M. A. Winch	18.38		1964	P. J. Piercy	1 27.3

WAAA Champions (Post-War)
(No championships in 1968)

				880 Yards		min. sec.
				1965	M. T. Campbell	2 22.1
				1966	M. T. Campbell	2 16.6
60 Yards		sec.		1967	S. J. Carey	2 14.8
1962	D. Slater	7.1		*800 Metres*		min. sec.
1963	D. Slater	7.1		1969	S. J. Carey	2 10.8
1964	D. Slater	7.1		1970	R. O. Wright	2 06.5
1965	E. A. Gill	6.9		1971	R. O. Wright	2 08.0
1966	D. Slater	7.1		1972	M. A. Beacham	2 09.4
				1973	N. D. Braithwaite	2 10.4
				1974	R. O. Wright	2 07.2
60 Metres		sec.		1975	M. Barrett	2 11.5
1967	D. P. James	7.5		1976	M. Stewart	2 08.2
1969	V. M. Cobb	7.5		1977	S. E. Smith	2 08.4
1970	J. Stroud	7.4		1978	V. M. Elder	2 08.4
1971	S. M. Lannaman	7.5		1979	G. Dainty	2 08.9
1972	V. M. Cobb	7.4		1980	C. Hanson	2 05.8
1973	J. A. C. Lynch	7.4		1981	K. M. McDermott	2 07.1
1974	S. M. Lannaman	7.5				
1975	J. A. C. Lynch	7.3		*Mile*		min. sec.
1976	J. A. C. Lynch	7.3		1966	J. Smith	5 03.6
1977	W. P. Hoyte	7.4		1967	D. I. Elliott	5 02.1
1978	H. R. Hunte	7.39				
1979	E. Thomas	7.34		*1500 Metres*		min. sec.
1980	W. P. Hoyte	7.34		1969	C. T. Gould	4 42.4
1981	W. P. Hoyte	7.30		1970	G. A. Tivey	4 32.8

INDOOR ATHLETICS

1971	M. A. Beacham	4	20.5
1972	J. M. Lochhead	4	26.9
1973	J. M. Lochhead	4	30.6
1974	N. D. Braithwaite	4	37.4
1975	M. Stewart	4	21.0
1976	L. K. Harvey	4	29.8
1977	M. Stewart	4	15.9
1978	J. White	4	16.2
1979	M. Stewart	4	18.7
1980	S. A. Arthurton	4	21.2
1981	A. J. Wright	4	16.7

3000 Metres — min. sec.
1973	E. Connors	9	36.0
1975	C. Haskett	9	40.2
1976	M. Stewart	9	07.6
1977	M. Stewart	9	09.4
1979	S. A. Harris	9	57.6
1980	T. Bateman	9	37.4
1981	T. Bateman	9	44.7

60 Yards Hurdles — sec.
1962	D. J. Window	8.2
1963	P. A. Nutting	8.1
1964	M. Y. Botley	7.9
1965	M. Y. Botley	7.9
1966	M. D. Rand	7.8

60 Metres Hurdles — sec.
1967	P. Whitehead	8.9
1969	C. Perera	8.8
1970	M. E. Peters	8.5
1971	A. S. Wilson	8.9
1972	A. S. Wilson	8.6
1973	J. A. Vernon	8.6
1974	J. A. Vernon	8.3
1975	L. M. Boothe	8.5
1976	E. A. Sutherland	8.3
1977	L. M. Boothe	8.5
1978	L. M. Boothe	8.36
1979	L. M. Boothe	8.46
1980	Y. J. Wray	8.33
1981	Y. J. Wray	8.33

High Jump — metres
1962	F. M. Slaap	1.70
1963	L. Y. Knowles	1.62
1964	F. M. Slaap	1.67
1965	D. A. Shirley	1.62
1966	M. D. Rand	1.65
1967	L. Y. Knowles	1.69
1969	B. J. Inkpen	1.73
1970	B. J. Inkpen	1.69
1971	A. S. Wilson	1.70
1972	R. Few	1.71
1973	B. J. Inkpen	1.86
1974	A. S. Wilson	1.75
1975	R. Few	1.80
1976	D. Cooper	1.74
1977	R. Few	1.78
1978	G. Hitchen	1.80
1979	L. A. Miller	1.75
1980	L. A. Miller	1.82
1981	L. A. Miller	1.80

Long Jump — metres
1962	S. Parkin	5.81
1963	S. Parkin	5.77
1964	L. A. Jamieson	6.08
1965	S. Parkin	5.86
1966	M. D. Rand	6.14
1967	B. Inkpen	5.74
1969	S. D. Reeve	5.87
1970	A. S. Wilson	5.99
1971	R. Martin-Jones	6.02
1972	M. A. Chitty	6.35
1973	B-A. Barrett	6.02
1974	M. A. Chitty	5.79
1975	J. M. Jay	5.78
1976	S. D. Reeve	6.28
1977	S. D. Reeve	6.09
1978	S. D. Reeve	6.20
1979	S. Colyear	6.05
1980	A. P. Manley	6.13
1981	S. J. Longden	5.85

Shot — metres
1962	S. Allday	13.76
1963	S. Allday	14.13
1964	M. E. Peters	14.97
1965	M. E. Peters	14.10
1966	M. E. Peters	15.30
1967	B. R. Bedford	13.90
1969	B. R. Bedford	14.49
1970	M. E. Peters	15.86
1971	B. R. Bedford	14.14
1972	M. E. Peters	16.26
1973	B. R. Bedford	14.59
1974	J. A. Kerr	13.23
1975	B. R. Bedford	15.08
1976	J. A. Kerr	15.80
1977	J. M. Oakes	15.87
1978	J. M. Oakes	16.41
1979	J. M. Oakes	16.44
1980	J. M. Oakes	16.45
1981	A. M. Littlewood	16.90

1½ Miles Walk — min. sec.
1966	J. U. Farr	12 29.2
1967	D. Cotterill	12 33.8

INTERNATIONAL AMATEUR ATHLETIC FEDERATION

The IAAF is the supreme governing body controlling international athletics throughout the world. It was founded in Stockholm in July of

1912 to draw up and enforce rules and regulations and a common amateur definition, and to recognise world records. Seventeen countries were represented at the meeting: Australia, Austria, Belgium, Canada, Chile, Denmark, Egypt Finland, France, Germany, Greece, Hungary, Norway, Russia, Sweden, United Kingdom of Great Britain and Ireland and the United States of America.

Member countries now number 169, the only notable absentee being South Africa which was expelled in 1976.

The IAAF promotes several important events, notably the World Cup, the World Cross-Country Championships, the Lugano Cup for walking, and—from 1983—the eagerly awaited World Track & Field Championships. A recent innovation has been the organising of IAAF Golden Events, sponsored high quality international invitation contests. Winners: (1978) Mile: Steve Ovett (GB) 3 min. 55.5 sec. (1979) 100/200 m: James Sanford (USA) 10.15/20.39 sec.; Mile: Sebastian Coe (GB) 3 min. 49.0 sec.; 10,000 m: Mike McLeod (GB) 27 min. 39.8 sec.; Javelin: Arto Harkonen (Fin) 90.18 m. (1980) Mile: Steve Ovett (GB) 3 min. 52.9 sec., Pole Vault: Serge Ferreira (Fra) 5.70 m.

INTERNATIONAL MATCHES

The earliest instance of an international match occurred in 1876 when an England team (all but one of the athletes being members of London Athletic Club) competed against Ireland in Dublin. However, it was not until 1921 that full-scale matches were instituted. The pioneers were France and Britain (styled "England" prior to 1933) who met in Paris. The following month, again in Paris, the same countries fought out the first (unofficial) women's international match.

British Men's Matches

Britain—the United Kingdom of Great Britain and Northern Ireland to be precise—has won 80 of her 165 men's matches from 1921 to 1980 inclusive. Highlights have included victories over Russia in 1963 (112–99) and 1979 (221–219), and the full USSR team in 1977 (111–98).

The most "capped" British international is pole vaulter and decathlete Mike Bull with 69 appearances (including 23 indoors) between 1965 and 1977, a total that reduces to 66 if one discounts three appearances in the 'European Indoor Games' (i.e. before they became official Championships). Shot putter Geoff Capes has notched up 67 internationals (including 25 indoors) between 1969 and 1980, and scored more points in matches than any other British athlete. Hammer thrower Howard Payne competed in 61 internationals (all outdoors, naturally!) between 1960 and 1974. Athlete with the longest span as a British international was high hurdler Don Finlay (1929–49).

Results of Britain's matches since 1977 (for earlier match scores see 4th edition of 'Encyclopaedia of Athletics'):—

1977 v.	Italy*	lost	43 —	74
1977 v.	Spain*	lost	59½—	61¼
1977 v.	W. Germany*	lost	59½—	67½
1977 v.	France*	lost	50 —	78
1977 v.	Finland	lost	110 —	113
1977 v.	Sweden	won	114 —	96
1977 v.	Poland	lost	93 —	118
1977 v.	USSR	won	111 —	98
1977 v.	W. Germany	won	125 —	86
1978 v.	W. Ger.*	won	65½—	62½
1978 v.	E. Germany*	lost	52 —	90
1978 v.	Spain*	won	58 —	48
1978 v.	E. Germany	lost	96 —	104
1978 v.	Finland	won	111 —	101
1979 v.	W. Ger.*	won	74½—	63¼
1979 v.	Spain*	lost	62 —	70
1979 v.	Italy*	lost	64 —	68
1979 v.	E. Germany*	lost	47 —	74
1979 3rd (153½) v. W. Germany (232), Poland (205½), Switzerland (108)				
1979 v.	Russian FSR (3) won		221 —	219
1980 v.	W. Ger.*	lost	59 —	79
1980 v.	Hungary	won	121 —	99
1980 v.	Greece	won	129 —	93
1980 v.	Sweden	won	128 —	95
1981 v.	W. Ger.*	lost	59 —	79
1981 v.	E. Ger.*	lost	48 —	72

* Indoor match (3) 3-a-side

British Women's Matches

Britain has notched up 83 wins in 132 matches from 1923 to 1980 inclusive. Famous victories were achieved

INTERNATIONAL MATCHES

over USSR in 1977 (80–74) and Russia in 1979 (156–151).

The most "capped" international is shot putter and discus thrower Brenda Bedford, with 66 appearances (including 9 indoors) between 1961 and 1978. Two athletes have spanned 20 years as internationals: high jumper Dorothy Tyler (1936–56) and middle/long distance runner Joyce Smith, who started at 800 m. in 1960 and was representing Britain in the marathon in 1980.

Results of Britain's matches since 1977:—

1977	v.	Italy*	won	28	— 27
1977	v.	W. Germany*	lost	47	— 48
1977	v.	France*	won	51	— 44
1977	v.	Finland	won	98	— 59
1977	v.	Sweden	won	105	— 49
1977	v.	Poland	won	94	— 58
1977	v.	USSR	won	80	— 74
1977	v.	W. Germany	won	94	— 63
1978	v.	W. Ger.*	won	53	— 40
1978	v.	E. Germany*	lost	32	— 78
1978	v.	E. Germany	lost	52½	—100½
1978	v.	France (3)	won	167½	—132½
1978	v.	Bulgaria	won	91	— 66
1978	v.	Finland	won	104	— 53
1979	v.	W. Ger.*	lost	45¼	— 59¼
1979	v.	France*	won	64	— 31
1979	v.	E. Germany*	lost	37	— 50
1979	1st (147), v. W. Germany (140), Poland (135), Switzerland (64)				
1979	v. Russian FSR (3)		won	156	—151
1980	v.	W. Ger.*	won	59	— 54
1980	v.	W. Germany	won	78	— 67
1980	v.	Sweden	won	91	— 75
1981	v.	W. Ger.*		lost 41	— 65
1981	v.	E. Ger.*		lost 41	— 57

* Indoor match (3) 3-a-side

USA Matches

The USA's first full-scale international match was in Berlin in 1938, the American men's team defeating Germany 122–92. The second took place a full 20 years later in Moscow, the occasion being the first of several "summit meetings" with the USSR. Results of this series: 1958 (Moscow) men won 126–109, women lost 44–63; 1959 (Philadelphia) men won 127–108, women lost 40–67; 1961 (Moscow) men won 124–111, women lost 39–68; 1962 (Stanford) men won 128–107, women lost 41–66; 1963 (Moscow) men won 119–114, women lost 28–75; 1964 (Los Angeles) men won 139–97, women lost 48–59; 1965 (Kiev) men lost 112–118, women lost 43½–63½; 1969 (Los Angeles) men won 125–111, women won 70–67; 1970 (Leningrad) men lost 114–122, women lost 59–78; 1971 (Berkeley) men won 126–110, women lost 60–76; 1973 (Minsk) men lost 112–121, women lost 51–95; 1974 (Durham) men won 115–102, women lost 67–90; 1975 (Kiev) men lost 89–129, women lost 49–96; 1976 (College Park) men won 115–107, women lost 42–104; 1977 (Sochi) men lost 115–118, women lost 66–89; 1978 (Berkeley) men won 119–102, women lost 71–75. Apart from the USSR, no team has beaten the USA in a men's match.

Jesse Owens (USA), winner of four gold medals, in action at the 1936 Olympic Games in Berlin

Italy's Pietro Mennea (433) wins the 1980 Olympic 200 metres from Britain's 100 metres champion Allan Wells (290)

Left: Irena Szewinska (Poland), left, and Marita Koch (East Germany)—both world record breakers at 200 and 400 metres—clash in 1977 World Cup

Right: World's fastest ever 400 metres runner on the flat, Lee Evans (USA), winning 1968 Olympic 4 × 400 metres relay

Left: Alberto Juantorena (Cuba), the winner in world record time, leads in the 1976 Olympic 800 metres final from Rick Wohlhuter (USA), Ivo Van Damme (Belgium), 103, and Willi Wulbeck (West Germany)

Right: World's fastest ever 400 metres runner over hurdles, Edwin Moses (USA), on the way to his Montreal Olympic triumph

Left: Steve Ovett (GB) storms to victory in the 1980 Olympic 800 metres as world record holder Sebastian Coe (GB), 254, overtakes Nikolay Kirov (USSR) for second

Right: Herb Elliott (Australia), during one of his 17 sub-four minute miles; he never lost a mile or 1500 metres race from the age of 16

Left: Two of the greatest figures in miling history: Sir Roger Bannister and Sebastian Coe pictured a week after Coe's Olympic 1500 Metres triumph

Right: Tatyana Kazankina (USSR), Olympic champion at 800 metres (1976) and 1500 metres (1976 and 1980)

Left: Paavo Nurmi (Finland), the most successful Olympic competitor in history

Right: Emil Zatopek, left, Chris Chataway (GB), 180, and Herbert Schade (West Germany) in the 1952 Olympic 5000 Metres—one of three titles won by the Czech in Helsinki

Left: Australian distance record breakers Ron Clarke (1) and Derek Clayton (18)

Left: Two laps to go in the 1976 Olympic 5000 metres final and out in front are Brendan Foster (GB), 364, and successful defending champion Lasse Viren (Finland), 301. Just behind are Ian Stewart (GB), left, and Dick Quax (New Zealand)

Miruts Yifter (Ethiopia), 5000 and 10,000 metres gold medallist at the Moscow Olympics

Henry Rono (Kenya), world record breaker at 3000, 5000, 10,000 metres and steeplechase

JAHL, Evelin (East Germany)

Evelin Schlaak, as she was then, created a major surprise at the Montreal Olympics when she unleashed a personal best of 69.00 metres to defeat a great field of discus throwers and bring to a halt the all-conquering progress of Faina Melnik. In subsequent seasons she won everything of note—the 1978 European title, the 1979 European and World Cup—and took over from Melnik as world record holder with a throw of 70.72 metres in 1978. After improving to 71.50 metres in May 1980 she lost the record to Bulgaria's Maria Vergova a few weeks before the Moscow Olympics but gained ample consolation in the Games by winning another gold medal, with a good two metres to spare over Vergova, to become the first woman in her event to gain two consecutive titles.

Success came early for her. She began discus throwing at the age of 13 and within four years was European junior champion. The following season (1974) she established a world junior record. Her annual progress: 1969—23.70 m.; 1970—43.14; 1971—49.38; 1972—50.00; 1973—60.00; 1974—63.26; 1975—63.44; 1976—69.00; 1977—65.14; 1978—70.22; 1979—69.82; 1980—71.50. She was born at Annaberg on March 28th, 1956.

JAVELIN

A javelin weighs a minimum of 800 grammes (1 lb. 12¼ oz.) and consists of three parts: a pointed metal head, a shaft and a cord grip. The shaft may be constructed of either wood or metal. The complete javelin measures between 2.60 m. (8 ft. 6¼ in.) and 2.70 m. (8 ft. 10¼ in.) in length.

It is thrown following a running approach. It must be thrown over the shoulder or upper part of the throwing arm and must not be slung nor hurled. At no time after preparing to throw until the javelin has been discharged into the air may the competitor turn completely around, so that his back is towards the throwing arc. (This rule was introduced when, in 1956, a Spanish athlete achieved phenomenal distances by spinning round with the javelin in the manner of a discus thrower). A throw is not valid unless the tip of the metal head strikes the ground before any other part of the javelin.

The event has largely been dominated by throwers from the Nordic lands. Erik Lemming (Sweden) led the way towards and beyond the 60 metre marker in the early years of the century, and was Olympic champion in 1908 and 1912. Jonni Myyra (Finland) was the next outstanding figure, raising the record to 66.10 metres in 1919 and taking Olympic honours in 1920 and 1924.

Sweden's Erik Lundqvist topped 70 metres in 1928, and it was Matti Jarvinen (Finland) who transformed the event in the 30s. He pushed the record up from 71.56 metres in 1930 to 77.22 metres in 1936 and collected the 1932 Olympic gold medal on the way. Two years later Jarvinen's protégé, Yrjo Nikkanen (Finland), carried the mark out to 78.70 metres and there the record stood for almost 15 years until an American, Franklin "Bud" Held, took over the world leadership with the first 80 metre throw in 1953.

It was his brother, Dick Held, who was chiefly responsible for the spectacular advance in javelin distances during the 1950's. Following research into the characteristics of flight and landing attitudes of javelins, he designed the first aerodynamic model.

Terje Pedersen (Norway) improved the record almost 5 m. during 1964, reaching 91.72 metres, and he was succeeded in 1968 by Janis Lusis (USSR), the greatest javelin thrower of all time. Olympic champion in 1968, four times European gold medallist, he held the world record with 93.80 metres. That mark was beaten by Klaus Wolfermann (W. Germany) with 94.08 metres in 1973, and at the 1976 Olympics Miklos Nemeth (Hungary), son of the 1948 Olympic hammer champion, unleashed a throw of 94.58 metres. Another Hungarian, Ferenc Paragi, took over as world record holder in 1980 (96.72 metres).

Britain has a poor record internationally, the highest ever Olympic placing being 14th.

See also under KULA, DAINIS; LUSIS, JANIS; NEMETH, MIKLOS and PARAGI, FERENC.

Women

The women's javelin weighs a minimum of 600 grammes (1 lb. 5¼ oz.) and is between 2.20 m. (7 ft. 2½ in.) and 2.30 m. (7 ft. 6½ in.) in length.

The first woman to reach 60 m. was Yelena Gorchakova (USSR), with 62.40 metres in the 1964 Olympic qualifying round. This stood as the world record until, on one day in 1972, it was broken almost simultaneously by Ewa Gryziecka (Poland), 62.70 metres and Ruth Fuchs (E. Germany), 65.06 metres. The latter became one of the sport's legends, winning everything of note until her demise in the 1980 Olympics. The first 70-metre thrower was Tatyana Biryulina (USSR) in 1980.

Britain's most distinguished throwers have been Susan Platt, who would have gained the Olympic silver medal in 1960 had she not stepped across the line in her excitement, and Tessa Sanderson, 1978 European silver medallist, who threw a near world record 69.70 metres in 1980.

See also under BIRYULINA, TATYANA; COLON, MARIA and FUCHS, RUTH.

JENNER, Bruce (USA)

Bruce Jenner made good his claim to be considered the world's greatest all-round athlete by winning the 1976 Olympic decathlon title with a record-shattering score. In two days of competition he never put a foot wrong against the finest field ever assembled and in event after event he reached out to personal best performances in this the final competition of his career. His score at the end, 8, 618 pts., added no fewer than 164 pts. to Nikolay Avilov's Munich Olympic score, the previous world record using fully automatic timing, and itself hailed as a monumental achievement.

Far from being a world-class performer in any of the ten individual events which make up the decathlon, Jenner's strength was his lack of weakness in any department. Running, jumping, throwing—he was competent at all of them. In Montreal he ended the first day in third place and then let rip with the most devastating second day display in decathlon history, to finish over 200 pts. clear of his nearest rival.

Jenner, with his film star looks and " All American " personality, has cashed in on his fame to a greater degree than any other athlete and is reputed to be a millionaire.

Personal bests: 10.7 sec. for 100 m., 47.5 sec. for 400 m., 4 min. 12.6 sec. for 1500 m., 14.3 sec. for 110 m. hurdles, 2.03 m. high jump, 4.90 m. pole vault, 7.32 m. long jump, 15.35 m. shot, 51.70 m. discus, 69.48 m. javelin and 8,618 pts. decathlon (later revised to 8,617 due to change in scoring tables). He was born at Mt. Kisco, New York, on Oct. 28th, 1949.

JOHNSON, Rafer (USA)

Despite being handicapped by the after effects of an injury sustained in 1948 when he caught his left foot in a conveyor belt (necessitating 23 stitches and several weeks on crutches) and a knee injury in 1956 which caused him to divert his attention from hurdling and long jumping to the throwing events, Rafer Johnson was the most gifted all-round athlete of his, and perhaps any other, time.

He made his decathlon debut in 1954 (5,874 points), yet only the following year he set world record figures of 7,985! Standing 1.90 m. and weighing 90 kg., he placed second in the 1956 Olympic decathlon and triumphed in 1960. His best score was 8,683 points (8,063 when converted to 1962 Tables) in his final season, 1960. He competed in eleven decathlons during his career, winning nine.

His best marks, probably the finest series by any athlete, were 10.3 sec. for 100 m., 21.0 sec. for 220 yds. (straight), 47.9 sec. for 400 m., 4 min.

49.7 sec. for 1500 m., 13.8 sec. for 110 m. hurdles, 22.7 sec. for 220 yd. hurdles (straight), 1.90 m. high jump, 4.10 m. pole vault, 7.76 m. long jump, 16.75 m. shot, 52.50 m. discus and 76.74 m. javelin. He was born at Hillsboro, Texas, on Aug. 18th, 1934.

JUANTORENA, Alberto (Cuba)

In the view of many, Alberto Juantorena was the most exciting star of the Montreal Olympics. The muscular Cuban with the huge stride made a tremendous impression as, firstly, he won the 800 m. in the world record time of 1 min. 43.50 sec. (this was an event he had never seriously attempted prior to Olympic year!), then triumphed in the 400 m. in 44.26 sec.—the fastest non-altitude time on record—to complete a unique Olympic double.

Still Juantorena hadn't finished: he returned for the 4 x 400 m. relay and in the final (his eighth race of the Games) ran the first 200 m. flat out in 20.1 sec! He maintained a savage pace for another 100 m. but even he has limits and he trod water in the closing stages, finishing where he had started—in 7th place.

He began his sports career as a basketball player but, happily for athletics, his coach thought he would fare better as a runner. He switched in 1971, aged 20, and improved his 400 m. time from 51.0 sec. to 48.2 sec. that first season. Next year he reached the fringe of world class, breaking 46 sec. and missing the Olympic final by five-hundredths of a second. He defeated Britain's David Jenkins for the 1973 World Student Games title and in 1974 he topped the world rankings with 44.7 sec. Two operations on his foot caused him to sit out most of the 1975 season but he came back better than ever in time for the Olympics. "He's phenomenal", gasped Mal Whitfield after watching him in Montreal. "He's what the future's going to be like in running."

Juantorena trimmed the world 800 m. record to 1 min. 43.44 sec. and gained a World Cup 400/800 m. double (plus a 43.7 sec. relay leg) in 1977, but injuries and ill health played havoc with his running in later seasons. In the circumstances, he did well to finish 4th in the 1980 Olympic 400 m.

Best marks: 20.7 sec. for 200 m., 44.26 sec. for 400 m. and 1 min. 43.44 sec. for 800 m. Annual progress: 1971—48.2; 1972—45.94; 1973—45.36, 1:49.8; 1974—44.7, 1:50.9; 1975—44.80; 1976—44.26, 1:43.5; 1977—44.65, 1:43.44; 1978—44.27, 1:44.4; 1979—45.24, 1:46.4; 1980—45.09. He was born at Santiago on Nov. 21st, 1950.

JUNIORS

See EUROPEAN JUNIOR CHAMPIONSHIPS and APPENDIX.

KAZANKINA, Tatyana (USSR)

Small, skinny and pale, Tatyana Kazankina may not look like a superathlete but her track exploits in 1976 and 1980 were truly remarkable. Indeed, no female middle distance runner in history has ever achieved so much.

Prior to 1976 her best times were 2 min. 01.7 sec. for 800 m. and 4 min. 05.9 sec. for 1500 m., the latter recorded when she finished 4th in the 1974 European Championships. It wasn't until June 1976 that she firmly established herself as a prospective Olympic medallist at 1500 m.: running in Helsinki, she covered the last 800 m. in a sharp 2 min. 03.6 sec. for a personal best of 4 min. 02.8 sec. A few days later, in Podolsk, she shook the athletics world by passing 400 m. in an unheard of 59.5 sec., 800 m. in 2 min. 05.5 sec. and 1200 m. in 3 min. 09.5 sec. on the way to a 3 min. 56.0 sec. timing—an astonishing 5.4 sec. improvement on the world record! Just prior to the Games Mrs. Kazankina hacked her best 800 m. time to 1 min. 56.6 sec. and, contrary to her own wishes, she was picked for that event too.

In Montreal she showed, perhaps to her own surprise, that the selectors' faith in her was justified. She sprinted from fifth to first in the final 50 m. to win the 800 m. in a world record 1 min. 54.94 sec. and four days later her deadly kick carried her to victory in the 1500 m. (4 min. 05.5 sec.). The final time may have been on the slow side, but the closing stages certainly weren't—she covered the last 400 m. in 56.9 sec!

Little was seen of her until the next Olympic year when—having given birth to a daughter in November 1978—she re-emerged better than ever. Twice she smashed the world record for 1500 m. (3 min. 55.0 sec. and 3 min. 52.47 sec.), and in between she successfully defended her Olympic title, covering the final 800 m. in under two minutes. In her fabulous record run in Zurich 12 days after the Olympic final she passed 400 m. in 58.6, 800 m. in 2 min. 04.7 sec. and 1200 m. in 3 min. 07.1 sec. Her final time—faster than Paavo Nurmi's 1924 world record figures—equates to around 4:10 for a mile.

Annual progress: 1971—4:19.0; 1972—2:05.2, 4:13.6; 1973—2:03.5, 4:14.2; 1974—2:03.1, 4:05.9; 1975—2:01.7, 4:07.9; 1977—1:58.6, 4:04.2; 1979—2:00.4, 4:07.8; 1980—1:56.5, 3:52.47. She has run 400 m. in 54.0 and 3000 m. in 8:57.8. She was born at Petrovsk on Dec. 17th, 1951.

KEINO, Kip (Kenya)

Although inspired as a schoolboy by the deeds of his country's first great runner, Nyandika Maiyoro (7th in the 1956 Olympic 5000 m.), it was not until 1962 that Kipchoge Keino began to take athletics seriously. He started with 3 mi. in 14 min. 17.0 sec. and within a few months was Kenyan and East African champion. International competition brought the best out of him even in those early days for at the 1962 Commonwealth Games in Australia he finished 11th in the 3 mi. (in 13 min. 50.0 sec.) and set a national record of 4 min. 07.0 sec. in the mile heats.

At the 1964 Olympics he finished 5th in the 5000 m., less than a dozen metres behind the winner.

Keino set Europe's tracks alight in 1965. He beat Ron Clarke in two races out of three over 5000 m., set a 3000 m. world record of 7 min. 39.6 sec. and came close to the mile record with 3 min. 54.2 sec. Also during the year he won the 1500 m. and 5000 m. at the first African Games and, in New Zealand, temporarily relieved Clarke of the 5000 m. world record with 13 min. 24.2 sec. He carried all before him in 1966, his most notable successes including a magnificent double in the Commonwealth Games (12 min. 57.4 sec. 3 mi., 3 min. 55.3

sec. mile) and the then second fastest mile in history (3 min. 53.4 sec.).

During the next six years Kip raced incessantly throughout the world, exciting crowds everywhere with his fabulous loping stride and displaying his talent to good effect at all distances from 800 m. to 10,000 m. plus —in 1972—the steeplechase. Gold medals came his way in the 1968 Olympic 1500 m. (a sensational 3 min. 34.9 sec. at high altitude), 1970 Commonwealth 1500 m. (3 min. 36.6 sec.) and 1972 Olympic steeplechase (8 min. 23.6 sec.), an event he had not previously taken seriously. He did lose some important events—1968 Olympic 5000 m., 1970 Commonwealth 5000 m. and 1972 Olympic 1500 m., but still finished among the medals each time.

His best times include 1 min. 46.4 sec. for 800 m., 3 min. 34.9 sec. for 1500 m., 3 min. 53.1 sec. for the mile, 7 min. 39.6 sec. for 3000 m., 12 min. 57.4 sec. for 3 mi., 13 min. 24.2 sec. for 5000 m., 28 min. 06.4 sec. for 10,000 m. and 8 min. 23.6 sec. for 3000 m. steeplechase. He was born at Kipsamo on Jan. 17th, 1940.

KIRSZENSTEIN, Irena (Poland)

See under SZEWINSKA, IRENA

KISILYEV, Vladimir (USSR)

He showed good competitive qualities early in his career by winning the European junior championship in 1975 at the age of 18, but Vladimir Kisilyev hardly set the world of shot putting alight between then and the Olympic Games of five years later. Prior to 1980 his best stood at a solid but unremarkable 20.71 metres and he had never even won a Soviet senior title. He progressed to 21.13 metres in the run-up to Moscow but that ranked him only sixth among Olympic contenders and few would have considered him for victory. However, he enjoyed the form of his life on the day it counted most. His opening put of 21.10 metres projected him into a lead he was never to lose, and his final Olympic record-breaking effort of 21.35 metres placed the issue beyond doubt.

Annual progress: 1973—14.92 m. 1974—17.75; 1975—19.12; 1976—19.

71; 1977—19.39; 1978—20.07; 1979— 20.71; 1980—21.35. He was born at Myski on Jan. 1st, 1957.

KOCH, Marita (East Germany)

If ever an athlete looked destined to become an Olympic champion it was Marita Koch. She burst onto the international stage in 1975, aged 18, clocking 51.60 sec. for 400 m. (an improvement of nearly 4 sec. over her 1974 peak) in gaining the silver medal in the European Junior Championships. Next year she made the Olympic team only to suffer the misfortune of having to scratch, injured, from the 400 m. semi-finals . . . which also cost her the chance of being a member of East Germany's gold medal winning relay team.

Some consolation came in taking the 1977 European indoor crown with a world indoor best of 51.14 sec. while that summer she improved to 49.53 sec. when winning at the European Cup Final. Absent from that race was the legendary Irena Szewinska, Olympic champion and world record holder at 49.28 sec., but their paths crossed three weeks later in the World Cup. It was a classic duel, the experience and determination of Szewinska (31) proving just too much for the youthful exuberance of Koch (20), 49.52 to 49. 76 sec. But the writing was on the wall, and at the 1978 European Championships she demolished her Polish rival in a scintillating 48.94 sec. That was her fourth world record of the season, having earlier clocked 49.19 and 49.03 sec. plus a 22.06 sec. 200 m.

Marita scaled even greater heights in 1979 as she set further world records at 200 m. of 22.02 and an astonishing 21.71 sec., and at 400 m. with 48.89 and 48.60 sec. Her only reverse came in the World Cup where she was beaten over 200 m. by Evelyn Ashford (USA), 21.83 to 22.02 sec. Injury hampered her build-up to the 1980 Olympics, where to the relief of the 200 m. specialists she concentrated on the one-lap event, but all was well on the day in Moscow and she sped to victory in the second fastest time ever of 48.88 sec. She later ran a fabulous anchor leg in the relay (48.27 sec.!) but had to settle for the silver as her Soviet rival took over too far ahead

to be caught.
Annual progress at 200 and 400 m.: 1972—25.5, 60.3; 1973—24.5; 1974—24.2, 55.5; 1975—23.92, 51.60; 1976—22.70, 50.19; 1977—22.38, 49.53; 1978 22.06, 48.94; 1979—21.71, 48.60; 1980—22.34, 48.88. Her fastest 100 m. time is 10.99, which ranks her third fastest of all time as at the start of 1981. She was born at Wismar on Feb. 18th, 1957.

KOLEHMAINEN, Hannes (Finland)

Hannes Kolehmainen was the first of the long line of Finnish distance running masters. He won three Olympic gold medals in 1912: at 5000 m., 10,000 m. and cross-country. His most celebrated race was the 5000 m. in which he defeated Jean Bouin (France) in a desperate finish in 14 min. 36.6 sec. No man had previously beaten 15 min.!

The time lasted ten years until broken by Paavo Nurmi, who as a boy had been inspired to take up running because of that very performance. Kolehmainen won the 1920 Olympic marathon on a course which was 605 yd. over the standard distance of 26 mi. 385 yd. in 2 hr. 32 min. 35.8 sec.—equivalent of close to 2¼ hr. for the normal distance—and held world records at numerous events from 3000 to 30,000 m.

His best marks: 8 min. 36.9 sec. for 3000 m., 14 min. 36.6 sec. for 5000 m., 30 min. 20.4 sec. for 6 mi., 31 min. 20.4 sec. for 10,000 m., 51 min. 03.4 sec. for 10 mi. He was born on Dec. 9th, 1889 and died in Jan. 1966. His brothers, Tatu and Willie, were also distinguished marathon runners, the latter—as a professional—being the first to break 2½ hours with a 2 hr. 29 min. 39.2 sec. timing in 1912.

KOLPAKOVA, Tatyana (USSR)

Few athletes have rocketed from obscurity to Olympic stardom quite as quickly as long jumper Tatyana Kolpakova. She came from nowhere as a 19-year-old to place equal 12th on the 1979 world list with a leap of 6.63 metres . . . and the following season she triumphed in Moscow in as exciting a competition as one could hope to see.

Kolpakova was, based on pre-Olympic best performance (6.83 metres), only the Soviet third string in the event and hadn't won a major competition all year, but she quickly demonstrated excellent form when she opened with a career best of 6.84 metres and improved to 6.87 metres in the fourth round. Such was the standard that, going into the last round, Kolpakova was just out of the medals in fourth place, as team-mate Tatyana Skatchko led with 7.01 metres. But Kolpakova chose just the right moment to launch the jump of her life . . . 7.06 metres, just 3 cm. short of the world record. It was close, though, for the next jumper—East Germany's Brigitte Wujak— finished with 7.04 metres.

Kolpakova was born at Frunze (Kirghiz SSR) on Oct. 15th, 1959.

KOMISOVA, Vera (USSR)

Vera Komisova (née Nikitina) astonished everyone—not least herself—by capturing the 1980 Olympic 100 m. hurdles title in 12.56 sec. Her previous fastest was 12.67 sec. in the previous day's heats, and before that it was 12.84 sec. Thus she improved by the massive margin of some 2¼ metres during the Games. Significantly, she cut her 100 m. flat time by a similar margin in 1980, from 11.53 to 11.26 sec.

Her only previous international medal as a hurdler was a bronze in the 1977 World Student Games. Like team-mate Kolpakova she timed her peak just right; both had finished only fifth in their events at the European Indoor Championships some five months before the Olympics.

Komisova, whose best 200 m. time is 22.96 sec., has shown the following annual progress over the hurdles: 1973—14.3; 1974—13.9; 1975—13.6; 1976—13.45; 1977—13.0; 1978—13.41; 1979—12.87; 1980—12.39. She was born in Leningrad on June 11th, 1953.

KONDRATYEVA, Lyudmila (USSR)

Lyudmila Kondratyeva's first recorded athletic achievement was winning a 500 m. cross-country race, then she turned to the high jump with some success as a 14-year-old. The following season (1973) she switched to the 100 m., long jump and pentathlon. "I was good enough in many events but did not excel in any of them," she was to reflect.

It was in 1975 that she began to concentrate on sprinting, placing fourth in that season's European junior 200 m., but it took another three years before she made the transition to world class. In 1978 she cut her 200 m. time from 23.12 sec. to the 22.52 sec. she recorded in the European Championships final, snatching a shock victory—by one-hundredth of a second—over Marlies Gohr. The East German had previously won the 100 m. easily, with Kondratyeva sixth.

The Soviet speedster handed her another defeat in the 1979 European Cup 200 m. but despite a personal best of 11.15 sec. she was well beaten by Gohr in the 100. Three weeks later, in the World Cup, Kondratyeva was trounced in both events (Evelyn Ashford of the USA scoring a sensational double) but after working hard on improving her start she emerged a much better sprinter in 1980. Discounting a 10.87 timing which at first was claimed as breaking Gohr's world record of 10.88 but in fact was 'merely' a hand-timed 10.9, she trimmed her 100 m. time to 11.06—and that was precisely the time that gained her the Olympic gold medal. Gohr, the favourite, was beaten again by just one-hundredth of a second. An injury sustained in the 100 m. final caused Kondratyeva to withdraw from the 200 m. and 4 x 100 m. relay . . . and the chance of two further gold medals.

Personal bests: 11.06 and 10.9 sec. for 100 m., 22.31 sec. for 200 m., 52.9 sec. for 400 m. and 6.31 metres long jump. Annual progress at 100 m.: 1969—9.8 (60 m.); 1970—13.6; 1971 —12.4; 1972—12.1; 1973—11.5; 1974 —11.81; 1975—11.6; 1976—11.72; 1977—11.3; 1978—11.35; 1979—11.15; 1980—11.06. She was born at Shakhty on Apr. 11th, 1958.

KOZAKIEWICZ, Wladyslaw (Poland)

Prior to 1980 only one pole vaulter in history had achieved the dream result of winning an Olympic title with a world record performance: Frank Foss, who had lifted the 1920 gold medal with a vault of 4.09 metres. Sixty years later, the American's feat was emulated by Wladyslaw Kozakiewicz thanks to a breathtaking clearance of 5.78 metres.

It set the seal on an extraordinary season of pole vaulting, one which saw the world record—which had stood at 5.70 metres to the credit of Dave Roberts (USA)—raised on several occasions: first by 'Kozak' with 5.72 metres, then by the French pair of Thierry Vigneron (5.75 metres twice) and Philippe Houvion (5.77 metres), and finally by the muscular Pole again in Moscow.

Kozakiewicz, whose vaulting career had begun 16 years earlier as an 11-year-old, deserved his success. Injury had cost him his big chance at the 1976 Olympics (where he had the galling experience of watching the title go to a compatriot, Tadeusz Slusarski, who had long played second fiddle to himself) and he had been the world's most consistently brilliant performer for several seasons in a notoriously unstable event. Before 1980 he had chalked up 12 clearances of 5.60 metres or higher, whereas no one else had accumulated more than three.

In Moscow, Kozakiewicz couldn't put a foot wrong, despite unsporting attempts by some Soviet fans to distract him during the competition. Just five vaults clinched the title for him: first time clearances at 5.35, 5.50, 5.60, 5.65 and 5.70 metres. He then went on to make 5.75 metres without failure and 5.78 metres (18 ft. 11¼ in.) at the second try.

A fine all-round athlete (like his international decathlete brother Eduard), he has scored 7683 pts. for the ten-event test. His annual pole vault progress: 1964—1.80 m.; 1965 —2.00; 1966—2.40; 1967—2.60; 1968 —2.95; 1969—3.85; 1970—4.26; 1971 —4.65; 1972—5.02; 1973—5.35; 1974 —5.38; 1975—5.60; 1976—5.62; 1977 —5.66; 1978—5.62; 1979—5.61; 1980 —5.78. He was born at Soletshnika (Lithuania) on Dec. 8th, 1953.

KRATSCHMER, Guido (West Germany)

Who is the world's greatest all-round athlete? When Bruce Jenner won the 1976 Olympic decathlon title by a huge margin with a world record score the situation was clear-cut, but in 1980 there were two legitimate claimants to Jenner's mantle. Olympic champion Daley Thompson was one, world record holder Guido Kratschmer the other.

In Thompson's favour was the fact that he soundly defeated Kratschmer in their one confrontation, in Austria in May (8622 pts. to 8421), as well as his Olympic triumph. The case for Kratschmer is that in June he eclipsed Thompson's pending world record score with a total of 8649 pts. and, because of the West German Olympic boycott, he was unable to try to go one better than in Montreal where he took the silver medal behind Jenner.

On the basis of comparing lifetime best marks in the ten decathlon events, Kratschmer comes out on top over Thompson with a 'perfect' score of 8921 pts. as against the Briton's 8902, although Thompson's tally rises to 8947 if one takes into account wind-assisted marks in the 100 m. and long jump. Kratschmer's personal bests: 10.54 for 100 m., 7.84 metres long jump, 16.56 metres shot, 2.03 metres high jump, 47.64 sec. for 400 m., 13.85 sec. for 110 m. hurdles, 49.74 metres discus, 4.70 metres pole vault, 69.64 metres javelin and 4 min. 24.2 sec. for 1500 m.

His annual decathlon progress: 1972—7550; 1973—7488; 1974—8132; 1975—8005; 1976—8411; 1977—8088; 1978—8498; 1979—8484; 1980—8649. He was born at Grossheubach on Jan. 10th, 1953.

KULA, Dainis (USSR)

Just what constitutes a flat, and therefore foul, throw in the javelin has often generated controversy. The IAAF rule stipulates that "no throw shall be valid in which the tip of the metal head does not strike the ground before any other part of the javelin" —but borderline cases are common and the judges have to make an instant decision. A classic case occurred in the Moscow Olympics. As a result of the judges accepting Dainis Kula's third-round throw as valid (many observers alleged it landed flat) he went on to win the gold medal. Had, instead, the red flag been raised then the Soviet athlete would have finished last of the twelve finalists with a zero against his name.

After fouling his first two attempts, all depended on that third throw; Kula needed a distance of at least 80.60 metres to qualify for three further trials. The alternative . . . oblivion. The judges' decision to allow Kula's debatable third throw not only granted the Latvian a reprieve but, with the measurement at 88.88 metres, it gave him the lead. A 91.20 metres delivery in the next round clinched the title for the tall, little known 21-year-old who was competing in his first major Games.

The annual javelin progress of Kula, who is a 2.06 metres high jumper, has been: 1974—37.00 m.; 1975—54.00; 1976—73.38; 1977—75.42; 1978—80.48; 1979—86.04; 1980—92.06. He was born on Apr. 28th, 1959.

KUTS, Vladimir (USSR)

It was Vladimir Kuts who succeeded Emil Zatopek as the world's fastest and most effective distance runner. He began running in 1949, when he was 22, and broke into world class in 1953 when he won his first national titles and was unofficially timed at 13 min. 31.4 sec. for 3 mi.— a second faster than Gunder Hagg's world record—during a 5000 m. race.

He quickly made a reputation for himself by the way he would try to run his rivals into the ground in the early stages of a race, often " blowing up " himself instead. However, in 1954 he scored a dramatic *coup* in the European 5000 m. championship when he did not come back to the field and proceeded to win by a wide margin from Chris Chataway and Zatopek in the world record time of 13 min. 56.6 sec.

Later in the season he lost a 5000 m. race (and the record) to Chataway in a classic duel in London, but recaptured it only ten days afterwards with 13 min. 51.2 sec.

His next major defeat occurred in June 1956 when Gordon Pirie beat him in world record time over 5000 m. in Norway. He obtained adequate revenge a few months later at the Melbourne Olympics when he killed off the Englishman in the 10,000 m. and came back to complete a double by winning the 5000, with Pirie a distant second.

Just prior to the Olympics he had set a world record for 10,000 m. of 28 min. 30.4 sec. and to this he added a 5000 m. mark of 13 min. 35.0 sec. in 1957, which survived for as long as seven years.

His best marks: 1500 m. in 3 min. 50.8 sec., 3000 m. in 8 min. 01.4 sec., 5000 m. in 13 min. 35.0 sec., 10,000 m. in 28 min. 30.4 sec. and 3000 m. steeplechase in 9 min. 13.0 sec. He was born at Aleksino on Feb. 7th, 1927 and died of a heart attack on Aug. 16th, 1975.

LIDDELL, Eric (GB)

The 1924 Olympic Games was a wonderful occasion for British sprinting. Harold Abrahams upset the form book by taking the 100 m. and the Scot, Eric Liddell, did likewise by scoring a memorable victory in the 400 m.

Liddell, who opted out of the 100 m. because the heats were run on a Sunday, directed all his religious fervour to winning that 400 m. Though he had not previously bettered 49 sec. for the quarter-mile he won his semi-final in 48.2 sec. In the final he amazed everyone by shooting off in the outside lane at unprecedented speed. He flashed by 200 m. in an unofficial 22.2 sec. and hit the straight four metres ahead. Though fading somewhat in the closing stages he held on to win by three metres in the glorious time of 47.6 sec. Two days earlier he had gained a bronze medal in the 200 m.

Liddell never raced seriously again after 1925, though in 1928 he is reputed to have recorded 47.8 sec. for 400 m. in China, where he was a missionary.

This Scottish rugby international was an exceptional performer at the short sprint, too. His 100 yd. time of 9.7 sec. in 1923 stood unbeaten as the UK record for 35 years. Other best times were 21.6 sec. for 220 yd. and 49.2 sec. for 440 yd. He was born at Tientsin, China, on Jan. 16th, 1902 and died in a Japanese internment camp in China on Feb. 21st, 1945.

LONG DISTANCE RUNNING

Opinions vary as to where middle-distance running leaves off and long-distance takes over. For the purpose of this section, long-distance comprises events from 5000 metres upwards.

The following track events in this category are included in the IAAF's current schedule of world records: 5000 m., 10,000 m., 20,000 m. 1 hour run, 25,000 m. and 30,000 m. Two of these events, the 5000 and 10,000 m. feature in the Olympic programme.

Walter George, Sid Thomas and Alf Shrubb were the pre-eminent long distance runners of the late 19th and early 20th centuries, but British supremacy was terminated by the Finns. Hannes Kolehmainen led the way with his double at the 1912 Olympics and from then until 1948 only twice did the Olympic title at 5000 and 10,000 m. slip from Finland's possession.

Kolehmainen's successor as the individual champion of champions was Paavo Nurmi, the most prolific of all Olympic gold medallists and holder of countless world records.

Emil Zatopek (Czechoslovakia), winner of an unprecedented Olympic treble (5000, 10,000 and marathon) in 1952, was an even more comprehensive record breaker.

The outstanding competitors of the post-Zatopek era have been Vladimir Kuts (USSR), Lasse Viren one of a great new wave of Finnish runners, and Ethiopia's Miruts Yifter—all winners of the Olympic 5000 and 10,000 double. Viren went on to make history by retaining both titles in 1976.

A dominating figure in the 1960s, even though he won no major title, was Ron Clarke (Australia). Among his 21 world records, indoors and out, from 2 miles to the hour were such landmarks as the first 3 mi. inside 13 min., the first 6 mi. inside 27 min. and the first 10,000 m. inside 28 min. A more recent world record collector has been Henry Rono of Kenya, who in 1978 set phenomenal times in the 3000 m., 5000 m., 10.000 m. and steeplechase.

Although no Briton has ever won the Olympic 5000 or 10,000, several UK distance runners have performed with great credit since the war—including Sydney Wooderson, famous as a half-miler and miler but who spreadeagled a fine field in the 1946 European 5000 m. championship;

Gordon Pirie, the man who by his own example lifted British distance running to its present position; Chris Chataway, conqueror of Kuts in a never to be forgotten 5000 m. race; Bruce Tulloh, who ran a flawless tactical race to win the European 5000 m. in 1962; Ian Stewart, European 5000 m. champion at the age of 20 (1969) and Commonwealth winner the next year; Dave Bedford, world record breaker at 10,000 m., and Brendan Foster, the 1974 European 5000 m. and 1978 Commonwealth 10,000 m. champion.

Official world records for the women's 5000 m. and 10,000 m. will be recognised by the IAAF from Dec. 31st, 1981. The best times prior to the 1981 season were, respectively, 15 min. 08.8 sec. and 31 min. 45.4 sec. by Loa Olafsson (Denmark) in 1978. Kath Binns set UK best marks of 15 min. 49.6 sec. and 32 min. 57.2 sec. in 1980.

See also under BEDFORD, DAVE; CHATAWAY, CHRIS; CLARKE, RON; FOSTER, BRENDAN; GEORGE, W. G.; HAGG, GUNDER; IBBOTSON, DEREK; KEINO, KIP; KOLEHMAINEN, HANNES; KUTS, VLADIMIR; NURMI, PAAVO; PIRIE, GORDON; ROELANTS, GASTON; RONO, HENRY; SHRUBB, ALF; VIREN, LASSE; WOODERSON, SYDNEY; YIFTER, MIRUTS and ZATOPEK, EMIL.

LONG JUMP

The long jump take-off is marked by a board sunk level with the runway and the surface of the landing area. The board's edge which is nearer to the landing area is called the take-off line. A competitor can take off wherever he pleases before the line but if he oversteps the line the jump is counted as a failure. Jumps are measured from the nearest break in the sand made by any part of the athlete's body or limbs to the take-off line and at right angles to such line.

As was the case in so many events, British, Irish and American athletes tended to dominate the proceedings in the formative years of modern athletics—say from 1870 to the outbreak of the First World War.

It is recorded that one Chionis, of Sparta jumped 7.05 metres in 656 B.C., a mark equalled just 2,530 years later by John Lane, of Ireland.

Charles Fry (C. B. Fry of cricketing fame) entered his name in the record books with a leap of 7.17 metres in 1893.

The inaugural Olympic title in 1896 went for a paltry 6.35 metres, but the standard was much more respectable in 1900, with Alvin Kraenzlein (USA) winning by a single centimetre from his Polish-born team-mate, Myer Prinstein, the world record holder with 7.50 metres—both men leaping over 7.17 metres. Later that season Peter O'Connor (Ireland) took possession of the world record which he lengthened to 7.61 metres in 1901.

That was that so far as records were concerned for 20 years, until Ed Gourdin (USA) achieved 7.69 metres First to surpass 26 ft. (7.92 m.) was Silvio Cator, Haiti's sole but distinguished contribution to international athletics, in 1928, though William DeHart Hubbard (USA) was unfortunate when in 1927 he jumped 7.98 metres only to find the take-off board was one inch higher than the pit's surface, and thus a record was ruled out.

The next landmark in view was 8 metres (26 ft. 3 in.) and this duly fell in 1935 to the incomparable Jesse Owens with 8.13 metres. The record stood inviolate for 25 long years until Ralph Boston (USA) assumed world leadership. It was Boston who became the first 27-footer. Both the 28 and 29-foot barriers were broken simultaneously when Bob Beamon (USA) touched down at 8.90 metres at the 1968 Olympics—perhaps the most sensational exploit in the entire history of athletics. The nearest approach to that mighty leap has been 8.54 metres by Lutz Dombrowski (E. Germany) at the 1980 Olympics.

A newly developed backward somersault style, dubbed the 'flip', was banned by the IAAF in 1974.

Rather depressingly, Harold Abrahams' English record of 7.38 metres (a fine performance in 1924) stood up for 32 years, but in 1964 Lynn Davies added a new dimension to British long jumping history by defeating Ralph Boston for the Olympic title. Davies, a 10.4 sec. sprinter, proved himself one of the greatest competitors of all time by adding the Commonwealth (for Wales) and European Championships in 1966—a unique treble. He retained his Commonwealth title in 1970 and became, in 1968, Britain's first and only 27-footer (8.23 m.).

See also under BEAMON, BOB; BOSTON, RALPH; DAVIES, LYNN; DOMBROWSKI, LUTZ and OWENS, JESSE.

Women

The long jump made its Olympic debut as late as 1948. The two big names in the event's history before then were Kinue Hitomi (Japan), an astonishing all-rounder who raised the world record by 38 cm. to 5.98 metres in 1928, and an even more distinguished example of athletic versatility in Fanny Blankers-Koen (Netherlands), who leapt 6.25 metres in 1943.

Mary Rand's victory in Tokyo, with a world record distance of 6.76 metres, was the first ever Olympic gold medal success by a British woman athlete. In spite of the advantage of all-weather runways in later years, the world record had progressed only to 6.84 metres prior to 1976, when Sigrun Siegl (E. Germany) came within a centimetre of 7 metres. That barrier fell to Vilma Bardauskiene (USSR) in 1978.

See also under BARDAUSKIENE, VILMA; BLANKERS-KOEN, FANNY; KOLPAKOVA, TATYANA; RAND, MARY; ROSENDAHL, HEIDE and SZEWINSKA, IRENA.

LOWE, Douglas (GB)

A remarkable anomaly in Douglas Lowe's glorious career is that he became Olympic 800 m. champion in 1924 before he ever managed to win an AAA title. Four years later he made history by retaining his gold medal, on that occasion lowering the Olympic record to 1 min. 51.8 sec.

Midway between his Olympic triumphs Lowe was defeated in one of the most celebrated track duels of all time. The event was the 1926 AAA 880 yd., and after a tremendous scrap (in which Lowe led at the bell in 54.6 sec.) Germany's Dr. Otto Peltzer won by three yards in 1 min. 51.6 sec. with Lowe (untimed, but estimated at 1 min. 52.0 sec.) also inside the world record figures of 1 min. 52.2 sec. Only the previous week Lowe had set up a world record of 1 min. 10.4 sec. for 600 yd., a distance then recognised by the IAAF.

His final race was run in Berlin shortly after the 1928 Olympics and he closed his career with a brilliant four metres victory over Peltzer in his fastest 800 m. time of 1 min. 51.2 sec. He was also a capable performer at 440 yd. (best of 48.8 sec.) and 1500 m. (fourth at 1924 Olympics in 3 min. 57.0 sec.). Later he became a leading administrator of the sport, serving as honorary secretary of the AAA from 1931 to 1938. He was born in Manchester on Aug. 7th, 1902 and died on March 30th, 1981.

LUGANO CUP

This coveted trophy (for the IAAF Walking Team Competition) is contested every other year by the world's top walkers. Points are awarded for placings in the two road races, 20 km. and 50 km. and added together to determine the team positions.

Britain won the inaugural Cup Final in Lugano in 1961, scoring 54 pts. as did Sweden. The Cup was awarded to Britain as, under the competition rules, the formula to decide a tie was the position of the first competitor in the 50 km. Don Thompson finished 2nd in that race, one place ahead of the first Swede. Ken Matthews won the 20 km. on that occasion and in 1963 when Britain scored an easy team victory. The East Germans, Russians and Mexicans have subsequently dominated the tournament.

1961: 1, GB 54 pts; 2, Sweden 54; 3, Italy 28. Individual winners: 20 km: K. Matthews (GB) 1 hr. 30 min. 54.2 sec.; 50 km: A. Pamich (Italy) 4 hr. 25 mins. 38 sec.

1963: 1, GB 93; 2, Hungary 64; 3, Sweden 63. 20 km: K. Matthews (GB) 1 hr. 30 min. 10 sec.; 50 km: I. Havasi (Hungary) 4 hr. 14 min. 24 sec.

1965: 1, East Germany 117; 2, GB 89; 3, Hungary 64. 20 km: D. Lindner (E. Ger) 1 hr. 28 min. 09 sec.; 50 km: C. Hohne (E. Ger) 4 hr. 03 min. 14 sec.

1967: 1, East Germany 128; 2, USSR 107; 3, GB 104. 20 km: N. Smaga (USSR) 1 hr. 28 min. 38 sec.; 50 km: C. Hohne (E. Ger) 4 hr. 09 min. 09 sec.

1970: 1, East Germany 134; 2, USSR 125; 3, West Germany 88; 4,

GB 65. 20 km: H-G. Reimann (E. Ger) 1 hr. 26 min. 54 sec.; 50 km: C. Hohne (E. Ger) 4 hr. 04 min. 35 sec.

1973: 1, East Germany 139; 2, USSR 134; 3, Italy 104; 4, West Germany 95; 5, USA 95; 6, GB 81. 20 km: H-G. Reimann (E. Ger) 1 hr. 29 min. 31 sec.; 50 km: B. Kannenberg (W. Ger) 3 hr. 56 min. 51 sec.

1975: 1, USSR 117; 2, East Germany 105; 3, West Germany 102; 4, GB 102; 5, Italy 100; 6, Hungary 76. 20 km: K-H. Stadtmuller (E. Ger) 1 hr. 26 min. 12 sec.; 50 km: Y. Lyungin (USSR) 4 hr. 03 min. 42 sec.

1977: 1, Mexico 185; 2, East Germany 180; 3, Italy 160; 4, USSR 128; 5, Poland 112; 6, West Germany 99. 20 km.: D. Bautista (Mex) 1 hr. 24 min. 02 sec. 50 km.: R. Gonzales (Mex) 4 hr. 04 min. 16 sec. Women's 5 km. (non-scoring): S. Gustavsson (Swe) 23 min. 19 sec.

1979: 1, Mexico 240; 2, USSR 235; 3, East Germany 201; 4, Italy 152; 5, Czechoslovakia 142; 6, Poland 127. 20 km.: D. Bautista (Mex) 1 hr. 18 min. 49 sec. 50 km.: M. Bermudez (Mex) 3 hr. 43 min. 36 sec. Women's 5 km. (non-scoring): M. Fawkes (GB) 22 min. 51 sec. Team: GB.

LUSIS, Janis (USSR)

In an event—the javelin—in which an athlete's performance often fluctuates wildly, Janis Lusis has been the personification of consistency. A combination of outstanding competitive ability over a period of many years plus a smattering of world record throws makes him the greatest javelin artist of all time—surpassing even the achievements of Finland's Matti Jarvinen.

Lusis is the only man, in any event, to have won four consecutive European titles (1962, 1966, 1969, 1971); on top of that he can point to Olympic gold (1968), silver (1972) and bronze (1964) medals . . . and that silver in Munich would have been a gold had his final throw of 90.46 metres travelled just 2 cm. farther. He was the second man to reach the 300 ft. line, seizing the world record in 1968 from Terje Pedersen (Norway) with 91.98 metres. He lost it to Finland's Jorma Kinnunen the following year but regained the record temporarily in 1972 with 93.80 metres.

In his younger and lighter days he was an excellent all-rounder, having scored 7,483 pts. in the decathlon, high jumped 1.92 m., long jumped 7.22 m. and triple jumped 14.41 m.

He was born at Jelgava (Latvia) on May 19th, 1939. His wife, Elvira (née Ozolina) was Olympic javelin champion in 1960.

MALINOWSKI, Bronislaw (Poland)

Tough and rugged, with an excellent turn of speed (he's a 3 min. 55.4 sec. miler), Bronislaw Malinowski has been one of the world's most respected steeplechasers ever since winning the European junior title at 2000 m. in 1970.

A noted front runner, this son of a Polish father and Scottish mother is the only athlete to have won the European 3000 m. steeplechase twice (1974 and 1978), but it was the Olympic title he had his eye on. At his first attempt, in 1972, he placed fourth; in 1976 he smashed the previous world record with a time of 8 min. 09.2 sec. but still had to settle for the silver medal behind arch-rival Anders Garderud of Sweden.

It was a case of third time lucky, for in Moscow Malinowski landed the title with a cool, self-confident display. Trusting to his own instincts and pace judgement, he allowed Filbert Bayi to blaze away at world record pace. Fully 35 metres down at the 2000 m. mark, the powerfully built Pole narrowed the gap to 20 m. by the bell and overtook his spent rival just before the final water jump to win by a handsome margin in 8 min. 09.7 sec.

Personal bests: 1 min. 49.8 sec. for 800 m., 3 min. 37.4 sec. for 1500 m., 3 min. 55.4 sec. for the mile, 7 min. 42.4 sec. for 3000 m., 13 min. 17.7 sec. for 5000 m., 28 min. 25.2 sec. for 10,000 m. and 8 min. 09.2 sec. for the steeplechase. Annual progress: 1969—9:08.8; 1970—8.45.2; 1971—8:28.2; 1972—8:22.2; 1973—8:21.6; 1974—8.15.1; 1975—8:12.7; 1976—8:09.2; 1977—8:17.0; 1978—8:11.7; 1979—8:22.0; 1980—8:09.7. He was born at Nowe on June 4th, 1951.

MARATHON

The marathon is the longest of all running events in such international celebrations as the Olympic Games, European Championships and Commonwealth Games. The race, all but a few hundred yards of which is contested on the road, was run over 26 mi. 385 yd. (42, 195 m.) at the 1908 Olympics, and that is recognised as the standard distance for a marathon course.

No other athletics event has given rise to so much drama. The history of the sport is littered with marathon race incidents, some inspiring, many heartbreaking.

Under the latter category the two most notable victims were an Italian, Dorando Pietri, and an Englishman, Jim Peters. Pietri was the first to reach the White City Stadium at the 1908 Olympics but was in a dire state. After collapsing several times during the final lap of the track he was finally helped over the finish—and thus disqualified as a competitor may not be physically assisted during a race.

Nearly half a century later—the occasion being the 1954 Commonwealth Games in Vancouver—Britain's champion, Jim Peters, was brought down by a combination of the heat and his own uncompromising speed. He entered the stadium literally miles in front but, staggering and falling like a drunken man, he took eleven minutes to cover half a lap and was carried off the track when he collapsed just 200 yards from the end. These two men will never be forgotten, yet the victors of those two races, Johnny Hayes (USA) and Joe McGhee (Scotland), are virtually unknown.

As for the inspiring occasions, none was more so than Spiridon Louis' win at Athens in the first modern Olympic marathon in 1896. How appropriate that he, a Greek, should triumph over the same route (as legend has it) covered by Pheidippides or Philippides 2,386 years earlier.

The first of the great marathon runners was Hannes Kolehmainen whose time of 2 hr. 32 min. 35.8 sec. in winning the 1920 Olympic title on

MARATHON

an over-distance course was worth very close to 2½ hours for the correct distance. Nevertheless, he won by less than 13 sec. from the Estonian, Juri Lossman—the closest result in Olympic marathoning history.

Kitei Son, a Korean running for Japan, brought the Olympic record under 2½ hr. in 1936. That record was beaten by Emil Zatopek, who in 1952 followed up his track double with a marathon in 2 hr. 23 min. 03.2 sec. He was succeeded in 1956 by his former track shadow, Alain Mimoun (France), who like Zatopek four years earlier was making his competitive debut in the event. The 1960 gold medal went to a previously unknown, barefooted Ethiopian, Abebe Bikila, in the then world's fastest time of 2 hr. 15 min. 16.2 sec. and it was he who triumphed again (wearing shoes this time) in Tokyo—winning by the remarkable margin of 4 minutes in 2 hr. 12 min. 11.2 sec. East Germany's Waldemar Cierpinski emulated that feat of two Olympic marathon gold medals in 1976 and 1980.

Owing to the disparity in the nature, if not distance, of various courses, marathon times should not be taken too seriously. No official records are recognised but the man who revolutionised the event was Britain's Jim Peters who in 1953 became the first runner to break 2 hr. 20 min. in acceptable conditions. Ten years later British-based American, Buddy Edelen, was the first to better 2 hr. 15 min., and in 1967 the English-born Australian, Derek Clayton, led the way under 2 hr. 10 min. Clayton improved to 2 hr. 08 min. 33.6 sec. in 1969, which remains the fastest on record, although there are lingering doubts as to whether the course was of the full distance. The next best time is the European record at 2 hr. 09 min. 01 sec. by Holland's Gerard Nijboer in 1980.

Though yet to provide an Olympic winner, Britain has a fine record in marathon running. Silver medals have been gained by Sam Ferris (1932), who won the famous Polytechnic marathon from Windsor to Chiswick eight times in eight attempts, Ernie Harper (1936), Tom Richards (1948) and Basil Heatley (1964). Jack Holden, at the age of 43, won both Commonwealth and European titles in 1950, a feat achieved also by Brian Kilby in 1962, Ron Hill in 1969/70 and Ian Thompson in 1974. The latter's Commonwealth Games time of 2 hr. 09 min. 12.0 sec. is the fastest ever recorded under championship conditions.

Although there are reports that a Greek woman named Melopene ran unofficially in the 1896 Olympic race, finishing in about 4½ hours, it is only in recent years—thanks mainly to the example and campaigning of the Americans—that women's marathon running has become widely accepted throughout the world. Progress has been rapid, and only eight years after the first sub-3 hour time Norway's Grete Waitz cracked the 2½ hour barrier.

Evolution of marathon 'records' (rounded up to full second above), with acknowledgments to the research of early performances by Dr. David E. Martin and Roger W. H. Gynn, authors of " The Marathon Footrace ".

WORLD MEN

Time	Athlete	Date
2:55:19	Johnny Hayes (USA)	24.7.08
2:52:46	Robert Fowler (USA)	1.1.09
2:46:53	James Clark (USA)	12.2.09
2:46:05	Albert Raines (USA)	8.5.09
2:42:31	Fred Barrett (GB)	26.5.09
2:38:17	Harry Green (GB)	12.5.13
2:36:07	Alexis Ahlgren (Swe)	31.5.13
2:32:36	Hannes Kolehmainen (Fin)	22.8.20
2:29:02	Al Michelsen (USA)	12.10.25
2:27:49	Fusashige Suzuki (Jap)	31.3.35
2:26:44	Yasuo Ikenaka (Jap)	4.4.35
2:26:42	Kitei Son (Jap)	23.11.35
2:25:39	Yun Bok Suh (Kor)	19.4.47
2:20:43	Jim Peters (GB)	11.6.52
2:18:41	Peters	13.6.53
2:18:35	Peters	4.10.53
2:17:40	Peters	26.6.54
2:15:17	Sergey Popov (USSR)	24.8.58
2:15:17	Abebe Bikila (Eth)	10.9.60
2:15:16	Toru Terasawa (Jap)	17.2.63
2:14:28	Buddy Edelen (USA)	15.6.63
2:13:55	Basil Heatley (GB)	13.6.64
2:12:12	Abebe Bikila	21.10.64

2:12:00	Morio Shigematsu (Jap)	
		12.6.65
2:09:37	Derek Clayton (Aus)	
		3.12.67
2:08:34	Clayton	30.5.69

UK MEN

2:42:31	Fred Barrett	8.5.09
2:38:17	Harry Green	12.5.13
2:37:41	Arthur Mills	17.7.20
2:35:59	Sam Ferris	30.5.25
2:35:27	Ferris	28.9.27
2:34:34	Harry Payne	6.7.28
2:33:00	Ferris	26.9.28
2:30:58	Payne	5.7.29
2:29:28	Jim Peters	16.6.51
2:20:43	Peters	11.6.52
2:18:41	Peters	13.6.53
2:18:35	Peters	4.10.53
2:17:40	Peters	26.6.54
2:14:43	Brian Kilby	6.7.63
2:13:55	Basil Heatley	13.6.64
2:13:45	Alastair Wood	9.7.66
2:12:17	Bill Adcocks	19.5.68
2:10:48	Adcocks	8.12.68
2:10:30	Ron Hill	20.4.70
2:09:28	Hill	23.7.70
2:09:12	Ian Thompson	31.1.74

WORLD WOMEN

3:40:22	Violet Piercy (GB)	3.10.26
3:27:45	Dale Greig (GB)	23.5.64
3:19:33	Millie Sampson (NZ)	21.7.64
3:15:22	Maureen Wilton (Can)	
		6.5.67
3:07:26	Anni Pede-Erdkamp	
	(W.Ger)	16.9.67
3:02:53	Caroline Walker	
	(USA)	28.2.70
3:01:42	Beth Bonner (USA)	9.5.71
2:46:30	Adrienne Beames	
	(Aus)	31.8.71
2:46:24	Chantal Langlace	
	(Fra)	27.10.74
2:43:55	Jackie Hansen	
	(USA)	1.12.74
2:42:24	Liane Winter	
	(W. Ger)	21.4.75
2:40:16	Christa Vahlensieck	
	(W. Ger)	3.5.75
2:38:19	Hansen	12.10.75
2:35:16	Langlace	1.5.77
2:34:48	Vahlensieck	10.9.77
2:32:30	Grete Waitz (Nor)	22.10.78
2:27:33	Waitz	21.10.79
2:25:42	Waitz	26.10.80

UK WOMEN

3:40:22	Violet Piercy	3.10.26
3:27:45	Dale Greig	23.5.64
3:11:54	Anne Clarke	19.10.75
3:07:47	Margaret Thompson	
		26.10.75
2:50:55	Christine Readdy	16.4.76
2:50:54	Rosemary Cox	3.9.78
2:41:37	Joyce Smith	17.6.79
2:41:03	Gillian Adams	9.9.79
2:36:27	Smith	22.9.79
2:33:32	Smith	22.6.80
2:30:27	Smith	16.11.80
2:29:57	Smith	29.3.81

See also under ABEBE BIKILA; CIERPINSKI, WALDEMAR; CLAYTON, DEREK; KOLEHMAINEN, HANNES; PETERS, JIM; SMITH, JOYCE; THOMPSON, IAN; WAITZ, GRETE and ZATOPEK, EMIL.

MARKIN, Viktor (USSR)

For more than 20 years, following the retirement of 1956 Olympic bronze medallist Ardalion Ignatyev, the men's 400 m. event obstinately remained one of the USSR's weakest. Miraculously, all was changed in 1980 and at the Moscow Olympics gold medals in both the 400 m. and 4 x 400 m. relay were won by Soviet athletes. The boycott, which removed strong American, West German and Kenyan contenders, made it easier for the Russians to succeed but by any standards Viktor Markin's performance in taking the individual title in a European record of 44.60 sec. was formidable running.

It represented an astonishing breakthrough by the internationally untested 23-year-old medical student from Siberia—who, prior to 1980, had run no faster than 47.20 sec. for the distance. Before the Games he had improved to 45.33 sec., which ranked him fourth among those entered. He ran a finely judged race in the 400 m. final and came back to anchor the relay squad to victory in controversial circumstances. He was withdrawn from the heats on medical grounds but had 'recovered' in time for the final next day. A similar occurrence happened in the women's 4 x 400 m. relay where two of the USSR's star runners appeared, rested, in the final after missing the heats.

Markin's best performances: 10.4 sec. for 100 m., 21.1 sec. for 200 m., 44.60 sec. for 400 m. Annual progress:

1976—49.5; 1979—47.20; 1980—44.60. He was born at Oktobrsk Ust-Tarskovo on Feb. 23rd, 1957.

MATHIAS, Bob (USA)

Bob Mathias was only 17¼ when he won a gold medal at Wembley in 1948 to become the youngest male Olympic champion (in the sphere of athletics). What made the feat doubly astonishing was that Mathias' success came in the most searching test of the track and field programme, the decathlon. He went on to break the world record three times and successfully defend his laurels in 1952.

Mathias was one of that extraordinary number of outstanding athletes who overcame the most gigantic odds to become world champion. He suffered from anaemia as a boy, but so successful was his fight to become strong that by the time he was 16 he held the California schoolboy discus record.

He made his decathlon debut in June 1948 and won all ten of the competitions he contested from then until 1956. Actually he forfeited his amateur status in 1953 but continued to compete in the Services for the following three years.

His best marks included 10.8 sec. for 100 m., 50.2 sec. for 400 m., 4 min. 50.8 sec. for 1500 m., 13.8 sec. for 110 m. hurdles, 1.90 m. high jump, 4.00 m. pole vault, 6.98 m. long jump, 16.05 m. shot, 52.84 m. discus, 62.20 m. javelin and 7,731 point decathlon (on 1962 tables). Mathias, who starred in the Hollywood version of his own life story and later became a US Congressman, was born at Tulare, California, on Nov. 17th, 1930.

MATSON, Randy (USA)

It took 38 years for the world record in the shot-put to advance from 40ft. to 50ft., and a further 45 years before Parry O'Brien opened the 60ft. era in 1954. At that rate of progress 70ft. looked a long way off but a young Texan by the name of Randy Matson had other ideas. He was barely 18 and still at school when he crashed the 60ft. barrier in 1963—and this before he concentrated on weight training and with little coaching.

H

Matson's improvement in 1964 was sensational: he bettered his season's target of 62ft. during the indoor season, then topped 63 . . . 64 . . . 65ft. He defeated Dallas Long for the American title and came close to repeating the dose in the Olympics with a silver medal winning 20.20 metres. Matson, by now standing 1.99 metres and weighing 117 kg., succeeded Long as world record holder in April 1965 with 20.71 metres. Within a month the record stood at the fabulous distance of 21.52 metres (70 ft. 7¼ in.)—nearly a metre further than any other man had yet achieved.

He improved to 21.78 metres during 1967, the year he threw the discus 65.16 metres for an American record. He won the 1968 Olympic title as expected but, sensationally, failed to qualify for the 1972 Olympic team and announced his retirement from amateur competition. He was born at Kilgore (Texas) on March 5th, 1945.

MATTHEWS, Ken (GB)

Superbly consistent, Ken Matthews won four of his five major international 20 kilometres (12mi. 753yd.) walk tests: the European title in 1962, the Lugano Trophy finals of 1961 and 1963 . . . and the ultimate, an Olympic gold medal to seal his career in 1964.

His one slip in an otherwise brilliant record occurred at the 1960 Olympics where he led for eight kilometres before the heat and his own imprudent speed took their toll. A scrupulously fair walker and winner of countless style prizes. Matthews held the unofficial world's best for 5 and 10 mi. and the UK records at all events from 5 mi. to 2 hrs.

Best marks included 2 mi. in 13 min. 09.6 sec., 5 mi. in 34 min. 21.2 sec., 10,000 m. in 42 min. 35.6 sec., 7 mi. in 48 min. 22.2 sec., 13,927 metres in the hour, 10 mi. in 69 min. 40.6 sec., 20 kilometres (road) in 88 min. 15 sec., and 20 mi. (road) in 2 hr. 38 min. 39 sec. He was born in Birmingham on June 21st, 1934.

MELNIK, Faina (USSR)

In just two seasons Faina Melnik achieved enough to justify being considered one of the greatest female discus throwers of all time.

She made her international championship debut at the 1971 European Championships a memorable one, for she crushed the opposition with her final throw of 64.22 metres, a world record. A few weeks later, in Munich, she improved to 64.88 metres. Three times in 1972 she extended the world record and on the basis of her 66.76 metres performance she was rated a strong favourite for the Olympic title. She won it all right, but not without some anxious moments on the way. After three rounds she was only fifth but a magnificent fourth-round throw of 66.62 metres drew her clear of Argentina Menis of Romania.

She went on to better the world record several more times and broke through the 70-metre barrier in 1975, but her reputation as an invincible competitor was shattered at the 1976 Olympics where she was surprisingly shunted into fourth place. Worse was to come—fifth at the 1978 European (she was the winner in 1974) and an ignominious non-qualifier at the 1980 Olympics—even though she was still producing the occasional throw of around 70 metres. Also a first-class shot-putter, with a best of 20.03 metres, her longest discus throw was 70.50 metres in 1976. Born at Bakota (Ukraine) on June 9th, 1945, she was for a time married to Bulgaria's world class discus thrower Velko Velev.

MENNEA, Pietro (Italy)

Whichever way you look at it, Pietro Mennea has a strong case for being considered the greatest 200 m. runner who ever drew breath. Take first of all the question of world records. For 11 years the fastest time stood to the name of Tommie Smith with his 19.83 sec. mark when winning the 1968 Olympic title at high-altitude Mexico City. Competing in the World Student Games on the same track in 1979, Mennea blasted his way to the fantastic time of 19.72 sec. Some will argue that high altitude sprint times, being grossly flattering, should be ignored or at least listed separately— so what about the fastest 200 m. mark at or near sea level? That belonged to Valeriy Borzov with his 20.00 sec. time at the 1972 Olympics . . . until Mennea registered 19.96 sec. in his native Barletta shortly after the 1980 Olympics.

At those Games, Mennea had won the 200 m. gold medal in 20.19 sec., after overhauling 100 m. champion Allan Wells, to succeed at his third attempt. He had placed third in 1972, fourth in 1976. Other evidence of his flair for the big occasion is his hat-trick of European titles: the 100 m. in 1978, the 200 m. in 1974 and 1978. On the basis of high level consistency Mennea has no rival. Of the 13 fastest times ever recorded up to the start of 1981, Mennea was responsible for eight of them: 19.72, 19.96, 19.96, 20.01, 20.03, 20.03, 20.04 and 20.05!

A brilliant all-round sprinter, he holds the European 100 m. record of 10.01 sec. (high altitude), has clocked a world best 300 m. time of 32.23 sec., run 400 m. in 45.87 sec. (plus a 44.2 sec. relay stint) and was European indoor 400 m. champion in 1978. Annual progress at 200 m.: 1970 —21.5; 1971—20.88; 1972—20.30; 1973—20.56; 1974—20.53; 1975—20.23; 1976—20.23; 1977—20.11; 1978—20.16; 1979—19.72; 1980—19.96. He was born at Barletta on June 28th, 1952.

MIDDLE DISTANCE RUNNING

The province of middle distance running may be said to stretch from 800 m. to 3000 m. Olympic and European championships are staged at 800 m. and 1500 m. (120 yd. less than a mile); world records are officially recognised at 800 m. 1000 m., 1500 m., mile, 2000 m. and 3000 m.

800 Metres & 880 Yards

The first of the "modern" half-milers is generally acknowledged to be Mel Sheppard (USA), winner of the 1908 Olympic 800 m. in a world record of 1 min. 52.8 sec. after covering the first 400 m. in a sparkling 53.0 sec. He was succeeded by James "Ted" Meredith, another American, who not only won the 1912 gold medal in the world record time of 1 min. 51.9 sec. but carried on for another five yards to complete 880 yd. in 1 min. 52.5 sec.—another record.

Albert Hill, the 800 and 1500 m. champion in 1920, began a wonderful string of Olympic successes for Britain. Douglas Lowe triumphed in 1924 and 1928, and Tom Hampson carried on the tradition in 1932, in the process clocking 1 min. 49.7 sec. to become the first man to run two laps inside 1 min. 50 sec. Two years later Ben Eastman (USA) lowered the 880 yd. record to 1 min. 49.8 sec.

John Woodruff (USA) took the 1936 title but though he never officially broke any world records his amazing 880 yd. time of 1 min. 47.7 sec. on a 264 yd. indoor track in 1940 testifies to his tremendous ability. Sydney Wooderson (GB) captured both the 800 m. and 880 yd. records in 1938 but was relieved of the metric standard within a year by Rudolf Harbig (Germany), whose time of 1 min. 46.6 sec. would today still be reckoned as international class.

Mal Whitfield (USA), who broke Wooderson's half-mile record in 1953, equalled Lowe's feat by winning the Olympic crown in 1948 and 1952, on both occasions clocking 1 min. 49.2 sec. and defeating Jamaica's Arthur Wint by a metre. Harbig's record finally tumbled in 1955 when Roger Moens (Belgium) was timed in 1 min. 45.7 sec. ahead of the Norwegian, Audun Boysen (1 min. 45.9 sec.).

Tom Courtney (USA), who narrowly defeated British record holder Derek Johnson in the 1956 Olympics, recorded a 1 min. 46.8 sec. 880 yd. in 1957, yet even this seemed pedestrian when in 1962 Peter Snell (New Zealand) stopped the watches at 1 min. 45.1 sec. after passing 800 m. in 1 min. 44.3 sec. Snell was Olympic champion in 1960 and 1964.

The next gold medallist, Ralph Doubell (Australia), ran a record equalling 1 min. 44.3 sec. in winning his title and in turn his successor, Dave Wottle (USA) also clocked that time in 1972.

Alberto Juantorena (Cuba) set a world record of 1 min. 43.5 sec. when winning the 1976 Olympic gold medal (he later triumphed also in the 400 m. for an unprecedented double) and he was succeeded as world record holder by Sebastian Coe with a scintillating 1 min. 42.33 sec. in 1979. The 1980 Olympic title, however, went to other great British middle-distance star Steve Ovett.

See also under COE, SEBASTIAN; HAMPSON, TOM; HARBIG, RUDOLF; HILL ALBERT; JUANTORENA, ALBERTO; LOWE, DOUGLAS; MYERS,LON; OVETT, STEVE; RYUN, JIM; SNELL, PETER; WHITFIELD, MAL and WOODERSON, SYDNEY.

Women

Among the greatest names in the realm of women's 800 m. running: Nina Otkalenko (USSR), who in five seasons (1951-55) hacked down the world record for 800 m. from 2 min. 12.0 sec. to 2 min. 05.0 sec.; the almost legendary Sin Kim Dan (North Korea), who became the first woman to break two minutes with a breathtaking 1 min. 59.1 sec. for the distance in 1963 (and improved to 1 min. 58.0 sec, in 1964); Britain's Ann Packer, who in her first and only season at the event won the 1964 Olympic 800m. crown in 2 min. 01.1 sec.; Hildegard Falck (W. Germany), first woman officially to break 2 minutes (Sin Kim Dan's times were not ratified) in 1971; Tatyana Kazankina (USSR), 1976 Olympic winner in a world record 1 min. 54.94 sec.; and Nadyezhda Olizaryenko (USSR), 1980 Olympic champion in a world record 1 min. 53.42 sec.

See also under KAZANKINA, TATYANA; OLIZARYENKO, NADYEZHDA and PACKER, ANN.

1500 Metres & Mile

See under MILE

MILBURN, Rod (USA)

For a whole decade the world high hurdles record of 13.2 sec. by Martin Lauer (W. Germany) in 1959 stood unbroken. Then along came Rod Milburn to astonish the track world with a 1971 season that ranks among the most momentous of any athlete. He went through 28 races unbeaten; and two of them were sensational. On June 4th he was timed at 13.0 sec. with wind assistance over the limit, and three weeks later—at the AAU Championships—he clocked 13 seconds flat again for the 120 yd. hurdles, and this time legally. No less an authority than Lee Calhoun expressed the opinion that Milburn was capable of 12.7 sec.

He encountered some problems in 1972, barely qualifying for the Olympic team, but he struck top form on the big day in Munich and won the gold medal in 13.24 sec. for a world record for the 110 m. event which is some ten inches longer than 120 yd. Milburn, who became a professional in 1974, was reinstated in 1980 and made a brilliant comeback to rank sixth in the world for the year with 13.40 sec. He was born at Opelousas, Louisiana, on May 18th, 1950.

MILE

No other athletic event has captured the public's imagination to quite the same degree as the mile. Even men and women who could not tell a discus from a javelin are aware of the worth of a mile covered in four minutes. That figure four—4 minutes to run 4 laps—developed a mystical quality over the years and even now, when the four-minute " barrier " has been broken hundreds of times, the magic persists.

The first great miler was Englishman Walter George, who set an amateur best of 4 min. 18.4 sec. in 1884 and a professional record of 4 min. 12.75 sec. two years later. He is said to have run 4 min. 10.2 sec. in a time trial. So far ahead of his time was George that it was not until 1931 that 4 min. 10 sec. was officially beaten in competition . . . by the Frenchman, Jules Ladoumegue (4 min. 09.2 sec.).

The Swedish pair, Gunder Hagg and Arne Andersson, beat 4 min. 03 sec. five times between 1943 and 1945 but they were disqualified in the latter year for professionalism. It was left to Britain's Roger Bannister to earn immortality in three minutes and fifty nine point four seconds at Oxford on May 6th, 1954. The lap times on that historic occasion were 57.5, 60.7, 62.3 and 58.9 sec.

John Landy (Australia) and Derek Ibbotson (GB) succeeded Bannister as world record holder but it was left to Herb Elliott (Australia), the greatest mile competitor in history, to drag the record under 3 min. 55 sec. Peter Snell (New Zealand) and Michel Jazy (France) knocked off a few tenths each before Jim Ryun (USA), aged only 19, brought 3 min. 50 sec. within range with 3 min. 51.3 sec. in 1966. He improved to 3 min. 51.1 sec. in 1967 and there the record stopped until Filbert Bayi of Tanzania ran 3 min. 51.0 sec. in 1975. Less than three months later John Walker (NZ) opened the sub-3:50 era with a time of 3 min. 49.4 sec.

The years of 1979 and 1980 saw Britain's Sebastian Coe reduce the record to 3 min. 49.0 sec. (splits of 57.8, 57.5, 58.1 and 55.6 sec.) and Steve Ovett to 3 min. 48.8 sec. (55.7, 58.1, 57.2 and 57.8 sec.).

The metric, and therefore Olympic, equivalent of the mile is 1500 m.—a little under 120 yd. short of the English distance. Approximately 17.5 sec. is the usual conversion factor for top-class performances.

Winning an Olympic crown in world record time is just about the supreme achievement possible for a runner, and Elliott's 1960 win emulated that of New Zealand's Jack Lovelock, who in 1936 stormed home in 3 min. 47.8 sec.

The first man to break 3 min. 40 sec. was Stanislav Jungwirth (Czechoslovakia), who once handed Roger Bannister a defeat in the latter's great 1954 season, with an almost unbelievable 3 min. 38.1 sec. in 1957, roughly two seconds faster than John Landy's then record mile of 3 min. 57.9 sec. Even the Czech's time lasted barely a year, for Elliott clocked 3 min. 36.0 sec. in 1958 and 3 min. 35.6 sec. in 1960. Ryun smashed that record with his 3 min. 33.1 sec. timing in 1967, although some believe that Kip Keino's 1968 Olympic victory in 3 min. 34.9 sec. at high altitude was an even greater run. Bayi lowered the record to 3 min. 32.2 sec. when winning the 1974 Commonwealth title, leading all the way.

Coe chipped the record down to 3 min. 32.1 sec. in 1979 and succeeded Walker as Olympic champion in 1980, but the world mark passed to arch-rival Ovett with 3 min. 31.4 sec. a few weeks after the Games.

See also under BANNISTER, ROGER; BAYI, FILBERT; CHATAWAY, CHRIS; COE, SEBASTIAN; ELLIOTT, HERB; FOSTER, BRENDAN; GEORGE, W. G.; HAGG, GUNDER; HILL, ALBERT; IBBOT-

SON, DEREK; KEINO, KIP; NURMI, PAAVO; OVETT, STEVE; RYUN, JIM; SNELL, PETER; WALKER, JOHN and WOODERSON, SYDNEY.

Women

Diane Leather (GB) was the first to break 5 min., in 1954. The present best mile times are 4 min. 17.6 sec. indoors and 4 min. 21.7 sec. outdoors by Mary Decker (USA) in 1980 but they bear no comparison to the world 1500 m. record of 3 min. 52.5 sec. by Tatyana Kazankina (USSR) in 1980 —the equivalent of around 4 min. 10 sec. for a mile! The 1500 m. became an Olympic distance in 1972. Lyudmila Bragina (USSR) winning the inaugural title and Kazankina succeeding on the two subsequent occasions.

See also under BRAGINA, LYUDMILA and KAZANKINA, TATYANA.

MOSES, Edwin (USA)

Edwin Moses went down in history on three counts when he won the Olympic 400 m. hurdles title in 1976: his time of 47.64 sec. broke John Akii-Bua's world record of 47.82 sec.; his winning margin of over a second was the widest ever in this event at the Olympics; and he became the first to win the Olympic title using a thirteen-stride pattern throughout the race.

Rarely has an athlete catapulted from total obscurity to the ultimate in athletic achievement so quickly. At high school, Moses had broken neither 50 sec. for the flat quarter nor 15 sec. for the high hurdles, yet by 1975 (aged 19) he was running 45.5 sec. for 440 yd. in a relay and 14.0 sec. for 120 yd. hurdles. His coach realised that this combination of talents pointed towards the longer hurdles event and a start was made with a 52.0 sec. timing over 440 yd. hurdles.

He began the 1976 season with 50.1 sec. for 400 m. hurdles in March and his rise towards greatness was relentless: 49.8 sec. in April, 48.8 sec. in May, an American record of 48.30 sec. in June. He was in peak form for the Olympics, clocking 48.29 sec. in his semi and the world record shattering 47.64 sec. in the final, which he won by the gaping margin of some eight metres.

But that was only the start of an international career of such brilliance that Ed Moses is not only the dominant name in his event's history but must be rated as one of the sport's all-time greats. Because of the USA's Moscow boycott he was unable to equal Glenn Davis's feat of winning a second Olympic title, but his 1980 campaign was such that the authoritative American magazine, "Track & Field News" named him world athlete of the year. During the season he lowered his 1977 world record of 47.45 sec. to a resounding 47.13 sec. (the Olympic title went in 48.70 sec.), he extended his three-year sequence of victories to 55, and by year's end he owned 12 of the 14 sub-48 sec. marks ever recorded!

In other events he has run 45.60 sec. in a rare excursion at the flat 400 m. (and 44.1 sec. in a relay) and 13.64 sec. for 110 m. hurdles. He was born at Dayton, Ohio, on Aug. 31st, 1955.

MUNKELT, Thomas
(East Germany)

Fine, consistent competitor that he is, Thomas Munkelt could count himself lucky that the USA Olympic boycott in 1980 removed world record holder Renaldo Nehemiah from the running in Moscow. Barring accidents, Nehemiah was considered a near-certainty for victory in the 110 m. hurdles; in the absence of him and his US team-mates, the battle for the gold was expected to be fought out by European champion Munkelt and Cuba's ex-world record holder Alejandro Casanas. So it proved. Munkelt, who had placed fifth in the 1976 final, held a narrow lead throughout with the dynamic run-in of Casanas taking him to within one-hundredth of a second of the East German at the finish as Munkelt won in 13.39 sec.

Munkelt, who didn't start training seriously as an athlete until the relatively late age of 18, has personal bests of 10.37 sec. for 100 m. and 13.37 sec. for 110 m. hurdles. Annual progress: 1970—15.6; 1971—14.5; 1972—14.0; 1973—13.77; 1974—13.72; 1975—13.45; 1976—13.44; 1977—13.37;

1978—13.50; 1979—13.42; 1980—13.39. He was born at Zedtletz on Aug. 3rd, 1952.

MYERS, Lon (USA)

Just as Walter George was clearly the outstanding middle and long distance runner of the 19th century, so Laurence "Lon" Myers was undisputed master of the short distances. Standing 1.73 metres and weighing a mere 50 kg., but possessed of disproportionately long legs, Myers began racing in Nov. 1878. The following year he set the first of his numerous world records.

From 1880 to 1888 he held the world records for 100 yd. (equal), 440 yd. and 880 yd.—a feat that, needless to add, has never been duplicated. The quarter-mile was his best event and he was responsible for reducing the best on record from 50.4 sec. to 48.8 sec. In 1880 he succeeded in winning eight national titles in a week: first the American and then the Canadian championships at 100, 220, 440 and 880 yd.

As an amateur his best times included 5.5 sec. for 50 yds., 10.0 sec. for 100 yd., 22.5 sec. for 220 yd., 48.8 sec. for 440 yd., 1 min. 55.4 sec. for 880 yd., 3 min. 13.0 sec. for ¾ mi. He turned professional in 1885 and the following year defeated even George over 880 yd., ¾ mi. and mile. He was born at Richmond, Virginia, on Feb. 16th, 1858, and died of pneumonia on Feb. 15th, 1899.

NEHEMIAH, Renaldo (USA)

The records show that Thomas Munkelt is the reigning Olympic 110 m. hurdles champion, but no one could dispute that the dominant figure in the event is Renaldo 'Skeets' Nehemiah. Denied by the US boycott of his chance for Olympic glory, Nehemiah sought consolation by reeling off a series of fast times throughout Europe in 1980. By the end of the season he was able to claim 11 of the 15 fastest times in history—topped by his fabulous world record of 13.00 sec. in 1979, and not counting a wind-assisted 12.91 sec. and a hand timed 12.8 sec. the same year. Nehemiah's predecessor as world record holder, Cuba's Alejandro Casanas, ranked second on the all-time performer list with 13.21 sec. which means that Nehemiah is a full two metres faster than anyone else in the world—a colossal margin of supremacy.

Nehemiah was a high school sensation, clocking a stunning 12.9 sec. for 120 yd. hurdles over 3 ft. 3 in. hurdles in 1977 and setting another US high school record of 35.8 sec. for 330 yd. hurdles. In 1978 he broke the world junior 110 m. hurdles record five times, ending with 13.23 sec., and the following year he dispossessed Casanas with a time of 13.16 sec. prior to his phenomenal 13-dead, and went on to win at the Pan-American Games and World Cup.

Additionally he has run 100 m. in 10.24 sec., 200 m. in 20.37 sec. and clocked 44.3 sec. for a 400 m. relay leg, as well as long jumping 7.61 metres while at high school. Annual high hurdles progress: 1976—14.2; 1977—13.89; 1978—13.23; 1979—13.00; 1980—13.21. He was born at Newark, New Jersey, on March 24th, 1959.

NEMETH, Miklos (Hungary)

The javelin throwing son of 1948 Olympic hammer champion Imre Nemeth, Miklos Nemeth spent much of his career in his father's shadow. Sometimes a brilliant performer when the pressure was off, he was often a disappointment in major competition —falling far short of the high level consistency attained by Nemeth senior. From the time he reached top world class in 1967, at the age of 20, his record in the big championships was exceedingly modest: he failed to qualify for the 1968 Olympic final (suffering from an elbow injury) and placed 7th in 1972, while in the European Championships he finished 9th in 1971 and 7th in 1974.

It wasn't until 1975 that he began to tap his obvious potential; that year he topped the world list with a throw of 91.38 metres, though even then he was only ranked fifth on merit due to wildly fluctuating form. The moment of truth came at the Montreal Olympics: would he confirm the widely held opinion that he was a rotten competitor, or would he seize the opportunity to show the world his true form? His very first throw said it all —as the spear sailed on and on to touch down at the remarkable world record distance of 94.58 metres. That knocked the stuffing out of his rivals and his winning margin of more than 6¼ metres was the widest in Olympic field event history. Miklos Nemeth had emerged from his father's shadow at last.

Although he topped the 1977 world list with another mighty throw of 94.10 metres, his competitive record slumped again following the dizzy heights scaled in Montreal. He was 3rd in the 1977 World Cup, 6th in the 1978 European and 8th in the 1980 Olympics, having by then been relieved of the world record by his compatriot Ferenc Paragi. Nemeth, who once long jumped 7.27 metres, was born in Budapest on Oct. 23rd, 1946.

NURMI, Paavo (Finland)

Over 50 years after his great exploits, Paavo Nurmi remains a household name. No other athlete has won such wide and lasting fame. During his long career he amassed practically every honour open to him, notably nine Olympic gold medals (six individual and three team) collected over three Olympiads and a score of world records over distances ranging from 1500 to 20,000 m.

He opened his Olympic account in 1920 by succeeding his idol, Hannes Kolehmainen, as 10,000 m. and cross-country champion, and he also won a silver medal in the 5000 m. In 1924 he won all four of his races—1500 m., 5000 m. (these two within 1½ hours!), cross-country and 3000 m. team race. Four years later he recaptured his 10,000 m. crown and placed second in the 5000 m. and 3000 m. steeplechase.

But for an untimely disqualification for professionalism he might well have climaxed his career with victory in the 1932 Olympic marathon, for earlier that year he ran 40,200 m. (24 mi. 1,506 yd.) in 2 hr. 22 min. 03.8 sec., the equivalent of under 2¼ hr. for the full marathon distance. The Olympic race was won in 2 hr. 31 min. 36 sec.

As for world records, his first came at 6 mi. in 1921 and his last at 2 mi. in 1931. His most spectacular achievement in this department was his pair of world records within one hour a few weeks before the 1924 Olympics —3 min. 52.6 sec. for 1500 m. and 14 min. 28.2 sec. for 5000 m. Another indication of his greatness was the longevity of his world records. His 6 mi. mark stood 15 years, that for 10 mi. almost 17 years.

Even American indoor racing, the downfall of many a European champion, came naturally to him. During his epic campaign of 1925 he won all but one of his numerous races and among his crop of indoor records was a mark of 8 min. 58.2 sec. for 2 mi.— which was over 11 sec. faster than the official outdoor record of the time.

He ran his last important race in 1933, aged 36, winning the Finnish 1500 m. title as a " national amateur " in 3 min. 55.8 sec. A statue of him stands outside Helsinki's Olympic Stadium and it was he who was given the honour of carrying the Olympic torch at the opening ceremony of the 1952 Games. He was born at Turku on June 13th, 1897 and died on Oct. 2nd, 1973.

His best marks were 1 min. 56.3 sec. for 800 m., 3 min. 52.6 sec. for 1500 m., 4 min. 10.4 sec. for the mile, 5 min. 24.6 sec. for 2000 m., 8 min. 20.4 sec. for 3000 m., 8 min. 59.5 sec. for 2 mi., 14 min. 02.0 sec. for 3 mi., 14 min. 28.2 sec. for 5000 m., 19 min. 18.7 sec. for 4 mi., 29 min. 07.1 sec. for 6 mi., 30 min. 06.1 sec. for 10,000 m., 50 min. 15.0 sec. for 10 mi., 19,210 metres in the hour, 64 min. 38.4 sec. for 20,000 m. and 9 min. 30.8 sec. for 3000 m. steeplechase.

O'BRIEN, Parry (USA)

Without question the most significant individual in the history of shot-putting is Parry O'Brien, who revolutionised the event by the introduction of the technique that bears his name. He developed this new method following the 1951 season, during which he had terminated Jim Fuchs' long supremacy by beating him for the USA title. Ridiculed at first, O'Brien quickly silenced all criticism by winning the 1952 Olympic title.

For many years he utterly dominated the speciality. Between July 7th, 1952 and June 15th, 1956 he won 116 consecutive competitions; in 1953 he broke Fuchs' world record of 17.95 metres and in 14 instalments carried the record out to 19.25 metres in 1956, thus being the first man to achieve 18 metres, 60 feet and 19 metres. He successfully defended his Olympic crown in 1956 and also won the Pan-American title in 1955 and 1959.

Dallas Long relieved him of the world mark for two months in 1959 before O'Brien came back with records of 19.26 and 19.30 metres. Experience finally gave way to youth when Long recaptured the standard in 1960, in which year O'Brien took the Olympic silver medal behind Bill Nieder after leading until the penultimate round.

He made the Olympic team yet again in 1964 and placed 4th, but this was not the signal to retire. Although unable to reach the distances of Long and Randy Matson, O'Brien continued to be a formidable competitor and in 1966, his 19th season, he improved to 19.69 metres. Fast (10.8 sec. 100 m. in 1953) as well as strong (1.90 metres, 114 kg.), he was also a top-flight discus thrower—American champion in 1955. He was born at Santa Monica, California, on Jan. 28th 1932.

OERTER, Al (USA)

Four times acclaimed Olympic champion, the first man to exceed 200 ft. in competition: Al Oerter is the nonpareil of discus throwing.

He seemed destined for greatness when he set an American schoolboy discus (3 lb. 9 oz.) record of 56.14 metres in 1954 but few could have anticipated he would develop so speedily that only two years later he won an Olympic gold medal. His repeat victory in 1960 was less surprising. Oerter's third triumph in 1964 ranks among the greatest competitive efforts in athletics history for he was in acute pain throughout.

His achievement in winning an unprecedented fourth Olympic title in 1968 made him the most outstanding competitor in the annals of athletics. On paper, his fellow-American Jay Silvester—who had recently set a world record of 68.40 metres—should have won but once again Oerter rose splendidly to the occasion, unleashing a personal best of 64.78 metres. As Silvester once remarked: "When you throw against Oerter, you don't expect to win. You just hope."

It was not until 1962 that he laid claim to the world record. He made history by throwing 200 ft. 5 in. (61.10 m.), lost the record 17 days later to Vladimir Trusenyov (USSR) and recaptured it with 62.44 metres after a further lapse of 27 days. He improved to 62.62 metres in 1963 and 62.94 metres in 1964 for further world records, but distances were always secondary to him. He was the competitor supreme, and it was a relief to those with 1972 Olympic aspirations that Oerter decided not to try for a fifth victory. However, in 1976—aged 39—he resumed throwing after a seven-year lay-off . . . hoping to make the 1980 Olympic team!

That might have seemed a far-fetched notion, but Oerter was deadly serious. Starting off with a modest 53.40 metres in 1976, he set a world veterans record of 62.52 metres in

1977 and improved to 62.62 metres in 1978, a personal best of 67.46 metres in 1979, and an extraordinary 69.46 metres—which ranked second in the world for the year—in 1980, aged 43!

He was born at Astoria, New York, on Sept. 19th, 1936.

OLDEST

Men

Oldest Olympic champion was Pat McDonald (USA), winner of the 56 lb. weight in 1920 at the age of 42. Tommy Green (GB) won the 50 km. walk in 1932 aged 39.

Oldest European champion: Jack Holden (GB), Marathon in 1950, aged 43.

Oldest Commonwealth champion: Jack Holden (England), Marathon in 1950, aged 42.

Oldest British champion: T. Lloyd Johnson, RWA 50 km. walk in 1949, aged 49.

Oldest British internationals: T. Lloyd Johnson (1948 Olympic 50 km. walk) and Harold Whitlock (1952 Olympic 50 km. walk), aged 48.

Oldest world record breakers: John Flanagan (USA), hammer in 1909, and Gerhard Weidner (W. Germany), 20 mi. walk in 1974, aged 41.

Oldest UK record breaker in a track and field event: Don Finlay, 120 yd. hurdles in 1949, aged 40.

Women

Oldest Olympic champion: Lia Manoliu (Romania), discus in 1968, aged 36.

Oldest European champion and world record breaker: Dana Zatopkova (Czechoslovakia), javelin in 1958, aged 35.

Oldest Commonwealth champion: Rosemary Payne (Scotland), discus in 1970, aged 37.

Oldest UK record breaker: Joyce Smith, Marathon in 1981, aged 43.

Oldest British champion: Joyce Smith, Marathon in 1980, aged 42.

Oldest British international: Joyce Smith, Marathon in 1980, aged 43.

OLDFIELD, Brian (USA)

Brian Oldfield, who once described himself as "a drifter (have shot, will travel)", is a larger than life personality who shocked the world of shot putting—to his undisguised glee —in 1975. Prior to that season the longest distance ever achieved was an indoor put of 22.02 metres by George Woods, while the official world record (i.e. outdoors) stood to the credit of Al Feuerbach with 21.82 metres. Oldfield, whose personal best before turning professional in 1973 was 20.97 metres (he placed 6th in the Munich Olympics), paved the way with an indoor mark of 22.11 metres in April but it was outdoors at El Paso, Texas, on May 10th 1975 that he uncorked his sensational performance. In the second round he reached 21.94 metres, in the fifth he sent the shot 22.25 metres and with his final put he produced 22.86 metres (75 feet exactly), a mark greeted by such comments as 'fantastic', 'unbelievable' and 'incredible' from fellow shot-putters.

Oldfield uses the discus-style rotational style, but it took him three years of perseverance before he learned how to handle the technique effectively without falling out of the circle. With the demise in 1976 of the ITA professional troupe of which he was a member his active career might have been brought to an end but he kept in training and in 1980, the year he was reinstated, he won the American title with 21.82 metres—his best in amateur competition. He was born at Elgin, Illinois, on June 1st, 1945.

OLIVEIRA, Joao Carlos de (Brazil)

See under DE OLIVEIRA, JOAO CARLOS

OLIZARYENKO, Nadyezhda (USSR)

Recording a time that was equal to Albert Hill's winning mark in the 1920 Olympics and fast enough to have secured third place in the 1936 Games, Nadyezhda Olizaryenko (neé Mushta) achieved immortality at the Moscow Olympics by front-running to victory in the 800 m. in an astonishing 1 min. 53.42 sec. Passing the 400 m. mark in 56.41 sec. she added a 57.01 sec. second lap to win the title by ten metres and achieve a breakthrough in the event comparable to Sebastian Coe's the previous year. She held the previous record at

1 min. 54.9 sec., set the previous month. At the age of 26 she had emerged as a star of the greatest magnitude, but she had served a long apprenticeship. She first made the USSR national team as a 400 m. runner as long ago as 1970, and it took another seven years before she reached the fringe of world class at 800 m. by running just inside two minutes. She made spectacular progress the following season, coming very close to winning the European title as she shared the winning time of team colleague Tatyana Providokhina. She won another silver medal in the 4 x 400 m. relay, covering her lap in a speedy 50.39 sec. In 1979 her top achievements were finishing second in the World Cup and victory in the World Student Games. With her speed (best 400 m. of 50.96 sec.), endurance (3 min. 56.8 sec. for 1500 m. and Olympic bronze medal) and determination, Nadyezhda blossomed forth in 1980 as the most brilliant female two-lapper ever seen.

Born at Bryansk on Nov. 28th, 1953, she is married to Olympic steeplechaser Sergey Olizaryenko. Annual progress: 1970—2:11.4; 1972—2:08.6; 1974—2:05.0; 1975—2:03.3; 1976—2:05.8; 1977—1:59.8; 1978—1:55.9; 1979—1:57.5; 1980—1:53.42.

OLYMPIC GAMES

The precise origins of the Olympic Games are shrouded by the mists of Greek antiquity. As the most famous of a cycle which included the Pythian, Nemean and Isthmian Games, the ancient Olympic Games have been traced back as far as the 13th century B.C. The first Olympic champion known to posterity was one **Coroebus**, winner of the stade foot-race in the Games of 776 B.C.

From that date, for the next 1,170 years, the Games were staged every four years (an Olympiad). In deference to the Olympic Games and its ideals all battles were halted for the five-days duration of each celebration. The Games, which featured track and field events, wrestling, boxing and chariot racing, were held at Olympia, situated on a plain in the Elis province of Southern Greece. **The horseshoe-shaped stadium**, some 210 metres long and 31 metres wide, held 40,000 spectators. As the Greek civilisation declined so, too, did the Olympic Games and in A.D. 393 they were abolished altogether by the decree of the Roman emperor Theodosius.

Nearly 15 centuries were to pass before the Olympic Games were brought back to life. The revival was the brainchild of an English surgeon, William Penny Brookes, who founded an annual Games at Much Wenlock in Shropshire in 1850 and whose ideas greatly influenced the French baron, Pierre de Coubertin who was the driving force behind the first modern international Olympic Games held in Athens in 1896.

Subsequent venues: 1900—Paris; 1904—St. Louis; 1908—London; 1912—Stockholm; 1920—Antwerp; 1924—Paris; 1928—Amsterdam; 1932—Los Angeles; 1936—Berlin; 1948—London; 1952—Helsinki; 1956—Melbourne; 1960—Rome; 1964—Tokyo; 1968—Mexico City; 1972—Munich; 1976—Montreal; 1980—Moscow. War has caused the cancellation of the Games on three occasions: in 1916 (scheduled for Berlin), 1940 (awarded first to Tokyo, then to Helsinki) and 1944 (London). The 1984 Games will be held in Los Angeles.

The Games have grown steadily since their modest beginnings in Athens, where 59 athletes from 10 countries contested the track and field events. No fewer than 104 countries sent athletic teams to the 1972 Games but the number of competing nations fell in 1976 to 78 due to the withdrawal of some thirty countries (principally African) in protest against New Zealand's sporting links with South Africa, and to 69 at Moscow in 1980 as a result of boycotts over the Soviet invasion of Afghanistan. Among the nations absent were the USA, West Germany, Kenya, Japan, China, Canada and New Zealand.

The athletics events of the Olympics are officially designated "World Championships" by the IAAF, the body which is delegated by the IOC to supervise and control all the technical arrangements. Events for women were introduced in 1928, but Britain did not send a ladies' team on that occasion.

British Medallists

The following athletes, listed in alphabetical order, have won Olympic medals while representing Great Britain & Northern Ireland or, prior to 1924, Great Britain & Ireland. G signifies gold (1st), S silver (2nd) and B bronze (3rd).

Abrahams, H. M., 1924, 100 m. (G) and 4 x 100 m. (S).
Ahearne, T. J., 1908, triple jump (G).
Ainsworth-Davis, J. C., 1920, 4 x 400 m. (G).
Applegarth, W. R., 1912, 4 x 100 m. (G) and 200 m. (B).
Archer, J., 1948, 4 x 100 m. (S).
Bailey, E. McD., 1952, 100 m. (B).
Baker, P. J. (Noel-), 1920, 1500 m. (S).
Bennett, C., 1900, 1500 m. (G), 5000 m. team (G) and 4000 m. steeplechase (S).
Blewitt, C. E., 1920, 3000 m. team (S).
Brasher, C. W., 1956, 3000 m. steeplechase (G).
Brightwell, R. I., 1964, 4 x 400 m. (S).
Brown, A. G. K., 1936, 4 x 400 m. (G) and 400 m. (S).
Burghley, Lord, 1928, 400 m. hurdles (G); 1932, 4 x 400 m. (S).
Butler, G. M., 1920, 4 x 400 m. (G) and 400 m. (S); 1924, 400 m. (B) and 4 x 400 m. (B).
Coales, W., 1908, 3 mi. team (G).
Coe, S. N., 1980, 1500 m. (G) and 800 m. (S).
Cooper, J. H., 1964, 400 m. hurdles (S); 4 x 400 m. (S).
Cornes, J. F., 1932, 1500 m. (S).
Cottrill, W., 1912, 3000 m. team (B).
d'Arcy, V. H. A., 1912, 4 x 100 m. (G).
Davies, L., 1964, long jump (G).
Deakin, J. E., 1908, 3 mi. team (G).
Disley, J. I., 1952, 3000 m. steeplechase (B).
Edward, H. F. V., 1920, 100 m. (B) and 200 m. (B).
Evenson, T., 1932, 3000 m. steeplechase (S).
Ferris, S., 1932, Marathon (S).
Finlay, D. O., 1932, 110 hurdles (B); 1936, 110 hurdles (B).
Foster, B., 1976, 10,000 m. (B).
Gill, C. W., 1928, 4 x 100 m. (B).
Glover, E., 1912, Cross-country team (B).
Goodwin, G. R., 1924, 10,000 m. walk (S).
Goulding, G. T. S., 1896, 110 m. hurdles (S).
Graham, T. J. M., 1964, 4 x 400 m. (S).
Green, T. W., 1932, 50 km. walk (G).
Gregory, J. A., 1948, 4 x 100 m. (S).
Griffiths, C. R., 1920, 4 x 400 m. (G).
Gunn, C. E. J., 1920, 10,000 m. walk (B).
Hallows, N. F., 1908, 1500 m. (B).
Halswelle, W., 1908, 400 m. (G).
Hampson, T., 1932, 800 m. (G) and 4 x 400 m. (S).
Harper, E., 1936, Marathon (S).
Heatley, B. B., 1964, Marathon (S).
Hegarty, A., 1920, Cross-country team (S).
Hemery, D. P., 1968, 400 m. hurdles (G); 1972, 400 m. hurdles (B) and 4 x 400 m. (S).
Henley, E. J., 1912, 4 x 400 m. (B).
Herriott, M., 1964, 3000 m. steeplechase (S).
Hibbins, F. N., 1912, Cross-country team (B).
Higgins, F. P., 1956, 4 x 400 m. (B).
Hill, A. G., 1920, 800 m. (G), 1500 m. (G) and 3000 m. team (S).
Hodge, P., 1920, 3000 m. steeplechase (G).
Horgan, D., 1908, Shot (S).
Humphreys, T., 1912, Cross-country team (B).
Hutson, G. W., 1912, 5000 m. (B) and 3000 m. team (B).
Ibbotson, G. D., 1956, 5000 m. (B).
Jackson, A. N. Strode-, 1912, 1500 m. (G).
Jacobs, D. H., 1912, 4 x 100 m. (G).
Jenkins, D. A., 1972, 4 x 400 m. (S).
Johnson, D. J. N., 1956, 800 m. (S) and 4 x 400 m. (B).
Johnson, T. Lloyd, 1948, 50 km. walk (B).
Johnston, H. A., 1924, 3000 m. team (S).
Jones, D. H., 1960, 4 x 100 m. (B).
Jones, K. J., 1948, 4 x 100 m. (S).
Larner, G. E., 1908, 3500 m. walk (G) and 10 mi. walk (G).
Leahy, C., 1900, long jump (B); 1908, high jump (S).
Leahy, P. J., 1900, high jump (S).
Liddell, E. H., 1924, 400 m. (G) and 200 m. (B).
Lindsay, R. A., 1920, 4 x 400 m. (G).
London, J. E., 1928, 100 m. (S) and 4 x 100 m. (B).

OLYMPIC GAMES

Lowe, D. G. A., 1924, 800 m. (G); 1928, 800 m. (G).
McCorquodale, A., 1948, 4 x 100 m. (S).
MacDonald, B., 1924, 3000 m. team (S).
Macintosh, H. M., 1912, 4 x 100 m. (G).
Matthews, K. J., 1964, 20 km. walk (G).
Metcalfe, A. P., 1964, 4 x 400 m. (S).
Nichol, W. P., 1924, 4 x 100 m. (S).
Nichols, A. H., 1920, Cross-country team (S).
Nicol, G., 1912, 4 x 400 m. (B).
Nihill, V. P., 1964, 50 km. walk (S).
Nokes, M. C., 1924, hammer (B).
Oakes, G. J., 1980, 400 m. hurdles (B).
Ovett, S. M. J., 1980, 800 m. (G) and 1500 m. (B).
Owen, E., 1908, 5 mi. (S).
Pascoe, A. P., 1972, 4 x 400 m. (S).
Pirie, D. A. G., 1956, 5000 m. (S).
Porter, C. H. A., 1912, 3000 m. team (B).
Radford, P. F., 1960, 100 m. (B) and 4 x 100 m. (B).
Rampling, G. L., 1932, 4 x 400 m. (S); 1936, 4 x 400 m. (G).
Rangeley, W., 1924, 4 x 100 m. (S); 1928, 200 m. (S) and 4 x 100 m. (B).
Renwick, G. R., 1924, 4 x 400 m. (B).
Reynolds, M. E., 1972, 4 x 400 m. (S).
Richards, T., 1948, Marathon (S).
Rimmer, J. T., 1900, 4000 m. steeplechase (G) and 5000 m. team (G).
Ripley, R. N., 1924, 4 x 400 m. (B).
Roberts, W., 1936, 4 x 400 m. (G).
Robertson, A. J., 1908, 3 mi. team (G) and 3200 m. steeplechase (S).
Robinson, S. J., 1900, 5000 m. team (G), 2500 m. steeplechase (S) and 4000 m. steeplechase (B).
Royle, L. C., 1924, 4 x 100 m. (S).
Russell, A., 1908, 3200 m. steeplechase (G).
Salisbury, J. E., 1956, 4 x 400 m. (B).
Seagrove, W. R., 1920, 3000 m. team (S).
Seedhouse, C. N., 1912, 4 x 400 m. (B).
Segal, D. H., 1960, 4 x 100 m. (B).
Sherwood, J., 1968, 400 m. hurdles (B).
Smouha, E. R., 1928, 4 x 100 m. (B).
Soutter, J. T., 1912, 4 x 400 m. (B).
Spencer, E. A., 1908, 10 mi. walk (B).
Stallard, H. B., 1924, 1500 m. (B).
Stewart, I., 1972, 5000 m. (B).
Stoneley, C. H., 1932, 4 x 400 m. (S).
Thompson, D. J., 1960, 50 km. walk (G).
Thompson, F. M., 1980, decathlon (G).
Toms, E. J., 1924, 4 x 400 m. (B).
Tremeer, L. F., 1908, 400 m. hurdles (B).
Tysoe, A. E., 1900, 800 m. (G) and 5000 m. team (G).
Vickers, S. F., 1960, 20 km. walk (B).
Voigt, E. R., 1908, 5 mi. (G).
Webb, E. J., 1908, 3500 m. walk (S) and 10 mi. walk (S); 1912, 10,000 m. walk (S).
Webber, G. J., 1924, 3000 m. team (S).
Wells, A. W., 1980, 100 m. (G) and 200 m. (S).
Wheeler, M. K. V., 1956, 4 x 400 m. (B).
Whitehead, J. N., 1960, 4 x 100 m. (B).
Whitlock, H. H., 1936, 50 km. walk (G).
Wilson, H. A., 1908, 1500 m. (S).
Wilson, J., 1920, Cross-country team (S) and 10,000m. (B).
Wolff, F., 1936, 4 x 400 m. (G).

Women

Arden, D., 1964, 4 x 100 m. (B).
Armitage, H. J., 1952, 4 x 100 m. (B); 1956, 4 x 100 m. (S).
Board, L. B., 1968, 400 m. (S).
Brown, A., 1936, 4 x 100 m. (S).
Burke, B., 1936, 4 x 100 m. (S).
Cawley, S., 1952, long jump (B).
Cheeseman, S., 1952, 4 x 100 m. (B).
Desforges, J. C., 1952, 4 x 100 m. (B).
Gardner, M. A. J., 1948, 80 m. hurdles (S).
Goddard, B. L., 1980, 4 x 100 m. (B).
Halstead, N., 1932, 4 x 100 m. (B).
Hartley, D-M. L., 1980, 4 x 400 m. (B).
Hiscock, E. M., 1932, 4 x 100 m. (B); 1936, 4 x 100 m. (S).
Hopkins, T. E., 1956, high jump (S).
Hoyte-Smith, J. Y., 1980, 4 x 400 m. (B).
Hunte, H. R., 1980, 4 x 100 m. (B).
Hyman, D., 1960, 100 m. (S) and 200 m. (B), 1964, 4 x 100 m. (B).
Lannaman, S. M., 1980, 4 x 100 m. (B).
Lerwill, S., 1952, high jump (S).
Macdonald, L. T., 1980, 4 x 400 m. (B).

Manley, D. G., 1948, 100 m. (S).
Olney, V., 1936, 4 x 100 m. (S).
Packer, A. E., 1964, 800 m. (G); 400 m. (S).
Pashley, A., 1956, 4 x 100 m. (S).
Paul, J. F., 1952, 4 x 100 m. (B); 1956, 4 x 100 m. (S).
Peters, M. E., 1972, Pentathlon (G).
Porter, G. A., 1932, 4 x 100 m. (B).
Probert, M., 1980, 4 x 400 m. (B).
Quinton, C. L., 1960, 80 m. hurdles (S).
Rand, M. D., 1964, long jump (G); Pentathlon (S); 4 x 100 m. (B).
Scrivens, J. E., 1956, 4 x 100 m. (S).
Sherwood, S. H., 1968, long jump (S).
Shirley, D. A., 1960, high jump (S).
Simpson, J. M., 1964, 4 x 100 m. (B).
Smallwood, K. J., 1980, 4 x 100 m. (B).
Tyler, D. J. B., 1936, high jump (S); 1948, high jump (S).
Webb, V., 1932, 4 x 100 m. (B).
Williamson, A. D., 1948, 200 m. (S).

Champions

60 Metres

		sec.
1900	A. C. Kraenzlein (USA)	7.0
1904	A. Hahn (USA)	7.0

100 Metres

		sec.
1896	T. E. Burke (USA)	12.0
1900	F. W. Jarvis (USA)	11.0
1904	A. Hahn (USA)	11.0
1908	R. E. Walker (S. Africa)	10.8
1912	R. C. Craig (USA)	10.8
1920	C. W. Paddock (USA)	10.8
1924	H. M. Abrahams (GB)	10.6
1928	P. Williams (Canada)	10.8
1932	T. E. Tolan (USA)	10.3
1936	J. C. Owens (USA)	10.3
1948	W. H. Dillard (USA)	10.3
1952	L. J. Remigino (USA)	10.79
1956	B. J. Morrow (USA)	10.62
1960	A. Hary (Germany)	10.32
1964	R. L. Hayes (USA)	10.05
1968	J. R. Hines (USA)	9.95
1972	V. Borzov (USSR)	10.14
1976	H. Crawford (Trinidad)	10.06
1980	A. W. Wells (GB)	10.25

200 Metres

		sec.
1900	J. W. B. Tewksbury (USA)	22.2
1904*	A. Hahn (USA)	21.6
1908	R. Kerr (Canada)	22.6
1912	R. C. Craig (USA)	21.7
1920	A. Woodring (USA)	22.0
1924	J. V. Scholz (USA)	21.6
1928	P. Williams (Canada)	21.8
1932	T. E. Tolan (USA)	21.2
1936	J. C. Owens (USA)	20.7
1948	M. E. Patton (USA)	21.1
1952	A. W. Stanfield (USA)	20.81
1956	B. J. Morrow (USA)	20.75
1960	L. Berruti (Italy)	20.62
1964	H. Carr (USA)	20.38
1968	T. C. Smith (USA)	19.83
1972	V. Borzov (USSR)	20.00
1976	D. Quarrie (Jamaica)	20.23
1980	P. Mennea (Italy)	20.19

* straight course

400 Metres

		sec.
1896	T. E. Burke (USA)	54.2
1900	M. W. Long (USA)	49.4
1904	H. L. Hillman (USA)	49.2
1908*	W. Halswelle (GB)	50.0
1912	C. D. Reidpath (USA)	48.2
1920	B. G. D. Rudd (S. Africa)	49.6
1924	E. H. Liddell (GB)	47.6
1928	R. J. Barbuti (USA)	47.8
1932	W. A. Carr (USA)	46.2
1936	A. F. Williams (USA)	46.5
1948	A. S. Wint (Jamaica)	46.2
1952	V. G. Rhoden (Jamaica)	46.09
1956	C. L. Jenkins (USA)	46.86
1960	O. C. Davis (USA)	45.07
1964	M. D. Larrabee (USA)	45.15
1968	L. Evans (USA)	43.86
1972	V. Matthews (USA)	44.66
1976	A. Juantorena (Cuba)	44.26
1980	V. Markin (USSR)	44.60

* walk-over

800 Metres

		min.	sec.
1896	E. H. Flack (Australia)	2	11.0
1900	A. E. Tysoe (GB)	2	01.2
1904	J. D. Lightbody (USA)	1	56.0
1908	M. W. Sheppard (USA)	1	52.8
1912	J. E. Meredith (USA)	1	51.9
1920	A. G. Hill (GB)	1	53.4
1924	D. G. A. Lowe (GB)	1	52.4
1928	D. G. A. Lowe (GB)	1	51.8
1932	T. Hampson (GB)	1	49.7
1936	J. Y. Woodruff (USA)	1	52.9
1948	M. G. Whitfield (USA)	1	49.2
1952	M. G. Whitfield (USA)	1	49.2
1956	T. W. Courtney (USA)	1	47.7
1960	P. G. Snell (New Zealand)	1	46.3
1964	P. G. Snell (New Zealand)	1	45.1
1968	R. Doubell (Australia)	1	44.3
1972	D. Wottle (USA)	1	45.9
1976	A. Juantorena (Cuba)	1	43.5
1980	S. M. J. Ovett (GB)	1	45.4

1500 Metres

Year	Athlete	min. sec.
1896	E. H. Flack (Australia)	4 33.2
1900	C. Bennett (GB)	4 06.2
1904	J. D. Lightbody (USA)	4 05.4
1908	M. W. Sheppard (USA)	4 03.4
1912	A. N. S. Jackson (GB)	3 56.8
1920	A. G. Hill (GB)	4 01.8
1924	P. J. Nurmi (Finland)	3 53.6
1928	H. E. Larva (Finland)	3 53.2
1932	L. Beccali (Italy)	3 51.2
1936	J. E. Lovelock (New Zealand)	3 47.8
1948	H. Eriksson (Sweden)	3 49.8
1952	J. Barthel (Luxembourg)	3 45.1
1956	R. M. Delany (Ireland)	3 41.2
1960	H. J. Elliott (Australia)	3 35.6
1964	P. G. Snell (New Zealand)	3 38.1
1968	K. Keino (Kenya)	3 34.9
1972	P. Vasala (Finland)	3 36.3
1976	J. Walker (New Zealand)	3 39.2
1980	S. N. Coe (GB)	3 38.4

3000 Metres Team

Year	Team	
1912	USA (T. S. Berna, N. S. Taber, G. V. Bonhag)	8:44.6
1920	USA (H. H. Brown, A. A. Schardt, I. C. Dresser)	8:45.4
1924	Finland (P. J. Nurmi, V. J. Ritola, E. Katz)	8:32.0

3 Miles Team

Year	Team	
1908	GB (J. E. Deakin, A. J. Robertson, W. Coales)	14:39.6

5000 Metres Team

Year	Team	
1900	GB (C. Bennett, J. T. Rimmer, A. E. Tysoe, S. J. Robinson, S. Rowley)	15.20.0

5000 Metres

Year	Athlete	min. sec.
1912	H. Kolehmainen (Finland)	14 36.6
1920	J. Guillemot (France)	14 55.6
1924	P. J. Nurmi (Finland)	14 31.2
1928	V. J. Ritola (Finland)	14 38.0
1932	L. A. Lehtinen (Finland)	14 30.0
1936	G. Hockert (Finland)	14 22.2
1948	G. E. G. Reiff (Belgium)	14 17.6
1952	E. Zatopek (Czechoslovakia)	14 06.6
1956	V. Kuts (USSR)	13 39.6
1960	M. G. Halberg (New Zealand)	13 43.4
1964	R. K. Schul (USA)	13 48.8
1968	M. Gammoudi (Tunisia)	14 05.0
1972	L. Viren (Finland)	13 26.4
1976	L. Viren (Finland)	13 24.8
1980	M. Yifter (Ethiopia)	13 21.0

4 Miles Team

Year	Team	
1904	New York A.C., USA (A. L. Newton, G. Underwood, P. H. Pilgrim, H. Valentine, D. C. Munson)	21:17.8

5 Miles

Year	Athlete	min. sec.
1908	E. R. Voigt (GB)	25 11.2

10,000 Metres

Year	Athlete	min. sec.
1912	H. Kolehmainen (Finland)	31 20.8
1920	P. J. Nurmi (Finland)	31 45.8
1924	V. J. Ritola (Finland)	30 23.2
1928	P. J. Nurmi (Finland)	30 18.8
1932	J. Kusocinski (Poland)	30 11.4
1936	I. Salminen (Finland)	30 15.4
1948	E. Zatopek (Czechoslovakia)	29 59.6
1952	E. Zatopek (Czechoslovakia)	29 17.0
1956	V. Kuts (USSR)	28 45.6
1960	P. Bolotnikov (USSR)	28 32.2
1964	W. M. Mills (USA)	28 24.4
1968	N. Temu (Kenya)	29 27.4
1972	L. Viren (Finland)	27 38.4
1976	L. Viren (Finland)	27 40.4
1980	M. Yifter (Ethiopia)	27 42.7

Marathon

Year	Athlete	hr. min. sec.
1896*	S. Louis (Greece)	2 58 50.0
1900*	M. Theato (France)	2 59 45.0
1904*	T. J. Hicks (USA)	3 28 53.0
1908(1)	J. J. Hayes (USA)	2 55 18.4
1912*	K. K. McArthur (S. Africa)	2 36 54.8
1920	H. Kolehmainen (Finland)	2 32 35.8
1924	A. O. Stenroos (Finland)	2 41 22.6
1928	B. El Ouafi (France)	2 32 57.0
1932	J. C. Zabala (Argentine)	2 31 36.0
1936	K. Son (Japan)	2 29 19.2
1948	D. Cabrera (Argentine)	2 34 51.6
1952	E. Zatopek (Czechoslovakia)	2 23 03.2
1956	A. Mimoun (France)	2 25 00.0
1960	Abebe Bikila	

	(Ethiopia)	2 15 16.2
1964	Abebe Bikila	
	(Ethiopia)	2 12 11.2
1968	M. Wolde (Ethiopia)	2 20 26.4
1972	F. Shorter (USA)	2 12 19.8
1976	W. Cierpinski	
	(E. Germany)	2 09 55.0
1980	W. Cierpinski	
	(E. Germany)	2 11 03.0

* under standard distance of 26 mi. 385 yd. (42,195 m.)

(1) D. Pietri (Italy), 1st in 2:54:46.4, disqualified.

2500 Metres Steeplechase min .sec.
1900 G. W. Orton (Canada) 7 34.4
1904 J. D. Lightbody (USA) 7 39.6

3000 Metres Steeplechase min. sec.
1920 P. Hodge (GB) 10 00.4
1924 V. J. Ritola (Finland) 9 33.6
1928 T. A. Loukola (Finland) 9 21.8
1932* V. Iso-Hollo (Finland) 10 33.4
1936 V. Iso-Hollo (Finland) 9 03.8
1948 T. Sjostrand (Sweden) 9 04.6
1952 H. Ashenfelter (USA) 8 45.4
1956 C. W. Brasher (GB) 8 41.2
1960 Z. Krzyszkowiak
   (Poland) 8 34.2
1964 G. Roelants (Belgium) 8 30.8
1968 A. Biwott (Kenya) 8 51.0
1972 K. Keino (Kenya) 8 23.6
1976 A. Garderud (Sweden) 8 08.0
1980 B. Malinowski (Poland) 8 09.7

* 450 metres over distance

3200 Metres Steeplechase min. sec.
1908 A. Russell (GB) 10 47.8

4000 Metres Steeplechase min. sec.
1900 J. T. Rimmer (GB) 12 58.4

Cross-Country
1912 Sweden (H. Andersson, J. Eke, J. Ternstrom). Winner: H. Kolehmainen (Finland).
1920 Finland (P. J. Nurmi, winner; H. Liimatainen, T. Koskenniemi)
1924 Finland (P. J. Nurmi, winner; V. J. Ritola, H. Liimatainen).

110 Metres Hurdles (3ft. 6in.)   sec.
1896 T. P. Curtis (USA) 17.6
1900 A. C. Kraenzlein (USA) 15.4
1904 F. W. Schule (USA) 16.0
1908 F. C. Smithson (USA) 15.0
1912 F. W. Kelly (USA) 15.1
1920 E. J. Thomson (Canada) 14.8
1924 D. C. Kinsey (USA) 15.0
1928 S. J. M. Atkinson (S. Africa) 14.8
1932 G. J. Saling (USA) 14.6
1936 F. G. Towns (USA) 14.2
1948 W. F. Porter (USA) 13.9
1952 W. H. Dillard (USA) 13.91
1956 L. Q. Calhoun (USA) 13.70
1960 L. Q. Calhoun (USA) 13.98
1964 H. W. Jones (USA) 13.6
1968 W. Davenport (USA) 13.33
1972 R. Milburn (USA) 13.24
1976 G. Drut (France) 13.30
1980 T. Munkelt (E. Germany) 13.39

200 Metres Hurdles (2ft. 6in.)   sec.
1900 A. C. Kraenzlein (USA) 25.4
1904 H. L. Hillman (USA) 25.4

400 Metres Hurdles (2ft. 6in.)   sec.
1904 H. L. Hillman (USA) 53.0

400 Metres Hurdles (3ft. 0in.)   sec.
1900 J. W. B. Tewksbury
   (USA) 57.6
1908 C. J. Bacon (USA) 55.0
1920 F. F. Loomis (USA) 54.0
1924 F. M. Taylor (USA) 52.6
1928 Lord Burghley (GB) 53.4
1932 R. M. N. Tisdall (Ireland) 51.7
1936 G. F. Hardin (USA) 52.4
1948 L. V. Cochran (USA) 51.1
1952 C. H. Moore (USA) 51.06
1956 G. A. Davis (USA) 50.29
1960 G. A. Davis (USA) 49.51
1964 W. J. Cawley (USA) 49.6
1968 D. P. Hemery (GB) 48.12
1972 J. Akii-Bua (Uganda) 47.82
1976 E. Moses (USA) 47.64
1980 V. Beck (E. Germany) 48.70

4 x 100 Metres Relay   sec.
1912 GB (D. H. Jacobs, H. M. Macintosh, V. H. A. d'Arcy, W. R. Applegarth) 42.4
1920 USA (C. W. Paddock, J. V. Scholz, L. C. Murchison, M. M. Kirksey) 42.2
1924 USA (F. Hussey, L. A. Clarke, L. C. Murchison, J. A. Leconey) 41.0
1928 USA (F. C. Wykoff, J. F. Quinn, C. E. Borah, H. A. Russell) 41.0
1932 USA (R. A. Kiesel, E. Toppino, H. M. Dyer, F. C. Wykoff) 40.0

1936	USA (J. C. Owens, R. H. Metcalfe, F. Draper, F. C. Wykoff)	39.8		1936	Warner, W. A. Carr) GB (F. F. Wolff, G. L. Rampling, W. Roberts, A. G. K. Brown)	3 08.2 3 09.0
1948	USA (H. N. Ewell, L. C. Wright, W. H. Dillard, M. E. Patton)	40.6		1948	USA (A. H. Harnden, C. F. Bourland, L. V. Cochran, M. G. Whitfield)	3 10.4
1952	USA (F. D. Smith, W. H. Dillard, L. J. Remigino, A. W. Stanfield)	40.26		1952	Jamaica (A. S. Wint, L. A. Laing, H. H. McKenley, V. G. Rhoden)	3 03.9
1956	USA (I. J. Murchison, L. King, W. T. Baker, B. J. Morrow)	39.59		1956	USA (L. W. Jones, J. W. Mashburn, C. L. Jenkins, T. W. Courtney)	3 04.7
1960*	Germany (B. Cullmann, A. Hary, W. Mahlendorf, K. M. Lauer)	39.66		1960	USA (J. L. Yerman, E. V. Young, G. A. Davis, O. C. Davis)	3 02.2
1964	USA (O. P. Drayton, G. H. Ashworth, R. V. Stebbins, R. L. Hayes)	39.0		1964	USA (O. C. Cassell, M. D. Larrabee, U. C. Williams, H. Carr)	3 00.7
1968	USA (C. Greene, M. Pender, R. R. Smith, J. R. Hines)	38.23		1968	USA (V. Matthews, R. Freeman, L. James, L. Evans)	2 56.1
1972	USA (L. Black, R. Taylor, G. Tinker, E. Hart)	38.19		1972	Kenya (C. Asati, H. Nyamau, R. Ouko, J. Sang)	2 59.8
1976	USA (H. Glance, J. Jones, M. Hampton, S. Riddick)	38.33		1976	USA (H. Frazier, B. Brown, F. Newhouse, M. Parks)	2 58.7
1980	USSR (V. Muravyov, N. Sidorov, A. Aksinin, A. Prokofiev)	38.26		1980	USSR (R. Valiulis, M. Linge, N. Chernetsky, V. Markin)	3 01.1

* USA (F. J. Budd, O. R. Norton, S. E. Johnson, D. W. Sime) 1st in 39.59, disqualified.

1600 Metres Medley Relay   min. sec.

1908	USA (W. F. Hamilton, N. J. Cartmell, J. B. Taylor, M. W. Sheppard)	3 29.4

4 x 400 Metres Relay
                         min. sec.

1912	USA (M. W. Sheppard, E. F. J. Lindberg, J. E. Meredith, C. D. Reidpath)	3 16.6
1920	GB (C. R. Griffiths, R. A. Lindsay, J. C. Ainsworth-Davis, G. M. Butler)	3 22.2
1924	USA (C. S. Cochrane, W. E. Stevenson, J. O. McDonald, A. B. Helffrich)	3 16.0
1928	USA (G. Baird, E. M. Spencer, E. P. Alderman, R. J. Barbuti)	3 14.2
1932	USA (I. Fuqua, E. A. Ablowich, K. D.	

High Jump   metres

1896	E. H. Clark (USA)	1.81
1900	I. K. Baxter (USA)	1.90
1904	S. S. Jones (USA)	1.80
1908	H. F. Porter (USA)	1.90
1912	A. W. Richards (USA)	1.93
1920	R. W. Landon (USA)	1.93
1924	H. M. Osborn (USA)	1.98
1928	R. W. King (USA)	1.94
1932	D. McNaughton (Canada)	1.97
1936	C. C. Johnson (USA)	2.03
1948	J. A. Winter (Australia)	1.98
1952	W. F. Davis (USA)	2.04
1956	C. E. Dumas (USA)	2.12
1960	R. Shavlakadze (USSR)	2.16
1964	V. Brumel (USSR)	2.18
1968	R. Fosbury (USA)	2.24
1972	J. Tarmak (USSR)	2.23
1976	J. Wszola (Poland)	2.25
1980	G. Wessig (E. Germany)	2.36

Standing High Jump   metres

1900	R. C. Ewry (USA)	1.65
1904	R. C. Ewry (USA)	1.50

OLYMPIC GAMES

1908	R. C. Ewry (USA)	1.57
1912	P. Adams (USA)	1.63

Pole Vault — metres
1896	W. W. Hoyt (USA)	3.30
1900	I. K. Baxter (USA)	3.30
1904	C. E. Dvorak (USA)	3.50
1908	E. T. Cooke (USA) and A. C. Gilbert (USA)	3.71
1912	H. S. Babcock (USA)	3.95
1920	F. K. Foss (USA)	4.09
1924	L. S. Barnes (USA)	3.95
1928	S. W. Carr (USA)	4.20
1932	W. W. Miller (USA)	4.31
1936	E. E. Meadows (USA)	4.35
1948	O. G. Smith (USA)	4.30
1952	R. E. Richards (USA)	4.55
1956	R. E. Richards (USA)	4.56
1960	D. G. Bragg (USA)	4.70
1964	F. M. Hansen (USA)	5.10
1968	R. Seagren (USA)	5.40
1972	W. Nordwig (E. Germany)	5.50
1976	T. Slusarski (Poland)	5.50
1980	W. Kozakiewicz (Poland)	5.78

Long Jump — metres
1896	E. H. Clark (USA)	6.35
1900	A. C. Kraenzlein (USA)	7.18
1904	M. Prinstein (USA)	7.34
1908	F. C. Irons (USA)	7.48
1912	A. L. Gutterson (USA)	7.60
1920	W. Pettersson (Sweden)*	7.15
1924	W. De H. Hubbard (USA)	7.44
1928	E. B. Hamm (USA)	7.73
1932	E. L. Gordon (USA)	7.64
1936	J. C. Owens (USA)	8.06
1948	W. S. Steele (USA)	7.82
1952	J. C. Biffle (USA)	7.57
1956	G. C. Bell (USA)	7.83
1960	R. H. Boston (USA)	8.12
1964	L. Davies (GB)	8.07
1968	R. Beamon (USA)	8.90
1972	R. Williams (USA)	8.24
1976	A. Robinson (USA)	8.35
1980	L. Dombrowski (E. Ger.)	8.54

* later known as Bjorneman

Standing Long Jump — metres
1900	R. C. Ewry (USA)	3.21
1904	R. C. Ewry (USA)	3.47
1908	R. C. Ewry (USA)	3.33
1912	C. Tsiclitiras (Greece)	3.37

Triple Jump — metres
1896*	J. V. Connolly (USA)	13.71
1900	M. Prinstein (USA)	14.47
1904	M. Prinstein (USA)	14.35
1908	T. J. Ahearne (GB/Ire)	14.91
1912	G. Lindblom (Sweden)	14.76
1920	V. Tuulos (Finland)	14.50
1924	A. W. Winter (Australia)	15.52
1928	M. Oda (Japan)	15.21
1932	C. Nambu (Japan)	15.72
1936	N. Tajima (Japan)	16.00
1948	A. P. Ahman (Sweden)	15.40
1952	A. F. da Silva (Brazil)	16.22
1956	A. F. da Silva (Brazil)	16.35
1960	J. Szmidt (Poland)	16.81
1964	J. Szmidt (Poland)	16.85
1968	V. Sanyeyev (USSR)	17.39
1972	V. Sanyeyev (USSR)	17.35
1976	V. Sanyeyev (USSR)	17.29
1980	J. Uudmae (USSR)	17.35

* two hops and one jump

Standing Triple Jump — metres
1900	R. C. Ewry (USA)	10.58
1904	R. C. Ewry (USA)	10.55

Shot — metres
1896*	R. S. Garrett (USA)	11.22
1900*	R. Sheldon (USA)	14.10
1904	R. W. Rose (USA)	14.81
1908	R. W. Rose (USA)	14.21
1912	P. J. McDonald (USA)	15.34
1920	V. Porhola (Finland)	14.81
1924	C. L. Houser (USA)	14.99
1928	J. Kuck (USA)	15.87
1932	L. J. Sexton (USA)	16.00
1936	H. Woellke (Germany)	16.20
1948	W. M. Thompson (USA)	17.12
1952	W. P. O'Brien (USA)	17.41
1956	W. P. O'Brien (USA)	18.57
1960	W. H. Nieder (USA)	19.68
1964	D. C. Long (USA)	20.33
1968	J. R. Matson (USA)	20.54
1972	W. Komar (Poland)	21.18
1976	U. Beyer (E. Germany)	21.05
1980	V. Kiselyev (USSR)	21.35

* from 7 ft. square

Shot (Both Hands) — metres
1912	R. W. Rose (USA)	27.70

Discus — metres
1896	R. S. Garrett (USA)	29.14
1900	R. Bauer (Hungary)	36.04
1904	M. J. Sheridan (USA)	39.28
1908	M. J. Sheridan (USA)	40.88
1912	A. R. Taipale (Finland)	45.20
1920	E. Niklander (Finland)	44.68
1924	C. L. Houser (USA)	46.14

1928	C. L. Houser (USA)	47.32
1932	J. F. Anderson (USA)	49.48
1936	K. K. Carpenter (USA)	50.48
1948	A. Consolini (Italy)	52.78
1952	S. G. Iness (USA)	55.02
1956	A. A. Oerter (USA)	56.36
1960	A. A. Oerter (USA)	59.18
1964	A. A. Oerter (USA)	61.00
1968	A. A. Oerter (USA)	64.78
1972	L. Danek (Czech)	64.40
1976	M. Wilkins (USA)	67.50
1980	V. Rashchupkin (USSR)	66.64

Discus (Greek Style) — metres
1908 M. J. Sheridan (USA) 38.00

Discus (Both Hands) — metres
1912 A. R. Taipale (Finland) 82.86

Hammer — metres
1900*	J. J. Flanagan (USA)	49.72
1904	J. J. Flanagan (USA)	51.22
1908	J. J. Flanagan (USA)	51.92
1912	M. J. McGrath (USA)	54.74
1920	P. J. Ryan (USA)	52.86
1924	F. D. Tootell (USA)	53.28
1928	P. O'Callaghan (Ireland)	51.38
1932	P. O'Callaghan (Ireland)	53.92
1936	K. Hein (Germany)	56.48
1948	I. Nemeth (Hungary)	56.06
1952	J. Csermak (Hungary)	60.34
1956	H. V. Connolly (USA)	63.18
1960	V. Rudenkov (USSR)	67.10
1964	R. Klim (USSR)	69.74
1968	G. Zsivotzky (Hungary)	73.36
1972	A. Bondarchuk (USSR)	75.50
1976	Y. Sedykh (USSR)	77.52
1980	Y. Sedykh (USSR)	81.80

* from 9 ft. circle

Javelin — metres
1908	E. V. Lemming (Sweden)	54.82
1912	E. V. Lemming (Sweden)	60.64
1920	J. J. Myyra (Finland)	65.78
1924	J. J. Myyra (Finland)	62.96
1928	E. H. Lundkvist (Sweden)	66.60
1932	M. H. Jarvinen (Finland)	72.70
1936	G. Stock (Germany)	71.84
1948	K. T. Rautavaara (Finland)	69.76
1952	C. C. Young (USA)	73.78
1956	E. Danielsen (Norway)	85.70
1960	V. Tsibulenko (USSR)	84.64
1964	P. L. Nevala (Finland)	82.66
1968	J. Lusis (USSR)	90.10
1972	K. Wolfermann (W. Germany)	90.48
1976	M. Nemeth (Hungary)	94.58
1980	D. Kula (USSR)	91.20

Javelin (Free Style) — metres
1908 E. V. Lemming (Sweden) 54.44

Javelin (Both Hands) — metres
1912 J. Saaristo (Finland) 109.42

56 lb. Weight — metres
1904 E. Desmartreau (Canada) 10.46
1920 P. McDonald (USA) 11.26

Pentathlon
1912* F. Bie (Norway)
1920 E. Lehtonen (Finland)
1924 E. Lehtonen (Finland)
* J. H. Thorpe (USA), 1st, subsequently debarred.

Decathlon (1962 Tables) — Pts.
1912*	H. Wieslander (Sweden)	6161
1920	H. Lovland (Norway)	5970
1924	H. M. Osborn (USA)	6668
1928	P. I. Yrjola (Finland)	6774
1932	J. A. B. Bausch (USA)	6896
1936	G. E. Morris (USA)	7421
1948	R. B. Mathias (USA)	6825
1952	R. B. Mathias (USA)	7731
1956	M. G. Campbell (USA)	7708
1960	R. L. Johnson (USA)	8001
1964	W. Holdorf (Germany)	7887
1968	W. Toomey (USA)	8193
1972	N. Avilov (USSR)	8456†
1976	B. Jenner (USA)	8617†
1980	F. M. Thompson (GB)	8495†

* J. H. Thorpe (USA), 1st with 6756, subsequently debarred.
† scored on 1977 Tables

3000 Metres Walk — min. sec.
1920 U. Frigerio (Italy) 13 14.2

3500 Metres Walk — min. sec.
1908 G. E. Larner (GB) 14 55.0

10,000 Metres Walk — min. sec
1912 G. H. Goulding (Canada) 46 28.4
1920 U. Frigerio (Italy) 48 06.2
1924 U. Frigerio (Italy) 47 49.0

| 1948 | J. F. Mikaelsson (Sweden) | 45 13.2 |
| 1952 | J. F. Mikaelsson (Sweden) | 45 02.8 |

10 Mile Walk — hr. min. sec.
| 1908 | G. E. Larner (GB) | 1 15 57.4 |

20,000 Metres Walk — hr. min. sec.
1956	L. Spirin (USSR)	1 31 27.4
1960	V. Golubnichiy (USSR)	1 34 07.2
1964	K. J. Matthews (GB)	1 29 34.0
1968	V. Golubnichiy (USSR)	1 33 58.4
1972	P. Frenkel (E. Germany)	1 26 42.4
1976	D. Bautista (Mexico)	1 24 40.6
1980	M. Damilano (Italy)	1 23 35.5

50,000 Metres Walk — hr. min. sec.
1932	T. W. Green (GB)	4 50 10.0
1936	H. H. Whitlock (GB)	4 30 41.4
1948	J. A. Ljunggren (Sweden)	4 41 52.0
1952	G. Dordoni (Italy)	4 28 07.8
1956	N. R. Read (New Zealand)	4 30 42.8
1960	D. J. Thompson (GB)	4 25 30.0
1964	A. Pamich (Italy)	4 11 12.4
1968	C. Hohne (E. Germany)	4 20 13.6
1972	B. Kannenberg (W. Germany)	3 56 11.6
1976	Not held	
1980	H. Gauder (E. Ger)	3 49 24.0

WOMEN CHAMPIONS

100 Metres — sec.
1928	E. Robinson (USA)	12.2
1932	S. Walasiewicz (Poland)	11.9
1936	H. H. Stephens (USA)	11.5
1948	F. E. Blankers-Koen (Netherlands)	11.9
1952	M. Jackson (Australia)	11.65
1956	B. Cuthbert (Australia)	11.82
1960	W. G. Rudolph (USA)	11.18
1964	W. Tyus (USA)	11.4
1968	W. Tyus (USA)	11.08
1972	R. Stecher (E. Germany)	11.07
1976	A. Richter (W. Germany)	11.08
1980	L. Kondratyeva (USSR)	11.06

200 Metres — sec.
1948	F. E. Blankers-Koen (Netherlands)	24.4
1952	M. Jackson (Australia)	23.89
1956	B. Cuthbert (Australia)	23.55
1960	W. G. Rudolph (USA)	24.13
1964	E. M. McGuire (USA)	23.0
1968	I. Szewinska (Poland)	22.58
1972	R. Stecher (E. Germany)	22.40
1976	B. Wockel (E. Germany)	22.37
1980	B. Wockel (E. Germany)	22.03

400 Metres — sec.
1964	B. Cuthbert (Australia)	52.0
1968	C. Besson (France)	52.03
1972	M. Zehrt (E. Germany)	51.08
1976	I. Szewinska (Poland)	49.29
1980	M. Koch (E. Germany)	48.88

800 Metres — min. sec.
1928	L. Radke (Germany)	2 16.8
1960	L. Lysenko (USSR)	2 04.3
1964	A. E. Packer (GB)	2 01.1
1968	M. Manning (USA)	2 00.9
1972	H. Falck (W. Germany)	1 58.6
1976	T. Kazankina (USSR)	1 54.9
1980	N. Olizaryenko (USSR)	1 53.5

1500 Metres — min. sec.
1972	L. Bragina (USSR)	4 01.4
1976	T. Kazankina (USSR)	4 05.5
1980	T. Kazankina (USSR)	3 56.6

80 Metres Hurdles — sec.
1932	M. Didrikson (USA)	11.7
1936	T. Valla (Italy)	11.7
1948	F. E. Blankers-Koen (Netherlands)	11.2
1952	S. B. De La Hunty (Australia)	11.03
1956	S. B. De La Hunty (Australia)	10.96
1960	I. Press (USSR)	10.94
1964	K. Balzer (Germany)	10.5
1968	M. Caird (Australia)	10.3

100 Metres Hurdles — sec.
1972	A. Ehrhardt (E. Germany)	12.59
1976	J. Schaller (E. Germany)	12.77
1980	V. Komissova (USSR)	12.56

4 x 100 Metres Relay — sec.
1928	Canada (F. Rosenfeld, E. Smith, F. Bell, M. Cook)	48.4
1932	USA (M. L. Carew, E. Furtsch, A. J. Rogers, W. von Bremen)	47.0
1936	USA (H. C. Bland, A. J. Rogers, E. Robinson, H. H. Stephens)	46.9
1948	Netherlands (X. Stad-de-Jongh, J. M. Witziers, G. J. M. Koudijs, F. E. Blankers-Koen)	47.5

Year	Team/Athletes	Result
1952	USA (M. E. Faggs, B. P. Jones, J. T. Moreau, C. Hardy)	46.14
1956	Australia (S. B. De La Hunty, N. W. Croker, F. N. Mellor, B. Cuthbert)	44.65
1960	USA (M. Hudson, L. Williams, B. P. Jones, W. G. Rudolph)	44.72
1964	Poland (T. B. Ciepla, I. Szewinska, H. Gorecka, E. Klobukowska)	43.6
1968	USA (B. Ferrell. M. Bailes, M. Netter, W. Tyus)	42.87
1972	W. Germany (C. Krause, I. Mickler, A. Richter, H. Rosendahl)	42.81
1976	E. Germany (M. Gohr, R. Stecher, C. Bodendorf, B. Wockel)	42.55
1980	E. Germany (R. Muller, B. Wockel, I. Auerswald, M. Gohr)	41.60

4 x 400 Metres Relay min. sec.

Year	Team	Time
1972	E. Germany (D. Kasling, R. Kuhne, H. Seidler, M. Zehrt)	3 23.0
1976	E. Germany (D. Maletzki, B. Rohde, E. Streidt, C. Brehmer)	3 19.2
1980	USSR (T. Prorochenko, T. Goitchik, N. Zyuskova, I. Nazarova)	3 20.2

High Jump metres
1928	E. Catherwood (Canada)	1.59
1932	J. H. Shiley (USA)	1.65
1936	I. Csak (Hungary)	1.60
1948	A. Coachman (USA)	1.68
1952	E. C. Brand (S. Africa)	1.67
1956	M. I. McDaniel (USA)	1.76
1960	I. Balas (Romania)	1.85
1964	I. Balas (Romania)	1.90
1968	M. Rezkova (Czechoslovakia)	1.82
1972	U. Meyfarth (W. Germany)	1.92
1976	R. Ackermann (E. Germany)	1.93
1980	S. Simeoni (Italy)	1.97

Long Jump metres
1948	V. O. Gyarmati (Hungary)	5.69
1952	Y. W. Williams (New Zealand)	6.24
1956	E. Krzesinska (Poland)	6.35
1960	V. Krepkina (USSR)	6.37
1964	M. D. Rand (GB)	6.76
1968	V. Viscopoleanu (Romania)	6.82
1972	H. Rosendahl (W. Germany)	6.78
1976	A. Voigt (E. Germany)	6.72
1980	T. Kolpakova (USSR)	7.06

Shot metres
1948	M. O. M. Ostermeyer (France)	13.75
1952	G. I. Zybina (USSR)	15.28
1956	T. A. Tyshkevich (USSR)	16.59
1960	T. Press (USSR)	17.32
1964	T. Press (USSR)	18.14
1968	M. Gummel (E. Germany)	19.61
1972	N. Chizhova (USSR)	21.03
1976	I. Khristova (Bulgaria)	21.16
1980	I. Slupianek (E. Ger)	22.41

Discus metres
1928	H. Konopacka (Poland)	39.62
1932	L. Copeland (USA)	40.58
1936	G. Mauermayer (Germany)	47.62
1948	M. O. M. Ostermeyer (France)	41.92
1952	N. Ponomaryeva (USSR)	51.42
1956	O. Fikotova (Czechoslovakia)	53.68
1960	N. Ponomaryeva (USSR)	55.10
1964	T. Press (USSR)	57.26
1968	L. Manoliu (Romania)	58.28
1972	F. Melnik (USSR)	66.62
1976	E. Jahl (E. Germany)	69.00
1980	E. Jahl (E. Germany)	69.96

Javelin metres
1932	M. Didrikson (USA)	43.68
1936	T. Fleischer (Germany)	45.18
1948	H. Bauma (Austria)	45.56
1952	D. Zatopkova (Czechoslovakia)	50.46
1956	I. Jaunzeme (USSR)	53.86
1960	E. Ozolina (USSR)	55.98
1964	M. Penes (Romania)	60.54
1968	A. Nemeth (Hungary)	60.36
1972	R. Fuchs (E. Germany)	63.88
1976	R. Fuchs (E. Germany)	65.94
1980	M. Colon (Cuba)	68.40

Pentathlon

		pts.
1964	I. Press (USSR)	5246
1968	I. Mickler (W. Germany)	5098
1972†	M. E. Peters (GB & NI)	4801
1976†	S. Siegl (E. Germany)	4745

† Scored on 1970 Tables.
With 800 metres:
1980 N. Tkachenko (USSR)   5083

Record Achievements (Men)

Most gold medals won is nine by Paavo Nurmi (Finland), who between 1920 and 1928 was victorious in six individual and three team races.

Most individual wins is eight by Ray Ewry (USA) in the standing jump events between 1900 and 1908. His tally rises to ten if the Games of 1906 are included.

Most gold medals at one Olympics is five by Nurmi in 1924 (1500 m., 3000 m. team, 5000 m., cross-country team and individual winner).

Most individual gold medals at one Olympics is four by Alvin Kraenzlein (USA)—60 m., 110 and 200 m. hurdles and long jump champion in 1900.

Most gold medals in one event is four by Al Oerter (USA) in the discus, 1956-1968 inclusive.

Most medals of any denomination is 12 by Nurmi.

Most medals by a British athlete is four by Guy Butler: 400 m. and 4 x 400 m. relay in 1920 and 1924.

Record Achievements (Women)

Most gold medals won is four by Fanny Blankers-Koen (Netherlands): the 100 m., 200 m., 80 m. hurdles and 4 x 100 m. relay in 1948; and Betty Cuthbert (Australia): the 100m., 200 m. and 4 x 100 m. relay in 1956 and the 400 m. in 1964.

Most gold medals at one Olympics is four by Blankers-Koen as above.

Most individual gold medals at one Olympics is three by Blankers-Koen as above.

Most gold medals in one individual event is two by Shirley De La Hunty, Australia (80 m. hurdles in 1952 and 1956); Nina Ponomaryeva, USSR (discus in 1952 and 1960); Iolanda Balas, Romania (high jump in 1960 and 1964); Tamara Press, USSR (shot in 1960 and 1964); Wyomia Tyus, USA (100 m. in 1964 and 1968); Ruth Fuchs, E. Germany (Javelin in 1972 and 1976); Barbel Wockel, E. Germany (200 m. in 1976 and 1980); Tatyana Kazankina, USSR (1500 m. in 1976 and 1980); and Evelin Jahl, E. Germany (discus in 1976 and 1980).

Most medals of any denomination is seven by De La Hunty between 1948 and 1956, and Irena Szewinska (Poland) between 1964 and 1976. The latter is the only woman athlete to have gained a medal in four successive Games.

Most individual medals by a British athlete is three by Dorothy Hyman (100 m. and 200 m. in 1960, 4 x 100 m. relay in 1964) and Mary Rand (long jump, pentathlon and 4 x 100 m. relay in 1964).

Most appearances in an Olympics is six by Romanian discus thrower Lia Manoliu: 6th in 1952, 9th in 1956, 3rd in 1960, 3rd in 1964, 1st in 1968 and 9th in 1972.

Unofficial Olympics

An unofficial Olympic celebration was staged in Athens in 1906. For the record, the winners were as follows:

100 m., A. Hahn (USA) 11.2 sec.; 400 m., P. H. Pilgrim (USA) 53.2 sec.; 800 m., P. H. Pilgrim (USA) 2 min. 11.2 sec.; 1500 m., J. D. Lightbody (USA) 4 min. 12.0 sec.; 5 mi., H. Hawtrey (GB) 26 min. 26.2 sec.; Marathon, W. J. Sherring (Canada) 2 hr. 51 min. 23.6 sec.; 110 m. hurdles, R. G. Leavitt (USA) 16.2 sec.; High jump, C. Leahy (Ireland) 1.75 metres; Standing high jump, R. C. Ewry (USA) 1.57 metres; Pole vault, F. Gonder (France) 3.50 metres; long jump, M. Prinstein (USA) 7.20 metres; Standing long jump, R. C. Ewry (USA) 3.30 metres; Triple jump, P. J. O'Connor (Ireland) 14.07 metres; Shot, M. J. Sheridan (USA) 12.32 metres; Discus, M. J. Sheridan (USA) 41.46 metres; Discus (Greek Style), W. Jarvinen (Finland) 35.16 metres; Javelin, E. Lemming (Sweden) 53.50 metres; throwing the stone (14 lb.), Georgeantas (Greece) 19.92 metres; pentathlon, Mellander (Sweden).

OVETT, Steve (GB)

After winning the Olympic 800 m. title in Moscow, Steve Ovett could well be considered the greatest competitive athlete Britain has ever produced, for that success—achieved at the age of 24—completed a remarkable decade of major triumphs.

It all started in 1970 when he won the English Schools Junior (under-15) 400 m. title, and that here was a runner physically endowed beyond his years became evident in 1973 when, only 17, he won the European Junior 800 m. and recorded such notable times as 1 min. 47.3 sec. for that distance and exactly four minutes for the mile. In 1974 he distinguished himself by finishing second in the European 800 m. championship with a European junior record of 1 min. 45.8 sec. but Ovett's attitude—one of dismay that by being boxed in at the crucial moment when Luciano Susanj (Yug) made his strike for home with 200 m. to go he lost his own chance of victory—earmarked this tall, strongly built young man as a very special breed of athlete.

Another aspect of Ovett's unique talent was his versatility. He had in 1974 improved his 400 m. time to 47.5 sec. and yet he opened his 1975 campaign by winning the English Junior cross-country title with 200 m. to spare! Highlight of the summer season was a resounding victory in the European Cup Final 800 m. Considered a possible Olympic medallist at the distance he did produce a personal best of 1 min. 45.4 sec in the Montreal final but, too slow into his running, he was never in the hunt and placed fifth some 15 m. behind Alberto Juantorena's world record 1 min. 43.5 sec. Ovett later picked up another personal best as he won his Olympic 1500 m. heat in 3 min. 37.9 sec. but was eliminated in the semi-finals.

It was from 1977 onwards that Ovett's trademarks, the unmatched burst of acceleration 200 m. from the finish and his cheeky waves to the crowd well before the race was over, made him a charismatic and controversial figure known the world over. His first serious track race of 1977, in Jamaica on May 13th, resulted in a narrow 1500 m. defeat by Steve Scott (USA)—but that was to prove Ovett's last loss at either 1500 m. or mile until the Olympic final on Aug. 1st 1980! In June 1977 he claimed his first UK senior record (3 min. 54.7 sec. mile), in August he played with the field in the European Cup Final 1500 m. and in September he ran a devastating race to obliterate some very classy opposition in the World Cup 1500 m. with a UK record of 3 min. 34.5 sec. Ever unpredictable, Ovett had—just a fortnight before the World Cup—turned up on impulse for a half-marathon and won it in 65 min. 38 sec!

A further indication of his endurance came in the 1978 English cross-country championship, in which he placed fourth, but his speed remained intact as was evident in the European Championships where he took the silver medal in the 800 m. with a short-lived UK record of 1 min. 44.1 sec. Third in the race, won by East Germany's Olaf Beyer, was Sebastian Coe; this was the first ever track clash between the two British stars. Ovett's main target in Prague, though, was the 1500 m. and that he duly won in 3 min. 35.6 sec., covering the last 200 m. in an unanswerable 24.8 sec. Twelve days later he strung together miles of 4 min. 09.1 sec. and 4 min. 04.4 sec. to defeat Henry Rono in a world outdoor 2 miles best of 8 min. 13.5 sec. Previously scornful of the chasing of records, Ovett made a specific attack in very unhelpful conditions in Norway and came away with a UK mile mark of 3 min. 52.8 sec.

Coe's record-breaking binge in 1979 tempted Ovett to dispense with the low profile he had earlier promised for pre-Olympic year, and he went after Coe's figures of 3 min. 49.0 sec. and 3 min. 32.1 sec. He fell short, but only just, with times of 3 min. 49.6 sec. and 3 min. 32.2 sec.

That situation he rectified in 1980. In Oslo on July 1st he gained his first official world record—a 3 min. 48.8 sec. mile made up of quarters of 55.7, 58.1, 57.2 and 57.8 sec.—and on the same Bislett track 14 days later he equalled the 3 min. 32.1 sec. 1500 m. record, although on hundredths his time of 3 min. 32.09 sec. was slower than Coe's 3 min. 32.03 sec.

At the Olympics he created a double sensation; first by triumphing over Coe in the 800 m. (1 min. 45.4 sec.) and then by suffering a reaction to finish a jaded third in the 1500 m. behind Coe and East Germany's Jurgen Straub. That reverse ended a run of

45 consecutive 1500 m. or mile victories. Undaunted, he bounced back with a series of fast runs, crowned by a 3 min. 31.36 sec. 1500 m. at Koblenz on Aug. 27th which removed any lingering confusion over the world record. The first lap took 55.6 sec., the second 57.4, the third 57.7, and Ovett completed the final 300 m. in 40.7.

His best marks: 47.5 sec. for 400 m., 1 min. 44.09 sec. for 800 m., 2 min. 15.91 sec. for 1000 m., 3 min. 31.36 sec. for 1500 m., 3 min. 48.8 sec. for the mile, 4 min. 57.8 sec. for 2000 m., 7 min. 41.3 sec. for 3000 m., 8 min. 13.5 sec. for 2 miles and 13 min. 25.0 sec. for 5000 m. Annual progress at 800 & 1500 m: 1970—2:00.0, 4:10.7; 1971—1:55.3; 1972—1:52.5, 4:02.0; 1973—1:47.3, 3:44.8 (& 4:00.0 mile); 1974—1:45.8, 3:46.2 (& 3:59.4); 1975—1:46.1, 3:39.5 (& 3:57.0); 1976—1:45.4, 3:37.9; 1977—1:48.3, 3:34.5 (& 3:54.7); 1978—1:44.09, 3:35.6 (& 3:52.8); 1979—1:45.0, 3:32.11 (& 3:49.6); 1980—1:45.4, 3:31.36 (& 3:48.8). He was born in Brighton on Oct. 9th, 1955.

OWENS, Jesse (USA)

That Jesse Owens was the supreme physical genius of his age is less an opinion than a statement of fact. His sparkling career culminated in his quadruple success at the 1936 Olympic Games yet it is open to debate whether even that superlative achievement (winning the 100 m., 200 m., long jump and 4 x 100 m. relay) eclipses his feat at Ann Arbor, Michigan, on May 25th, 1935.

The sequence of events on that afternoon was as follows: 3.15—Owens equals 100 yd. world record of 9.4 sec.; 3.25—Owens takes one long jump . . . a very long jump of 8.13 metres, a world record destined to survive for quarter of a century; 3.45—Owens sets new world record of 20.3 sec. for the straight 220 yd., automatically collecting the 200 metres mark *en route;* 4.00—Owens covers the straight 220 yd. hurdles in 22.6 sec. for new world figures at that event and 200 m. hurdles . . . and two of the three watches showed 22.4 sec. Six records in 45 minutes! The world will never again witness the like.

Perhaps his finest single competitive performance was winning the Olympic long jump in Berlin. He began disastrously, managing to qualify on his third and last try. In the final, after a thrilling struggle, he pulled out a magnificent leap of 8.06 metres to which the inspired German, Luz Long (7.87 metres), had no reply. Ever the sportsman, Owens even massaged his rival's leg during the competition at a vital stage.

He displayed his athletic gifts at an early age, recording 9.9 sec. for 100 yd., high jumping 1.90 metres and long jumping 7.01 metres when he was 15. In 1932, aged 18, he ran a wind-aided 100 m. in 10.3 sec. and next year, still at school, clocked 9.4 sec. for 100 yd., 20.7 sec. for the straight furlong and jumped 7.61 metres.

Had he not turned professional shortly after the Olympics, he might have developed into the world's fastest quarter-miler, for he ran an effortless 29.5 sec. for 300 yd. in a time trial in 1936. His natural ability (he once high jumped 1.98 metres in training without any special preparation) stayed with him for many years. He claims to have run 100 yd. in 9.7 sec. and long jumped 7.90 metres in 1948, and 9.8 sec. in 1955 (aged 41).

His best marks were 9.4 sec. for 100 yd., 10.2 sec. for 100 m., 20.7 sec. for 200 m. (turn), 20.3 sec. for 220 yd. (straight), 22.6 sec. for 220 yd. hurdles (straight) and 8.13 m. long jump. He was born at Danville, Alabama, on Sept. 12th, 1913 and died on March 31st, 1980.

PACKER, Ann (GB)

Whereas Fanny Blankers-Koen began her sparkling career as an 800 m. runner and found lasting fame as a sprinter, hurdler and jumper, Ann Packer started as a sprinter, hurdler and jumper and found lasting fame as an 800 m. runner. And whereas Fanny was 30 when she achieved Olympic immortality and continued in serious competition for a further eight years, Ann decided to retire immediately after her Olympic success aged only 22.

She can look back upon an extraordinarily varied career. She won the 100 yd. at the 1959 English Schools Championships, took the Women's AAA long jump title (in Mary Rand's absence) in 1960 and gained her first international in that event. Against all odds she reached the 200 m. final at the 1962 European Championships and later that year placed sixth in the Commonwealth Games 80 m. hurdles final and won a silver medal in the relay. In 1963 she moved up to the quarter-mile and, in only her fourth race, burst into the highest world class with 53.4 sec. for 400 m. Finally, in 1964, she added yet another string to her bow by taking up the 800 m.—with astonishing results.

She travelled to Tokyo with only five two-lap races behind her, the main objective being to win the Olympic 400 m. Despite returning a superb 52.2 sec. (a European record) she had to settle for second place in that event behind Betty Cuthbert but three days later she ran in simply inspired fashion to win the 800 m. in the world record time of 2 min. 01.1 sec.

Her best marks were 10.9 sec. for 100 yd., 12.0 sec. (and wind-assisted 11.7 sec.) for 100 m., 23.7 sec. for 200 m., 52.2 sec. for 400 m., 2 min. 01.1 sec. for 800 m., 11.4 sec. for 80 m. hurdles, 1.60 metres high jump, 5.92 metres long jump, and 4,294 point pentathlon (old tables). Ann, who is married to 1962 European 400 m. champion Robbie Brightwell, was born at Moulsford (Berkshire) on March 8th, 1942.

PAN-AMERICAN GAMES

The Pan-American Games were instituted in 1951, the first being held in Buenos Aires. Subsequent venues have been Mexico City (1955), Chicago (1959), Sao Paulo (1963), Winnipeg (1967), Cali (1971), Mexico City (1975) and San Juan, Puerto Rico (1979). Past winners:—

100 Metres sec.
1951 R. Fortun (Cuba) 10.6
1955 R. Richard (USA) 10.3
1959 R. Norton (USA) 10.3
1963 E. Figuerola (Cuba) 10.3
1967 H. Jerome (Canada) 10.2
1971 D. Quarrie (Jamaica) 10.2
1975 S. Leonard (Cuba) 10.15
1979 S. Leonard (Cuba) 10.13

200 Metres sec.
1951 R. Fortun (Cuba) 21.3
1955 R. Richard (USA) 20.7
1959 R. Norton (USA) 20.6
1963 R. Romero (Venezuela) 21.2
1967 J. Carlos (USA) 20.5
1971 D. Quarrie (Jamaica) 19.86
1975 J. Gilkes (Guyana) 20.43
1979 S. Leonard (Cuba) 20.37

400 Metres sec.
1951 M. Whitfield (USA) 47.8
1955 L. Jones (USA) 45.4
1959 G. Kerr (West Indies) 46.1
1963 J. Johnson (USA) 46.7
1967 L. Evans (USA) 44.9
1971 J. Smith (USA) 44.6
1975 R. Ray (USA) 44.45
1979 T. Darden (USA) 45.11

800 Metres min. sec.
1951 M. Whitfield (USA) 1 53.2
1955 A. Sowell (USA) 1 49.7
1959 T. Murphy (USA) 1 49.1
1963 D. Bertoia (Canada) 1 48.3
1967 W. Bell (USA) 1 49.2
1971 K. Swenson (USA) 1 48.0

PAN-AMERICAN GAMES

1975	L. Medina (Cuba)	1	48.0
1979	J. Robinson (USA)	1	46.3

1500 Metres		min.	sec.
1951	B. Ross (USA)	4	00.4
1955	J. Miranda (Argentina)	3	53.2
1959	D. Burleson (USA)	3	49.1
1963	J. Grelle (USA)	3	43.5
1967	T. Von Ruden (USA)	3	43.4
1971	M. Liquori (USA)	3	42.1
1975	A. Waldrop (USA)	3	45.1
1979	D. Paige (USA)	3	40.5

5000 Metres		min.	sec.
1951	R. Bralo (Arg)	14	51.2
1955	O. Suarez (Arg)	15	30.6
1959	W. Dellinger (USA)	14	28.4
1963	O. Suarez (Arg)	14	25.8
1967	V. Nelson (USA)	13	47.4
1971	S. Prefontaine (USA)	13	52.6
1975	D. Tibaduiza (Col)	14	02.0
1979	M. Centrowitz (USA)	14	01.0

10,000 Metres		min.	sec.
1951	C. Stone (USA)	31	08.6
1955	O. Suarez (Arg)	32	42.6
1959	O. Suarez (Arg)	30	17.2
1963	P. McArdle (USA)	29	52.2
1967	V. Nelson (USA)	29	17.4
1971	F. Shorter (USA)	28	50.8
1975	L. Hernandez (Mex)	29	19.4
1979	R. Gomez (Mex)	29	02.4

Marathon		hr. min.	sec.
1951	D. Cabrera (Arg)	2 25	00.2
1955	D. Flores (Guatemala)	2 59	09.2
1959	J. Kelley (USA)	2 27	54.2
1963	F. Negrete (Mexico)	2 27	55.6
1967	A. Boychuk (Canada)	2 22	00.4
1971	F. Shorter (USA)	2 22	40.4
1975	R. Mendoza (Cuba)	2 25	02.8
1979	R. Gonzalez (Cuba)	2 24	09.0

3000 m. Steeplechase		min.	sec.
1951	C. Stone (USA)	9	32.0
1955	G. Sola (Chile)	9	46.8
1959	P. Coleman (USA)	8	56.4
1963	J. Fishback (USA)	9	08.0
1967	C. McCubbins (USA)	8	38.2
1971	M. Manley (USA)	8	42.2
1975	M. Manley (USA)	9	04.4
1979	H. Marsh (USA)	8	43.6

110 Metres Hurdles		sec.
1951	R. Attlesey (USA)	14.0
1955	J. Davis (USA)	14.3
1959	H. Jones (USA)	13.6
1963	B. Lindgren (USA)	13.8
1967	E. McCullouch (USA)	13.4
1971	R. Milburn (USA)	13.4
1975	A. Casanas (Cuba)	13.44
1979	R. Nehemiah (USA)	13.20

400 Metres Hurdles		sec.
1951	J. Aparicio (Colombia)	53.4
1955	J. Culbreath (USA)	51.5
1959	J. Culbreath (USA)	51.2
1963	J. Dyrzka (Arg)	50.2
1967	R. Whitney (USA)	50.7
1971	R. Mann (USA)	49.1
1975	J. King (USA)	49.60
1979	J. Walker (USA)	49.66

4 x 100 Metres		sec.
1951	United States	41.0
1955	United States	40.7
1959	United States	40.4
1963	United States	40.4
1967	United States	39.0
1971	Jamaica	39.2
1975	United States	38.31
1979	United States	38.85

4 x 400 Metres		min.	sec.
1951	United States	3	09.9
1955	United States	3	07.2
1959	The West Indies	3	05.3
1963	United States	3	09.6
1967	United States	3	02.0
1971	United States	3	00.6
1975	United States	3	00.8
1979	United States	3	03.8

High Jump		metres
1951	V. Severns (USA)	1.95
1955	E. Shelton (USA)	2.01
1959	C. Dumas (USA)	2.10
1963	G. Johnson (USA)	2.11
1967	E. Caruthers (USA)	2.19
1971	P. Matzdorf (USA)	2.10
1975	T. Woods (USA)	2.25
1979	F. Jacobs (USA)	2.26

Pole Vault		metres
1951	R. Richards (USA)	4.50
1955	R. Richards (USA)	4.50
1959	D. Bragg (USA)	4.62
1963	D. Tork (USA)	4.90
1967	R. Seagren (USA)	4.90
1971	J. Johnson (USA)	5.33
1975	E. Bell (USA)	5.40
1979	B. Simpson (Can)	5.15

Long Jump		metres
1951	G. Bryan (USA)	7.14
1955	R. Range (USA)	8.03
1959	I. Roberson (USA)	7.97
1963	R. Boston (USA)	8.11
1967	R. Boston (USA)	8.29

1971	A. Robinson (USA)	8.02	1971	R. Wanamaker (USA)	7,648*
1975	J. C. de Oliveira (Braz)	8.19	1975	B. Jenner (USA)	8,045*
1979	J. C. de Oliveira (Braz)	8.18	1979	B. Coffman (USA)	8,078*

1962 tables

Triple Jump — metres
- 1951 A. F. da Silva (Brazil) 15.19
- 1955 A. F. da Silva (Braz) 16.56
- 1959 A. F. da Silva (Braz) 15.90
- 1963 W. Sharpe (USA) 15.15
- 1967 C. Craig (USA) 16.54
- 1971 P. Perez (Cuba) 17.40
- 1975 J. C. de Oliveira (Braz) 17.89
- 1979 J. C. de Oliveira (Braz) 17.27

20 Kilometres Walk — h. min. sec.
- 1963 A. Oakley (Canada) 1 42 43.2
- 1967 R. Laird (USA) 1 33 05.2
- 1971 G. Klopfer (USA) 1 37 30.0
- 1975 D. Bautista (Mex) 1 33 06.0
- 1979 D. Bautista (Mex) 1 28 15.0

Shot — metres
- 1951 J. Fuchs (USA) 17.25
- 1955 P. O'Brien (USA) 17.59
- 1959 P. O'Brien (USA) 19.04
- 1963 D. Davis (USA) 18.52
- 1967 R. Matson (USA) 19.83
- 1971 A. Feuerbach (USA) 19.76
- 1975 B. Pirnie (Canada) 19.28
- 1979 D. Laut (USA) 20.22

50 Kilometres Walk — h. min. sec
- 1951 S. Idanez (Arg) 5 06 06.8
- 1967 L. Young (USA) 4 26 20.8
- 1971 L. Young (USA) 4 38 31.0
- 1975 not held
- 1979 R. Gonzalez (Mex) 4 05 17.0

Women's Events

60 Metres — sec.
- 1955 B. Diaz (Cuba) 7.5
- 1959 I. Daniels (USA) 7.4

Discus — metres
- 1951 J. Fuchs (USA) 48.90
- 1955 F. Gordien (USA) 53.10
- 1959 A. Oerter (USA) 58.12
- 1963 R. Humphreys (USA) 57.82
- 1967 G. Carlsen (USA) 57.50
- 1971 R. Drescher (USA) 62.26
- 1975 J. Powell (USA) 62.36
- 1979 M. Wilkins (USA) 63.30

100 Metres — sec.
- 1951 J. Sanchez (Peru) 12.2
- 1955 B. Jones (USA) 11.5
- 1959 L. Williams (USA) 12.1
- 1963 E. McGuire (USA) 11.5
- 1967 B. Ferrell (USA) 11.5
- 1971 I. Davis (USA) 11.2
- 1975 P. Jiles (USA) 11.38
- 1979 E. Ashford (USA) 11.07

Hammer — metres
- 1951 G. Ortiz (Arg) 48.04
- 1955 R. Backus (USA) 54.90
- 1959 A. Hall (USA) 59.70
- 1963 A. Hall (USA) 62.74
- 1967 T. Gage (USA) 65.32
- 1971 A. Hall (USA) 65.84
- 1975 L. Hart (USA) 66.56
- 1979 S. Nielsen (Can) 69.64

200 Metres — sec.
- 1951 J. Patton (USA) 25.3
- 1959 L. Williams (USA) 24.2
- 1963 V. Brown (USA) 23.9
- 1967 W. Tyus (USA) 23.7
- 1971 S. Berto (Canada) 23.5
- 1975 C. Cheeseborough (USA) 22.77
- 1979 E. Ashford (USA) 22.24

Javelin — metres
- 1951 R. Heber (Arg) 68.08
- 1955 F. Held (USA) 69.76
- 1959 B. Quist (USA) 70.50
- 1963 D. Studney (USA) 75.60
- 1967 F. Covelli (USA) 74.28
- 1971 C. Feldmann (USA) 81.52
- 1975 S. Colson (USA) 83.82
- 1979 D. Atwood (USA) 84.16

400 Metres — sec.
- 1971 M. Neufville (Jamaica) 52.3
- 1975 J. Yakubowich (Canada) 51.62
- 1979 S. Dabney (USA) 51.81

800 Metres — min. sec.
- 1963 A. Hoffman (Canada) 2 10.2
- 1967 M. Manning (USA) 2 02.3
- 1971 A. Hoffman (Canada) 2 05.5
- 1975 K. Weston (USA) 2 04.9
- 1979 E. Kelley (USA) 2 01.2

Decathlon (1950 Tables) — Pts.
- 1951 H. Figueroa (Chile) 6,610
- 1955 R. Johnson (USA) 7.985
- 1959 D. Edstrom (USA) 7,245
- 1963 J. D. Martin (USA) 7.335
- 1967 W. Toomey (USA) 8,044*

1500 Metres — min. sec.
- 1975 J. Merrill (USA) 4 18.3
- 1979 M. Decker (USA) 4 05.7

3000 Metres	min. sec.
1979 J. Merrill (USA)	8 53.6

80 Metres Hurdles	sec.
1951 E. Gaete (Chile)	11.9
1955 E. Gaete (Chile)	11.7
1959 B. Diaz (Cuba)	11.2
1963 J. A. Terry (USA)	11.3
1967 C. Sherrard (USA)	10.8

100 Metres Hurdles	sec.
1971 P. Johnson (USA)	13.1
1975 E. Noeding (Peru)	13.56
1979 D. La Plante (USA)	12.90

4 x 100 Metres	sec.
1951 United States	48.7
1955 United States	47.0
1959 United States	46.4
1963 United States	45.6
1967 Cuba	44.6
1971 United States	44.5
1975 United States	42.90
1979 United States	43.30

4 x 400 Metres	min. sec.
1971 United States	3 32.4
1975 Canada	3 30.4
1979 United States	3 29.4

High Jump	metres
1951 J. Sandiford (Ecuador)	1.46
1955 M. McDaniel (USA)	1.68
1959 A. Flynn (USA)	1.61
1963 E. Montgomery (USA)	1.68
1967 E. Montgomery (USA)	1.78
1971 D. Brill (Canada)	1.85
1975 J. Huntley (USA)	1.89
1979 L. Ritter (USA)	1.93

Long Jump	metres
1951 B. Kretschmer (Chile)	5.42
1959 A. Smith (USA)	5.73
1963 W. White (USA)	6.15
1967 I. Martinez (Cuba)	6.33
1971 B. Eisler (Canada)	6.43
1975 A. Alexander (Cuba)	6.63
1979 K. McMillan (USA)	6.46

Shot	metres
1951 I. de Preiss (Arg)	12.45
1959 E. Brown (USA)	14.68
1963 N. McCredie (Can)	15.32
1967 N. McCredie (Can)	15.18
1971 L. Graham (USA)	15.75
1975 M. Sarria (Cuba)	18.03
1979 M. Sarria (Cuba)	18.81

Discus	metres
1951 I. de Preiss (Arg)	38.54
1955 I. Pfuller (Arg)	43.18
1959 E. Brown (USA)	49.30
1963 N. McCredie (Can)	50.18
1967 C. Moseke (USA)	49.24
1971 C. Romero (Cuba)	57.20
1975 C. Romero (Cuba)	60.16
1979 C. Romero (Cuba)	60.58

Javelin	metres
1951 H. Garcia (Mex)	39.44
1955 K. Anderson (USA)	49.14
1959 M. Ahrens (Chile)	45.38
1963 M. Ahrens (Chile)	49.92
1967 B. Friedrich (USA)	53.26
1971 A. Nunez (Cuba)	54.00
1975 S. Calvert (USA)	54.70
1979 M. Colon (Cuba)	62.30

Pentathlon	Pts.
1967* P. Winslow (USA)	4860
1971 D. Van Kiekebelt (Can)	4290
1975 D. Konihowski (Can)	4673
1979 D. Konihowski (Can)	4605

* Old tables

PARAGI, Ferenc (Hungary)

One of the early-season sensations of 1980 was the massively strong Hungarian javelin thrower Ferenc Paragi. He started off a spree of world records in the field events in Europe when, as early as April, he reached the phenomenal distance of 96.72 metres to add over two metres to the record set at the 1976 Olympics by his compatriot Miklos Nemeth . . . and renew calls for the amending of javelin specifications on the grounds of safety. Paragi's monster throw was no flash in the pan, for in an international match in Wales the following month he again exceeded Nemeth's mark with 96.20 metres.

However, a knee injury ruined his Olympic hopes in Moscow. He led the qualifiers with a throw of 88.76 metres, but in the final he was unable to reach even 80 metres and was buried in tenth place. Thus the major competitive record of Paragi, who back in 1972 became the first European junior to top 80 metres, remains unimpressive; he failed to make the the final at the 1976 Olympics and was ninth in the 1978 European Championships.

Annual progress: 1968—59.68 m.; 1969—67.70; 1970—70.06; 1971—74.36; 1972—80.06; 1973—81.24; 1974—82.02; 1975—89.92; 1976—87.98; 1977—91.92; 1978—86.04; 1979—92.14; 1980—96.72. He was born in Budapest on Aug. 21st, 1953.

PENTATHLON

The pentathlon is a five-event test of all-round ability. The men's version comprises the long jump, javelin, 200 m., discus and 1500 m. in that order on one day. The event is staged occasionally in West Germany, the Soviet Union and United States but is rarely held elsewhere. Scoring is on the same basis as the decathlon.

The pentathlon was for long a most popular women's event, and was introduced into the Olympic schedule in 1964. The events were 100 m. hurdles, shot, high jump, long jump, and 800 m. (re-placing the 200 m. held prior to 1977).

Alexandra Chudina broke the world record four times between 1949 and 1955; Galina Bystrova, European champion in 1958 and 1962, pushed the record up twice in 1957 and 1958; and from 1959 to 1966 the event was controlled by Irina Press, the inaugural Olympic champion in 1964. All three athletes were from the USSR.

The event was modified in 1969 when the 100 m. hurdles (2ft. 9in.) replaced the 80 m. hurdles (2ft. 6in.), and there was a further change in scoring when revised points tables came into force in 1972. Mary Peters (GB and NI) broke all previous records with her score of 4801 pts. in winning the 1972 Olympic title. The 1980 Olympic version of the event was won by Nadyezhda Tkachenko (USSR) with a world record 5083 pts. As from 1981, the pentathlon was replaced as the standard women's all-round test by the seven-event heptathlon.

See also under BLANKERS-KOEN, FANNY; PETERS, MARY; RAND, MARY; ROSENDAHL, HEIDE; and TKACHENKO, NADYEZHDA.

PETERS, Jim (GB)

Jim Peters was largely responsible for the radical advance in marathon times during the 1950s. Until he appeared on the scene the marathon was regarded as an ultra-long distance race in which one's resources had to be very carefully husbanded. Peters, by virtue of his spartan training regime and forceful racing tactics, did for marathon running what Emil Zatopek did for long distance track racing a few years earlier.

Between 1952 and 1954 he lowered the world's best time of 2 hr. 25 min. 39 sec. by eight minutes, and his fastest time of 2 hr. 17 min. 39.4 sec. represented an average of about 5¼ minutes per mile—which only a few years earlier was considered good speed for a 10 miles race.

Peters had two careers. In 1946 he won the AAA 6 mi., next year added the 10 mi. title and in 1948 (aged 29) clocked 30 min. 07.0 sec. for 6 mi. and placed ninth in the Olympic 10,000 m.

Little was heard of him in the next two seasons but in 1951, coached by "Johnny" Johnston, he burst back as a marathon runner, winning the Windsor to Chiswick event in the British record time of 2 hr. 29 min. 24 sec. In 1952 he travelled to Helsinki as favourite after setting his first "world record" of 2 hr. 20 min. 42.2 sec., but in the Olympics—after leading for about 10 miles—he was forced out of the race by cramp at 20 miles while in fourth place.

He carried all before him in 1953: twice he lowered the world's best (2:18:40.2 and 2:18:34.8), he captained England's cross-country team, broke Walter George's 69-year-old English hour record and represented Britain on the track.

His final season, 1954, was notable for his final record-shattering run of 2 hr. 17 min. 39.4 sec. and his tragic experience in the Commonwealth Games at Vancouver. Refusing to compromise with the hot, humid conditions he entered the stadium with a 17 minutes lead—but was unable to complete those last few hundred yards, so weak was he. Later he received a special gold medal from the Duke of Edinburgh inscribed "To J. Peters as a token of admiration for a most gallant marathon runner."

His best track marks included 14 min. 09.8 sec. for 3 mi. and 28 min.

57.8 sec. for 6 mi. He was born at Homerton (London), on Oct. 24th, 1918.

PETERS, Mary (GB & NI)

After 17 years of pentathlon competition, Mary Peters " overnight " became one of the world's great sports stars and a household name throughout the British Isles when in Munich in 1972 she joined the immortals by winning an Olympic title with a world record performance—in the tradition established by Britain's only previous female Olympic champions. Mary Rand and Ann Packer.

Her story is one of perseverance. Overshadowed as a pentathlete by Mary Rand (now Mrs. Bill Toomey) and never quite making world class as a shot-putter, her career might well have ended after a disappointing showing at the 1968 Olympics where, hampered by an injured ankle, she placed 9th. She was already 29 and had she quit then she would have been remembered as a very good and big hearted athlete (4th in the 1964 Olympics) but not truly a great one.

Instead she took off 1969 in order to regain her zest and at her fourth Commonwealth Games, in 1970, she won gold medals in both the shot and pentathlon — representing Northern Ireland. Her score of 5,148 pts. (4,524 on the new tables) re-established her among the world's elite after a gap of six years.

Mary again passed up competition in 1971, but the following indoor season saw her transformed as a high jumper. Previously just a competent straddle jumper with a best of 1.67 metres, she was now a Fosbury-flopper of close to world class. This dramatic improvement was worth over 100 pts. in that one event and was the key to her Olympic pentathlon aspirations.

During the Olympic build-up period she raised her UK record to 4,630 pts., which ranked her fifth among the pentathlon contenders. From the very first event in Munich it was apparent she was in superb form and afraid of nobody. She clocked 13.3 sec. for the hurdles, her fastest without wind assistance; put the shot 16.20 metres which was only a few inches below her UK record; and ended the first day with an inspired high jump of 1.82 metres, another personal best. Her overnight score of 2,969 pts., a " world record ", gave her a lead of 97 pts.

On the second day she reached a near personal best long jump of 5.98 metres and just held off the tremendous challenge of Heide Rosendahl (W. Germany) by clocking her fastest ever 200 m. time of 24.1 sec. Her final score of 4,801 pts. (5,430 on the old tables), a world record, was ten points more than Rosendahl's.

Her best marks were 11.1 sec. for 100 yd., 24.1 sec. for 200 m., 11.0 sec. for 80 m. hurdles, 13.3 sec. for 100 m. hurdles (and 13.1 sec. wind assisted), 1.82 metres high jump, 6.04 metres long jump, 16.40 metres shot (indoors), 38.72 metres discus (standing throw) and 4,801 pentathlon. The British women's team manager at the 1980 Olympics, she was born at Halewood (Lancs) on July 6th, 1939.

PETKOVA, Maria (Bulgaria)

See under VERGOVA, MARIA.

PIRIE, Gordon (GB)

While Jim Peters was transforming the face of marathon running, his young countryman Gordon Pirie was leading British track distance running from the depths into which it had plunged following Sydney Wooderson's retirement to unprecedented heights.

He reached top class in 1951, winning his first AAA 6 mi. title in the English record time of 29 min. 32.0 sec. He broke more national records in 1952 but was not quite ready for success in Olympic competition and placed seventh in the 10,000 and fourth in the 5000 m.

In 1953, during a fabulously successful season, he captured the first of his three successive English cross-country titles, set a 6 mi. world record of 28 min. 19.4 sec., helped a British team to a world 4 x 1500 m. relay record and even defeated America's star miler Wes Santee in 4 min. 06.8 sec. He predicted that one day he would run 5000 m. in 13 min. 40 sec., although the world record then existing stood at 13 min. 58.2 sec. Statements like this infuriated his detractors—but three years later he seized the record with a time of 13 min. 36.8 sec. in defeating Vladimir Kuts.

Within five days of this remarkable achievement he tied the 3000 m. world record of 7 min. 55.6 sec. and won over 1500 m. in 3 min. 43.7 sec. against Klaus Richtzenhain, the German who was destined to win the Olympic silver medal later in the year. Pirie reduced the 3000 m. mark to 7 min. 52.8 sec. against the combined forces of the Hungarian trio of Istvan Rozsavolgyi, Sandor Iharos and Laszlo Tabori.

At the Olympics, though, Kuts avenged his earlier defeat. He took both the 5000 and 10,000 m., with Pirie finishing eighth in the longer event (after cracking in the last mile following a murderous duel) and second in the 5000 m. Pirie's record was somewhat spotty in the seasons that followed but in 1960 he recaptured his dashing form of old, only to feature in one of the most sensational upsets in track history by failing even to qualify for the Olympic 5000 m. final. He came back for one last season in 1961 and succeeded in breaking the British 3 mi. record once more and turning in his fastest 1500 m. Later he became a professional and was reinstated in 1980 to allow him to compete as a veteran. Late that year he ran a marathon in 2 hr. 49 min. 02 sec.

His best marks included 1 min. 53.0 sec. for 880 yd., 3 min. 42.5 sec. for 1500 m., 3 min. 59.9 sec. for the mile, 5 min. 09.8 sec. for 2000 m., 7 min. 52.8 sec. for 3000 m., 8 min. 39.0 sec. for 2 mi., 13 min. 16.4 sec. for 3 mi., 13 min. 36.8 sec. for 5000 m., 28 min. 09.6 sec. for 6 mi., 29 min. 15.2 sec. for 10,000 m. 35,659 metres in two hours, and 3000 m. steeplechase in 9 min. 06.6 sec. Pirie, who married the international sprinter Shirley Hampton in 1956, was born in Leeds on Feb. 10th, 1931.

POLE VAULT

Pole vaulting was practised by King Henry VIII and was well established as a gymnastic event by the end of the 18th century in England and Germany. Instances of competitive vaulting date from 1843 at Penrith (Cumbria)

For some 25 years there were two schools of vaulting in existence: the English (Ulverston) style entailed the athlete climbing up the heavy ash, cedar or hickory pole and levering himself over the bar in a sitting position, while the method used elsewhere was similar to that practised today in that the athlete was forbidden to move his upper hand once he had left the ground.

The heavy poles in use in the 19th century were equipped with three iron spikes in the base. Light bamboo poles were introduced from Japan in the early years of this century. In place of spikes, the base of the pole was equipped with a plug that fitted into a box sunk level with the ground. The next development was the advent of aluminium poles and then of the fibre-glass models that have revolutionised the event.

Apart from knocking off the bar, a failure is registered when the athlete places his lower hand above the upper one or moves the upper hand higher on the pole after leaving the ground, when he leaves the ground for the purpose of making a vault and fails to clear the bar, or when before taking off he touches with any part of his body or with the pole the ground beyond the vertical plane of the upper part of the stopboard. It is not counted a failure if the athlete's pole breaks while making an attempt.

The IAAF rule decrees that "the pole may be of any material or combination of materials and of any length or diameter, but the basic surface must be smooth."

In the years when both styles were flourishing, the slightly greater heights were achieved by the British vaulters, most of whom hailed from the Lake District. Edwin Woodburn (GB) was the first to exceed 11 ft. (3.35 metres) in 1876, seven years before Hugh Baxter (USA) did so with the fixed hand style. When the English technique fell into disuse the record stood to the credit of Richard Dickinson at 3.58 metres in 1891. Marc Wright (USA) was the first to vault over 4 metres, in 1912.

American supremacy was broken in the early 1920s by Charles Hoff (Norway), who held the world record from 1922 to 1927 with a best of 4.25 metres. A foot injury prevented his challenging for the 1924 Olympic title —though he managed to reach the 800 m. final!

The 1937 season was particularly notable, the Americans Earle Meadows and William Sefton between them lifting the record six times. Finally the "Heavenly Twins," as they were dubbed, tied at 4.54 metres and were prevented from trying 15 feet (4.57 metres) because the bar could not be raised any higher.

The first 15-footer was posted by Cornelius Warmerdam (USA) in 1940. Although no other man cleared 15 ft. until 1951 Warmerdam totalled 43 such clearances during the war years and his final world marks of 4.77 metres (outdoors) and 4.79 metres (indoors) lasted many years. The next great figure was Bob Richards (USA), who never beat Warmerdam's records but became the first vaulter successfully to defend his Olympic title.

Bob Gutowski (USA), who died while in his prime, and the 1960 Olympic champion Don Bragg (USA) led the way to 16 feet (4.87 m.)—an honour that befell John Uelses, a German-born American, in 1962. Uelses used a glass pole, as do all the world's leading vaulters now, and the record has been climbing steeply since athletes have been learning to take full advantage of the glass pole's catapult-like properties. During 1963 the record rose ten times in the hands of Americans Brian Sternberg (first to clear 5 metres) whose career was cut short when he suffered a grave injury while training, and John Pennel, the inaugural 17-footer (5.18 metres). Chris Papanicolaou (Greece) opened the 18 feet (5.48 metres) era in 1970, and by 1980 the record stood at 5.78 metres by Wladyslaw Kozakiewicz of Poland.

Britain's record in this event has been modest during this century. Only four vaulters have achieved anything of international significance: Richard Webster, who tied with ten others for sixth place in the 1936 Olympics; Geoff Elliott, the Commonwealth champion in 1954 and 1958; Mike Bull, of Northern Ireland, who won the 1970 Commonwealth title and was the first Briton to top 5 metres; and Brian Hooper, twice an Olympic finalist and UK record holder at 5.59 metres.

See also under KOZAKIEWICZ, WLADYSLAW and WARMERDAM, CORNELIUS.

PROFESSIONAL ATHLETICS

Until an American-organised circuit began operations in 1973, professional athletics—particularly popular during much of the 19th century—had dwindled into insignificance. However, the International Track Association, by signing up such big names as Jim Ryun, Randy Matson, Lee Evans and Bob Seagren, hoped to rekindle the public's interest in this side of the sport. The novelty quickly wore off, and following a curtailed season in 1976 the ITA operation was wound up. In view of the increasingly lucrative pickings to be made 'under the counter' in so-called amateur competition, the organisation had been unable to recruit more recent topliners. In the words of one big star approached: "I just can't afford to turn professional!"

Only one professional world record is superior to the amateur equivalent: the 22.86 metres shot put by Brian Oldfield (USA) in 1975.

Discussions by governing bodies of 'open' athletics, which would involve cash prizes and other financial benefits for athletes, were taking place in 1981.

QUARRIE, Don (Jamaica)

A precocious sprint talent, Don Quarrie had won six important gold medals by the time he was 20. He won the 100 m. and 200 m. and was a member of the victorious Jamaican 4 x 100 m. relay team at both the 1970 Commonwealth and 1971 Pan-American Games. His performance in the Pan-Am Games at Cali (Colombia) was all the more notable for his time in the 200 m. Taking half a second off his previous fastest, he clocked the second fastest ever electrically timed 200 m. of 19.86 sec.

His first two Olympics brought Quarrie disappointment. In 1968, as a 17-year-old who had already run 10.3 sec. for 100 m., he injured himself in training in Mexico City and was unable to take his place in the relay team; while in 1972 he pulled a muscle during his 200 m. semi-final.

Happily all went well at the Montreal Olympics, for after finishing second in the 100 m. a mere 1/100th sec. behind Hasely Crawford, he triumphed in his parade event, the 200 m. He had, in 1974, retained both his individual titles at the Commonwealth Games.

Quarrie picked up yet another gold medal when defeating Allan Wells for the 1978 Commonwealth 100 m. title but had to forfeit the 200 m. (won by Wells) when suffering a mid-race attack of cramp in the semi-finals. He lost his Olympic 200 m. title also in 1980, but not without a spirited defence as he placed third behind Pietro Mennea and Wells.

A former co-holder of hand-timed world records for 100 m. (9.9 sec.) 200 m. (19.8 sec.) and 220 yd. (19.9 sec.), his best marks are 10.07 sec. for 100 m. and 19.86 sec. for 200 m. He was born in Kingston (where a statue has been erected in his honour) on Feb. 25th, 1951.

RABSZTYN, Grazyna (Poland)

On the basis of world records and fast times generally, Grazyna Rabsztyn ranks as one of the all-time greats of women's hurdling, but in terms of placings in major championships the Pole has been a great disappointment.

Victory in the 1970 European Junior 100 m. hurdles championship got her career off to a good start, but a decade later that remained her only medal in the most important outdoor championships. At the Olympics she finished 8th (1972), 5th (1976) and 5th (1980), despite being favourite on the last two occasions, and her record in the European Championships has been worse: 8th in 1974 and a disqualification in 1978. She has had her moments—as when she won the European indoor title three years running (1974–76) and the World Cup races of 1977 and 1979—but she has tended to be somewhat disaster-prone on the supreme occasions.

In the stopwatch department she has reigned supreme for three seasons. She set her first world record, 12.48 sec., in 1978; she duplicated that time in 1979 and reduced it to 12.36 sec. in 1980. The brilliance of her hurdling technique can be gauged from the fact that her fastest 100 m. time on the flat is 11.42 sec. Younger sister Elzbieta Rabsztyn is also a world-class hurdler, with a best of 12.80 sec.

Annual progress: 1967—13.4 (80 m.); 1968—11.0 (80 m.); 1969—13.9; 1970—13.6; 1971—13.2; 1972—12.7; 1973—12.7; 1974—13.1; 1975—12.82; 1976—12.69; 1977—12.70; 1978—12.48; 1979—12.48; 1980—12.36. She was born at Wroclaw on Sept. 20th, 1952.

RAND, Mary (GB)

" The greatest thing of all would be to do a world record at the Olympics —like Herb Elliott, for instance. That would be wonderful. Needless to say, that's what I would like to do in Tokyo!" Those were the words of Mary Rand when interviewed by the author on Sept. 22nd, 1964. Twenty-two days later her hopes were translated into deeds in Tokyo's Olympic stadium . . . victory, a world record of 6.76 metres, the greatest series of jumps on record (the *worst* of her six leaps was 6.56 metres), the first Olympic gold medal to be won by a British woman athlete. And that was by no means all, for later in the Games she performed brilliantly in the pentathlon for a silver medal and second place on the world all-time list with 5,035 points, and later still contributed to the British team's third place in the 4 x 100m. relay.

Long before her marriage she had achieved fame as Mary Bignal. She set her first national record in the pentathlon (4,046 pts.) as early as 1957, when she was 17. Next year she gained a silver medal in the Commonwealth Games long jump and finished a creditable seventh in the European pentathlon championship.

An attack of nerves ruined her chances in the 1960 Olympic long jump. She led the qualifiers with a magnificent UK record of 6.33 metres but in the final placed no higher than ninth—one of the very rare occasions on which she failed to do herself justice in major competition. She made partial amends by unexpectedly taking fourth place in the hurdles.

Only a few months after the birth of her daughter in 1962 she made a remarkable comeback to earn the bronze medal in the European long jump. She enjoyed a glorious season in 1963 (including a share in a world relay record) and reached the summit of athletic endeavour in 1964.

She won the 1966 Commonwealth long jump title but was frustrated by injury in her attempt to make the British Olympic team in 1968 and retired. Her second marriage, to Olympic decathlon champion Bill Toomey (USA), took place in 1969.

Best marks: 10.6 sec. for 100yd., 11.7 sec. for 100m., 23.9 (and wind-assisted 23.6) for 200m., 56.5 sec. for 440 yd., 10.8 sec. for 80m. hurdles, 13.4 sec. (and 13.3 sec. wind-assisted) for 100m. hurdles, 1.72 metres high jump, 6.76 metres long jump, 12.25 metres shot and 5,035 pt. pentathlon (old tables). She was born at Wells, Somerset, on Feb. 10th, 1940.

RASHCHUPKIN, Viktor (USSR)

A relative nonentity by top world standards, Viktor Rashchupkin kept his nerve while all around were losing theirs and chose the perfect moment to deliver the longest discus throw of his life: the Olympic final in Moscow. He was holding fourth place until, with his fourth throw, he reached 66.64 metres to take the lead. The mark survived, and Rashchupkin was Olympic champion.

A slow developer who between 1973 and 1979 had improved only from 60.00 metres to 64.28 metres, he had not previously competed in a major international championship. His best performance before the Olympics was 65.98 metres, which had ranked him only eighth among those competing in Moscow.

A 19.08 metres shot putter, he has progressed thus with the discus: 1968 —41.00 m.; 1969—45.52; 1970—50.22; 1971—47.90; 1972—54.20; 1973—60.00; 1974—60.24; 1975—61.74; 1976—61.94; 1977—61.36; 1978—63.32; 1979—64.28; 1980—66.64. He was born at Kamensk-Uralsk on Oct. 16th, 1950.

RECORDS

See APPENDIX.

RELAYS

There are nine relay events included in the IAAF's world record schedule —ranging from 4 x 100 m. to 4 x 1500 m. for men and 4 x 800 m. for women. Olympic, European and Commonwealth championships are staged at 4 x 100 m. and 4 x 400 m.

Lines are drawn across the track to mark the distances of the stages and to denote the scratch line. Other lines are drawn 10 m. before and after the scratch line, denoting the take-over zone within which the baton must be passed. Under a rule brought into force in 1963, in races up to 4 x 200 m. the second, third and fourth runners may start running up to 10 m. outside the take-over zone. The passing of the baton is completed at the moment it is in the hand of the receiving runner only.

The baton, which is passed from athlete to athlete, must be carried in the hand throughout the race. Should it be dropped, it must be recovered by the athlete who dropped it. Disqualification is incurred when the baton is passed outside the 20 m. take-over zone.

The first relay race recorded was a two miles event at Berkeley, California, on Nov. 17th, 1883, nearly 12 years before the first relay held in Britain. Relay events entered the Olympic programme from 1908.

RIEHM, Karl-Hans (West Germany)

Surely the greatest hammer thrower never to win an Olympic medal, Karl-Hans Riehm first made a big impact on the event in 1975 when he became the first athlete ever to break the previous world record six times in a single competition. With the record standing at 76.66 metres, Riehm opened with 76.70 metres and followed with 77.56, 77.10, 78.50, 77.16 and 77.28 metres. Later in the season he triumphed in the European Cup Final but the following year he had to give best to the Soviet trio of throwers in the Montreal Olympics, finishing fourth. However, he came back into his own in 1977 when he topped the world rankings as well as filling first place in both the European Cup and World Cup.

In 1978 he was foiled in his bid to be the world's first 80-metre thrower by Boris Zaichuk (USSR), but later seized the world record with a toss of 80.32 metres, only to end up third in a close fought competition at the European Championships. A third European Cup victory came his way in 1979 but Riehm's big chance for Olympic glory came to nought in 1980 when West Germany boycotted the Moscow Games. Whether he would have beaten Yuriy Sedykh who, on the big day, set a tremendous new world record of 81.80 metres, is open to question, but Riehm—who himself registered a personal best of 80.80 metres the day before the Olympic final—did defeat Sedykh in both their clashes after the Olympics and went through the season undefeated.

His annual progress: 1967—52.46 m.; 1968—57.00; 1969—60.38; 1970—64.50; 1971—70.22; 1972—73.92; 1973—73.98; 1974—71.10; 1975—78.50; 1976—78.52; 1977—77.60; 1978—80.32; 1979—79.82; 1980—80.80. He was born at Konz on May 31st, 1951.

ROELANTS, Gaston (Belgium)

Until 1972 it was unusual for Ron Clarke to lose a world record; yet in Oct. 1966 Gaston Roelants slashed over a minute off the Australian's figures for 20,000m. and carried on to add over 400 metres to his one hour record!

It is as a steeplechaser, though, that he is best known. Famed for his front running, Roelants was a runaway winner of the 1962 European title after having placed fourth at the 1960 Olympics. He scored another great victory at the 1964 Olympics but was defeated at the 1966 European Championships, thus terminating an unbeaten steeplechase record stretching back all of five years. He was the first to run the distance inside 8¼ minutes.

On the flat, Roelants is a former European 10,000m. record holder, and in 1972—the year in which he won his fourth International Cross-Country Championship—he broke his own world records for 20,000m. and the hour. As a marathon runner he won European medals in 1969 and 1974. In 1977 he won five World Masters (Veterans) titles and set an exceptional world age-40 steeplechase best of 8 min. 41.5 sec.

Best marks: 3 min. 44.4 sec. for 1500m., 7 min. 48.6 sec. for 3000m., 13 min. 34.6 sec. for 5000m., 28 min. 03.8 sec. for 10,000m., 57 min. 44.4 sec. for 20,000 m., 20,784 metres in the hour, 8 min. 26.4 sec. for the steeplechase, and 2 hr. 16 min. 30 sec. for the marathon. He was born at Opvelp on Feb. 5th, 1937.

RONO, Henry (Kenya)

A member of the Nandi sub-group of the Kalenjin tribe which has produced so many great runners, Kipwambok (but known as Henry) Rono accomplished in the space of less than three months in 1978 what no athlete before him had ever done . . . he set world records for 3000, 5000, 10,000 m. and steeplechase. By smashing the previous marks, he made nonsense of the claims of some of the sport's academics that records, at least in the men's events, were now so close to the ultimate in human endeavour that if they were broken at all it would be by very small margins.

Record number one came at Berkeley on April 8th when, competing for Washington State University, he slashed 4.5 sec. from Dick Quax's 5000 m. figures with 13 min. 08.4 sec. His kilometre splits were 2:41.4, 2:37.4, 2:36.5, 2:39.4 and 2:33.7. Next he turned his attention to the steeplechase and in Seattle on May 13th, despite windy conditions and none too efficient a hurdling technique, he clocked 8 min. 05.4 sec. (kilometres of 2:42.0, 2:42.8 and 2:40.6) to carve 2.6 sec. from Anders Garderud's time. Over in Europe he removed 8.2 sec. from the 10,000 m. record held by his compatriot Samson Kimobwa with 27 min. 22.4 sec. in Vienna on June 11th, covering the first half of the race in 13 min. 48.2 sec. and the second in a remarkable 13 min. 34.2 sec.—a time which would have constituted a world 5000 m. record only 13 years earlier! Finally, in Oslo on June 27th, he relieved Brendan Foster of the 3000 m. record, running 3.1 sec. faster at 7 min. 32.1 sec. Again he achieved a 'negative split' (i.e. ran the second half faster than the first) for after clocking 3 min. 49.5 sec. at halfway he ripped through the second 1500 m. in a personal best of 3 min. 42.6 sec., taking under four minutes for the last mile of the race!

Those four runs alone would qualify Rono for a place in any pantheon of all-time great athletes, but in addition he was unpressed in gaining the 5000 m. and steeplechase double at both the African and Commonwealth Games, and he went unbeaten in 31 outdoor races in 1978, including a half-marathon victory (64 min. 46 sec.) over Bill Rodgers (USA).

Rono, who was inspired to become

an athlete by Kip Keino, was born and raised at an altitude of 6000 ft., a built-in physiological advantage for a distance runner. He first reached international standard in 1976 and would have competed in the Montreal Olympic steeplechase but for the African withdrawal. He missed out again in 1980 when Kenya boycotted the Moscow Games, although illness and injuries in any case have hampered his attempts to regain that breathtaking form of 1978.

In addition to the world records, his best marks are 3 min. 43.1 sec. for 1500 m. and 4 min. 00.9 sec. for the mile (although unofficially faster during the 3000 m. world record). Annual progress at 5000 m., 10,000 m. and steeplechase: 1975—13:37.0, 28:58.0, 8:34.4; 1976—13:30.8, 8:29.0; 1977—13:22.1, 27:37.1, 8:31.1; 1978—13:08.4, 27:22.4, 8:05.4; 1979—13:19.7; 8:18.0; 1980—13:19.8, 27:31.4, 8:37.4. He was born at Kaprirsang in the Nandi Hills on Feb. 12th, 1952.

ROSENDAHL, Heide
(West Germany)

Few could have begrudged Heide Rosendahl her success at the Munich Olympics. The greatest long jumper in the world and one of the finest all-rounders, she had been plagued by misfortune on several major occasions. All she had to show in terms of gold medals for several years of brilliant endeavour was the 1971 European pentathlon crown.

She gave an early glimpse of her potential when, aged 19, she placed 2nd in the 1966 European pentathlon only 22 pts. behind the winner, but she was right out of luck at the 1968 Olympics—illness reduced her to 8th in the long jump and after pulling a muscle warming up she wasn't even able to start in the pentathlon. Another setback came at the 1969 European Championships; the West German team withdrew from all individual events as a protest against Jurgen May being ruled ineligible to run for West Germany.

A momentous season in 1970 was capped by a world record long jump of 6.84 metres and the following year she gained that elusive gold medal. Her luck was turning and at the 1972 Olympics she endeared herself still further with an adoring public. After winning the long jump she ran Mary Peters to ten points in the pentathlon, breaking the former world record herself, and on the anchor leg of the 4 x 100 m. relay she outpaced East Germany's Renate Stecher to bring West Germany in first in world record equalling time. Two golds and a silver!

The daughter of a German discus champion, Heide can point to a staggering range of personal bests: 11.3 sec. (11.2 sec. wind assisted) 100 m., 22.96 sec. 200 m., 13.1 sec. 100 m. hurdles, 1.70 metres high jump, 6.84 metres long jump (and over 7 metres from take-off to landing), 14.27 metres shot, 48.18 metres javelin and 4,791 pts. pentathlon. She was born at Huckeswagen on Feb. 14th, 1947.

ROSSLEY, Karin
(East Germany)

In the brief history of women's 400 m. hurdling, the name of Karin Rossley (née Regel) looms large. She it was who won the first ever major international race at the distance, at the 1977 European Cup Final. Aged 20 and running the event for only the third time in her life, she set a world record of 55.63 sec. into the bargain. Before her emergence as a hurdler she had been a good, though not outstanding, 400 m. flat runner who ranked 11th on the East German list for 1976 with 52.21 sec.

In 1978 the women's 400 m. hurdles was added to the European Championships programme, and although she improved to 55.36 sec. Rossley finished third as Tatyana Zelentsova (USSR) captured the title in a world record 54.89 sec. Another Soviet athlete, Marina Makeyeva (who had lowered the record to 54.78 sec. the previous week), beat her in the 1979 European Cup Final, but Rossley reclaimed number one spot in 1980 when she smashed that world record by a full half second with 54.28 sec. Injury caused her to miss the IAAF World Championship (staged in lieu of an Olympic event) later in the season.

Her best flat times are 11.88 sec. for 100 m., 23.67 sec. for 200 m., 51.31 sec. for 400 m. and 2 min. 10.2 sec.

for 800 m. Annual progress in the hurdles: 1977—55.63; 1978—55.36; 1979—55.01; 1980—54.28. She was born at Cottbus on April 5th, 1957.

RUDOLPH, Wilma (USA)

Born with polio, it was not until she was twelve that she was able to dispense with a steel brace on her right leg. Yet at 16 Wilma Rudolph won a bronze medal as a member of the United States sprint relay team at the Melbourne Olympics and four years later she developed into the fastest female runner up till that time.

Her speed, grace and three gold medals combined to make her the outstanding personality of the 1960 Olympic Games. She had come to Rome as world record holder for 200 m. (22.9 sec.) but something of an unknown quantity though by no means a novice. She won both individual sprints with some three metres to spare, her time for the 100 m. (with the following wind just over the permissible limit) being what was then considered a phenomenal 11.0 sec. (or 11.18 sec. on electrical timing).

The following year she gained sole possession of the 100 m. world record with a time of 11.2 sec. The tall, slim American did not run the 200 metres after 1960 and she announced her retirement in 1964. She was born at Clarksville, Tennessee, on June 23rd, 1940—the twentieth of a family of 22 children.

RYUN, Jim (USA)

Who could have guessed when Peter Snell broke Herb Elliott's world mile record in Jan. 1962 that a then 14-year-old American who had never run a mile in his life would, 4½ years later, be timed at 3 min. 51.3 sec. The rise to fame of Jim Ryun was indeed bewilderingly swift.

His very first mile race, on Sept. 7th, 1962, occupied as long as 5 min. 38 sec., but shortly before his 16th birthday he returned a highly promising 4 min. 26.4 sec. Here is how he cut down his mile time subsequently (with age in years and months in brackets):—

4:16.2	May 3rd, 1963	(16.0)
4:08.2	May 25th, 1963	(16.0)
4:07.8	June 8th, 1963	(16.1)
4:06.4	May 16th, 1964	(17.0)
4:01.7	May 23rd, 1964	(17.0)
3:59.0	June 5th, 1964	(17.1)
3:58.3	May 15th, 1965	(18.0)
3:58.1	May 29th, 1965	(18.1)
3:56.8	June 4th, 1965	(18.1)
3:55.3	June 27th, 1965	(18.1)
3:53.7	June 4th, 1966	(19.1)
3:51.3	July 17th, 1966	(19.2)
3:51.1	June 23rd, 1967	(20.1)

Ryun also claimed world records of 1 min. 44.9 sec. for 880 yd. and 3 min. 33.1 sec. for 1500 m. He was unlucky, though, in his three Olympic appearances. In 1964, at 17 the youngest member of the USA team, he was hampered by a heavy cold and failed to reach the final; in 1968 he ran brilliantly to clock 3 min. 37.8 sec. at high altitude but found Kip Keino 20 m. ahead, and in 1972 he tripped over in his heat. He turned professional shortly afterwards.

His best marks were 21.6 sec. for 220 yd. relay leg, 47.0 sec. for 440 yd. relay leg, 1 min. 44.9 sec. for 880 yd., 3 min. 33.1 sec. for 1500 m., 3 min. 51.1 sec. for the mile, 8 min. 25.2 sec. for 2 mi. and 13 min. 38.2 secs. for 5000 m. He was born at Wichita, Kansas, on Apr. 29th, 1947.

SANYEYEV, Viktor (USSR)

A knee injury caused Viktor Sanyeyev to switch from his first love, the high jump, but success in other fields came quickly. He placed second in both long and triple jumps at the 1964 European Junior Games.

After reaching 7.90 metres and 16.67 metres in 1967 he decided to concentrate on the triple jump for the following year's Olympics. It was a wise choice. No one would have beaten Bob Beamon at those Games, but in the greatest and most thrilling triple jump competition of all time Sanyeyev emerged the champion with his final effort of 17.39 metres—a massive improvement on the pre-Games world record of 17.03 metres by Poland's Jozef Szmidt.

He scored another brilliant victory at the 1969 European Championships (17.34 metres) and though he lost this title in 1971 to his keenest rival, Jorg Drehmel (E. Germany), he was again in exceptional form for the Olympics —his opening leap of 17.35 metres proved 4 cm. too much for Drehmel. Later in 1972 Sanyeyev regained the world record he had lost the previous year to Pedro Perez (Cuba) by registering 17.44 metres in his Georgian birthplace.

Sanyeyev continued to dominate the event, winning back the European title in 1974 (17.23 metres) and scoring an unprecedented triple jump triple in 1976 by winning the Olympic gold medal for the third time (17.29 metres). He easily defeated Joao Carlos de Oliveira, the Brazilian who seized the world record in 1975.

Despite repeated injuries from an event which takes a heavy toll of the legs, this former 10.5 sec. sprinter had no intention of retiring before the Moscow Olympics. He was beaten by a single centimetre in the 1978 European Championships but believed, even in his 35th year, that he could emulate the great Al Oerter by winning an Olympic title for the fourth time. And how close he came, for his final jump in Moscow of 17.24 metres brought him the silver medal. It was his longest jump since the 1976 Games. A 17 metre-plus performer in 12 of the 13 seasons between 1968 and 1980, he was born at Sukhumi on Oct. 3rd, 1945.

SCHLAAK, Evelin (East Germany)

See JAHL, EVELIN.

SCHMIDT, Wolfgang (East Germany)

With his two main rivals, Mac Wilkins (USA) and Knut Hjeltnes (Norway), out of the running due to their nations' boycott of the Games, the gold medal in the discus at the Moscow Olympics seemed destined to be won by the event's world record holder and dominant competitor—Wolfgang Schmidt. But, hampered by a foot injury, he fell several metres short of his best and although he did hold the lead for a while he eventually finished fourth.

The son of Ernst Schmidt (who won ten East German shot, discus and decathlon titles between 1950 and 1954), Wolfgang was an outstanding thrower from an early age and in 1973 won the European junior discus title and finished second to team-mate Udo Beyer (later to become Olympic champion and world record holder) in the shot. As a senior his first big success was in the 1975 European Cup Final, while in 1976 he became European record holder and Olympic silver medallist behind Wilkins.

During the next three seasons he won all the major honours: European Cup and World Cup victories (defeating Wilkins both times) in 1977 and 1979, the European title in 1978 and a world record of 71.16 metres also that year. He has kept his hand in as a shot putter, gaining a European bronze medal in 1978 and boasting a personal best of 20.76 metres.

His annual progress: 1970—48.52 m.; 1971—54.40; 1972—57.90; 1973—61.30; 1974—64.10; 1975—66.80; 1976—68.60; 1977—68.26; 1978—71.16; 1979—69.08; 1980—68.48. He was born in Berlin on Jan. 16th, 1954.

SEDYKH, Yuriy (USSR)

For the first time since an Irish-American clean sweep in 1908, one nation monopolised the Olympic hammer medals when, in Montreal, the youthful Yuriy Sedykh won ahead of his Soviet compatriots Aleksey Spiridonov and Anatoliy Bondarchuk (his own coach).

Hammer throwers tend to mature at a later age than athletes in most other events, so it's unusual for an Olympic hammer title to fall to a 21-year-old. However, Sedykh could look back on a career of eight years in the event, for his first competition was in 1968 when he threw the 5 kg. implement 38 metres. Four years later, his personal best with the full-size 7.26 kg. hammer standing at 62.50 metres, he came under the coaching influence of Bondarchuk, the 1972 Olympic champion and former world record holder. The partnership quickly bore fruit, for in 1973 Sedykh set a world junior record of 69.04 metres and won the European junior title.

Sedykh went on to surpass the achievements even of his distinguished mentor, for in 1978 he won the European title and in 1980 became the first hammer thrower since Ireland's Pat O'Callaghan (1932) to defend the Olympic crown successfully. With the very first throw of the competition in Moscow he whirled the ball and chain out to the prodigious world record distance of 81.80 metres and, as in Montreal, led a Soviet clean sweep of the medals.

His annual progress: 1971—57.02 m., 1972—62.96; 1973—69.04; 1974—70.86; 1975—75.00; 1976—78.86; 1977—76.60; 1978—79.76; 1979—77.58; 1980—81.80. He was born at Novocherkassk on June 11th, 1955.

SHOT

A shot is a ball made of solid iron, brass or any metal not softer than brass, or a shell of such metal filled with lead or other material. The men's shot weighs 16 lb. (7.26 kg.). It is delivered from a circle of 7 feet (2.135 metres) diameter (the same as for the hammer.) A stop board, firmly fastened to the ground, is placed at the middle of the circumference in the front half of the circle. The shot must land within a sector of 40 degrees.

The shot must not be thrown; it is put from the shoulder with one hand only. The IAAF rule states: "At the time the competitor takes a stance in the ring to commence a put, the shot shall touch or be in close proximity to the chin and the hand shall not be dropped below this position during the action of putting. The shot must not be brought behind the line of the shoulders." A competitor is allowed to touch the inside of the stop board but it is a foul if he touches the top of the stop board or the ground outside.

Three names are especially prominent in the early history of the event. George Gray (Canada) took the record to 14.32 metres in 1893 and he was succeeded by the remarkable Irish athlete Denis Horgan, who in 1904 improved to 14.88 metres from a seven foot square—the custom in Britain from 1882 to 1907. Horgan is noted for his string of 13 AAA titles between 1893 and 1912, a record number for one event. The third man was 1.98 metres tall Ralph Rose (USA), who pushed the record out to 15.54 metres in 1909 and was Olympic champion in 1904 and 1908 and runner-up in 1912. He had the bad luck of tying for first in the 1904 discus, only to lose the gold medal in a throw-off with countryman Martin Sheridan.

Rose's record stood until 1928 and progress was slow until 1934, a season that drastically altered all previous concepts of shot-putting standards. The man responsible was the giant American, Jack Torrance. He began with 16.30 metres in Apr. and finished with 17.40 metres in Aug. There the world record stayed until Charles Fonville (USA) reached 17.68 metres in 1948.

Jim Fuchs (USA) ruled the roost for the next few seasons—he recorded 17.95 metres in 1950—but even his performances were made to look puny by comparison with those of his successor, Parry O'Brien (USA), the inventor of a technique that permitted distances far in excess of 60 feet (18.29 metres). O'Brien, winner of two Olympic titles, improved the world record 16 times between 1953 (18.00 metres) and 1959 (19.30 metres).

Bill Nieder was the first to reach 20 metres, in 1960, and another American, Randy Matson, passed the 70 feet (21.33 metres) milestone in 1965. The current world record is 22.15 metres by Udo Beyer (E. Germany), although Brian Oldfield (USA) was credited with 22.86 metres in professional competition—using a rotational technique.

The two outstanding figures in British shot-putting have been Arthur Rowe, the 1958 European champion whose distance of 19.56 metres in 1961 lasted as a UK record until 1972, and Geoff Capes—six times a European indoor medallist (twice champion)—who raised the national record to 21.68 metres in 1980.

See also under BEYER, UDO; KISILYEV, VLADIMIR; MATSON, RANDY; O'BRIEN, PARRY; and OLDFIELD, BRIAN.

Women

Women use a shot weighing 4 kg. (8 lb. 13 oz.) Leading individuals have been Gisela Mauermayer (Germany), the 1936 Olympic discus champion (there was no Olympic shot until 1948) whose 14.38 metres in 1934 stood unmolested for 11 years; Galina Zybina (USSR), the O'Brien of women's putting who set a dozen world records between 1952 (15.19 metres) and 1956 (16.76 metres) and was Olympic champion in 1952; Tamara Press (USSR), the first to reach such landmarks as 17 and 18 metres; Nadyezhda Chizhova (USSR) whose world records ranged from 18.67 metres in 1968 to 21.45 metres in 1973; the current world record holder (22.45 metres) and Olympic champion Ilona Slupianek of East Germany; and her contemporary Helena Fibingerova (Czechoslovakia), who has reached 22.50 metres indoors.

See also under CHIZHOVA, NADYEZHDA; FIBINGEROVA, HELENA; and SLUPIANEK, ILONA.

SHRUBB, Alf (GB)

During his heyday in the early years of the century, Alf Shrubb held just about every British running record from 1¼ miles to one hour—many of them surviving over 30 years, the last for all of 49 years. Not only was he outstanding from a British point of view; he was certainly the greatest in the world in the years prior to the rise of Jean Bouin (France) and the line of "Flying Finns."

World records can be judged by their longevity. Shrubb's 10 mi. time of 50 min. 40.6 sec. lasted 24 years, his 9 min. 09.6 sec. 2 mi. stood 22 years, 14 min. 17.2 sec. 3 mi. for 18 years, 18,742 metres hour run for nine years, 29 min. 59.4 sec. 6 mi. and 31 min. 02.4 sec. 10,000 m. for seven years. All these performances were established in 1904, but unfortunately he was deprived of certain Olympic victory because Britain did not send a team to St. Louis.

He began running in 1898 and won his first national titles at cross-country, 4 mi. and 10 mi. in 1901. He won each of these championships four years running and also won the AAA mile and the International cross-country titles in 1903 and 1904.

He was declared a professional in Oct. 1905 and enjoyed a varied career in the paid ranks, his contests including a 10 miles race against a horse! Later he became Oxford University's first professional coach (1920-1926) and he lived in Canada from 1928. At the age of 75 he was reinstated by the AAA. He was born at Slinfold, Sussex, on Dec. 12th, 1878, and died in Canada on Apr. 23rd, 1964.

SIMEONI, Sara (Italy)

Ballet's loss was athletics' gain when Sara Simeoni grew too tall to pursue her dream of becoming a classical dancer. So instead she took to athletics at the age of 12 and developed gradually into the *prima ballerina assoluta* of high jumping.

What was noticeable from early in her international career was her fighting competitive spirit—the priceless ability to produce her best when it mattered the most. Thus, in the 1971

European Championships, in which she finished 9th, she jumped her own physical height of 1.78 metres for the first time; when placing 6th in the 1972 Olympics she raised her personal best to 1.85 metres; and she broke new ground at the 1974 European Championships by flopping over 1.89 metres for a bronze medal.

She did it again at the 1976 Olympics, where she cleared 1.91 metres for the silver medal after a great battle with the favourite, Rosi Ackermann. With her great East German rival injured, Sara won her first major title at the 1977 European Indoor Championships with—surprise, surprise—a personal best of 1.92 metres, but outdoors Ackermann continued to reign supreme.

The turning point came in 1978 when the Italian took over as number one. After yet another of their epic and sporting duels, Simeoni captured the European title with a leap of 2.01 metres, which equalled the world record she had established a few weeks earlier. Not that Ackermann, for all her injuries, was ready to step down and in 1979 she notched up a great victory in the European Cup Final. Simeoni got the better of her in the World Cup though, albeit in second place as Canada's Debbie Brill pulled off the most stunning win of her career. However, Simeoni returned to her best form in 1980 and scored a most popular and deserved success in her third Olympic bid.

Annual progress: 1965—1.25 m.; 1966—1.45; 1967—1.48; 1968—1.55; 1969—1.65; 1970—1.75; 1971—1.80; 1972—1.85; 1973—1.86; 1974—1.90; 1975—1.89; 1976—1.91; 1977—1.93; 1978—2.01; 1979—1.98; 1980—1.98. She was born at Rivoli Veronese on Apr. 19th, 1953.

SLUPIANEK, Ilona (East Germany)

Ilona Slupianek (née Schoknecht) shares with Soviet pentathlete Nadyezhda Tkachenko the dubious distinction of being caught out as a cheat, suspended and reinstated by the IAAF, and going on to become an Olympic champion. Her fall from grace occurred in 1977 when, after winning the shot at the European Cup Final, a doping test proved she had been taking anabolic steroids. Those in the sport who feel that known drug offenders should be severely penalised were dismayed to find the statuesque East German eligible for the European Championships just after a year later—a title she duly lifted.

Her dominance of the event was overwhelming in 1980: she raised the world record first to 22.36 metres and then to 22.45 metres, topped 22 metres roughly fifty times during the season, and won in Moscow (22.41 metres) by the biggest margin in Olympic women's shot putting history.

Also a 64.60 metres discus thrower, she has shown the following annual progress: 1970—12.50 m.; 1971—13.32; 1972—14.40; 1973—17.05; 1974—19.23 1975—20.12; 1976—21.30; 1977—21.79; 1978—22.06; 1979—22.04; 1980—22.45. She was born at Demmin on Sept. 24th, 1956.

SMITH, Joyce (GB)

Still improving at the age of 43, Joyce Smith (née Byatt) gained her first international badge, as reserve for the England cross-country team, way back in 1956—and 24 years later recorded the fastest ever marathon time by a woman either in a females-only race or on a loop course.

There have been three distinct phases to Joyce's career. In the first she became English cross-country champion in 1959 and 1960, and in the latter year won her British international track colours in the 800 m. However, she didn't like the nervousness involved with competing at international level and settled back to being primarily a club runner.

The second era began in 1971 (she was then 33) when her daughter started at play school, leaving Joyce with more time in which to train. Setting her sights on the newly developing 3000 m. event she won the WAAA title that year in an unofficial world record of 9 min. 23.4 sec., and the following winter she became the first British woman to win the International Cross-Country Championship. Her next target was the 1500 m., which was making its bow on the Olympic programme in 1972. Her best time prior to 1972 was a modest 4 min. 25.2 sec., but she made astonishing progress to qualify for the team and, in Munich, she set UK records of 4 min. 11.3 sec. (heat) and 4 min. 09.4 sec. (semi-final). The next big goal was the inaugural European 3000 m. championship in 1974, in which she finished third.

The third and most successful segment of Joyce's running career started in 1977 after the birth of her second daughter: she took to the road. An early indication of what was to come was provided when she set a UK best for 10 miles of 56 min. 27 sec., and in 1979 she graduated to the event which was to prove her forte . . . the marathon. She made a spectacular debut in June that year, knocking nine minutes off the previous UK best with 2 hr. 41 min. 37 sec., and three months later she won the Avon international race in Germany in 2 hr. 36 min. 27 sec. for a Commonwealth record. That mark she lowered to 2 hr. 33 min. 32 sec. in June 1980, while in November she won the Tokyo international women's race for the second year running—this time in 2 hr. 30 min. 27 sec. Joyce improved again, to 2 hrs. 29 min. 57 sec., in the London Marathon in March 1981—to become the third woman in the world to break 2½ hours.

Her best marks include: (track) 2 min. 08.8 sec. for 800 m., 4 min. 09.4 sec. for 1500 m. and 8 min. 55.6 sec for 3000 m.; (road) 53 min. 17 sec. for 10 miles, 1 hr. 13 min. 40 sec. for half marathon, 1 hr. 25 min. 08 sec. for 15 miles, 1 hr. 53 min. 55 sec. for 20 miles and 2 hr. 29 min. 57 sec. for the marathon. She was born in London on Oct. 26th, 1937.

SMITH, Tommie (USA)

It was thought, when Henry Carr retired in 1964, that the world would have to wait many years for another 200 cum 400 metres runner of his calibre. In fact, Tommie Smith almost immediately stepped into Carr's shoes and quickly bettered his records. During his great 1966 season he set four world records (200 m. and 220 yd. straight and turn), was timed to run a lap (43.8 sec. 400 m. relay leg) faster than any man until then, missed the 100 m. world record by only a tenth of a second and casually long jumped 7.90 metres (actually measured at 8.18 metres from point of take-off)!

He collected further world records in 1967 (44.5 400 m. and 44.8 440 yd.) and 1968 (19.83 200 m. when winning the Olympic title). He later turned professional.

His best performances were 9.3 sec. (and 9.2 sec. wind-assisted) for 100 yd., 10.1 sec. for 100 m., 19.5 sec. for 220 yd. straight, 19.83 sec. for 200 m. turn, 44.5 sec. for 400 m., 44.8 sec. for 440 yd. and 7.90 metres long jump. He was born at Acworth, Texas, on Jan. 12th, 1944.

SNELL, Peter (New Zealand)

Early in 1962 Peter Snell clipped a tenth of a second from Herb Elliott's mile world record of 3 min. 54.5 sec. and followed up one week later with an even more dazzling exploit—records at 800 m. (1 min. 44.3 sec.) and 880 yd. (1 min. 45.1 sec.). If he achieved nothing else these records would suffice to earn Snell immortality.

In fact, Snell can boast of an enviable competitive record. He lost several unimportant races but was undefeated in his five major championship outings: the 1960 Olympic 800 m., 1962 Commonwealth 880 yd. and mile, and 1964 Olympic 800 m. and 1500 m. His double in Tokyo was the first at those events since Albert Hill in 1920.

Snell travelled to Rome in 1960 as New Zealand half-mile record holder at 1 min. 49.2 sec. and an unknown quantity. At the Olympics he scored a sensational upset victory over Belgium's Roger Moens in 1 min. 46.3 sec. and shortly afterwards was timed in a scorching 1 min. 44.9 sec. (50.0 sec. first lap!) for an 880 yd. relay leg in London, the official world record standing then at 1 min. 46.8 sec. He retired in 1965.

His best marks were 47.9 sec. for 440 yd. (relay leg), 1 min. 44.3 sec. for 800 m., 1 min. 45.1 sec. for 880 yd., 2 min. 06.0 sec. for 1000 yd. (an indoor world's best), 2 min. 16.6 sec. for 1000 m., 3 min. 37.6 sec. for 1500 m., 3 min. 54.1 sec. for the mile, 5 min. 12.6 sec. for 2000 m., 2 hr. 41 min. 11 sec. for the marathon and 9 min. 38.8 sec. for 3000 m. steeplechase. He was born at Opunake on Dec. 17th, 1938.

SPRINTS

The sprinting events are those races up to and including 400 m., the three Olympic distances in this category being 100 m., 200 m. and 400 m. As from May 1977 only performances timed by an approved fully automatic electrical timing device have been eligible for world records at distances up to and including 400 m.

The start is a vital part of a sprint race, and there have been two major advances in this department in the last century.

Until 1888 amateur sprinters invariably used a standing start. They would lean forward with the front foot on the starting line, the other seven or eight inches behind. The crouch start was invented by Charles Sherrill (later General Sherrill, US Ambassador to Turkey), the American 100 yd. champion in 1887, and his coach Mike Murphy, and was used in competition for the first time by Sherrill in May 1888. It was introduced into England later that year by T. L. Nicholas.

The second significant advance occurred in 1927 when starting blocks were invented by the American coach, George Bresnahan. In 1929 George Simpson (USA) ran 100 yd. in 9.4 sec. from blocks but the performance, though genuine in every respect, was rejected as a world record since blocks were then still against the rules. Tests have indicated that the advantage of blocks over holes amounts to about one thirtieth of a second—roughly a foot in terms of distance. They were not used in the Olympic Games until 1948.

100 Yards and 100 Metres

The first recorded instance of an " even time " (10.0 sec.) 100 yd. under regular conditions was by C. A. Absalom (GB) in 1868. Since then the record has been reduced, as distinct from equalled, on eight occasions: John Owen, 9.8 sec. in 1890; Arthur Duffey, 9.6 sec. in 1902; Charley Paddock, 9.5 sec. in 1926; George Simpson, 9.4 sec. in 1929; Mel Patton, 9.3 sec. in 1948; Frank Budd, 9.2 sec. in 1961; Bob Hayes, 9.1 sec. in 1963; and Ivory Crockett, 9.0 sec. in 1975. All these athletes are American.

Harald Andersson, later Arbin (Sweden) clocked 11.0 sec. for 100 m. in 1890. There have been seven subsequent record breakers: Luther Cary (USA), 10.8 sec. in 1891; Knut Lindberg (Sweden), 10.6 sec. in 1906; Richard Rau (Germany), 10.5 sec. in 1911; Charley Paddock (USA), 10.4 sec. and 10.2 sec. in 1921; Lloyd La Beach (Panama), 10.1 sec. in 1950; Armin Hary (W. Germany), 10.0 sec. in 1960; and Jim Hines (USA), 9.9 sec. in 1968. Hines holds the fastest electrical time of 9.95 sec. at high altitude. Quickest time at or near sea level is 10.02 sec. by James Sanford (USA) in 1980.

Of the men named above only four won Olympic titles at 100 m.—Paddock in 1920, Hary in 1960, Hayes in 1964 and Hines in 1968, though Duffey was unfortunate to pull a tendon while leading in the 1900 final. Most Olympic finals have been won by a foot or less, the " easiest " victor being Hayes, who won in 1964 by some two metres.

The highest speed ever attained by a sprinter may be 27.89 m.p.h. by Hayes during a 100 yd. race in 1963.

Britain has produced two winners of the Olympic 100 m. crown: Harold Abrahams in 1924 and Allan Wells in 1980.

200 Metres

James Carlton (Australia) was the first to break 21 sec. around a turn, although his timing of 20.6 sec. in 1932 is treated with reserve by some. Nineteen years elapsed before Andy Stanfield (USA) tied the record. Peter Radford (GB) broke new ground with 20.5 sec. in 1960 and there the record stood until Henry Carr (USA) clocked 20.3 sec. in 1963, and 20.2 sec. in 1964. Tommie Smith (USA) ran 20.0 sec. in 1966; and in 1968 he won the Olympic title at altitude in 19.83 sec.—a mark broken in 1979 by Italy's Pietro Mennea (19.72 sec.), who also holds the " sea-level " best of 19.96 sec. (1980).

No Briton has won the 200 m. at the Olympics but medals were obtained in each final between 1912 and 1928 and Allan Wells was a close second in 1980. On the world record plane, Radford had two predecessors in Charles Wood, who in 1887 became the first man to crack 22.0 sec., and Willie Applegarth, whose 21.2 sec. for 220 yd. in 1914 survived until Carlton's feat in 1932.

400 Metres

Apart from the intrusion of two Germans (Rudolf Harbig and Carl Kaufmann, both of whom posted world records for 400 m.) the history of one-lap running is bound up mainly with the United States, Britain and the Caribbean.

Lon Myers (USA) was the first to duck under 50 sec. with 49.2 sec. for 440 yd. in 1879. The record was whittled down little by little until suddenly in 1932 Ben Eastman (USA) sliced a complete second off the previous best with 46.4 sec. Jamaican Herb McKenley (who in two Olympics finished second to a team-mate) ran 46.0 sec. flat in 1948 and Adolph Plummer (USA) broke 45 seconds for 440 yd. for the first time with 44.9 sec. in 1963—thus duplicating the metric world record which had been set by Otis Davis (USA) and Kaufmann in their epic duel at the 1960 Olympics. Lee Evans (USA) became the first to break 44 sec. when winning the 1968 Olympic crown in 43.86 sec. The fastest at or near sea level is 44.26 sec. by Cuba's Alberto Juantorena, the 1976 champion.

Britain has a grand record in this event. Wyndham Halswelle won the 1908 Olympic title in a walk-over after his two American rivals scratched in protest against one of their colleagues being disqualified in a heat. Fellow Scotsman Eric Liddell ran away with the 1924 gold medal, and silver medals were secured by Guy Butler in 1920 and Godfrey Brown in 1936. The European title has been won by a Briton five times since 1938.

See also under ABRAHAMS, HAROLD; BORZOV, VALERIY; DAVIS, GLENN; EVANS, LEE; HARBIG, RUDOLF; HAYES, BOB; HINES, JIM; JUANTORENA, ALBERTO; LIDDELL, ERIC; MARKIN, VIKTOR; MENNEA, PIETRO; MYERS, LON; OWENS, JESSE; QUARRIE, DON; SMITH, TOMMIE; and WELLS, ALLAN.

Women

From 1948, when the 200 m. was added to the schedule, until 1960 the winner of the Olympic 100 m. always went on to score in the longer event also. Fanny Blankers-Koen (Netherlands) was the first to gain this sprint double and she was followed by Marjorie Jackson (Australia) in 1952, Betty Cuthbert (Australia) in 1956 and Wilma Rudolph (USA) in 1960. The sequence was broken in 1964 but in 1972 Renate Stecher (E. Germany) also achieved the double. In the 100 m. she succeeded Wyomia Tyus (USA), who with Barbel Wockel (E. Germany), 200 m. winner in 1976 and 1980, is the only sprinter ever to retain an Olympic title.

The first woman to break 11 sec. for 100 m. with electrical timing was Marlies Gohr (E. Germany) with 10.88 sec., while her compatriot Marita Koch led the way under 22 sec. for 200 m.

Britain has produced a string of accomplished sprinters over the years, the most successful being Dorothy Hyman with two Olympic medals, two Commonwealth Games gold medals, and a European title.

The first to break 53 sec and 52 sec. for 400 m. was the mysterious Sin Kim Dan of North Korea, whose unratified time of 51.2 sec. in 1964 was not bettered until Marilyn Neufville (Jamaica) ran 51.0 sec in 1970, a mark tied by Monika Zehrt (E. Germany) in 1972. Irena Szewinska (Poland), in 1974, was the first under 50 sec. and Marita Koch took the record under 49 sec. in 1978.

Among the greatest names in British quarter-miling history are Nellie Halstead, who held the 440 yd. world best for nearly quarter of a century; Ann Packer, the 1964 Olympic silver medallist and European record breaker at 400 m., Lillian Board, who was so narrowly beaten for the 1968 Olympic title; and Verona Elder, three times European indoor champion.

See also under BLANKERS-KOEN, FANNY; CUTHBERT, BETTY; DE LA HUNTY, SHIRLEY; GOHR, MARLIES; KOCH, MARITA; KONDRATYEVA, LYUDMILA; PACKER, ANN; RUDOLPH, WILMA; STECHER, RENATE; SZEWINSKA, IRENA; TYUS, WYOMIA; and WOCKEL, BARBEL.

STECHER, Renate
(East Germany)

One of the strongest as well as fleetest of all the great women sprinters, Renate Stecher (née Meissner) amassed the impressive total of six Olympic medals (three gold) between 1972 and 1976, and eight European medals (four gold) from 1969 to 1974—not counting four European indoor titles.

Her international career actually began in 1966 when, only 16, she won a gold medal in the 4 x 100 m. relay at the European Junior Games. At the next Games, two years later, she gained silver medals in the 100, 200 and relay. A late addition to the team, she increased her medal tally with a gold in the relay and a silver in the 200 in the senior European Championships of 1969.

The first of several world records (11.0 sec. for 100 m.) came in 1970 and the following season she won both European titles with ease. Superbly consistent, she was predictably at her very best for the 1972 Olympics and there she won the 100 m. in 11.07 sec. and the 200 m. in 22.40 sec., both electrical world records. Only an inspired run by West Germany's Heide Rosendahl prevented her collecting a third gold medal in the 4 x 100 m. relay.

She made further history in 1973 by clocking 10.8 sec. (hand timed) but she was below her best at the 1974 European Championships where she was 2nd to Irena Szewinska in both sprints. Her career came to an end in 1976 after gaining three more medals (including the relay gold this time) in Montreal.

Best marks: 10.8 sec. and 11.07 sec. for 100 m., 22.1 sec. and 22.38 sec. for 200 m., 5.65 metres long jump and 4,297 pts. pentathlon (old tables).

She was born at Suptitz on May 12th, 1950.

STEEPLECHASE

The standard steeplechasing distance is 3000 m. The race comprises 28 hurdles and seven water jumps. All the obstacles are 3 ft. (91.4 cm.) in height. Unlike those used in conventional hurdle races, the steeplechase barriers are solid and weigh between 80 and 100 kg. The width of the top of the hurdle is 5 in. (127 mm.), which enables an athlete to step on and off if he chooses. The water jump is 12 ft. (3.66 m.) in length and width, the water being 2 ft. 3½ in. (70 cm.) deep immediately in front of the hurdle. The trough slopes to ground level at the further end.

The first steeplechase to be traced was held in Edinburgh in 1828. The event was introduced into the Oxford University sports in 1860 for a few years and two races (2500 and 4000 m.) were held at the 1900 Olympics.

The distance was internationally standardised at 3000 m. in 1920—Percy Hodge (GB) winning the first Olympic title over that length course. An official's error at the 1932 Olympics resulted in the runners covering one lap (460 m.) too many! The winner, Volmari Iso-Hollo (Finland) successfully defended his title in 1936 and is regarded as the father of modern steeplechasing.

Nine minutes was beaten for the first time in 1944 by Erik Elmsater (Sweden). Nineteen years later Gaston Roelants (Belgium) broke 8¼ minutes and the record now stands at 8 min. 05.4 sec. by Henry Rono (Kenya) in 1978. Because of variations in the placing and number of hurdles, official world records were not recognised until 1954. The event is now fully standardised, although the design of hurdles and water jumps varies from stadium to stadium and at some tracks the water jump is located inside the main track, outside at others.

Steeplechasing for women has been staged in Finland since 1979. In 1980 a time of 4 min. 41.8 sec. for 1500 m. was set by Marjo Riitta Lakka.

Welshman John Disley, the 1952 Olympic bronze medallist, was the first Briton to break nine minutes. In 1956 Chris Brasher won Britain's first individual Olympic gold medal on the track since 1932 with a time of 8 min. 41.2 sec.—six seconds faster than he had ever run before. Maurice Herriott was 2nd in the 1964 Olympics.

See also under BRASHER, CHRIS; GARDERUD, ANDERS; KEINO, KIP; MALINOWSKI, BRONISLAW; ROELANTS, GASTON; and RONO, HENRY.

STRICKLAND, Shirley (Australia)

see DE LA HUNTY, SHIRLEY

SZEWINSKA, Irena (Poland)

Even before her 21st birthday Irena Szewinska (née Kirszenstein) had established herself as one of the most distinguished of all women athletes. As an inexperienced 18-year-old at the Tokyo Olympics she captured silver medals in the long jump (with a national record of 6.60 metres) and 200 m. (in a European record of 23.1 sec.) and ran in Poland's winning and world record-breaking 4 x 100 m. relay team.

The following season, 1965, she really showed her paces with world record sprints of 11.1 sec for 100 m. and 22.7 sec for 200 m. Again, at the 1966 European Championships, she produced her best form at the opportune time by winning the 200 m. and long jump, finishing a close second in the 100 m. and helping Poland win the sprint relay.

Even better was to come: she won the Olympic 200 m. crown in 1968 with a world record 22.58 sec. and took third place in the 100 m. Following the birth of her baby she picked up two more bronze medals in the 200 m. at the 1971 European Championships and 1972 Olympics.

In 1973 she made her long awaited debut at 400 m., clocking 52.0 sec., and the following year she enjoyed a fabulously successful season which included such gems as world records of 22.0 sec. (manually timed) and 22.21 sec. (electrical) for 200 m. and a revolutionary 49.9 sec. for 400 m., plus victories over Renate Stecher in the European 100 and 200 m. Most astonishing of all was a 400 m. relay leg timed at 48.5 sec! She concentrated on the 400 m. at the 1976 Olympics to superb effect—triumphing by 10 metres in a world record 49.28 sec. to strengthen claims that she should be considered the greatest woman athlete of all time.

Szewinska maintained her position as world's number one in the 200 and 400 m. in 1977. At the World Cup she first disposed of Olympic champion Barbel Wockel in the 200 m. and then prevailed over up and coming Marita Koch in the 400 m. But youth was not to be denied, and at the 1978 European Championships the winner of the 400 m. was Koch in a world record 48.94 sec., with the Pole third in 50.40 sec. Another bronze in the 4 x 400 m. relay brought Szewinska's tally of European medals to ten. Her final fling, aged 34, came at the Moscow Games—her fifth Olympics—but an achilles tendon injury caused her to be eliminated at the semi-final stage.

Best marks: 10.9 sec. and 11.13 sec. for 100 m., 22.0 sec. and 22.21 sec. for 200 m., 35.70 sec. for 300 m., 49.28 sec. for 400 m., 14.0 sec. for 100 m. hurdles, 56.62 sec. for 400 m. hurdles, 1.68 metres high jump, 6.67 metres long jump and 4,705 pts. pentathlon (old tables).

She was born in Leningrad (USSR) on May 24th, 1946.

SZMIDT, Jozef (Poland)

Jozef Szmidt is one of those enviable sportsmen who always seemed to be at their very best on the occasions that mattered most. In his prime he won four major triple jump titles: the European championship in 1958 and 1962 and the Olympic gold medal in 1960 and 1964.

He became the first man to exceed the classic distance of 17 metres when he established a new world record of 17.03 metres in 1960, despite an awkward landing—an outstanding performance for the era before all-weather runways which stood unbroken for eight years. In spite of a series of leg injuries he maintained a high standard for many years and in placing 7th at the 1968 Games he bettered his previous Olympic winning marks with 16.89 metres. Aged 37 he was still in international class in 1972.

His other best marks were 10.4 sec. for 100 m. (equalling the personal best of his elder brother Edward) and long jumps of 7.84 metres and wind-assisted 7.96 metres. He was born at Michalkowice on March 28th, 1935.

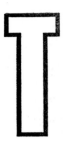

THOMPSON, Daley (GB)

Ever since, at the age of 16, he scored the remarkable total of 6685 pts. in his decathlon debut in 1975, Francis Morgan (Daley) Thompson appeared destined to become the world's greatest all-round athlete. Barely a year after that precocious start he was British senior and world junior record holder with 7905 pts., having earlier made a promising showing in the Montreal Olympics where (placing 18th) he impressed gold medallist and world record smasher Bruce Jenner as a likely successor to himself.

Over the next four years Thompson gradually approached, and then surpassed, Jenner's monumental score of 8617 pts. He topped 8000 for the first time in 1977 (the year he won the European junior title), and the following season—at the Commonwealth Games, a week after his 20th birthday—he piled up the third highest score (using electrical timing) in decathlon history. His total of 8467 pts. couldn't be ratified as a Commonwealth record because of excessive wind assistance in the long jump, where he achieved the spectacular distance of 8.11 metres, but three weeks later he put together a valid record total of 8289 pts. in placing second to Aleksandr Grebenyuk (USSR) in the European Championships.

Although he didn't feature in any decathlon ranking lists in 1979, he made good use of the pre-Olympic season by making considerable progress in the 100 m., hurdles and throws, and further evidence that Daley was already capable of a world record score was provided in Germany in July 1979 when, having run up a magnificent seven-event total of 6169 pts. (on course for over 8600 pts.), he failed three times in the pole vault.

Sometimes spending up to eight hours a day training to perfect the diverse skills required of the decathlete, Thompson is one of a new breed of full-time athlete, unable due to training demands to contemplate a job and therefore existing on officially channelled sponsorship money. He prepared for the Olympics brimming with self-confidence. It wasn't misplaced for in a competition in Austria in May 1980 he not only comfortably beat Guido Kratschmer, who would have been his main rival in Moscow but for the West German boycott, but he broke Jenner's world record with a score of 8622 pts. His individual performances were 10.55 sec. for 100 m., 7.72 metres long jump, 14.46 metres shot, 2.11 metres high jump, 48.04 sec. for 400 m. (halfway score of 4486 pts.), 14.37 sec. for 110 m. hurdles, 42.98 metres discus, 4.90 metres pole vault, 65.38 metres javelin and 4 min. 25.5 sec. for 1500 m.

The record lasted only a month, for Kratschmer went on to amass 8649 pts., but of more immediate concern to Thompson was the Olympics—and in Moscow he proved unstoppable. After enjoying an enormous overnight lead with 4542 pts. he looked set to regain the record, but hampered by the weather on the second day he was content practically to jog home in the final event for a score of 8495 pts.

Thompson, with his awesome physical talent and cheery personality, will be delighting the world of track and field for many years to come if his plans come to fruition. "I intend to compete in the next two Olympics," he said in Moscow. "No decathlete has ever won three golds so I couldn't wish for a better incentive. I won't even be 30 at the 1988 Games. Why stop doing something that's fun?"

His best individual marks: 10.45 sec. (and wind assisted 10.36 sec.), 8.00 metres (and wind assisted 8.11 metres), 15.45 metres, 2.11 metres, 47.30 sec., 14.37 sec., 46.64 metres, 5.00 metres, 65.38 metres and 4 min. 20.3 sec. for the decathlon events, plus 20.88 sec. for 200 m. and 52.6 sec. for 400 m. hurdles. Annual decathlon progress:

The legendary Abebe Bikila (Ethiopia), here heading for his second Olympic marathon victory in 1964

Grete Waitz (Norway) finishes the 1980 New York marathon in a women's world best of 2 hours 25 minutes 42 seconds

Left: David Hemery (GB) on his way to winning the 1968 Olympic 400 metres hurdles in world record time

Right: Fanny Blankers-Koen (Netherlands), nearest camera, on the way to winning the 1948 Olympic 80 metres hurdles from Maureen Gardner (GB) and Shirley Strickland (Australia), number 668.

Left: Bronislaw Malinowski (Poland) takes the water jump during his 1980 Olympic steeplechase success

Right: Neck and neck in the 1979 World Cup 110 Metres hurdles: Thomas Munkelt (East Germany), left, who won the Olympic title in 1980, and world record holder Renaldo Nehemiah (USA)

Left: Sara Simeoni (Italy), 1980 Olympic champion and world record holder

Right: Bob Beamon (USA) leaping to his sensational world record long jump of 8.90 metres at Mexico City in 1968

Left: Gerd Wessig (East Germany), 1980 Olympic champion and world record holder

Right: Mary Rand (now Mrs Bill Toomey) the first Briton to win an Olympic women's athletics title

Wladyslaw Kozakiewicz (Poland) clearing 5.78 metres for a world record and Olympic gold medal in Moscow

Daley Thompson (GB) showing the speed and strength that have made him the world's greatest all-rounder

Viktor Sanyeyev (USSR), three times Olympic triple jump champion and silver medallist in Moscow

Vladimir Golubnichiy (USSR), the greatest name in Olympic walking

The astonishing Al Oerter (USA), the only athlete to win four successive Olympic titles. In 1980, aged 43, he was throwing the discus further than ever!

Mary Peters (GB & NI), left, and Burglinde Pollak (East Germany) in the 1972 Olympic Pentathlon 200 metres. Mary Peters won the gold medal

1975—7648; 1976—7905; 1977—8190; 1978—8467; 1980—8622. He was born of a Nigerian father and Scottish mother in London on July 30th, 1958.

THOMPSON, Don (GB)

Britain's hero at the Rome Olympic Games of 1960 was diminutive (1.68 metres, 57 kg.) Don Thompson, winner of the 50,000 m. road walk in the Olympic record time of 4 hr. 25 min. 30 sec. This popular victory wiped out the memory of Thompson's greatest disappointment: dropping out 5000 m. from the finish of the 1956 Olympic event.

He took up walking in 1951 by accident . . . literally. A strained achilles tendon prevented his running, so he trained as a walker instead, won his first race and continued. His first major success came in 1955 when he won the London to Brighton (52 mi.) race for the first of eight successive years. The next season he chalked up his first national 50,000 m. title (an event he was to win for the following six years). On the track he set UK records at 20 mi., 30 mi. and 50,000 m.

He competed in three European Championships, finishing fifth in 1958, third in 1962 and ninth in 1966. Illness caused him to miss much of the 1963 season but he made a gallant comeback in 1964 to finish 10th in the Olympics

His best marks included 94 min. 45 sec. for 20,000 m. (road), 2 hr. 41 min. 43.8 sec. for 20 mi. (track), 4 hr. 08 min. 11.6 sec. for 30 miles (track), 4 hr. 12 min. 19 sec. for 50,000 m. (road), 4 hr. 17 min. 29.8 sec. for 50,000 m. (track) and 7 hr. 35 min. 12 sec. for London to Brighton. He was born at Hillingdon, Middlesex, on Jan. 20th, 1933.

THOMPSON, Ian (GB)

Ian Thompson was just an ordinary club athlete . . . until he discovered marathon running. Prior to that fateful day (Oct. 27th, 1973) he was primarily a 5000 m. runner and had never raced beyond 10 miles on the road. Only in August had he stepped up his training mileage, after agreeing to run in the AAA marathon championship to make up the team for his club. His target of 2 hr. 20 min. was, for such a novice, ambitious. In fact, he won the race in sensational fashion, clocking a world-class 2 hr. 12 min. 40 sec. (the fastest first attempt at that time) and thus qualifying for England's team at the Commonwealth Games three months later.

Fluke? Far from it. Thompson went on to capture the Commonwealth title by a margin of two minutes in a European 'record' of 2 hr. 9 min. 12 sec., the fastest ever in a championship race. Further victories in 1974 followed in Athens (2hr. 13 min. 50 sec.) and at the European Championships (2 hr. 13 min. 19 sec.). Unknown a year earlier, he was unquestionably the best marathoner in the world.

Thompson took it easy in 1975, running only one marathon (which he won in a slow 2 hr. 24 min. 30 sec.), but was unable to recapture the former magic when he needed it—in the Olympic year of 1976. Cramp in his thighs during the Olympic trial race, in which he finished 7th in 2 hr. 19 min. 7 sec., put paid to his dreams.

Although he has shown the occasional glimpse of his early form, Thompson's racing record has been wildly erratic ever since. He did succeed in 1980 where he failed in 1976, making the Olympic team, but in Moscow he had to drop out at halfway, victim of a virus infection. However, he ended 1980 on a high note by winning the London to Brighton 54¼ mile classic in a record 5 hr. 15 min. 15 sec. in his ultra long distance debut.

His best marks: 3 min. 51.0 sec. for 1500 m., 14 min. 05.4 sec. for 5000 m., 29 min. 33.0 sec. for 10,000 m. and 2 hr. 09 min. 12 sec. for the marathon. Annual progress: 1973—2:12:40; 1974—2:09:12; 1975—2:24:30; 1976—2:12:54; 1977—2:14:32; 1978—2:13:49; 1979—2:13:42; 1980—2:14:00. He was born at Birkenhead on Oct. 16th 1949.

THORPE, Jim (USA)

Although nearly seventy years have passed and the great man has long been dead, the disqualification of Jim Thorpe for professionalism and the resulting forfeiture of his two hard earned Olympic titles still provokes indignation. It is true that Thorpe did receive money playing baseball in 1909 and 1910 but he was not aware that this would debar him from amateur athletics.

It was not until Jan. 1913, several months after his Olympic victories in the pentathlon and decathlon, that the story of his baseball activities came to light. Thorpe was stripped of his medals and records along with his amateur status but the fact remains he was the outstanding all-round athlete of his generation, and for many years to follow.

His best marks included 10.0 sec. for 100 yd., 51.0 sec. for 440 yd., 4 min. 40.1 sec. for 1500 m., 15.0 sec. for 110 m. hurdles, 23.8 sec. for 220 yd. hurdles (straight), 1.95 metres high jump, 3.25 metres pole vault, 7.16 metres long jump, 14.55 metres shot, 38.30 metres discus, 49.68 metres javelin and 6,756 points decathlon (under 1964 scoring tables.)

Following his disqualification, Thorpe played professional baseball and football until he was 41 and was voted the greatest football player of the half-century. Of part American Indian ancestry, he was born in Oklahoma in 1888 and died in 1953. Burt Lancaster played him in a film biography, 'Man of Bronze'.

TKACHENKO, Nadyezhda (USSR)

Although she was stripped of the 1978 European pentathlon title after a dope test showed she had been using anabolic steroids, and despite competing domestically during her 18-month period of suspension by the IAAF, Nadyezhda Tkachenko mounted the dais to be crowned Olympic champion in 1980. She had just compiled literally the ultimate in pentathlon scores (the event was replaced by the heptathlon in 1981) ... a world record of 5083 pts., a massive improvement of 227 pts. over the previous mark. It was her third attempt at the title: she was 9th in 1972 (when Mary Peters won) and a tearful 5th in 1976 after leading prior to the final event.

She re-emerged officially after her suspension in May 1980 with a score of 4880 pts. which exceeded her own world record of 4839 pts. but couldn't count as the hurdles and 800 m. were hand timed. Compatriot Olga Kuragina raised the record to 4856 pts. before the Games, but at the Olympics there was no holding Tkachenko who clocked 13.29 sec. for 100 m. hurdles, put the shot 16.84 metres, high jumped 1.84 metres, long jumped 6.73 metres and ran 800 m. in 2 min. 05.2 sec.— an amazing time for such a heavily muscled athlete. All but the shot mark (she has reached 16.86 metres) were personal bests.

Annual progress: 1971—4398; 1972 —4579; 1973—4711; 1974—4776; 1975 —4698; 1976—4772; 1977—4839; 1978 —4746; 1979—4711; 1980—5083. She was born at Kremenchug (Ukraine) on Sept. 19th, 1948.

TOOMEY, Mary (GB)
See RAND, MARY.

TRIPLE JUMP

Basically, the rules for the triple jump (formerly known as the hop, step and jump) are identical with those governing the long jump. Specific regulations are that in the hopping phase of the event the competitor must land upon the same foot from which he took off; in the step he lands on the other foot, from which subsequently the jump is performed. If the competitor while jumping touches the ground with the " sleeping " leg it is counted as a failure.

The early history of the event is somewhat confused, since more often than not the pioneers took two hops and a jump. James Connolly (USA) performed in this manner to win the first Olympic title in 1896.

Americans and Irishmen (who competed for Britain) had things much their own way until just before the First World War. Myer Prinstein (USA) gained Olympic honours in 1900 and 1904 and he was succeeded in 1908 by Ireland's Tim Ahearne, whose winning jump of 14.91 metres was a world record. His brother Dan Ahearn relieved him of the record two years later in becoming the first man to exceed 15 metres.

Keen competition seems to bring out the best in triple jumpers, for on no fewer than five other occasions the Olympic title has been won at a world record distance. Tony Winter (Australia) scored in 1924 with 15.52 metres, Chuhei Nambu (Japan) in 1932 with 15.72 metres, Naoto Tajima (Japan) in 1936 with 16.00 metres, Adhemar da Silva (Brazil) in 1952 with 16.22 metres and Viktor Sanyeyev (USSR) in 1968 with 17.39 metres. Sanyeyev retained the Olympic title in 1972 and 1976 to become only the third athlete ever to win any Olympic title three times running—and added a silver medal in 1980 for good measure. Joao Carlos de Oliveira of Brazil has held the world record since 1975.

British triple jumpers have been rather quiet internationally. However, Fred Alsop jumped 16.46 metres for 4th place at the 1964 Olympics and the same position was filled in the 1980 Olympics by Keith Connor, the first Briton to exceed 17 metres. Connor set a world indoor best of 17.31 metres in 1981.

See also under DA SILVA, A. F., DE OLIVEIRA, JOAO CARLOS; SANYEYEV, VIKTOR; SZMIDT, JOZEF; and UUDMAE, JAAK.

TYLER, Dorothy (GB)

Dorothy Odam high jumped over 5 ft. (1.52 metres) for the first time in 1935; as Mrs. Tyler she was still clearing close to that height in 1966, aged 46! Her long career was strewn with medals and records, but the supreme competitive honours narrowly eluded her.

At both the 1936 and 1948 Olympics she cleared the height of the winner only to take second place in accordance with the rules then in operation for deciding ties. Under later rules, both times Dorothy would have been declared champion. She competed in four Olympics in all, covering a span of 20 years, finishing equal seventh in 1952 and equal 12th in 1956. She placed second also in the 1950 European and 1954 Commonwealth Games competitions.

Her three major successes (not that the foregoing can be considered as failures!) were winning the Commonwealth title in 1938 and 1950 and setting a world record of 1.66 metres in 1939. Between 1936 and 1956 she won eight outdoor and four indoor WAAA high jump titles, and also took the long jump and pentathlon in 1951.

It was in that year, aged 31, that she changed her style from the outmoded scissors to the western roll. In 1957 she cleared her own physical height of 1.67 metres, only a centimetre below her all-time best of nine years earlier. She was born at Stockwell (London) on Mar. 14th, 1920.

TYUS, Wyomia (USA)

Wyomia Tyus showed promise for a 17-year-old on a European tour in 1963 and created a minor sensation when in Feb. 1964 she set an indoor 70 yd. best performance of 7.5 sec. Outdoors, however, she was overshadowed by Edith McGuire . . . until she arrived in Tokyo for the Olympics. There she hacked three-tenths of a second off her best 100 m. time to equal Wilma Rudolph's world record of 11.2 sec. in a heat and went on to win the final by a good two metres. The following season she tied the world records for 100 yd. (10.3 sec.) and 100 m. (11.1 sec.) and in 1968 she clocked a world record 11.0 sec. (11.08 electrical) at the Olympics where she became the first sprinter to defend successfully. Her best 200 m. time was 23.0 sec She was born at Griffin, Georgia, on Aug 29th, 1945.

UNITED KINGDOM CHAMPIONSHIPS

UK National Championships, not to be confused with the long-established AAA and Women's AAA Championships (which are open to foreign athletes and staged separately), were inaugurated by the BAAB in 1977. Only athletes eligible to represent Great Britain & Northern Ireland in international competition are allowed to enter.

100 Metres		sec.
1977	A. Bennett	10.63
1978	A. W. Wells	10.15
1979	T. J. Hoyte	10.40
1980	R. C. Sharp	10.60

200 Metres		sec.
1977	A. Bennett	21.2
1978	A. W. Wells	20.70
1979	E. G. Tulloch	21.06
1980	R. C. Sharp	21.02

400 Metres		sec.
1977	W. C. Taylor	47.5
1978	R. J. Ashton	46.35
1979	S. Scutt	47.01
1980	D. A. Jenkins	45.29

800 Metres		min. sec.
1977	D. M. J. Warren	1 50.4
1978	S. N. Coe	1 47.1
1979	D. L. Joseph	1 49.2
1980	D. M. J. Warren	1 48.6

1500 Metres		min. sec.
1977	S. M. J. Ovett	3 37.5
1978	J. Robson	3 43.9
1979	A. D. Mottershead	3 43.4
1980	D. R. Moorcroft	3 41.5

5000 Metres		min. sec.
1977	N. H. Rose	13 20.6
1978	M. J. McLeod	13 25.2
1979	S. J. Emson	13 36.6
1980	D. R. Moorcroft	13 41.8

10,000 Metres		min. sec.
1977	I. Stewart	27 51.3
1978	D. J. Black	28 34.8
1979	D. J. Black	28 46.1
1980	G. Smith	28 20.3

3000 Metres Steeplechase		min. sec.
1977	A. R. Staynings	8 31.0
1978	D. Coates	8 26.0
1979	G. Rimmer	8 39.2
1980	A. R. Staynings	8 27.3

110 Metres Hurdles		sec.
1977	B. Price	14.19
1978	B. Price	13.93
1979	J. M. Holtom	13.95
1980	W. E. Greaves	14.05

400 Metres Hurdles		sec.
1977	P. Kelly	51.74
1978	W. J. Hartley	51.03
1979	G. J. Oakes	50.76
1980	G. J. Oakes	50.24

High Jump		metres
1977	M. Butterfield	2.10
1978	M. Naylor	2.15
1979	B. Burges	2.13
1980	M. Naylor	2.22

Pole Vault		metres
1977	J. Gutteridge	5.00
1978	K. F. Stock	5.25
1979	B. R. L. Hooper	5.40
1980	K. F. Stock	5.30

Long Jump		metres
1977	T. Henry	7.66
1978	K. D. Cocks	7.56
1979	F. M. Thompson	7.69
1980	R. R. Mitchell	7.74

Triple Jump		metres
1977	A. L. Moore	15.80
1978	K. L. Connor	16.66
1979	A. L. Moore	15.72
1980	K. L. Connor	16.77

Shot		metres
1977	G. L. Capes	20.04
1978	G. L. Capes	19.80
1979	G. L. Capes	19.00
1980	M. A. Winch	18.96

UNITED KINGDOM RECORDS

Discus		metres
1977	P. A. Tancred	55.44
1978	P. Gordon	54.66
1979	R. C. Slaney	55.32
1980	P. A. Tancred	56.42

Hammer		metres
1977	P. Dickenson	64.88
1978	C. F. Black	69.10
1979	C. F. Black	66.68
1980	P. Dickenson	71.34

Javelin		metres
1977	P. De Kremer	75.82
1978	D. C. Ottley	76.62
1979	D. C. Ottley	74.72
1980	D. C. Ottley	84.10

10,000 Metres Walk		min. sec.
1980	A. James	43 26.3

Women's Events

100 Metres		sec.
1977	S. M. Lannaman	11.30
1978	S. M. Lannaman	11.24
1979	H. R. Hunte	11.30
1980	H. R. Hunte	11.33

200 Metres		sec.
1977	S. M. Lannaman	23.16
1978	S. M. Lannaman	23.16
1979	H. R. Hunte	23.15
1980	K. J. Smallwood	22.62

400 Metres		sec.
1977	D-M. L. Hartley	51.88
1978	K. J. Colebrook	53.80
1979	J. Y. Hoyte-Smith	52.24
1980	L. T. Macdonald	51.16

800 Metres		min. sec.
1977	L. Kiernan	2 01.5
1978	K. J. Colebrook	2 03.3
1979	C. T. Boxer	2 01.6
1980	C. T. Boxer	2 02.2

1500 Metres		min. sec.
1977	H. J. Hollick	4 13.0
1978	H. J. Hollick	4 14.1
1979	G. Dainty	4 15.7
1980	J. White	4 19.5

3000 Metres		min. sec.
1977	G. C. Penny	9 20.0
1978	P. Fudge	8 53.6
1979	G. C. Penny	9 08.4
1980	K. M. Binns	9 01.7

100 Metres Hurdles		sec.
1977	S. Colyear	13.5
1978	S. Colyear	13.67
1979	S. E. Strong	13.28
1980	S. E. Strong	13.48

400 Metres Hurdles		sec.
1977	C. A. Warden	57.6
1978	E. A. Sutherland	58.52
1979	C. A. Warden	56.93
1980	S. M. Dalgoutte	57.79

High Jump		metres
1977	B. M. Gibbs	1.78
1978	G. Hitchen	1.85
1979	A-M. Devally	1.86
1980	L. A. Miller	1.88

Long Jump		metres
1977	S. Colyear	6.42
1978	S. D. Reeve	6.43
1979	S. D. Reeve	6.30
1980	S. C. Hearnshaw	6.47

Shot		metres
1977	V. A. Head	15.72
1978	J. M. Oakes	15.96
1979	A. M. Littlewood	16.43
1980	A. M. Littlewood	17.17

Discus		metres
1977	M. E. Ritchie	53.92
1978	M. E. Ritchie	57.20
1979	M. E. Ritchie	56.80
1980	M. E. Ritchie	62.16

Javelin		metres
1977	T. I. Sanderson	60.24
1978	T. I. Sanderson	59.52
1979	J. Zaslona	53.32
1980	D. Royle	49.52

5000 Metres Walk		min. sec.
1980	C. Tyson	23 48.7

UNITED KINGDOM RECORDS

For current records, see APPENDIX.

Evolution of UK Records

These lists show how British best performances (not necessarily official records) in the standard events have improved over the past 20 years. The first performance shown in most events is the UK best on record as at the beginning of 1961.

UNITED KINGDOM RECORDS

100 Metres
sec.
10.2	McDonald Bailey	Aug. 25	1951
10.2	Menzies Campbell	May 20	1967
10.2	Campbell	May 27	1967
10.1	David Jenkins	May 20	1972
10.1	Brian Green	June 3	1972

Electrical timing:
10.29	Peter Radford	Sept. 13	1958
10.29	Allan Wells	July 9	1978
10.15	Wells	July 15	1978
10.11	Wells	July 24	1980

200 Metres
sec.
20.5	Peter Radford	May 28	1960
20.3	David Jenkins	Aug. 19	1972

Electrical timing:
21.04	Radford	Sept 3	1960
20.66	Dick Steane	Oct. 15	1968
20.66	Jenkins	Aug. 27	1973
20.66	Greg Colin	May 1	1978
20.61	Allan Wells	Aug. 8	1978
20.56	Wells	June 24	1979
20.42	Wells	Aug. 15	1979
20.42	Ainsley Bennett	Sept 12	1979
20.35	Wells	July 1	1980
20.21	Wells	July 28	1980

400 Metres
sec.
46.1	Robbie Brightwell	Sept. 5	1960
45.8	Adrian Metcalfe	July 7	1961
45.7	Metcalfe	Sept. 2	1961
45.7	Brightwell	Oct. 18	1964
45.7	Brightwell	Oct. 19	1964
45.5	David Jenkins	Aug. 13	1971
45.3	Jenkins	June 27	1972
45.2	Jenkins	Aug. 4	1973
45.18	Jenkins	Aug. 16	1974
44.93	Jenkins	June 21	1975

800 Metres
min. sec.
1:46.6	Derek Johnson	Aug. 9	1957
1:46.6	Chris Carter	Sept 5	1965
1:46.5	John Boulter	June 18	1966
1:46.3	C. Carter	Sept. 4	1966
1:46.2	Andy Carter	Aug. 12	1971
1:46.1	Colin Campbell	July 26	1972
1:45.5	A. Carter	July 6	1973
1:45.1	A. Carter	July 14	1973
1:45.0	Sebastian Coe	Sept. 9	1977
1:44.3	Coe	Aug. 18	1978
1:44.1	Steve Ovett	Aug. 31	1978
1:44.0	Coe	Sept. 15	1978
1:42.4	Coe	July 5	1979

1500 Metres
min. sec.
3:41.1	Brian Hewson	Aug. 22	1958
3:40.4	John Boulter	June 28	1964
3:39.1	Alan Simpson	Aug. 15	1964
3:39.1	Ian Stewart	Sept. 1	1969
3:39.0	Peter Stewart	Sept. 12	1970
3:38.7	Jim Douglas	June 27	1972
3:38.2	P. Stewart	July 15	1972
3:38.2	Brendan Foster	Sept. 9	1972
3:37.6	Foster	Feb. 2	1974
3:37.4	Frank Clement	July 30	1974
3:36.8	Mike Kearns	July 26	1977
3:34.5	Steve Ovett	Sept 3	1977
3:32.8	Sebastian Coe	July 17	1979
3:32.1	Coe	Aug. 15	1979
3:32.1	Ovett	July 15	1980
3:31.4	Ovett	Aug. 27	1980

Mile
min. sec.
3:57.2	Derek Ibbotson	July 19	1957
3:56.6	Alan Simpson	June 7	1965
3:55.7	Simpson	Aug. 30	1965
3:55.3	Peter Stewart	June 10	1972
3:55.0	Frank Clement	June 30	1975
3:54.7	Steve Ovett	June 26	1977
3:54.2	Clement	June 20	1978
3:52.8	Ovett	Sept. 20	1978
3:49.0	Sebastian Coe	July 17	1979
3:48.8	Ovett	July 1	1980

5000 Metres
min. sec.
13:36.8	Gordon Pirie	June 19	1956
13:33.0	Mike Wiggs	June 30	1965
13:29.0	Dick Taylor	Aug. 13	1969
13:26.2	Taylor	June 13	1970
13:22.8	Ian Stewart	July 25	1970
13:22.2	Dave Bedford	June 12	1971
13:17.2	Bedford	July 14	1972
13:14.6	Brendan Foster	Jan. 29	1974

10,000 Metres
min. sec.
28:53.0	John Merriman	Sept. 8	1960
28:52.4	Don Taylor	Aug. 23	1963
28:50.0	Jim Hogan	Aug. 14	1965
28:37.6	Mike Freary	Sept. 4	1965
28:26.0	Freary	Sept. 17	1966
28:24.4	Dave Bedford	Apr. 19	1969
28:06.6	Dick Taylor	June 22	1969
28:06.2	Bedford	Sept. 12	1970
27:47.0	Bedford	July 10	1971
27:30.8	Bedford	July 13	1973
27:30.3	Brendan Foster	June 23	1978

Marathon
see under MARATHON

3000 Metres Steeplechase
min. sec.
8:41.2	Chris Brasher	Nov. 29	1956
8:40.4	Maurice Herriott	Aug. 5	1963
8:36.6	Herriott	Sept. 14	1963
8:36.2	Herriott	Sept. 29	1963
8:35.4	Herriott	Oct. 2	1963
8:33.0	Herriott	Oct. 15	1964
8:32.4	Herriott	Oct. 17	1964
8:30.8	Gerry Stevens	Sept. 1	1969
8:28.6	Dave Bedford	Sept. 10	1971
8:26.4	Andy Holden	Sept. 15	1972
8:24.8	John Davies	Jan. 26	1974
8:22.6	Davies	Sept. 13	1974
8:19.0	Dennis Coates	July 25	1976

110 Metres Hurdles
sec.
14.3	Don Finlay	Sept. 4	1938
14.3	Peter Hildreth	Sept. 15	1957
14.3	Hildreth	Aug. 26	1958
14.3	Hildreth	Aug. 28	1958
14.3	Hildreth	Sept. 14	1958
14.3	Hildreth	July 9	1960
14.3	Bob Birrell	Aug. 13	1960
14.2	Mike Parker	Sept. 3	1961
14.2	Birrell	Sept. 6	1961
14.1	Parker	May 19	1963
14.1	Mike Hogan	Sept. 5	1963
14.1	Parker	Sept. 28	1963
13.9	Parker	Oct. 2	1963
13.9	David Hemery	July 2	1966
13.9	Alan Pascoe	Aug. 2	1967
13.9	Pascoe	Oct. 16	1968
13.9	Pascoe	May 17	1969
13.9	Hemery	May 25	1969
13.8	Pascoe	June 2	1969
13.6	Hemery	July 5	1969
13.6	Hemery	Sept. 13	1970
13.5	Berwyn Price	July 1	1973
13.5	Price	May 14	1976

Electrical timing:
13.76	Hemery	Sept. 6	1970
13.69	Price	Aug. 18	1973

400 Metres Hurdles
sec.
51.0	Tom Farrell	June 15	1960
51.0	Chris Surety	Sept 2	1961
51.0	John Cooper	Aug. 14	1963
50.5	Cooper	Sept. 29	1963
50.5	Cooper	Oct. 14	1964
50.4	Cooper	Oct. 15	1964
50.1	Cooper	Oct. 16	1964
49.8	David Hemery	June 15	1968
49.6	Hemery	Aug. 24	1968
49.3	John Sherwood	Oct. 14	1968
49.3	Hemery	Oct. 14	1968
48.12	Hemery	Oct. 15	1968

High Jump
metres
2.05	Crawford Fairbrother	Oct. 10	1959
2.05	Gordon Miller	July 16	1960
2.06	Fairbrother	July 15	1961
2.06	Fairbrother	June 23	1962
2.07	Miller	May 13	1964
2.08	Miller	May 18	1964
2.08	Mike Campbell	Aug. 6.	1971
2.08	Dave Livesey	June 27	1972
2.10	Alan Lerwill	July 18	1973
2.11	Colin Boreham	June 20	1974
2.12	Mike Butterfield	May 4	1975
2.14	Butterfield	May 31	1975
2.14	Angus McKenzie	May 31	1975
2.14	McKenzie	June 8	1975
2.14	McKenzie	June 14	1975
2.15	Brian Burgess	June 26	1976
2.17	Mark Naylor	June 11	1978
2.17	Burgess	June 11	1978
2.20	Burgess	June 11	1978
2.20	Naylor	June 14	1980
2.22	Naylor	June 14	1980
2.24	Naylor	June 28	1980
2.24	Naylor	Aug. 25	1980

Pole Vault
metres
4.30	Geoff Elliott	Aug. 28	1954
4.30	Elliott	July 3	1957
4.30	Elliott	Aug. 27	1958
4.30	Elliott	Sept. 12	1959
4.30	Elliott	Sept. 30	1959
4.32	Rex Porter	June 22	1963
4.37	Trevor Burton	Aug. 5	1963
4.39	Porter	Aug. 30	1963
4.40	Dave Stevenson	Sept. 14	1963
4.41	Stevenson	Sept. 21	1963
4.42	Stevenson	Sept. 25	1963
4.43	Burton	May 16	1964
4.46	Burton	June 20	1964
4.57	Burton	July 11	1964
4.60	Stevenson	July 25	1964
4.61	Stevenson	Aug. 29	1964
4.65	Stevenson	May 25	1966
4.67	Stevenson	May 28	1966
4.72	Mike Bull	Aug. 13	1966
4.80	Bull	Sept. 2	1967
4.94	Bull	June 26	1968
5.03	Bull	Sept. 12	1968
5.07	Bull	Sept. 14	1968
5.10	Bull	July 23	1970
5.11	Bull	June 4	1972
5.20	Bull	June 21	1972
5.20	Bull	July 3	1972

UNITED KINGDOM RECORDS

5.21	Bull	July 15 1972	20.27	Capes	July 14 1973
5.25	Bull	Sept. 22 1973	20.34	Capes	July 19 1973
5.29	Brian Hooper	Apr. 19 1976	20.47	Capes	July 31 1973
5.30	Hooper	May 14 1976	20.59	Capes	Jan. 6 1974
5.31	Hooper	Aug. 7 1976	20.64	Capes	Jan. 19 1974
5.32	Hooper	Aug. 22 1976	20.74	Capes	Feb. 2 1974
5.32	Hooper	July 30 1977	20.81	Capes	May 22 1974
5.37	Hooper	July 30 1977	20.90	Capes	May 26 1974
5.40	Hooper	Aug. 29 1977	21.00	Capes	June 19 1974
5.41	Hooper	Aug. 19 1978	21.37	Capes	Aug. 10 1974
5.42	Hooper	Sept. 17 1978	21.55	Capes	May 28 1976
5.45	Hooper	Aug. 8 1980	21.68	Capes	May 18 1980
5.50	Hooper	Aug. 16 1980			
5.51	Hooper	Aug. 20 1980	*Discus*		
5.52	Keith Stock	Sept. 6 1980	metres		
5.54	Hooper	Sept 6 1980	55.32	Mike Lindsay	May 4 1960
5.55	Stock	Sept. 6 1980	56.70	Roy Hollingsworth	
5.56	Hooper	Sept. 6 1980			Sept. 14 1963
5.57	Stock	Sept. 6 1980	57.00	Gerry Carr	July 17 1965
5.58	Hooper	Sept. 6 1980	57.26	Bill Tancred	May 18 1968
5.59	Hooper	Sept. 6 1980	57.78	John Watts	Sept. 2 1968
			58.00	Tancred	May 1 1971
Long Jump			59.02	Tancred	Apr. 7 1972
metres			59.16	Tancred	Apr. 10 1972
			59.22	Tancred	Apr. 26 1972
7.63	John Howell	Aug. 14 1960	59.42	Tancred	May 10 1972
7.72	Lynn Davies	Nov. 26 1962	59.58	Tancred	May 10 1972
7.73	John Morbey	Aug. 23 1963	59.80	Tancred	June 3 1972
8.01	Davies	May 16 1964	60.56	Tancred	June 7 1972
8.02	Davies	July 25 1964	61.94	Tancred	June 7 1972
8.07	Davies	Oct. 18 1964	61.96	Tancred	May 27 1973
8.13	Davies	Apr. 6 1966	62.10	Tancred	Aug. 11 1973
8.18	Davies	Apr. 9 1966	62.92	Tancred	Aug. 12 1973
8.23	Davies	June 30 1968	63.98	Tancred	Oct. 13 1973
			64.40	Tancred	July 20 1974
			64.94	Tancred	July 21 1974
Triple Jump			*Hammer*		
metres			metres		
15.66	Fred Alsop	Oct. 16 1960	64.96	Mike Ellis	June 4 1959
15.78	Alsop	Sept. 7 1961	65.28	Howard Payne	Aug. 7 1968
16.03	Alsop	Nov. 29 1962	65.68	Payne	Sept. 14 1968
16.13	Alsop	Sept. 11 1964	65.98	Payne	Oct. 5 1968
16.46	Alsop	Oct. 16 1964	68.06	Payne	Oct. 16 1968
16.52	Aston Moore	June 11 1976	68.20	Payne	June 20 1970
16.68	Moore	June 23 1978	68.82	Payne	July 11 1970
16.76	Keith Connor	Aug. 12 1978	69.24	Payne	Sept. 26 1970
17.16	Connor	Jan. 17 1980	69.28	Barry Williams	Aug. 19 1972
Indoor mark:			69.42	Williams	Sept. 16 1972
17.31	Connor	Mar. 13 1981	69.56	Williams	June 2 1973
			70.14	Williams	June 16 1973
Shot			70.28	Ian Chipchase	July 1 1973
metres			71.20	Williams	July 28 1973
19.11	Arthur Rowe	Oct. 16 1960	71.26	Williams	Sept. 8 1973
19.44	Rowe	Aug. 5 1961	72.36	Paul Dickenson	Mar. 26 1976
19.56	Rowe	Aug. 7 1961	73.20	Dickenson	May 22 1976
19.56	Geoff Capes	Apr. 26 1972	73.58	Chris Black	June 26 1976
19.75	Capes	July 26 1972	73.86	Williams	July 1 1976
19.82	Capes	July 26 1972	74.12	Black	Aug. 6 1976
20.18	Capes	July 26 1972	74.98	Black	Aug. 21 1976

UNITED KINGDOM RECORDS

Javelin
metres

75.16	Colin Smith	Sept. 14	1957
78.06	John McSorley	June 30	1962
79.26	McSorley	July 14	1962
79.26	John Greasley	Sept. 14	1963
79.78	John FitzSimons	Aug. 5	1966
81.92	FitzSimons	March 23	1969
82.22	Dave Travis	July 5	1970
83.44	Travis	Aug. 2	1970
84.92	Charles Clover	Feb. 2	1974
85.52	Dave Ottley	May 28	1980

Decathlon (* old tables)
pts.

6177*	Colin Andrews	July 8/9	1960
6184*	George McLachlan	Aug. 10/11	1962
6699	Derek Clarke	July 23/24	1964
6736	Norman Foster	June 11/12	1965
6791	Dave Travis	Aug. 6/7	1965
6840	Foster	Aug. 6/7	1965
7002	Clarke	Sept. 4/5	1965
7200	Clive Longe	June 20/21	1967
7392	Longe	July 8/9	1967
7451	Longe	June 28/29	1969
7486	Barry King	May 31/June 1	1970
7639	Peter Gabbett	May 22/23	1971
7903	Gabbett	June 5/6	1971
7905	Daley Thompson	Sept. 4/5	1976
7921	Thompson	May 21/22	1977
8190	Thompson	June 25/26	1977
8238	Thompson	May 27/28	1978
8289	Thompson	Aug. 30/31	1978
8622	Thompson	May 17/18	1980

20 Kilometres Walk
h. mi. sec.

1	28 15	Ken Matthews	July 23	1960
1	27 34	Paul Nihill	Aug. 10	1971
1	24 50	Nihill	July 30	1972

50 Kilometres Walk
h. mi. sec.

4	12 19	Don Thompson	June 20	1959
4	11 31	Paul Nihill	Oct. 18	1964
4	11 22	Bob Dobson	Aug. 10	1974
4	10 20	Dobson	Sept. 18	1976
4	09 39	Dobson	Oct. 23	1976
4	08 39	Dobson	Oct. 29	1978
4	07 22	Dobson	Oct. 20	1979
4	06 43	Chris Maddocks	Apr. 20	1980
4	05 14	Maddocks	Sept. 13	1980

Evolution of UK Women's Records

100 Metres
sec.

11.5	Dorothy Hyman	Sept. 2	1960
11.5	Jennifer Smart	Sept. 1	1961
11.5	Hyman	June 20	1962
11.5	Hyman	Aug. 25	1962
11.5	Hyman	Sept. 28	1963
11.3	Hyman	Oct. 2	1963
11.3	Hyman	Oct. 3	1963
11.3	Val Peat	Oct. 14	1968
11.3	Della James	Oct. 14	1968
11.3	Anita Neil	May 3	1971
11.2	Andrea Lynch	June 30	1973
11.1	Lynch	June 29	1974
11.1	Lynch	May 18	1975
10.9	Lynch	May 28	1977

Electrical timing:

11.36	James	Oct. 14	1968
11.36	Lynch	Jan. 25	1974
11.31	Lynch	Jan. 26	1974
11.27	Lynch	July 20	1974
11.16	Lynch	June 11	1975

200 Metres
sec.

23.7	Dorothy Hyman	Sept. 3	1960
23.6	Jennifer Smart	Sept. 1	1961
23.5	Hyman	Aug. 4	1962
23.4	Hyman	Aug. 18	1962
23.4	Hyman	Sept. 29	1963
23.2	Hyman	Oct. 3	1963
23.2	Margaret Critchley	Aug. 2	1970
23.1	Helen Golden	Sept. 7	1973
23.0	Golden	June 30	1974
22.8	Sonia Lannaman	May 2	1976
22.8	Lannaman	June 22	1977

Electrical timing:

23.42	Lillian Board	Oct. 17	1968
23.34	Val Peat	Sept. 19	1969
23.14	Golden	Sept. 7	1973
22.81	Lannaman	May 2	1976
22.75	Donna Hartley	June 17	1978
22.70	Kathy Smallwood	Sept. 12	1979
22.58	Lannaman	May 18	1980
22.31	Smallwood	Aug. 8	1980

400 Metres
sec.

54.0	Molly Hiscox	Sept. 12	1959
53.9	Joy Grieveson	Sept. 14	1962
53.16	Grieveson	Sept. 14	1963
53.1	Ann Packer	Oct. 15	1964
52.7	Packer	Oct. 16	1964
52.2	Packer	Oct. 17	1964

UNITED KINGDOM RECORDS

52.12	Lillian Board	Oct. 16	1968
52.1	Verona Elder	May 31	1973
51.94	Elder	Jan. 26	1974
51.77	Donna Hartley	July 30	1974
51.28	Hartley	July 12	1975
51.16	Linsey Macdonald	June 15	1980
51.06	Joslyn Hoyte-Smith	June 27	1980
50.88	Hoyte-Smith	July 1	1980

800 Metres
min. sec.

2:06.1	Joy Jordan	Sept. 24	1960
2:05.0	Jordan	Sept. 16	1962
2:04.8	Anne Smith	Oct. 19	1964
2:01.1	Ann Packer	Oct. 20	1964
2:00.2	Rosemary Stirling	Sept. 3	1972
1:59.1	Christina Boxer	Aug. 4	1979

1500 Metres
min. sec.

4:29.7	Diane Leather	July 19	1957
4:17.3	Anne Smith	June 3	1967
4:15.9	Rita Ridley	Sept. 20	1969
4:15.4	Ridley	June 20	1970
4:14.3	Ridley	July 17	1971
4:12.7	Ridley	Aug. 15	1971
4:11.3	Joyce Smith	Sept. 4	1972
4:09.4	J. Smith	Sept. 7	1972
4:07.4	Sheila Carey	Sept. 7	1972
4:04.8	Carey	Sept. 9	1972
4:04.7	Christine Benning	Aug. 5	1979
4:01.6	Benning	Aug. 15	1979

Mile
min. sec.

4:45.0	Diane Leather	Sept. 21	1955
4:41.4	Anne Smith	June 4	1966
4:39.2	Smith	May 13	1967
4:37.0	Smith	June 3	1967
4:36.2	Joan Allison	Sept. 14	1973
4:36.1	Mary Stewart	May 18	1977
4.30.2	Christina Boxer	July 8	1979

3000 Metres
min. sec.

9:59.6	Rita Ridley	Dec. 15	1968
9:54.4	Barbara Banks	July 5	1969
9:52.2	Joyce Smith	Dec. 16	1970
9:43.8	Smith	June 12	1971
9:23.4	Smith	July 16	1971
9:22.6	Ridley	Aug. 12	1972
9:05.8	Smith	Sept. 19	1972
9:04.4	Smith	June 20	1974
8:55.6	Smith	July 19	1974
8:52.8	Ann Ford	Aug. 28	1977
8:52.3	Christine Benning	Aug. 19	1978
8:48.7	Paula Fudge	Aug. 29	1978

Marathon
See under **MARATHON**.

100 Metres Hurdles
sec.

13.7	Chris Bell	June 3	1967
13.7	Bell	July 19	1968
13.5	Bell	July 19	1968
13.4	Bell	Aug. 2	1970
13.2	Judy Vernon	July 26	1972
13.2	Vernon	June 9	1974
13.2	Vernon	June 22	1974
13.0	Vernon	June 29	1974
13.0	Blondelle Thompson	June 29	1974

Electrical timing:

13.29	Mary Peters	Sept. 2	1972
13.21	Sharon Colyear	June 22	1976
13.11	Colyear	June 22	1976
13.08	Lorna Boothe	June 11	1978
13.06	Shirley Strong	July 11	1980

400 Metres Hurdles
sec.

61.1	Sandra Dyson	May 15	1971
60.4	Judy Vernon	March 21	1973
60.3	Christine Warden	May 27	1973
59.87	Vernon	Sept. 14	1973
58.86	Warden	May 26	1974
58.0	Warden	June 30	1974
57.84	Warden	Aug. 21	1976
57.6	Warden	June 11	1977
57.59	Liz Sutherland	Aug. 25	1977
57.0	Warden	May 20	1978
56.80	Warden	June 23	1979
56.06	Warden	July 28	1979

High Jump
metres

1.74	Thelma Hopkins	May 5	1956
1.75	Frances Slaap	Aug. 15	1964
1.76	Slaap	Sept. 26	1964
1.76	Barbara Lawton	Apr. 19	1969
1.76	Linda Hedmark	May 24	1969
1.78	Lawton	June 7	1969
1.79	Hedmark	June 17	1969
1.79	Lawton	July 11	1970
1.83	Hedmark	July 4	1971
1.85	Lawton	Aug. 12	1971
1.85	Lawton	Sept. 4	1971
1.85	Lawton	Sept. 4	1972
1.86	Lawton	Sept. 15	1972
1.87	Lawton	Sept. 22	1973
1.87	Moira Maguire	May 11	1980
1.88	Louise Miller	May 17	1980
1.90	Miller	May 18	1980

1.92	Miller	May 25	1980
1.94	Miller	May 25	1980

Long Jump
metres
6.33	Mary Rand	Aug. 31	1960
6.35	Rand	July 13	1963
6.44	Rand	Aug. 5	1963
6.58	Rand	July 4	1964
6.76	Rand	Oct. 14	1964

Shot
metres
14.96	Suzanne Allday	Aug. 8	1959
15.18	Allday	May 18	1964
16.31	Mary Peters	June 1	1966
16.40	Meg Ritchie	May 14	1978
16.72	Judy Oakes	June 3	1979
16.84	Ritchie	March 28	1980
17.17	Angela Littlewood	June 14	1980
17.53	Littlewood	July 24	1980

Indoor mark:
17.65	Venissa Head	Feb. 22	1981

Discus
metres
47.70	Suzanne Allday	June 7	1958
48.06	Rosemary Payne	Sept. 19	1964
48.24	Payne	Sept 20	1964
50.68	Payne	June 14	1965
50.94	Payne	June 17	1966
51.04	Payne	June 18	1969
51.88	Payne	June 28	1969
52.22	Payne	July 26	1969
52.22	Payne	Aug. 16	1969
52.30	Payne	Apr. 29	1970
55.04	Payne	May 17	1970
56.90	Payne	May 7	1972
58.02	Payne	June 3	1972
59.88	Meg Ritchie	Sept. 3	1977
60.80	Ritchie	Apr. 15	1978
61.88	Ritchie	March 1	1980
62.76	Ritchie	March 15	1980
63.74	Ritchie	March 18	1980
64.30	Ritchie	March 22	1980
65.08	Ritchie	Apr. 26	1980
65.96	Ritchie	July 19	1980
67.48	Ritchie	Apr. 26	1981

Javelin
metres
51.60	Susan Platt	Aug. 20	1960
54.44	Platt	Aug. 24	1961
54.82	Platt	Aug. 3	1964
55.60	Platt	June 15	1968
56.14	Tessa Sanderson	June 11	1976
57.18	Sanderson	July 23	1976
57.20	Sanderson	Aug. 30	1976
58.90	Sanderson	June 4	1977
60.24	Sanderson	June 12	1977
64.42	Sanderson	July 1	1977
67.20	Sanderson	July 17	1977
69.70	Sanderson	June 5	1980

Pentathlon (* old tables)
pts. (with 80 Metres Hurdles)
4679*	Mary Rand	Aug. 8	1959
4712*	Rand	July 13	1963
4726*	Rand	Aug. 23/24	1963
4801*	Mary Peters	May 30	1964
4815*	Rand	June 20/21	1964
4823*	Peters	Aug. 19	1964
4435	(5035*) Rand	Oct. 16/17	1964

(With 100 Metres Hurdles)
4527	(5148*) Peters	July 21/22	1970
4630	Peters	May 7	1972
4801	Peters	Sept. 2/3	1972

(With 800 Metres)
4385	Sue Longden	July 31	1977
4409	Longden	May 24	1980

5000 Metres Track Walk
min. sec.
26 47.0	Judy Farr	May 30	1964
26 27.0	Barbara Fisk	Aug. 24	1969
25 09.2	Betty Jenkins	Sept. 16	1972
25 02.0	Marion Fawkes	Aug. 4	1974
24 59.2	Fawkes	Aug. 24	1974
24 47.8	Fawkes	Sept. 7	1975
24 10.0	Fawkes	Aug. 21	1976
23 59.6	Fawkes	July 26	1977
23 58.4	Carol Tyson	Aug. 20	1977
23 42.4	Tyson	Oct. 1	1977
23 11.2	Tyson	June 30	1979

10,000 Metres Track Walk
min. sec.
52 50.0	Christine Coleman	Aug. 21	1973
50 03.0	Marion Fawkes	March 26	1977
49 59.0	Carol Tyson	March 25	1978
48 37.6	Fawkes	March 31	1979
48 11.4	Fawkes	July 8	1979

UNITED STATES CHAMPIONSHIPS

The first American Championships, organised by the New York AC, were held in 1876. Three years later they were taken over by the National Association of Amateur Athletes of America. The inaugural AAU Championships were staged in 1888, and have continued without break—even during the war years—ever since, although from 1980 they have been conducted by the AAU's successor as the governing body for track and field: The Athletics Congress.

The most titles won in any single men's event is ten by Henry Laskau in the 3000 m. or 2 miles walk from 1948 to 1957 and by George Gray in the shot between 1887 and 1902. The most by a woman is 11 by Stella Walsh in the 200 m. between 1930 and 1948, Maren Seidler in the shot between 1967 and 1980, and Dorothy Dodson in the javelin from 1939 to 1949.

American Championship records— 100 m: 10.03 sec. J. Hines 1968; 200 m: 20.08 sec. L. King 1980; 400 m: 44.82 sec. M. Parks 1976; 800 m: 1 min 43.9 sec. R. Wohlhuter 1974; 1500 m: 3 min. 36.4 sec. S. Scott 1979; 5000 m: 13 min. 29.0 sec. M. Liquori 1975; 10,000 m: 27 min. 39.4 sec. C. Virgin 1979; 3000 m. Steeplechase: 8 min. 21.6 sec. J. Munyala (Kenya) 1977; 110 m. Hurdles: 13.19 sec. R. Nehemiah 1979; 400 m. Hurdles: 47.45 sec. E. Moses 1977; High Jump: 2.30 m. D. Stones 1978; Pole Vault: 5.56 m. D. Ripley 1978; Long Jump: 8.32 m. A. Robinson 1976; Triple Jump: 17.36 m. W. Banks 1980; Shot: 21.82 m. B. Oldfield 1980; Discus: 70.66 m. M. Wilkins 1979; Hammer: 76.58 m. G. Urlando (Italy) 1980; Javelin: 86.64 m. J. Murro 1969; Decathlon: 8444 pts. B. Jenner 1976. (*Women*) 100 m: 10.97 sec. E. Ashford 1979; 200 m: 22.60 sec. B. Morehead 1978; 400 m. 51.04 sec. L. Forde 1978; 800 m: 1 min. 58.8 sec. M. Manning 1980; 1500 m: 4 min. 06.6 sec. F. Larrieu 1979; 3000 m: 8 min. 53.8 sec. F. Larrieu 1979; 100 m. Hurdles: 12.86 sec. D. LaPlante 1979; 400 m. Hurdles: 56.3 sec. E. Mahr 1980; High Jump: 1.93 m. D. Brill (Canada) 1979 & C. Rienstra 1980; Long Jump: 6.89 m. J. Anderson 1978; Shot: 19.09 m. M. Seidler 1979; Discus: 58.44 m. L. Griffin 1980; Javelin: 66.52 m. K. Schmidt 1976; Pentathlon: 4506 pts. J. Frederick 1979.

UUDMAE, Jaak (USSR)

In Moscow, for the fourth consecutive Olympics, the triple jump gold medal went to a Soviet athlete —not, this time, to the legendary Viktor Sanyeyev, champion since 1968, but to the gangling Estonian Jaak Uudmae. It was a competition which aroused much controversy due to allegations of unfair judging, but what cannot be disputed is that on the day Uudmae produced the longest jump of his life and was a worthy successor to Sanyeyev, who on this occasion finished second. Uudmae's leap of 17.35 metres, achieved into a slight headwind, brought him up to fourth place on the world all-time list, or third if one discounts high altitude marks.

Uudmae's own previous best of 17.20 metres was set at altitude in Mexico City when placing second in the 1979 World Student Games. His only other significant medals prior to the Olympics were two silvers and a bronze in the European Indoor Championships.

His annual progression: 1970— 10.73 m.; 1971—11.77; 1972—13.82; 1973—14.32; 1974—15.60; 1975—16.03; 1976—16.54; 1977—16.72; 1978—16.86; 1979—17.20; 1980—17.35. He was born in Tallin on Sept. 3rd, 1954.

VERGOVA, Maria (Bulgaria)

It's never happened before in the entire history of Olympic women's track and field, but in Moscow gold and silver medals in an event went to the same athletes for the second Games running. It occurred in the discus: Evelin Jahl won in both 1976 (69.00 metres) and 1980 (69.96 metres), while runner-up each time was Maria Vergova (or Petkova as she's sometimes referred to) with 67.30 and 67.90 metres respectively. The difference is that whereas the Bulgarian was reasonably content with her placing in Montreal, that wasn't the case in Moscow where she entered the competition as brand-new world record holder, having unleashed a mighty throw of 71.80 metres just a couple of weeks earlier.

The statuesque Vergova (she is 1.82 metres tall and weighs over 100 kg.) who missed the 1978 European Championships to give birth to a son, will be 33 then but is confident it will be a case of third time lucky for her at the 1984 Olympics.

Her annual progress: 1968—35.60 m.; 1969—38.90; 1970—42.60; 1971—50.40; 1972—53.20; 1973—60.72; 1974—68.48; 1975—66.98; 1976—68.62; 1977—68.20; 1979—65.02; 1980—71.80. She was born at Plovdiv on Nov. 3rd, 1950.

VETERANS

One of the fastest growing areas in athletics in recent years has been competition for veterans (or masters, as they are known in the USA), i.e. male athletes aged 40 or over and women of 35 or over on the day of the meeting. Inaugural World Championships were staged with great success in Toronto in 1975, and have subsequently been held in Gothenburg (1977), Hanover (1979) and Christchurch (1981), with the next Championships scheduled for Puerto Rico in 1983. Athletes compete within five-year age bands, up to 80 and over.

Several past Olympic medallists and world record holders have gone on to make their mark as veterans, as will be seen from this list of champions (40-44 age group for men, 35-39 for women, unless otherwise noted in the case of a superior performance in an older age category).

100 Metres		sec.
1975	T. Baker (USA)	11.1
1977	R. Austin (Aus)	10.8
1979	K-H. Schroder (W. Ger)	10.95
1981	D. Smith (USA)	11.25

200 Metres		sec.
1975	M. Garbisch (W. Ger)	22.7
1977	R. Austin (Aus)	21.9
1979	R. Austin (Aus)	22.50
1981	R. Austin (Aus)	22.53

400 Metres		sec.
1975	M. Garbisch (W. Ger)	50.7
1977	N. Clough (Aus)	49.5
1979	B. Bianchi (Ita)	49.57
1981	G. Mathe (Hol)	50.46

800 Metres		min. sec.
1975	L. Means (USA)	2 00.2
1977	A. Blue (Aus)	1 54.8
1979	E. Billups (USA)	1 56.6
1981	G. Cohen (USA)	1 55.5

1500 Metres		min. sec.
1975	A. Thomas (Aus)	3 59.5
1977	C. Huyssen (Bel)	3 56.7
1979	M. Schleime (W. Ger)	4 00.8
1981	A. Bradford (Aus)	4 02.4

3000 Metres		min. sec
1975	A. Thomas (Aus)	8 26.8

5000 Metres		min. sec.
1975	R. Fowler (GB)	14 52.0
1977	G. Roelants (Bel)	14 03.0
1979	J. Kessler (W. Ger)	15 16.6
1981	M. Connolly (Ire)	14 54.7

VETERANS

10,000 Metres	min. sec.
1975 R. Fowler (GB)	31 19.6
1977 R. Fowler (GB)	31 45.7
1979 D. Macgregor (GB)	30 04.2
1981 A. Villanueva (Mex)	29 52.2

Cross-Country	min. sec.
1975 R. Fowler (GB)	32 51
1977 G. Roelants (Bel)	28 57
1979 T. Davies (GB)	33 22
1981 R. Robinson (NZ)	32 14

Marathon	hr. min. sec.
1975 E. Austin (GB)	2 28 23
1977 E. Austin (GB)	2 25 57
1979 J. Robinson (NZ)	2 22 52
1981 R. de Palmas (Ita)	2 19 34

3000 m. Steeplechase	min. sec.
1975 H. Higdon (USA)	9 18.6
1977 G. Roelants (Bel)	8 56.6
1979 T. Davies (GB)	9 03.5
1981* D. Worling (Aus)	9 41.5
* 45–49 winner	

110 m. Hurdles (3' 3")	sec.
1975 L. Marien (Bel)	14.7
1977 H. Mandl (Aut)	15.2
1979* V. Thorlaksson (Ice)	14.86
1981* L. Marien (Bel)	15.95
* 45–49 winner	

400 m. Hurdles	sec.
1975* J. Greenwood (USA)	57.8
1977 N. Clough (Aus)	54.3
1979 L. Hacker (Rho)	54.08
1981 G. Mathe (Hol)	55.28
* 45–49 winner	

High Jump	metres
1975 S. Pettersson (Swe)	1.95
1977 H. Mandl (Aut)	2.00
1979 F. Schmitz (W. Ger)	1.89
1981* H. Wyatt (USA)	1.83
* 45–49 winner	

Pole Vault	metres
1975 W. Kostric (Can)	4.42
1977 M. Houvion (Fra)	4.50
1979 W. Kostric (Can)	4.20
1981 W. Sokolowski (USA)	4.60

Long Jump	metres
1975* S. Davisson (USA)	6.52
1977 T. Chilton (USA)	7.03
1979 P. Pinto (Por)	6.91
1981 H. Thomann (W. Ger)	6.40
* 45–49 winner	

Triple Jump	metres
1975 D. Jackson (USA)	13.63
1977 H. Mandl (Aut)	14.31
1979 G. Swakala (Rho)	14.40
1981 H. Thomann (W. Ger)	13.20

Shot	metres
1975 E. McComas (USA)	16.23
1977 I. Ivancic (Yug)	18.03
1979 F. Schladen (W. Ger)	18.30
1981 K. Flocke (W. Ger)	15.38

Discus	metres
1975 E. McComas (USA)	49.90
1977 A. Oerter (USA)	60.36
1979 F. Schladen (W. Ger)	54.22
1981* P. Speckens (W. Ger)	45.56
* 45–49 winner	

Hammer	metres
1975 H. Payne (GB)	63.22
1977 H. Potsch (Aut)	61.32
1979* H. Potsch (Aut)	61.14
1981* H. Potsch (Aut)	61.36
* 45–49 winner	

Javelin	metres
1975 P. Conley (USA)	62.78
1977 U. von Wartburg (Swi)	78.66
1979 U. von Wartburg (Swi)	78.98
1981 U. von Wartburg (Swi)	74.06

Pentathlon	pts.
1975 P. Conley (USA)	2704
1977 D. Clarke (GB)	3789
1979 W. Schallau (W. Ger)	3903
1981* R. Williams (NZ)	4038
* 45–49 winner	

5000 Metres Walk	min. sec.
1977 S. Ladany (Isr)	23 15.6
1981 R. Mee (Aus)	23 04.0

10,000 Metres Walk	min. sec
1979* G. Weidner (W. Ger)	43 50.1
* 45–49 winner	

20 Kilometres Walk	hr. min. sec.
1977 S. Ladany (Isr)	1 38 08
1979* G. Weidner (W. Ger)	1 31 58
1981 J. Smith (Aus)	1 34 10
* 45–49 winner	

25 Kilometres Walk	hr. min. sec.
1975 R. Thorpe (GB)	2 02 45

Women

100 Metres — sec.
1975* R. Payne (GB) 12.3
1977 T. Rautanen (Fin) 12.1
1979 E. Wandscher (W. Ger) 12.10
1981 V. Lund (Aus) 12.55
* 40–44 winner

200 Metres — sec.
1979 E. Wandscher (W. Ger) 24.99
1981* K. Holland (Aus) 26.12
* 40–44 winner

400 Metres — sec.
1975* C. Mills (NZ) 58.9
1977 K. Holland (Aus) 56.5
1979 K. Holland (Aus) 58.19
1981 P. Kenny (NZ) 59.11
* 40–44 winner

800 Metres — min. sec.
1979 M. Hoffman (W. Ger) 2 13.2
1981 P. Kenny (NZ) 2 18.7

1500 Metres — min. sec.
1975* M. Klopfer (USA) 5 05.7
1977 T. Syrjala (Fin) 4 30.6
1979 M. Hoffmann (W. Ger) 4 31.9
1981 D. Browne (Aus) 4 40.5
* 40–44 winner

3000 Metres — min. sec.
1977 S. Larsson (Swe) 9 49.1

5000 Metres — min. sec.
1975* D. Stock (USA) 19 26.4
1979* M. Gorman (USA) 17 39.2
1981 V. Foltz (USA) 17 37.0
* 40–44 winner

10,000 Metres — min. sec.
1977 Konings-Rypers (Hol) 37 12.2
1979 L. Winter (W. Ger) 36 20.2
1981* B. Shingles (NZ) 36 28.4
* 40–44 winner

Cross-Country — min. sec.
1977* M. Gorman (USA) 35 28
1979 T. Tammisto (Fin) 39 49
1981 V. Foltz (USA) 39 10
* 40–44 winner

Marathon — hr. min. sec.
1975* R. Anderson (USA) 3 17 34
1977* M. Gorman (USA) 2 57 05
1979 L. Winter (W. Ger) 2 47 31
1981 R. Haynes (NZ) 2 54 59
* 40–44 winner

100 m. Hurdles — sec.
1979 C. Voss (W. Ger) 14.46
1981 P. McNab (GB) 15.18

High Jump — metres
1975* R. Payne (GB) 1.55
1979 C. Voss (W. Ger) 1.73
1981* H. Searle (Aus) 1.51
* 40–44 winner

Long Jump — metres
1977 T. Rautanen (Fin) 5.53
1979 D. Breul (W. Ger) 5.59
1981 D. Breul (W. Ger) 5.65

Shot — metres
1979 I. Wehmonen (Swe) 15.15
1981* E. Huber (W. Ger) 13.40
* 45–49 winner

Discus — metres
1975 (1) R. Payne (GB) 52.18
1977 I. Wehmonen (Swe) 44.12
1979 G. Johansson (Swe) 47.02
1981 (2) O. Domingos (Bra) 48.24
(1) 40–44   (2) 45–49

Javelin — metres
1979 C. Peters (W. Ger) 47.32
1981 M. Thomas (Aus) 43.60

Pentathlon — pts.
1979 C. Voss (W. Ger) 4503
1981* H. Searle (Aus) 3732
* 40–44 winner

5000 Metres Walk — min. sec.
1975* M. Ohlsson (Swe) 30 30.0
1977 J. Farr (GB) 24 37.7
1979 J. Farr (GB) 24 28.1
1981 S. Miller (Aus) 26 55.0
* 40–44 winner

10,000 Metres Walk — min. sec.
1979* Broders (W. Ger) 51 26.2
1981 S. Miller (Aus) 54 05.0
* 40–44 winner

VIREN, Lasse (Finland)

Between 1912 and 1936 there was a total of twelve Olympic 5000 m. or 10,000 m. races; ten of them were won by Finnish runners! Names like Hannes Kolehmainen, Paavo Nurmi and Ville Ritola are still revered in Finland and the country long awaited an heir to this great tradition. Juha Vaatainen's double at the 1971 European Championships in Helsinki was hailed with emotion, but it was Lasse Viren in Munich in 1972 who brought Finnish distance running

Olympic honours again after such a long interval. And what honours! Not only did he win both the 5000 m. and 10,000 m., but his time in the latter event of 27 min. 38.4 sec. broke Ron Clarke's world record . . . in spite of his having fallen over just before halfway! He covered the final 800 m. in an amazing 1 min. 56.6 sec., and produced another remarkable display in the 5000 m. (13 min. 26.4 sec.) in zipping through the last four laps in 3 min. 59.8 sec.

Viren, who was barely noticed in the 1971 European meet where he placed 7th in the 5000 m. and 17th in the 10,000 m., claimed a world 2 mile record with 8 min. 14.0 sec. shortly before the 1972 Olympics and set a short-lived 5000 m. record of 13 min. 16.4 sec. in the late season.

Apart from placing 3rd in the 5000 m. at the 1974 European Championships (he was 7th in the 10,000 m.), at a time when he was unfit following injury, he achieved little of note until the 1976 Olympics. There he made history by not only retaining both his titles (27 min. 40.4 sec. followed by 13 min. 24.8 sec.), the first man ever to do so, but placing a remarkable 5th in his marathon debut —the day after the 5000 m. final!

The pattern repeated itself during the next four years. Although a living legend on account of his Olympic triumphs, Viren displayed mediocre form in countless races all over the world. Persistent injury was one reason, but so was a lack of motivation: for him only the Olympics really mattered. Sure enough, the 1980 Games found him in his best condition since Montreal and some of the old magic was still there as he strode into the lead with three laps of the 10,000 m. remaining. He was run out of it in the closing stages, finishing 5th in 27 min. 50.5 sec., but at least he lost his title with honour.

His best marks: 3 min. 41.8 sec. for 1500 m., 7 min. 43.2 sec. for 3000 m., 8 min. 14.0 sec. for 2 miles, 13 min. 16.4 sec. for 5000 m., 27 min. 38.4 sec. for 10,000 m., and 2 hr. 13 min. 11 sec. for the marathon. He was born at Myrskyla on July 22nd, 1949.

WAITZ, Grete (Norway)

Interviewed at the end of 1974, the season she became European 1500 m. bronze medallist, Grete Andersen—as she was then—was asked whether she would be moving up to the 3000 m. in view of her moderate basic speed. "No," she replied. "I've raced the distance once and thought it far too long." Ironic, considering the future Grete Waitz was to develop into the greatest long distance runner in women's athletics history!

That 3000 m. debut, in 1973, took a less than earth-shattering 9 min. 34.2 sec., but when she tried the event again two years later her time was a world record cracking 8 min. 46.6 sec. Whether she liked it or not, she had found the track event which suited her best. Shortly before the 1976 Olympics she trimmed the record to 8 min. 45.4 sec., but at the Games she failed to reach the final of the 1500 m.—the longest race for women on the programme. To make matters worse, her 3000 m. record was wiped out just after the Games by Lyudmila Bragina, whose revolutionary time of 8 min. 27.2 sec. remains unchallenged.

There was some compensation for the tall, majestic Norwegian in 1977 when first she reduced her own best time to 8 min. 36.8 sec. and then she trounced Bragina (8 min. 43.5 sec. to 8 min. 46.3 sec.) in the World Cup. Her prospects for success in the 1978 European Championships were looking bright, particularly after an amazing 30 sec. margin of victory in her first attempt at the World Cross-Country Championship and the second fastest ever 3000 m. time of 8 min. 32.1 sec., but in Prague she was outsprinted to finish third behind Svetlana Ulmasova (USSR), who clocked 8 min. 33.2 sec., and Natalia Marasescu of Romania.

That disappointment was put firmly behind her when, in October 1978, she made an astonishing marathon debut in New York—slicing over two minutes from the previous world best with a time of 2 hr. 32 min. 30 sec.

Another momentous but flawed season followed in 1979. Over the country (winner of the World title by 26 sec.) and on the road, where she set breathtaking world bests of 31 min. 15.4 sec. for 10,000 m., 53 min. 05 sec. for 10 miles and 2 hr. 27 min. 33 sec. in the New York Marathon, she reigned supreme. But on the track, despite trimming her personal bests for 1500 and 3000 m. to 4 min. 00.6 sec. and 8 min. 31.8 sec., she was again outkicked by Ulmasova in the biggest event of the year—the World Cup 3000 m.

Grete completed a hat-trick of World cross-country titles in 1980 (this time with all of 40 sec. to spare), but wasn't seen much on the track. There was little incentive, with the 1500 m. still the longest Olympic event for her, but in the end the decision on whether to compete or not in Moscow was taken for her when Norway boycotted the Games. The inaugural World 3000 m. championship would have been a natural target but injury caused her to miss the event. On the USA road circuit, however, she showed phenomenal form with world bests of 30 min. 59.8 sec. for 10,000 m. and 2 hr. 25 min. 42 sec. for the marathon. Placing 74th out of 14,012 starters in New York, she thus notched up her third world record in three tries at the marathon! It was a time which would have won every Olympic marathon title up to and including 1948 and been good enough for a silver medal as recently as 1956. She passed 10 miles in 54 min. 53 sec., halfway in 1 hr 12 min. 37 sec. and 20 miles in another world's best of 1 hr 51 min. 23 sec.

Grete's best track times are 57.6 sec. for 400 m., 2 min. 03.1 sec. for 800 m., 4 min. 00.6 sec. for 1500 m.

and 8 min. 31.8 sec for 3000 m; and she high jumped 1.61 metres at the age of 17. She was born in Oslo on Oct. 1st, 1953.

WALKER, John (New Zealand)

Like his fellow New Zealanders Jack Lovelock and Peter Snell, John Walker has scaled two of the most glamorous peaks in athletics: he has broken the world record for the mile and won the Olympic 1500 m. title.

Walker's first truly great race was one he lost . . . the 1974 Commonwealth Games 1500 m. That was the memorable occasion on which Filbert Bayi led from start to finish in the world record time of 3 min. 32.2 sec., but Walker was only a couple of metres behind at the end and his time of 3 min. 32.5 sec. also smashed Jim Ryun's previous mark. Later in the year, in a re-match in Helsinki, Bayi blew up after reaching 1200 m. in 2 min. 50.4 sec., leaving Walker to win with ease in 3 min. 33.4 sec.

He really came into his own on a European tour in 1975. He narrowly missed Bayi's 1500 m. record with 3 min. 32.4 sec. (passing 1200 m. in 2 min. 50.9 sec.); and a fortnight later he became the first man to break 3 min. 50 sec. for the mile. He followed a pacemaker through 440 yd. in 55.8 sec. and 880 yd. in 1 min. 55.1 sec., and from then on he was on his own. He covered the third quarter in 57.9 sec. to reach three-quarters in 2 min. 53.0 sec., and sped around the last lap in 56.4 sec. for a final time of 3 min. 49.4 sec.,—exactly ten seconds faster than Roger Bannister's historic run of 21 years earlier.

Another world record fell to him prior to the 1976 Olympics when he chopped no less than 4.8 sec. off Michel Jazy's highly rated 2000 m. figures with a time of 4 min. 51.4 sec. His lap times were 60.1, 58.5, 57.7, 57.9 and 57.2 sec., and he must have run the final mile in around 3 min. 53 sec! With Bayi a non-starter in Montreal due to the African boycott, Walker was deprived of the Olympic clash he had been preparing for and in a slow race he turned in a 52.7 sec. last lap for a narrow but confident victory in 3 min. 39.2 sec.

Hampered by injury since 1977, Walker has never quite recaptured his old form while at the same time remaining a formidable competitor. He clocked 3 min. 33.4 sec. for 1500 m. in 1980 but was unable, because of New Zealand's boycott, to defend his Olympic crown.

Best marks.: 48.9 sec. for 400 m., 1 min. 44.9 sec. for 800 m., 3 min. 32.4 sec. for 1500 m., 3 min. 49.4 sec. for the mile, 4 min. 51.4 sec. for 2000 m., 7 min. 40.6 sec. for 3000 m. He has also placed 4th in the 1975 IAAF cross-country championship and has run 21 miles at 2 hr. 19 min. marathon pace. He was born at Papukura on Jan. 12th, 1952.

WALKING

The IAAF defines walking as " progression by steps so taken that unbroken contact with the ground is maintained. At each step, the advancing foot of the walker must make contact with the ground before the rear foot leaves the ground. During the period of each step in which a foot is on the ground, the leg must be straightened (i.e. not bent at the knee) at least for one moment, and in particular, the supporting leg must be straight in the vertically upright position." The judges have the power to disqualify any competitor whose mode of progression they consider fails to comply with the definition of walking.

When an athlete is moving at a speed of around 9 m.p.h. it can be difficult for the judges to decide whether he is " lifting " (having both feet off the ground for a split second). Several controversial decisions over the years led to the removal of track walking from the Olympic programme in 1928, 1932, 1936 and since 1952. The two international championship distances on the road are 20 kilometres and 50 kilometres. The latter event was dropped from the Olympic programme in 1976, the IAAF instituting a world championship to fill the gap, but the 50 km. was reinstated at the 1980 Games. The world track records for these two events are held by the Mexicans, Daniel Bautista and Raul Gonzalez.

Britain has an enviable record at both these events, having supplied the winner of the 20 km. at the 1958, 1962 and 1969 European Championships and 1964 Olympic Games, and of the 50 km. in the 1932, 1936 and 1960 Olympic Games. Norman Read (New Zealand), the 1956 Olympic 50 km. champion, is English by birth.

The Race Walking Association (known as the Road Walking Association until 1954), which came into existence in 1907, is the governing body for road walking in England and Wales and their annual road races are recognised as English Championships. Winners (from 1956) :—

10 Miles min. sec.
1956 R. Hardy 74 31.0
1957 S. F. Vickers 76 51.0
1958 S. F. Vickers 73 44.0
1959* K. J. Matthews 71 00.4
1960 K. J. Matthews 70 57.0
1961 K. J. Matthews 74 21.0
1962 K. J. Matthews 76 10.0
1963 K. J. Matthews 73 00.0
1964 K. J. Matthews 70 22.0
1965 V. P. Nihill 74 55.0
1966 P. McCullagh (Australia)
 74 05.0
1967 R. Wallwork 75 06.0
1968 V. P. Nihill 72 28.0
1969 V. P. Nihill 71 14.0
1970 W. Wesch (W. Germany)
 72 07.0
1971 P. B. Embleton 69 29.0
1972 V. P. Nihill 73 33.0
1973 J. A. Webb 72 43.0
1974 P. Marlow 72 58.0
1975 O. T. Flynn 71 15.0
1976 O. T. Flynn 69 59.0
1977 R. G. Mills 72 36.0
1978* O. T. Flynn 67 29.0
1979 C. J. Harvey 71 25.0
1980* R. G. Mills 68 45.0
1981 M. Parker (NZ) 73 37.0
 * short course

20 Miles hr. min. sec.
1956 R. Hardy 2 38 27.0
1957 E. W. Hall 2 45 12.0
1958 L. Allen 2 43 21.0
1959 T. W. Misson 2 45 19.0
1960 S. F. Vickers 2 41 41.0
1961 D. J. Thompson 2 44 49.0
1962 K. J. Matthews 2 38 39.0
1963 V. P. Nihill 2 39 43.0
1964 V. P. Nihill 2 40 13.0
1965 V. P. Nihill 2 44 03.0
1966 N. R. Read
 (New Zealand) 2 39 33.0
1967 R. J. Lodge 2 42 43.0
1968 V. P. Nihill 2 35 07.0
1969 V. P. Nihill 2 44 51.0
1970 W. Wesch
 (W. Germany) 2 38 15.0
1971 V. P. Nihill 2 30 35.0
1972 J. Warhurst 2 35 19.0
1973 R. W. Dobson 2 40 07.0
1974 R. S. Thorpe 2 39 47.0
1975 R. W. Dobson 2 36 26.0
1976 R. G. Mills 2 32 13.0
1977 A. Seddon 2 35 15.0

20 Kilometres hr. min.sec.
1965 V. P. Nihill 1 33 33.0
1966 V. P. Nihill 1 33 45.0
1967 R. E. Wallwork 1 37 21.0
1968 V. P. Nihill 1 31 19.0
1969 V. P. Nihill 1 30 07.0
1970 W. Wesch
 (W. Germany) 1 31 47.0
1971 V. P. Nihill 1 32 06.0
1972 V. P. Nihill 1 28 45.0
1973 R. G. Mills 1 31 13.0
1974 O. T. Flynn 1 32 06.0
1975 O. T. Flynn 1 28 58.0
1976 O. T. Flynn 1 30 00.0
1977 O. T. Flynn 1 28 42.0
1978 O. T. Flynn 1 28 44.0
1979 C. P. Lawton 1 32 25.0
1980 M. Parker (NZ) 1 29 20.0

30 Kilometres hr.min.sec.
1978 O. T. Flynn 2 21 54

35 Kilometres hr.min.sec.
1979 R. G. Mills 2 52 08
1980 A. Seddon 2 40 04

50 Kilometres hr. min.sec.
1956 D. J. Thompson 4 24 39
1957 D. J. Thompson 4 41 48
1958 D. J. Thompson 4 21 50
1959 D. J. Thompson 4 12 19
1960 D. J. Thompson 4 32 55
1961 D. J. Thompson 4 22 51
1962 D. J. Thompson 4 27 26
1963 R. C. Middleton 4 16 44
1964 V. P. Nihill 4 17 10
1965 R. C. Middleton 4 17 23
1966 D. J. Thompson 4 28 26
1967 S. Lightman 4 26 56
1968 V. P. Nihill 4 18 59
1969 B. Eley 4 19 13
1970 R. W. Dobson 4 20 22
1971 V. P. Nihill 4 15 05
1972 J. Warhurst 4 18 31
1973 R. W. Dobson 4 14 29
1974 R. W. Dobson 4 16 58
1975 J. Warhurst 4 20 32
1976 R. S. Thorpe 4 23 43

50 Kilometres		hr. min. sec.
1977	B. Adams	4 25 28
1978	D. Cotton	4 14 25
1979	M. Parker (NZ)	4 14 26
1980	T. Erickson (Aus)	4 10 33

100 Kilometres		hr. min. sec.
1979	P. Hodkinson	9 46 36
1980	I. W. Richards	9 45 46

Women

Winners of English women's road walking titles:—

1956	D. Williams
1957	J. Williams
1958	P. Myatt
1959	B. E. M. Randle
1960	S. Jennings
1961	S. Jennings
1962	J. Farr
1963	J. Farr
1964	J. Farr
1965	J. Farr
1966	S. Jennings
1967	B. A. Jenkins
1968	J. Farr
1969	B. A. Jenkins
1970	J. Farr
1971	B. A. Jenkins
1972	B. A. Jenkins
1973	M. Fawkes
1974	M. Fawkes
1975	J. Farr
1976	J. Farr
1977	C. Tyson
1978	C. Tyson
1979	E. Cox
1980	C. Tyson

See also under BAUTISTA, DANIEL; DAMILANO, MAURIZIO; GAUDER, HARTWIG; GOLUBNICHIY, VLADIMIR; MATTHEWS, KEN; THOMPSON, DON, and LUGANO CUP.

WARMERDAM, Cornelius (USA)

A 15 ft. (4.57 m.) pole vault may be routine in this fibre-glass era but it was not until 1940 that Cornelius Warmerdam registered the first such leap. Utilising a bamboo pole, the American-born son of Dutch parents raised the world record several more times, finishing with 4.77 metres outdoors (1942) and 4.79 metres indoors (1943).

He cleared 15 ft. or over on 43 occasions before withdrawing from amateur competition in 1944. No other man up to that time had vaulted higher than 4.54 metres and it was only in 1951 that another athlete managed to scale 15 ft.

Warmerdam would almost certainly have won the Olympic gold medals of 1940 and 1944 had the world not been preoccupied with war. As it was, he had to settle for the American title every year from 1937 to 1944 except for 1939. In 1952 he made an exhibition vault of 4.37 metres . . . and in 1975 he returned to competition at the age of 60, vaulting 3.20 metres! He was born at Long Beach, California, on June 22nd, 1915.

WELLS, Allan (GB)

Who could have predicted that the lad raking the long jump pit at Edinburgh's 1970 Commonwealth Games, enabling him to watch close up his idol Lynn Davies, would—precisely ten years later—become an Olympic champion himself? At the time, Allan Wells was 18 and the reigning Scottish junior triple jump champion.

He made progress primarily as a long jumper, reaching 7.32 metres in 1972, but was handicapped by a lack of blazing speed. His best legal 100 metres mark at that time was a mere 11.1 sec. (a far cry from Lynn Davies' 10.4 sec.), and indeed another three seasons were to pass before he so much as broke 11 sec. in authentic conditions.

What irony too that at the start of 1978, when Harold Abrahams died, British sprinting was at its lowest ebb for years. The selectors hadn't even bothered to send any 100 m. men to the Montreal Olympics and the picture wasn't much brighter in 1977. Had anyone, at the time of Harold's passing, forecast that two years hence in Moscow a Briton would emulate his Olympic 100 m. victory, that person would surely have been regarded as crazy! But in July 1978 it became apparent that an exciting new sprint talent had been unearthed in the muscular frame of the 'Flying Scot'. In the space of a week Wells first equalled Peter Radford's UK 100 m. record of 10.29 sec. and then smashed it with a world class clocking of 10.15 sec. on his home track in Edinburgh.

Wells, who went on that season to win two gold medals (200 m. and 4 x 100 m. relay) and a silver (100 m.) in the Commonwealth Games, where he was credited with sensational if wind-aided times of 10.07 sec. and 20.12 sec., was quite the most unorthodox as well as the fleetest sprinter Britain had ever turned out. A product of the Scottish professional running school of training with great importance attached to speedball (a boxer's punchball) work, Wells was unusual also for the fact that he scorned the use of starting blocks. He argued that he could get eight inches nearer to the start line without blocks, which could make all the difference in a close race.

As a result of an IAAF rule which made blocks compulsory at the Moscow Olympics (they were fitted with an electronic device to register false starts), Wells adapted hastily but successfully to them in 1980. Despite injury problems he peaked perfectly for the Games, trimming his UK record to 10.11 sec. in the heats of the 100 m. The final, run in less favourable conditions, was one of the closest in Olympic history as Wells and Cuba's Silvio Leonard—drawn the width of the track apart—crossed the line simultaneously. Neither was sure who had won, until the TV action replay suggested what the photo finish was to confirm: that Wells' lunge had won him the race by the narrowest of margins. It was so close that the two men could not be separated even by 1/100 of a second at 10.25 sec. Aged 28, Wells had become the oldest man ever to win this particular title, and the first Scot to lift any Olympic athletics gold medal since Eric Liddell's 400 m. triumph in 1924.

One fancied contender who didn't even make the final was European record holder Pietro Mennea, but the flamboyant Italian's moment of glory was to come in the 200 m.—at the expense of Wells, who had the previous year inflicted a very rare defeat on Mennea, and in Italy at that, in the European Cup Final 200 m. Wells ran a scorchingly fast turn to enter the straight well clear but Mennea chased after him and forged ahead in the final ten metres to win by 2/100ths. Wells' time of 20.21 sec. was a UK record.

After the Games, Wells conjectured that with suitable preparation he could go close to Lynn Davies' UK long jump record of 8.23 metres, but said it was unlikely that he would revert to his old event. Another intriguing aspect of Wells' athletic potential that probably would never be fulfilled was as a 400 m. runner. He was timed at 47.8 sec. in a relay in 1973, when he was just an 11.1/22.4 sec. sprinter.

His annual progress as a sprinter: 1971—11.1; 1972—10.9w, 22.1w; 1973—11.1, 22.4; 1975—11.0, 22.2; 1976—10.55, 21.42; 1977—10.62, 21.10; 1978—10.15, 20.61; 1979—10.19, 20.42; 1980—10.11 (& 10.05w), 20.21 (20.11w). He was born in Edinburgh on May 3rd, 1952, and his wife Margot is also a British international sprinter with best wind-free times of 11.68 sec. and 24.12 sec.

WESSIG, Gerd (E. Germany)

The meteoric rise to fame of Gerd Wessig was one of the big talking points of the 1980 Olympics. His outdoor best in 1979 of 2.21 metres didn't even rank him among the world's top fifty high jumpers, and yet in Moscow he not only won the gold medal but also took possession of the world record as he flopped over 2.36 metres.

The 1.96 metres tall East German went to these, his first major Games, with personal bests of 2.27 metres (outdoors) and 2.29 metres (indoors) to his name. His competitive temperament in Moscow was remarkable as he repeatedly jumped higher than ever before and one rival after another dropped by the wayside. Not until he cleared 2.31 metres was he assured of a medal, but at the next height (2.33 metres) the gold medal became his as he cleared on the second attempt and his two remaining opponents were eliminated. It would have been understandable if all incentive had drained away in the excitement of winning as the bar was raised to 2.36 metres, but at his second try Wessig succeeded with something to spare.

A talented all-rounder, capable of a good decathlon, he has pole vaulted 4.40 m., long jumped 7.40 m., and thrown the javelin 60 m. His high jump progress: 1976—2.06 m.; 1977—2.13; 1978—2.19; 1979—2.23 (indoors); 1980—2.36. He was born at Lubz on July 16th, 1959.

WHITFIELD, Mal (USA)

Mal Whitfield, one of the supreme racers of all-time, won the Olympic 800 m. twice—in 1948 and 1952—clocking 1 min. 49.2 sec. both times. He collected three other Olympic medals: gold in the 1948 4 x 400 m. relay, silver in the 1952 relay and bronze in the 1948 400 m.

A beautiful stylist, he was always more interested in simply winning than setting fast times, though he held world records at 880 m. and 1000 m. His km. record of 2 min. 20.8 sec. in 1953 was followed just an hour later by an American 440 yd. standard of 46.2 sec.!

Between June 1948 and the end of 1954 he lost only three of his 69 races at 800 m. and 880 yd. He made an unsuccessful attempt at miling in 1955 and retired in 1956 after failing to qualify for the Olympic team.

His best marks: 10.7 sec. for 100 m., 45.9 sec. for 400 m., 46.2 sec. for 440 yd., 1 min. 17.3 sec. for 660 yd., 1 min. 47.9 sec. for 800 m., 1 min. 48.6 sec. for 880 yd., 2 min. 20.8 sec. for 1000 m., and 4 min. 12.6 sec. for the mile. He was born at Bay City, Texas, on Oct. 11th, 1924.

WILKINS, Mac (USA)

Mac Wilkins, the 1976 Olympic discus champion and the first man to throw the platter beyond 70 metres in official conditions, has another claim to fame: he is the greatest all-round thrower in history. Nicknamed 'Multiple Mac' by his college teammates when he used to indulge in all four throws, he can claim marks of 78.44 metres for the javelin (which was his main event until an elbow injury forced him to drop it), 61.36 metres for the hammer (an event he never took seriously) and 21.06 metres for the shot.

His first world discus record came unexpectedly in April 1976 when he threw 69.16 metres despite a back injury. One week later he took full advantage of helpful wind conditions to smash the record on three successive throws: 69.80, 70.24 and 70.86 metres. He was over 70 metres again in the American Championships where he *averaged* 69.22 metres for his six-throw series. He was far below that form in Montreal but his second-round effort of 67.50 metres sufficed for the Olympic title.

Wilkins lost both his world record and competitive supremacy to Wolfgang Schmidt in subsequent seasons (he lost to the East German in the World Cup of 1977 and 1979), but showed excellent form in 1980—including a throw of 70.98 metres, the second longest ever—but the USA boycott deprived him of the opportunity of defending his Olympic title. He was born at Eugene, Oregon, on Nov. 15th, 1950.

WOMEN'S AMATEUR ATHLETIC ASSOCIATION

The WAAA, which was founded in 1922, is the governing body for women's athletics in England and Wales. The Association promotes annual Championships.

The most titles gained in one event is ten by walker Judy Farr, including nine in succession, 1962–1970. Dorothy Tyler won the high jump eight times over a 20-year period, 1936–1956.

Champions
(From 1956)

100 Yards		sec.
1956	J. F. Paul	10.6
1957	H. J. Young	10.9
1958	V. M. Weston	10.6
1959	D. Hyman	10.8
1961	J. Smart	10.7
1962	D. Hyman	10.6
1963	D. Hyman	10.9
1964	D. Slater	10.6
1965	I. Kirszenstein (Poland)	10.6
1966	D. Slater	10.5
1967	J. Cornelissen (S. Africa)	10.5

100 Metres		sec.
1960	D. Hyman	11.7
1968	V. Peat	11.5
1969	Chi Cheng (Taiwan)	11.9

WAAA CHAMPIONS

1970	D. A. Neil	11.6
1971	S. Berto (Canada)	11.4
1972	D. P. Pascoe	11.9
1973	J. A. C. Lynch	11.7
1974	R. Boyle (Australia)	11.23
1975	J. A. C. Lynch	11.68
1976	J. A. C. Lynch	11.22
1977	S. M. Lannaman	11.24
1978	K. J. Smallwood	11.66
1979	H. R. Hunte	11.58
1980	K. J. Smallwood	11.45

200 Metres		sec.
1968	V. Peat	23.6
1969	D. Hyman	23.7
1970	M. A. Critchley	23.8
1971	S. Berto (Canada)	23.5
1972	D-M. L. Murray	24.0
1973	H. Golden	24.3
1974	R. Boyle (Australia)	23.2
1975	H. Golden	24.17
1976	D. I. Ramsden	23.48
1977	S. M. Lannaman	23.06
1978	K. J. Smallwood	23.24
1979	K. J. Smallwood	23.39
1980	K. J. Smallwood	23.14

220 Yards		sec.
1956	J. F. Paul	23.8
1957	H. J. Young	24.2
1958	H. J. Young	24.5
1959	D. Hyman	24.5
1960	D. Hyman	24.0
1961	J. Smart	24.0
1962	D. Hyman	23.8
1963	D. Hyman	24.3
1964	D. Slater	23.6
1965	J. M. Simpson	23.9
1966	J. M. Simpson	24.1
1967	J. Cornelissen (S. Africa)	24.0

400 Metres		sec.
1968	H. van der Hoeven (Netherlands)	53.6
1969	J. B. Pawsey	54.3
1970	M. F. Neufville	52.6
1971	J. V. Roscoe	53.9
1972	V. M. Elder	53.2
1973	J. V. Roscoe	53.8
1974	Y. Saunders (Canada)	51.9
1975	D. M. L. Murray	51.88
1976	V. M. Elder	52.08
1977	V. M. Elder	52.3
1978	J. T. Hoyte-Smith	52.66
1979	J. T. Hoyte-Smith	51.90
1980	M. Probert	51.94

440 Yards		sec.
1956	J. E. Ruff	56.5
1957	J. E. Ruff	56.4
1958	S. Pirie	56.4
1959	M. J. Pickerell	55.9
1960	P. Piercy	57.2
1961	M. E. E. Kyle (Ireland)	56.3
1962	J. Sorrell	55.1
1963	E. J. Grieveson	55.9
1964	A. E. Packer	54.3
1965	E. J. Grieveson	55.1
1966	H. Slaman (Netherlands)	54.7
1967	L. B. Board	55.3

800 Metres		min. sec.
1968	V. Nikolic (Yugoslavia)	2 00.5
1969	P. B. Lowe	2 03.3
1970	S. J. Carey	2 03.6
1971	A. Hoffman (Canada)	2 04.8
1972	M. Purcell (Ireland)	2 03.0
1973	M. Purcell (Ireland)	2 03.3
1974	L. Kiernan	2 05.1
1975	A. M. Creamer	2 05.1
1976	A. M. Creamer	2 04.6
1977	C. T. Boxer	2 03.8
1978	C. T. Boxer	2 03.1
1979	C. M. Benning	2 01.3
1980	A. R. Clarkson	2 01.9

880 Yards		min. sec.
1956	P. E. M. Perkins	2 13.2
1957	D. S. Leather	2 09.4
1958	J. W. Jordan	2 13.3
1959	J. W. Jordan	2 09.5
1960	J. W. Jordan	2 09.1
1961	J. W. Jordan	2 11.0
1962	J. W. Jordan	2 08.0
1963	P. E. M. Perkins	2 12.2
1964	A. R. Smith	2 08.0
1965	A. R. Smith	2 07.2
1966	A. R. Smith	2 04.2
1967	A. R. Smith	2 04.8

1500 Metres		min. sec.
1968	R. Ridley	4 25.3
1969	M. Gommers (Netherlands)	4 16.0
1970	R. Ridley	4 15.4
1971	R. Ridley	4 14.3
1972	E. Tittel (W. Germany)	4 17.2
1973	J. F. Allison	4 15.8
1974	G. Andersen (Norway)	4 10.0
1975	M. Stewart	4 14.7
1976	P. A. Yule	4 15.1
1977	P. A. Yule	4 12.7
1978	C. Hanson	4 11.6
1979	M. Stewart	4 14.8
1980	G. Dainty	4 14.1

Mile		min. sec.
1956	D. S. Leather	5 01.0
1957	D. S. Leather	4 55.3
1958	M. A. Bonnano	5 02.6
1959	J. S. Briggs	5 02.2
1960	R. Ashby	4 54.2

WAAA CHAMPIONS

1961	R. Ashby	5 01.8
1962	J. Beretta (Australia)	4 57.0
1963	P. Davies	5 10.8
1964	A. Leggett	4 56.0
1965	J. Smith	4 53.5
1966	R. Ridley	4 47.9
1967	R. Ridley	4 51.4

3000 Metres — min. sec.

1968	C. T. Gould	10 06.4
1969	A. O'Brien (Ireland)	9 47.6
1970	A. O'Brien (Ireland)	9 34.4
1971	J. Smith	9 23.4
1972	A. Ford	9 30.8
1973	I. Knutsson (Sweden)	9 08.0
1974	J. Smith	9 07.2
1975	M. Purcell (Ireland)	9 08.0
1976	M. Purcell (Ireland)	9 08.0
1977	C. T. Gould	9 20.7
1978	C. M. Benning	8 52.3
1979	D. Nagle (Ireland)	9 13.3
1980	R. Joyce	9 13.9

Marathon — hr min sec

1978	M. Lockley	2 55 08
1979	J. Smith	2 41 37
1980	J. Smith	2 41 22

80 Metres Hurdles — sec.

1956	P. G. Elliott	11.1
1957	T. E. Hopkins	11.4
1958	C. L. Quinton	10.9
1959	M. D. Rand	11.3
1960	C. L. Quinton	10.8
1961	B. R. H. Moore (Australia)	10.8
1962	B. R. H. Moore (Australia)	10.7
1963	P. A. Pryce	11.2
1964	P. A. Pryce	10.7
1965	P. A. Jones	11.2
1966	D. Straszynska (Poland)	10.9
1967	P. A. Jones	11.0
1968	P. A. Pryce	10.9

100 Metres Hurdles (2ft. 6in) — sec.

1963	P. A. Pryce	14.1
1964	P. A. Pryce	13.4
1965	P. A. Jones	13.8
1966	M. D. Rand	13.7

100 Metres Hurdles (2ft. 9in.) — sec.

1967	P. A. Jones	13.8
1968	C. Bell	13.5
1969	Chi Cheng (Taiwan)	13.5
1970	M. E. Peters	14.0
1971	V. Bufanu (Romania)	13.5
1972	P. Ryan (Australia)	13.4
1973	J. A. Vernon	14.0
1974	L. Drysdale	13.45
1975	E. Damman (Canada)	13.93
1976	S. Colyear	13.47
1977	L. M. Boothe	13.48
1978	S. Colyear	13.51
1979	S. E. Strong	13.67
1980	S. E. Strong	13.57

200 Metres Hurdles — sec.

1961	P. A. Pryce	28.3
1962	P. A. Pryce	28.9
1963	P. A. Pryce	28.9
1964	P. A. Jones	27.9
1965	S. M. Hayward	28.0
1966	P. A. Jones	27.7
1967	P. A. Jones	27.3
1968	C. Bell	27.8
1969	S. M. Hayward	28.5
1970	C. Bell	27.4
1971	S. Colyear	26.7
1972	P. Ryan (Australia)	26.8

400 Metres Hurdles — sec.

1973	S. E. Howell	61.4
1974	H. de Lange (S. Africa)	58.4
1975	J. V. Roscoe	58.31
1976	C. A. Warden	57.84
1977	E. Sutherland	57.93
1978	M. Appleby (Ireland)	57.46
1979	C. A. Warden	56.06
1980	S. A. J. Morley	58.76

High Jump — metres

1956	D. J. B. Tyler	1.60
1957	T. E. Hopkins	1.65
1958	M. D. Rand	1.65
1959	N. Zwier (Netherlands)	1.65
1960	D. A. Shirley	1.67
1961	D. A. Shirley	1.70
1962	I. Balas (Romania)	1.83
1963	I. Balas (Romania)	1.70
1964	F. M. Slaap	1.72
1965	F. M. Slaap	1.70
1966	D. A. Shirley	1.70
1967	L. Y. Knowles	1.70
1968	D. A. Shirley	1.67
1969	B. J. Inkpen	1.72
1970	D. A. Shirley	1.67
1971	D. Brill (Canada)	1.83
1972	R. Few	1.74
1973	I. Gusenbauer (Austria)	1.85
1974	V. J. Harrison	1.82
1975	D. Brown	1.75*
1976	D. Brown	1.79
1977	B. M. Gibbs	1.85
1978	C. Mathers	1.76
1979	B. A. Simmonds	1.81
1980	A-M. Devally	1.88

* 1.79 in jump-off

WAAA CHAMPIONS

Long Jump		metres
1956	S. H. Hoskin	5.65
1957	C. M. Cops	5.87
1958	S. H. Hoskin	5.96
1959	M. D. Rand	6.04
1960	A. E. Packer	5.68
1961	M. D. Rand	5.95
1962	J. Bijleveld (Netherlands)	6.21
1963	M. D. Rand	5.91
1964	M. D. Rand	6.58
1965	M. D. Rand	6.40
1966	B. Berthelsen (Norway)	6.30
1967	B. Berthelsen (Norway)	6.47
1968	S. H. Sherwood	6.42
1969	S. H. Sherwood	6.23
1970	I. Mickler (W. Germany)	6.50
1971	S. H. Sherwood	6.52
1972	S. H. Sherwood	6.37
1973	M. Nimmo	6.33
1974	R. Martin-Jones	6.26
1975	M. Nimmo	6.30
1976	S. D. Reeve	6.28
1977	S. D. Reeve	6.31
1978	J. Davies	6.19
1979	S. C. Hearnshaw	6.55
1980	S. D. Reeve	6.55

Shot		metres
1956	S. Allday	13.39
1957	J. Cook	12.60
1958	S. Allday	14.15
1959	S. Allday	13.19
1960	S. Allday	14.30
1961	S. Allday	13.73
1962	S. Allday	13.88
1963	M. Klein (W. Germany)	15.48
1964	M. E. Peters	14.22
1965	G. Schafer (W. Germany)	14.81
1966	B. R. Bedford	14.52
1967	B. R. Bedford	15.18
1968	M. Gummel (E. Germany)	16.99
1969	B. R. Bedford	15.22
1970	M. E. Peters	14.85
1971	J. E. Roberts (Australia)	15.81
1972	J. E. Roberts (Australia)	15.34
1973	B. R. Bedford	14.82
1974	J. Haist (Canada)	15.03
1975	B. R. Bedford	14.89
1976	J. A. Kerr	15.88
1977	B. R. Bedford	15.79
1978	A. M. Littlewood	15.97
1979	J. M. Oakes	16.38
1980	J. M. Oakes	16.85

Discus		metres
1956	S. Allday	47.02
1957	S. J. Needham	40.22
1958	S. Allday	47.70
1959	S. Allday	45.22
1960	S. Allday	45.24
1961	S. Allday	45.30
1962	L. Boling (Netherlands)	47.28
1963	L. Manoliu (Romania)	49.40
1964	K. Limberg (W. Germany)	50.92
1965	E. Ricci (Italy)	50.56
1966	C. R. Payne	49.88
1967	C. R. Payne	46.66
1968	K. Illgen (E. Germany)	57.22
1969	L. Manoliu (Romania)	55.58
1970	C. R. Payne	52.58
1971	L. Westermann (W. Germany)	58.44
1972	C. R. Payne	53.78
1973	C. R. Payne	56.40
1974	J. Haist (Canada)	56.38
1975	M. E. Ritchie	53.12
1976	J. F. Thompson	51.38
1977	M. E. Ritchie	53.98
1978	J. F. Thompson	49.80
1979	J. F. Thompson	53.56
1980	L. K. Mallin	51.24

Javelin		metres
1956	D. Orphall	40.82
1957	A. M. Williams	40.24
1958	A. M. Williams	43.48
1959	S. Platt	49.04
1960	S. Platt	50.84
1961	S. Platt	47.88
1962	S. Platt	50.72
1963	A. Gerhards (W. Germany)	50.30
1964	A. Gerhards (W. Germany)	51.82
1965	A. Koloska (W. Germany)	53.16
1966	S. Platt	45.18
1967	S. Platt	49.16
1968	S. Platt	53.26
1969	S. Platt	49.32
1970	A. Koloska (W. Germany)	54.14
1971	I. Fallo (Norway)	47.68
1972	P. E. French	51.00
1973	S. J. Corbett	53.88
1974	E. Janko (Austria)	61.56
1975	T. I. Sanderson	54.40
1976	T. I. Sanderson	56.98
1977	T. I. Sanderson	59.96
1978	A. Farquhar	49.20
1979	T. I. Sanderson	61.82
1980	T. I. Sanderson	64.08

Pentathlon		pts.
1956	M. Rowley	3812
1957	M. Rowley	4183
1958	J. P. Gaunt	3887
1959	M. D. Rand	4679
1960	M. D. Rand	4568
1961	C. A. Hamby	3986
1962	M. E. Peters	4190
1963	M. E. Peters	4385
1964	M. E. Peters	4801
1965	M. E. Peters	4413
1966	M. E. Peters	4625
1967	J. L. Honour	3965
1968	M. E. Peters	4723
1969	M. L. Walls	4591
1970	M. E. Peters	4841
1971	J. L. Honour	4571

New tables:

1972	A. S. Wilson	†4292
1973	M. E. Peters	†4429
1974	A. S. Wilson	†4248
1975	S. J. Longden	†4196
1976	S. J. Longden	†4337

With 800 Metres:

1977	S. J. Longden	4152
1978	Y. J. Wray	4140
1979	M. M. Marriott	3897
1980	S. J. Longden	4409

Mile Walk		min. sec.
1956	D. Williams	7 47.6
1957	D. Williams	8 08.4
1958	B. A. Jenkins	8 09.4

1½ Miles Walk		min. sec.
1959	B. A. Jenkins	12 56.4
1960	J. Farr	12 31.2
1961	S. Jennings	12 18.4
1962	J. Farr	12 20.0
1963	J. Farr	12 26.4
1964	J. Farr	12 06.8
1965	J. Farr	12 14.2
1966	J. Farr	12 09.2
1967	J. Farr	12 09.2
1968	J. Farr	12 39.0

2500 Metres Walk		min.sec.
1969	J. Farr	12 45.8
1970	J. Farr	12 34.0
1971	B. J. Cook	12 39.8
1972	B. A. Jenkins	12 31.2

3000 Metres Walk		min. sec.
1973	B. A. Jenkins	14 59.4
1974	M. Fawkes	14 33.6

5000 Metres Walk		min. sec.
1975	V. C. Lovell	25 02.8
1976	M. Fawkes	24 10.0
1977	M. Fawkes	24 50.6
1978	C. Tyson	24 08.2
1979	M. Fawkes	23 31.5
1980	I. L. Bateman	24 09.0

10,000 Metres Walk		min. sec.
1978	C. Tyson	49 59.0
1979	M. Fawkes	48 37.6
1980	C. Tyson	49 30.4
1981	I. L. Bateman	49 54.3

Cross-Country

1956	D. S. Leather
1957	J. Bridgland
1958	R. Ashby
1959	J. Smith
1960	J. Smith
1961	R. Ashby
1962	R. Ashby
1963	M. C. Ibbotson
1964	M. C. Ibbotson
1965	P. Davies
1966	P. Davies
1967	P. Davies
1968	P. Davies
1969	R. Ridley
1970	R. Ridley
1971	R. Ridley
1972	R. Ridley
1973	J. Smith
1974	R. Ridley
1975	D. Nagle (Ireland)
1976	A. Ford
1977	G. C. Penny
1978	M. Stewart
1979	K. M. Binns
1980	R. P. Smeeth
1981	W. Smith

WOMEN'S ATHLETICS

Barred on pain of death from even watching the Olympic Games, the women of Ancient Greece held their own Heraea Games every four years —named after their reputed founder Hera, wife of Zeus. The events included foot races of about 150 m.

Women took part from the 17th century in the sports meetings held at English fairs and wakes but the "modern" history of women's athletics stretches back only to 1895 when sprints, hurdles and jumps were staged at America's exclusive Vassar College. The first governing body to come into existence was the French Women's Sports Federation in 1917. Two years later women's athletics began to be held on an organised basis in England.

The year of 1921 marked the beginning of international competition. Five nations were represented at the Monte Carlo Games, at which British athletes scored six wins in 11 events, and later in the year was an unofficial British team met France in Paris and won six of the eight events.

An international governing body called the Fédération Sportive Féminine Internationale was formed in Paris on Oct. 31st, 1921. Britain, Czechoslovakia, France, Italy, Spain and the USA were the co-founders. The FSFI requested the International Olympic Committee to add women's athletics to the 1924 Olympic programme. The request was refused, and consequently the FSFI organised their own "Women's Olympic Games" in Paris in August 1922. Five nations sent teams, with Britain emerging the most successful.

Winners: — 60 m. M. Mejzlikova (Czechoslovakia) 7.6 sec.; 100 yd., N. E. Callebout (GB) 12.0 sec.; 300 m., M. Lines (GB) 44.8 sec.; 1000 m., L. Breard (France) 3 min. 12.0 sec.; 100 yd. hurdles, C. Sabie (USA) 14.4 sec.; High jump, H. Hatt (GB) and N. Voorhees (USA), 1.46 metres; Long jump, M. Lines (GB) 5.06 metres; Standing long jump, C. Sabie (USA) 2.48 metres; 8 lb. Shot (aggregate of both hands), L. Godbold (USA) 20.22 metres; 800 gr. Javelin (aggregate), F. Pianzola (Switzerland) 43.24 metres; 4 x 110 yd. relay, GB (Lines, Callebout, Leach, Porter) 51.8 sec.

The second "Women's Olympics"—now entitled the "Women's World Games" following protests by the IAAF and IOC—were held in Gothenburg in 1926. Britain again fared best of the ten participating nations.

Winners:—60 m., M. Radideau (France) 7.8 sec.; 100 yd., Radideau 11.8 sec.; 250 m., E. Edwards (GB) 33.4 sec.; 1000 m., E. Trickey (GB) 3 min. 08.8 sec.; 100 yd. hurdles, L. Sychrova (Czechoslovakia) 14.4 sec.; High jump, Bons (France) 1.50 metres; Long jump, K. Hitomi (Japan) 5.50 metres; Standing long jump, Hitomi 2.49 metres; Shot (aggregate), Vidiakova (Czechoslovakia) 19.54 metres; Discus H. Konopacka (Poland) 37.70 metres; Javelin (aggregate), A. L. Adelskold (Sweden) 49.14 metres; 1000 m. Walk, D. E. Crossley (GB) 5 min. 10 sec.; 4 x 100 m. relay, GB (D. E. Scouler, F. C. Haynes, E. Edwards, R. Thompson) 49.8 sec.

Five women's events were included in the 1928 Olympics but Britain was not one of the 21 competing nations.

For a list of all Olympic champions, see under OLYMPIC GAMES.

Meanwhile the FSFI, with British support, continued to promote their "Women's World Games." Winners in Prague in 1930:—60 m., S. Walasiewicz (Poland) 7.7 sec.; 100 m., Walasiewicz 12.5 sec.; 200 m. Walasiewicz 25.7 sec.; 800 m., G. Lunn (GB) 2 min. 21.9 sec.; 80 m. hurdles, M. Jacobson (Sweden) 12.4 sec.; High Jump, I. Braumuller (Germany) 1.57 metres; Long jump, K. Hitomi (Japan) 5.90 metres; Shot, G. Heublein (Germany) 12.49 metres; Discus, H. Konopacka (Poland), 36.80 metres; Javelin, L. Schumann (Germany), 42.32 metres; Triathlon (Javelin, high jump, 100 m.), Braumuller; 4 x 100 m. relay, Germany (Kellner, Karrer, Holger, L. Gelius), 49.9 sec.

Britain made her debut in Olympic competition in Los Angeles in 1932. Women's events were introduced into the Commonwealth Games in 1934 (see COMMONWEALTH GAMES for list of winners).

The fourth and final "Women's World Games" were held in London in 1934. Winners:—60 m., S. Walasiewicz (Poland) 7.6 sec.; 100 m., K. Krauss (Germany) 11.9 sec.; 200 m., Krauss 24.9 sec.; 800 m., Z. Koubkova (Czechoslovakia) 2 min. 12.8 sec.; 80 m. hurdles, R. Englehardt (Germany) 11.6 sec.; High jump, S. Grieme (Germany) 1.55 metres; Long jump, G. Koppner (Germany) 5.80 metres; Shot, G. Mauermayer (Germany) 13.67 metres; Discus, J. Wajsowna (Poland) 43.80 metres; Javelin, G. Gelius (Germany) 42.44 metres; Pentathlon, Mauermayer; 4 x 100 m. relay, Germany (M. Grieme, Krauss, M. Dollinger, I. Dorffeldt) 48.6 sec.

In 1936 the FSFI handed over full control of international women's athletics to the IAAF. Two years later the first European Championships were staged by the IAAF in Vienna (see EUROPEAN CHAMPIONSHIPS for list of all European champions.)

WOODERSON, Sydney (GB)

No man looked less like the popular image of a world champion athlete than small (1.68 metres, 57 kg.), bespectacled Sydney Wooderson. He was not even possessed of good health. Yet this was the man who won his way into the hearts of a whole nation with his world records and courageous racing at distances ranging from 440 yd. to 10 mi. cross-country.

Wooderson never won an Olympic title or medal, for a cracked bone in his ankle put paid to his chances in Berlin, but he did win two European championships: the 1500 m. in 1938 and the 5000 m. in 1946.

This latter performance was probably the finest of a superlative career. At the age of 32 (less one week) he drew clean away from a notable field to win by 30 m. in 14 min. 08.6 sec., the second fastest time on record at that date. Placing fifth and sixth in the race were two rising stars of whom much more was to be heard, Emil Zatopek and Gaston Reiff.

When he was 18 Sydney ran a mile in 4 min. 29.8 sec. Today this would be regarded as rather slow but in 1933 this time was the fastest ever recorded by a schoolboy and it made his name. He never looked back. In 1934 he improved drastically to 4 min. 13.4 sec. and even managed to finish in front of Jack Lovelock in one race.

He set his first British record in 1936, a 4 min. 10.8 sec. mile—a time he cut to 4 min. 06.4 sec. in 1937 for a new world record. In 1938 he prepared for the European Championships by concentrating on the half-mile . . . to such good effect that he posted world records of 1 min. 48.4 sec. for 800 m. and 1 min. 49.2 sec. for 880 yd. and in an earlier race defeated the great Mario Lanzi, of Italy.

Wooderson raced Arne Andersson (Sweden) twice in 1945, losing both times but clocking his fastest mile of 4 min. 04.2 sec. on the second occasion after leading at 1500 m. in 3 min. 48.4 sec. The European 5000 m. victory marked the end of his track career but in 1948 he set the final seal on a remarkable athletic lifetime by winning the English cross-country title.

His best marks were 49.3 sec. for 440 yd., 1 min. 48.4 sec. for 800 m., 1 min. 49.2 sec. for 880 yd., 2 min. 59.5 sec. for ¾ mi., 3 min. 48.4 sec. for 1500 m., 4 min. 04.2 sec. for the mile, 9 min. 05.0 sec. for 2 mi., 13 min. 53.2 sec. for 3 mi. and 14 min. 08.6 sec. for 5000 m. He was born in London on Aug. 30th, 1914.

WORLD CHAMPIONSHIPS

The IAAF has traditionally held its World Championships every four years in the form of the Olympic Games athletics programme. Consequently every Olympic champion is by definition World champion also. The IAAF has also staged annual World Cross-Country Championships since 1973 and its Lugano Cup, held every other year, is in effect a World team championship for walking. In 1976, as a result of the 50 km. walk having been dropped from that year's Olympic programme, a World Championship was organised by the IAAF instead—the winner being Veniamin Soldatenko (USSR) in 3 hr. 54 min. 40 sec. Similarly, as there was no provision for women's 3000 m. and 400 m. hurdles at the 1980 Olympics, specific World Championships were held after the Games. The winners were Birgit Friedmann (W. Germany) in 8 min. 48.1 sec. and Barbel Broschat (E. Germany) in 54.55 sec.

A major development is scheduled for 1983 when the IAAF will organise its own World Championships in Helsinki from Aug. 7th to 14th. Each country will be entitled to enter one athlete per event who has met the 'B' entry standard (corresponding to the 100th best performer in 1981) during the 12 months prior to entries closing; two or three competitors per event will be permitted if all have achieved the higher 'A' entry standard. The World Championships are thereafter to be held every four years.

WORLD CUP

The IAAF's inaugural World Cup competition, held in Dusseldorf in 1977, was hailed as a great success both as an athletics spectacular and as a means of attracting extra income for the IAAF to use in helping develop the sport in the Third World in particular. Eight continental or national teams were involved. Result of the men's contest was: 1, East Germany 127 pts; 2, USA 120; 3, West Germany 112; 4, Europe Select 111; 5, Americas 92; 6, Africa 78; 7, Oceania 48; 8, Asia 44. The women's result was: 1, Europe Select 109; 2, East Germany 93; 3, USSR 90; 4, USA 60; 5, Americas 56; 6, Oceania 46; 7, Africa 32; 8, Asia 30.

Individual winners—100 m: S. Williams (USA) 10.13 sec.; 200 m: C. Edwards (USA) 20.17 sec.; 400 m: A. Juantorena (Am) 45.36 sec.; 800 m: A. Juantorena (Am) 1 min. 44.0 sec.; 1500 m: S. Ovett (GB) 3 min. 34.5 sec.; 5000 m: M. Yifter (Afr) 13 min. 13.8 sec.; 10,000 m: M. Yifter (Afr) 28 min. 32.3 sec.; 3000 m. Steeplechase: M. Karst (W. Ger) 8 min. 21.6 sec.; 110 m. Hurdles: T. Munkelt (E. Ger) 13.41 sec.; 400 m. Hurdles: E. Moses (USA) 47.58 sec.; High Jump: R. Beilschmidt (E. Ger) 2.30 m.; Pole Vault: M. Tully (USA) 5.60 m.; Long Jump: A. Robinson (USA) 8.19 m.; Triple Jump: J. C. de Oliveira (Am) 16.68 m.; Shot: U. Beyer (E. Ger) 21.74 m.; Discus: W. Schmidt (E. Ger) 67.14 m.; Hammer: K-H. Riehm (W. Ger) 75.64 m.; Javelin: M. Wessing (W. Ger) 87.46 m.; 4 x 100 m. Relay: USA 38.03 sec.; 4 x 400 m. Relay: W. Germany 3 min. 01.3 sec. (*Women*) 100 m: M. Gohr (E. Ger) 11.16 sec.; 200 m: I. Szewinska (Eur) 22.72 sec.; 400 m: I. Szewinska (Eur) 49.52 sec.; 800 m: T. Petrova (Eur) 1 min. 59.2 sec.; 1500 m: T. Kazankina (USSR) 4 min. 12.7 sec.; 3000 m: G. Waitz (Eur) 8 min. 43.5 sec.; 100m. Hurdles: G. Rabsztyn (Eur) 12.70 sec.; High Jump: R. Ackermann (E. Ger) 1.98 m.; Long Jump: L. Jacenko (Oce) 6.54 m.; Shot: H. Fibingerova (Eur) 20.63 m. (I. Slupianek, E. Ger, won with 20.93 m. but was subsequently disqualified for failing dope test at earlier European Cup Final); Discus: F. Melnik (USSR) 68.10 m.; Javelin: R. Fuchs (E. Ger) 62.36 m.; 4 x 100 m. Relay: Europe 42.51 sec. (team included GB's A. Lynch and S. Lannaman); 4 x 400 m. Relay: E. Germany 3 min. 24.0 sec.

World Cup II, in Montreal in 1979, was much less of a popular success with an aggregate three-day attendance of only about 55,000 as against Dusseldorf's 130,000. Men's team result: 1, USA 119 pts.; 2, Europe Select 112; 3, E. Germany 108; 4, USSR 102; 5, Americas 98; 6, Africa 84; 7, Oceania 58; 8, Asia 36. Women's result: 1, E. Germany 106; 2, USSR 98; 3, Europe Select 88; 4, USA 76; 5, Americas 68; 6, Oceania 47; 7, Africa 30; 8, Asia 26.

Individual winners—100 m: J. Sanford (USA) 10.17 sec.; 200 m: S. Leonard (Am) 20.34 sec.; 400 m: K. Hassan (Afr) 45.39 sec.; 800 m: J. Maina (Afr) 1 min. 47.7 sec.; 1500 m: T. Wessinghage (Eur) 3 min. 46.0 sec.; 5000 m: M. Yifter (Afr) 13 min. 35.9 sec.; 10,000 m: M. Yifter (Afr) 27 min. 53.1 sec.; 3000 m. Steeplechase: K. Rono (Afr) 8 min. 26.0 sec.; 110 m. Hurdles: R. Nehemiah (USA) 13.39 sec.; 400 m. Hurdles: E. Moses (USA) 47.53 sec.; High Jump: F. Jacobs (USA) 2.27 m.; Pole Vault: M. Tully (USA) 5.45 m.; Long Jump: L. Myricks (USA) 8.52 m.; Triple Jump: J .C. de Oliveira (Am) 17.02 m.; Shot: U. Beyer (E. Ger) 20.45 m.; Discus: W. Schmidt (E. Ger) 66.02 m.; Hammer: S. Litvinov (USSR) 78.70 m.; Javelin: W. Hanisch (E. Ger) 86.48 m.; 4 x 100 m. Relay: Americas 38.70 sec.; 4 x 400 m. Relay: USA 3 min. 00.7 sec. (*Women*) 100 m: E. Ashford (USA) 11.06 sec.; 200 m: E. Ashford (USA) 21.83 sec.; 400 m: M. Koch (E. Ger) 48.97 sec.; 800 m: N. Shtereva (Eur) 2 min. 00.6 sec.; 1500 m: C. Wartenberg (E. Ger) 4 min. 06.9 sec. (T. Petrova, Eur, won in 4 min. 06.5 sec. but was subsequently disqualified for failing dope test at earlier Balkan Games); 3000 m: S. Ulmasova (USSR) 8 min. 36.4 sec.; 100 m. Hurdles: G. Rabsztyn (Eur) 12.67 sec.; 400 m. Hurdles: B. Klepp (E. Ger) 55.83 sec.; High Jump: D. Brill (Am) 1.96 m.; Long Jump: A. Stukane (USSR) 6.64 m.; Shot: I. Slupianek (E. Ger) 20.98 m.; Discus: E. Jahl (E. Ger) 65.18 m.; Javelin: R. Fuchs (E. Ger) 66.10 m.; 4 x 100 m. Relay: Europe Select 42.19 sec. (team included GB's H. Hunte); 4 x 400 m. Relay: E. Germany 3 min. 20.4 sec.

The third edition of the World Cup is being held in Rome in 1981, with nine teams (including the Italian hosts) participating.

WORLD RECORDS
See APPENDIX.

Evolution of World Records

These lists show how the world's best performances in the standard events have been improved during the past 20 years. Many marks listed have never been officially accepted as world records by the International Amateur Athletic Federation (which began recognising records in 1913) but have satisfied statisticians as to their authenticity. Performances marked by an asterisk have been accorded official status by the IAAF.

For earlier records, see previous editions of "Encyclopaedia of Athletics".

100 Metres
sec.
10.0* Armin Hary (W. Germany) June 21 1960
10.0* Harry Jerome (Canada) July 15 1960
10.0* Horacio Esteves (Venezuela) Aug. 15 1964
10.0* Bob Hayes (USA) Oct. 15 1964
10.0 Chen Chia-chuan (China) Oct. 24 1965
10.0* Jim Hines (USA) May 27 1967
10.0 Willie Turner (USA) May 27 1967
10.0* Enrique Figuerola (Cuba) June 17 1967
10.0* Paul Nash (S. Africa) Apr. 2 1968
10.0 Nash Apr. 6 1968
10.0 Charlie Greene (USA) Apr. 20 1968
10.0* Oliver Ford (USA) May 31 1968
10.0* Greene June 20 1968
10.0* Roger Bambuck (France) June 20 1968
9.9* Hines June 20 1968
9.9* Ronnie Ray Smith (USA) June 20 1968
9.9* Greene June 20 1968
9.9* Hines Oct. 14 1968
9.9* Eddie Hart (USA) July 1 1972
9.9* Rey Robinson (USA) July 1 1972
9.9* Steve Williams (USA) June 21 1974
9.9* Silvio Leonard (Cuba) June 5 1975
9.9* Williams July 16 1975
9.9* Williams Aug. 22 1975
9.9* Williams March 27 1976
9.9* Harvey Glance (USA) Apr. 3 1976
9.9* Glance May 1 1976
9.9* Don Quarrie (Jamaica) May 22 1976
9.9 Leonard March 27 1977
9.9 Johnny Jones (USA) Apr. 2 1977
9.8 Glance Apr. 9 1977
9.8 Glance Mar. 28 1981

100 Metres (Electrical)
10.06 Bob Hayes (USA) Oct. 15 1964
9.95* Jim Hines (USA) Oct. 14 1968

200 Metres
20.5* Peter Radford (GB) May 28 1960
20.5* Stone Johnson (USA) July 2 1960
20.5* Ray Norton (USA) July 2 1960
20.5* Livio Berruti (Italy) Sept. 3 1960
20.5* Berruti Sept. 3 1960
20.5* Paul Drayton (USA) June 23 1962
20.5 Bob Hayes (USA) Feb. 10 1963
20.5 Hayes Mar. 2 1963
20.3* Henry Carr (USA) Mar. 23 1963
20.2* Carr Apr. 4 1964
20.0* Tommie Smith (USA) June 11 1966
19.7 John Carlos (USA) Sept. 12 1968
IAAF records not shown above:
19.8 Tommie Smith (USA) Oct. 16 1968
19.8 Don Quarrie (Jamaica) Aug. 3 1971
19.8 Quarrie June 7 1975

200 Metres (Electrical)
20.36 Henry Carr (USA) Oct. 17 1964
20.26 Tommie Smith (USA) June 17 1967
19.92 John Carlos (USA) Sept. 12 1968
19.83* Smith Oct. 16 1968
19.72* Pietro Mennea (Italy) Sept. 12 1979

400 Metres
sec.
44.9* Otis Davis (USA) Sept. 6 1960

44.9* Carl Kaufmann (W.
   Germany)   Sept. 6 1960
44.9* Adolph Plummer
   (USA)   May 25 1963
44.9* Mike Larrabee (USA)
                 Sept. 12 1964
44.5* Tommie Smith (USA)
                 May 20 1967
44.4 Vince Matthews (USA)
                 Aug. 31 1968
44.0 Lee Evans (USA) Sept. 14 1968
43.8* Evans   Oct. 18 1968

IAAF record not shown above:
44.1 Larry James (USA)
                 Sept. 14 1968

400 Metres (Electrical)
45.07 Otis Davis (USA)
                 Sept. 6 1960
44.97 Lee Evans (USA)
                 Sept. 13 1968
44.06 Evans   Sept. 14 1968
43.86* Evans   Oct. 18 1968

800 Metres
min. sec.
1:45.7* Roger Moens
   (Belgium)   Aug. 3 1955
1:44.3* Peter Snell (New
   Zealand)   Feb. 3 1962
1:44.3* Ralph Doubell
   (Australia)   Oct. 15 1968
1:44.3* Dave Wottle (USA)
                 July 1 1972
1:43.7* Marcello Fiasconaro
   (Italy)   June 27 1973
1:43.50* Alberto Juantorena
   (Cuba)   July 25 1976
1:43.44* Juantorena Aug. 21 1977
1:42.33* Sebastian Coe (GB)
                 July 5 1979

1000 Metres
2:16.7* Siegfried Valentin
   (E. Germany) July 19 1960
2:16.6* Peter Snell (New
   Zealand)   Nov. 12 1964
2:16.2* Jurgen May
   (E. Germany) July 20 1965
2:16.2* Franz-Josef Kemper
   (W. Germany) Sept. 21 1966
2:16.0* Danie Malan (S.
   Africa)   June 24 1973
2:13.9* Rick Wohlhuter
   (USA)   July 30 1974
2:13.4* Sebastian Coe (GB)
                 July 1 1980

1500 Metres
min. sec.
3:35.6* Herb Elliott (Australia)
                 Sept. 6 1960
3:33.1* Jim Ryun (USA)
                 July 8 1967
3:32.2* Filbert Bayi (Tanzania)   Feb. 2 1974
3:32.1* Sebastian Coe (GB)
                 Aug. 15 1979
3:32.1* Steve Ovett (GB)
                 July 15 1980
3:31.4* Ovett   Aug. 27 1980

Mile
min. sec.
3:54.5* Herb Elliott
   (Australia)   Aug. 6 1958
3:54.4* Peter Snell (New
   Zealand)   Jan. 27 1962
3:54.1* Snell   Nov. 17 1964
3:53.6* Michel Jazy (France)
                 June 9 1965
3:51.3* Jim Ryun (USA)
                 July 17 1966
3:51.1* Ryun   June 23 1967
3:51.0* Filbert Bayi (Tanzania)   May 17 1975
3:49.4* John Walker (New
   Zealand)   Aug. 12 1975
3:49.0* Sebastian Coe (GB)
                 July 17 1979
3:48.8* Steve Ovett (GB)
                 July 1 1980

2000 Metres
min. sec.
5:02.2* Istvan Rozsavolgyi
   (Hungary)   Oct. 2 1955
5:01.5* Michel Jazy (France)
                 June 14 1962
5:01.1* Josef Odlozil (Czechoslovakia)   Sept. 8 1965
4:57.8* Harald Norpoth (W
   Germany)   Sept. 10 1966
4:56.2* Jazy   Oct. 12 1966
4:51.4* John Walker (New
   Zealand)   June 30 1976

3000 Metres
min. sec.
7:52.8* Gordon Pirie (GB)
                 Sept. 4 1956
7:49.2* Michel Jazy (France)
                 June 27 1962
7:49.0* Jazy   June 23 1965
7:46.0* Siegfried Herrmann
   (E. Germany) Aug. 5 1965
7:39.5* Kipchoge Keino (Kenya)
                 Aug. 27 1965

7:37.6* Emiel Puttemans
  (Belgium)   Sept. 14 1972
7:35.2* Brendan Foster (GB)
           Aug. 3 1973
7:32.1* Henry Rono (Kenya)
           June 27 1978

5000 Metres
min. sec.
13:35.0* Vladimir Kuts (USSR)
           Oct. 13 1957
13:34.8* Ron Clarke (Australia)
           Jan. 16 1965
13.33.6* Clarke   Feb. 1 1965
13:25.8* Clarke   June 4 1965
13:24.2* Kipchoge Keino (Kenya)
           Nov. 30 1965
13:16.6* Clarke   July 5 1966
13:16.4* Lasse Viren
  (Finland)   Sept. 14 1972
13:13.0* Emiel Puttemans
  (Belgium)   Sept. 20 1972
13:12.9* Dick Quax (New Zealand)
           July 5 1977
13:08.4* Henry Rono (Kenya)
           Apr. 8 1978

10,000 Metres
min. sec.
28:18.8* Pyotr Bolotnikov
  (USSR)   Oct. 15 1960
28:18.2* Bolotnikov   Aug. 11 1962
28:15.6* Ron Clarke (Australia)
           Dec. 18 1963
27:39.4* Clarke   July 14 1965
27:38.4* Lasse Viren
  (Finland)   Sept. 3 1972
27:30.8* Dave Bedford (GB)
           July 13 1973
27:30.5* Samson Kimobwa (Kenya)
           June 30 1977
27:22.4* Henry Rono (Kenya)
           June 11 1978

20,000 Metres
min. sec.
59:51.8* Emil Zatopek (Czechoslovakia)   Sept. 29 1951
59:28.6* Bill Baillie (New
  Zealand)   Aug. 24 1963
59:22.8* Ron Clarke (Australia)
           Oct. 27 1965
58:06.2* Gaston Roelants (Belgium)
           Oct. 28 1966
57:44.4* Roelants   Sept. 20 1972
57:31.6* Jos Hermens
  (Netherlands)   Sept. 27 1975
57:24.2* Hermens   May 1 1976

1 Hour
metres
20,052* Emil Zatopek
  (Czechoslovakia) Sept. 29 1951
20,190* Bill Baillie
  (New Zealand)   Aug. 24 1963
20,232* Ron Clarke
  (Australia)   Oct. 27 1965
20,664* Gaston Roelants
  (Belgium)   Oct. 28 1966
20,784* Roelants   Sept. 20 1972
20,907* Jos Hermens
  (Netherlands)   Sept. 27 1975
20,944* Hermens   May 1 1976

25,000 Metres
hr. min. sec.
1:16:36.4* Emil Zatopek
  (Czechoslovakia) Oct. 29 1955
1:15:22.6* Ron Hill (GB)
           July 21 1965
1:14:55.6* Seppo Nikkari
  (Finland)   Oct. 14 1973
1:14:16.8* Pekka Paivarinta
  (Finland)   May 15 1975
1:14:11.8* Bill Rodgers (USA)
           Feb. 21 1979

30,000 Metres
hr. min. sec.
1:35:01.0* Albert Ivanov
  (USSR)   June 6 1957
1:34:41.2* Aurel Vandendriessche (Belgium)   Oct. 3 1962
1:34:32.2* Viktor Baikov
  (USSR)   June 22 1963
1:34:01.8* Jim Alder (GB)
           Oct. 17 1964
1:32:34.6* Tim Johnston (GB)
           Oct. 16 1965
1:32:25.4* Jim Hogan (GB)
           Nov. 12 1966
1:31:30.4* Alder   Sept. 5 1970

Marathon
  See under MARATHON.

3000 Metres Steeplechase
min. sec.
8:31.3* Zdzislaw Krzyszkowiak
  (Poland)   June 26 1960
8:31.2* Grigoriy Taran (USSR)
           May 28 1961
8:30.4* Krzyszkowiak   Aug. 10 1961
8:29.6* Gaston Roelants
  (Belgium)   Sept. 7 1963
8:26.4* Roelants   Aug. 7 1965
8:24.2* Jouko Kuha
  (Finland)   July 17 1968

8:22.2* Vladimir Dudin
 (USSR) Aug. 19 1969
8:22.0* Kerry O'Brien
 (Australia) July 4 1970
8:20.8* Anders Garderud
 (Sweden) Sept. 14 1972
8:20.8 Ben Jipcho (Kenya)
 Jan. 15 1973
8:19.8* Jipcho June 19 1973
8:13.9* Jipcho June 27 1973
8:10.4* Garderud June 25 1975
8:09.7* Garderud July 1 1975
8:08.0* Garderud July 28 1976
8:05.4* Henry Rono (Kenya)
 May 13 1978

110 Metres Hurdles
sec.
13.2* Martin Lauer (W.
 Germany) July 7 1959
13.2* Lee Calhoun (USA)
 Aug. 21 1960
13.2* Earl McCullouch
 (USA) July 16 1967
13.2* Willie Davenport
 (USA) July 4 1969
13.2* Rod Milburn (USA)
 Sept. 7 1972
13.1* Milburn July 6 1973
13.1* Milburn July 22 1973
13.1 Guy Drut (France)
 June 29 1975
13.1* Drut July 23 1975
13.0* Drut Aug.22 1975
12.8 Renaldo Nehemiah (USA)
 May 11 1979

110 Metres Hurdles (Electrical)
13.56 Martin Lauer (W.
 Germany) July 7 1959
13.50 Willie Davenport (USA)
 June 25 1966
13.43 Earl McCullouch
 (USA) July 16 1967
13.38 Ervin Hall (USA)
 Oct. 17 1968
13.33 Davenport Oct. 17 1968
13.24* Rod Milburn (USA)
 Sept. 7 1972
13.21* Alejandro Casanas (Cuba)
 Aug. 21 1977
13.16* Renaldo Nehemiah (USA)
 Apr. 14 1979
13.00* Nehemiah May 6 1979

400 Metres Hurdles
sec.
49.2* Glenn Davis (USA)
 Aug. 6 1958
49.2* Salvatore Morale (Italy)
 Sept. 14 1962
49.1* Rex Cawley (USA)
 Sept. 13 1964
48.8* Geoff Vanderstock (USA)
 Sept. 11 1968
48.1* David Hemery (GB)
 Oct. 15 1968
47.8* John Akii-Bua (Uganda)
 Sept. 2 1972
47.6 Edwin Moses (USA)
 July 25 1976

400 Metres Hurdles (Electrical)
48.94 Geoff Vanderstock
 (USA) Sept. 11 1968
48.12 David Hemery (GB)
 Oct. 15 1968
47.82* John Akii-Bua (Uganda)
 Sept. 2 1972
47.63* Edwin Moses (USA)
 July 25 1976
47.45* Moses June 11 1977
47.13* Moses July 3 1980

High Jump
metres
2.22* John Thomas (USA)
 July 1 1960
2.23* Valeriy Brumel (USSR)
 June 18 1961
2.24* Brumel July 16 1961
2.25* Brumel Aug. 31 1961
2.26* Brumel July 22 1962
2.27* Brumel Sept. 29 1962
2.28* Brumel July 21 1963
2.29* Pat Matzdorf (USA)
 July 3 1971
2.30* Dwight Stones (USA)
 July 11 1973
2.31* Stones June 5 1976
2.32* Stones Aug. 4 1976
2.33* Vladimir Yashchenko
 (USSR) July 3 1977
2.34* Yashchenko June 16 1978
2.35* Jacek Wszola (Poland)
 May 25 1980
2.35* Dietmar Mogenburg
 (W. Germany) May 26 1980
2.36* Gerd Wessig
 (E. Germany) Aug. 1 1980

Pole Vault
metres
4.82 Bob Gutowski (USA)
 June 15 1957
4.83* George Davies (USA)
 May 20 1961
4.89* John Uelses (USA)
 Mar. 31 1962

4.93*	Dave Tork (USA)	Apr. 28 1962
4.94*	Pentti Nikula (Finland)	June 22 1962
4.95	John Pennel (USA)	Mar. 22 1963
4.98	Pennel	Apr. 10 1963
5.00*	Brian Sternberg (USA)	Apr. 27 1963
5.05	Pennel	Apr. 30 1963
5.05	Sternberg	May 25 1963
5.08*	Sternberg	June 7 1963
5.10	Pennel	July 13 1963
5.10	Pennel	July 26 1963
5.13*	Pennel	Aug. 5 1963
5.20*	Pennel	Aug. 24 1963
5.20	Fred Hansen (USA)	June 5 1964
5.23*	Hansen	June 13 1964
5.28*	Hansen	July 25 1964
5.32*	Bob Seagren (USA)	May 14 1966
5.32	Seagren	July 2 1966
5.34*	Pennel	July 23 1966
5.36*	Seagren	June 10 1967
5.38*	Paul Wilson (USA)	June 23 1967
5.41*	Seagren	Sept. 12 1968
5.44*	Pennel	June 21 1969
5.45*	Wolfgang Nordwig (E. Germany)	June 17 1970
5.46*	Nordwig	Sept. 3 1970
5.49*	Chris Papanicolaou (Greece)	Oct. 24 1970
5.51*	Kjell Isaksson (Sweden)	Apr. 8 1972
5.54*	Isaksson	Apr. 15 1972
5.59	Seagren	May 23 1972
5.59	Isaksson	May 23 1972
5.63*	Seagren	July 2 1972
5.65*	Dave Roberts (USA)	March 28 1975
5.67*	Earl Bell (USA)	May 29 1976
5.70*	Roberts	June 22 1976
5.72*	Wladyslaw Kozakiewicz (Poland)	May 11 1980
5.75*	Thierry Vigneron (France)	June 1 1980
5.75*	Vigneron	June 29 1980
5.77*	Philippe Houvion (France)	July 17 1980
5.78*	Kozakiewicz	July 30 1980

IAAF records not shown above:

4.80	Don Bragg (USA)	July 2 1960
5.55	Kjell Isaksson (Sweden)	June 12 1972

Long Jump
metres

8.21*	Ralph Boston (USA)	Aug. 12 1960
8.24*	Boston	May 27 1961
8.28*	Boston	July 16 1961
8.31*	Igor Ter-Ovanesyan (USSR)	June 10 1962
8.31*	Boston	Aug. 15 1964
8.34*	Boston	Sept. 12 1964
8.35*	Boston	May 29 1965
8.35*	Ter-Ovanesyan	Oct. 19 1967
8.90*	Bob Beamon (USA)	Oct. 18 1968

Triple Jump
metres

17.03*	Jozef Szmidt (Poland)	Aug. 5 1960
17.10*	Giuseppe Gentile (Italy)	Oct. 16 1968
17.22*	Gentile	Oct. 17 1968
17.23*	Viktor Sanyeyev (USSR)	Oct. 17 1968
17.27*	Nelson Prudencio (Brazil)	Oct. 17 1968
17.39*	Sanyeyev	Oct. 17 1968
17.40*	Pedro Perez (Cuba)	Aug. 5 1971
17.44*	Sanyeyev	Oct. 17 1972
17.89*	Joao Carlos de Oliveira (Brazil)	Oct. 15 1975

Shot
metres

19.45*	Bill Nieder (USA)	Mar. 19 1960
19.67*	Dallas Long (USA)	Mar 26 1960
19.99*	Nieder	Apr. 2 1960
20.06*	Bill Nieder (USA)	Aug. 12 1960
20.08*	Long	May 18 1962
20.10*	Long	Apr. 4 1964
20.30	Long	May 9 1964
20.68*	Long	July 25 1964
20.71	Randy Matson (USA)	Apr. 9 1965
21.05	Matson	Apr. 30 1965
21.52*	Matson	May 8 1965
21.78*	Matson	Apr. 22 1967
21.82*	Al Feuerbach (USA)	May 5 1973
21.85*	Terry Albritton (USA)	Feb. 21 1976
22.00*	Aleksandr Baryshnikov (USSR)	July 10 1976
22.15*	Udo Beyer (E. Germany)	July 6 1978

IAAF record not shown above:
20.20 Dallas Long (USA)
                    May 29 1964

Discus
metres
59.90* Edmund Piatkowski
       (Poland)   June 14 1959
60.56* Jay Silvester (USA)
                     Aug. 11 1961
60.72* Silvester   Aug.20 1961
61.10* Al Oerter (USA)
                     May 18 1962
61.64* Vladimir Trusenyov
       (USSR)   June 4 1962
62.44* Oerter   July 1 1962
62.62* Oerter   Apr. 27 1963
62.94* Oerter   Apr. 25 1964
64.54* Ludvik Danek
       (Czechoslovakia) Aug. 2 1964
65.22* Danek   Oct. 12 1965
66.06 Danek   June 7 1966
66.54* Silvester   May 25 1968
68.40* Silvester   Sept. 18 1968
68.40* Ricky Bruch
       (Sweden)   July 5 1972
68.48* John Van Reenen
       (S. Africa)   March 14 1975
69.08* John Powell (USA)
                     May   4 1975
69.18* Mac Wilkins (USA)
                     Apr. 24 1976
69.80* Wilkins   May   1 1976
70.24* Wilkins   May   1 1976
70.86* Wilkins   May   1 1976
71.16* Wolfgang Schmidt
       (E. Germany)   Aug. 9 1978

IAAF record not shown above:
59.90 Rink Bakba (USA)
                     Aug. 12 1960

Hammer
metres
70.32* Hal Connolly (USA)
                     Aug. 12 1960
70.66* Connolly   July 21 1962
71.06* Connolly   May 29 1965
71.26* Connolly   June 20 1965
73.74* Gyula Zsivotzky
       (Hungary)   Sept 4 1965
73.76* Zsivotzky   Sept. 14 1968
74.52* Romuald Klim
       (USSR)   June 15 1969
74.68* Anatoliy Bondarchuk
       (USSR)   Sept. 20 1969
75.48* Bondarchuk   Oct. 12 1969
76.40* Walter Schmidt (W.
       Germany)   Sept. 4 1971
76.60* Reinhard Theimer (E.
       Germany)   July   4 1974
76.66* Aleksey Spiridonov
       (USSR)   Sept. 11 1974
76.70* Karl-Hans Riehm
       (W. Germany)   May 19 1975
77.56* Riehm   May 19 1975
78.50* Riehm   May 19 1975
79.30* Schmidt   Aug. 14 1975
80.14* Boris Zaichuk (USSR)
                     July   9 1978
80.32* Riehm   Aug.   6 1978
80.38* Yuriy Sedykh (USSR)
                     May 16 1980
80.46* Juri Tamm (USSR)
                     May 16 1980
80.64* Sedykh   May 16 1980
81.66* Sergey Litvinov (USSR)
                     May 24 1980
81.80* Sedykh   July 31 1980

Javelin
metres
86.04* Al Cantello (USA)
                     June 5 1959
86.74* Carlo Lievore (Italy)
                     June 1 1961
87.12* Terje Pedersen (Norway)
                     July 1 1964
91.72* Pedersen   Sept. 1 1964
91.98* Janis Lusis (USSR)
                     June 23 1968
92.70* Jorma Kinnunen
       (Finland)   June 18 1969
93.80* Lusis   July 6 1972
94.08* Klaus Wolfermann
       (W. Germany)   May   5 1973
94.58* Miklos Nemeth
       (Hungary)   July 26 1976
96.72* Ferenc Paragi
       (Hungary)   Apr. 23 1980

Decathlon (1962 tables)
8063* Rafer Johnson (USA)
                     July 8/9 1960
8089* Yang Chuan-kwang
       (Taiwan)   Apr. 27/28 1963
8234 Bill Toomey (USA)
                     July 2/3 1966
8319* Kurt Bendlin (W.
       Germany)   May 13/14 1967
8417* Toomey   Dec. 10/11 1969
8454* Nikolay Avilov (USSR)
       (elec)   Sept. 7/8 1972
8524* Bruce Jenner (USA)
                     Aug. 9/10 1975
8538* Jenner   June 25/26 1976
8618* (elec) Jenner   July 29/30 1976
8622* (elec) Daley Thompson
       (GB)   May 17/18 1980
8649* (elec) Guido Kratschmer

(W. Germany) June 13/14 1980
IAAF record not shown above:
8230 Russ Hodge (USA)
July 23/24 1966

Walking records as ratified by IAAF

20,000 Metres Walk
1:27:05.0 Vladimir Golubnichiy
(USSR) Sept. 23 1958
1:26:45.8 Gennadiy Agapov
(USSR) Apr. 6 1969
1:25:50.0 Peter Frenkel (E.
Germany) July 4 1970
1:25:19.4 Frenkel June 24 1972
1:25:19.4 Hans-Georg Reimann
(E. Germany) June 24 1972
1:24:45.0 Bernd Kannenberg
(W. Germany) May 25 1974
1:23:31.9 Daniel Bautista
(Mexico) May 14 1977
1:22:59.4 Anatoliy Solomin
(USSR) Apr. 26 1979
1:22:19.4 Gerard Lelievre
(France) Apr. 29 1979
1:20:58.6 Domingo Colin
(Mexico) May 26 1979
1:20:06.8 Bautista Oct. 17 1979

2 Hours Walk
metres
25,595 Josef Dolezal
(Czechoslovakia) Oct. 12 1952
25,701 Dolezal May 14 1955
25,865 Anatoliy Vedyakov
(USSR) Oct. 7 1955
26,117 Ted Allsop
(Australia) Sept. 22 1956
26,429 Anatoliy Yegorov
(USSR) July 15 1959
26,658 Peter Frenkel
(E. Germany) Apr. 11 1971
26,911 Karl-Heinz Stadt-
muller (E. Germany)
Apr. 16 1972
26,930 Frenkel Apr. 14 1974
27,153 Bernd Kannenberg
(W. Germany) May 11 1974
27,247 Raul Gonzalez
(Mexico) May 19 1978
28,165 Jose Marin (Spain)
Apr. 8 1979

30,000 Metres Walk
hr. min. sec.
2:17:16.8 Anatoliy Yegorov (USSR)
July 15 1959
2:15:16.0 Christoph Hohne (E.
Germany) Apr. 11 1971
2:14:45.6 Karl-Heinz Stadtmuller
(E. Germany) Apr. 16 1972
2:14:21.2 Peter Frenkel
(E. Germany) Apr. 14 1974
2:12:58.0 Bernd Kannenberg
(W. Germany) May 11 1974
2:11:53.4 Raul Gonzalez
(Mexico) May 19 1978
2:08:00 Jose Marin (Spain)
Apr. 8 1979

50,000 Metres Walk
hr. min. sec.
4:16:08.6 Sergey Lobastov (USSR)
Aug. 23 1958
4:14:02.4 Abdon Pamich (Italy)
Nov. 19 1961
4:10:51.8 Christoph Hohne
(E. Germany) May 16 1965
4:08:05.0 Hohne Oct. 18 1969
4:04:19.8 Peter Selzer
(E. Germany) Oct. 3 1971
4:03:42.6 Veniamin Soldatenko
(USSR) Oct. 5 1972
4:00:27.2 Gerhard Weidner
(W. Germany) Apr. 8 1973
3:56:51.4 Bernd Kannenberg
(W. Germany) Nov. 16 1975
3:56:38.2 Enrique Vera
(Mexico) May 16 1977
3:52:23.5 Raul Gonzalez
(Mexico) May 19 1978
3:41:39.0 Gonzalez May 25 1979

Evolution of Women's World Records

100 Metres
sec.
11.3* Shirley De La Hunty
(Australia) Aug. 4 1955
11.3* Vyera Krepkina (USSR)
Sept. 13 1958
11.3* Wilma Rudolph (USA)
Sept. 2 1960
11.3 Rudolph July 15 1961
11.2* Rudolph July 19 1961
11.2* Wyomia Tyus (USA)
Oct. 15 1964
11.1* Irena Szewinska (Poland)
July 9 1965
11.1* Tyus July 31 1965
11.1* Barbara Ferrell (USA)
July 2 1967
11.1 Tyus Apr. 21 1968
11.1* Ludmila Samotyosova
(USSR) Aug. 15 1968
11.1 Margaret Bailes (USA)
Aug. 18 1968
11.1* Szewinska Oct. 14 1968
11.1 Ferrell Oct. 14 1968

11.0* Tyus   Oct. 15 1968
11.0* Chi Cheng (Taiwan)
                            July 18 1970
11.0* Renate Stecher (E.
      Germany)   Aug. 2 1970
11.0* Stecher   July 31 1971
11.0* Stecher   June 3 1972
11.0* Ellen Stropahl (E.
      Germany)   June 15 1972
11.0* Eva Gleskova (Czecho-
      slovakia)   July 1 1972
11.0 Stecher   Aug. 19 1972
10.9* Stecher   June 7 1973
10.9 Stecher   June 30 1973
10.9 Stecher   July 20 1973
10.8* Stecher   July 20 1973
10.8 Annegret Richter (W.
      Germany)   June 27 1976

100 Metres (Electrical)
11.07* Wyomia Tyus (USA)
                            Oct. 15 1968
11.07* Renate Stecher (E.
       Germany)   Sept. 2 1972
11.07 Stecher   July 20 1973
11.04* Inge Helten (W.
       Germany)   June 13 1976
11.01* Annegret Richter (W.
       Germany)   July 25 1976
10.88* Marlies Gohr
       (E. Germany)   July 1 1977

200 Metres
sec.
22.9* Wilma Rudolph (USA)
                            July 9 1960
22.9* Margaret Burvill (Australia)
                            Feb. 22 1964
22.7* Irena Szewinska (Poland)
                            Aug. 8 1965
22.7 Szewinska   July 2 1967
22.5* Szewinska   Oct. 18 1968
22.4* Chi Cheng (Taiwan)
                            July 12 1970
22.4* Renate Stecher (E.
      Germany)   Sept. 7 1972
22.4 Stecher   July 1 1973
22.1* Stecher   July 21 1973
22.0 Szewinska   June 13 1974

200 Metres (Electrical)
22.62 Chi Cheng (Taiwan)
                            July 12 1970
22.40 Renate Stecher (E.
       Germany)   Sept. 2 1972
22.38 Stecher   July 21 1973
22.21* Irena Szewinska
       (Poland)   June 13 1974
22.06* Marita Koch
       (E. Germany)   May 28 1978

22.02* Koch   June 3 1979
21.71* Koch   June 10 1979

400 Metres
sec.
53.0 Sin Kim Dan (N. Korea)
                            Oct. 22 1960
53.0 Sin Kim Dan   June 30 1962
51.9* Sin Kim Dan   Oct. 23 1962
51.4 Sin Kim Dan   Nov. 12 1963
51.2 Sin Kim Dan   Oct. 21 1964
51.0* Marilyn Neufville
      (Jamaica)   July 23 1970
51.0* Monika Zehrt
      (E. Germany)   July 4 1972
49.9* Irena Szewinska
      (Poland)   June 22 1974
49.8 Christina Brehmer (E.
      Germany)   May   9 1976
49.8 Szewinska   June 22 1976
49.3 Szewinska   July 29 1976

400 Metres (Electrical)
51.02 Marilyn Neufville
       (Jamaica)   July 23 1970
50.98 Jelica Pavlicic (Yugo-
       slavia)   Aug. 3 1974
50.78 Riitta Salin (Finland)
                            Aug. 17 1974
50.14* Salin   Sept. 4 1974
49.77* Christina Brehmer (E.
       Germany)   May   9 1976
49.75* Irena Szewinska
       (Poland)   June 22 1976
49.28* Szewinska   July 29 1976
49.19* Marita Koch
       (E. Germany)   July 2 1978
49.03* Koch   Aug. 19 1978
48.94* Koch   Aug. 31 1978
48.89* Koch   July 29 1979
48.60* Koch   Aug. 4 1979

IAAF records not shown above:
sec.
53.4 Maria Itkina (USSR)
                            Sept. 12 1959
53.4 Itkina   Sept. 14 1962
51.7 Nicole Duclos (France)
                            Sept. 18 1969
51.7 Colette Besson (France)
                            Sept. 18 1969

800 Metres
min. sec.
2:04.3* Lyudmila Shevtsova
        (USSR)   July 3 1960
2:04.3* Shevtsova   Sept. 7 1960
2:01.2 Sin Kim Dan (N. Korea)
                            May   1 1961

WORLD RECORDS

2:01.2* Dixie Willis (Australia)
    Mar. 3 1962
1:59.1 Sin Kim Dan Nov. 12 1963
1:58.0 Sin Kim Dan Sept. 5 1964
1:57.5* Svetla Zlateva (Bulgaria)
    Aug. 24 1973
1:56.0* Valentina Gerassimova
    (USSR) June 12 1976
1:54.9* Tatyana Kazankina
    (USSR) July 26 1976
1:54.85* Nadyezhda Olizaryenko
    (USSR) June 12 1980
1:53.42* Olizaryenko July 27 1980

IAAF records not shown above:
2:01.1 Ann Packer (GB)
    Oct. 20 1964
2:01.0 Judy Pollock (Australia)
    June 28 1967
2:00.5 Vera Nikolic (Yugo-
    slavia) July 20 1968
1:58.5 Hildegard Falck (W.
    Germany) July 11 1971

1500 Metres
min. sec.
4:29.7 Diane Leather (GB)
    July 19 1957
4:19.0 Marise Chamberlain
    (NZ) Dec. 8 1962
4:17.3* Anne Smith (GB)
    June 3 1967
4:15.6* Maria Gommers
    (Netherlands) Oct. 24 1967
4:12.4* Paola Pigni (Italy)
    July 2 1969
4:10.7* Jaroslava Jehlickova
    (Czechoslovakia) Sept. 20 1969
4:09.6* Karin Burneleit (E.
    Germany) Aug 15 1971
4:06.9* Lyudmila Bragina
    (USSR) July 18 1972
4:06.5* Bragina Sept. 4 1972
4:05.1* Bragina Sept. 7 1972
4:01.4* Bragina Sept. 9 1972
3:56.0* Tatyana Kazankina
    (USSR) June 28 1976
3:55.0* Kazankina July 6 1980
3:52.5* Kazankina Aug. 13 1980

Mile
min. sec.
4:45.0 Diane Leather (GB)
    Sept. 21 1955
4:41.4 Marise Chamberlain
    (NZ) Dec. 8 1962
4:39.2 Anne Smith (GB)
    May 13 1967
4:37.0* Smith June 3 1967

4:36.8* Maria Gommers
    (Netherlands) June 14 1969
4:35.3* Ellen Tittel (W.
    Germany) Aug. 20 1971
4:29.5* Paola Cacchi (Italy)
    Aug. 8 1973
4:23.8* Natalia Marasescu
    (Romania) May 21 1977
4:22.1* Marasescu Jan. 27 1979
4:21.7* Mary Decker (USA)
    Jan. 26 1980
Indoor mark:
4:17.6 Decker Feb. 16 1980

3000 Metres
min. sec.
9:23.4 Joyce Smith (GB)
    July 16 1971
9:09.2 Paola Cacchi (Italy)
    May 11 1972
8:53.0 Lyudmila Bragina
    (USSR) Aug. 12 1972
8:52.7* Bragina July 6 1974
8:46.6* Grete Waitz (Norway)
    June 24 1975
8:45.4* Waitz June 21 1976
8:27.2* Bragina Aug. 7 1976

Marathon
See under MARATHON.

100 Metres Hurdles
sec.
13.3* Karin Balzer (E.
    Germany) June 20 1969
13.3* Teresa Sukniewicz
    (Poland) June 20 1969
13.0* Balzer July 27 1969
12.9* Balzer Sept. 5 1969
12.8* Sukniewicz June 20 1970
12.8* Chi Cheng (Taiwan)
    July 12 1970
12.7* Balzer July 26 1970
12.7* Sukniewicz Sept. 20 1970
12.7 Sukniewicz Sept. 27 1970
12.7* Balzer July 25 1971
12.6* Balzer July 31 1971
12.5* Annelie Ehrhardt (E.
    Germany) June 15 1972
12.5* Pam Ryan (Australia)
    June 28 1972
12.5 Ehrhardt Aug. 13 1972
12.3* Ehrhardt July 22 1973

100 Metres Hurdles (Electrical)
12.93 Chi Cheng (Taiwan)
    July 12 1970
12.70 Annelie Ehrhardt (E.
    Germany) Sept. 4 1972
12.59* Ehrhardt Sept. 8 1972

WORLD RECORDS

12.48* Grazyna Rabsztyn
(Poland) June 10 1978
12.48* Rabsztyn June 18 1979
12.36 Rabsztyn June 13 1980

400 Metres Hurdles
sec.
61.1 Sandra Dyson (GB)
May 15 1971
60.7 Libuse Macounova
(Czechoslovakia) Sept. 29 1971
60.4 Judy Vernon (GB)
March 21 1973
59.1 Wendy Koenig (USA)
March 25 1973
58.6 Maria Sykora (Austria)
May 27 1973
58.5 Sykora June 16 1973
57.3 Sykora June 23 1973
56.7 Danuta Piecyk (Poland)
Aug. 11 1973
56.5* Krystyna Kacperczyk
(Poland) July 13 1974

400 Metres Hurdles (Electrical)
56.51* Krystyna Kacperczyk
(Poland) July 13 1974
55.74* Tatyana Storozheva
(USSR) June 26 1977
55.63* Karin Rossley
(E. Germany) Aug. 13 1977
55.44* Kacperczyk Aug. 18 1978
55.31* Tatyana Zelentsova
(USSR) Aug. 19 1978
54.89* Zelentsova Sept. 2 1978
54.78* Marina Makeyeva
(USSR) July 27 1979
54.28* Rossley May 18 1980

High Jump
metres
1.86* Iolanda Balas
(Romania) July 9 1960
1.87* Balas Apr. 15 1961
1.88* Balas June 18 1961
1.90* Balas July 8 1961
1.91* Balas July 16 1961
1.92* Ilona Gusenbauer
(Austria) Sept. 4 1971
1.92* Ulrike Meyfarth (W.
Germany) Sept. 4 1972
1.94* Yordanka Blagoeva
(Bulgaria) Sept. 24 1972
1.94* Rosi Ackermann (E.
Germany) Aug. 24 1974
1.95* Ackermann Sept. 8 1974
1.96* Ackermann May 8 1976
1.96* Ackermann July 3 1977
1.97* Ackermann Aug. 14 1977
1.97* Ackermann Aug. 26 1977
2.00* Ackermann Aug. 26 1977

2.01* Sara Simeoni (Italy)
Aug 4 1978
2.01* Simeoni Aug. 31 1978

Long Jump
metres
6.40* Hildrun Claus (E.
Germany) Aug. 7 1960
6.42* Claus June 23 1961
6.48* Tatyana Shchelkanova
(USSR) July 16 1961
6.53* Shchelkanova June 10 1962
6.70* Shchelkanova July 4 1964
6.76* Mary Rand (GB)
Oct. 14 1964
6.82* Viorica Viscopoleanu
(Romania) Oct. 14 1968
6.84* Heide Rosendahl (W.
Germany) Sept. 3 1970
6.92* Angela Voigt (E.
Germany) May 9 1976
6.99* Sigrun Siegl (E.
Germany) May 19 1976
7.07* Vilma Bardauskiene
(USSR) Aug. 18 1978
7.09* Bardauskiene Aug. 29 1978

Shot
metres
17.78* Tamara Press
(USSR) Aug. 13 1960
18.55* Press June 10 1962
18.55* Press Sept. 12 1962
18.59* Press Sept. 19 1965
18.67* Nadyezhda Chizhova
(USSR) Apr. 28 1968
18.87* Margitta Gummel (E.
Germany) Sept. 22 1968
19.07* Gummel Oct. 20 1968
19.61* Gummel Oct. 20 1968
19.72* Chizhova May 30 1969
20.09* Chizhova July 13 1969
20.10* Gummel Sept. 11 1969
20.10* Chizhova Sept. 16 1969
20.43* Chizhova Sept. 16 1969
20.43* Chizhova Aug. 29 1971
20.63* Chizhova May 19 1972
21.03* Chizhova Sept. 7 1972
21.20* Chizhova Aug. 28 1973
21.45 Chizhova Sept. 29 1973
21.57 Helena Fibingerova
(Czechoslovakia) Sept. 21 1974
21.60* Marianne Adam (E.
Germany) Aug. 6 1975
21.67* Adam May 30 1976
21.87* Ivanka Khristova
(Bulgaria) July 3 1976
21.89* Khristova July 4 1976
21.99* Fibingerova Sept. 26 1976
22.32* Fibingerova Aug. 20 1977

22.36*	Ilona Slupianek (E. Germany)	May 2	1980
22.45*	Slupianek	May 11	1980

Indoor mark:
22.50   Fibingerova   Feb. 19 1977

Discus
metres
57.14*	Tamara Press (USSR)	Sept. 12	1960
57.42*	Press	July 15	1961
58.06*	Press	Sept. 1	1961
58.98*	Press	Sept. 20	1961
59.28*	Press	May 19	1963
59.70*	Press	Aug. 11	1965
61.26*	Liesel Westermann (W. Germany)	Nov. 5	1967
61.64*	Christine Spielberg (E. Germany)	May 26	1968
62.54*	Westermann	July 24	1968
62.70*	Westermann	June 18	1969
63.96*	Westermann	Sept. 27	1969
64.22*	Faina Melnik (USSR)	Aug. 12	1971
64.88*	Melnik	Sept. 4	1971
65.42*	Melnik	May 31	1972
65.48*	Melnik	June 24	1972
66.76*	Melnik	Aug. 4	1972
67.32*	Argentina Menis (Romania)	Sept. 23	1972
67.44*	Melnik	May 25	1973
67.58*	Melnik	July 10	1973
69.48*	Melnik	Sept. 7	1973
69.90*	Melnik	May 27	1974
70.20*	Melnik	Aug. 20	1975
70.50*	Melnik	Apr. 24	1976
70.72*	Evelin Jahl (E. Germany)	Aug. 12	1978
71.50*	Jahl	May 10	1980
71.80*	Maria Vergova (Bulgaria)	July 13	1980

Javelin
metres
59.54*	Elvira Ozolina (USSR)	June 4	1960
59.78*	Ozolina	July 3	1963
61.38	Ozolina	Aug. 27	1964
62.40*	Yelena Gorchakova (USSR)	Oct. 16	1964
62.70*	Ewa Gryziecka (Poland)	June 11	1972
65.06*	Ruth Fuchs (E. Germany)	June 11	1972
66.10*	Fuchs	Sept. 7	1973
67.22*	Fuchs	Sept. 3	1974
69.12*	Fuchs	July 10	1976
69.32*	Kate Schmidt (USA)	Sept. 11	1977
69.52*	Fuchs	June 13	1979
69.96*	Fuchs	Apr. 29	1980
70.08*	Tatyana Biryulina (USSR)	July 12	1980

Pentathlon (1954 tables)
4972*	Irina Press (USSR)	Oct. 17/18	1960
5020	Press	Aug. 16/17	1961
5137*	Press	Oct. 8/9	1961
5194	Press	Aug. 29/30	1964
5246*	Press	Oct. 16/17	1964

With 100 m. hurdles
5352*	Liese Prokop (Austria)	Oct.4/5	1969
5406*	Burglinde Pollak (E. Germany)	Sept. 5/6	1970

New Tables
4791	Heide Rosendahl (W. Germany)	Sept. 2/3	1972
4801*	Mary Peters (GB & NI)	Sept. 2/3	1972
4831*	Pollak	Aug 12	1973
4932*	Pollak	Sept. 22	1973

With 800 metres
4765*	Eva Wilms (W. Germany)	May 14	1977
4823*	Wilms	June 19	1977
4839*	Nadyezhda Tkachenko (USSR)	Sept. 18	1977
4856*	Olga Kuragina (USSR)	June 20	1980
4875*	Kuragina	July 24	1980
4937*	Olga Rukavishnikova (USSR)	July 24	1980
5083*	Tkachenko	July 24	1980

WSZOLA, Jacek (Poland)

The youngest individual champion in the men's events of the 1976 Olympics, 19-year-old Jacek Wszola mastered the damp conditions which brought about the downfall of favourite Dwight Stones to win the high jump with an Olympic record of 2.25 metres. His victory elicited this characteristic tribute from Stones: "He's the greatest competitor around in high jump—next to me, that is".

Wszola's competitive qualities became known in 1974 when, at 17, he was placed 5th in the European Championships. He leapt 2.22 metres in 1975 to become European junior champion, but he was really put to the test in Montreal. He flopped over 2.23 metres at the first attempt and despite the pressure of more than 60,000 fans willing his last surviving opponent, Canada's Greg Joy, to beat him, the Pole succeeded in clearing 2.25 metres on his second try to place the issue beyond doubt. Some weeks later he broke Valeriy Brumel's European record (which had stood since 1963) by a centimetre with 2.29 metres.

Wszola lost his supremacy during the next three seasons and there was talk of his concentrating on the triple jump instead (he has reportedly cleared over 16 metres in training), but in 1980 he reached new heights—including a short lived world record of 2.35 metres. He cleared 2.31 metres in Moscow for the silver medal to join Valeriy Brumel as the only male high jumper ever to win Olympic gold and silver medals.

Annual progress: 1971—1.60 m; 1972—1.80; 1973—2.08; 1974—2.20; 1975—2.23; 1976—2.29; 1977—2.30; 1978—2.24; 1979—2.29; 1980—2.35. He was born in Warsaw on Dec. 30th, 1956.

YASHCHENKO, Vladimir (USSR)

His name isn't on the roll of Olympic champions, and he no longer holds the world record, but—in the opinion of many—Vladimir Yashchenko is the greatest high jump talent yet seen. Alas his career, of such brilliance, may have been prematurely ended by injury, but no one who saw him in action will forget the excitement and exuberance he generated.

It all happened so quickly. At the age of 14 his best was a fairly humdrum 1.70 metres, yet one year later he had shot up to 2.03 metres and at 18 he was world record holder! That first world record, set in the USA v USSR junior match in July 1977, came as a thunderbolt. True, he had created a world junior indoor best of 2.26 metres the previous winter, but who could have anticipated the sequence of events at Richmond, Virginia. In quick succession, he straddled clear at 2.27 metres for a world junior record, 2.31 metres for a European record and then an astounding 2.33 metres to add a centimetre to the world mark held by Dwight Stones (USA). Later in the season he won the European junior title at 2.30 metres.

Yashchenko's next dramatic breakthrough occurred in March 1978 at the European Indoor Championships in Milan. The 1.93 metres tall Ukrainian teenager captivated the audience as he jumped 2.33 metres for a world indoor record, and the crowd went delirious when he followed with a third-time clearance at 2.35 metres. It was Yashchenko's twentieth jump of the evening, he having entered the competition with the bar at a lowly 2.10 metres—which he proceeded to knock down at his first attempt! Rolf Beilschmidt, the East German who finished a gallant second, said of Yashchenko: " He is the greatest jumper of all time. His technique is not perfect, but he has phenomenal spring. He will certainly be the first one day to clear 2.40 metres ". Other athletes and coaches agreed.

After raising the official world record to 2.34 metres in his first outdoor appearance of the 1978 season he looked to be on course, but injuries began to bedevil him although he did capture the European title that year with 2.30 metres in poor conditions. He competed only rarely in 1979, and not at all in 1980 following a series of knee operations. It remained to be seen whether he would ever jump again.

His annual progress: 1970—1.40 m.; 1971—1.45; 1972—1.60; 1973—1.70; 1974—2.03; 1975—2.12; 1976—2.22; 1977—2.33; 1978—2.35 (indoors) & 2.34; 1979—2.29 (indoors) & 2.24. He was born at Zaporozhye on Jan. 12th, 1959.

YIFTER, Miruts (Ethiopia)

No world famous athlete has remained as mysterious and enigmatic for as long as Miruts Yifter. For a start, no one—not even himself—knows exactly how old he is. At first it was claimed that his year of birth was 1947, but 1943 or 1944 would seem more likely, although in Moscow he looked even older than 36 or 37. Little is known about his lifestyle (the father of six children, he is an officer in the Ethiopian Air Force) or even his training methods, although he does have the inborn advantage of living at high altitude. What we do know is that he is one of the most remarkable long distance competitors the world has ever seen, possessor of perhaps the deadliest finishing kick in the game. Any sympathy the fans might have had at the start of a race when they see this tiny, balding figure lining up with much more athletic looking opponents will almost certainly have been transferred to the

African's luckless rivals by the finish!

It was in 1970 that he began to make a name for himself, first by defeating Olympic marathon champion Mamo Wolde over 10,000 m. and then by scoring a shock victory over Kenya's Kip Keino in a 5000 m. race in Israel. He became an international celebrity in 1971 on the occasion of the USA v Africa match at Durham, North Carolina. Miscounting the laps in the 5000 m., he sprinted to what he thought was victory over Steve Prefontaine—only to discover to his horror that there was another lap to go. The race went to the American, but the next day Yifter defeated Frank Shorter in the 10,000 m. and a new star was born.

He encountered mixed fortunes at the 1972 Olympics. He ran bravely to come within 2 sec. of Ron Clarke's previous world record in finishing third in the 10,000 m. (27 min. 41.0 sec., which is still his best time) behind Lasse Viren and Emiel Puttemans, but his 5000 m. hopes were dashed when he spent too long in the toilet and missed the start of the final.

The African boycott prevented Yifter from challenging the all-conquering Viren at the 1976 Games, but the following year he demonstrated what might have been as he uncorked spectacular finishes to clock under 54 sec. for the last lap in both 5000 m. (in which he just missed the world record) and 10,000 m. at the World Cup. Two years later, in 1979, he repeated that World Cup double in equally convincing fashion.

'Yifter the Shifter' as he is affectionately and admiringly dubbed, seized his belated chance of Olympic glory in Moscow, sprinting away to victory in both the 10,000 m. (27 min. 42.7 sec., with the second half covered in an exceptional 13 min. 39.2 sec.) and the 5000 m. (13 min. 21.0 sec.). He thus joined such immortals as Hannes Kolehmainen, Paavo Nurmi, Emil Zatopek, Vladimir Kuts and Lasse Viren as a winner of both Olympic long distance track events. Had the timetable allowed, he would have gone for the marathon too . . . but that may have to wait now until Los Angeles in 1984.

His best marks include unconfirmed times of 48.0 sec. for 400 m. and 1 min. 48.8 sec. for 800 m., plus 13 min. 13.9 sec. for 5000 m., 27 min. 41.0 sec. for 10,000 m. and 62 min. 56 sec. for half marathon. His annual progress: 1970—14:25.8; 1971—13:52.6, 28:53.2; 1972—13:33.8, 27:41.0; 1973—13:54.0, 29:04.8; 1974—14:11.0, 29:57.4; 1975—13:39.0, 28:09.2; 1976—13:24.4, 28:26.4; 1977—13:13.9, 27:50.4; 1978—13:41.6, 28:47.1; 1979—13:20.8, 27:44.2; 1980—13:16.4, 27:42.7.

YOUNGEST
Men

Youngest Olympic champion was Bob Mathias (USA), 1948 decathlon winner at the age of 17 yr. 8 mth.

Youngest British champion: Charles Lockton, winner of Amateur Athletic Club (English Championships) long jump in 1873, aged 16 yr. 9 mth.

Youngest British international: Ross Hepburn, high jump in 1977, aged 15 yr. 10 mth.

Youngest world record holder: John Thomas (USA) was 10 days short of his 18th birthday when in 1959 he jumped 2.16 metres for an indoor world best—superior to the existing outdoor record.

Youngest British record holder: Alan Paterson, high jump in 1946, aged 17 yr. 11 mth.

Women

Youngest Olympic champion: Barbara Jones (USA), member of winning 4 x 100 m. relay team in 1952, aged 15 yr. 4 mth. Youngest individual gold medallist: Ulrike Meyfarth (W. Germany), high jump in 1972, aged 16 yr. 4 mth. These two girls are also the youngest world record setters.

Youngest British champion: Betty Lock, WAAA 60 m. in 1936, aged 15.

Youngest British international: Janis Walsh, indoor 60 m. in 1975, 41 days before her 15th birthday.

Youngest British record holder: Dorothy Tyler, high jump in 1936, aged 16 yr. 2 mth.

ZATOPEK, Emil
(Czechoslovakia)

In the eyes of many athletics experts, Emil Zatopek's triple triumph at the 1952 Olympics represents the sport's supreme achievement. Even to attempt the 5000 m., 10,000 m. and marathon against the cream of the world's athletes is startling; to win all three—each in Olympic record time—is well nigh incredible.

This was the measure of Zatopek's feat in Helsinki: July 20th, first in 10,000 m. in 29 min. 17.0 sec. (won by 100 m.); July 22nd, third in 5000 m. heat in 14 min. 26.0 sec.; July 24th, first in 5000 m. final in 14 min. 06.6 sec. (won by 5 metres); July 27th, first in marathon in 2 hr. 23 min. 03.2 sec. (won by 700 m.). What is more, he had never before run a marathon in competition!

The only athlete who has remotely approached this treble is Lasse Viren, who in 1976 placed fifth in the marathon after winning the 10,000 m. and 5000 m.

Zatopek made his Olympic bow in London in 1948, winning the 10,000 m. (only two months after his debut in the event) and placing a close second in the 5000 m. His final Olympic appearance in 1956 only weeks after a hernia operation, resulted in his finishing sixth in the second marathon race of his career.

On the European Championship plane, he won both titles in 1950, the 10,000 m. in 1954 and was third in the 5000 m. He set world records at several distances between 5000 and 30,000 m. from 1949 to 1955 and was the first man to leap such barriers as 29 min. for 10,000 m. and 60 min. for 20,000 m.

Zatopek made himself the greatest runner of his generation, if not all-time, by virtue of his capacity for training longer and harder than anyone had previously attempted. He possessed little natural ability. For the record, his first race was a 1400 m. event in 1941 (at the age of 18) for which he was timed in an unimpressive 4 min. 24.6 sec.

His best marks included 3 min. 52.8 sec. for 1500 m.; 8 min. 07.8 sec. for 3000 m.; 13 min. 57.0 sec. for 5000 m.; 28 min. 54.2 sec. for 10,000 m.; 44 min. 54.6 sec. for 15 km.; 48 min. 12.0 sec. for 10 mi.; 59 min. 51.8 sec. for 20 km.; 20,052 m. in one hour; 1 hr. 14 min. 01 sec for 15 mi.; 1 hr. 16 min. 36.4 sec. for 25 km.; 1 hr. 35 min. 23.8 sec. for 30 km. and 2 hr. 23 min. 03.2 sec for the marathon.

Emil's wife, Dana Zatopkova (*née* Ingrova), was herself an Olympic champion—winner of the javelin in 1952. She won the silver medal in 1960 and was European champion in 1954 and 1958. She held the world record briefly in 1958.

Curiously, she and Emil were born on the same day: Sept. 19th, 1922—he at Koprivnice, she at Tryskat. He is the elder by six hours!

APPENDIX 1

BIOGRAPHIES FEATURED IN PREVIOUS EDITIONS

Date shown is the most recent edition of *Encyclopaedia of Athletics* in which the athlete was featured. Athletes whose biographies appear in this edition are not listed here.

Alder, Jim	1967	Herriott, Maurice	1967
Applegarth, Willie	1967	Hewson, Brian	1967
Avilov, Nikolay	1973	Hill, Ron	1973
Baillie, Bill	1964	Hogan, Jim	1967
Balzer, Karin	1973	Holden, Jack	1967
Baryshnikov, Aleksandr	1977	Holdorf, Willi	1967
Batty, Mel	1964	Hopkins, Thelma	1967
Birkemeyer, Gisela	1964	Hyman, Dorothy	1973
Blagoeva, Yordanka	1973	Iharos, Sandor	1967
Board, Lillian	1973	Iso-Hollo, Volmari	1967
Bolotnikov, Pyotr	1967	Itkina, Maria	1964
Bondarchuk, Anatoliy	1973	Jackson, Marjorie	1967
Brightwell, Robbie	1967	Jarvinen, Matti	1977
Brown, Godfrey	1967	Jazy, Michel	1967
Budd, Frank	1964	Jenkins, David	1973
Burvill, Margaret	1964	Jerome, Harry	1967
Butler, Guy	1967	Jipcho, Ben	1973
Carlos, John	1973	Johnson, Derek	1967
Carr, Henry	1967	Johnston, Tim	1967
Cawley, Rex	1967	Jones, Hayes	1967
Chi Cheng	1973	Jordan, Joy	1967
Chudina, Alexandra	1964	Kannenberg, Bernd	1973
Connolly, Harold	1964	Kaufmann, Carl	1964
Consolini, Adolfo	1967	Khristova, Ivanka	1977
Cooper, John	1967	Kilby, Brian	1967
Crawford, Hasely	1977	Klim, Romuald	1967
Danek, Ludvik	1973	Klobukowska, Ewa	1967
Davis, Otis	1967	Komar, Wladyslaw	1973
Didrikson, 'Babe'	1967	Kraenzlein, Alvin	1967
Doubell, Ralph	1973	Krzyszkowiak, Zdzislaw	1964
Drut, Guy	1977	Kuznyetsov, Vasiliy	1964
Dumbadze, Nina	1967	Landy, John	1967
Eastman, Ben	1967	Larrabee, Mike	1967
Edelen, 'Buddy'	1964	Lauer, Martin	1967
Falck, Hildegard	1973	Leather, Diane	1967
Finlay, Donald	1973	Lerwill, Sheila	1967
Flanagan, John	1967	Lievore, Carlo	1964
Frenkel, Peter	1973	Long, Dallas	1967
Gardner, Maureen	1967	Lovelock, Jack	1977
Gorchakova, Yelena	1967	McGuire, Edith	1967
Grieveson, Joy	1964	McKenley, Herb	1967
Halberg, Murray	1977	Matthews, Vince	1973
Halstead, Nellie	1964	Matzdorf, Pat	1973
Hansen, Fred	1967	Menis, Argentina	1973
Hary, Armin,	1967	Meyfarth, Ulrike	1973
Heatley, Basil	1967	Mills, Billy	1967
Hermens, Jos	1977	Moens, Roger	1964

Moore, Betty	1964	Schmidt, Walter	1977
Morale, Salvatore	1964	Schul, Bob	1967
Morrow, Bobby	1973	Seagren, Bob	1973
Neufville, Marilyn	1973	Shchelkanova, Tatyana	1967
Nevala, Pauli	1967	Shorter, Frank	1977
Nieder, Bill	1964	Sidlo, Janusz	1964
Nihill, Paul	1973	Siegl, Sigrun	1977
Nordwig, Wolfgang	1973	Silvester, Jay	1973
O'Callaghan, Pat	1964	Sime, Dave	1964
Otkalenko, Nina	1967	Simpson, Alan	1967
Ozolina, Elvira	1964	Sin Kim Dan	1967
Paddock, Charley	1973	Slusarski, Tadeusz	1977
Pamich, Abdon	1967	Stephens, Helen	1967
Pascoe, Alan	1977	Stones, Dwight	1977
Patton, Mel	1964	Tarmak, Juri	1973
Pedersen, Terje	1967	Ter-Ovanesyan, Igor	1964
Penes, Mihaela	1967	Thomas, John	1964
Pennel, John	1967	Toomey, Bill	1973
Plummer, Adolph	1967	Towns, Forrest	1977
Pollak, Burglinde	1977	Tulloh, Bruce	1967
Pollock, Judy	1967	Vasala, Pekka	1973
Ponomaryeva, Nina	1967	Voigt, Angela	1977
Potgieter, Gert	1967	Walasiewicz, Stanislawa	1977
Press, Irina	1967	Whitlock, Harold	1967
Press, Tamara	1967	Willard, Marlene	1964
Puttemans, Emiel	1977	Williams, Randy	1973
Quinton, Carole	1967	Willis, Dixie	1964
Radford, Peter	1967	Wolfermann, Klaus	1973
Richards, Bob	1967	Woodruff, John	1967
Richter, Annegret	1977	Wottle, Dave	1973
Roberts, Dave	1977	Yang, C. K.	1964
Robinson, Arnie	1977	Zehrt, Monika	1973
Rowe, Arthur	1967	Zsivotzky, Gyula	1967
Ryan, Pam	1973	Zybina, Galina	1967
Schaller, Johanna	1977		

APPENDIX 2

LIST OF RECORDS

Below are the best recorded performances, as at May 5th 1981, in as many as 13 different categories per event. Abbreviations used:
Eur = European; Comm = Commonwealth; WJ = World Junior; EJ = European Junior; UKJ = UK Junior; WV = World Veteran (40 & over); UKV = UK Veteran; WI = World Indoor; EI = European Indoor; UKI = UK Indoor.

60 METRES (INDOORS)
World 6.54 sec. Houston McTear (USA) 1978. *Eur* 6.55 Christian Haas (W. Ger) 1980. *UK* 6.68 Allan Wells 1978.

100 METRES
World/USA 9.95 sec. Jim Hines (USA) 1968. *Eur* 10.01 Pietro Mennea (Ita) 1979. *Comm* 10.04 Lennox Miller (Jam) 1968. *UK* 10.11 Allan Wells 1980. *WJ* 10.07 Stanley Floyd (USA) 1980. *EJ* 10.29 Peter Radford (UK) 1958. Indoors: 10.16 Eugen Ray (E. Ger) 1976. *UKJ* 10.29 Peter Radford 1958. *WV* 10.7 Thane Baker (USA) 1972. *UKV* 10.9 Ron Taylor 1978.

200 METRES
World/Eur 19.72 sec. Pietro Mennea (Ita) 1979. *Comm* 19.86 Don Quarrie (Jam) 1971. *UK* 20.21 Allan Wells 1980. *USA* 19.83 Tommie Smith 1968. *WJ* 20.22 Dwayne Evans (USA) 1976. *EJ* 20.59 Bernhard Hoff (E. Ger) 1977. *UKJ* 20.67 David Jenkins 1971. *WV* 21.9 Reg Austin (Aus) 1977. *UKV* 22.2 Ron Taylor 1975.

400 METRES
World/USA 43.86 sec. Lee Evans (USA) 1968. *Eur* 44.60 Viktor Markin (USSR) 1980. *Comm* 44.84 Rick Mitchell (Aus) 1980. *UK* 44.93 David Jenkins 1975. *WJ* 45.04 Wayne Collett (USA) 1968. *EJ/UKJ* 45.45 David Jenkins 1971. *WV* 49.5 Noel Clough (Aus) 1977. *UKV* 49.7 Jim Dixon 1973. *WI/EI* 45.96 Hartmut Weber (W. Ger) 1981. *UKI* 46.56 Glen Cohen 1980.

800 METRES
World/Eur/Comm/UK 1 min. 42.33 sec. Sebastian Coe (UK) 1979. *USA* 1:43.9 Rick Wohlhuter 1974. *WJ* 1:44.9 (880 yards) Jim Ryun (USA) 1966. *EJ* 1:45.45 Andreas Busse (E. Ger) 1978. *UKJ* 1:45.77 Steve Ovett 1974. *WV* 1:54.5 Klaus Mainka (W. Ger) 1977. *UKV* 1:56.3 Ronnie Anderson 1977. *WI/EI/UKI* 1:46.0 Sebastian Coe 1981.

1000 METRES
World/Eur/Comm/UK 2 min. 13.40 sec. Sebastian Coe (UK) 1980. *USA* 2:13.9 Rick Wohlhuter 1974. *WJ* 2:18.3 Andreas Busse (E. Ger) 1977, Johan Fourie (S. Afr) 1979. *EJ* 2:18.3 Andreas Busse (E. Ger) 1977. *UK* 2:19.92 Graham Williamson 1979.

1500 METRES
World/Eur/Comm/UK 3 min. 31.36 sec. Steve Ovett (UK) 1980. *USA* 3:33.1 Jim Ryun 1967. *WJ* 3:36.1 Jim Ryun (USA) 1966. *EJ/UKJ* 3:36.6 Graham Williamson 1979. *WV* 3:52.0 Michel Bernard (Fra) 1972. *UKV* 3:56.6 Nat Fisher 1977. *WI/EI* 3:35.6 Eamonn Coghlan (Ire) 1981. *UKI* 3:41.9 Phil Banning 1975.

1 MILE

World/Eur/Comm/UK 3 min. 48.8 sec. Steve Ovett (UK) 1980. *USA* 3:51.1 Jim Ryun 1967. *WJ* 3:51.3 Jim Ryun (USA) 1966. *EJ/UKJ* 3:53.15 Graham Williamson 1979. *WI/EI* 3:50.6 Eamonn Coghlan (Ire) 1981. *UKI* 3:59.5 Bob Maplestone 1972.

2000 METRES

World/Comm 4 min. 51.4 sec. John Walker (NZ) 1976. *Eur* 4:56.2 Michel Jazy (Fra) 1966. *UK* 4:57.82 Steve Ovett 1978. *USA* 5:01.4 Steve Prefontaine 1975. *WJ/EJ* 5:04.4 Harald Hudak (W. Ger) 1976. *UKJ* 5:10.1 Julian Goater 1972.

3000 METRES

World/Comm 7 min. 32.1 sec. Henry Rono (Ken) 1978. *Eur/UK* 7:35.2 Brendan Foster 1974. *USA* 7:37.70 Rudy Chapa 1979. *WJ/EJ* 7:43.2 Ari Paunonen (Fin) 1977. *UKJ* 7:51.84 Steve Binns 1979. *WV* 8:17.4 Jack Foster (NZ) 1976. *UKV* 8:22.0 Laurie O'Hara 1974. *WI/EI* 7:39.2 Emiel Puttemans (Bel) 1973. *UKI* 7:46.7 Nick Rose 1979.

2 MILES
(no official world record)

World/Eur/Comm/UK 8 min. 13.51 sec. Steve Ovett (UK) 1978. *WJ* 8:25.2 Jim Ryun (USA) 1966. *EJ/UKJ* 8:28.31 Steve Binns 1979. *WI/EI* 8:13.2 Emiel Puttemans (Bel) 1973. *UKI* 8:18.4 Nick Rose 1978.

5000 METRES

World/Comm 13 min. 08.4 sec. Henry Rono (Ken) 1978. *Eur* 13:13.0 Emiel Puttemans (Bel) 1972. *UK* 13:14.6 Brendan Foster 1974. *USA* 13:15.06 Marty Liquori 1977. *WJ/EJ/UKJ* 13:27.04 Steve Binns 1979. *WV* 13:45.8 Lucien Rault (Fra) 1976. *UKV* 14:22.0 Mike Turner 1980.

10,000 METRES

World/Comm 27 min. 22.4 sec. Henry Rono (Ken) 1978. *Eur/UK* 27:30.3 Brendan Foster 1978. *USA* 27:29.16 Craig Virgin 1980. *WJ* 28:32.7 Rudy Chapa (USA) 1976. *EJ* 29:08.0 Konstantin Lebedyev (USSR) 1976. *UKJ* 29:38.6 Ray Crabb 1973. *WV* 28:33.4 Lucien Rault (Fra) 1976. *UKV* 29:47.0 Mike Freary 1978.

10 MILES
(no official world record)

World/Eur 45 min. 57.2 sec. Jos Hermens (Hol) 1975. *Comm/UK* 46:44.0 Ron Hill 1968.

20,000 METRES

World/Eur 57 min. 24.2 sec. Jos Hermens (Hol) 1976. *Comm/UK* 58:39.0 Ron Hill 1968. *USA* 58:15.0 Bill Rodgers 1977.

1 HOUR

World/Eur 20,944 m. Jos Hermens (Hol) 1976. *Comm/UK* 20,472 Ron Hill 1968. *USA* 20, 547 Bill Rodgers 1977.

25,000 METRES

World/USA 1 hr. 14 min. 11.8 sec. Bill Rodgers (USA) 1979. *Eur* 1:14:16.8 Pekka Paivarinta (Fin) 1975. *Comm/UK* 1:15:22.6 Ron Hill 1965.

30,000 METRES

World/Eur/Comm/UK 1 hr. 31 min. 30.4 sec. Jim Alder (UK) 1970. *USA* 1:31:49.0 Bill Rodgers 1979.

50 KILOMETRES
(no official world record)

World/Eur/Comm/UK 2 hr. 48 min. 06 sec. Jeff Norman (UK) 1980.

50 MILES
(no official world record)
World/Eur/Comm/UK 4 hr. 53 min. 28 sec. Don Ritchie (UK) 1978.

100 KILOMETRES
(no official world record)
World/Eur/Comm/UK 6 hr. 10 min. 20 sec. Don Ritchie (UK) 1978.

100 MILES
(no official world record)
World/Eur/Comm/UK 11 hr. 30 min. 51 sec. Don Ritchie (UK) 1977.

MARATHON (ROAD)
(no official world record)
World/Comm 2 hr. 08 min. 34 sec. Derek Clayton (Aus) 1969. *Eur* 2:09:01 Gerard Nijboer (Hol) 1980. *UK* 2:09:12 Ian Thompson 1974. *USA* 2:09:27 Bill Rodgers 1979. *WJ* 2:17:44 Kirk Pfeffer (USA) 1975. *WV* 2:11:19 Jack Foster (NZ) 1974. *UKV* 2:15:46 Ron Hill 1979.

2000 METRES STEEPLECHASE
(no official world record)
World/Comm 5 min. 20.3 sec. Filbert Bayi (Tan) 1980. *Eur/WJ/EJ* 5:27.5 Graetano Erba (Ita) 1979. *UK/UKJ* 5:29.7 Colin Reitz 1979.

3000 METRES STEEPLECHASE
World/Comm 8 min. 05.37 sec. Henry Rono (Ken) 1978. *Eur* 8:08.02 Anders Garderud (Swe) 1976. *UK* 8:18.95 Dennis Coates 1976. *USA* 8:15.68 Henry Marsh 1980. *WJ/EJ* 8:29.50 Ralf Ponitzsch (E. Ger) 1976. *UKJ* 8:42.75 Colin Reitz 1979. *WV* 8:41.5 Gaston Roelants (Bel) 1977. *UKV* 9:03.5 Tacwyn Davies 1979.

60 METRES HURDLES (INDOORS)
World/Eur 7.54 sec. Andrey Prokofiev (USSR) 1979, Yuriy Chervanyov (USSR) 1980. *UK* 7.80 Berwyn Price 1976.

110 METRES HURDLES
World/USA 13.00 sec. Renaldo Nehemiah (USA) 1979. *Eur* 13.28 Guy Drut (Fra) 1975. *Comm* 13.69 Berwyn Price (UK) 1973, Fatwell Kimaiyo (Ken) 1974, Godwin Obasogie (Nig) 1976. *UK* 13.69 Berwyn Price 1973. *WJ* 13.23 Renaldo Nehemiah (USA) 1978. *EJ* 13.66 Arto Bryggare (Fin) 1977. *UKJ* 14.06 Mark Holtom 1977. *WV/UKV* 14.4 Don Finlay 1949.

400 METRES HURDLES
World/USA 47.13 sec. Edwin Moses (USA) 1980. *Eur* 47.85 Harald Schmid (W. Ger) 1979. *Comm* 47.82 John Akii-Bua (Uga) 1972. *UK* 48.12 David Hemery 1968. *WJ/EJ* 49.61 Harald Schmid (W. Ger) 1976. *UKJ* 51.15 Andy Todd 1967. *WV* 54.08 Leon Hacker (Zimbabwe) 1980. *UKV* 54.8 Jim Dixon 1973.

HIGH JUMP
World/Eur 2.36 m. Gerd Wessig (E. Ger) 1980. *Comm* 2.26 Greg Joy (Can) 1976 (and 2.31 indoors, 1978). *UK* 2.24 Mark Naylor 1980. *USA* 2.32 Dwight Stones 1976, Jeff Woodard 1980. Indoors: 2.33 Woodard 1981. *WJ/EJ* 2.35 Dietmar Mogenburg (W. Ger) 1980. Indoors: 2.35 Vladimir Yashchenko (USSR) 1978. *UKJ* 2.18 Ossie Cham 1980. *WV* 2.05 Egon Nilsson (Swe) 1966. *UKV* 1.80 Gordon Hickey 1978. *WI/EI* 2.35 Vladimir Yashchenko (USSR) 1978. *UKI* 2.22 Mark Naylor 1979.

POLE VAULT
World/Eur 5.78 m. Wladyslaw Kozakiewicz (Pol) 1980. *Comm/UK* 5.59 Brian Hooper 1980. *USA* 5.70 Dave Roberts 1976. *WJ/EJ* 5.61 Thierry Vigneron (Fr) 1979. *UKJ* 5.10 Brian Hooper 1972. *WV* 4.80 Rudolf Tomasek

(Cze) 1977. *UKV* 4.15 Robert Brown 1979. *WI/EI* 5.71 Thierry Vigneron (Fra) 1981. *UKI* 5.50 Brian Hooper 1981.

LONG JUMP
World/USA 8.90 m. Bob Beamon (USA) 1968. *Eur* 8.54 Lutz Dombrowski (E. Ger) 1980. *Comm* 8.23 Lynn Davies (UK) 1968. Indoors: 8.26 Charlton Ehizuelen (Nig) 1975. *UK* 8.23 Lynn Davies 1968. *WJ* 8.34 Randy Williams (USA) 1972. *EJ* 8.09 Antonio Corgos (Spa) 1979. *UKJ* 7.72 Daley Thompson 1977. *WV* 7.43 Tom Chilton (USA) 1978. *UKV* 6.62 Ron Taylor 1975. *WI* 8.49 Carl Lewis (USA) 1981. *EI* 8.23 Igor Ter-Ovanesyan (USSR) 1968. *UKI* 7.97 Lynn Davies 1966.

TRIPLE JUMP
World 17.89 m. Joao Carlos de Oliveira (Bra) 1975. *Eur* 17.44 Viktor Sanyeyev (USSR) 1972. *Comm/UK* 17.16 Keith Connor 1980 (17.31 indoors, 1981). *USA* 17.31 Willie Banks 1981. *WJ* 17.40 Pedro Perez (Cub) 1971. *EJ* 16.83 Aleksandr Beskrovniy (USSR) 1979. *UKJ* 16.24 Aston Moore 1975. *WV* 14.70 S. Backlund (Fin) 1980. *UKV* 13.67 David Smith 1977. *WI/EI/UKI* 17.31 Keith Connor 1981.

SHOT
World 22.15 m. Udo Beyer (E. Ger) 1978. Professional: 22.86 Brian Oldfield (USA) 1975. *Eur* 22.15 Udo Beyer (E. Ger) 1978. *Comm/UK* 21.68 Geoff Capes 1980. *USA* 21.85 Terry Albritton 1976. *WJ* 20.38 Terry Albritton (USA) 1974. *EJ* 20.20 Udo Beyer (E. Ger) 1974. *UKJ* 16.80 Geoff Capes 1968. Indoors: 16.87 Tony Zaidman 1981. *WV* 19.77 Pierre Colnard (Fra) 1970. *UKV* 16.56 Sid Clark 1975. *WI* 22.01 George Woods (USA) 1974. Professional: 22.11 Brian Oldfield (USA) 1975. *EI* 21.10 Udo Beyer (E. Ger) 1978. *UKI* 20.98 Geoff Capes 1976.

DISCUS
World/Eur 71.16 m. Wolfgang Schmidt (E. Ger) 1978. *Comm* 65.40 Boris Chambul (Can) 1976. *UK* 64.94 Bill Tancred 1974, *USA* 70.98 Mac Wilkins (USA) 1980. *WJ/EJ* 63.64 Werner Hartmann (W. Ger) 1978. *UKJ* 53.40 Bob Weir 1980. *WV* 69.46 Al Oerter (USA) 1980. *UKV* 48.36 Konstanty Maksimczyk 1957.

HAMMER
World/Eur 81.80 m. Yuriy Sedykh (USSR) 1980. *Comm* 75.90 Peter Farmer (Aus) 1979. *UK* 74.98 Chris Black 1976. *USA* 71.90 Ed Burke 1967. *WJ/EJ* 78.14 Roland Steuk (E. Ger) 1978. *UKJ* 66.14 Martin Girvan 1979. *WV* 70.90 Romuald Klim (USSR) 1973. *UKV* 70.88 Howard Payne 1974.

JAVELIN
World/Eur 96.72 m. Ferenc Paragi (Hun) 1980. *Comm* 89.58 Mike O'Rourke (NZ) 1981. *UK* 85.52 Dave Ottley 1980. *USA* 91.44 Mark Murro 1970. *WJ* 87.76 Phil Olsen (Can) 1976. *EJ* 85.70 Arto Harkonen (Fin) 1978. *UKJ* 84.92 Charles Clover 1974. *WV* 78.98 Urs von Wartburg (Swi) 1979. *UKV* 61.50 John James 1980.

DECATHLON
World/Eur 8649 pts. Guido Kratschmer (W. Ger) 1980. *Comm/UK* 8622 Daley Thompson 1980. *USA* 8617 Bruce Jenner 1976. *WJ/EJ/UKJ* 8124 Daley Thompson 1977. *WV* 6402 Valbjorn Thorlaksson (Ice) 1975.

4 x 100 METRES RELAY
World/USA 38.03 sec. USA 1977. *Eur* 38.26 USSR 1980. *Comm* 38.39 Jamaica 1968. *UK* 38.62 in 1980. *WJ* 39.32 USA 1979. *EJ* 39.67 USSR 1978. *UKJ* 40.06 in 1979

4 x 200 METRES RELAY
World/USA 1 min 20.26 sec. Univ. of S. California (USA) 1978. *Eur* 1:21.5 Italy 1972. *Comm* 1:22.5 Trinidad 1972. *UK* 1:24.1 in 1971.

4 x 400 METRES RELAY
World/USA 2 min. 56.16 sec. USA 1968. *Eur/UK* 3:00.46 UK 1972. *Comm* 2:59.64 Kenya 1968. *WJ* 3:04.75 USA 1976. *EJ* 3:06.8 E. Germany 1973, W. Germany 1979, USSR 1979. *UKJ* 3:07.3 in 1973.

4 x 800 METRES RELAY
World/Eur 7 min. 08.1 sec. USSR 1978. *Comm* 7:11.6 Kenya 1970. *UK* 7:14.6 in 1966. *USA* 7:10.4 (4 x 880 yd.) Univ. of Chicago Track Club 1973.

4 x 1500 METRES RELAY
*World/*Eur 14 min. 38.8 sec. W. Germany 1977. *Comm* 14:40.4 New Zealand 1973. *UK* 14:56.8 in 1979. *USA* 14:46.3 in 1979.

3000 METRES WALK
(no official world record)
World/Comm 11 min. 11.5 sec. David Smith (Aus) 1981. Indoors: 11.05.1 Reima Salonen (Fin) 1977. *Eur* 11:13.2 Jozef Pribilinec (Cze) 1979. *UK* 11:51.1 Paul Nihill 1971.

10,000 METRES WALK
(no official world record)
World/Eur 38 min. 54.3 sec. Roland Wieser (E. Ger) 1980. Indoors: 38:31.4 Werner Heyer (E. Ger) 1980. *Comm* 40:54.7 David Smith (Aus) 1980. *UK* 41:55.6 Phil Embleton 1971. *WJ/EJ* 39:41.2 Ralf Kowalski (E. Ger) 1980. *UKJ* 42:33.8 Gordon Vale 1981.

20,000 METRES WALK
World 1 hr. 20 min. 06.8 sec. Daniel Bautista (Mex) 1979. *Eur* 1:20:57.0 Erling Andersen (Nor) 1980. Indoors: 1:20:40.0 Ronald Weigel (E. Ger) 1980. *Comm* 1:27:15.8 Marcel Jobin (Can) 1979. *UK* 1:28:45.8 Ken Matthews 1964. *USA* 1:28:32.7 Todd Scully 1979.

20,000 METRES ROAD WALK
(no official world record)
World 1 hr. 18 min. 49 sec. Daniel Bautista (Mex) 1979. *Eur* 1:19:11 Gennadiy Terekhov (USSR) 1980. *Comm* 1:23:16 David Smith (Aus) 1979. *UK* 1:24:50 Paul Nihill 1972. *USA* 1:26:26 Dan O'Connor 1980. *WJ* 1:22:44 Josef Pribilinec (Cze) 1979. *WV* 1:23:55 Vladimir Golubnichiy (USSR) 1976. *UKV* 1:33:18 Roy Thorpe 1976.

2 HOURS WALK
World/Eur 28,165 m. Jose Marin (Spa) 1979. *Comm* 26,118 Ted Allsopp (Aus) 1956. *UK* 26,037 Ron Wallwork 1971.

30,000 METRES WALK
World/Eur 2 hr. 08 min. 00 sec. Jose Marin (Spa) 1979. *Comm* 2:23:10 Noel Freeman (Aus) 1969. *UK* 2:24:18.2 Roy Thorpe 1974. USA 2:23:14 Goetz Klopfer 1970.

50 KILOMETRES WALK
World 3 hr. 41 min. 39 sec. Raul Gonzalez (Mex) 1979. *Eur* 3:48:59 Vladimir Rezayev (USSR) 1980. *Comm* 4:06:39 Willi Sawall (Aus) 1976. *UK* 4:11:22 Bob Dobson 1974. *USA* 4:13:36 Bob Kitchen 1972.

50 KILOMETRES ROAD WALK
(no official world record)
World 3 hr. 41 min. 20 sec. Raul Gonzalez (Mex) 1978. *Eur* 3:43:35 Jose Marin (Spa) 1980. *Comm* 3:46:33 Willi Sawall (Aus) 1980. *UK* 4:05:14 Chris Maddocks 1980. *USA* 3:59:33 Carl Schueler 1980. *WV* 3:50:24 Yevgeniy Ivchenko (USSR) 1979. *UKV* 4:22:41 (track) Charles Fogg 1975.

100 KILOMETRES ROAD WALK
(no official world record)
World/Eur 9 hr. 15 min. 58 sec. Christoph Hohne (E. Ger) 1967. *Comm/UK* 9:34:25 Anthony Geal 1979.

WOMEN'S EVENTS

60 METRES (INDOORS)
World/Eur 7.10 sec. Marlies Gohr (E. Ger) 1980, Marita Koch (E. Ger) 1981. *UK* 7.17 Andrea Lynch 1975.

100 METRES
World/Eur 10.88 sec. Marlies Gohr (E. Ger) 1977. *Comm* 11.14 Lileith Hodges (Jam) 1978. *UK* 11.16 Andrea Lynch 1975. *USA* 10.97 Evelyn Ashford 1979. *WJ* 11.13 Chandra Cheeseborough (USA) 1976. *EJ* 11.17 Marlies Gohr (E. Ger) 1976. *UKJ* 11.45 Sonia Lannaman 1972. *UKV* (40 and over) 12.0 Maeve Kyle 1970.

200 METRES
World/Eur 21.71 sec. Marita Koch (E. Ger) 1979. *Comm* 22.20 Merlene Ottey (Jam) 1980. *UK* 22.31 Kathy Smallwood 1980. *USA* 21.83 Evelyn Ashford 1979. *WJ/EJ* 22.19 Natalya Botchina (USSR) 1980. *UKJ* 22.99 Kathy Smallwood 1978. *UKV* 25.1 Maeve Kyle 1969.

400 METRES
World/Eur 48.60 sec. Marita Koch (E. Ger) 1979. *Comm/UK* 50.88 Joslyn Hoyte-Smith 1980. *USA* 50.62 Rosalyn Bryant 1976. *WJ/EJ* 49.77 Christine Brehmer (E. Ger) 1976. *UKJ* 51.16 Linsey Macdonald 1980. *UKV* 55.3 Maeve Kyle 1970. *WI/EI* 49.64 Jarmila Kratochvilova (Cze) 1981. *UKI* 51.80 Verona Elder 1979.

800 METRES
World/Eur 1 min. 53.43 sec. Nadyezhda Olizaryenko (USSR) 1980. *Comm* 1:59.0 Charlene Rendina (Aus) 1976. *UK* 1:59.05 Chris Boxer 1979. *USA* 1:57.90 Madeline Manning 1976. *WJ/EJ* 1:59.7 Marion Hubner (E. Ger) 1979. *UKJ* 2:02.0 Jo White 1977. *UKV* 2:32.0 Hazel Rider 1977. *WI/EI* 1:58.4 Olga Vakrusheva (USSR) 1980. *UKI* 2:01.1 Jane Colebrook 1977.

1000 METRES
(no official world record)
World/Eur 2 min. 30.6 sec. Tatyana Providokhina (USSR) 1978. *Comm* 2:36.9 Francine Gendron (Can) 1978. *UK* 2:37.43 Chris Boxer 1980. *WJ/EJ* 2:35.4 Irina Nikitina (USSR) 1979. *UKJ* 2:38.58 Jo White 1977.

1500 METRES
World/Eur 3 min. 52.47 sec. Tatyana Kazankina (USSR) 1980. *Comm/UK* 4:01.53 Chris Benning 1979. *USA* 3:59.43 Mary Decker 1980. *WJ/EJ* 4:06.02 Birgit Friedmann (W. Ger) 1978. *UKJ* 4:14.55 Ruth Smeeth 1978. *UKV* 4:20.8 Joyce Smith 1978. *WI* 4:00.8 Mary Decker (USA) 1980. *EI* 4:03.0 Natalia Marasescu (Rom) 1979. *UKI* 4:08.1 Mary Stewart 1977.

1 MILE
World/USA 4 min. 21.68 sec. Mary Decker 1980. Indoors (oversized track): 4:17.55 Mary Decker 1980. *Eur* 4:22.09 Natalia Marasescu (Rom) 1979. *Comm/UK* 4:30.2 Chris Boxer 1979.

3000 METRES
World/Eur 8 min. 27.12 sec. Lyudmila Bragina (USSR) 1976. *Comm/UK* 8:48.74 Paula Fudge 1978. *USA* 8:38.73 Mary Decker 1980. *WJ/EJ* 8:58.36 Inger Knutsson (Swe) 1973. *UKJ* 9:15.82 Ruth Smeeth 1978. *UKV* 9:11.2 Joyce Smith 1978. *WI* 8:50.8 Grete Waitz (Nor) 1980. *UKI* 8:56.4 Paula Fudge 1981.

5000 METRES
World/Eur 15 min. 08.8 sec. Loa Olafsson (Den) 1978. *Comm/UK* 15:49.6 Kathryn Binns 1980. *USA* 15:30.6 Jan Merrill 1980.

10,000 METRES
World/Eur 31 min. 45.4 sec. Loa Olafsson (Den) 1978. *Comm/UK* 32:57.2 Kathryn Binns 1980. *USA* 32:52.5 Mary Shea 1979.

MARATHON (ROAD)
(no official world record)
World/Eur 2 hr. 25 min. 42 sec. Grete Waitz (Nor) 1980. *Comm* 2:26:45 Allison Roe (NZ) 1981. *UK/UKV* 2:29:57 Joyce Smith 1981. *USA* 2:27:51 Patti Catalano 1981. *WJ* 2:41:48 Celia Peterson (USA) 1978.

60 METRES HURDLES (INDOORS)
World/Eur 7.77 sec. Zofia Bielczyk (Pol) 1980. *UK* 8.21 Sharon Colyear 1981.

100 METRES HURDLES
World/Eur 12.36 sec. Grazyna Rabsztyn (Pol) 1980. *Comm* 12.93 Pam Ryan (Aus) 1972. *UK* 13.06 Shirley Strong 1980. *USA* 12.86 Deby LaPlante (USA) 1979. *WJ* 12.95 Candy Young (USA) 1979. *EJ* 13.24 Lena Spoof (Fin) 1979. *UKJ* 13.65 Wendy McDonnell 1978. *UKV* 15.1 Maeve Kyle 1969.

400 METRES HURDLES
World/Eur 54.28 sec. Karin Rossley (E. Ger) 1980. *Comm/UK* 56.06 Chris Warden 1979. *USA* 56.16 Esther Mahr 1980. *WJ/EJ* 56.68 Anne-Louise Skoglund (Swe) 1980. *UKJ* 59.00 Diane Heath 1975.

HIGH JUMP
World/Eur. 2.01 m. Sara Simeoni (Ita) 1978. *Comm* 1.97 Debbie Brill (Can) 1980. *UK* 1.94 Louise Miller 1980. *USA* 1.95 Louise Ritter 1980. Indoors: 1.95 Joni Huntley 1981. *WJ/EJ* 1.93 Kerstin Dedner (E. Ger) 1979. *UKJ* 1.86 Barbara Simmonds 1979. *UKV* 1.63 Dorothy Tyler 1961. *WI/EI* 1.98 Andrea Matay (Hun) 1979. *UKI* 1.86 Barbara Lawton 1973.

LONG JUMP
World/Eur. 7.09 m. Vilma Bardauskiene (USSR) 1978. *Comm/UK* 6.76 Mary Rand 1964. *USA* 7.00 Jodi Anderson 1980. *WJ/EJ* 6.77 Marianne Voelzke (E. Ger) 1974. *UKJ* 6.68 Sue Hearnshaw 1979. *UKV* 5.28 Maeve Kyle 1969. *WI/EI* 6.77 Karin Hanel (W. Ger) 1981. *UKI* 6.53 Mary Rand 1966, Sue Reeve 1978.

SHOT
World/Eur. 22.45 m. Ilona Slupianek (E. Ger) 1980. *Comm* 18.55 Gael Mulhall (Aus) 1980. *UK* 17.53 Angela Littlewood 1980. *USA* 19.09 Maren Seidler 1979. *WJ/EJ* 19.23 Ilona Slupianek (E. Ger) 1974. *UKJ* 15.94 Judy Oakes 1976. *UKV* 15.72 Brenda Bedford 1978. *WI/EI* 22.50 Helena Fibingerova (Cze) 1977. *UKI* 17.65 Venissa Head 1981.

DISCUS
World/Eur 71.80 m. Maria Vergova (Bul) 1980. *Comm/UK* 67.48 Meg Ritchie 1981. *USA* 63.22 Lorna Griffin 1980. *WJ/EJ* 64.86 Irina Meszynski (E. Ger) 1980. *UKJ* 49.60 Fiona Condon 1979. *UKV* 56.40 Rosemary Payne 1973.

JAVELIN
World/Eur 70.08 m. Tatyana Biryulina (USSR) 1980. *Comm/UK* 69.70 Tessa Sanderson 1980. *USA* 69.32 Kate Schmidt 1977. *WJ/EJ* 66.40 Antoaneta Todorova (Bul) 1980. *UKJ* 58.20 Fatima Whitbread 1979. *UKV* 39.68 Averil Williams 1979.

PENTATHLON
World/Eur 5083 pts. Nadyezhda Tkachenko (USSR) 1980. *Comm* 4768

Diane Konihowski (Can) 1978. *UK* 4409 Sue Longden 1981. *USA* 4708 Jane Frederick 1979. *WJ/EJ* 4594 Sabine Everts (W. Ger) 1979. *UKJ* 3987 Judy Livermore 1978.

HEPTATHLON
World 6166 pts. Jane Frederick (USA) 1981. *Eur* 6144 Yekaterina Gordienko (USSR) 1980. *Comm* 5724 Chris Stanton (Aus) 1981. *UK* 5383 Allison Manley 1981.

4 x 100 METRES RELAY
World/Eur 41.60 sec. E. Germany 1980. *Comm/UK* 42.43 in 1980. *USA* 42.87 in 1968. *WJ/EJ* 43.95 E. Germany 1979. *UKJ* 44.71 in 1977.

4 x 200 METRES RELAY
...*World/Eur* 1 min. 28.15 sec. E. Germany 1980. *Comm/UK* 1:31.57 in 1977.

4 x 400 METRES RELAY
World/Eur 3 min. 19.23 sec. E. Germany 1976. *Comm* 3:25.56 Australia 1976. *UK* 3:26.6 in 1975. *USA* 3:22.81 in 1976. *WJ/EJ* 3:31.7 E. Germany 1979. *UKJ* 3:36.98 in 1973.

4 x 800 METRES RELAY
World/Eur 7 min 52.3 sec. USSR 1976. *Comm/UK* 8:23.8 in 1971. *USA* 8:19.9 in 1979.

3000 METRES WALK
(no official world record)
World/Comm 13 min. 20.7 sec. Sue Cook (Aus) 1980. *Eur/UK* 13 min. 25.2 sec. Carol Tyson 1979.

5000 METRES WALK
World/Comm 22 min. 53.2 sec. Sue Cook (Aus) 1981. *Eur/UK* 23:11.2 Carol Tyson 1979.

10,000 METRES WALK
World/Eur/Comm/UK 48 min. 11.4 sec. Marion Fawkes (UK) 1979.

LATE AMENDMENTS TO RECORD LIST (APPENDIX 2)
(as at May 20th 1981)

25,000 METRES
World 1hr. 13min. 55.8sec. Toshihiko Seko (Japan).

30,000 METRES
World 1hr. 29min. 18.8sec. Toshihiko Seko (Japan).

SHOT
USA 22.02m. Brian Oldfield. *UK* Junior 16.94m. Tony Zaidman.

DISCUS
World/USA 71.20m. Ben Plucknett.

WOMEN'S SHOT
UK 17.54m. Venissa Head.

WOMEN'S HEPTATHLON
World/Europe 6212pts. Nadyezhda Vinogradova (USSR). *Comm/UK* 5852 Judy Livermore.

APPENDIX 3
DISTINGUISHED IN OTHER FIELDS

Most top-class athletes retire from active competition during their twenties or thirties, and set about living the rest of their lives away from the glare of publicity. For a significant number, though, the fame gained as athletes has proved a stepping stone to careers in coaching, journalism, broadcasting or films. Others have gone on to make a name for themselves in areas far removed from sport: as politicians, judges, novelists etc. In this unique compilation we list some of the celebrated athletes who have achieved considerable distinction in other fields, together with famous personalities who, although not world-beaters as athletes, did exhibit some degree of athletic prowess in their youth.

Politicians

Philip Noel-Baker (now Lord Noel-Baker): Olympic 1500 m. silver medallist 1920. An MP from 1929 to 1970, he served as Minister of Fuel & Power in the Labour Government 1950/51. He won the Nobel Peace Prize in 1959.

Elaine Burton (now Baroness Burton of Coventry): Self-described "world's sprint champion 1920" (at age 16), she was the winner of a 100 yd. event in 12.0 sec. in the pioneering days of women's athletics. MP from 1950 to 1959.

Frank Byers (now Lord Byers): Oxford 'Blue' at 220 yd hurdles in 1937 and British Universities 440 yd. hurdles record holder. Former MP and, since 1967, Liberal leader in House of Lords.

Chris Chataway: Commonwealth 3 miles champion and world 5000 m. record breaker (13 min. 51.6 sec.) in 1954. MP from 1959 to 1966 and from 1969 to 1974, he was Minister of Posts & Telecommunications in the Conservative Government 1970-72.

Terence Higgins: Silver medallist in 1950 Commonwealth Games 4 x 440 yd. relay. MP since 1964; a former Minister of State, Treasury, in Conservative Government.

Jeffrey Archer: Represented Britain in 200 m. in 1966. MP from 1969 to 1974. See also under writers.

Sir Harold Wilson: The former Labour Prime Minister clocked 53.8 sec. for 440 yd. while an Oxford undergraduate in 1938.

President Kekkonen of Finland: Urho Kekkonen was Finnish high jump champion in 1925 and once held what was claimed to be a world record for the standing triple jump of 9.71 m.

Norman Manley: The former Prime Minister of Jamaica set a Jamaican junior 100 yd. record of 10.0 sec. in 1911.

Habib Thiam: Prime Minister of Senegal since January 1981, he was a former French 200 m. champion with sprint marks of 10.6/21.5 sec.

Pandit Nehru: India's first Prime Minister was a noted 880 yd. runner at Harrow School in 1906.

Estes Kefauver: A leading discus thrower at college in 1924, he became a US Senator and was a presidential candidate in 1952.

Ralph Metcalfe: Silver medallist in the 1932 and 1936 Olympic 100 m. and gold medallist in the 1936 4 x 100 m. relay, he became a US Congressman.

Bob Mathias: Olympic decathlon champion in 1948 (at age 17 still the youngest ever male Olympic athletics champion) and 1952, he became a US Congressman. See also under actors.

Lawyers

Richard E. Webster (later Viscount Alverstone): Set an amateur 2 miles world best of 10 min. 05.5 sec. in 1865. Became Lord Chief Justice of England

(1900–1913) and was Judge of the Dr Crippen case.
Sir Montague Shearman: AAA 440 yd. champion in 1880 and one of the founders (and first honorary secretary) of the AAA. Became a Judge and a member of the Privy Council.
Sir Sidney Abrahams: AAA long jump champion 1913, and brother of 1924 Olympic 100 m. champion Harold Abrahams (himself a qualified barrister), he was appointed Chief Justice in various former British colonies.
Rt. Hon. W. R. (Bill) Milligan: Member of Oxford/Cambridge team which set a world 4 x 880 yd. relay record in 1920. A former Solicitor-General for Scotland and Lord Advocate.
Mr. Justice Kilner Brown (Hon. Sir Ralph Kilner Brown): Bronze medallist in 1934 Empire Games 440 yd. hurdles, he is a present Judge of the High Court. His brother Godfrey Brown (1936 Olympic 4 x 400 m. relay gold medallist) was headmaster of Worcester Royal Grammar School 1950–1978.
Thomas Curry, QC. Joint editor of "Palmer's Company Law", was AAA steeplechase champion 1948.

Governors and Diplomats

Field Marshal Earl Alexander of Tunis: The Irish mile champion of 1914 was the man who led the Allied invasion of Italy in the 2nd World War and was Governor-General of Canada from 1946 to 1952.
Arthur Porritt (now Lord Porritt): Bronze medallist in 1924 Olympic 100 m., representing New Zealand. Surgeon to King George VI and the Queen, he was Governor-General of New Zealand from 1967 to 1972.
Lord Burghley (now 6th Marquess of Exeter): Olympic 400 m. hurdles champion in 1928. A former MP, he was appointed Governor and Commander-in-Chief of Bermuda during the 2nd World War.
Dr Arthur Wint: Jamaica's Olympic 400 m. champion 1948 and 4 x 400 m. relay gold medallist 1952 was Jamaican High Commissioner in the UK from 1974 to 1978. He is a surgeon by profession.

Actors

Among renowned American athletes who have appeared in Hollywood films are *Herman Brix, later known as Bruce Bennett* (2nd 1928 Olympic shot) and *Glenn Morris* (1936 Olympic decathlon champion), both of whom played Tarzan; *Bob Mathias* (1948 and 1952 Olympic decathlon champion) who starred in "The Bob Mathias Story"; *Rafer Johnson* (1960 Olympic decathlon champion); *Floyd Simmons* (3rd 1948 Olympic decathlon); *Parry O'Brien* (1952 and 1956 Olympic shot champion); *Fortune Gordien* (world record discus thrower); *Dean Smith* (gold medallist in 1952 Olympic 4 x 100 m. relay); *Bob Seagren* (1968 Olympic pole vault champion); *O. J. Simpson* (member of world record breaking 4 x 110 yd. relay team); and *Bruce Jenner* (1976 Olympic decathlon champion). Others to make screen appearances include *C. K. Yang* of Taiwan (world record decathlete); *Giuseppe Tosi* (2nd 1948 Olympic discus) and *Giuseppe Gentile* (world record triple jumper) of Italy; *Tapio Rautavaara* of Finland (1948 Olympic javelin champion); and *Adhemar Ferreira da Silva* of Brazil (1952 and 1956 Olympic triple jump champion).

Among American actors first and foremost who were good athletes are the following—*Roscoe Lee Browne*, who was the world's fastest 800 m. runner in 1951 with a time of 1 min. 49.3 sec.; *Dennis Weaver*, well known to TV fans from the "Gunsmoke" and "McCloud" series, was 6th in the 1948 US Olympics Trials decathlon (6488 pts.); *Bruce Dern*, nominated for an Academy Award for his role in "Coming Home", was a 1 min. 56.8 sec. half miler in college and has run 50 miles in 7 hr. 6 min; *Jack Lemmon*, Oscar winner for "Mister Roberts" and "Save The Tiger", was a New England high school record holder as a distance runner. *Oliver Reed* was one of the best schoolboy cross-country runners in Britain; and *Bernard Miles (now Lord Miles)* was prominent in athletics while at Oxford University.

Singers

The legendary *Paul Robeson* was a distinguished high jumper (1.93 m.) at college, as was pop singer *Johnny Mathis* (1.96 m.). *Anne Pashley*, Olympic silver medallist with the British 4 x 100 m. relay team in 1956 and 3rd in the 1954 European 100 m., is a well known operatic soprano who has appeared at Covent Garden, Sadlers Wells, Glyndebourne etc. *Moira Kerr*, a leading Scottish folk singer, was a British shot-put international.

Writers

Jeffrey Archer, former British international sprinter, is a best-selling author ("Not A Penny More, Not A Penny Less" etc), as is *Erich Segal* ("Love Story"), a 2 hr. 42 min. marathon runner. Another experienced American marathoner is playwright *Israel Horovitz*. Prize winning science fiction author *Philip Jose Farmer* was reserve for the 1936 US Olympic team as a long jumper. *Ian Fleming*, creator of James Bond, was twice Victor Ludorum at Eton and shone particularly in the 120 yd. hurdles.

Miscellaneous

Julian Huxley, the distinguished biologist and zoologist (and first Director-General of UNESCO), was an Oxford high jump 'Blue' in 1908/09. *Captain Noel Godfrey Chavasse*, who represented Britain in the 1908 Olympics, won the Victoria Cross in the 1st World War but did not survive the conflict. *Arnold Strode-Jackson*, 1912 Olympic 1500 m. champion, was one of only seven officers to win a quadruple DSO in the 1st World War and at 26 was the youngest temporary brigadier-general in the British Army. *Professor George Carstairs*, a professor of psychiatry and former President of the World Federation for Mental Health, was Scottish 3 miles champion and 6th in the 1938 European 5000 m. *Ottavio Missoni*, head of the Italian knitwear fashion house of Missoni, was 6th in the 1948 Olympic 400 m. hurdles. *Ed. White*, the USA's first 'space walker', competed in the US Olympic 400 m. hurdles trials in 1952. *Norris McWhirter*, co-founder with his late twin brother Ross of that publishing phenomenon, "The Guinness Book of Records", was a Scottish international sprinter.

INDEX

Abascal, J., 72
Abbas, A., 21
Abbyasov, S., 69
Abebe Bikila, 11, 34, 111, 127, 128
Abehi, A., 13
Ablowich, E. A., 129
Abrahams, H. M., 11, 76, 86, 106, 107, 124, 126, 156, 180
Abrahams, S. S., 76, 216
Abramovich, O., 24
Absalom, C. A., 156
Achurch, J. D., 40
Aciro, J., 14
Ackermann, R., 11, 12, 62, 67, 71, 85, 86, 133, 154, 189, 199
Adam, M., 67, 71, 199
Adams, B. (GB), 21, 180
Adams, B. (USA), 76
Adams, G., 112
Adams, P., 76, 130
Adams, R. A., 38
Adams, R. S., 91
Adcocks, W. A., 17, 42, 112
Addy, E. C., 39
Addy, J. A., 39
Adelskold, A. L., 187
Adema, M., 62
Adey, J. A., 42
Afriyie, H., 13
Agapov, G., 196
Agbebaku, A., 13
Agostini, M. G. R., 37
Ahearn, D. F., 76, 162
Ahearne, T. J., 49, 76, 124, 130, 162
Ahey, M., 39
Ahlgren, A., 111
Ahman, A. P., 130
Ahrens, M., 140
Ainsworth-Davis, J. C., 124, 129
Ajit Singh, 22
Ajmer Singh, 21
Akagi, K., 21
Akii-Bua, J., 12, 14, 89, 117, 128, 193, 209
Akika, E., 13
Akremi, K., 13

Aksinin, A., 129
Albritton, D., 85
Albritton, T., 194, 210
Albus, E., 62
Alder, J. N. C., 17, 38, 45, 56, 192, 208
Alderman, E. P., 129
Aldridge, A., 47
Alexander, A., 140
Alexander, Earl, of Tunis, 216
Alexander, S. W., see LERWILL, S. W.
Alfeyeva, L., 67, 71
Alford, J. W., Ll., 37, 46
Allday, P. C., 19, 42
Allday, S., 44, 94, 171, 185
Allen, C. K., 42
Allen, L., 179
Allison, J. F., 44, 170, 183
Allotey, S. F., 37, 39
Allsop, E. J., 196, 211
Almen, R., 86
Al-Saffar, T. F., 22
Alsop, F. J., 19, 42, 92, 163, 168
Amin, I., 14
Anders, H., 74
Andersen, E., 211
Andersen, G., see WAITZ, G.
Anderson, J., 172, 213
Anderson, J. F., 131
Anderson, K., 140
Anderson, R. (GB), 207
Anderson, R. (USA), 175
Anderson, T. D., 39, 42
Andersson, A., 25, 82, 116, 188
Andersson, H. (CC), 128
Andersson, H. (DT), 60
Andersson, O., 196
Andersson-Arbin, H., 156
Andrews, C. J., 20, 169
Andrews, T., 16
Andreyeva, A., 62
Anisimova, T., 66
Anisimova, V., 62
Ankio, R., 18
Annum, A., 13
Antao, S., 15, 37

Antenen, M., 71, 74, 75
Anyakun, C., 13
Aparacio, J., 138
Appleby, M., 184
Applegarth, W. R., 86, 124, 128, 157
Apps, C. J. S., 39
Arame, J., 59
Arbin, H., see ANDERSSON-ARBIN, H.
Archer, J., 42, 56, 57, 124, 215, 217
Arden, A., 77
Arden, D., see SLATER, D.
Arese, F., 58, 65
Arizmendi, F., 48
Armitage, H. J., see YOUNG, H. J.
Arop, J., 13
Arthurton, S. A., 94
Arzhanov, Y., 58, 65, 68
Asaad, N., 13
Asati, C., 12, 37, 39, 129
Ashby, R., 183, 184, 186
Ashenfelter, H., 128
Ashford, E., 81, 101, 103, 139, 172, 189, 212
Ashmarin, Y., 73
Ashton, R. J., 164
Ashworth, G. H., 129
Atkinson, S. J. M., 128
Atterberry, W., 18
Atterwall, A. L. F., 60
Attlesey, R. H., 138
Atwood, D., 139
Auerswald, I., 133
Aukett, J. W., 65, 91
Austin, E., 174
Austin, R., 173, 207
Avilov, N., 51, 98, 131, 195
Aye, J., 13

Baba, T., 22
Babcock, H. S., 130
Babka, R., 195
Babu, S., 23
Backlund, S., 210
Backus, R., 139
Bacon, C. J., 128
Badana, V., 24
Badenski, A., 59, 64, 68

Baghbanbashi, A., 22
Bahadur Singh, 23
Baikov, V., 192
Bailes, M., 133, 196
Bailey, E. McD., 15, 124, 166
Bailey, G. W., 38, 42
Baillie, W. D., 192
Baird, D., 39
Baird, G., 129
Bakari, G., 13
Baker, P. J. Noel-, 86, 124, 215
Baker, W. T., 129, 173, 207
Bakhtawar Singh, 23
Baklanov, N., 72
Bakosi, B., 69
Balachowski, J., 68
Balas, I., 25, 62, 70, 86, 133, 134, 184, 199
Balcha, R., 12
Baldwin, A. G., 56
Balikhin, V., 65
Balkar, Singh, 23
Bally, E., 57
Balzer, K., 55, 62, 66, 70, 132, 198
Bambuck, R., 58, 59, 190
Banks, B., 170
Banks, W., 172, 210
Banning, P. A., 91, 207
Bannister, R. G., 25, 31, 33, 37, 42, 56, 58 116, 178
Banthorpe, R., 91
Barbuti, R. J., 126, 129
Bardauskiene, V., 26, 62, 108, 199, 213
Bariban, M., 73
Barkusky, A., 70, 74
Barnard, A., 20
Barnes, E. A., 68, 93
Barnes, J. G., 56
Barnes, L. S., 130
Barrett, B-A., 94
Barrett, F., 111, 112
Barrett, M., 93
Barry, S. J., 21
Barthel, J., 83, 127
Barthel, W., 73
Bartholomew, P., 41, 44
Barua, B. S., 21
Baryshnikov, A., 194
Bastians, W., 72
Bateman, I. L., 186
Bateman, T., 94
Batter, D., 44
Batty, M. R., 17, 46
Bauer, R., 130

Bauma, H., 133
Baumgartl, F., 72, 80
Baumgartner, H., 69
Bausch, J. A. B., 131
Bautista, D., 26, 49, 109, 132, 139, 178, 196, 211
Baxter, H., 143
Baxter, I. K., 129, 130
Baxter, M. I., 17
Bayi, F., 12, 26, 27, 35, 37, 78, 110, 116, 178, 191, 209
Beacham, M. A., 68, 70, 93, 94
Beacham, P. J., 91
Beames, A., 112
Beamon, R., 15, 27, 30, 49, 51, 53, 107, 130, 151, 194, 210
Beasley, G., 41
Beaven, P. M., 71, 72
Beavers, W. J., 38, 42
Beccali, L., 58, 127
Beck, V., 27, 28, 65, 128
Becker, I., see MICKLER, I.
Bedford, B. R., 94, 96, 185, 213
Bedford, D. C., 17, 28, 47, 48, 107, 166, 167, 192
Bednarek, E., 62, 74
Bednarski, J., 48
Beer, K., 69
Begier, Z., 66
Beilschmidt, R., 65, 189, 202
Belfaa, O., 12
Bell, C., 44, 68, 94, 170, 184
Bell, D. R., 42
Bell, E., 138, 194
Bell, F., 132
Bell, G. C., 130
Bell, W., 137
Bell-Gam, B., 13, 14
Bell-Gam, J., 13
Benabid, J., 13
Bender, H-J., 59, 90
Bendlin, K., 195
Ben Hamo, A., 63
Ben Hassine, A., 13
Ben Saad, M., 13
Benn, R. J., 71
Bennett, A., 91, 164, 166
Bennett, C., 124, 127
Bennett, J., 41
Benning, C. M., 44, 170, 183, 184, 212
Beretta, J., 184
Berger, C. D., 57

Berger, M., 59
Berkes, E., 69
Bermudez, M., 109
Berna, T. S., 127
Bernard, K., 39
Bernard, M., 16, 207
Bernard, V. M., see ELDER, V. M.
Bernhard, R., 69
Berruti, L., 126, 190
Berthelsen, B., 71, 185
Berto, S., 139, 183
Bertoia, D., 137
Bertould, G., 59
Beskrovniy, A., 73, 210
Besson, C., 70, 132, 197
Bettridge, P., 92
Bexell, O., 61
Beyer, G., 29, 76
Beyer, O., 36, 58, 135
Beyer, U. (E. Ger), 28, 29, 60, 66, 71, 73, 76, 130, 151, 153 189, 194, 210
Beyer, U. (W. Ger), 60
Bhim Singh, 22
Bianchi, B., 173
Bickle, T. S., 39
Bie, F., 131
Bielczyk, Z., 70, 213
Biffle, J. C., 130
Bignal, M. D., see RAND, M. D.
Bijleveld, J., 185
Bikila Abebe, see ABEBE BIKILA
Bilham, M., 16, 42
Billups, E., 173
Binks, J., 86
Binns, K. M., 107, 165, 186, 213
Binns, S. J., 71, 72, 208
Birlenbach, H., 70
Birnbaum, W., 74
Birrell, R., 167
Biryulina, T., 29, 36, 98, 200, 213
Biwott, A., 128
Bjorneman, W., see PETTERSSON, W.
Black, C. F., 20, 45, 83, 168, 210
Black, D. J., 17, 42, 47, 164
Black, L., 129
Blackburn, P., 93
Blagoeva, Y., 67, 71, 86, 199
Blake, G. N., 39, 42
Blakeley, B. D., 92

Bland, H. C., 132
Blankers-Koen, F. E., 29, 61, 62, 63, 108, 132, 134, 137, 157
Blazejezak, H., 59
Blewitt, C. E., 47, 124
Blinston, J. A., 56
Blinyayev, A., 73
Bliznyetsov, G., 69
Blodniece, L., 75
Blomqvist, J. E., 73
Blue, A., 173
Boak, R., 41
Board, L. B., 56, 61, 62, 66, 125, 157, 169, 170, 183
Bochkaryeva, L., 61, 62
Bodendorf, C., 133
Bodunrin, J., 13
Bogdanova, V., 62
Boggis, J. L. A., 71
Boguszewicz, L., 16
Bohman, L., 59
Boit, M., 12, 37
Bolding, J., 18
Boldt, A., 86
Bolinder, A., 59
Boling, L., 185
Bolotnikov, P., 58, 127, 192
Bondarchuk, A., 60, 66, 83, 131, 152, 195
Bonhag, G. V., 127
Bonheme, J-F., 69
Bonnano, M. A., 183
Bonner, B., 112
Bonnet, F., 73
Bons, 187
Boosey, D. C. J., 92, 93
Boot, V. P., 37
Boothe, L. M., 41, 44, 94, 170, 184
Booysen, D., 19
Borah, C. E., 128
Borchmeyer, E., 59
Boreham, C. A. J., 92, 167
Borowski, E., 59
Borsenko, A., 73
Borzov, V., 29, 30, 57, 58, 64, 67, 68, 71, 72, 114, 126
Boston, R. H., 27, 30, 33, 49, 107, 130, 138, 194
Botchina, N., 212
Botha, J., 19
Botley, M. Y., 94
Boubekeur, A., 13
Bouchta, A., 48
Bouin, J., 47, 102, 153

Boulter, J. P., 16, 166
Bourbeillon, P., 59
Bourland, C. F., 129
Boutamine, S., 13
Box, K. J., 15, 56
Boxberger, J., 68
Boxer, C. T., 165, 170, 183, 212
Boychuk, A., 138
Boyd, D., 41
Boyd, I. H., 42
Boyd, R., 18
Boyes, M. G., 18
Boyle, R. A., 40, 41, 183
Boysen, A., 115
Brabec, J., 70
Bradford A., 173
Bragg, D. G., 130, 138, 144, 194
Bragina, L., 30, 117, 132, 177, 198, 212
Braithwaite, N. D., 93, 94
Bralo, R., 138
Brand, E. C., 133
Brangwin, K. C., 39, 42
Brasher, C. W., 25, 30, 31, 124, 128, 158, 167
Bratanov, J., 68
Bratchikov, A., 68, 72
Braumuller, I., 187
Breacker, A., 39, 42, 56
Breard, L., 187
Brehmer, C., 62, 74, 133, 197, 212
Bresnahan, G., 156
Breul, D., 175
Bridgland, J., 186
Briesenick, H., 60, 66, 70, 73
Briggs, J. S., 183
Brightwell A. E., see PACKER, A. E.
Brightwell, R. I., 16, 42, 56, 58, 124, 137, 166
Brill, D., 41, 140, 154, 172, 184, 189, 213
Brix, H., 216
Broders, 175
Brookes, W. P., 123
Brooks, M. J., 85
Broschat, B., 188
Brown, A., 76, 125
Brown, A. G., 20
Brown, A. G. K., 56, 58, 76, 124, 129, 157, 216
Brown, B., 129
Brown, D. (GB), 184
Brown, D. (USA), 48
Brown, E., 140
Brown, H., 39

Brown, H. H., 127
Brown, J. (Can), 38
Brown, J. (GB), 48
Brown, J. (USA), 48
Brown, J. R., 38
Brown, M. M., 41
Brown, P. A., 71, 91
Brown, R., 210
Brown, R. K., 42, 76, 216
Brown, V., 139
Browne, D., 175
Browne, P. M., 16, 91
Browne, R. L., 216
Brownlee, D. A., 45
Bruch, R., 66, 195
Brumel, V., 32, 60, 65, 86, 129, 193, 201
Bruns, U., 70
Bruzsenyak, I., 62
Bryan, G., 138
Bryan, T. J. B., 91
Bryan-Jones, D. G., 17
Bryant, R., 212
Brydenbach, A., 68, 72
Bryggare, A., 69, 73, 209
Bryngeirsson, T., 60
Budd, F. J., 84, 129, 156
Bues, M., 59
Bufanu, V., 184
Bulanchik, Y., 59
Bull, M. A., 18, 39, 40, 46, 90, 92, 95, 144, 167, 168
Bullivant, M. J., 17
Burge, D., 40, 41
Burger, M. D., 20
Burgess, B., 45, 164, 167
Burgess, S., 44
Burghley, Lord, 32, 38, 39, 42, 88, 89, 124, 128, 216
Burke, B., 41, 125
Burke, E., 20, 210
Burke, T. E., 126
Burleson, D., 138
Burneleit, K., 61, 70, 198
Burns, J. A., 42
Burton, E., 215
Burton, T. P., 92, 167
Burvill, M. J., 197
Buryakov, V., 73
Busse, A., 72, 207
Bussmann, G., 74
Butler, G. M., 124, 129, 134, 157
Butt, M. S., 21
Butterfield, D., 44
Butterfield, M., 86, 92, 164, 167
Bychkova, T., 74

Byers, F., 215
Bystrova, G., 62, 63, 141
Cabrera, D., 127, 138
Cacchi, P., *see* PIGNI, P.
Caird, M., 132
Calhoun, L. Q., 33, 88, 115, 128, 193
Callan, R. J., 92
Callebout, N. E., 187
Calvert, S., 140
Camien, J., 16
Campbell, C. W. A., 91, 166
Campbell, M. C., 18, 92, 167
Campbell, M. G., 131
Campbell, M. T., 93
Campbell, W. M., 15, 16, 166
Cannon, D. A., 17
Cantello, A., 195
Capes, G. L., 19, 40, 42, 56, 66, 68 70, 93, 95, 153, 164, 168, 210
Carette, J., 59
Carew, M. L., 132
Carey, S. J., 93, 170, 183
Carlos, J., 137, 190
Carlsen, G., 139
Carlton, J., 156
Carpenter, K. K., 131
Carr, E. W., 37, 39
Carr, G. A., 42, 168
Carr, H., 126, 129, 155, 156, 190
Carr, S. W., 130
Carr, W. A., 126, 129
Carrigan, C., 18
Carroll, N., 16, 68
Carstairs, G., 217
Carter, A., 93
Carter, A. W., 16, 42, 56, 65, 166
Carter, C. S., 166
Carter, L. W., 39, 42
Cartmell, N. J., 129
Caruthers, E., 138
Cary, L. H., 156
Casanas, A., 117, 119, 138, 193
Cassell, O. C., 129
Catalano, P., 213
Catherwood, E., 133
Catineanu, D., 71
Cator, S., 107
Cawley, S., 125
Cawley, W. J., 18, 89, 128, 193
Centrowitz, M., 138

Cerrada, F., 72
Cerutty, P. W., 55
Chairsuvaparb, S., 21
Chalmers, L., 44
Cham, O., 209
Chamberlain, M., *see* STEPHEN, M.
Chambul, B., 40, 210
Chand, H., 22
Chang Hoon Lee, 22
Chapa, R., 208
Chataway, C. J., 25, 28, 33, 38, 42, 56 104, 107, 215
Chauvelot, D., 59
Chavasse, N. G., 217
Cheeseborough, C., 139, 212
Cheeseman, S., 44, 125
Chee Swee Lee, 23
Chefd'hotel, R., 59
Chelnikov, V., 73
Chemabwai, T., 13
Chemweno, M., 13
Chen Chia-chuan, 190
Chenchik, T., 62, 67, 70
Chen Hsin, 24
Cheng Ta-chen, 24
Chernetsky, N., 68, 129
Chernuck, P., 72
Cherrier, B., 59
Chervanyov, Y., 69, 209
Chhota Singh, 22
Chi Cheng, 23, 24, 182, 184, 197, 198
Chilton, T., 174, 210
Chionis, 87, 107
Chipchase, I. A., 40, 42, 168
Chitty, M. A., 94
Chivers, A. H., 42
Chivers, J., 91
Chizhova, N., 33, 62, 63, 67, 71, 74, 133, 153, 199
Chmelkova, A., 61
Choi Chung Sik, 22
Chou Mao-chia, 24
Chouri, M., 48
Christie, L., 91
Chromik, J., 58
Chudina, A., 63, 141
Chuhan, V. S., 23
Ciepla, T. B., 62, 133
Cierpinski, W., 34, 111, 128
Ciochina, S., 19, 69
Cioltan, V., 54
Clark, D. McD. M., 40, 45, 56, 83
Clark, E. H., 129, 130

Clark, J., 111
Clark, M. R., 41
Clark, S., 210
Clarke, A., 112
Clarke, D. S., 20, 169, 174
Clarke, L. A., 128
Clarke, M., 35
Clarke, R. W., 14, 16, 17, 34, 100, 106, 148, 176, 192, 203
Clarke, S., 91
Clarke, W., 72
Clarkson, A. R., 72, 183
Claus, H., 199
Claus, K., 74
Clausnitzer, K., 74
Clayton, D., 35, 111, 112, 209
Clement, F. J., 65, 91, 166
Clerc, P., 58
Clough, N. S., 37, 173, 174, 207
Clover, C. P., 40, 42, 169, 210
Coachman, A., 133
Coales, W., 124, 127
Coates, D., 209
Coates, D. M., 17, 92, 164, 167
Cobb, V. M., 41, 44, 57, 68, 93, 182
Cochran, L. V., 128, 129
Cochrane, C. S., 129
Cocks, K. D., 164
Coe, P., 35
Coe, S. N., 35, 36, 56, 65, 68, 71, 91, 92, 95, 115, 116, 122, 124, 127, 135, 164, 166, 191, 207
Coetzee, W., 18
Coffman, B., 139
Coghlan, E., 16, 17, 69, 207, 208
Cohen, G., 173
Cohen, G. H., 56, 59, 65, 71, 91, 207
Cohen H. J., 42
Colchen, A., 62
Colebrook, K. J., 44, 68, 70, 165, 212
Coleman, C., 171
Coleman, G. W., 21
Coleman, J., 41
Coleman, J. L., 38
Coleman, P., 138
Colin, D., 196
Colin, G., 166
Collett, W., 75, 207
Colman, C. P., 93
Colnard, P., 210

Colon, M., 29, 36, 133, 140
Colson, S., 139
Colyear, S., 41, 44, 57, 93, 94, 165, 170, 184, 213
Commandeur, O., 74
Condon, F., 213
Conley, P., 174
Connolly, H. V., 83, 131, 195
Connolly, J. V., 130, 162
Connolly, M., 173
Connolly, O., 133
Connor, K. L., 19, 40, 42, 68, 93, 163, 164, 168, 210
Connors, E., 94
Consolini, A., 60, 131
Cook, B. J., 93, 186
Cook, J., 185
Cook, M., 132
Cook, S., 214
Cooke, E. T., 130
Cooke, J. E., 91
Cooke, P. J., 71
Cooper, A., 37
Cooper, A. A., 15
Cooper, D., 94
Cooper, J. H., 18, 89, 124, 167
Cooper, S. A., 57
Copeland, L., 133
Cops, C. M., 185
Corbett, S. J., 44, 185
Corbu, C., 69
Corden, M., 20
Corgos, A., 210
Cornelissen, J., 182, 183
Cornes, J. F., 42, 124
Coroebus, 87, 123
Costache, G., 73
Cotterell, W. M., 47
Cotterill, D., 94
Cotton, D., 180
Cottrill, W., 124
Courtney, T. W., 115, 126, 129
Courtwright, J. A., 40
Covelli, F., 139
Cox, B., 41
Cox, E., 180
Cox, M., 44
Cox, R., 112
Coy, E. E., 40
Crabb, R., 208
Craig, C., 139
Craig, R. C., 126
Cram, S., 71, 72
Cramerotti, R., 73
Crampton, J., 21
Crawford, H., 126, 145

Creamer, A. M., 183
Cripps, W., 41
Critchley, M. A., 44, 169, 183
Crockett, I., 156
Croker, N. W., 133
Croome, A. C. M., 88
Cropper, D., 16
Cropper, P. B., 45, 57, 62, 183
Cros, Y., 59
Crossley, D. E., 187
Crothers, W. F., 16, 91
Crowther, B., 44, 57
Cruttenden, A. R., 19
Csak, I., 62, 133
Csanyi, G., 59
Csermak, J., 83, 131
Culbreath, J., 138
Cullen, P. S., 20
Cullmann, B., 129
Cummings, W., 80
Cunningham, J., 46
Curry, T. P. E., 216
Curtis, T. P., 128
Cusick, C. F., 91
Cuthbert, B., 41, 48, 132, 133, 134, 137, 157
Cybulski G., 66

Dadney, S., 139
Dahl, R., 60
Dainton, A. R., 18
Dainty, G., 93, 165, 183
Dale, W., 39
Dalgoutte, S. M., 165
Dalhauser, R., 69
Dalins, J., 61
Damilano, G., 49, 77
Damilano, M., 49, 77, 132
Damilano S., 49
Damman, E., 184
Danek, L., 53, 60, 131, 195
Daniels I., 139
Danielsen, E., 131
Danielsson, S., 59
Danilova, T., 63
D'Arcy, L., 39
D'Arcy, V. H. A., 124, 128
Darden, T., 137
Da Silva, A. F., 49, 51, 130, 139, 163, 216
Davenport W., 128, 193
Davies, G., 193
Davies, J. (800m), 91
Davies, J. (Steep), 17, 46, 167
Davies, J. (LJ), 185

Davies, L., 19, 30, 39, 46, 49, 56, 60, 68, 69, 92, 107, 124, 130, 168, 180, 181, 210
Davies P., 184, 186
Davies, T., 174, 209
Davin, P., 76
Davin, T., 76
Davis, D., 139
Davis, E. I., 38, 42
Davis, G. A., 50, 89, 117, 128, 129, 193
Davis, I., 139
Davis, J., 88, 138
Davis, O. C., 126, 129, 157, 190, 191
Davis, W. F., 129
Davisson, S., 174
Day, G. R., 39
Deakin, J. E., 124, 127
Dear, D. G., 16, 42, 91
Dearnley A., 41
De Beck, E., 48
Decker, E., 70
Decker, M., 117, 139, 198, 212
De Coubertin, P., 123
Dedner, K., 74, 213
Degats, J., 59
De Gruchy, A. W., 38
De Kremer, P., 165
De La Hunty, S. B., 41, 51, 132, 133, 134, 196
De Lange, H., 184
Delany, R. M., 16, 90, 127
De La Vina, J., 24
Delecour, J., 59
Dellinger, W., 138
Demec, J., 59
De Oliveira, J. C., 15, 51, 139, 151, 163, 189, 194, 210
De Palmas, R., 174
De Pauw, E., 48
De Preiss, I., 140
Dern, B., 216
Desforges, J. C., *see* PICKERING, J. C.
Desmartreau, E., 131
Desruelles, R., 19, 69
Devally, A-M., 165, 184
De Villiers, P., 20
Dew, M. C., 57
Dia, M., 13
Diaz, B., 139, 140
Dick, A., 39, 42, 59
Dickenson, P., 165, 168
Dickinson, R. D., 143
Didrikson, M., 132, 133

Dietsch, W., 62
Dillard, W. H., 33, 52, 88, 126, 128, 129
Dima, I., 72
Dionisi, R., 18, 69
Disley, J. I., 17, 124, 158
Disley, S., see CHEESEMAN, S.
Ditta, A., 18
Dixon, J., 207, 209
Dixon, R. (Can), 40
Dixon, R. (NZ), 16
Dobbie, S., 46
Dobson, R. W., 169, 179, 211
Dodson, D., 172
Dolezal, J., 61, 196
Dolgi, M., 73
Dolgov, A., 73
Dollinger, M., 187
Dombrowski, L., 53, 66, 107, 130, 210
Domingos, O., 175
Dominik, R., 72
Doms, J., 47
Dorando, see PIETRI, D.
Dordoni, G., 49, 61, 132
Dorffeldt, I., 187
Doubell, R. D., 115, 126, 191
Douglas, E. C. K., 45
Douglas, J., 166
Dourass, G., 93
Draper, F., 129
Drayton, A. W., 20, 42
Drayton, O. P., 129, 190
Drehmel, J., 60, 66, 151
Drescher, R., 139
Dresser, I. C., 127
Driver, P. B., 38, 42
Drut, G., 59, 65, 69, 88, 128, 193, 209
Drysdale, L., 184
Duclos, N., 61, 197
Dudin, V., 65, 193
Dudkin, N., 69
Dudziak, M., 64
Duffey, A. F., 156
Dumas, C. E., 54, 85, 129, 138
Dumbadze, N., 53, 63
Dumke, J., 73
Dumon, J., 48
Dumshev, Y., 73
Duncan, K. S., 42
Dunecki, L., 59, 73
Dunn, C., 18
Du Plessis, A. S., 39
Du Plessis, S. J., 19, 40
Dutov, N., 65

Dvorak, C. E., 130
Dyer, H. M., 128
Dyrzka, J. C., 138
Dyson, M. A. J., see GARDNER, M. A. J.
Dyson, S., 170, 199

Eastman, B. B., 115, 157
Eaton, W. E., 47
Eckersley, H., 47
Eckert, B., see WOCKEL, B.
Eddy, E. M., 93
Ede, D. R., 56
Edelen, L. G., 17, 111
Edinburgh, Duke of, 141
Edstrom, D., 139
Edward, H. F. V., 15, 124
Edwards, C., 15, 16, 189
Edwards, E. W., 187
Edwards, M. R., 91
Edwards, P. A., 37, 83
Efimovich, M., 73
Ehizuelen, C., 13, 210
Ehrhardt, A., 55, 62, 66, 70, 71, 74, 132, 198
Eigenherr, J., 72
Eisler, B., 140
Eke, J., 128
Elder, V. M., 41, 44, 68, 70, 90, 93, 157, 170, 183, 212
Eldon, S. E., 16, 17, 18
Eley, B., 179
Elfaquir, F., 13
El Ghazi, A., 48
Elliott, B. W., 56
Elliott, D. I., 93
Elliott, G. M., 39, 42, 51, 56, 144, 167
Elliott, H. J., 37, 55, 116, 127, 146, 150, 155, 191
Elliott, P. G., 57, 184
Ellis, G. S., 56
Ellis, M. J., 19, 20, 40, 42, 83, 168
Elloe, B., 13
Elmsater, E., 158
El Ouafi, B., 127
Elvin, A. E., 93
Elze, G., 73
Embleton, P. B., 21, 179, 211
Emery, C. A. J., 47
Emson, S. J., 92, 164
England, D. M., 46
Englehardt, R., 187
Englehart, S. E., 37, 42
Erba, G., 73, 209
Erickson, T., 180

Ericson, B., 60
Erik, L., 66
Eriksson, H., 127
Erinle, F., 12
Esteves, H., 190
Ethirveerasingam, N., 22
Etolu, P., 18
Evans, D., 207
Evans, G. G., 39
Evans, L. E., 75, 126, 129, 137, 144, 157, 191, 207
Evenson, T., 42, 47, 124
Everett, G. E., 16
Everts, S., 75, 214
Ewell, H. N., 129
Ewry, R. C., 129, 130, 134
Exeter, Marquess of, see BURGHLEY, Lord
Eyre, L., 38, 42

Faggs, M. E., 133
Fairbrother, C. W., 18, 92, 167
Faircloth, D. K., 17, 42
Falck, H., 66, 70, 115, 132, 198
Fallo, I., 185
Fanning, J., 92
Farmer, P., 20, 40, 210
Farmer, P. J., 217
Farquhar, A., 44, 185
Farr, J. U., 94, 171, 175, 180, 182, 186
Farrell, T. F., 16
Farrell, T. S., 16, 18, 167
Farrington, J., 48
Fawkes, M., 109, 171, 180, 186, 214
Fayolle, J–C., 48
Fedorchuk, A., 74
Fejer, G., 73
Feld, I., 69
Feldmann, C., 139
Fenouil, G., 59, 72
Ferragne, C., 39
Ferreira, S., 95
Ferrell, B., 133, 139, 196
Ferris, S., 42, 103, 111, 112, 124
Feuerbach, A., 19, 122, 139, 194
Few, R., 94, 184
Fiasconaro, M., 191
Fibingerova, H., 71, 77, 153, 189, 199, 200, 213
Fiedler, A., 70
Figueroa, H., 139
Figuerola, E., 15, 137, 190
Fikotova, O., see CON-

NOLLY, O.
Filiput, A., 59
Finlay, D. O., 15, 38, 43, 56, 59, 88, 95, 122, 124, 167, 209
Fischer, H., 66
Fishback, J., 138
Fisher, N., 207
Fisk, B., 171
Fitzpatrick, J. R., 38
FitzSimons, J. H. P., 20, 40, 43, 169
Flack, E. H., 126, 127
Flanagan, J. J., 82, 122, 131
Fleischer, T., 133
Fleming, I., 217
Fleming-Smith, J. C., 17
Fleschen, K., 69
Flocke, K., 174
Flockhart, J. C., 47
Flores, D., 138
Floyd, S., 207
Flynn, A., 140
Flynn, O. T., 40, 43, 179
Fogarty, N. A., 41
Fogg, C., 211
Foldessy, O., 60
Foltz, V., 175
Fonville, C., 152
Forbes, A., 45
Forbes, H. J., 56
Forbes, P., 91
Ford, A., 44, 77, 170, 184, 186
Ford, B. W., 47
Ford, H., 43
Ford, O., 190
Forde, L., 172
Foreman, P., 39
Fortun, R., 137
Fosbury, R., 77, 85, 129
Foss, F. K., 103, 130
Foster, B., 17, 38, 43, 47, 56, 58, 65, 78, 107, 124, 148, 166, 192, 208
Foster, J., 208, 209
Foster, N., 20, 169
Fouche, L. A., 40
Foulds, J. F., see PAUL, J. F.
Fourie, J., 207
Fowell, W. M., 71
Fowler, H. R., 17, 48, 56, 111, 173, 174
Francis, M., 71
Franco, A., 22
Fraser, B., 43
Frazer, J., 39
Frazier, H., 129

Freary, M., 166, 208
Frederick, J., 172, 214
Freeman, N. F., 40, 211
Freeman, R., 129
Freeman, W., 47
French, P. E., 185
Frenkel, P., 26, 81, 132, 196
Frese, C., 70
Friedel, H., 74
Friedmann, B., 188, 212
Friedrich, B., 140
Frigerio, U., 49, 131
Frinolli, R., 59
Frith, R. M., 68, 90
Fromm, D., 58, 68
Fry, C. B., 107
Fryer, P. G., 39, 43, 59
Fuchs, J., 121, 139, 152
Fuchs, R., 29, 36, 63, 67, 78, 98, 133, 134, 189, 200
Fudge, P., 41, 44, 77, 165, 170, 212
Fuqua, I., 129
Furtsch, E., 132
Furze, A. F., 43
Futterer, H., 57, 59

Gabbett, P. J., 20, 43, 169
Gabrielli, G., 72
Gaby, F. R., 43
Gadjadoum, N., 12
Gaete, E., 140
Gage, T., 139
Galant, H., 72
Gammoudi, M., 14, 17, 48, 127
Gamper, P., 59
Garbisch, M., 173
Garcia, H., 140
Garcia, J., 48
Garderud, A., 71, 72, 80, 110, 128, 148, 193, 209
Gardner, D. K., 44
Gardner, K.A.St.H., 18, 37, 38
Gardner, M. A. J., 57, 125
Gardner, P. J., 38
Garrett, R. S., 130
Gauder, H., 71, 73, 80, 132
Gaunt, J. P., 186
Gavrilenko, Y., 73
Gavrilov, V., 60, 65, 69
Geal, A., 212
Gedge, G. V., 39
Gelius, G., 187
Gelius, L., 63, 187

Gendron, F., 212
Gentile, G., 194, 216
George, W. G., 15, 80, 81, 106, 116, 118, 141
Georgeantas, 134
Gerassimova, V., 198
Gerhards, A., 185
Germar, M., 57, 59
Gerschler, W., 83
Gerstenberg, D., 73
Gervasini, R., 72
Geyer, B., 74
Gheita, A., 13
Ghiassi, T., 22
Ghipu, G., 72
Giannattasio, P., 68
Gibbs, B. M., 165, 184
Gibbs, K., 41
Gibson, A. K., 91
Gilbert, A. C., 130
Gildemeister, R., 74
Gilkes, J., 137
Gill, C. W., 124
Gill, E. A., 93
Gillmeister, E., 59
Gilmour, I. W., 92
Gingell, J., 91
Girke, W., 69
Girvan, M., 20, 210
Glance, H., 129, 190
Gleskova, E., 197
Glover, E., 124
Gnanasekharan, R., 21
Goater, J. N., 47, 208
Godbold, L., 187
Goddard, B. L., 41, 44, 57, 125
Gohr, M., 61, 66, 70, 81, 103, 133, 157, 189, 197, 212
Goitchik, T., 133
Golden, H., 72, 74, 169, 183
Goldovanyi, B., 59
Golubnichaya, M., 62
Golubnichiy, V., 61, 81, 132, 196, 211
Gomez, R., 138
Gommers, M., 183, 198
Gonder, F., 134
Gonzalez, A., 69
Gonzalez, F., 68
Gonzalez, R. (Cuba), 138
Gonzalez, R. (Mex), 109, 139, 178, 196, 211
Goodall, R. F., 20
Goodwin, G. R., 124
Gora, L., 73
Gorchakova, Y., 67, 78, 98, 200

Gordien, F. E., 139, 216
Gordienko, Y., 85
Gordon, A. K., 38
Gordon, E. L., 130
Gordon, P., 165
Gorecka, H., 133
Gorman, M., 175
Gorski, Y., 73
Gosper, R. K., 37
Goudeau, J-P., 59
Goudge, C. E., 18
Gould, C. T., 93, 184
Goulding, G. H., 131
Goulding, G. T. S., 124
Gourdin, E., 107
Gower, G. J., 92
Graham, L., 140
Graham, T. J. M., 16, 43, 124
Gray, G. R., 152, 172
Graybehl, R., 18
Greasley, J., 169
Greaves, W. E., 164
Grebenyuk, A., 61, 67, 160
Grebnyev, N., 66
Gredzinski, S., 58, 59
Green, A. R., 16
Green, B. W., 15, 43, 90, 166
Green, E. E., 44
Green, F., 43
Green, H., 111, 112
Green, I. D., 43
Green, P., 86
Green, S. M., 91
Green, T. W., 122, 124, 132
Greene, C., 87, 129, 190
Greenwood, J., 174
Gregory, J. A., 124
Greig, D., 112
Grelle, J., 138
Grieme, M., 187
Grieme, S., 187
Grieveson, E. J., 57, 169. 183
Griffin, L., 172, 213
Griffiths, C. R., 124, 129
Griffiths, D. G., 16, 91
Grigoryev, A., 65
Gromov, I., 73
Grustinsh, Y., 69
Gryziecka, E., 78, 98, 200
Guillemot, J., 47, 127
Gummel, M., 71, 133, 185, 199
Gunn, C. E. J., 124
Gurbachan Singh, 23
Gusenbauer, I., 62, 70,

P

86, 184, 199
Gushiken, K., 23
Gustafsson, R., 58
Gustavsson, S., 109
Gutowski, R., 144, 193
Gutteridge, J., 164
Gutterson, A. L., 130
Gyarmati, V. O., 133
Gynn, R. W. H., 111

Haarhoff, P., 59
Haas, C., 77, 207
Haas, K-F., 77
Haase, J., 17, 58, 65, 72
Habib Thiam, 215
Hacker, L., 174, 209
Hackney, R., 17, 91
Hagg, G., 25, 82, 104, 116
Haglund, L. G., 19, 70
Hahn, A., 126, 134
Haisley, E., 39
Haist, J., 42, 185
Hakam Singh, 23
Hakansson, S., 59
Halberg, M. G., 38, 127
Haley, P., 38
Hall, A., 139
Hall, D. G., 44, 57, 62, 126
Hall, E., 193
Hall, E. W., 179
Hall, J. A., 44
Halldorsson, H., 70
Halliday, D. G., 15, 90
Hallows, N. F., 124
Halstead, E., 44, 77
Halstead, N., 41, 44, 77, 125, 157
Halswelle, W., 124, 126, 157
Hamada, Y., 22
Hamann, H., 59
Hamby, C. A., 186
Hamilton, C., 91
Hamilton, W. F., 129
Hamm, E. B., 130
Hampson, T., 37, 43, 83, 115, 124, 126
Hampton, M., 129
Hampton, S., see PIRIE, S.
Handley, F. R., 43
Handt, A., 62
Hanel, K., 71, 213
Hanisch, W., 66, 189
Hanlon, J. A. T., 43
Hannon, G. P., 17
Hansen, F. M., 18, 130, 194
Hansen, J., 112

225

Hanson, C., 93, 183
Harbig, R., 58, 59, 83, 115, 157
Hardin, G. F., 83, 84, 89, 128
Hardin, W., 84
Hardy, C., 133
Hardy, R., 179
Harkonen, A., 95, 210
Harnden, A. H., 129
Harper, E., 43, 47, 111, 124
Harris, R., 92
Harris, S. A., 94
Harrison, V. J., 184
Hart, E., 30, 129, 190
Hart, H. B., 40
Hart, L., 139
Hart, R., 13, 14
Hartley, D-M. L., 41, 44, 72, 125, 165, 169, 170, 183
Hartley, W. J., 18, 43, 56, 59, 65, 164
Hartmann, W., 210
Hartnett, J., 48
Harvey, C. J., 179
Harvey, L. K., 94
Hary, A., 57, 59, 126, 129, 156, 190
Haskell, G., 39
Haskett, C., 72, 94
Hassan, K., 12, 16, 189
Hatt, H. M., 187
Hauck, M. A., 43
Havasi, I., 108
Hawtrey, H., 134
Hay, E., 57, 62
Hayes, J. J., 110, 111, 127
Hayes, R. L., 84, 126, 129, 156, 190
Haynes, F. C., 187
Haynes, R., 175
Hayward, B., 92
Hayward, S. M., 184
Head, V. A., 165, 171, 213
Heap, J. C., 43
Hearnshaw, S. C., 72, 76, 165, 185, 213
Heath, D., 72, 213
Heath, E., 33
Heatley, B. B., 17, 46, 48, 111, 112, 124
Hebauf, A., 84
Heber, R., 139
Hebert, B., 72
Hedmark, L., 67
Hedmark, L. Y., 57, 68, 86, 94, 170, 184
Hegarty, A., 124

Hein, K., 60, 131
Heine, J., 61
Heinich, C., 62, 74
Heino, V. J., 58
Heinrich, I., 61
Held, F. D., 97, 139
Held, R., 97
Helffrich, A. B., 129
Helten, I., 62, 197
Hemery, D. P., 14, 18, 38, 43, 56, 84, 85, 88, 89, 124, 128, 167, 193, 209
Henley, E. J., 124
Hennige, G., 65
Henning, H., 70
Henry, A., 92, 164
Henry VIII, King, 87, 143
Hepburn, R., 203
Hera, 186
Hermens, J., 192, 208
Hernandez, L., 138
Herriott, M., 15, 17, 43, 124, 158, 167
Herrmann, B., 59, 65
Herrmann, S., 80, 191
Heublein, G., 187
Hewson, B. S., 16, 43, 56, 58, 166
Heyer, W., 211
Hibbins, F. N., 124
Hickey, G., 209
Hicks, H. J., 17
Hicks, T. J., 127
Hietanen, M., 58
Higdon, H., 174
Higdon, M. R., 92
Higgins, F. P., 16, 39, 43, 59, 124
Higgins, R., 42
Higgins, T. L., 43, 215
Higham, C. E. E., 43
Hignett, G. J., 19
Hildreth, P. B., 18, 56, 88, 167
Hill, A. G., 30, 86, 114, 122, 124, 126, 127, 155
Hill, R., 17, 38, 43, 46, 47, 56, 58, 111, 112, 192, 208, 209
Hill, W., 72
Hillier, J. N., 43
Hillman, H. L., 126, 128
Hines, H., 19
Hines, J. R., 87, 126, 129, 156, 172, 190, 207
Hirota, T., 22
Hirscht, J., 68
Hiscock, E. M., 40, 41, 44, 125
Hiscox, M. E., 57, 169

Hitchen, G., 94, 165
Hitomi, K., 108, 187
Hjeltnes, K., 151
Hobson, P. F., 39
Hockert, G., 127
Hodge, P., 124, 128, 158
Hodge, R., 77, 196
Hodges, L., 212
Hodkinson, P., 180
Hofer, R., 62
Hoff, B., 72, 207
Hoff, C., 143
Hoffman, A., 41, 139, 183
Hoffman, M., 41
Hoffmann, D., 60
Hoffmann, M., 175
Hoffmann, P. R. W., 71, 91
Hoffmeister, G., 61, 66, 70
Hofmeister, F-P., 58, 59, 72
Hogan, J. J., 56, 58, 166, 192
Hogan, J. M. W., 92, 167
Hohne, C., 61, 108, 109, 132, 196, 212
Holden, J. A., 17, 167
Holden, J. T., 38, 43, 47, 56, 58, 111, 122
Holdorf, W., 131
Holger, 187
Holland, K., 175
Hollick, H. J., 165
Hollings, S. C., 17
Hollingsworth, R. A., 19, 168
Holmen, N., 62
Holmer, G., 81
Holmes, C. B., 37, 43
Holmvang, G., 61
Holst-Sorensen, N., 58
Holtom, J. M., 18, 71, 92, 164, 209
Holzapfel, B., 75
Honour, J. L., 186
Honz, K., 58, 65
Hooper, B. R. L., 18, 19, 43, 92, 144, 164, 168, 209, 210
Hopkins, T. E., 41, 46, 57, 62, 86, 125, 170, 184
Horgan, D., 15, 124, 152
Horine, G., 85
Hornberger, G., 59
Horovitz, I., 217
Hoskin, S. H., 42, 44, 185
Houser, C. L., 52, 130, 131
Houvion, M., 174

Houvion, P., 103, 194
Howell, J., 168
Howell, S. E., 184
Howland, R. L., 15, 43
Hoyt, W. W., 130
Hoyte, T. J., 164
Hoyte, W. P., 93
Hoyte-Smith, J. Y., 41, 44, 125, 165, 170, 183, 212
Hsiao Chieh-ping, 24
Huang Liang-cheng, 22
Hubbard, W. de H., 107, 130
Huber, E., 175
Hubner, M., 74, 212
Hudak, H., 17, 208
Hudson, M., 133
Hulst, E., 48
Humphreys, J. W., 39
Humphreys, R., 139
Humphreys, T., 124
Hunt, T., 48
Hunte, H. R., 72, 93, 125, 165, 183, 189
Hunter, F. A. R., 38, 45
Huntley, J., 140, 213
Huseby, G., 60
Hussey, F., 128
Hutchings, T. H., 91
Hutson, G. W., 124
Hutton, L., 39
Huxley, J., 217
Huyssen, C., 173
Hyman, D., 40, 41, 44, 57, 61, 63, 125, 134, 157, 169, 182, 183
Hyytiainen, T., 60

Ibbotson, G. D., 16, 90, 91, 116, 124, 166
Ibbotson, M. C., 186
Idanez, S., 139
Ifeajuna, E. A., 39
Ignatyev, A., 58, 112
Igun, S., 12, 13, 40
Iharos, S., 143
Iimura, Y., 23
Ikenaka, Y., 111
Illgen, K., 67, 185
Inaoko, M., 24
Iness, S. G., 131
Inkpen, B. J., see LAWTON, B. J.
Inoue, K., 22
Inoue, O., 22
Inoue, T., 19, 23
Ionesco, C., 42
Iqbal, M., 23, 40
Irons, F. C., 130

Irrgang, I., 62
Isaksson, K., 194
Ishii, T., 22
Iso-Hollo, V., 128, 158
Issakov, Y., 65, 73
Itkina, M., 61, 62, 66, 197
Itokowa, T., 23
Ivancic, I., 174
Ivanov, A., 192
Ivchenko, Y., 211
Iwai, H., 23
Iwamoto, M., 24

Jacenko, L., 189
Jackson, A. N. Strode-, 124, 127, 217
Jackson, B. D., 43, 56
Jackson, C., 46
Jackson, D., 174
Jackson, J. M., 17
Jackson, M., see NELSON, M.
Jacob, B., 72
Jacobi, H-J., 73
Jacobi, L., 62
Jacobs, D. H., 124, 128
Jacobs, F., 18, 86, 138, 189
Jacobsson, M., 187
Jahl, E., 63, 67, 71, 74, 97, 133, 134, 173, 189, 200
Jahns, A., see EHRHARDT, A.
James, A., 165
James, D. P., see PASCOE, D. P.
James, J., 210
James, L., 129, 191
Jamieson, L. A., 94
Janko, E., 185
Januchta, J., 70
Jarmrich, M., 18
Jarvinen, A., 50, 76
Jarvinen, K., 76
Jarvinen, M. H., 50, 60, 76, 97, 109, 131
Jarvinen, W., 76, 134
Jarvinen, Y., 76
Jarvis, F. W., 126
Jaskulka, S., 73
Jaunzeme, I., 133
Jaworska, D., 63, 67
Jay, J. M., 94
Jazy, M., 58, 116, 178, 191, 208
Jegathesan, M., 21
Jehlickova, J., 61, 198
Jellinghaus, M., 59
Jenkins, B. A., 171, 180,

186
Jenkins, C. L., 126, 129
Jenkins, D. A., 16, 39, 45, 56, 58, 59, 65, 99, 124, 164, 166, 207
Jenkins, R. A., 71
Jenner, B., 51, 98, 104, 131, 139, 160, 172, 195, 210, 216
Jennings, S., 180, 186
Jerbi, F., 14
Jerome, H. W., 15, 37, 137, 190
Jessee, L., 19
Jiles, P., 139
Jinno, M., 21
Jipcho, B., 12, 27, 38, 78, 193
Joachimowski, M., 69
Jobin, M., 211
Joginder Singh, 23
Johansson, G., 175
Johnson, C. C., 85, 129
Johnson, D., 38
Johnson, D. C., 19, 93
Johnson, D. J. N., 37, 39, 43, 59, 115, 124, 166
Johnson, E., 44
Johnson, G., 138
Johnson, J. (400m), 137
Johnson, J. (PV), 138
Johnson, P., 140
Johnson, R. L., 51, 98, 131, 139, 195, 216
Johnson, S. E., 129, 190
Johnson, T. Ll., 122, 124
Johnston, H. A., 124, 141
Johnston, T. F. K., 17, 192
Johnston, V., 41
Jones, A. J., 21
Jones, B. P., 133, 139, 203
Jones, D., see KONIHOWSKI, D.
Jones, D. H., 15, 39, 43, 56, 90, 124
Jones, H. W., 128, 138
Jones, I., 44
Jones, J., 129, 190
Jones, K. J., 46, 56, 124
Jones, L. W., 129, 137
Jones, P. A., 184
Jones, R., 15, 46, 56
Jones, S. S., 129
Jones, T. B., 15, 46, 56
Jonsson, B., 73
Jonsson, O., 57
Jordan, J. W., 45, 170, 183
Jordan, P., 19

Jordan, T., 59
Jordan, W. S., 45, 57
Joseph, D. L., 164
Jowett, D. W., 37
Joy, G., 201, 209
Joyce, R., 184
Joye, P., 59
Juantorena, A., 28, 36, 99, 115, 126, 135, 157, 189, 191
Jungwirth, S., 90, 116
Justus, K-P., 58, 72

Kachkoube, B., 13
Kacperczyk, K., 199
Kadhum, H., 22
Kadiri, J. S. O., 18
Kahma, P., 60, 66
Kainov, A., 73
Kalliomaki, A., 65, 69, 73
Kalliwoda, E., 74
Kalyayev, L., 59
Kamamoto, F., 23
Kamiya, E., 24
Kampfert, M., 74
Kane, H., 43
Kannenberg, B., 109, 132, 196
Kantanen, T., 65
Kao Yu-kuei, 24
Kapisheva, T., 74
Karakulov, N., 57, 59
Karasyov, N., 66, 70
Karbanova, M., 71
Karikari, O., 12
Karrer, 187
Karst, M., 65, 189
Karvonen, V. L., 58
Kasling, D., 133
Katayama, M., 24
Katolik, E., 70
Katz, E., 127
Kaufmann, C., 157, 191
Kawano, N., 23
Kazankina, T., 30, 66, 100, 115, 117, 132, 134, 189, 198, 212
Kearns, M., 166
Kefauver, E., 215
Keino, K., 12, 26, 37, 38, 100, 101, 116, 127, 128, 149, 150, 191, 192, 203
Kekkonen, U., 215
Kelley, E., 139
Kelley, J. J., 138
Kellner, 187
Kelly, B. H., 15, 68, 90
Kelly, F. W., 128
Kelly, P. C., 92, 164
Kemball, C. K., 17

Kemper, F-J., 65, 72, 191
Kennedy, R., 41, 45, 72
Kenny, P., 175
Kepp, L., 62
Kerner, H., 74
Kerr, A. C., 71
Kerr, G. E., 16, 37, 39, 137
Kerr, J. A., 94, 185
Kerr, M., 217
Kerr, R., 126
Kersch, M., 59
Keshmiri, D. A., 23
Kesiime, P., 13
Kessler, J., 173
Kessler, K., 70
Khalifa, O., 16
Khaligh, M., 22
Khaliq, A., 21
Khan, L., 39
Khristova, I., 71, 133, 199
Khristova, T., 75
Kidd, B., 38, 91
Kidner, D. F., 20
Kiernan, L., 165, 183
Kiesel, R. A., 128
Kigawa, Y., 22
Kilborn, P., see RYAN, P.
Kilby, B. L., 17, 38, 43, 56, 58, 111, 112
Kimaiyo, D., 12, 38, 39
Kimaiyo, F., 12, 38, 209
Kimball, R., 48
Kimihara, K., 22
Kimobwa, S., 148, 192
Kim Ok Sun, 23
Kinder, M., 59, 68
Kindermann, W., 59
King, B. J., 20, 43, 169
King, J., 18, 138
King, Lamonte, 172
King, Leamon, 129
King, R. W., 129
Kinnunen, J. V. P., 20, 109, 195
Kinsella, E. F., 18
Kinsey, D. C., 128
Kipkurgat, J., 37
Kiprugut, W., 12
Kirkpatrick, C. J., 92
Kirkpatrick, W. A., 92
Kirksey, M. M., 128
Kirkup, E., 17
Kirst, J., 61
Kirszenstein, I., see SZEWINSKA, I.
Kishimoto, S., 24
Kishkun, V., 60
Kisilyev, V., 71, 73, 101, 130
Kitchen, R., 211
Klauss, M., 60, 69, 73
Kleiber, J., 67
Klein, M., 185
Klepp, B., 189
Klepsch, W., 69
Klier, J., 62, 66, 70, 132
Klim, R., 60, 66, 131, 195, 210
Klimaszewski, A., 73
Klink, H., 73
Klobukowska, E., 61, 62, 66, 74, 133
Klopfer, G., 139, 211
Klopfer, M., 175
Knarr, O., 72
Knebel, A., 68
Knight, G., 17
Knowles, L. Y., see HEDMARK, L. Y.
Knox, E., 48
Knutsson, I., 74, 184, 212
Koba, T., 70
Kobayashi, Y., 23
Kobuszewski, J., 73
Koch, H., 68
Koch, M., 61, 62, 66, 70, 101, 132, 157, 159, 189, 197, 212
Koenig, W., 199
Kogo, B., 12
Kohl, F., 62
Kohler, H., 59, 68
Kojima, Y., 23
Kolar, K., 68
Kolehmainen, H., 76, 102, 106, 110, 111, 120, 127, 128, 175, 203
Kolehmainen, T., 102
Kolehmainen, W., 76, 102
Kolesnikov, N., 68
Koloska, A., 185
Kolpakova, T., 102, 133
Komar, W., 130
Komisova, V., 102, 132
Kondratyeva, L., 61, 62, 66, 81, 102, 103, 132
Kone, G., 12
Konihowski, D., 42, 140, 214
Konings-Rypers, 175
Konopacka, H., 133, 187
Konow, M., 73
Koppetsch, P., 74
Koppner, G., 187
Koskei, W., 39
Koskenniemi, T., 128
Kostric, W., 174
Kostuchenko, L., 74
Kotei, R. E., 18
Kotkas, K., 59
Koubkova, Z., 187
Koudijs, G. J. M., 62, 132
Kovacs, J., 59
Kowalski, R., 211
Koyama, T., 22
Kozakiewicz, E., 103
Kozakiewicz, W., 65, 69, 103, 130, 144, 194, 209
Kraan, G., 61
Kraenzlein, A. C., 88, 107, 126, 128, 130, 134
Kragbe, S., 13
Kratochvilova, J., 70, 212
Kratschmer, G., 51, 103, 104, 160, 195, 210
Kraus, A., 24
Kraus, B., 70
Krause, C., 133
Krauss, K., 62, 187
Kreek, A., 60
Krenz, E. C. W., 52
Krepkina, V., 62, 133, 196
Kretschmer, B., 140
Krivonosov, M., 60
Krivozub, S., 73
Kriz, L., 59
Krug, B., 62
Krumm, D., 73
Krupinski, W., 73
Krzesinska, E., 133
Krzyszkowiak, Z., 58, 128, 192
Kuck, J., 130
Kudinskiy, V., 58, 65, 69
Kuha, J., 192
Kuhne, R., 62, 133
Kuhnel, I., 62
Kuhse, A., 74
Kula, D., 104, 131
Kumar, P., 23
Kunze, H-J., 65
Kuragina, O., 162, 200
Kurihara, A., 24
Kurrat, K-D., 72
Kuryan, A., 65
Kuschmann, M., 58
Kusocinski, J., 127
Kuts, V., 28, 33, 58, 90, 104, 106, 127, 143, 192, 203
Kuznyetsov, V., 61
Kyle, M. E. E., 183, 212, 213
Kynos, J., 59

Laayouni, Z., 14
La Beach, L. B., 156
Ladany, S., 174

Ladoumegue, J., 116
Laeesker, O., 59, 60
Laing, L. A., 129
Laird, R., 139
Lakka, M. R., 158
Lal, M., 23
Lamitie, B., 66
Lamy, J., 41
Lancaster, B., 162
Landon, R. W., 129
Landstrom, E., 60
Landy, J. M., 25, 33, 116
Lane, J., 107
Lange, J., 73
Langlace, C., 112
Lannaman, S. M., 40, 41, 45, 57, 68, 72, 74, 93, 125, 165, 169, 183, 189, 212
Lansdell, E., 18
Lanzi, M., 83, 188
Laopinkarn, U., 23
LaPlante, D., 140, 172, 213
Larder, S., 91
Larner, G. E., 124, 131, 132
Larrabee, M. D., 16, 126, 129, 191
Larrieu, F., 172
Larsson, L. A., 58
Larsson, S., 175
Larva, H. E., 127
Laskau, H., 90, 172
Lattany, M., 16
Lauer, K. M., 59, 88, 115, 129, 193
Laukkanen, V., 73
Launela, K., 75
Laut, D., 139
Lavery, T. P., 38
Lawlor, J. F., 20
Lawson, C. P., 39, 179
Lawton, B. J., 41, 45, 57, 94, 170, 184, 213
Lay, S. A., 40
Leach, 187
Leahy, C., 76, 86, 124, 134
Leahy, P. J., 76, 86, 124
Lean, D. F., 18, 38
Leather, D. S., 57, 117, 170, 183, 186, 198
Leavitt, R. G., 134
Lebeau, L., 74
Lebedyev, K., 208
Leconey, J. A., 128
Lees, N., 71
Leggett, A., 184
Lehtinen, L. A., 127

Lehtonen, E., 131
Leichum, W., 60
Leigh-Wood, R., 39, 43
Leiteritz, K-H., 65
Lelievre, G., 196
Lemming, E. V., 97, 131, 134
Lemmon, J., 216
Leonard, S., 137, 181, 189, 190
Lepik, T., 69
Lerwill, A. L., 19, 39, 43, 92, 167
Lerwill, S. W., 57, 62, 86, 125
Lewis, Carl, 76, 209
Lewis, Carol, 76
Lewis, G., 39
Lewis, L. C., 43, 56, 59
Lewis, P. J., 68, 91
Licznerski, Z., 59
Liddell, E. H., 106, 124, 126, 157, 181
Lidman, E., 59
Liebetrau, C., 66
Lievore, C., 195
Lightbody, J. D., 126, 127, 128, 134
Lightman, S., 179
Li Hsiao-hui, 24
Liimatainen, H., 128
Limberg, K., 185
Lindberg, A., 60
Lindberg, E. F. J., 129
Lindberg, K., 156
Lindblom, G., 130
Lindgren, B., 18, 138
Lindner, D., 61, 108
Lindsay, M. R., 19, 45, 93, 168
Lindsay, R. A., 124, 129
Lines, M., 187
Linge, M., 129
Linnhoff, E., 59
Lipowski, L., 73
Liquori, M., 17, 138, 172, 208
Lismont, K., 58
Little, P. D., 91
Littlewood, A. M., 94, 165, 171, 185, 213
Lituyev, Y., 59, 89
Litvinov, S., 189, 195
Litvinyenko, L., 67, 73
Livermore, J., 214
Livesey, D. J., 92, 167
Li Wei-nan, 23
Ljunggren, J. A., 61, 132
Llopart, J., 61
Lloyd-Johnson, T., see

JOHNSON, T. Ll.
Loaring, J. W., 38, 39
Lobastov, S., 196
Lochhead, J. M., 94
Lock, B., 203
Lockhoff, B., 74
Lockley, M., 184
Lockton, C. L., 203
Lodge, R. J., 179
Lohse, I., 62
Loikkanen, A., 69
London, J. E., 124
Long, D. C., 113, 121, 130, 194, 195
Long, L., 136
Long, M. W., 126
Longden, S. J., 94, 171, 186, 214
Longe, C. C. O., 46, 169
Loomis, F. F., 128
Lopes, C., 48
Losch, H., 60
Lossman, J., 111
Louis, S., 110, 127
Loukola, T. A., 128
Lovasz, L., 20
Lovell, V. C., 186
Lovelock, J. E., 37, 82, 116, 127, 178, 188
Lovland, H., 131
Lowe, D. G. A., 108, 115, 125, 126
Lowe, P. B., see CROPPER, P. B.
Lucking, M. T., 40, 43, 93
Lund, V., 175
Lundberg, R. L., 60
Lundmark, K., 18, 65
Lundqvist, E. H., 97, 131
Lundqvist, K., 59
Lunis, J., 59
Lunn, G. A., 41, 42, 45, 48, 187
Lusis, E., see OZOLINA, E.
Lusis, J., 60, 61, 63, 66, 97, 109, 131, 195
Luttge, M., 63
Lutz, M., 16
Lynch, J. A. C., 45, 57, 68, 70, 72, 93, 169, 183, 189, 212
Lysenko L., see SHEVTSOVA, L.
Lyungin, Y., 109

Mabuza, R., 12
McAndrew, R., 92
McArdle, P., 138

McArthur, K. K., 127
McCabe, B. F., 43
McCafferty, I., 45, 48, 91
McComas, E., 174
McCorquodale, A., 125
McCredie, N., 140
McCubbins, C., 138
McCullagh, P. J., 179
McCullouch, E., 138, 193
McDaniel, M. I., 133, 140
McDermott, K. M., 93
MacDonald, B., 125
McDonald, J. O., 129
Macdonald, L. T., 93, 125, 165, 170, 212
McDonald, P. J., 122, 130, 131
McDonnell, W., 213
Macfarlane, J. D., 39
McFarlane, M. A., 71, 72, 91
McGhee, J., 38, 45, 110
McGibbon, C. C., 42
McGrath, M., 19
McGrath, M. J., 82, 131
Macgregor, D., 174
MacGregor, J., 72
McGuiness, J., 91
McGuire, E. M., 132, 139, 163
Machura, R., 73
Macintosh, H. M., 125, 128
MacIsaac, J., 56, 59
McIver, A. D., 92
McKenley, H. H., 129, 157
McKenzie, A. C. A., 71, 167
Mackenzie, M., 46
Mackenzie, W., 45
McLachlan, G., 169
McLean, T., 16
McLeod, M. J., 43, 47, 95 164
McMaster, A. E., 39, 45, 91
McMeekin, E., 72
McMillan, K., 140
McNab, P., 175
McNaughton, D., 129
Macounova, L., 199
Macquet, M., 20
McSorley, J. V., 20, 43, 169
McStravick, B. S., 20
McTear, H., 207
McWhirter, A. R., 217
McWhirter, N. D., 217
Maddocks, C., 169, 211

Madubost, J., 60
Maguire, E., 41, 45
Maguire, M. L., 46, 72, 170, 186
Mahlendorf, W., 59, 129
Mahr, E., 172, 213
Mahy, M., 72
Maina, J., 12, 189
Mainka, K., 207
Maiyoro, N., 100
Major, I., 69
Makeyeva, M., 149, 199
Makhan Singh, 23
Maki, T. A., 58
Maksimczyk, K., 210
Malan, D., 16, 191
Malan, E., 19
Maletzki, D., 62, 133
Malinowski, B., 27, 59, 71, 72, 80, 110, 128
Mallin, L. K., 185
Maly, V., 69
Mamo Wolde, 11, 12, 128, 203
Mandl, H., 174
Maniak, W. J., 57
Manley, A. P., 85, 94, 214
Manley, D. G., see HALL, D. G.
Manley, M., 138
Manley, N., 215
Mann, R., 14, 138
Manning, A. P., 38
Manning, M., 132, 139, 172,, 212
Manoliu, L., 122, 133, 134, 185
Manolov, T., 73
Maplestone, R., 208
Mapstone, S. L., 45, 72
Marasescu, N., 54, 70, 177, 198, 212
Marie, A. J., 59
Marien, L., 174
Marin, J., 196, 211
Markin, V., 112, 126, 129, 207
Markus, D., 23
Marlow, P., 21, 179
Marquardt, C., 62
Marriott, M. M., 186
Marsh, H., 138, 209
Martin, B. A., 45, 72
Martin, D. E., 111
Martin, J. D., 139
Martin du Gard, J-P., 59
Martinez, I., 140
Martin-Jones, R., 46, 94, 185
Martynek, W., 73

Mashburn, J. W., 129
Maskell, E. M., 41
Maskinskov, Y., 61
Maslakova, L., 62
Maslovskaya, V., 62
Mason, M. M., see BROWN, M. M.
Matay, A., 71, 77, 213
Mathe, G., 173, 174
Mathers, C., 184
Mathews, M. J., see WILLARD, M. J.
Mathias, R. B., 51, 113, 131, 203, 215, 216
Mathis, J., 216
Matson, J. R., 113, 121, 130, 139, 144, 153, 194
Matthews, C. H., 38
Matthews, K. J., 20, 21, 56, 61, 81, 108, 113, 125, 132, 169, 179, 211
Matthews, V., 75, 126, 129
Matthews, V. C., 18, 191
Matuschewski, M., 58, 65
Matveyev, I., 73
Matzdorf, P., 86, 138, 193
Mauermayer, G., 53, 63, 133, 153, 187
May, J., 56, 149, 191
May, P. J., 40
Maync, P., 20
Mayuchaya, K., 63
Mazepa, Y., 73
Meadows, E. E., 130, 144
Meagher, A. A., 41
Meakin, A. F., 39, 43, 56, 90
Means, L., 173
Medina, L., 138
Mee, R., 174
Megnin, C., 56
Meite, A., 12
Mejzlikova, M., 187
Mellander, 134
Mellor, F. N., 133
Melnik, F., 53, 63, 67, 97, 113, 133, 189, 200
Melopene, 111
Mendenhall, D., 18
Mendoza, R., 138
Mends, B. K., 39
Menis, A., 114, 200
Mennea, P., 15, 57, 58, 64, 68, 114, 126, 145, 156, 181, 190, 207
Meredith, J. E., 114, 126, 129
Meredith, K., 91
Merrill, J., 139, 140, 213

Merriman, J. L., 46, 166
Meszynski, I., 74, 213
Metcalf, J., 18
Metcalfe, A. P., 16, 43, 56, 125, 166
Metcalfe, J. P., 39
Metcalfe, R. H., 129, 215
Metzner, A., 58, 59
Meyfarth, U., 133, 199, 203
Michel, S., 74
Michelsen, A., 111
Michie, J. F., 45
Mickler, I., 62, 66, 67, 133, 134, 185
Middleton, A. D., 91
Middleton, R. C., 43, 179
Mignon, H., 72
Mihalic, F., 48
Mikaelsson, J. F., 61, 132
Mikhailov, A., 59, 65
Miki, T., 23
Milburn, R., 18, 88, 115, 116, 128, 138, 193
Miles, B., 216
Milhau, R., 68
Milkha Singh, 16, 21, 37
Miller, G. A., 92, 167
Miller, L. (Can), 38
Miller, L. (Jam), 39, 207
Miller, L. A., 94, 165, 170, 171, 213
Miller, S., 175
Miller, W. W., 130
Milligan, W. R., 216
Mills, A., 112
Mills, C. (NZ), 175
Mills, C. (USA), 75
Mills, L. R., 19, 40
Mills, R. G., 21, 56, 179
Mills, W. M., 127
Milne, R. B. W., 16
Mimoun, A., 47, 48, 111, 127
Miranda, J., 138
Mirza Khan, 22
Misson, T. W., 179
Missoni, O., 217
Mistoul, O., 14
Mitchell, A. E., 40
Mitchell, R., 37, 207
Mitchell, R. R., 19, 39, 43, 92, 164
Miura, N., 22
Moens, R., 83, 115, 155, 191
Mogenburg, D., 65, 69, 73, 193, 209
Mohamed, Y., 12
Mohinder Singh (1500),

22
Mohinder Singh (TJ), 23
Mohinder Singh Gill, 23
Monk, C. L., 16, 64, 91
Montgomery, E., 140
Moody, H. E. A., 43
Moorcroft, D. R., 16, 27, 37, 43, 56, 91, 164
Moore, A. L., 19, 43, 68, 71, 73, 92, 93, 164, 168, 210
Moore, B. R. H., 45, 184
Moore, C. H., 128
Morale, S., 18, 59, 89, 193
Morbey, J., 168
Moreau, J. T., 133
Morehead, B., 172
Morgan, R., 45
Morgan, V. E., 43
Morimoto, M., 21
Morita, M., 22
Morita, N., 24
Moritz, G., 74
Moritz, S., 75
Morley, S. A. J., 184
Moroz, A., 69
Morris, B. H. A., 91
Morris, G. E., 50, 131, 216
Morris, M., 71, 72
Morris, P. A., 92
Morrison, P. J. A., 15
Morrow, B. J., 87, 126, 129
Morton, M. A., 48
Moseke, C., 140
Moses, E., 14, 18, 27, 28, 89, 117, 128, 172, 189, 193, 209
Moseyev, L., 58
Moshiashvili, A., 69
Mottershead, A. D., 91, 164
Mottley, W., 16, 37, 39, 91
Mubarak Shah, 22
Muench, A., 73
Muinonen, V., 58
Muir, N., 71, 72
Mulhall, G., 213
Muller, B., 75
Muller, E., 73,
Muller, R., 133
Mundinger, E., 74
Munkelt, T., 59, 65, 69, 117, 119, 128, 189
Munson, D. C., 127
Munyala, J., 172
Muraki, M., 19
Murase, K., 24

Muravyov, V., 129
Murchison, I. J., 129
Murchison, L. C., 128
Murdoch, R. L., 45
Murofushi, S., 23
Muroya, Y., 21
Murphy, F., 16
Murphy, T., 137
Murray, D-M. L., see HARTLEY, D-M. L.
Murro, M., 172, 210
Mussabini, S. A., 86
Musyoki, F., 39
Myasnikov, V., 69
Myatt, P., 180
Myers, L. E., 118, 157
Myricks, L., 53, 189
Myyra, J. J., 97, 131

Nabein, K., 72
Naessens, Y., 72
Nagata, M., 22
Nagayasu, H., 23
Nagle, D., 184, 186
Naidenko, V., 73
Nakanishi, M., 23
Nallet, J-C., 59, 64, 65
Nambu, A., 23
Nambu, C., 130, 163
Nankeville, G. W., 56
Nash, P., 15, 16, 190
Nashatur Singh Sidhu, 23
Nawaz, M., 20, 23
Naylor, M., 92, 164, 167, 209
Nazarova, I., 133
Nazhimov, A., 23
Neame, D. M. L., 43
Neckermann, K., 59
Needham, S. J., 185
Negrete, F., 138
Nehemiah, R., 88, 117, 119, 138, 172, 189, 193, 209
Nehru, P., 215
Neil, D. A., 45, 57, 169, 183
Nekesa, E., 14
Nelson, H., 39
Nelson, M., 40, 41, 46, 132, 157
Nelson, V., 138
Nelson, W. H., 38
Nemeshazi, M., 70
Nemeth, A., see RANKY, A.
Nemeth, I., 76, 119, 131
Nemeth, M., 20, 76, 98, 119, 131, 140, 195
Nemsovsky, P., 69

231

Netter, M., 133
Neufville, M. F., 41, 68, 70, 93, 139, 157, 183, 197
Nevala, P. L., 131
Newhouse, F., 129
Newton, A. L., 127
Ngetich, J., 39
Niare, N., 13
Ni Chih-chin, 86
Nichol, W. P., 125
Nicholas, T. L., 156
Nichols, A. H., 47, 125
Nickel, G., 69
Nicol, G., 125
Nicolau, C., 59
Nieder, W. H., 121, 130, 153, 194
Nielson, S., 139
Nihill, V. P., 21, 56, 61, 125, 169, 179, 211
Nijboer, G., 111, 209
Nikiciuk, W., 20, 66
Nikitenko, L., 70
Nikitina, I., 74, 212
Nikitina, V., see KOMISOVA, V.
Nikkanen, Y., 97
Nikkari, S., 192
Nikka Singh, 22
Niklander, E., 130
Nikolic, V., 61, 74, 183, 198
Nikula, P. K., 18, 60, 194
Nikulin, I., 73
Nilsson, B., 60
Nilsson, E., 209
Nilsson, I., 59
Nilsson, K-A., 18
Nimmo, M., 185
Nishiuchi, F., 23
Nitzsche, C., 74, 75
Niwa, K., 18
Njiri, W., 39
Noeding, E., 140
Noel-Baker, P. J., see BAKER, P. J. Noel-
Nokes, M. C., 40, 43, 83, 125
Nordwig, W., 60, 65, 69, 130, 194
Norman, D., 40, 41, 46
Norman, G. J., 17, 208
Noro, S., 22
Norpoth, H., 65, 69, 191
Norris, A. J., 43
Norris, D. S., 19
Norris, F., 17, 46, 48, 56
Norris, K. L., 17, 346
North G. A., 46

Norton, O. R., 129, 137, 190
Nowosz, Z., 59, 64, 68
Nsenu, O., 13
Nuckles, G., 68
Nunez A., 140
Nurmi, P. J., 30, 34, 100, 102, 106, 120, 127, 128, 134, 175, 203
Nutting, P. A., see PRYCE, P. A.
Nyamau, H., 39, 129
Nygrynova, J., 71, 74

Oakes, G. J., 12, 209
Oakes, J. M., 45, 68, 94, 165, 171, 185, 213
Oakley, A., 139
Obasogie, G., 12, 209
Obeng, E., 12
Obonai, S., 24
O'Brien, A., 184
O'Brien, K., 193
O'Brien, W. P., 113, 121, 130, 139, 153, 216
O'Callaghan, P., 82, 131, 152
Ochola, Y., 13
O'Connor, D., 211
O'Connor, L. G., 38
O'Connor, P. J., 107, 134
Oda, M., 130
Odam, D. J. B., see TYLER, D. J. B.
Odlozil, J., 191
Oelsner, M., see GOHR, M.
Oerter, A. A., 52, 53, 121, 131, 134, 139, 151, 174, 195, 210
Ofili, E., 12
Ogura, S., 23
Ogushi, K., 22
O'Hara, L., 208
Ohlert, H-H., 72
Ohlsson, M., 175
Okamoto, K., 23
Okamoto, M., 24
Okamoto, N., 20, 23
Okano, E., 21, 22
Okazaki, T., 23
Okeke, E., 14
Ok Ja Paik, 24
Okoli, A., 13
Okorokova, A., 67
Okuwobi, O., 18
Okwara, H., 14
Oladitan, O., 19, 92
Olafsson, L., 107, 213
Olausson, G., 74

Oldfield, B., 19, 122, 144, 153, 172, 210
Oliver, B. T., 40
Olivier, W., 91
Olizaryenko, N., 115, 122, 123, 132, 198, 212
Olizaryenko S., 123
Olney, V., 126
Olowu, K. A. B., 19
Olsen, P., 40, 210
Omagbemi. J. S. O., 15
Onizuka, J., 23
O'Rourke, M., 210
Orphall, D., 185
Orr, J., 39
Orthmann, H-J., 72
Ortis, V., 58
Ortiz, C., 139
Orton, G. W., 128
Osborn, H. M., 129, 131
Osborne, S. R., 20
Osendarp, M. B., 57
Oshikoya, M., 13, 42
Ostermeyer, M. O. M., 133
Ota, T., 19
Otkalenko, N., 61, 115
Ottey, M., 212
Ottley, D. C., 20, 165, 169, 210
Ottoz, E., 18, 59, 69
Ouko, R., 37, 39, 129
Ovett, S. M. J., 16, 36, 56, 58, 65, 71, 72, 95, 115, 116, 125, 126, 134, 135, 136, 164, 166, 189, 191, 207, 208
Owen, E. 125
Owen, J., 156
Owens, J. C., 27, 30, 52, 107, 126, 129, 130, 136
Owusu, J., 13, 40
Oyakhire, A., 13
Ozolina, E., 63, 109, 133, 200

Pack, H. E., 43
Packer, A. E., 45, 57, 115, 126, 132, 137, 142, 157, 169, 183, 185, 198
Paddock, C. W., 126, 128, 156
Paez, A., 68
Page, E. L., 43, 56
Paige, D., 138
Paivarinta, P., 48, 192, 208
Palkowsky, J., 73
Palmer, L., 41
Palmer, M. G., 18

Palmer, W. B. L., 19
Pamich, A., 49, 61, 108, 132, 196
Pangelova, T., 70
Pani, J., 66
Panzo, H., 72
Papageorgopoulos, V., 15
Papanicolaou, C., 144, 194
Papp, M., 63
Paragi, F., 98, 119, 140, 195, 210
Parduman Singh, 23
Parker, F. J., 56
Parker, J. M., 18, 43, 68, 88, 92, 167
Parker, M. (Aus) 42
Parker, M. (NZ), 179, 180
Parkin, S. H., see SHERWOOD, S. H.
Parks, M., 129, 172
Parlett, H. J., 37, 43, 56, 58
Parnell, C. W., 37
Pascoe, A. P., 16, 18, 38, 43, 56, 59, 63, 65, 68, 69, 88, 89, 92, 125, 167
Pascoe, D. P., 93, 169, 183
Pashley, A., 45, 57, 126, 216
Paterson, A. S., 45, 56, 59, 86, 203
Patton, J., 139
Patton, M. E., 84, 126, 129, 156
Paul, J. F., 41, 45, 57, 62, 126, 182, 183
Paunonen, A., 72, 208
Pavlicic, J., 70, 197
Pawsey, J. B., 93, 183
Payne, A. H., 20, 40, 43, 46, 83, 95, 168, 174, 210
Payne, C. R., 46, 122, 171, 175, 185, 213
Payne, H., 112
Payne, L., 47
Pazera, A., 42
Peake, T., 41
Peat, V., 45, 57, 169, 182, 183
Pechenkina, N., 70
Peckham, J., 41
Peckham, L., 39
Pede-Erdkamp, A., 112
Pedersen, T., 97, 109, 195
Pedraza, J., 26, 81
Peikert M., 75
Peltzer, O., 108

Pender, M., 129
Penes, M., 71, 75, 133
Pennel, J. T., 18, 144, 194
Pennington, A., 56
Penny, A. W., 38, 43
Penny, G. C., 165, 186
Peoples, M., 16
Perera, C., see BELL, C.
Perez, P., 139, 151, 194, 210
Perka, D., 70
Perkins, A. F., 46
Perkins, P. E. M., 93, 183
Peter, J., 65
Peters, C., 175
Peters, J. H., 43, 110, 111, 112, 141, 142
Peters M. E., 42, 46, 94, 126, 134, 141, 142, 162, 170, 171, 184, 185, 186, 200
Peters, W., 60
Peterson, C., 213
Petkova, M., see VERGOVA, M.
Petnjaric, L., 74
Petrova, Tonka, 66, 70
Petrova, Totka, 54, 66, 189
Petrovsky V., 30
Pettersson, S., 174
Pettersson, W., 130
Pettet, S., 41, 45, 72
Pfeffer, K., 209
Pfuller, I., 140
Pharaoh, M., 19, 43, 53
Pheidippides, 110
Philipp, L., 17
Philippides, 110
Philps, R. T., 93
Pianzola, F., 187
Piatkowska, M., 62
Piatkowski, E., 60, 66, 195
Pickard, V. W., 39
Pickerell, M. J., 183
Pickering, J. C., 45, 57, 62, 125
Piecyk, D., 199
Piercy, P. J., 93, 183
Piercy, V., 112
Pietri, D., 110, 128
Pietrzyk, J., 73
Pigni, P., 48, 198
Pike, M. W., 56, 59
Pilbrow, A. G., 43
Pilgrim, P. H., 127, 134
Pinnington, P., 90
Pinto, L., 21
Pinto, P., 174

Piquemal, C., 57, 59
Pirie, A., 76
Pirie, D. A. G., 16, 17, 56, 76, 83, 90, 104, 105, 106, 125, 142, 143, 166, 191
Pirie, S., 45, 57, 183
Pirnie, B., 139
Pishchulin, B., 73
Piskulin, A., 66, 69
Plachy, J., 68
Plain, B. J., 17
Platt, S. M., 42, 45, 98, 171, 185
Pletts, M., 76
Plummer, A. C., 157, 191
Podeswa, B., 62
Podluzhniy, V., 60, 66, 73
Pogyor, K., 74
Pohland, W., see STROTZER, W.
Poirier, R., 65
Polhill, A., 16
Pollak, B., 67, 75, 200
Pollock, J. F., 41, 198
Polyakov, V., 73
Polyakova, N., 62
Ponitzsch, R., 209
Ponomaryeva, N., 63, 133, 134
Popkova, V., 70
Popov, S., 58, 111
Popova, S., 79
Porhola, V., 60, 130
Porritt, A., 216
Porter, C. H. A., 125
Porter, G. A., 126
Porter, H. F., 129
Porter, S. R., 18, 167
Porter, W. F., 128
Possamai, A., 70
Potgieter, G. C., 38, 39
Potgieter, H., 20
Potsch, H., 174
Pouchkov, A., 73
Powell, J., 19, 139, 195
Powell, M., 71
Power, W. D., 17, 38
Prackova, A., 74
Praetz, I., 62
Prasad, M., 23
Prefontaine, S., 138, 203, 208
Press, I., 66, 70, 77, 132, 134, 141, 200
Press T., 62, 63, 67, 77, 133, 134, 153, 199, 200
Pribilinec, J., 73, 211
Price, B., 18, 38, 46, 68, 71, 73, 92, 164, 167, 209

233

Price, N. G., 39
Price, R. E., 39
Pridie, K. H., 43
Prinstein, M., 107, 130, 134, 162
Probert, M., 72, 126, 183
Prokofiev, A., 129, 209
Prokhorenko, Y., 69
Prokop, L., 63, 200
Prorochenko, T., 133
Providokhina, T., 61, 123, 212
Prudencio, N., 51, 194
Pryce, P. A., 94, 184
Przesdzing, P., 73
Puce, G., 40
Pugh, D. C., 43, 56, 58, 59, 63
Pujazon, R., 47, 58
Pullard, R., 19
Purcell, M., 183, 184
Pusko, A., 73
Puttemans, E., 69, 78, 192, 203, 208

Quarrie, D., 15, 16, 37, 39, 46, 126, 137, 145, 190, 207
Quax D., 148, 192
Quinn, J. F., 128
Quinton, C. L., 45, 57, 126, 184
Quist, B., 139

Rabsztyn, E., 146
Rabsztyn, G., 70, 74, 89, 146, 189, 199, 213
Raby E. M., 45
Radford, P. F., 15, 39, 43, 56, 125, 156, 157, 166, 180, 207
Radideau, M., 187
Radke, L., 132
Radtke, H., 74
Raduly, E., 67
Rahal, L., 13
Raines, A., 111
Rajamani, M., 23
Rajasaari, O., 60
Ralph, M., 92
Rampling, G. L., 37, 39, 43, 125, 129
Ramsden, D. I., 57, 183
Rand, M. D., 42, 45, 57, 68, 94, 108, 126, 133, 134, 137, 142, 146, 171, 184, 185, 186, 199, 213
Randle, B. E. M., 180
Range, R., 138
Rangeley, W., 38, 43, 125

Ranjit Singh, 21
Ranky, A., 63, 133
Rashchupkin, V., 131, 147
Rasmussen, D., 74
Ratanapol, A., 21
Ratcliffe, A., 39
Rathbone, D. L., 39, 43
Ratjen, D., 62
Rau, R., 156
Rault, L., 208
Rautanen, T., 175
Rautavaara, K. T., 131, 216
Rautio, K. J. V., 60
Ravenscroft, J., 72
Rawson, M. A., 16, 43, 56, 58, 91
Ray, E., 64, 207
Ray, R., 137
Raziq, H. G., 18, 22, 38
Read, N. R., 132, 179
Readdy, C., 112
Reed, I. M., 40
Reed, O., 216
Reeve, S. D., 42, 45, 68, 94, 165, 185, 213
Reichenbach, I., 74
Reidpath, C. D., 126, 129
Reiff, G. E. G., 127, 188
Reimann, H-G., 26, 108, 109, 196
Reiser, G., 41
Reitz, C. R., 72, 209
Remigino, L. J., 126, 129
Rendina, C., 41, 212
Renwick, G. R., 125
Repser, H., 75
Reske, H-J., 59
Revans, R. W., 43
Reynolds, M. E., 16, 43, 125
Rezayev, V., 211
Rezkova, M., 62, 133
Rhadi, A., 48
Rhoden, V. G., 126, 129
Ricci, E., 185
Richard, R., 137
Richards, A. W., 129
Richards, I. W., 180
Richards, M. D., 18
Richards, R. E., 130, 138, 144
Richards, T., 111, 125
Richardson, K. J., 43
Richardson, S., 39
Richter, A., 70, 132, 133, 197
Richtzenhain, K., 143
Riddick, S., 15, 16, 129

Rider, H., 212
Ridley, R., 41, 45, 170, 183, 184, 186
Riehm, K-H., 66, 147, 148, 189, 195
Rienstra, C., 172
Rimmer, G., 164
Rimmer, J. T., 125, 127, 128
Rintamaki, J. A., 18
Ripley, D., 172
Ripley, R. N., 125
Ritchie, D., 209
Ritchie, M. E., 53, 165, 171, 185, 213
Ritola, V. J., 127, 128, 175
Ritter, L., 140, 213
Rivers, P., 42
Roberson, I., 138
Roberts, D., 103, 194, 209
Roberts, D. L., 91
Roberts, E., 39
Roberts, J. E., 185
Roberts, R. M., 18
Roberts, W., 37, 43, 56, 125, 129
Robertson, A. J., 47, 125, 127
Robertson, D.McN., 45
Robeson, P., 216
Robinson, A., 19, 130, 139, 172, 189
Robinson, C., 48
Robinson, E., 132
Robinson, J. (NZ), 174
Robinson, J. (USA), 138
Robinson, M. M., 37
Robinson, R. (NZ), 174
Robinson, R. (USA), 30, 190
Robinson, S. J., 47, 125, 127
Robinson, T. A., 37
Robson, J., 45, 68, 164
Rochard, R., 58
Roche, K. J., 38
Rodgers, W., 148, 192, 208, 209
Roe, A., 213
Roelants, G., 47, 48, 58, 128, 148, 158, 173, 174, 192, 209
Roesen, B., 71
Rogers, A. J., 132
Rogers, R., 18
Rohde, B., 62, 133
Roininen, L. J., 40
Romanova, G., 61
Romero, C., 140

Romero, R., 137
Rono, H., 12, 17, 38, 106, 135, 148, 158, 189, 192, 193, 208, 209
Rono, K., 12
Roper, I., 72
Rosa, L., 22
Rosani, D., 54
Roscoe, J. V., 41, 45, 93, 183, 184
Rose, N. H., 17, 47, 48, 65, 164, 208
Rose, R. W., 52, 130, 152
Rosendahl H., 63, 67, 71, 133, 142, 149, 158, 199, 200
Rosenfeld, F., 132
Ross, B., 138
Rossland, F., 73
Rossley, K., 89, 149, 199, 213
Rot, E., 23, 24 ,
Rothenburg, H-J., 28
Roudny, J., 58
Rousseau, J., 60, 66, 69
Rowe, A., 19, 40, 43, 56, 60, 153, 168
Rowley, M., 186
Rowley, S., 127
Royle, D., 165
Royle, L. C., 125
Rozsavolgyi, I., 143, 191
Rozsnyoi, S., 58
Rubsam, D., 74
Ruckborn, H-J., 66
Rudd, B. G. D'U., 126
Rudenkov, V., 131
Rudolph, W. G., 132, 133, 150, 157, 163, 196, 197
Ruff, J. E., 183
Rukavishnikova, O., 200
Rushmer, A. T., 44
Russell, A., 125, 128
Russell, H. A., 128
Rut, T., 60
Rwabiryage, C., 14
Ryan, P., 41, 42, 46, 184, 198, 213
Ryan, P. J., 82, 131
Ryffel, M., 69
Ryun, J. R., 36, 116, 144, 150, 178, 191, 207, 208

Saaristo, J., 131
Sabie, C., 187
Sagawa, N., 22, 23
Saik Oik Cam, 23
Saint-Gilles, F., 59
Sainte-Rose, L., 59

Sakamoto, M., 22
Sakamoto, T., 18, 22
Sakurai, K., 19, 23
Salin, R., 61, 197
Saling, G. J., 128
Salisbury, J. E., 16, 44, 56, 59, 125
Salminen, I., 58, 127
Salvat, F. G. J., 16
Salve, E., 68
Salzedo, A., 37
Samotyosova, L., 196
Sampson, E. J., 44, 57, 59
Sampson, M., 112
Sanadze, L., 59
Sanchez, J., 139
Sanderson, J. B., 20
Sanderson, T. I., 42, 45, 57, 98, 165, 171, 185, 213
Sandhu, K., 23
Sandiford, J., 140
Sando, F. D., 44, 46, 48, 57
Sandstrom, E. R., 39, 44, 57
Sanford, J., 15, 95, 156
Sang, J., 39, 129
San Romani, A. (Snr), 76
San Romani, A. (Jnr), 76
Santee, W. D., 14, 142
Santona, B., 59
Sanyeyev, V., 52, 60, 66, 69, 130, 151, 163, 172, 194, 210
Sapeya, V., 64
Sapka, K., 60, 69
Saracevic, Z., 70
Sarengat, M., 21, 22
Sarna, M., 62
Sarria, M., 140
Sarteur, A., 59
Saruwatari, T., 22
Sarwan Singh, 22
Sato, H., 24
Sato, M., 23
Saunders, D. S., 45
Saunders, G. B., 47
Saunders, G. T., 38, 44
Saunders, Y., 41, 183
Savel, I., 18
Savic, M., 16
Savidan, W. J., 38
Savidge, J. A., 40, 44
Sawada, B., 22
Sawaki, K., 22
Sawall, W., 211
Scarr, M. M., 57
Scarsbrook, S. C., 38, 44
Scartezzini, M., 65

Schafer, G., 185
Schallau, W., 174
Schaller, J., see KLIER, J.
Schardt, A. A., 127
Scheele, H., 59
Schein, E., 59
Schenke, S., 64
Scheuring, J., 59
Schiel, R., 18
Schigin, A., 73
Schittenhelm, E., 62
Schlaak, E., see JAHL, E.
Schladen, F., 174
Schleime, M., 173
Schloske, H-R., 59
Schmelz, R., 92
Schmid, H., 27, 28, 59, 65, 209
Schmidt, E., 151
Schmidt, K., 79, 172, 200, 213
Schmidt, R., 67, 70, 71
Schmidt, W. (E. Ger), 60, 66, 73, 151, 182, 189, 195, 210
Schmidt, W. (W. Ger), 195
Schmitt, J., 59
Schmitz, F., 174
Schmul, L., 74
Schneider, U., 72
Schoknecht, I., see SLUP-IANEK, I.
Scholz, J. V., 126, 128
Schots, L., 48
Schroder, H., 62
Schroder, K-H., 173
Schroder, T., 72
Schroeder, W., 60
Schueler, C., 211
Schul, R. K., 127
Schule, F. W., 128
Schult, J., 73
Schumann, L., 187
Schwab, F., 61
Schwarz, J., 64
Scott, A. W., 57, 59
Scott, P. N., 92
Scott, S., 16, 135, 172
Scott, S. D., see REEVE, S. D.
Scott-Oldfield, J. R. A., 18
Scouler, D. E., 187
Scrivens, J. E., 126
Scully, T., 211
Scutt, S., 91, 164
Seagren, R., 130, 138, 144, 194, 216
Seagrove, W. R., 125

235

Searle, H., 175
Sechenova, Y., 61
Seddon, A., 179
Sedykh, Y., 60, 71, 131, 147, 148, 152, 195, 210
Seedhouse, C. N., 125
Sefton, W. H., 144
Segal, D. H., 15, 39, 44, 57, 125
Seidler, H., 61, 62, 133
Seidler, M., 172, 213
Selvey, W. P., 40
Selzer, P., 196
Sensburg, I., 69
Senyukov, S., 69
Setti, R. E. F., 44
Severns, V., 138
Sevryukova, T., 62
Sexton, L. J., 130
Shahanga, G., 38
Shanley, A., 41
Sharp, R. C., 39, 45, 91, 164
Sharpe, W., 139
Shavlakadze, R., 32, 129
Shaw, R. D., 46
Shchelkanova, T., 62, 67, 71, 199
Shcherbakov, L., 60
Shea, M., 213
Shearman, M., 216
Sheldon, R., 130
Sheldrick, J. W., 44
Shelton, E., 138
Shen Li-chuan, 24
Shen Mao-mao, 23
Shenton, B., 15, 44, 57
Sheppard, M. W., 114, 126, 127, 129
Sheridan, M. J., 52, 130, 131, 134, 152
Sherrard, C., 140
Sherrill, C., 156
Sherring, W. J., 134
Sherwood, J., 18, 38, 44, 57, 125, 167
Sherwood, S. H., 42, 45, 94, 126, 185
Shevtsova, L., 132, 197
Shezifi, H., 23
Shida, Y., 24
Shidova, I., 74
Shigematsu, M., 35, 112
Shigeta, Y., 22
Shiley, J. H., 133
Shimizu, K., 24
Shingles, B., 175
Shintaku, M., 22
Shirley, D. A., 45, 57, 94, 126, 184

Shirley, E., 17
Shivnath Singh, 22
Shorter, F., 34, 128, 138, 203
Shrubb, A., 46, 47, 106, 153
Shtereva, N., 66, 70, 189
Sidlo, J., 60
Sidorov, N., 129
Sidorova, M., 70
Siebeck, F., 59, 69
Siegl, S., 71, 108, 134, 199
Sievert, H. H., 61
Siitonen, H., 61
Silai, I., 70
Silei, C., 12
Silvester, L. J., 19, 52, 121, 195
Sime, D. W., 129
Simeoni, S., 11, 12, 62, 71, 77, 85, 86, 133, 153, 154, 199, 213
Simmonds B. A., 72, 184, 213
Simmons, A. D., 17, 47, 57
Simmons, F., 216
Simpson, A., 16, 44, 91, 166
Simpson, B., 39, 138
Simpson, G., 156
Simpson, J. M., 45, 57, 62, 76, 126, 183
Simpson, O. J., 216
Simpson, R., 88
Sin Kim Dan, 115, 157, 197, 198
Sjostrand, T., 128
Skatchko, T., 102
Skobla, J., 60
Skoglund, A-L., 213
Skomorokhov, V., 59
Skowronek, R., 61
Skvortsov, V., 69
Slaap, F. M., 94, 170, 184
Slaman, H., 183
Slaney, R. C., 165
Slater, D., 45, 57, 93, 125, 182, 183
Slijkhuis, W. F., 58
Slupianek, L., 54, 63, 67, 71, 74, 133, 153, 154, 189, 200, 213
Slusarski, T., 69, 103, 130
Sly, C., 72
Smaga, N., 61, 108
Smallacombe, G. C., 39
Smallwood, K. J., 41, 45, 57, 72, 126, 165, 169,

183, 212
Smart, C. V., 93
Smart, J. A., 169, 182, 183
Smedley, R. J., 68, 91
Smeeth, R. P., 186, 212
Smirnitskaya, N., 63
Smirnova, Y., 67
Smith, A., 140
Smith, A. R., 45, 170, 183, 198
Smith, C. G., 20, 40, 44, 169
Smith, D. (Aus), 211
Smith, D. (GB)), 210
Smith, D. (USA), 173
Smith, Dean, 216
Smith, E., 132
Smith, F. D., 129
Smith, G., 164
Smith, G. J., 40
Smith, J. (Aus), 174
Smith, J. (GB), 48, 57, 93, 96, 112, 122, 154, 155, 170, 184, 186, 198, 212, 213
Smith, O. G., 130
Smith, R. R., 129, 190
Smith, S. E., 93
Smith, T. C., 75, 114, 126, 155, 156, 190, 191, 207
Smith, T. J., 91
Smith, W., 186
Smithson, F. C., 128
Smouha, E. R., 125
Smythe, T. F., 47
Sneazwell, A., 92
Snell, P. G., 37, 115, 116, 126, 127, 150, 155, 191
Snook, W., 15
Sobotta, B., 61, 62
Soeter, I., 18, 25
Sokolowski, W., 174
Sola, G., 138
Soldatenko, V., 61, 188, 196
Solis, I., 23
Solomin, A., 49, 196
Son, K., 111, 127
Songok, K., 12
Sorrell, J., 183
Sou, S., 77
Sou, T., 77
Soutter, J. T., 125
Sowell, A. N., 137
Spassov, V., 73
Speckens, P., 174
Spence, Mal, 39
Spence, M. C., 39
Spence, Mel, 39

236

Spencer, E. A., 125
Spencer, E. M., 129
Spielberg, C., 63, 200
Spiridonov, A., 60, 152, 195
Spirin, L., 132
Spoof, L., 74, 213
Springbett, B., 39
Srejovic, M., 60
Sri Ram Singh, 21
Stacey, N. D., 44
Stad-de-Jongh, X., 132
Stadtmuller, K-H., 109, 196
Stahlberg, R., 70
Stallard, H. B., 125
Stanfield, A. W., 126, 129, 156
Stankovits, S., 55
Stanton, C., 214
Stark, S., 67
Staynings, A. R., 17, 164
Steane, R., 166
Stebbins, R. V., 129
Stecher, R., 61, 62, 66, 70, 132, 133, 149, 157, 158, 159, 197
Steele, W. S., 130
Steen, D., 40
Steers, L., 85
Stenning, P. H., 46
Stenroos, A. O., 127
Stephen, M., 198
Stephens, H. H., 132
Sternberg, B. H., 144, 194
Steuk, R., 73, 210
Stevens, G., 167
Stevenson, D. D., 92, 167
Stevenson, W. E., 129
Stewart, C. R., 17
Stewart, E., 39
Stewart, G., 72
Stewart, I., 17, 38, 45, 48, 57, 58, 68, 69, 76, 91, 107, 125, 164, 166
Stewart, J. L., 17, 38, 45
Stewart, M., 41, 45, 68, 70, 76, 93, 94, 170, 183, 186, 212
Stewart, P. J., 16, 68, 69, 76, 91, 166
Stirling, R. O., see WRIGHT, R. O.
Stock, D., 175
Stock, G., 76, 131
Stock, J., 76
Stock, K. F., 92, 164, 168
Stoev, V., 70
Stoikovski, G., 60
Stokes, K., 45

Stolle, G., 68
Stone, C., 138
Stonehouse, D. R., 39
Stoneley, C. H., 39, 44, 125
Stones, D., 18, 86, 172, 193, 200, 202, 209
Storoshkova, L., 62
Storozhova, T., 199
Storskrubb, B., 59
Stothard, J. C., 45
Strand, L., 58
Strandli, S., 60
Straszynska, D., 62, 184
Straub, J., 36, 65, 69, 135
Straw, C. J., 47
Streidt, E., 62, 133, 197
Strickland, S. B., see DE LA HUNTY, S. B.
Strode-Jackson, A. N., see JACKSON, A. N.
Strode-Strong, S. E., 45, 165, 170, 184, 213
Stropahl, E., see STREIDT, E.
Strotzer, W., 66, 74
Stroud, J., 93
Studney, D., 139
Stukalov, D., 73
Stukane, A., 189
Sturm, M., 77
Suarez, O., 138
Sugawara, T., 20, 23
Sugimura, K., 23, 24
Sugioka, K., 18, 22
Sugiyama, R., 24
Suh Yang Joo, 22
Sukegawa, R., 24
Sukharyev, V., 59
Sukniewicz, T., 198
Sulaiman, M., 23
Suman, M., 66
Sumich, Z., 20
Sun Mei-hua, 23
Suppe, H., 66
Surety, C. W. E., 18, 167
Susanj, L., 58, 68, 135
Sutherland, E. A., 94, 165, 170, 184
Sutherland, G. W., 40
Sutherland, W. M. S., 21, 45
Sutter, K., 60
Suzuki, F., 111
Svara, M., 18
Sviridov, N., 65
Swakala, G., 174
Swanepoel, M. C., 42
Sweeney, A. W., 37, 38,

44, 57
Sweeney, M. F., 85
Swenson, K., 137
Sychrova, L., 187
Sykora, M., 70, 199
Symonds, R. G., 15
Syrjala, T., 175
Syromyatnikova, E., 74
Sysoyeva, M., 86
Szabo, M., 58
Szabo, Z., 70
Szajda, A., 73
Szalma, L., 69
Szentgali, L., 58
Szewinska, I., 61, 62, 63, 66, 70, 71, 74, 101, 132, 133, 134, 157, 158, 159, 189, 196, 197
Szmidt, E., 159
Szmidt, J., 19, 60, 130, 151, 159, 194
Szordykowski, H., 68
Szyroka, E., 62

Taber, N. S., 127
Tabori, L., 16, 143
Tafelmeier, K., 73
Tagg, M. J., 47, 48, 57
Taipale, A. R., 130, 131
Tait, R., 40
Taitt, J. L., 18, 44, 92
Tajima, M., 22
Tajima, N., 130, 163
Takahashi, S., 22
Takahashi, T., 22
Takahashi, Y., 24
Takeda, M., 24
Tamm, J., 195
Tammert, A., 73
Tammisto, T., 175
Tamoi, S., 22
Tanaka, C., 23
Tanaka, M., 23
Tancred, P. A., 19, 165
Tancred, W. R., 19, 44, 53, 93, 168, 210
Taran, G., 192
Tarlok Singh, 22
Tarmak, J., 129
Taskinen, M., 68
Tayler, R., 38
Taylor, D., 166
Taylor, F. M., 89, 128
Taylor, G. A. H., 17
Taylor, J. B., 129
Taylor, R. (GB), 207, 210
Taylor, R. (USA), 129
Taylor, R. G., 17, 44, 46, 166
Taylor, S. G., 16

Taylor, W. C., 164
Tchuinte, A., 14
Teale, J., 19, 44, 93
Tebroke, G., 17
Tegla, F., 73
Telliez, S., 70
Templeton, P. S., 92
Temu, N., 38, 127
Terasawa, T., 111
Terekhov, G., 211
Ternstrom, J., 128
Ter-Ovanesyan, I., 30, 49, 60, 66, 69, 194, 210
Terry, J. A., 140
Testoni, C., 62
Tewksbury, J. W. B., 126, 128
Thacker, E. T., 39
Theato, 127
Theimer, R., 195
Theodosius, 123
Theys, L., 47
Thomann, H., 174
Thomas, A., 173
Thomas, C. J., 91
Thomas, E., 93
Thomas, J. C., 32, 86, 193, 203
Thomas, M. (Aus), 175
Thomas, M. (GB), 47
Thomas, R. H., 37, 44
Thomas, S., 106
Thompson, B., 170
Thompson, D. J., 57, 108, 125, 132, 161, 169, 179
Thompson, F. M. (Daley), 19, 20, 40, 44, 51, 57, 71, 72, 73, 104, 125, 131, 160, 164, 169, 195, 210
Thompson, I. R., 17, 38, 44, 57, 58, 111, 112, 161, 209
Thompson, J. F., 185
Thompson, M., 112
Thompson, R., 187
Thompson, W. M., 130
Thomson, E. J., 88, 128
Thorith, D., 60
Thorlaksson, V., 174, 210
Thorpe, J. H., 50, 131, 161, 162
Thorpe, R. S., 44, 174, 179, 211
Thranhardt, C., 18
Thrower, N. C., 41
Tibaduiza, D., 138
Tietz, K., 72
Tikhomirova, V., 63
Timmer, N., 62

Tinker, G., 129
Tisdall, R. M. N., 84, 88, 89, 128
Tittel, E., 66, 70, 183, 198
Tivey, G. A., 94
Tkachenko, N., 54, 63, 67, 134, 141, 154, 162, 200, 213
Todd, A. C., 57, 209
Todorova, A., 213
Todten, J., 75
Toivonen, A. A., 58
Tolan, T. E., 126
Tolley, M. R., 21
Tomasek, R., 210
Tomasini, A., 48
Tomizawa, H., 18
Tomlin, S. A., 37, 44
Tomlinson, I. R., 40
Tomonaga, Y., 21
Tomova, L., 61
Toms, E. J., 125
Toomey, M. D., see RAND, M. D.
Toomey, W., 51, 131, 139, 142, 146, 195
Tootell, F. D., 131
Toppino, E., 128
Tork, D., 138, 194
Torrance, J., 152
Torring, J., 60
Tosi, G., 216
Townend, H. S., 39, 44
Towns, F. G., 88, 128
Tozzi, R., 72
Tracanelli, F., 69, 73
Tranter, M. D., 45, 93
Travis, D. H., 20, 40, 44, 169
Traykov, Z., 72
Treacy, J., 17, 48
Treloar, J. F., 37, 38
Tremeer, L. F., 125
Trickey, E. F., 187
Trofimenko, V., 60
Trusenyov, V., 60, 121, 195
Tsai Cheng Fu, 22
Tsai Chien-hua, 24
Tsciclitiras, C., 130
Tsepelev, V., 69
Tsibulenko, V., 131
Tsou Wa, 24
Tsuchiya, K., 22
Tsui Lin, 22
Tsutsumi, K., 24
Tuicakau, M., 40
Tulloch, E. G., 164
Tulloh, M. B. S., 16, 57,

58, 107
Tully, M., 18, 19, 189
Tummler, B., 58, 65
Tuokko, M., 66
Turishcheva, L., 30
Turner, A. D., 45
Turner, D. M., 208
Turner, W., 190
Tuulos, V., 130
Tuwei, H., 17
Tyler, D. J. B., 41, 45, 46, 57, 86, 96, 126, 163, 182, 184, 203, 213
Tyshkevich, T., 133
Tysoe, A. E., 125, 126, 127
Tyson, C., 165, 171, 180, 186, 214
Tyus, W., 132, 133, 134, 139, 157, 163, 196, 197

Uchida, H., 24
Uelses, J., 144, 193
Ukhov, V., 61
Ulitkina, R., 62
Ulmasova, S., 62, 177, 189
Ulonska, K., 59
Underwood, A., 47
Underwood, G., 127
Urlando, G., 172
Usami, J., 17
Uudmae, J., 130, 172

Vaatainen, J., 58, 175
Vahlensieck, C., 112
Vainio, M., 58
Vakrusheva, O., 212
Vale, G., 211
Valentin, S., 191
Valentine, H., 127
Valero, C., 48
Valiulis, R., 129
Valkama, J. R., 19
Valla, T., 132
Valyukevich, G., 69, 73
Vamvakas, G., 73
Van Damme, I., 68
Vandendriessche, A., 192
Van der Hoeven, H., 183
Vanderstock, G., 89, 193
Vandewattyne, M., 47
Van Doorn, M., 74
Van Kiekebelt, D., 140
Van Reenen, J., 19, 195
Van Rees, C., 72
Varasdi, G., 59
Varju, V., 19, 60, 66, 70
Vasala, P., 127
Vasselinova, V., 74

Vaughan, K., 13
Vedeneyeva, S., 74
Vedyakov, A., 196
Velev, V., 54, 114
Vera, E., 196
Vergova, M., 97, 173, 200, 213
Vernon, J. A., 41, 45, 94, 170, 184, 199
Vickers, S. F., 20, 21, 57, 61, 125, 179
Vidiakova, 187
Vigneron, T., 69, 103, 194, 209, 210
Viiding, A., 60
Viljoen, J. H., 39
Villain, J-P., 58
Villanueva, A., 174
Vincent, T. A., 38
Vine, P. A. L., 18
Vinnitchenko, M., 73
Viren, L., 28, 34, 78, 106, 127, 175, 176, 192, 203, 204
Virgin, C., 48, 172, 208
Viscopoleanu, V., 71, 133, 199
Voelzke, M., 213
Vogt, P., 61, 62
Voigt, A., 67, 133, 199
Voigt, E. R., 125, 127
Voigt, H., 59
Volkov, K., 65, 69
Von Bremen, W. 132
Von Moltke, W., 61
Von Ruden, T., 138
Von Wartburg, U., 174, 210
Voorhees, N., 187
Voss, C., 175

Wadhams, A. E., 19, 93
Wadsworth, H., 92
Waitz, G., 48, 111, 112, 177, 183, 189, 198, 212, 213
Wajsowna, J., 187
Walasiewicz, S., 61, 132, 172, 187
Waldrop, A., 16, 138
Walker, C., 112
Walker, D., 92
Walker, I. K., 45
Walker, J. (NZ), 26, 27, 78, 116, 127, 178, 191, 208
Walker, J. (USA), 138
Walker, M., 45
Walker, R. E., 126
Wallace, G., 41

Wallace, L. M., 44
Wallace, R. H. H., 45
Wallgren, K., 70
Walls, M. L., see MAGUIRE, M. L.
Wallwork, R. E., 21, 40, 44, 179, 211
Walsh, J., 203
Walsh, S., see WALASIEWICZ, S.
Walter, K., 74
Walters, L. B., 44
Wanamaker, R., 139
Wandscher, E., 175
Wang Hsun-hua, 22
Ward, I., 18
Ward, P. D. H., 44
Warden, C. A., 93, 165, 170, 184, 213
Warden, P., 44
Warhurst, J. 40, 44, 179
Warmerdam, C. A., 144, 180
Warner, K. D., 129
Warren, D. M. J., 164
Wartenberg, C., 189
Wartenberg, F., 73
Wasughe, A., 12
Watanabe, C., 22
Watkinson, D. A., 45
Watson, B. J., 17
Watts, J., 168
Wearne, A. E., 41
Weatherburn, R., 91
Weaver, D., 216
Webb, E. J., 125
Webb, J. A., 179
Webb, V., 45, 76, 126
Webber, G. J., 125
Weber, H., 72, 207
Webster, F. R., 144
Webster, H., 38
Webster, J. E., 47
Webster, R. E., 215
Wegner, G., 60
Wehmonen, I., 175
Weidner, G., 122, 174, 196
Weigel, R., 211
Weill, D., 19
Weir, R., 210
Weisiger, C., 16
Wellmann, P-H., 68
Wells, A. W., 15, 37, 39, 45, 64, 91, 114, 125, 126, 145, 156, 164, 166, 180, 181, 207
Wells, M., 181
Welsh, R. P., 38
Wentz, S., 73

Wenzel, K., 74
Weppler, M., 59
Werner, J., 58, 59, 65
Werner, M., 62
Wesch, W., 179
Wessig, G., 77, 85, 86, 129, 181, 193, 209
Wessing M., 61, 189
Wessinghage, T., 65, 68, 69, 189
Westermann, L., 53, 185, 200
Weston, K., 139
Weston, V. M., see COBB, V. M.
Whall, J. E. C., 19
Wheeler, M. K. V., 16, 125
Whetton, J. H., 16, 57, 58, 68, 91
Whitbread, F., 72, 75, 213
White, B., 41
White, D., 38
White, E., 217
White, J., 72, 94, 165, 212
White, W. B., 140
Whitehead, J. N., 46, 125
Whitehead, P., 94
Whitehead, T. R., 91
Whitfield, M. G., 99, 115, 126, 129, 137, 182
Whitlock, G. B. R., 76
Whitlock, H. H., 57, 61, 76, 122, 125, 132
Whitney, R., 138
Whittle, H., 15, 57
Whyte, D. J., 19
Wieck, B., 70, 74
Wieser, R., 61, 73, 211
Wieslander, H., 131
Wiggs, M., 166
Wilcock, K. J., 57
Wilde, R. S., 68, 69, 91
Wilden, R., 70
Wilkins, M., 53, 131, 139, 151, 172, 182, 195, 210
Wilkinson, P. A., 44
Wilkinson, W., 16, 68, 91
Willard, M. J., 40, 48
Williams, A. F., 126
Williams, A. M., 45, 185, 213
Williams, B., 20, 44, 83, 168
Williams, C., 21
Williams, D., 180, 186
Williams, H. L., 20
Williams, J., 180
Williams, K., 72
Williams, L., 133, 139

Williams, P., 37, 126
Williams, P. S., 91
Williams, R., 130, 210
Williams, R. A., 40, 76, 174
Williams, S., 15, 190
Williams, U. C., 129
Williams, Y. W., 42, 76, 133
Williamson, A. D., 126
Williamson, J. G., 72, 207, 208
Willis, D., 41, 198
Wilms, E., 67, 200
Wilmshurst, K. S. D., 18, 19, 39, 40, 44
Wilson, A., 37
Wilson, A. S., 45, 94, 186
Wilson, D. N., 92
Wilson, H., 215
Wilson, H. A., 125
Wilson, J., 47, 125
Wilson, J. A., 44
Wilson, P., 18, 194
Wilton, M., 112
Wiltshire, P., 91
Wimaladse, W., 21
Winbolt Lewis, M. J., 16, 44
Winch, M. A., 44, 93, 164
Windeyer, G., 39
Window, D. J., 94
Winfield, J. W., 44
Winslow, P., 140
Wint, A. S., 115, 126, 129, 216
Winter, A. W., 130, 163
Winter, J. A., 39, 129
Winter, L., 112, 175
Witschas, R., *see* ACKERMANN, R.
Witziers, J. M., 132
Wlodarczyk, A., 71
Wockel, B., 62, 71, 74, 132, 133, 134, 157, 159
Wodzynski, L., 69
Woellke, H., 130
Wohlhuter, R., 172, 191, 207
Wolde, Mamo, *see* MAMO WOLDE
Wolfermann, K., 66, 98, 131, 195
Wolff, F. F., 125, 129
Wolfrum, B., 74
Wood, A. E., 47, 112
Wood, C. G., 157
Wood, K., 16, 90
Woodard, J., 209

Woodburn, E., 143
Wooderson, S. C., 44, 57, 58, 83, 86, 106, 115, 142, 188
Woodhouse, R., 41
Woodland, J., 41
Woodring, A., 126
Woodruff, J. Y., 115, 126
Woods, G., 122, 210
Woods, T., 138
Worling, D., 174
Woronin, M., 59, 68
Wottle, D., 115, 126, 191
Wray, Y. J., 45, 94, 186
Wright, A. J., 94
Wright, D. McL., 38, 45
Wright, L. C., 129
Wright, M., 143
Wright, R. O., 41, 46, 57, 62, 68, 93, 170
Wright T., 17, 47, 57
Wrighton, J. D., 16, 44, 57, 58, 59
Wszola, J., 69, 71, 73, 129, 193, 200, 201
Wu Ah-min, 23
Wujak, B., 67, 102
Wulbeck, W., 65
Wursthorn, H., 68
Wyatt, H., 174
Wykoff, F. C., 128, 129
Wylde, R. B., 45
Wymark, S., 72

Yagi, T., 86
Yagishita, T., 24
Yakubowich, J., 139
Yamada, H., 23
Yamada, K., 23
Yamada, T., 23
Yamamoto, H., 23
Yamashita, H., 24
Yanagawa, S., 23
Yang, C. K., 23, 51, 195, 216
Yao Yui-ying, 24
Yarrow, S. S., 57
Yashchenko, V., 60, 69, 73, 85, 193, 202, 209
Yasuda, N., 22
Yates, P. D., 20, 44
Yearwood, L., 39
Yegorov, A., 196
Yeh, Pei-su, 24
Yeoman, A., *see* FORD, A.
Yeoman, P., *see* FUDGE, P.
Yerman, J. L., 129
Yermolayeva, Y., 61
Yifter, M., 12, 106, 127, 189, 202, 203
Ying Ya-ping, 23
Yoda, I., 24
Yohannan, T. C., 23
Yoneda, K., 24
Yoon Chil Choi, 22
Yordanova, S., 70
Yorgova, D., 71
Yoshino, T., 24
Young, C., 213
Young, C. C., 131
Young, D., 45
Young, E. V., 129
Young H. J., 41, 45, 57, 61, 125, 182, 183
Young, I. C., 45
Young, J. R. C., 15
Young, L., 139
Young, V. I., 42
Younis, M., 22
Yrjola, P. I., 131
Yui, K., 22
Yule, P. A., 183
Yulin, A., 59
Yum Bok Suh, 111

Zabala, J. C., 127
Zaichuk, B., 83, 147, 195
Zaidman, A., 210
Zarandi, L., 59
Zaslona, J., 165
Zatopek, E., 58, 104, 106, 111, 127, 141, 188, 192, 203, 204
Zatopkova, D., 63, 122, 133, 204
Zauli, B., 63
Zehrt, M., 62, 66, 71, 74, 132, 133, 157, 197
Zelentsova, T., 62, 149, 199
Zeniou, P., 20
Zeus, 186
Zharkova, L., 74
Zhelev, M., 58
Zlateva, S., 198
Zsivotzky, G., 20, 60, 131, 195
Zutchi, G., 23
Zuyeva, N., 74
Zwier, N., 184
Zybina, G., 62, 133, 153
Zyuskova, Z., 133